NOTES

ON THE

OLD TESTAMENT

EXPLANATORY AND PRACTICAL

BY

ALBERT BARNES

ENLARGED TYPE EDITION

EDITED BY

ROBERT FREW, D.D.

ISAIAH

VOL. II

BAKER BOOK HOUSE

GRAND RAPIDS, MICHIGAN

Library of Congress Catalog Card Number: 55-11630

ISBN: 0-8010-0539-6

First Printing, June 1950
Second Printing, January 1956
Third Printing, January 1959
Fourth Printing, February 1961
Fifth Printing, February 1963
Sixth Printing, October 1965
Seventh Printing, June 1967
Eighth Printing, September 1968
Ninth Printing, August 1969
Tenth Printing, June 1971
Eleventh Printing, September 1972
Twelfth Printing, March 1974
Thirteenth Printing, July 1975

PHOTOLITHOPRINTED BY CUSHING - MALLOY, INC.
ANN ARBOR, MICHIGAN, UNITED STATES OF AMERICA
1975

NOTE BY THE EDITOR.

In this Edition of Barnes on Isaiah, the "New Translation," given with the first Edition of the Work, is withheld, because the Author himself has suppressed it in his second and last Edition, and the Editor did not feel himself at liberty to disturb that arrangement. "My principal aim," says Mr. Barnes in his preface, "has been to *condense* the work as much as possible, by removing redundant words, and by excluding whatever did not contribute to the elucidation of the prophet. In revising it I have stricken out matter, besides the 'New Translation,' to the amount of about one hundred and twenty octavo pages." For the omission of the Translation in the recent Edition, the want of room was one reason, and probably the character of the Translation itself was another. The Author never claimed much for it, and his profound countryman, Alexander, observes regarding it, that "it seems to be wholly independent of the Commentary, and can hardly be considered an improvement, either on the Common Version or on that of Lowth." It is on the Commentary that the Author has rested his fame, and there assuredly it has a solid and lasting foundation.

For peculiarities of this Edition, see the Editor's Preface in the first volume.

THE BOOK

OF

THE PROPHET ISAIAH.

CHAPTER XXXVI.

ANALYSIS.

THIS chapter commences the historical portion of Isaiah, which continues to the close of the thirty-ninth chapter. The main subject is the destruction of Sennacherib and his army. It contains also an account of the sickness and recovery of Hezekiah; the song with which he celebrated his recovery; and an account of his ostentation in showing his treasures to the ambassadors of the king of Babylon. In 2 Chron. xxxii. 32, the following record occurs:—'Now the rest of the acts of Hezekiah, and his goodness, behold they are written in the vision of Isaiah, the son of Amoz;' and it is to this portion of Isaiah to which the author of the Book of Chronicles doubtless refers.

There was an obvious propriety in Isaiah's making a record of the invasion and destruction of Sennacherib. That event has occupied a considerable portion of his prophetic announcements; and as he lived to see them fulfilled, it was proper that he should record the event. The prophecy and its fulfilment can thus be compared together; and while there is the strongest internal testimony that the prophecy was uttered before the event, there is also the most striking and clear fulfilment of all the predictions on the subject.

A parallel history of these transactions occurs in 2 Kings xvii.-xx., and in 2 Chron. xxxii. The history in Chronicles, though it contains an account of the same transaction, is evidently by another hand, as it bears no further resemblance to this, than that it contains an account of the same transactions. But between the account here and in 2 Kings there is a most striking resemblance, so much so as to show that they were mainly by the same hand. It has been made a matter of inquiry whether Isaiah was the original author, or whether he copied a history which he found in the Book of Kings, or whether both he and the author of the Book of Kings copied from some original document which is now lost, or whether the collectors of the prophetic writings after the return from the captivity at Babylon, judging that such a history would appropriately explain the prophecies of Isaiah, copied the account from some historical record, and inserted it among his prophecies. This last is the opinion of Rosenmüller—an opinion which evidently lacks all historical evidence, and indeed all probability. The most obvious and fair supposition undoubtedly is, that this history was inserted here by Isaiah, or, that he made this record according to the statement in 2 Chron. xxxii. 32. Gesenius also accords substantially with Rosenmüller in supposing that this history is an *elaboration* of that in the Book of Kings, and that it was reduced to its present form by some one who collected and edited the Books of Isaiah after the Babylonish captivity. Vitringa supposes that both the accounts in Kings and in Isaiah have been derived from a common historical document, and have been adopted and somewhat abridged and modified by the author of the Book of Kings and by Isaiah.

It is impossible now to determine the truth in regard to this subject; nor is it of much importance. Those who are desirous of seeing the subject discussed more at length may consult Vitringa, Rosenmüller, and Gesenius. The view of Gesenius is chiefly valuable because he has gone into a comparison of the account in Isaiah with that in Kings. The following remarks are all that occur to me as desirable to make, and express the conclusion which I have been able to form on the subject:—

I. The two accounts have a common origin, or are substantially the production of the same hand. This is apparent on the face of them. The same course of the narrative is pursued, the same expressions occur, and the same style of composition is found. It is *possible*, indeed, that the Holy Spirit *might* have inspired two different authors to adopt the same style and expressions in recording the same events, but this is not the mode elsewhere observed in the Scriptures. Every sacred writer is allowed to pursue his own method of narration, and to express himself in a style and manner of his own.

2. There is no *evidence* that the two accounts were abridged from a more full narrative. Such a thing is *possible;* nor is there any impropriety in the supposition. But it lacks historical support. That there *were* histories among the Jews which are now lost; that there were public records which were the fountains whence the authors of the histories which we now have drew their information, no one can doubt who reads the Old Testament. Thus we have accounts of the writings of Gad, and Iddo the seer, and Nathan, and the prophecy of Ahijah the Shilonite, and of the Book of Jehu the prophet (2 Chron. ix. 29; xx. 34; 1 Kings xvi. 1), all of which are now lost, except so far as they are incorporated in the historical and prophetical books of the Old Testament. It is *possible,* therefore, that these accounts may have been abridged from some such common record, but there is no historical testimony to the fact.

3. There is no *evidence* that these chapters in Isaiah were inserted by Ezra, or the other inspired men who collected the Sacred Writings, and published a *recension,* or an edition of them after the return from Babylon. That there was such a work performed by Ezra and his contemporaries is the testimony of all the Jewish historians (see Dr. Alexander *On the Canon of Scripture*). But there is no historical evidence that they thus introduced into the writings of Isaiah an entire historical narrative from the previous histories, or that they composed this history to be inserted here. It is done nowhere else. And had it been done on this occasion, we should have had reason to expect that they would have inserted historical records of the fulfilment of *all* the other prophecies which had been fulfilled. We should have looked, therefore, for historical statements of the downfall of Damascus and Syria; of the destruction of Samaria, of Moab, of Babylon, and of Tyre, as proofs of the fulfilment of the predictions of Isaiah. There can be no reason why the account of the destruction of Sennacherib should have been singled out and inserted in preference to others. And this is especially true in regard to *Babylon.* The prophecy of Isaiah (ch. xiii., xiv.) had been most striking and clear; the fulfilment had also been most remarkable; Ezra and his contemporaries must have felt a much deeper interest in that than in the destruction of Sennacherib; and it is unaccountable, therefore, if they inserted this narrative respecting Sennacherib, that they did not give us a full account also of the overthrow of Babylon, and of their deliverance, as showing the fulfilment of the prophecies on that subject.

4. The author of the Books of Kings is unknown. There is reason to believe that these books, as well as the Books of Chronicles, and some other of the historical books of the Old Testament, were written *by* the prophets; or at least compiled and arranged by some inspired man, from historical sketches that were made by the prophets. To such sketches or narratives we find frequent reference in the books themselves. Thus Nathan the prophet, and Ahijah the Shilonite, and Iddo the seer, recorded the acts of Solomon (2 Chron. ix. 29); thus the same Iddo the seer, and Shemaiah the prophet, recorded the acts of Rehoboam (2 Chron. xii. 15); thus the acts of Jehoshaphat were written in the Book of Jehu (2 Chron. xx. 34); and thus Isaiah wrote the acts of king Uzziah (2 Chron. xxvi. 22), and also of Hezekiah (2 Chron. xxxii. 32). Many of these historical sketches or fragments have not come down to us; but all that was essential to us has been doubtless incorporated into the sacred narrative, and transmitted to our own times. It is not improbable that many of these histories were mere fragments or public documents; narratives or sketches of a single reign, or some important fact in a reign, which were subsequently revised and inserted in the more extended history, so that, after all, it may be that we have all, or nearly all, of these fragments incorporated in the histories which we now possess.

5. As Isaiah is thus known to have written some portions of the history of the kings, it is probable that his history would be incorporated into the record of the kings by whomsoever that record might be composed. Indeed, the composition of the entire Books of Kings has been ascribed by many writers to Isaiah, though Grotius and some others ascribe it to Jeremiah. The general, and the probable opinion is, however, that the Books of the Kings were digested into their present form by Ezra. It is probable, therefore, I think, that Isaiah wrote the chapters in Kings respecting the invasion of Sennacherib; that the compiler of the Books of Kings, whoever he might be, adopted the fragment as a part of his history, and that the portion which we have here in Isaiah is the same fragment revised, abridged in some places, and enlarged in others, to adapt it to his purpose in introducing it into his book of prophecy. But it is admitted that this is conjecture. Every consideration, however, must lead us to suppose that this is the work of Isaiah (comp. Introd. § 5).

The portion of history contained in these chapters differs from the record in the Kings in several respects. There is no difference in regard to the historical facts, but the difference has respect to the fulness of the narratives, and to the change of a few words. The most material difference is that a few sentences, and members of sentences, are omitted in Isaiah which are found in Kings. These variations will be noticed in the exposition, and it is not necessary more particularly to refer to them here.

The thirty-sixth chapter contains the following parts, or subjects:—1. Sennacherib, having taken most of the strongholds of Judea, sent Rabshakeh with a great force to besiege Jerusalem, and to summon it to surrender (1, 2). 2. Hezekiah sent an embassy to meet with Rabshakeh, evidently to induce him to depart from the city (3). 3. This embassy Rabshakeh addressed in a proud, insolent, and taunting speech, reproaching them with putting their trust in Egypt, and with their feebleness, and assuring them that Sennacherib had come up against the city at the command of JEHOVAH (4–10). 4. The Jewish embassy requested Rabshakeh to speak in the Aramean or Syrian language, that the common people on the wall might not hear (11). 5. To this he replied, that he came that *they might hear;* to endeavour to draw them off from trusting to Hezekiah, and to induce them to submit to Sennacherib, promising them abundance in the land to which he would take them (12–20). 6. To all this, the embassy of Hezekiah said nothing, but returned, as they had been instructed, into the city, with deep expressions of sorrow and grief (21, 22).

NOW [a]it came to pass in the fourteenth year of king Hezekiah, *that* Sennacherib king of Assyria came up against all the defenced cities of Judah, and took them.

a 2 Ki.18.13,&c.; 2 Ch.32.1,&c.

CHAPTER XXXVI.

1. *In the fourteenth year of Hezekiah.* Of his reign, B.C. 709. ¶ That *Sennacherib.* Sennacherib was son and successor of Shalmaneser, king of Assyria, and began to reign A.M. 3290, or B.C. 714, and reigned, according to Calmet, but four years, according to Prideaux eight years, and according to Gesenius eighteen years. The immediate occasion of this war against Judah was the fact that Hezekiah had shaken off the yoke of Assyria, by which his father Ahaz and the nation had suffered so much under Tiglath-pileser, or Shalmaneser (2 Kings xviii. 7). To reduce Judea again to subjection, as well as to carry his conquests into Egypt, appears to have been the design of this celebrated expedition. He ravaged the country, took the strong towns and fortresses, and prepared then to lay siege to Jerusalem itself. Hezekiah, however, as soon as the army of Sennacherib had entered Judea, prepared to put Jerusalem into a state of complete defence. At the advice of his counsellors he stopped the waters that flowed in the neighbourhood of the city, and that might furnish refreshment to a besieging army, built up the broken walls, enclosed one of the fountains within a wall, and prepared shields and darts in abundance to repel the invader (2 Chron. xxxii. 2–5). Sennacherib, seeing that all hope of easily taking Jerusalem was taken away, apparently became inclined to hearken to terms of accommodation. Hezekiah sent to him to propose peace, and to ask the conditions on which he would withdraw his forces. He confessed his error in not paying the tribute stipulated by his father, and his willingness to pay now what should be demanded by Sennacherib. Sennacherib demanded three hundred talents of silver, and thirty talents of gold. This was paid by Hezekiah, by exhausting the treasury, and by stripping even the temple of its gold (2 Kings xviii. 13–16). It was evidently understood in this treaty that Sennacherib was to withdraw his forces, and return to his own land. But this treaty he ultimately disregarded (see Note on ch. xxxiii. 8). He seems, however, to have granted Hezekiah some respite, and to have delayed his attack on Jerusalem until his return from Egypt. This war with Egypt he prosecuted at first with great success, and with a fair prospect of the conquest of that country. But having laid siege to Pelusium, and having spent much time before it without success, he was compelled at length to raise the siege, and to retreat. Tirhakah king of Ethiopia having come to the aid of Sevechus, the reigning monarch of Egypt, and advancing to the relief of Pelusium, Sennacherib was compelled to raise the siege, and retreated to Judea. Here, having taken Lachish, and disregarding his compact with He-

2 And the king of Assyria sent
Rabshakeh from Lachish to Jerusalem
unto king Hezekiah with a
great army. And he stood by the
conduit of the upper pool in the
highway of the fuller's field.
3 Then came forth unto him
Eliakim, Hilkiah's son, which was
over the house, and Shebna the
scribe, [1] and Joah, Asaph's son, the
recorder.
4 And Rabshakeh said unto
them, Say ye now to Hezekiah,
Thus saith the great king, the king
of Assyria, What confidence *is* this
wherein thou trustest?
5 I say, *sayest thou* (but *they are*

[1] or, *secretary*.

zekiah, he sent an army to Jerusalem under Rabshakeh to lay siege to the city. This is the point in the history of Sennacherib to which the passage before us refers (see Prideaux's *Connection*, vol. i. pp. 138–141; Jos. *Ant.* x. 1; Gesenius *in loco*; and Robinson's Calmet). ¶ *All the defenced cities.* All the towns on the way to Egypt, and in the vicinity of Jerusalem (see Notes on ch. x. 28–32).

2. *And the king of Assyria sent Rabshakeh.* In 2 Kings xviii. 17, it is said that he sent Tartan, and Rabsaris, and Rabshakeh. In regard to Tartan, see Note on ch. xx. 1. It is probable that Rabshakeh only is mentioned in Isaiah because the expedition may have been mainly under his direction, or more probably because he was the principal speaker on the occasion to which he refers. ¶ *From Lachish.* This was a city in the south of the tribe of Judah, and was south-west of Jerusalem (Josh. x. 23; xv. 39). It was situated in a plain, and was the seat of an ancient Canaanitish king. It was rebuilt and fortified by Rehoboam (2 Chron. xi. 9). It was in some respects a border town, and was a defence against the incursions of the Philistines. It was therefore situated between Jerusalem and Egypt, and was in the direct way of Sennacherib in his going to Egypt, and on his return. It lay, according to Eusebius and Jerome, seven Roman miles from Eleutheropolis towards the south. No trace of the town, however, is now to be found (see Robinson's *Bib. Researches*, vol. ii. pp. 388, 389). ¶ *With a great army.* Sennacherib remained himself for a time at Lachish, though he followed not long after. It is probable that he sent forward a considerable portion of his immense army, retaining only so many forces as he judged would be necessary to carry on the siege of Lachish. In 2 Chron. xxxii. 9, it is said that Sennacherib, while he sent his servants to Jerusalem, 'laid siege to Lachish and all his power with him;' but this must mean that he retained with him a considerable part of his army, and doubtless *all* that contributed to his magnificence and splendour. The word 'power' in 2 Chron. xxxii. 9, means also 'dominion' (see the margin), and denotes all the insignia of royalty; and this might have been retained while a considerable part of his forces had been sent forward to Jerusalem. ¶ *And he stood.* He halted; he encamped there; he intended to make that the point of attack. ¶ *By the conduit*, &c. (see Notes on ch. vii. 3.)

3. *Then came forth unto him.* Isaiah has here omitted what is recorded in 2 Kings xviii. 18, viz., that Rabshakeh and his companions 'called to the king,' and as the result of that probably Hezekiah sent out Eliakim. ¶ *Eliakim, Hilkiah's son, which was over the house.* Respecting Eliakim, and his character, see Notes on ch. xxii. 20–25. ¶ *And Shebna the scribe.* This may have been some other man than the one mentioned in ch. xxii. 15. He is there said to have been 'over the house,' and it is stated that he should be degraded from that office, and succeeded by Eliakim. It is possible, however, that Hezekiah retained him as *scribe*, or as *secretary* (see the analysis of ch. xxii. 15–25). ¶ *And Joah, Asaph's son, the recorder.* The *chronicler;* the officer to whom was intrusted the keeping of the records of state. The Hebrew word means 'the remembrancer;' him by whose means former events might be recalled and remembered, perhaps an officer such as would be called *historiographer*.

4. *What confidence.* What is the ground of your confidence? on what do

but vain [1]words) [2]*I have* counsel and strength for war: now on whom dost thou trust, that thou rebellest against me?

6 Lo, thou trustest in the staff of this broken reed, on Egypt; whereon if a man lean, it will go into his hand, and pierce it: so *is* Pharaoh king of Egypt to all that trust in him.

7 But if thou say to me, We trust in the LORD our God: *is it* not he whose high places and whose altars Hezekiah hath taken away, and[a] said to Judah and to Jerusalem, Ye shall worship before this altar?

1 *a word of lips.*
2 or, but *counsel and strength* are *for the war.*

a 2 Ki.18.4.

you trust? The appellation 'great king' was the customary title of the kings of the Persians and Assyrians.

5. *I say,* sayest thou. In 2 Kings xviii. 20, this is 'thou sayest;' and thus many MSS. read it here, and Lowth and Noyes have adopted that reading. So the Syriac reads it. But the sense is not affected whichever reading is adopted. It is designed to show to Hezekiah that his reliance, either on his own resources or on Egypt, was vain. ¶ *But* they are but *vain words.* Marg. as Heb. 'A word of lips;' that is, mere words; vain and empty boasting. ¶ *On whom dost thou trust, that thou rebellest against me?* Hezekiah had revolted from the Assyrian power, and had refused to pay the tribute which had been imposed on the Jews in the time of Ahaz (2 Kings xviii. 7).

6. *Lo, thou trustest.* It is possible that Sennacherib might have been apprised of the attempt which had been made by the Jews to secure the co-operation of Egypt (see Notes on ch. xxx. 1–7; xxxi. 1, *sq.*), though he might not have been aware that the negotiation was unsuccessful. ¶ *In the staff of this broken reed.* The same comparison of Egypt with a broken reed, or a reed which *broke* while they were trusting to it, occurs in Ezek. xxix. 6, 7. *Reeds* were doubtless used often for staves, as they are now. They are light and hollow, with long joints. The idea here is, that as a slender reed would break when a man leaned on it, and would pierce his hand, so it would be with Egypt. Their reliance would give way, and their trusting to Egypt would be attended with injury to themselves (comp. ch. xxx. 5, 7; xxxi. 3).

7. *But if thou say to me.* If you shall make this plea, that you believe JEHOVAH will protect you in your revolt. The word 'thou' here refers to Hezekiah, or to the ambassadors speaking in his name. In 2 Kings xviii. 22, it is, 'but if *ye* say unto me;' that is, you ambassadors. The sense is substantially the same. ¶ Is it *not he,* &c. This is given as a reason why they should not put their confidence in JEHOVAH. The reason is, that he supposed that Hezekiah had removed all the altars of JEHOVAH from all parts of the land, and that they could not calculate on the protection of a God whose worship had been abolished. It is probable that Sennacherib and Rabshakeh had heard of the reformation which had been effected by Hezekiah; of his destroying the groves and altars which had been consecrated in the reign of his father to idolatry, and perhaps of the fact that he had even destroyed the brazen serpent which Moses had made, and which had become an object of idolatrous worship (2 Kings xviii. 4), and he may have supposed that all these altars and groves had been devoted to JEHOVAH, and were connected with his worship. He did not seem to understand that all that Hezekiah had done was only to establish the worship of JEHOVAH in the land. ¶ *High places.* The worship of idols was usually performed in groves on high places; or on the tops of hills and mountains. It seems to have been supposed that worship in such places was more acceptable to the Deity. Perhaps it may have been because they thus seemed *nearer* the residence of the gods; or, perhaps, because there is sublimity and solemnity in such places—a stillness and elevation above the world which seem favourable to devotion (see 1 Sam. ix. 12; 1 Kings iii. 4; 2 Kings xii. 2; 1 Chron. xiii. 29). Chapels, temples, and

8 Now therefore give [1]pledges,
I pray thee, to my master the king
of Assyria, and I will give thee two
thousand [a]horses, if thou be able on
thy part to set riders upon them.
9 How then wilt thou turn away
the face of one captain of the least
of my master's servants, and put
thy trust on Egypt [b]for chariots
and for horsemen?
10 And am I now come up without
the LORD against this land to destroy
it? The LORD [c]said unto me, Go
up against this land, and destroy it.

1 or, *hostages*. a Ps.20.7,8; Hos.14.3. b Jer.2.36. c ch.45.7; Am.3.6.

altars, were erected on such places (1 Kings xiii. 22; 2 Kings xvii., xxix), and ministers and priests attended there to officiate (1 Kings xii. 32; 2 Kings xvii. 32). Even the kings of Judah, notwithstanding the express prohibition of Moses (Deut. xii.), were engaged in such acts of worship (2 Kings xii. 4; xiv. 4; xv. 4, 35; 2 Chron. xv. 17; xx. 33); and Solomon himself sacrificed in chapels of this kind (1 Kings iii. 2). These places Hezekiah had destroyed; that is, he had cut down the consecrated groves, and had destroyed the chapels and temples which had been erected there. The fact that Ahaz, the father of Hezekiah, had been distinguished for worshipping in such places had probably led the king of Assyria to suppose that this was the proper worship of the God of the Jews; and now that Hezekiah had destroyed them all, he seems to have inferred that he was guilty of gross irreligion, and could no longer depend on the protection of JEHOVAH. ¶ *And said to Judah and Jerusalem.* He had commanded them to worship only in Jerusalem, at the temple. This was in strict accordance with the law of Moses; but this seems to have been understood by Sennacherib as in fact almost or quite banishing the worship of JEHOVAH from the land. Probably this was said to alienate the minds of the people from Hezekiah, by showing them that he had taken away their rights and privileges of worshipping God where they chose.

8. *Now, therefore, give pledges.* Marg. 'Hostages.' The Hebrew verb (עָרַב) means properly *to mix* or *mingle;* then, to exchange commodities by barter or traffic; then, to become surety for any one, to exchange with him, to stand in his place; then, to pledge, to pledge one's life, or to give security of any kind. Here it is used in a spirit of *taunting* or *derision*, and is equivalent to what would be said among us, 'I will bet you, or I will lay a wager, that if we should give you only two thousand horses, you could not find men enough to ride them, or men that had knowledge of horsemanship enough to guide them.' There was much severity in this taunt. The Jews hoped to defend themselves. Yet here was an immense army coming up to lay siege against them. What hope had they of defence? So weak and feeble were they, that Rabshakeh said they could not furnish two even thousand horsemen to resist all the host of the Assyrians. There was also, doubtless, much *truth* in this taunt. It was not permitted by the law of Moses for the Jews to keep cavalry, nor for their kings to multiply horses. The reason of this may be seen in the Notes on ch. ii. 7. Though some of the kings, and especially Solomon, had disregarded this law of Moses, yet Hezekiah had endeavoured to restore the observance of the law, and it is probable that he *had* no cavalry, and that the art of horsemanship *was* little known in Jerusalem. As the Assyrians prided themselves on their cavalry, they consequently looked with contempt on a people who were destitute of this means of defence.

9. *How then wilt thou turn away the face.* The most unimportant captain in the army of Assyria commands more horsemen than this, and how can you expect to oppose even him, much more how can you be able to resist all the mighty army of the Assyrians? ¶ *One captain of the least.* The word 'captain' here (פַּחַת, construct state from פֶּחָה) denotes a *prefect* or *governor* of a province less than a satrap, an officer who was under the satrap, and subject to him. It is applied to an officer in the Assyrian empire (2 Kings xviii. 24); in the Chaldean empire (Jer.

11 Then said Eliakim, and Shebna, and Joah, unto Rabshakeh, Speak, I pray thee, unto thy servants in the Syrian language; for we understand *it:* and speak not to us in the Jews' language, in the ears of the people that *are* on the wall.

---

li. 23); the Persian (Esth. viii. 9; ix. 3); and to the prefects of Judea in the time of Solomon (1 Kings x. 15). The word is of foreign origin.

10. *And am I now come up without the* LORD. Am I come up without his permission or command? Rabshakeh here speaks in the name of his master; and he means to say that he had the express command of JEHOVAH to inflict punishment on the Jews. It is *possible* that there had been conveyed to Sennacherib a rumour of what Isaiah had said (see ch. x. 5, 6) that God would bring the Assyrians upon the Jewish people to punish them for their sins, and that Rabshakeh now pleads that as his authority, in order to show them that resistance would be vain. Or it may be that he uses the name JEHOVAH here as synonymous with the name of GOD, and means to say that he had been *divinely directed* to come up in that expedition. All the ancient warriors usually consulted the gods, and endeavoured by auguries to obtain the Divine approbation of their plans of conquest, and Rabshakeh may mean simply to say that his master came now under the divine sanction and direction. Or, which is more probable, he made use of this as a mere pretence for the purpose of influencing the people who heard him, and to whom he said he was sent (ver. 12), in order to alienate their minds from Hezekiah, and to induce them to surrender. He knew that it was one of the *principles* of the Jews, however little they regarded it in practice, to yield to his authority. Wicked men will be glad to plead Divine authority for their purposes and plans when they can have the slightest pretence for it.

11. *Speak, I pray thee, unto thy servants in the Syrian language.* Heb. אֲרָמִית—'Aramean.' Aram, or Aramea, properly meaning *a high region,* or the *highlands,* was of wider extent than Syria Proper, and comprehended not only Syria, but Mesopotamia. It usually denotes however Syria Proper, of which the capital was Damascus. The language of all this country was probably the same—the Syrian or Aramean, a language of the same family as the Hebrew, and having a strong resemblance to that and to the Chaldee. This was not properly the language of *Assyria,* where probably a dialect composed of the language of the Medes and Persians was employed. But the Syriac language was spoken in different parts of Assyria. It was spoken in Mesopotamia, and doubtless in some of the provinces of the Assyrian empire, and might be presumed to be understood by Rabshakeh, and those with him. The Jews had intercourse with the Syrians, and those who had been sent out by Hezekiah had learned to speak that. It is not probable that they understood the Medo-Persian tongue that was spoken by the Assyrians usually. The Syriac or Aramean was probably the most common language which was spoken in that region. Its knowledge prevailed in the time of the Saviour, and was that which he usually spoke. ¶ *In the Jews' language* (יְהוּדִית). The language of *Judah.* It is remarkable that they did not call it the *Hebrew* language. But there might have been some national pride in regard to this. The Hebrew language had been the common language of all the Jews, and had been spoken by those of the kingdom of Israel or Samaria, as well as by those of the kingdom of Judah. But after the revolt of the ten tribes it is possible that they might have claimed the *language* as their own, and regarded the Hebrew—the venerable language of their fathers—as belonging to them peculiarly, as they claimed everything that was sacred or venerable in the nation, and hence they spoke of it as the language of *Judah.* The name of *Judah,* or *Jews,* which is derived from Judah, was, after the removal of the ten tribes, given to the entire nation—a name which is retained to the present time. In Isa. xix. 18, it is called the language of Canaan (see Note on that

12 But Rabshakeh said, Hath my[a] master sent me to thy master and to thee to speak these words? *hath he* not *sent me* to the men that sit upon the wall, that they may eat their own dung and drink their own piss with you?

[a] Ps.31.18.

place). ¶ *In the ears of the people that are on the wall.* This conference took place evidently near the city, and within hearing distance. Doubtless the people of the city, feeling a curiosity to hear the message of the Assyrian, crowded the walls. The Jewish ambassadors were apprehensive that what was said by Rabshakeh would alienate their minds from Hezekiah, and requested that the conference might be conducted in a language which they could not understand.

12. *Hath my master sent me to thy master and to thee?* To Hezekiah, and to you *alone*. A part of my purpose is to address the *people*, to induce them to leave Hezekiah, and to offer no resistance to the Assyrian. ¶ *To the men that sit on the wall*, &c. The meaning of this is, that the inhabitants of the city, if they do not surrender, will be subjected to the severest evils of famine. If they did not surrender, it was the purpose of the Assyrian to lay siege to the city, and to reduce it. But it was often the work of years to reduce and take a city. Nebuchadnezzar spent thirteen years before Tyre, and the Greeks employed ten in reducing ancient Troy. The sense here is, therefore, that unless the people could be induced to surrender to Sennacherib, they would be subjected to all the horrors of a siege, when they would be reduced to the most deplorable state of necessity and want. The idea in the whole verse is clearly expressed in the parallel place in 2 Chron. xxxii. 11: 'Doth not Hezekiah persuade you to give over yourselves to die by famine and by thirst, saying, The LORD our God shall deliver us out of the hand of the king of Assyria?'—In regard to the indelicacy of this passage, we may observe—1. That the Masorites in the Hebrew text have so *pointed* the words used, that in reading it the offensiveness would be considerably avoided. It is common in the Hebrew Scriptures, when a word is used in the text that is indelicate, to place another word in the margin, and the vowel-points that belong to the word in the margin are applied to the word in the text, and the word in the margin is thus commonly read. In accordance with this custom among the Jews, it is evident that more delicacy might have been observed by our translators in this, and in some other places of the Scriptures. 2. The customs, habits, and modes of expression of people in different nations and times, differ. What appears indelicate at one time or in one country, may not only be tolerated, but common in another. Many things are esteemed indelicate among us which are not so in polite and refined France; many expressions are so regarded now which were not in the time when the Bible was translated into English. Many things may be to us offensive which were not so to the Syrians, the Babylonians, and the Jews; and many modes of expression which are common now, and consistent with all our notions of refinement, *may* appear improper in some other period of the world. There are many things in Shakspere, and in most of the old English writers, which cannot now be read without a blush. Yet need I say that those expressions will be heard with unconcern in *the theatre* by those whose delicacy is most offended by some expression in the Bible? There are things infinitely more offensive to delicacy in Byron, and Moore, and even Burns, than there are in the Scriptures; and yet are these not read without a murmur by those who make the loudest complaints of the slightest departure from delicacy in the Bible? 3. There is another remark to be made in regard to this. Isaiah is not at all responsible for the indelicacy of the language here. He is simply a historian. He did not *say* it; nor is he responsible for it. If there is indelicacy in it, it is not in *recording* it, but in *saying* it; and the responsibility is on Rabshakeh. If Isaiah undertook to make a record of an important transaction, what right

13 Then Rabshakeh stood, and
cried with [a] a loud voice in the Jews'
language, and said, Hear ye the
words of the [b] great king, the king
of Assyria.
14 Thus saith the king, Let not
Hezekiah deceive you: for he shall
not be able to deliver you.
15 Neither [c] let Hezekiah make
you trust in the LORD, saying,
The LORD will surely deliver us:
this city shall not be delivered into
the hand of the king of Assyria.
16 Hearken not to Hezekiah:
for thus saith the king of Assyria,
Make [1] *an agreement* with me *by* a
present, and come out to me: and
eat ye every one of his vine, [d] and
every one of his fig-tree, and drink
ye every one the waters of his own
cistern;

[a] Ps.17.10-13. [b] Ps.82.6,7; Dan.4.37. [c] Ps.71.10,11.

1 *with me a blessing*, or, *seek my favour by a present.*
[d] Zech.3.10.

had he to abridge it, or contract it, or to make it different from what it was? 4. And again: it was of importance to give the *true character* of the attack which was made on Jerusalem. The coming of Sennacherib was attended with pride, and insolence, and blasphemy; and it was important to state the true character of the transaction, and to record *just what was said and done.* Hence Isaiah, as a faithful historian, recorded the coming of the Assyrians; the expressions of their haughtiness, insolence, and pride; their vain boasting, and their reproaches of JEHOVAH; and for the same reason he has recorded the gross and indelicate *language* which they used to add to the trials of the Jews. Let him who *used* the language, and not him who *recorded* it, bear the blame.

13. *Then Rabshakeh stood.* Indicating the posture of a man who intends to speak to them at a distance. ¶ *And cried with a loud voice.* So that those on the wall could hear. ¶ *The words of the king,* &c. (see Note on ver. 4.)

14. *Let not Hezekiah deceive you.* By inducing you to put your trust in JEHOVAH or in himself, or with promises that you will be delivered. ¶ *Not be able to deliver you.* In 2 Kings xviii. 29, it is added, 'out of his hand;' but the sense is substantially the same.

15. *Make you trust in the* LORD. Rabshakeh knew that Hezekiah was professedly devoted to JEHOVAH, and that he would endeavour to induce the people to trust in him. The Jews had now no other refuge but God, and as long as they put their confidence there, even Rabshakeh knew that it was hazardous to attempt to take and destroy their city. It was his policy, therefore, first to endeavour to undermine their reliance on God, before he could have any hope of success. The enemies of God's people cannot succeed in their designs against them until they can unsettle their confidence in Him.

16. *Hearken not to Hezekiah.* Do not listen to his entreaties to confide in him, and in JEHOVAH; do not unite with him in endeavouring to make any resistance or opposition to us. ¶ *Make* an agreement *with me* by *a present.* The LXX. read this, Εἰ βούλεσθε εὐλογηθῆναι—'If you wish to be blessed, or happy, come out to me.' The Hebrew is literally, 'Make with me a blessing' (בְּרָכָה). The idea of its being done 'by a present,' is not in the Hebrew text. The word 'blessing' here probably means the same as *peace.* 'Make peace with me,' perhaps because peace was regarded as a blessing; and perhaps the word is used with a reference to one of the significations of בָּרַךְ, which is *to kneel down,* and this word may refer to their *kneeling down;* that is, to their offering allegiance to the king of Assyria. The former is, however, the more probable sense, that the word means *peace,* because this was an evident blessing, or would be the source of rich blessings to them. It is not, however, used in this sense elsewhere in the Bible. The Chaldee renders it, 'Make peace (שְׁלָמָא) with me.' ¶ *And come out to me.* Surrender yourselves to me. It is evident, however, that he did not mean that he would *then* remove them from their city and country, but he demanded a surrender, intending to come and re-

17 Until [a] I come and take you
away to a land like your own land,
a land of corn and wine, a land of
bread and vineyards.

18 *Beware* lest Hezekiah persuade you, saying, The LORD will
deliver us: [b] Hath any of the gods
of the nations delivered his land
out of the hand of the king of Assyria?

19 Where *are* the gods of Hamath and Arphad? where *are* the
gods of Sepharvaim? and have

[a] Prov.12.10. [b] Dan.3.15.

move them at some other period (ver. 17). ¶ *And eat ye every one of his own vine.* An emblem of safety, when every man might be permitted to partake of the fruit of his own labour. All that he now professed to desire was, that they should surrender the city, and give up their means of defence, and *then* he would leave them in security and quietness, *until* it should please his master to come and remove them to a land as fertile as their own. ¶ *And drink ye every one.* Another emblem of security and happiness. This promise was made to induce them to surrender. On the one hand, he threatened them with the dreadful evils of famine if they refused and allowed their city to be besieged (ver. 12); and on the other, he promised them, for a time at least, a quiet and secure residence in their own city, and then a removal to a land not inferior to their own.

17. *Until I come.* These are the words of the king of Assyria delivered by Rabshakeh. It was proposed that they should remain safely in Jerusalem until Sennacherib should himself come and remove them to his own land. He was now engaged in the siege of Lachish (ver. 2), and it is probable that he purposed to take some other of the unsubdued towns in that part of Palestine. ¶ *And take you away.* It was common for conquerors in ancient times to remove a vanquished people from their own country. They did this either by sending them forth in colonies to people some unsettled region, or by removing the body of them to the land of the conqueror. This was done for various purposes. It was sometimes to make slaves of them; sometimes for the purposes of triumph; but more commonly to secure them from revolt. In this manner the ten tribes were removed from the kingdom of Samaria; and thus also the Jews were carried to Babylon. Suetonius says (ch. xxi.) of Augustus, that he removed the Suevi and the Sicambri into Gaul, and stationed them on the Rhine. The same thing was also practised in Egypt, for the purpose of securing the people from revolt (Gen. xlvii. 21). ¶ *A land like your own land.* A fertile land, abounding in the same productions as your own. ¶ *And wine.* Palestine was celebrated for the vine. The idea is, that in the land to which he would remove them, they should not want.

18. *Hath any of the gods of the nations,* &c. This is said to show them the impossibility, as he supposed, of being delivered from the arm of the king of Assyria. He had conquered all before him, and not even the gods of the nations had been able to rescue the lands where they were worshipped from the hands of the victorious invader. He *inferred,* therefore, that JEHOVAH, the God of Palestine, could not save their land.

19. *Where* are *the gods of Hamath,* &c. In regard to these places, see Notes on ch. x. 9–11. ¶ *Where* are *the gods of Sepharvaim?* Sepharvaim was probably in Mesopotamia. Ptolemy mentions a city there of the name of *Sipphara,* as the most southern city of Mesopotamia, which is probably the same. It is evident that it was in the vicinity of Hamath and Arphad, and these are known to have been in Mesopotamia. When Shalmaneser carried Israel away captive from Samaria, he sent colonies of people into Palestine in their stead, among whom were the Sepharvaim (2 Kings xvii. 24, 31). ¶ *And have they delivered Samaria* (see Note on ch. x. 11). The author of the Books of Chronicles expresses this in a more summary manner, and says, that Rabshakeh joined JEHOVAH with the gods of the nations in the same language of reproach: 'And he

they delivered Samaria out [a] of my
hand?

20 Who *are they* among all the
gods [b] of these lands that have delivered their land out of my hand,
that the LORD should deliver Jerusalem out of my hand?

21 But they held their peace,
and answered him not a word: for
the king's commandment was, saying, Answer him [c] not.

22 Then came Eliakim the son
of Hilkiah, that *was* over the household, and Shebna the scribe, and
Joah the son of Asaph, the recorder, to Hezekiah with *their*
clothes rent, and told him the
words of Rabshakeh.

a 2 Ki.18.10. b ch.37.18,19; 45.16,17. c Prov.26.4.

spake against the God of Jerusalem, as against the gods of the people of the earth, which were the work of the hands of man' (2 Chron. xxxii. 19).

HAMATH, VIEW OF THE CITY AND AQUEDUCT.—From Laborde's Syria.

21. *But they held their peace.* Hezekiah had commanded them not to answer. They were simply *to hear* what Rabshakeh had to propose, and to report to him, that he might decide on what course to pursue. It was a case also in which it was every way proper that they should be silent. There was so much insolence, self-confidence, blasphemy, the proposals were so degrading, and the claims were so arrogant, that it was not proper that they should enter into conference, or listen a moment to the terms proposed. Their minds also were so horror-stricken with the language of insolence and blasphemy, and their hearts so pained by the circumstances of the city, that they would not feel like replying to him.—There *are* circumstances when it is proper to maintain a profound silence in the presence of revilers and blasphemers, and when we should withdraw from them, and go and spread the case before the LORD. This was done here (ch. xxxvii. 1), and the result showed that this was the course of wisdom.

22. *With* their *clothes rent.* This was a common mark of grief among the Jews (see 2 Sam iii. 21; 1 Kings xxi. 27; Ezra ix. 3; Job i. 20; ii. 12; Jer. xxxvi. 24; and Notes on Matt. xxvi. 65; Acts xiv. 14). The *causes* of their griefs were the insolence and arrogance of Rabshakeh; the proposal to surrender the city; the threatening of the siege on the one hand, and of the removal on the other, and the blasphemy of the name of their God, and the reproach of the king. All these things filled their hearts with grief, and they hastened to make report to Hezekiah.

CHAPTER XXXVII.

ANALYSIS.

THIS chapter contains a continuation of the historical narrative commenced in the previous chapter. Hezekiah went with expressions of grief to the temple, to spread the cause of his distress before the Lord (1). He sent an embassage to Isaiah to ask his counsel in the time of the general distress (2–5). Isaiah replied that he should not be afraid of the Assyrian, for that he should soon be destroyed (6, 7). The return of Rabshakeh to Sennacherib (8). Sennacherib heard that Tirhakah, king of Ethiopia, was preparing to make war upon him, and sent another embassay, with substantially the same message as the former, to induce him to surrender (9–13). Hezekiah having read the letter which he sent, went again to the temple, and spread it before the Lord (14). His prayer is recorded (15–20). Isaiah, in answer to his prayer, reproves the pride and arrogance of Sennacherib, and gives the assurance that Jerusalem shall be safe, and that the Assyrian shall be destroyed (21–35). The chapter closes with an account of the destruction of the army of the Assyrians, and the death of Sennacherib (36–38).

AND [a] it came to pass when king
Hezekiah heard *it*, that he
rent [b] his clothes, and covered himself with sackcloth, and went [c] into
the house of the LORD.
2 And he sent Eliakim, who *was*
over the household, and Shebna
the scribe, and the elders of the
priests, covered with [d] sackcloth,
unto Isaiah the prophet the son of
Amoz.
3 And they said unto him, Thus
saith Hezekiah, This day *is* a day
of [e] trouble, and of rebuke, [f] and of
blasphemy: [1] for the children are
come to the birth, and *there* [g] *is* not
strength to bring forth.

[a] 2 Ki.19.1,&c. [b] Job 1.20. [c] ver. 14. [d] Joel 1.13. [e] Ps.50.15. [f] ch.25.8; Rev.3.19. [1] or, *provocation.* [g] ch.66.9.

CHAPTER XXXVII.

1. *When king Hezekiah heard* it. Heard the account of the words of Rabshakeh (ch. xxxvi. 22). ¶ *That he rent his clothes* (see Note on ch. xxxvi. 22). ¶ *He covered himself with sackcloth* (see Note on ch. iii. 24). ¶ *And went into the house of the* LORD. Went up to the temple to spread out the case before JEHOVAH (ver. 14). This was in accordance with the usual habit of Hezekiah; and it teaches us that when we are environed with difficulties or danger, and when the name of our God is blasphemed, we should go and spread out our feelings before God, and seek his aid.

2. *And he sent Eliakim* (see Note on ch. xxxvi. 3). ¶ *And the elders of the priests.* It was a case of deep importance, and one that pertained in a special manner to the interests of religion; and he, therefore, selected the most respectable embassage that he could to present the case to the prophet. ¶ *Covered with sackcloth.* Religion had been insulted. The God whom the priests served had been blasphemed, and the very temple was threatened, and it was proper that the *priests* should go with the habiliments of mourning. ¶ *Unto Isaiah.* It was customary on occasions of danger to consult prophets, as those who had direct communication with God, and seek counsel from them. Thus Balak sent messengers to Balaam to consult him in a time of perplexity (Num. xxii. 5, *sq.*); thus Jehoshaphat and the king of Israel consulted Micaiah in time of danger from Syria (1 Kings xxii. 1–13); thus Ahaziah, when sick, sent to consult Elijah (2 Kings i. 1–9); and thus Josiah sent an embassage to Huldah the prophetess to inquire in regard to the book which was found in the temple of the Lord (2 Kings xxii. 14.)

3. *This* is *a day of rebuke.* This may refer either to the reproaches of Rabshakeh, or more probably to the fact that Hezekiah regarded the LORD as *rebuking* his people for their sins. The word which is here used (תּוֹכֵחָה), means more properly *chastisement* or *punishment* (Ps. cxlix. 7; Hos. v. 9). ¶ *And of blasphemy.* Marg. 'Provocation.' The word here used (נְאָצָה), means properly *reproach* or *contumely;* and the sense is, that God and his cause had been vilified by Rabshakeh, and it was proper to appeal to him to vindicate the honour of his own name (ver. 4). ¶ *For the children are come,* &c. The meaning of this figure is plain. There was

4 It may be the LORD thy God
will hear the words of Rabshakeh,
whom the king of Assyria his
master hath sent to reproach [a] the
living God, and will reprove the
words which the LORD thy God
hath heard: wherefore lift up *thy*
prayer for the [b] remnant that is
left.[1]
5 So the servants of king Hezekiah came to Isaiah.

[a] ver.23.24; ch.51.7,8. [b] Ro.9.27. [1] *found.*

6 And Isaiah said unto them,
Thus shall ye say unto your master,
Thus saith the LORD, Be not afraid
of [c] the words that thou hast heard,
wherewith the servants of the king
of Assyria have blasphemed me.
7 Behold, I will [2] send a blast
upon him, and he shall hear a
rumour, and return to his own
land; and I will cause him to fall
by the sword in his own land.

[c] ch.43.1,2; 51.12,13.
[2] or, *put a spirit into him;* 1 Ki.22.23.

---

the highest danger, and need of aid. It was as in childbirth in which the pains had been protracted, the strength exhausted, and where there was most imminent danger in regard to the mother and the child. So Hezekiah said there was the most imminent danger in the city of Jerusalem. They had made all possible preparations for defence. And now, in the most critical time, they felt their energies exhausted, their strength insufficient for their defence, and they needed the interposition of God.

4. *It may be the* LORD *thy God.* The God whom thou dost serve, and in whose name and by whose authority thou dost exercise the prophetic office. ¶ *Will hear the words.* Will come forth and vindicate himself in regard to the language of reproach and blasphemy which has been used. See a similar use of the word 'hear' in Ex. ii. 24; iii. 7. ¶ *To reproach the living God.* The revilings of Rabshakeh were really directed against the true God. The reproach of the 'living God' consisted in comparing him to idols, and saying that he was no more able to defend Jerusalem than the idol-gods had been able to defend their lands (see Note on ch. xxxvi. 18). The phrase 'the *living* God' is often applied to JEHOVAH in contradistinction from idols, which were mere blocks of wood or stone. ¶ *For the remnant that is left.* For those who survive; or probably for those parts of the land, including Jerusalem, that have not fallen into the hands of the Assyrian. Sennacherib had taken many towns, but there were many also that had not yet been subdued by him.

6. *Wherewith the servants,* &c Heb. נַעֲרֵי—The 'youth,' or the young men. The word properly denotes boys, youths, young men; and is used here probably by way of disparagement, in contradistinction from an embassy that would be truly respectable, made up of aged men. ¶ *Have blasphemed me.* God regarded these words as spoken against himself, and he would vindicate his own honour and name.

7. *Behold, I will send a blast upon him.* Marg. 'Put a spirit into him.' The word rendered 'blast' (רוּחַ) is commonly rendered 'spirit.' It *may* denote breath, air, soul, or spirit. There is no reason to think that the word is here used in the sense of *blast* of wind, as our translators seem to have supposed. The sense is probably, 'I will infuse into him a spirit of *fear*, by which he shall be alarmed by the rumour which he shall hear, and return to his own land.' The word is often used in this sense (comp. 1 Sam. xvi. 14; see also Isa. xxxi. 8, 9). Gesenius understands it here in the sense of *will* or *disposition.* 'I will change his will or disposition, so that he will return to his own land.' ¶ *And he shall hear a rumour.* The rumour or report here referred to, was doubtless that respecting Tirhakah king of Ethiopia (ver. 9). It was this which would alarm him, and drive him in haste from the cities which he was now besieging, and be the means of expelling him from the land. ¶ *And I will cause him,* &c. This is said in accordance with the usual statements in the Scriptures, that *all* events are under God's providential control (comp. Note on ch. x. 5, 6). ¶ *By the sword in his own land* (see Note on ver. 38).

8 So Rabshakeh returned, and
found the king of Assyria warring
against Libnah: [a] for he had heard
that he was departed from [b] Lachish.
9 And he heard say concerning
Tirhakah king of Ethiopia, He is
come forth to make war with thee.
And when he heard *it*, he sent
messengers to Hezekiah, saying,
10 Thus shall ye speak to Heze-

[a] Num.33.20,21; Jos.21.13; 2 Ch.21.10. [b] Jos.10.31-34.

8. *So Rabshakeh returned.* Returned from Jerusalem to the camp of his master. He had received no answer to his insulting message (ch. xxxvi. 21); he saw there was no prospect that the city would surrender; and he therefore returned again to the camp. ¶ *And found the king of Assyria warring against Libnah.* He had departed from Lachish. Why he had done this is unknown. It is possible that he had taken it, though this is not recorded anywhere in history. Or it is possible that he had found it impracticable to subdue it as speedily as he had desired; and had withdrawn from it for the purpose of subduing other places that would offer a more feeble resistance. Libnah was a city in the south of Judah (Josh. xv. 42), given to the priests, and declared a city of refuge (1 Chron. vi. 54, 57). Eusebius and Jerome say it was in the district of Eleutheropolis (Calmet). It was about ten miles to the north-west of Lachish. This city was taken by Joshua, and all its inhabitants put to the sword. After taking this, Joshua next assaulted and took Lachish (Josh. x. 29–32).

9. *And he heard say.* The report or rumour referred to in ver. 7. In what way he heard this is not intimated. It is probable that the preparations which Tirhakah had made, were well known to the surrounding regions, and that he was already on his march against Sennacherib. ¶ *Tirhakah.* This king, who, by Eusebius and by most ancient writers, is called Ταρακὸς (*Tarakos*), was a celebrated conqueror, and had subdued Egypt to himself. He reigned over Egypt eighteen years. When Sennacherib marched into Egypt, Sevechus or Sethon was on the throne. Sennacherib having laid siege to Pelusium, Tirhakah came to the aid of the city, and, in consequence of his aid, Sennacherib was compelled to raise the siege and returned to Palestine, and laid siege to Lachish. Tirhakah succeeded Sevechus in Egypt, and was the third and last of the Ethiopian kings that reigned over that country. He probably took advantage of the distracted state that succeeded the death of Sevechus, and secured the crown for himself. This was, however, after the death of Sennacherib. The capital which he occupied was Thebes (see Prideaux's *Connection*, vol. i. pp. 141, 145, 149. Ed. 1815). As he was celebrated as a conqueror, and as he had driven Sennacherib from Pelusium and from Egypt, we may see the cause of the alarm of Sennacherib when it was rumoured that he was about to follow him into Palestine, and to make war on him there. ¶ *He is come forth.* He has made preparations, and is on his way. ¶ *He sent messengers,* &c. With letters or despatches (ver. 14). Hezekiah was probably ignorant of the approach of Tirhakah, or at all events Sennacherib would suppose that he was ignorant of it; and as Sennacherib knew that there would be no hope that Hezekiah would yield if he knew that Tirhakah was approaching to make war on him, he seems to have resolved to anticipate the intelligence, and to see if it were possible to induce him to surrender. He, therefore, sent substantially the same message as before, and summoned him to capitulate.

10. *Let not thy God deceive thee.* The similar message which had been sent by Rabshakeh (ch. xxxvi. 14, 15) had been sent mainly *to the people* to induce them not to put confidence in Hezekiah, as if he would deceive them by leading them to rely on the aid of JEHOVAH. As that had failed, he, as a last resort, sent a similar message to Hezekiah himself, designed to alienate *his mind* from God, and assuring him that resistance would be vain. To convince him, he referred him (ver. 11–13) to the conquests of the Assyrians,

kiah king of Judah, saying, Let
not thy God, in whom thou trustest, deceive thee, saying, Jerusalem
shall not be given into the hand of
the king of Assyria.
11 Behold, thou hast heard
what the kings of Assyria have
done to [a]all lands by destroying
them utterly; and shalt thou be
delivered?
12 Have the gods of the nations
delivered them which my fathers
have destroyed, *as* [b]Gozan, and
Haran,[c] and Rezeph, and the
children of [d]Eden which *were* in
Telassar?

a ch.14.17. *b* 2 Ki.17.6; 18.11. *c* Gen.12.4; 28.10. *d* Amos 1.5

---

and assured him that it would be impossible to resist a nation that had subdued so many others. He had it not in his power to add *Egypt* to the list of subdued kingdoms, or it would have been done.

11. *And shalt thou be delivered?* How will it be possible for you to stand out against the conquerors of the world?

12. *My fathers.* My predecessors on the throne. ¶ *Gozan.* This was a region or country in the northern part of Mesopotamia, and on the river Chaboras. There was a river of the name of *Gozan* in Media, which ran through the province, and gave it its name. The river fell probably into the Chaboras. This region is known to have been under the dominion of Assyria, for Shalmaneser, when he had subdued the ten tribes, carried them away beyond the Euphrates to a country bordering on the river Gozan (2 Kings xvii. 6). According to Gesenius, the river which is referred to, is the Chaboras itself. He translates the passage in 2 Kings xvii. 6, thus: 'And placed them in Chaleitis (Halah), and on the Chabor (Habor), a river of Gozan, and in the cities of the Medes.' According to this, the river was the Chaboras, the Chabor of Ezekiel, and the region was situated on the Chaboras. This river falls into the Euphrates from the east. Ptolemy calls the region lying between the Chaboras and Laocoras by the name of *Gauzanitis,* which is doubtless the same as the Hebrew *Gozan.* Gozan is usually mentioned in connection with cities of Mesopotamia (2 Kings xix. 42; 1 Chron. v. 26). ¶ *And Haran.* This was a city of Mesopotamia, to which Abraham went after he left Ur of the Chaldees. His father died here; and from this place he was called to go into the land of promise (Gen. xi. 31, 32; comp. Notes on Acts vii. 4). It is now called *Harran,* and is situated in lat. 36° 52′ N.; lon. 39° 5′ E., in a flat and sandy plain, and is only peopled by a few wandering Arabs, who select it as the place of residence on account of the delicious waters it contains. It belonged by conquest to the Assyrian empire. ¶ *And Rezeph.* According to Abulfeda, there were many towns of this name. One, however, was more celebrated than the others, and is probably the one here referred to. It was situated about a day's journey west of the Euphrates, and is mentioned by Ptolemy by the name of Ῥησαφα (*Resapha*). ¶ *And the children of Eden.* Eden was evidently a country well known in the time of Isaiah, and was, doubtless, the tract *within* which man was placed when he was created. The garden or Paradise was *in* Eden, and was not properly itself called Eden (Gen. ii. 8). It is probable that Eden was a region or tract of country of considerable extent. Its situation has been a subject of anxious inquiry. It is not proper here to go into an examination of this subject. It is evident from the passage before us that it was either in Mesopotamia, or in the neighbourhood of that country, since it is mentioned in connection with cities and towns of that region. It is mentioned by Amos (B.C. 787), as a country then well known, and as a part of Syria, not far from Damascus:

I will break also the bar of Damascus,
And cut off the inhabitant from the plain of
  Aven,
And him that holdeth the sceptre *from the house
  of* Eden,
And the people of Syria shall go into captivity
  to Kir,
Saith the Lord. Amos i. 5.

In Isa. li. 3, Eden is referred to as a

13 Where *is* the king of [a] Hamath,
and the king of Arphad, and the
king of the city of Sepharvaim,
Hena, and Ivah?
14 And Hezekiah received the
letter from the hand of the messengers,
and read it: and Hezekiah
went up [b] unto the house of
the LORD, and spread it before the
LORD.
15 And Hezekiah prayed unto
the LORD, saying,
16 O LORD of hosts, God of
Israel, that dwellest [c] *between* the
cherubims, thou [d] *art* the God, *even*
thou [e] alone, of all the kingdoms of
the earth: thou hast made heaven
and earth.

a ch.x.9; Jer.49.23. b ver.1; Joel 2.17-20. c Ex.25.22; Ps.80.1; 99.1. d ch.43.10,11. e Ps.86.10.

country well known, and as distinguished for its fertility:

> For JEHOVAH shall comfort Zion;
> He will comfort all her waste places,
> And he will make her wilderness *like Eden*,
> And her desert like the garden of JEHOVAH.

Thus also in Ezek. xxvii. 23, we find Eden mentioned in connection with Haran and Canneh. Canneh was probably the same as Calneh (Gen. x. 10), the Calno of Isaiah (ch. x. 9), and was, doubtless, situated in Mesopotamia, since it is joined with cities that are known to have been there (comp. also Ezek. xxxi. 9, 16, 18). All these passages demonstrate that there was such a country, and prove also that it was either in Mesopotamia, or in a country adjacent to Mesopotamia. It is not, however, possible now to designate its exact boundaries. ¶ *In Telassar.* This place is nowhere else mentioned in the Scriptures. Nothing, therefore, is known of its situation. The connection demands that it should be in Mesopotamia. The names of ancient places were so often lost or changed that it is often impossible to fix their exact locality.

13. *The king of Hamath* (see Note on ch. xxxvi. 19). ¶ *Hena and Ivah.* Hena is mentioned in 2 Kings xviii. 34; xix. 13. It was evidently in Mesopotamia, and was probably the same which was afterwards called *Ana*, situated near a ford of the Euphrates. The situation of Ivah is not certainly known. It was under the Assyrian dominion, and was one of the places from which colonists were brought to Samaria (2 Kings xvii. 24, 31). Michaelis supposes that it was between Berytus and Tripoli, but was under the dominion of the Assyrians.

14. *And Hezekiah received the letter.* Heb. 'Letters' (*plural*). It is not mentioned in the account of the embassy (ver. 9), that a letter was sent, but it is not probable that an embassage would be sent to a monarch without a written document. ¶ *Went up into the house of the* LORD. The temple (ver. 1). ¶ *And spread it before the* LORD. Perhaps unrolled the document there, and spread it out; or perhaps it means simply that he spread out the contents of the letter, that is, made mention of it in his prayer. Hezekiah had no other resource. He was a man of God; and in his trouble he looked to God for aid. He, therefore, before he formed any plan, went up to the temple, and laid his case before God. What an example for all monarchs and rulers! And what an example for all the people of God, in times of perplexity!

16. *O* LORD *of hosts* (see Note on ch. i. 9). ¶ *That dwellest* between *the cherubims.* On the cherubim, see Note on ch. xiv. 13. The reference here is doubtless to the fact that the symbol of the Divine presence in the temple—the Shechinah (from שָׁכַן *shâkhân, to dwell, to inhabit;* so called because it was the symbol of God's *dwelling* with his people or *inhabiting* the temple)—rested on the cover of the ark in the temple. Hence God is frequently represented as dwelling between the cherubim (Ex. xxv. 22; Ps. lxxx. 1; xcix. 1). On the whole subject of the cherubim, the reader may consult an article in the *Quarterly Christian Spectator* for September 1836. ¶ *Thou* art *the God.* The only God (ch. xliii. 10, 11). ¶ Even *thou alone.* There is none besides thee —a truth which is often affirmed in the Scriptures (Deut. xxxii. 39; Ps. lxxxvi. 10; 1 Cor. viii. 4). ¶ *Thou hast made heaven and earth.* It was on the ground of this power and universal

17 Incline [a]thine ear, O Lord,
and hear; open thine eyes, [b] O
Lord, and see: and hear all the
words of Sennacherib, which hath
sent to reproach the living God.
18 Of a truth, Lord, the kings
of Assyria have laid waste all the
nations, [1] and their countries,
19 And have [2] cast their gods
into the fire: for they *were* no gods,
but [c] the work of men's hands, wood
and stone: therefore they have destroyed them.
20 Now, therefore, O Lord our
God, save us from his hand, that
all the kingdoms of the earth may
know [d]that thou *art* the Lord, *even*
thou only.

a Dan.9.18. b Job 36.7. 1 *lands.* 2 *given.*
c Ps.115.4,&c.; ch.40.19,20; 41.7; 44.9,&c. d ch.42.8; Ps.46.10.

dominion that Hezekiah pleaded that God would interpose.

17. *Incline thine ear.* This is evidently language taken from what occurs among men. When they are desirous of hearing distinctly, they incline the ear or apply it close to the speaker. Similar language is not unfrequently used in the Scriptures as applicable to God (2 Kings xix. 16; Ps. lxxxvi. 1; xxxi. 2; lxxxviii. 2; Dan. ix. 18). ¶ *Open thine eyes.* This is similar language applied to God, derived from the fact that when we wish to see an object, the eyes are fixed upon it (comp. Job xiv. 3; xxvii. 19). ¶ *And hear all the words.* That is, attend to their words, and inflict suitable punishment. This was the burden of the prayer of Hezekiah, that God would vindicate his own honour, and save his name from reproach. ¶ *Which he hath sent.* In the letters which he had sent to Hezekiah, as well as the words which he had sent to the people by Rabshakeh (ch. xxxvi. 18–20). ¶ *To reproach the living God* (see Note on ver. 4).

18. *Of a truth.* It is as he has said, that all the nations had been subjected to the arms of the Assyrian. He now intends to add Jerusalem to the number of vanquished cities and kingdoms, and to boast that he has subdued the nation under the protection of Jehovah, as he had done the nations under the protection of idol-gods. ¶ *Have laid waste all the nations.* Heb. as Marg. 'All the lands.' But this is evidently an elliptical form of expression, meaning all the inhabitants or people of the lands. In 2 Kings xix. 17, it is thus expressed: 'The kings of Assyria have destroyed the nations and their lands.'

19. *And have cast their gods into the fire.* This appears to have been the usual policy of the Assyrians and Babylonians. It was contrary to the policy which the Romans afterwards pursued, for they admitted the gods of other nations among their own, and even allowed them to have a place in the Pantheon. Their design seems not to have been to alienate the feelings of the vanquished, but to make them feel that they were a part of the same people. They supposed that a vanquished people would be conciliated with the idea that their gods were admitted to participate in the honours of those which were worshipped by the conquerors of the world. But the policy of the Eastern conquerors was different. They began usually by removing the people themselves whom they had subdued, to another land (see Note on ch. xxxvi. 17). They thus intended to alienate their minds as much as possible from their own country. They laid everything waste by fire and sword, and thus destroyed their homes, and all the objects of their attachment. They destroyed their temples, their groves, and their household gods. They well knew that the civil policy of the nation was founded *in religion*, and that, to subdue them effectually, it was necessary to abolish their religion. Which was the wisest policy, may indeed admit of question. Perhaps in each case the policy was well adapted to the particular end which was had in view. ¶ *For they* were *no gods.* They were not truly gods, and therefore they had no power of resistance, and it was easy to destroy them.

20. *That all the kingdoms of the earth may know.* Since he has been able to subdue all others; and since Judea alone, the land under the pro-

21 Then Isaiah the son of Amoz sent unto Hezekiah, saying, Thus saith the LORD God of Israel, Whereas thou hast prayed [a] to me against Sennacherib king of Assyria:

22 This *is* the word which the LORD hath spoken concerning him; The virgin, the daughter of Zion, hath despised [b] thee, *and* laughed thee to scorn; the daughter of Jerusalem hath shaken her head at thee.

23 Whom hast thou reproached and blasphemed? and against whom hast thou exalted *thy* voice, and lifted up thine eye on high? *even* against the Holy One of Israel.

[a] Prov.15.29; Lu.18.1. [b] Ps.31.18; 46.1,2.

---

tection of JEHOVAH, would be saved, all the nations would know that it could not be by the power of an idol. The desire of Hezekiah, therefore, was not primarily that of his own personal safety or the safety of his kingdom. It was that JEHOVAH might vindicate his great and holy name from reproach, and that the world might know that he was the only true God. A supreme regard to the glory of God influenced this pious monarch in his prayers, and we have here a beautiful model of the object which we should have in view when we come before God. It is not primarily that we may be saved; it is not, as the leading motive, that our friends or that the world may be saved; it is *that the name of God may be honoured.* This motive of prayer is one that is with great frequency presented in the Bible (comp. ch. xlii. 8; xliii. 10, 13, 25; Deut. xxxii. 39; Ps. xlvi. 10; lxxxiii. 18; Neh. ix. 6; Dan. ix. 18, 19).—Perhaps there could have been furnished no more striking proof that JEHOVAH was the true God, than would be by the defeat of Sennacherib. No other nation had been able to resist the Assyrian arms. The great power of that empire was now concentrated in the single army of Sennacherib. He was coming with great confidence of success. He was approaching the city devoted to JEHOVAH—the city where the temple was, and the city and people that were everywhere understood to be under his protection. The affairs of the world had arrived at a crisis; and the time had come when the great JEHOVAH could strike a blow which would be felt on all nations, and carry the terror of his name, and the report of his power throughout the earth. Perhaps this was one of the main motives of the destruction of that mighty army. God intended that his power should be felt, and that monarchs and people that arrayed themselves against him, and blasphemed him, should have a striking demonstration that he was God, and that none of the devices of his enemies could succeed.

21. *Whereas thou hast prayed.* Because thou hast come to me instead of relying on thy own resources and strength. In 2 Kings xix. 20, it is, 'That which thou hast prayed to me against Sennacherib, king of Assyria, I have heard.'

22. *The virgin, the daughter of Zion.* Jerusalem (see Note on ch. i. 8; comp. Note on ch. xxiii. 12). The parallelism in this and the following verses shows that the poetic form of speech is here introduced. ¶ *Hast despised thee.* That is, it is secure from thy contemplated attack. The idea is, that Jerusalem would exult over the ineffectual attempts of Sennacherib to take it, and over his complete overthrow. ¶ *Hath laughed thee to scorn.* Will make thee an object of derision. ¶ *Hath shaken her head at thee.* This is an indication of contempt and scorn (comp. Ps. xxii. 7; cix. 25; Jer. xviii. 16; Zeph. ii. 15; Matt. xxvii. 39).

23. *Whom hast thou reproached?* Not an idol. Not one who has no power to take vengeance, or to defend the city under his protection, but the living God. ¶ *Exalted thy voice.* That is, by thy messenger. Thou hast spoken in a loud, confident tone; in the language of reproach and threatening. ¶ *And lifted up thine eyes on high.* To lift up the eyes is an indication of haughtiness and pride. He had evinced arrogance in his manner, and he was yet to learn that it was against the living and true God.

24 By [1] thy servants hast thou reproached the LORD, and hast said, By the multitude of my chariots am I come up to the height of the mountains, to the sides of Lebanon; and I will cut down the [2] tall cedars thereof, *and* the choice fir-trees thereof: and I will enter into the height of his border, [3] *and* the forest of his Carmel.

1 *the hand of thy.*

2 *tallness of the cedars thereof, and the choice of the fir-trees thereof.* 3 or, and *his fruitful field.*

24. *By thy servants.* Heb. 'By the hand of thy servants.' That is, by Rabshakeh (ch. xxxvi.), and by those whom he had now sent to Hezekiah with letters (ver. 9, 14). ¶ *And hast said.* Isaiah does not here quote the precise *words* which Rabshakeh or the other messengers had used, but quotes the substance of what had been uttered, and expresses the real feelings and intentions of Sennacherib. ¶ *By the multitude of my chariots.* The word 'chariots' here denotes *war-chariots* (see Notes on ch. ii. 7; lxvi. 20). ¶ *To the height of the mountains.* Lebanon is here particularly referred to. Chariots were commonly used, as cavalry was, in plains. But it is probable that Lebanon was accessible by chariots drawn by horses. ¶ *To the sides of Lebanon.* On the situation of Lebanon, see Notes on ch. x. 34; xxix. 17. Sennacherib is represented as having carried desolation to Lebanon, and as having cut down its stately trees (see Note on

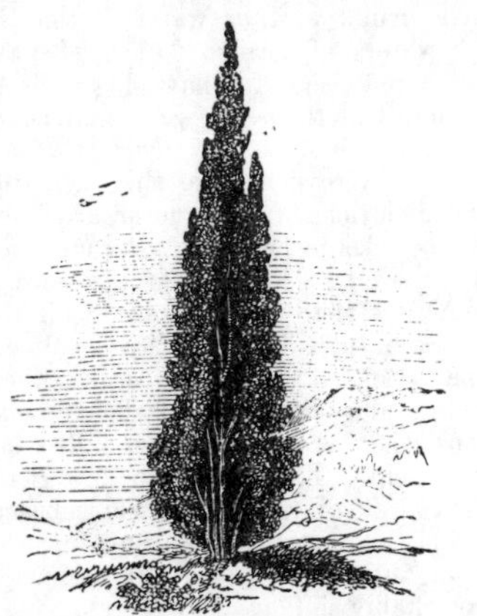

CYPRESS TREE (*Cupressus Sempervirens*).

ch. xxxiii. 9). ¶ *I will cut down the tall cedars thereof.* Marg. 'The tallness of the cedars thereof.' The boast of Sennacherib was that he would strip it of its beauty and ornament; that is, that he would lay the land waste. ¶ And *the choice fir-trees thereof* (see Note on ch. xiv. 8). The LXX. render it, Υϖαϱίσσου—'The beauty of the cypress.' The word here denotes the *cypress,* a tree resembling the white cedar. It grew on Lebanon, and, together with the cedar, constituted its glory. Its wood, like that of the cedar, was employed for the floors and ceilings of the temple (1 Kings v. 22, 24; vi. 15, 34). It was used for the decks and sheathing of ships (Ezek. xxvii. 5); for spears (Neh. ii. 4); and for musical instruments (2 Sam. vi. 5). ¶ *The height of his border.* The extreme retreats; the furthest part of Lebanon. In 2 Kings xix. 23, it is, 'I will enter the lodgings of his borders;' perhaps referring to the fact that on the ascent to the top of the mountain there was a place for the repose of travellers; a species of inn or caravansera which *bounded* the usual attempts of persons to ascend the mountain. Such a lodging-place on the sides or tops of mountains which are frequently ascended, is not uncommon. ¶ And *the forest of his Carmel.* On the meaning of the word Carmel, see Note on ch. xxix. 17. Here it means, as in that passage, a rich, fertile, and beautiful country. It is known that Lebanon was covered on the top, and far down the sides, with perpetual snow. But there was a region lying on its sides, between the snow and the base of the mountain, that was distinguished for fertility, and that was highly cultivated. This region produced grapes in abundance; and this cultivated part of the mountain, thick set with vines and trees, might be called a beautiful grove. This was doubtless the portion of Lebanon which is here intended. At a distance, this tract on the sides of Lebanon ap-

25 I have digged, and drunk water; and with the sole of my feet have I dried up all the rivers of the [1] besieged places.

1 or, *fenced and closed.*

peared doubtless as a *thicket* of shrubs and trees. The phrase 'garden-forest,' will probably express the sense of the passage. 'After leaving Baalbec, and approaching Lebanon, towering walnut-trees, either singly or in groups, and a rich carpet of verdure, the offspring of numerous streams, give to this charming district the air of an English park, majestically bordered with snow-tipped mountains. At Deir-el-Akmaar, the ascent begins—winding among dwarf oaks, hawthorns, and a great variety of shrubs and flowers. A deep bed of snow had now to be crossed, and the horses sunk or slipped at every moment. To ride was impracticable, and to walk dangerous, for the melting snow penetrated our boots, and our feet were nearly frozen. An hour and a half brought us to the cedars.'—(Hogg.)

25. *I have digged.* That is, I have digged wells. This was regarded among eastern nations as an important achievement. It was difficult to find water, even by digging, in sandy deserts; and in a country abounding with rocks, it was an enterprise of great difficulty to sink a well. Hence the possession of a well became a valuable property, and was sometimes the occasion of contention between neighbouring tribes (Gen. xxvi. 20). Hence also to stop up the wells of water, by throwing in rocks or sand, became one of the most obvious ways of distressing an enemy, and was often resorted to (Gen. xxvi. 15, 18; 2 Kings iii. 19, 25). To dig wells, or to furnish water in abundance to a people, became also an achievement which was deemed worthy to be recorded in the history of kings and princes (2 Chron. xxvi. 10). Many of the most stupendous and costly of the works of the Romans in the capital of their empire, and in the principal towns of their provinces, consisted in building aqueducts to bring water from a distance into a city. An achievement like this I understand Sennacherib as boasting he had performed; that he had furnished water for the cities and towns of his mighty empire; that he had accomplished what was deemed so difficult, and what required so much expense, as digging wells for his people; and that he had secured them from being stopped up by his enemies, so that he and his people drank of the water in peace. Gesenius, however, understands this as a boast that he had extended the bounds of his empire beyond its original limits, and unto regions that were naturally destitute of water, and where it was necessary to dig wells to supply his armies. Rosenmüller understands it as saying: 'I have passed over, and taken possession of foreign lands.' Drusius regards it as a proverbial saying, meaning 'I have happily and successfully accomplished all that I have undertaken, as he who digs a well accomplishes that which he particularly desires.' Vitringa regards it as saying, 'that to dig wells, and to drink the water of them, is to enjoy the fruit of our labours, to be successful and happy.' But it seems to me that the interpretation above suggested, and which I have not found in any of the commentators before me, is the correct exposition. ¶ *And drunk water.* In 2 Kings xix. 24, it is, 'I have drunk *strange* waters;' that is, the waters of foreign lands. I have conquered them, and have dug wells in them. But the sense is not materially changed. ¶ *And with the sole of my feet.* Expressions like this, denoting the desolations of a conqueror, are found in the classic writers. Perhaps the idea there is, that their armies were so numerous that they drank up all the waters in their march—a strong hyperbole to denote the number of their armies, and the extent of their desolations when even the waters failed before them. Thus Claudian (*De Bello Getico,* 526) introduces Alaric as boasting of his conquests in the same extravagant manner, and in language remarkably similar to this:

Cum cesserit omnis
Obsequiis natura meis. Subsidere nostris
Sub pedibus montes; arescere vidimus amnes—
Fregi Alpes, galeisque Padum victricibus hausi.

26 Hast thou not heard [1] long ago, *how* I have done it; *and* of ancient times, that I have formed it? now have I [a] brought it to pass, that thou shouldest be to lay waste defenced cities *into* ruinous heaps.

27 Therefore their inhabitants *were* [2] of small power, they were dismayed and confounded: they were *as* the grass of the field, and *as* the green herb, *as* the grass on the house-tops, and *as corn* blasted before it be grown up.

1 or, how *I have made it long ago, and formed it of ancient times? should I now bring it to be laid waste,* and *defenced cities* to be *ruinous heaps.*

a ch.10.5,6. 2 *short of hand.*

So Juvenal (*Sat.* x. 176), speaking of the dominion of Xerxes, says:

——credimus altos
Defecisse amnes, epotaque flumina Medo
Prandente.

The boast of drying up streams with the sole of the foot, is intended to convey the idea that he had not only supplied water for his own empire by digging wells, but that he had cut off the supplies of water from the others against whom he had made war. The idea perhaps is, that if such an army as his was, should pass through the streams of a country that they should invade, and should only take away the water that would adhere to the sole or the hollow of the foot on their march, it would dry up all the streams. It is strong hyperbolical language, and is designed to indicate the number of the forces which were under his command. ¶ *Of the besieged places.* Marg. ‘Fenced’ or ‘closed.’ The word rendered ‘rivers’ (יְאֹרֵי), may denote canals, or artificial streams, such as were common in Egypt. In ch. xix. 6, it is rendered ‘brooks,’ and is applied to the artificial canals of Egypt (see Note on that place). The word here rendered ‘besieged places’ (מָצוֹר *mâtzŏr*), may mean distress, straitness (Deut. xxviii. 53); siege (Ezek. iv. 2, 7); mound, bulwark, intrenchment (Deut. xx. 20); or it may be a proper name for Egypt, being one of the forms of the name מִצְרַיִם (*Mitzraim*) or Egypt. The same phrase occurs in ch. xix. 6, where it means Egypt (see Note on that place), and such should be regarded as its meaning here. It alludes to the conquests which Sennacherib is represented as boasting that he had made in Egypt, that he had easily removed obstructions, and destroyed their means of defence. Though he had been repulsed before Pelusium by Tirhakah king of Ethiopia (see Note on ch. xxxvi. 1), yet it is not improbable that he had taken many towns there, and had subdued no small part of the country to himself. In his vain boasting, he would strive to forget his repulse, and would dwell on the ease of conquest, and the facility with which he had removed all obstructions from his way. The whole language of the verse, therefore, is that of a proud and haughty Oriental prince, desirous of proclaiming his conquests, and forgetting his mortifying defeats.

26. *Hast thou not heard.* This is evidently the language of God addressed to Sennacherib. It is designed to state to him that he was under his control; that this was the reason (ver. 27) why the inhabitants of the nations had been unable to resist him; that he was entirely in his hands (ver. 28); and that he would control him as he pleased (ver. 29). ¶ *Long ago* how *I have done it.* You boast that all this is by your own counsel and power. Yet I have done it; *i.e.*, I have purposed, planned, arranged it long ago (comp. ch. xxii. 11). ¶ *That thou shouldest be to lay waste.* I have raised you up for this purpose, and you have been entirely under my control (see Note on ch. x. 5).

27. *Therefore.* Not because you have so great power; but because I have rendered them incapable of resisting you. ¶ Were *of small power.* Heb. ‘Short of hand;’ they were feeble, imbecile, unable to resist you. ¶ *They were dismayed.* Heb. ‘They were broken and ashamed.’ Their spirits sank; they were ashamed of their feeble powers of resistance; and they submitted to the ignominy of a surrender. ¶ *They were* as *the grass of the field.* The same idea is expressed by Sennacherib himself in ch. x. 15, though under a different image (see Note on that verse). The idea here is, as the grass of the

28 But I know thy [1]abode, and
thy going out, and thy coming in,
and thy rage against me.
29 Because thy rage against me,
and thy tumult, is come up into
mine ears, therefore will I put my
hook [a]in thy nose, and my bridle
in thy lips, and I will turn thee
back by the way by which thou
camest.
30 And this *shall be* a sign unto
thee, Ye shall eat this year such as
groweth of itself; and the second
year that which springeth of the
same: and in the third year sow ye,
and reap, and plant vineyards, and
eat the fruit thereof.

1 or, *sitting*. a ch.30.28; Eze.38.4.

field offers no resistance to the march of an army, so it was with the strongly fortified towns in the way of Sennacherib. ¶ As *the grass on the house-tops*. In eastern countries the roofs of houses are always flat. They are made of a mixture of sand, gravel, or earth; and on the houses of the rich there is a firmly constructed flooring made of coals, chalk, gypsum, and ashes, made hard by being beaten or rolled. On these roofs spears of wheat, barley, or grass sometimes spring up, but they are soon withered by the heat of the sun (Ps. cxxix. 6–8). The idea here, therefore, is that of the greatest feebleness. His enemies were not simply like the grass in the field, but they were like the thin, slender, and delicate blade that sprung up in the little earth on the roof of a house, where there was no room for the roots to strike down, and where it soon withered beneath the burning sun. ¶ As corn *blasted before it is grown up*. Before it acquires any strength. The idea in all these phrases is substantially the same—that they were incapable of offering even the feeblest resistance.

28. *But I know*. The language of God. 'I am well acquainted with all that pertains to you. You neither go out to war, nor return, nor abide in your capital without my providential direction' (see Notes on ch. x. 5–7). ¶ *Thy abode*. Marg. 'Sitting.' Among the Hebrews, sitting down, rising up, and going out, were phrases to describe the whole of a man's life and actions (comp. Deut. vi. 7; xxviii. 6; 1 Kings iii. 7; Ps. cxxi. 8). God here says that he knew the place where he dwelt, and he was able to return him again to it, ver. 29. ¶ *And thy rage against me* (see ver. 4).

29. *Because thy rage and thy tumult*. Or rather, thy pride, thy insolence, thy vain boasting. ¶ *Therefore will I put my hook in thy nose*. This is a most striking expression, denoting the complete control which God had over the haughty monarch, and his ability to direct him as he pleased. The *language* is taken from the custom of putting a ring or hook in the nose of a wild animal for the purpose of governing and guiding it. The most violent animals may be thus completely governed, and this is often done with those animals that are fierce and untameable. The Arabs often pursue this course in regard to the camel, and thus have it under entire control. A similar image is used in respect to the king of Egypt (Ezek. xxix. 4). The idea is, that God would control and govern the wild and ambitious spirit of the Assyrian, and that with infinite ease he could conduct him again to his own land. ¶ *And my bridle* (see Note on ch. xxx. 28). ¶ *And I will turn thee back* (see ver. 37).

30. *And this* shall be *a sign unto thee*. It is evident that the discourse here is turned from Sennacherib to Hezekiah. Such transitions, without distinctly indicating them, are common in Isaiah. God had in the previous verses, in the form of a direct personal address, foretold the defeat of Sennacherib, and the confusion of his plans. He here turns and gives to Hezekiah the assurance that Jerusalem would be delivered. On the meaning of the word 'sign,' see Note on ch. vii. 14. Commentators have been much perplexed in the exposition of the passage before us, to know how that which was to occur one, two, or three years after the event, could be a *sign* of the fulfilment of the prophecy. Many have supposed that the year in which this was spoken was a Sabbatic year, in which the lands were not cultivated, but were suffered

to lie still (Lev. xxxv. 2–7); and that the year following was the year of Jubilee, in which also the lands were to remain uncultivated. They suppose that the idea is, that the Jews might be *assured* that they would not experience the evils of famine which they had anticipated from the Assyrians, because the Divine promise gave them assurance of supply in the Sabbatic year, and in the year of Jubilee, and that although their fields had been laid waste by the Assyrian, yet their wants would be supplied, until on the third year they would be permitted in quietness to cultivate their land, and that this would be to them *a sign,* or a token of the Divine interposition. But to this there are two obvious objections—1. There is not the slightest evidence that the year in which Sennacherib besieged Jerusalem was a Sabbatic year, or that the following year was the Jubilee. No mention is made of this in the history, nor is it possible to prove it from any part of the sacred narrative. 2. It is still difficult to see, even if it were so, how that which was to occur two or three years after the event, could be a sign to Hezekiah then of the truth of what Isaiah had predicted. Rosenmüller suggests that the two years in which they are mentioned as sustained by the spontaneous productions of the earth were the two years in which Judea had been already ravaged by Sennacherib, and that the third year was the one in which the prophet was now speaking, and that the prediction means that in that very year they would be permitted to sow and reap. In the explanation of the passage, it is to be observed that the word 'sign' is used in a variety of significations. It may be used as an *indication* of anything unseen (Gen. i. 14); or as a military ensign (Num. ii. 2); or as a sign of something future, an omen (Isa. viii. 18); or as a token. argument, proof (Gen. xvii. 2; Exod. xxxi. 13). It may be used as a sign or token of the truth of a prophecy; that is, when some minor event furnishes a proof that the whole prophecy would be fulfilled (Ex. iii. 12; 1 Sam. ii. 34; x. 7, 9). Or it may be used as a wonder, a prodigy, a miracle (Deut. iv. 34; vi. 22). In the case before us, it seems to mean that, in the events predicted here, Hezekiah would have a token or argument that the land was *completely freed* from the invasion of Sennacherib. Though a considerable part of his army would be destroyed; though the monarch himself would be compelled to flee, yet Hezekiah would not from that fact alone have the assurance that he would not rally his forces, and return to invade the land. There would be every inducement arising from disappointment and the rage of defeat for him to do it. To compose the mind of Hezekiah in regard to this, this assurance was given, that the land would be quiet, and that the fact *that it would remain quiet during the remainder of that year, and to the third year, would be a* SIGN, *or demonstration that the Assyrian army was* ENTIRELY *withdrawn, and that all danger of an invasion was at an end.* The sign, therefore, does not refer so much to *the past,* as to the security and future prosperity which would be consequent thereon. It would be an evidence to them that the nation would be safe, and would be favoured with a high degree of prosperity (see ver. 31, 32). It is possible that this invasion took place when it was too late to sow for that year, and that the land was so ravaged that it could not that year be cultivated. The harvests and the vineyards had been destroyed; and they would be dependent on that which the earth had spontaneously produced in those parts which had been untilled. As it was now too late to sow the land, they would be dependent in the following year on the same scanty supply. In the third year, however, they might cultivate their fields securely, and the former fertility would be restored. ¶ *Such as groweth of itself.* The Hebrew word here (סָפִיחַ), denotes grain produced from the kernels of the former year, without new seed, and without cultivation. This, it is evident, would be a scanty supply; but we are to remember that the land had been ravaged by the army of the Assyrian. ¶ *That which springeth of the same.* The word here used (שָׁחִיס), in the parallel passage in 2 Kings xix. 29 (סָחִישׁ), denotes that

31 And [1] the remnant that is escaped of the house of Judah shall again take root downward, and bear fruit upward.

32 For out of Jerusalem shall go forth a remnant, and [2] they that escape out of mount Zion: the zeal of the LORD of hosts shall do this.

33 Therefore thus saith the LORD concerning the king of Assyria, He shall not come into this city, nor shoot an arrow there, nor come before it with [3] shields, nor cast a bank against it.

1 *the escaping of the house of Judah that remaineth.* 2 *the escaping.* 3 *shield.*

which grows of itself the third year after sowing. This production of the third year would be of course more scanty and less valuable than in the preceding year, and there can be no doubt that the Jews would be subjected to a considerable extent to the evils of want. Still, as the land would be quiet; as the people would be permitted to live in peace; it would be a *sign* to them that the Assyrian was finally and entirely withdrawn, and that they might return in the third year to the cultivation of their land with the assurance that this much-dreaded invasion was not again to be feared. ¶ *And in the third year.* Then you may resume your agricultural operations with the assurance that you shall be undisturbed. Your two years of quiet shall have been a full demonstration to you that the Assyrian shall not return, and you may resume your employments with the assurance that all the evils of the invasion, and all apprehension of danger, are at an end.

31. *And the remnant that is escaped* (see Marg.) Those that are left of the Jews. The ten tribes had been carried away; and it is not improbable that the inhabitants of the kingdom of Judah had been reduced by want, and by the siege of Lachish, Libnah, &c. It is not to be supposed that Sennacherib could have invaded the land, and spread desolation for so long a time, without diminishing the number of the people. The promise in the passage is, that those who were left should flourish and increase. The land should be at rest; and under the administration of their wise and pious king their number would be augmented, and their happiness promoted. ¶ *Shall again take root downward.* Like a tree that had been prevented by any cause from growing or bearing fruit. A tree, to bear well, must be in a soil where it can strike its roots deep. The sense is, that all obstructions to their growth and prosperity would be removed.

32. *Shall go forth a remnant.* The word 'remnant' means that which is left; and does not of necessity imply that it should be a small portion. No doubt a part of the Jews were destroyed in the invasion of Sennacherib, but the assurance is here given that a portion of them would remain in safety, and that they would constitute that from which the future prosperity of the state would arise. ¶ *And they that escape.* Marg. 'The escaping,' *i.e.*, the remnant. ¶ *The zeal* (see Note on ch. ix. 7).

33. *He shall not come into this city.* Sennacherib encamped probably on the north-east side of the city, and his army was destroyed there (see Notes on ch. x. 28, *sq.*) ¶ *Nor shoot an arrow there.* That is, nor shoot an arrow within the walls of the city. ¶ *Nor come before it with shields* (see Note on

ANCIENT EGYPTIAN BATTLEMENTS.
From Rosellini.

ch. xxi. 5). The meaning here is, that the army should not be permitted to

34 By the way that he came, by the same shall he return, and shall not come into this city, saith the LORD.

35 For I [a] will defend this city to save it for mine own sake, and for my servant David's sake.

36 Then [b] the angel of the LORD went forth, and smote in the camp of the Assyrians an hundred and fourscore and five thousand: and when they arose early in the morning, behold, they *were* all dead corpses.

a ch.38.6; Jer.17.25,26.

b ch.10.12,&c.

come before the city defended with shields, and prepared with the means of attack and defence. ¶ *Nor cast a bank against it.* A mound; a pile of earth thrown up in the manner of a fort to defend the assailants, or to give them an advantage in attacking the walls.

SIEGE TOWERS, FILLED WITH ARMED MEN.

Sieges were conducted by throwing up banks or fortifications, behind which the army of attack could be secure to carry on their operations. Towers filled with armed men were also constructed, covered with hides and other impenetrable materials, which could be made to approach the walls, and from which those who were within could safely conduct the attack.

34. *By the way that he came* (ver. 29; comp. ver. 37). ¶ *And shall not come into this city* (ver. 33; comp. ch. xxix. 6–8).

35. *For I will defend this city.* Notwithstanding all that Hezekiah had done to put it in a posture of defence (2 Chron. xxxii. 1, *sq.*) still it was JEHOVAH alone who could preserve it. ¶ *For mine own sake.* God had been reproached and blasphemed by Sennacherib. As his name and power had been thus blasphemed, he says that he would vindicate himself, and for the honour of his own insulted majesty would save the city. ¶ *And for my servant David's sake.* On account of the promise which he had made to him that there should not fail a man to sit on his throne, and that the city and nation should not be destroyed until the Messiah should appear (see Ps. cxxxii. 10–18).

36. *Then the angel of the* LORD *went forth.* This verse contains the record of one of the most remarkable events which have occurred in history. Many attempts have been made to explain the occurrence which is here recorded, and to trace the agencies or means which God employed. It may be observed that the use of the word 'angel' here does not determine the manner in which it was done. So far as the *word* is concerned, it might have been accomplished either by the power of an invisible messenger of God—a spiritual being commissioned for this purpose; or it might have been by some second causes under the direction of an angel—as the pestilence, or a storm and tempest; or it might have been by some agents *sent* by God whatever they were —the storm, the pestilence, or the simoom, to which the name *angel* might have been applied. The word 'angel' (מַלְאָךְ from לָאַךְ *to send*) means properly *one sent, a messenger,* from a private person (Job i. 14); from a king (1 Sam. xvi. 19; xix. 11, 14, 20). Then it means *a messenger of God,* and is applied (1) to an angel (Ex. xxiii. 20; 2 Sam. xiv. 16; *et al.*); (2) to a prophet (Hag. i. 13; Mal. iii. 1); (3) to a priest (Eccl. v. 5; Mal. ii. 7). The word may be applied to *any* messenger sent from God, whoever or whatever that may be. Thus, in Ps. civ. 4, the

winds are said to be his angels, or messengers:

> Who maketh the winds (רוּחוֹת) his angels (מַלְאָכָיו);
> The flaming fire his ministers.

The general sense of the word is that of ambassador, messenger, one sent to bear a message, to execute a commission, or to perform any work or service. It is known that the Jews were in the habit of tracing all events to the agency of invisible beings sent forth by God to accomplish his purposes in this world. There is nothing in this opinion that is contrary to reason; for there is no more improbability in the existence of a good angel than there is in the existence of a good man, or in the existence of an evil spirit than there is in the existence of a bad man. And there is no more improbability in the supposition that God employs invisible and heavenly messengers to accomplish his purposes, than there is that he employs man. Whatever, therefore, were the means used in the destruction of the Assyrian army, there is no improbability in the opinion that they were under the direction of a celestial agent sent forth to accomplish the purpose. The chief suppositions which have been made of the means of that destruction are the following:—1. It has been supposed that it was by the direct agency of an angel, without any second causes. But this supposition has not been generally adopted. It is contrary to the usual modes in which God directs the affairs of the world. His purposes are usually accomplished by some second causes, and in accordance with the usual course of events. Calvin supposes that it was accomplished by the direct agency of one or more angels sent forth for the purpose. 2. Some have supposed that it was accomplished by Tirhakah, king of Ethiopia, who is supposed to have pursued Sennacherib, and to have overthrown his army in a single night near Jerusalem. But it is sufficient to say in reply to this, that there is not the slightest historical evidence to support it; and had this been the mode, it would have been so recorded, and the fact would have been stated. 3. It has been attributed by some, among whom is Prideaux (*Connection*, vol. i. p. 143) and J. E. Faber (*Notes on Harmer's Obs.*, i. 65), to the hot pestilential wind which often prevails in the East, and which is often represented as suddenly destroying travellers, and indeed whole caravans. This wind, called *sam, simûm, samiel,* or *simoom,* has been usually supposed to be poisonous, and almost instantly destructive to life. It has been described by Mr. Bruce, by Sir R. K. Porter, by Niebuhr, and by others. Prof. Robinson has examined at length the supposition that the Assyrian army was destroyed by this wind, and has stated the results of the investigations of recent travellers. The conclusion to which he comes is, that the former accounts of the effects of this wind have been greatly exaggerated, and that the destruction of the army of the Assyrians cannot be attributed to any such cause. See the article WINDS, in his edition of Calmet's *Dictionary*. Burckhardt says of this wind, whose effects have been regarded as so poisonous and destructive, 'I am PERFECTLY CONVINCED that all the stories which travellers, or the inhabitants of the towns of Egypt and Syria, relate of the simoom of the desert are greatly exaggerated, and I *never could hear of a* SINGLE WELL-AUTHENTICATED INSTANCE *of its having proved mortal to either man or beast*.' Similar testimony has been given by other modern travellers; though it is to be remarked that the testimony is rather of a *negative* character, and does not entirely destroy the possibility of the supposition that this so often described pestilential wind may in some instances prove fatal. It is not, however, referred to in the Scripture account of the destruction of Sennacherib; and whatever may be true of it in the deserts of Arabia or Nubia, there is no evidence whatever that such poisonous effects are ever experienced in Palestine. 4. It has been attributed to a storm of hail, accompanied with thunder and lightning. This is the opinion of Vitringa, and seems to accord with the descriptions which are given in the prophecy of the destruction of the army in ch. xxix. 6; xxx. 30. To this opinion, as the most probable, I have been disposed to incline; for although these passages *may* be regarded as figurative, yet the more natural inter-

37 So Sennacherib king of Assyria departed, and went and returned, and dwelt at Nineveh.

pretation is to regard them as descriptive of the event. We know that such a tempest might be easily produced by God, and that violent tornadoes are not unfrequent in the East. One of the plagues of Egypt consisted in such a tremendous storm of hail accompanied with thunder, when 'the fire ran along the ground,' so that 'there was hail, and fire mingled with the hail,' and so that 'the hail smote throughout all the land of Egypt all that was in the field, both man and beast' (Ex. ix. 22-25). This description, in its terror, its suddenness, and its ruinous effects, accords more nearly with the account of the destruction of Sennacherib than any other which has been made. See Notes on ch. xxx. 30, for a remarkable description of the effect of a storm of hail. 5. It has been supposed by many that it was accomplished by the pestilence. This is the account which Josephus gives (*Ant.* x. 1. 5), and is the supposition which has been adopted by Rosenmüller, Döderlin, Michaelis, Hensler, and many others. But there are two objections to this supposition. One is, that it does not well accord with the description of the prophet (ch. xxix. 6; xxx. 30); and the other, and more material one is, that the plague does not accomplish its work so suddenly. This was done in a single night; whereas, though the plague appears suddenly, and has been known to destroy whole armies, yet there is no recorded instance in which it has been so destructive in a few hours as in this case. It may be added, also, that the plague does not often leave an army in the manner described here. One hundred and eighty-five thousand were suddenly slain. The survivors, if there were any, as we have reason to suppose (ver. 37), fled, and returned to Nineveh. There is no mention made of any who lingered, and who remained sick among the slain. Nor is there any apprehension mentioned, as having existed among the Jews, of going into the camp, and stripping the dead, and bearing the spoils of the army into the city. Had the army been destroyed by the plague, such is the fear of the contagion in countries where it prevails, that nothing would have induced them to endanger the city by the possibility of introducing the dreaded disease. The account leads us to suppose that the inhabitants of Jerusalem immediately sallied forth and stripped the dead, and bore the spoils of the army into the city (see Notes on ch. xxxiii. 4, 24). On the whole, therefore, the most probable supposition seems to be, that, if any secondary causes were employed, it was the agency of a violent tempest—a tempest of mingled hail and fire, which suddenly descended upon the mighty army. Whatever was the agent, however, it was the hand of God that directed it. It was a most fearful exhibition of his power and justice; and it furnishes a most awful threatening to proud and haughty blasphemers and revilers, and a strong ground of assurance to the righteous that God will defend them in times of peril.

It may be added, that Herodotus has given an account which was undoubtedly derived from some rumour of the entire destruction of the Assyrian army. He says (ii. 141) that when Sennacherib was in Egypt and engaged in the siege of Pelusium, an Egyptian priest prayed to God, and God heard his prayer, and sent a judgment upon him. 'For,' says he, 'a multitude of mice gnawed to pieces in one night both the bows and the rest of the armour of the Assyrians, and that it was on that account that the king, when he had no bows left, drew off his army from Pelusium.' This is probably a corruption of the history which we have here. At all events, the account in Herodotus does not conflict with the main statement of Isaiah, but is rather a confirmation of that statement, that the army of Sennacherib met with sudden discomfiture. ¶ *And when they arose.* At the time of rising in the morning; when the surviving part of the army arose, or when the Jews arose, and looked toward the camp of the Assyrians.

37. *So Sennacherib departed.* Probably with some portion of his army and retinue with him, for it is by no

38 And it came to pass, as he was worshipping in the house of Nisroch his god, that Adrammelech and Sharezer his sons smote [a] him with the sword; and they escaped into the land of [1] Armenia: and Esarhaddon his son reigned in his stead.

[a] ch.14.9-12.

[1] *Ararat.*

means probable that the whole army had been destroyed. In 2 Chron. xxxii. 21, it is said that the angel 'cut off all the mighty men of valour, and the leaders and captains in the camp of the king of Assyria.' His army was thus entirely disabled, and the loss of so large a part of it, and the consternation produced by their sudden destruction, would of course lead him to abandon the siege. ¶ *Went and returned.* Went from before Jerusalem and returned to his own land. ¶ *And dwelt at Nineveh.* How long he dwelt there is not certainly known. Berosus, the Chaldean, says it was 'a little while' (see Jos. *Ant.* x. 1. 5). Nineveh was on the Tigris, and was the capital of Assyria. For an account of its site, and its present situation, see the *American Biblical Repository* for Jan. 1837, pp. 139–159.

38. *As he was worshipping.* Perhaps this time was selected because he might be then attended with fewer guards, or because they were able to surprise him without the possibility of his summoning his attendants to his rescue. ¶ *In the house.* In the temple. ¶ *Of Nisroch his god.* The god whom he particularly adored. Gesenius supposes that the word *Nisroch* denotes *an eagle*, or *a great eagle.* The eagle was regarded as a sacred bird in the Persian religion, and was the symbol of Ormuzd. This god or idol had been probably introduced into Nineveh from Persia. Among the ancient Arabs the eagle occurs as an idol. Josephus calls the idol Araskes; the author of the book of Tobit calls it Dagon. Vitringa supposes that it was the Assyrian Bel, and was worshipped under the figure of Mars, the god of war. More probably it was the figure of the eagle, though it might have been regarded as the god of war. ¶ *That Adrammelech and Sharezer his sons smote him with the sword.* What was the cause of this rebellion and parricide is unknown. These two sons subsequently became, in Armenia, the heads of two celebrated families there, the Arzerunii, and the Genunii (see Jos. *Ant.* x. 1, 5, *note*). ¶ *And they escaped.* This would lead us to suppose that it was some *private* matter which led them to commit the parricide, and that they did not do it with the expectation of succeeding to the crown. ¶ *Into the land of Armenia.* Heb. as Marg. 'Ararat.' The Chaldee renders this, 'The land of קַרְדּוּ (*Kardoo*,' that is, *Kardianum*, or, the mountains of the Kurds. The modern Kurdistan includes a considerable part of the ancient Assyria and Media, together with a large portion of Armenia. This expression is generally substituted for Ararat by the Syriac, Chaldee, and Arabic translators, when they do not retain the original word *Ararat.* It is a region among the mountains of Ararat or Armenia. The Syriac renders it in the same way ܕܩܪܕܘܝܐ—'Of Kurdoya' (*the Kurds*). The LXX. render it, 'Into Armenia.' Jerome says that 'Ararat was a champaign region in Armenia, through which the Araxes flowed, and was of considerable fertility.' Ararat was a region or province in Armenia, near the middle of the country between the Araxes and the lakes Van and Oroomiah. It is still called by the Armenians *Ararat.* On one of the mountains in this region the ark of Noah rested (Gen. viii. 4). The name *Ararat* belongs properly to the region or country, and not to any particular mountain. For an account of this region, see Sir R. K. Porter's *Travels*, vol. i. p. 178, *sq.;* Smith and Dwight's *Researches in Armenia*, vol. ii. p. 73, *sq.;* and Morier's *Second Journey*, p. 312. For a very interesting account of the situation of Ararat, including a description of an ascent to the summit of the mountain which bears that name, see the *Bib. Rep.* for April, 1836, pp. 390–416. 'The origin of the name Armenia is unknown. The Armenians call themselves after their fabulous progenitor

CHAPTER XXXVIII.

ANALYSIS.

This chapter contains the record of an important transaction which occurred in the time of Isaiah, and in which he was deeply interested—the dangerous sickness, and the remarkable recovery of Hezekiah. It is introduced here, doubtless, because the account was drawn up by Isaiah (see Analysis of ch. xxxvi.); and because it records his agency at an important crisis of the history. A record of the same transaction, evidently from the same hand, occurs in 2 Kings xx. 1–11. But the account differs more than the records in the two previous chapters. It is *abridged* in Isaiah by omitting what is recorded in Kings in ver. 4, and in the close of ver. 6, it is *transposed* in the statement which occurs in regard to the application of the 'lump of figs;' and it is *enlarged* by the introduction of the record which Hezekiah made of his sickness and recovery (9–20).

The contents of the chapter are—1. The statement of the dangerous sickness of Hezekiah, and the message of God to him by the prophet (1). 2. The prayer which Hezekiah offered for his recovery (3). 3. The assurance which God gave to him by the prophet that his days should be lengthened out fifteen years, and the sign given to confirm it by the retrocession of the shadow on the sun-dial of Ahaz (5–8). 4. The record which Hezekiah made in gratitude to God for his recovery (9–20); and 5. The statement of the manner in which his recovery was effected (21, 22).

IN [a] those days was Hezekiah sick unto death. And Isaiah the prophet, the son of Amoz, came unto him, and said unto him, Thus saith the LORD, [1] Set thine house in order: for thou shalt die, and not live.

[a] 2 Ki.20.1,&c.; 2 Chron.32.24.
[1] *give charge concerning thy house.*

Haig, and derive the name *Armen* from the son of Haig, Armenag. They are probably a tribe of the ancient Assyrians; their language and history speak alike in favour of it. Their traditions say also that Haig came from Babylon.'

CHAPTER XXXVIII.

1. *In those days.* That is, his sickness commenced about the period in which the army of Sennacherib was destroyed. It has been made a question whether the sickness of Hezekiah was before or after the invasion of Sennacherib. The most natural interpretation certainly is, that it occurred *after* that invasion, and probably at no distant period. The only objection to this view is the statement in ver. 6, that God would deliver him out of the hand of the king of Assyria, which has been understood by many as implying that he was then threatened with the invasion. But this may mean simply that he would be *perpetually* and *finally* delivered from his hand; that he would be secure in that independence from a foreign yoke which he had long sought (2 Kings xviii. 7); and that the Assyrian should not be able again to bring the Jews into subjection (see Notes on ch. xxxvii. 30, 31; comp. Note on ver. 6). Jerome supposes that it was brought upon him lest his heart should be elated with the signal triumph, and in order that, in his circumstances, he might be kept humble. Josephus (*Ant.* x. 2. 1) says that the sickness occurred soon after the destruction of the army of Sennacherib. Prideaux (*Connection*, vol. i. p. 137) places his sickness *before* the invasion of the Assyrians. ¶ *Was sick.* What was the exact nature of this sickness is not certainly known. In ver. 21 it is said that it was 'a boil,' and probably it was a pestilential boil. The pestilence or plague is attended with an eruption or boil. 'No one,' says Jahn, 'ever recovered from the pestilence unless th boil of the pestilence came out upon hin and even then he could not always l cured' (*Biblical Antiquities*, § 19(The pestilence was, and is still, rapid its progress. It terminates the life those who are affected with it alm immediately, and at the furthest wit three or four days. Hence we see ground of the alarm of Hezekiah. other cause of his anxiety was, th had at this time no children, and sequently he had reason to appre that his kingdom would be throw contention by conflicting strifes f crown. ¶ *Unto death.* Ready t with a sickness which in the or course would terminate his life. *thine house in order.* Heb. 'Gi mand (צַו) to thy house,' *i.e.*, family. If you have any direc

give in regard to the succession to the crown, or in regard to domestic and private arrangements, let it be done soon. Hezekiah was yet in middle life. He came to the throne when he was twenty-five years old (2 Kings xviii. 2), and he had now reigned about fourteen years. It is possible that he had as yet made no arrangements in regard to the succession, and as this was very important to the peace of the nation, Isaiah was sent to him to apprize him of the necessity of leaving the affairs of his kingdom so that there should not be anarchy when he should die. The direction, also, may be understood in a more general sense as denoting that he was to make whatever arrangements might be necessary as preparatory to his death. We see here—1. The boldness and fidelity of a man of God. Isaiah was not afraid to go in and freely tell even a monarch that he must die. The subsequent part of the narrative would lead us to suppose that until this announcement Hezekiah did not regard himself as in immediate danger. It is evident here, that the *physician* of Hezekiah had not informed him of it—*perhaps* from the apprehension that his disease would be aggravated by the agitation of his mind on the subject. The duty was, therefore, left, as it is often, to a minister of religion—a duty which even many ministers are slow to perform, and which many physicians are reluctant to *have* performed. 2. No danger is to be apprehended commonly from announcing to those who are sick their true condition. Friends and relatives are often reluctant to do it, for fear of agitating and alarming them. Physicians often prohibit them from knowing their true condition, under the apprehension that their disease may be aggravated. Yet here was a case in which pre-eminently there might be danger from announcing the danger of death. The disease was deeply seated. It was making rapid progress. It was usually incurable. Nay, there was here a moral certainty that the monarch would die. And this was a case, therefore, which particularly demanded, it would seem, that the patient should be kept quiet, and free from alarms. But God regarded it as of great importance that he should know his true condition, and the prophet was directed to go to him and faithfully to state it. Physicians and friends often err in this. There is no species of cruelty greater than to suffer a friend to lie on a dying bed under a delusion. There is no sin more aggravated than that of designedly deceiving a dying man, and flattering him with the hope of recovery when there is a moral certainty that he will not, and cannot recover. And there is evidently no danger to be apprehended from communicating to the sick their true condition. It should be done tenderly, and with affection; but it should be done faithfully. I have had many opportunities of witnessing the effect of apprizing the sick of their situation, and of the moral certainty that they must die. And I cannot now recall an instance in which the announcement has had any unhappy effect on the disease. Often, on the contrary, the effect is to calm the mind, and to lead the dying to look up to God, and peacefully to repose on him. And the effect of THAT is *always* salutary. Nothing is more favourable for a recovery than a peaceful, calm, heavenly submission to God; and the repose and quiet which physicians so much desire their patients to possess, is often best obtained by securing confidence in God, and a calm resignation to his will. 3. Every man with the prospect of death before him should set his house in order. Death is an event which demands preparation—a preparation which should not be deferred to the dying moment. In view of it, whether it comes sooner or later, our peace should be made with God and our worldly affairs so arranged that we can leave them without distraction, and without regret. ¶ *For thou shalt die, and not live.* Thy disease is incurable. It is a mortal, fatal disease. The Hebrew is, 'for thou art *dead*' (מֵת); that is, you are a dead man. A similar expression occurs in Gen. xx. 3, in the address which God made to Abimelech: 'Behold thou art a dead man, on account of the woman which thou hast taken.' We have a similar phrase in our language, when a man is wounded, and when he says, 'I am a dead man.' This is all that we are required to understand here, that,

2 Then Hezekiah turned his face
toward the wall, and prayed unto
the LORD,
3 And said, Remember [a] now, O
LORD, I beseech thee, how I have
walked before thee in truth, and
with a perfect heart, and have done
that which is good in thy sight: and
Hezekiah wept [1] sore.

a Neh.13.14; Heb.6.10. 1 *with great weeping.*

according to the usual course of the disease, he must die. It is evident that Isaiah was not acquainted himself with the secret intention of God; nor did he know that Hezekiah would humble himself, and plead with God; nor that God would by a miracle lengthen out his life.

2. *Then Hezekiah turned his face toward the wall.* The wall of the room in which he was lying. He was probably lying on a couch next the wall of his room. Eastern houses usually have such couches or ottomans running along on the sides of the room on which they recline, and on which they lie when they are sick. Hezekiah probably turned his face to the wall in order that his emotion and his tears might not be seen by the bystanders, or in order that he might compose himself the better for devotion. His prayer he wished, doubtless, to be as secret as possible. The Chaldee renders this, 'Turned his face to the wall of the house of the sanctuary;' that is, of the temple, so that it might appear that he prayed toward the temple. Thus Daniel, when in Babylon, is said to have prayed with his windows opened towards Jerusalem (Dan. vi. 10). The Mahometans pray everywhere with their faces turned toward Mecca. But there is no evidence in the Hebrew text that Hezekiah prayed in that manner. The simple idea is, that he turned over on his couch toward the wall of his room, doubtless, for the greater privacy, and to hide his deep emotion.

3. *And said, Remember now, O* LORD, *I beseech thee.* The object which Hezekiah desired was evidently that his life might be spared, and that he might not be suddenly cut off. He therefore makes mention of the former course of his life, not with ostentation, or as a ground of his acceptance or justification, but *as a reason* why his life should not be cut off. He had not lived as many of the kings of Israel had done. He had not been a patron of idolatry. He had promoted an extensive and thorough reformation among the people. He had exerted his influence as a king in the service of JEHOVAH, and it was his purpose still to do it; and he, therefore, prayed that his life might be spared in order that he might carry forward and perfect his plans for the reformation of the people, and for the establishment of the worship of JEHOVAH. ¶ *How I have walked.* How I have lived. Life, in the Scriptures, is often represented as a journey, and a life of piety is represented as walking with God (see Gen. v. 24; vi. 9; 1 Kings ix. 4; xi. 33). ¶ *In truth.* In the defence and maintenance of the truth, or in sincerity. ¶ *And with a perfect heart.* With a heart sound, sincere, *entire* in thy service. This had been his leading aim; his main, grand purpose. He had not pursued his own ends, but his whole official royal influence had been on the side of religion. This refers to his *public* character rather than to his private feelings. For though, as a man, he might be deeply conscious of imperfection; yet as a king, his influence had been wholly on the side of religion, and he had not declined from the ways of God. ¶ *And have done* that which is *good.* This accords entirely with the account which is given of him in 2 Kings xviii. 3–5. ¶ *And Hezekiah wept sore.* Marg. as Heb. 'With great weeping.' Josephus (*Ant.* x. 2. 1) says, that the reason why Hezekiah was so much affected was that he was then childless, and saw that he was about to leave the government without a successor. Others suppose that it was because his death would be construed by his enemies as a judgment of God for his stripping the temple of its ornaments (2 Kings xviii. 16). It is possible that several things may have been combined in producing the depth of his grief. In his song, or in the record which he made to express his praise to God for his recovery, the main reason of his grief which he suggested was, the fact that he was in

4 Then came the word of the LORD to Isaiah, saying,
5 Go and say to Hezekiah, Thus saith the LORD, the God of David thy father, I have heard thy prayer, I have seen thy tears: behold, I will add unto thy days fifteen years.
6 And I will deliver thee and this city out of the hand of the king of Assyria: and I will defend this city.

---

danger of being cut off in the midst of his days; that the blessings of a long life were likely to be denied him (see ver. 10–12). We have here an instance in which even a good man may be surprised, alarmed, distressed, at the sudden announcement that he must die. The fear of death is natural; and even those who are truly pious are *sometimes* alarmed when it comes.

4. *Then came the word of the* LORD. In the parallel place in 2 Kings xx. 4, it is said, 'And it came to pass, afore Isaiah was gone out into the middle court, that the word of the Lord came unto him.' That is, the message of God came to Isaiah before he had left Hezekiah; or as soon as he had offered his prayer. This circumstance is omitted by Isaiah on the revision of his narrative which we have before us. But there is no contradiction. In this place it is implied that the message came to him soon, or immediately.

5. *The God of David thy father*. David is mentioned here, probably, because Hezekiah had a strong resemblance to him (2 Kings xviii. 3), and because a long and happy reign had been granted to David; and also because the promise had been made to David that there should not fail a man to sit on his throne (see Note on ch. xxxvii. 35). As Hezekiah resembled David, God promised that his reign should be lengthened out; and as he perhaps was then without a son and successor, God promised him a longer life, with the prospect that he might have an heir who should succeed him on the throne. ¶ *Behold, I will add unto thy days fifteen years*. This is perhaps the only instance in which any man has been told exactly how long he would live. Why God *specified* the time cannot now be known. It was, however, a full answer to the prayer of Hezekiah, and the promise is a full demonstration that God is the hearer of prayer, and that he can answer it at once.—We learn here, that it is right for a friend of God to pray for life. In times of sickness, and even when there are indications of a fatal disease, it is not improper to pray that the disease may be removed, and the life prolonged. If the desire be to do good; to advance the kingdom of God; to benefit others; or to perfect some plan of benevolence which is begun, it is not improper to pray that God would prolong the life. Who can tell but that he *often* thus spares useful lives when worn down with toil, and when the frame is apparently sinking to the grave, in answer to prayer? He does not indeed work miracles as he did in the case of Hezekiah, but he may direct to remedies which had not before occurred; or he may himself give a sudden and unlooked-for turn to the disease, and restore the sufferer again to health.

6. *And I will deliver thee and this city*. The purport of this promise is, that he and the city should be *finally* and *entirely* delivered from all danger of invasion from the Assyrians. It *might* be apprehended that Sennacherib would collect a large army, and return; or that his successor would prosecute the war which he had commenced. But the assurance here is given to Hezekiah that he had nothing more to fear from the Assyrians (see Notes on ch. xxxi. 4, 5; xxxvii. 35). In the parallel place in 2 Kings xx. 6, it is added, 'I will defend this city for mine own sake, and for my servant David's sake.' In the parallel passage also, in 2 Kings xx. 7, 8, there is inserted the statement which occurs in Isaiah at the end of the chapter (ver. 21, 22). It is evident that those two verses more appropriately come in here. Lowth conjectures that the abridger of the history omitted those verses, and when he had transcribed the song of Hezekiah, he saw that they were necessary to complete the narrative, and placed them at the end of the chapter,

7 And this *shall be* a sign [a] unto
thee from the LORD, that the LORD
will do this thing that he hath
spoken;
8 Behold, I will bring again the
shadow of the degrees, which is
gone down in the sun-dial [1] of Ahaz,
ten degrees backward. So the sun
returned ten degrees, by which degrees it was gone down.

[a] ch.7.11,14.

[1] *degrees by*, or, *with the sun.*

---

with proper marks to have them inserted in the right place, which marks were overlooked by transcribers. It is, however, immaterial *where* the statement is made; and it is now impossible to tell in what manner the transposition occurred.

7. *And this* shall be *a sign unto thee.* That is, a sign, or proof that God would do what he had promised, and that Hezekiah would recover and be permitted to go again to the temple of the Lord (ver. 22; 2 Kings xx. 8). On the meaning of the word 'sign,' see Notes on ch. vii. 11, 14; comp. Note on ch. xxxvii. 30. The promise was, that he should be permitted to go to the temple in three days (2 Kings xx. 5).

8. *Behold, I will bring again the shadow.* The shadow, or shade which is made by the interception of the rays of the sun by the gnomon on the dial. The phrase 'bring again' (Heb. מֵשִׁיב) means *to cause to return* (Hiphil, from שׁוּב, *to return*); that is, I will cause it retrograde, or bring back. LXX. Στρέψω—'I will turn back.' Few subjects have perplexed commentators more than this account of the sun-dial of Ahaz. The only other place where a sun-dial is mentioned in the Scriptures is in the parallel place in 2 Kings xx. 9, 10, where the account is somewhat more full, and the nature of the miracle more fully represented: 'This sign shalt thou have of the LORD, that the LORD will do the thing which he hath spoken:—Shall the shadow go forward ten degrees, or go back ten degrees? And Hezekiah answered, It is a light thing for the shadow to go down ten degrees; nay, but let the shadow return backward ten degrees.' That is, it would be in the usual direction which the shadow takes, for it to go *down*, and there would be less that would be decisive in the miracle. He therefore asked that it might be moved backward from its common direction, and then there could be no doubt that it was from God; 2 Kings xx. 11: 'And Isaiah the prophet cried unto JEHOVAH, and he brought the shadow ten degrees backward, by which it had gone down in the dial of Ahaz.' ¶ *The shadow of the degrees.* That is, the shadow made *on* the degrees; or indicated by the degrees on the dial. But there has been much difficulty in regard to the meaning of the word *degrees.* The Hebrew word (מַעֲלָה from עָלָה, *to ascend, to go up*) means properly *an ascent;* a going up from a lower to a higher region; then a *step* by which one ascends, applied to the steps on a staircase, &c. (1 Kings x. 19; Ezek. xl. 26, 31, 34.) Hence it may be applied to the ascending or descending figures or marks on a dial designating the ascent or descent of the sun; or the ascent or descent of the shadow going up or down by *steps* or hours marked on its face. The word is applied to a *dial* nowhere else but here. Josephus understands this as referring to the steps in the house or palace of Ahaz. 'He desired that he would make the shadow of the sun which he had already made to go down ten steps in his house, to return again to the same place, and to make it as it was before;' by which he evidently regarded Hezekiah as requesting that the shadow which had gone down on the steps of the palace should return to its place ten steps backward. It is possible that the time of day *may* have been indicated by the shadow of the sun on the steps of the palace, and that this may have constituted what was called the sun-dial of Ahaz; but the more probable interpretation is that which regards the dial as a distinct and separate contrivance. The LXX. render it by the word *steps,* yet understanding it as Josephus does, Ἀναβαθμοὺς τοῦ οἴκου τοῦ πατρός σου—'The steps of the house of thy father.' ¶ *Which is gone down on the sun-dial of Ahaz.* Marg. 'Degrees by,' or 'with the sun.' Heb. liter-

ally, 'which has descended on the steps, or degrees of Ahaz by, or with the sun' (בַּשֶּׁמֶשׁ), that is, by means of the sun, or caused by the progress of the sun. The shadow had gone down on the dial by the regular course of the sun. Ahaz was the father of Hezekiah; and it is evident from this, that the dial had been introduced by him, and had been used by him to measure time. There is no mention of any instrument for keeping time in the Bible before this, nor is it possible, perhaps, to determine the origin or character of this invention, or to know where Ahaz obtained it. Perhaps all that can be known on the subject has been collected by Calmet, to whose article [Dial] in his Dictionary, and to the Fragments of Taylor appended to his Dictionary (Fragments, ii., cii.) the reader may be referred for a more full statement on this subject than is consistent with the design of these Notes. The mention of the dial does not occur before the time of Ahaz, who lived B.C. 726; nor is it certainly known that even after his time the Jews generally divided their time by hours. The word 'hour' (καίρικός) occurs first in Tobit; and it has been supposed that the invention of *dials* came from beyond the Euphrates (Herod. ii. 109). But others suppose that it came from the Phenicians, and that the first traces of it are discoverable in what Homer says (*Odyss.* xv. 402) of 'an island called Syria lying above Ortygia, where the revolutions of the sun are observed.' The Phenicians are supposed to have inhabited this island of Syria, and it is therefore presumed that they left there this monument of their skill in astronomy. About three hundred years after Homer, Pherecydes set up a sun-dial in the same island to distinguish the hours. The Greeks confess that Anaximander, who lived B.C. 547, under the reign of Cyrus, first divided time by hours, and introduced sun-dials among them. This was during the time of the captivity at Babylon. Anaximander travelled into Chaldea, and it is not improbable that he brought the dial from Babylon. The Chaldeans were early distinguished for their attention to astronomy, and it is probable that it was in Babylon that the sun-dial, and the division of the day into hours, was first used, and that the knowledge of that was conveyed in some way from Chaldea to Ahaz. Interpreters have differed greatly in regard to the *form* of the sun-dial used by Ahaz, and by the ancients generally. Cyril of Alexandria and Jerome believed it was a staircase so disposed, that the sun showed the hours on it by the shadow. This, as we have seen, was the opinion of Josephus; and this opinion has been followed by many others. Others suppose it was an obelisk or pillar in the middle of a smooth pavement on which the hours were engraved, or on which lines were drawn which would indicate the hours. Grotius, in accordance with the opinion of Rabbi Elias Chomer, describes it thus: 'It was a concave hemisphere, in the midst of which was a globe, the shadow of which fell upon several lines engraved on the concavity of the hemisphere; these lines, they say, were eight-and-twenty in number.' This description accords nearly with the kind of dial which the Greeks called *scapha*, a boat, or *hemisphere*, the invention of which the Greeks ascribed to a Chaldean named Berosus (Vitruv. ix. 9). See the plate in Taylor's Calmet, 'Sun-dial of Ahaz' (Figs. 1 and 2). Berosus was a priest of Belus in Babylon, and lived indeed perhaps 300 years after Ahaz; but there is no necessity of supposing that he was the *inventor* of the dial. It is sufficient to suppose that he was reputed to be the first who introduced it into Greece. He went from Babylon to Greece, where he taught astronomy first at Cos, and then at Athens, where one of his dials is still shown. Herodotus expressly says (i. 109), 'the pole, the gnomon, and the division of the day into twelve parts, the Greeks received from the Babylonians.' This sun-dial was portable; it did not require to be constructed for a particular spot to which it should be subsequently confined; and therefore one ready-made might have been brought from Babylon to Ahaz. That he had commerce with these countries appears by his alliance with Tiglath-pileser (2 Kings xvi. 7, 8). And that Ahaz was a man who was desirous of availing himself of foreign inventions, and introducing them into his capital, appears evident from his desire to have an altar constructed in Jerusalem, similar to the one which he had seen in Damascus (2 Kings xvi. 10). The dial is now a well-known instrument, the *principle* of which is, that the hours are marked on its face by a *shadow* cast from the sun by a gnomon. In order to the understanding of this miracle, it is not necessary to be acquainted with the form of the ancient dial. It will be understood by a reference to *any* dial, and would have been substantially the same, whatever was the form of the instrument. The essential idea is, that the shadow of the gnomon which thus indicated a certain degree or hour of the day, was made to go back ten degrees or places. It may conduce, however, to the illustration of this subject to have before the eye a representation of the usual form of the ancient dial, and I therefore annex three forms of dials which have been discovered. 'The engraving represents—1. A concave dial of white marble, found at Civita, in the year 1762. 2. Another concave dial, found at mount Tusculum, near Rome, in 1726. 3. A compound dial, preserved in the Elgin collection in the British Museum. It was found at Athens, supposed to have been used in marking the hours on one of the crossways of the city. The first two are considered to resemble, if indeed they be not identical with the famous dial of Ahaz.'

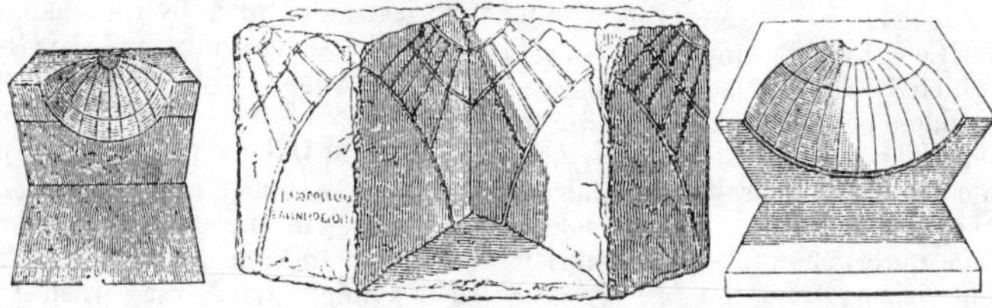

Ancient Sun Dials.—From Specimens in British Museum.

In regard to this miracle, it seems only necessary to observe that all that is indispensable to be believed is, that the shadow on the dial was made suddenly to recede from *any* cause. It is evident that this may have been accomplished in several ways. It may have been by arresting the motion of the earth in its revolutions, and causing it to retrograde on its axis to the extent indicated by the return of the shadow, or it may have been by a miraculous *bending*, or inclining of the rays of the sun. As there is no evidence that the event was observed elsewhere; and as it is not *necessary* to suppose that the earth was arrested in its motion, and that the whole frame of the universe was adjusted to this change in the movement of the earth, it is most probable that it was an inclination of the rays of the sun; or a miraculous causing of the *shadow* itself to recede. This is the whole statement of the sacred writer, and this is all that is necessary to be supposed. What Hezekiah desired was a miracle; a sign that he should recover. That was granted. The retrocession of the shadow in this sudden manner was not a natural event. It could be caused only by God; and *this* was all that was needed. A simple exertion of Divine power on the rays of the sun which rested on the dial, deflecting those rays, would accomplish the whole result. It may be added that it is not recorded, nor is it necessary to an understanding of the subject to suppose, that the bending of the rays was *permanent*, or that so much time was *lost*. The miracle was instantaneous, and was satisfactory to Hezekiah, though the rays of the sun casting the shadow may have again been soon returned to their regular position, and the shadow restored to the place in which it would have been had it not been interrupted. No infidel, therefore, can object to this statement, unless he can prove that this *could* not be done by him who made the sun, and who is himself the fountain of power. ¶ *By which degrees it was gone down.* By the same *steps*, or degrees on which the shadow had descended. So the

9 The writing of Hezekiah king
of Judah, when he had been sick,
and was recovered of his sickness:
10 I said [a]in the cutting off of
my days, I shall go to the gates of
the grave: I am deprived of the
residue of my years.
11 I said, I shall not see the

a Job 7.7,&c.; Ps.77.3,&c.

LXX. express it; 'so the sun re-ascended the ten steps by which the shadow had gone down.' It was the *shadow* on the dial which had gone down. The *sun* was *ascending*, and the consequence was, of course, that the shadow on a vertical dial would *descend*. The 'sun' here means, evidently, the sun *as it appeared;* the rays, or the shining of the sun. A return of the shadow was effected such as would be produced by the recession of the sun itself.

9. *The writing of Hezekiah.* This is the title to the following hymn—a record which Hezekiah made to celebrate the goodness of God in restoring him to health. The writing itself is *poetry*, as is indicated by the parallelism, and by the general structure. It is in many respects quite obscure—an obscurity perhaps arising from the brevity and conciseness which are apparent in the whole piece. It is remarkable that this song or hymn is not found in the parallel passage in the Book of Kings. The reason why it was omitted there, and inserted here, is unknown. It is *possible* that it was drawn up for Hezekiah by Isaiah, and that it is inserted here as a part of his composition, though adopted by Hezekiah, and declared to be *his*, that is, as expressing the gratitude of his heart on his recovery from his disease. It was common to compose an ode or hymn of praise on occasion of deliverance from calamity, or any remarkable interposition of God (see Notes on ch. xii. 1; xxv. 1; xxvi. 1). Many of the Psalms of David were composed on such occasions, and were expressive of gratitude to God for deliverance from impending calamity. The hymn or song is composed of two parts. In the first part (ver. 10–14), Hezekiah describes his feelings and his fears when he was suffering, and especially the apprehension of his mind at the prospect of death; and the second part (ver. 15–20) expresses praise to God for his goodness.

10. *I said.* Probably the words 'I said' do not imply that he said or spoke this openly or audibly; but this was the language of his heart, or the substance of his reflections. ¶ *In the cutting off of my days.* There has been considerable diversity of interpretation in regard to this phrase. Vitringa renders it as our translators have done. Rosenmüller renders it, 'In the meridian of my days.' The LXX. Ἐν τῷ ὕψει τῶν ἡμερῶν μου—'In the height of my days,' where they evidently read ברמי instead of בדמי, by the change of a single letter. Aquila, and the Greek interpreters generally, rendered it, 'In the silence of my days.' The word here used in Hebrew (דְּמִי) denotes properly *stillness*, quiet, rest; and Gesenius renders it, 'in the quiet of my days.' According to him the idea is, 'now when I might have rest; when I am delivered from my foes; when I am in the midst of my life, of my reign, and of my plans of usefulness, I must die.' The sense is, doubtless, that he was about to be cut off in middle life, and when he had every prospect of usefulness, and of happiness in his reign. ¶ *I shall go to the gates of the grave.* Heb. 'Gates of sheol.' On the meaning of the word *sheol*, and the Hebrew idea of the descent to it through gates, see Notes on ch. v. 14; xiv. 9. The idea is, that he must go down to the regions of the dead, and dwell with departed shades (see Note on ver. 11). ¶ *The residue of my years.* Those which I had hoped to enjoy; of which I had a reasonable prospect in the ordinary course of events. It is evident that Hezekiah had looked forward to a long life, and to a prosperous and peaceful reign. *This* was the means which God adopted to show him the impropriety of his desire, and to turn him more entirely to his service, and to a preparation for death.—Sickness often has this effect on the minds of good men.

11. *I shall not see the* Lord. In the

LORD, *even* the LORD, in [a] the land
of the living: I shall behold man
no more with the inhabitants of the
world.
12 Mine age is departed, and is
removed from me as a shepherd's
tent: I have cut off like a weaver
my life: he will cut me off [1] with
pining sickness: from day *even* to
night wilt thou make an end of me.

[a] Ps.27.13.

[1] or, *from the* thrum.

original, the Hebrew which is rendered 'LORD,' is not JEHOVAH, but יָהּ יָהּ (JAH, JAH.) On the meaning of it, see Note on ch. xii. 2 (comp. Note on ch. vii. 14). The *repetition* of the name here denotes *emphasis* or *intensity of feeling*—the deep desire which he had to see JEHOVAH in the land of the living, and the intense sorrow of his heart at the idea of being cut off from that privilege. The idea here is, that Hezekiah felt that he would not be spared to enjoy the tokens of Divine favour on earth; to reap the fruits of the surprising and remarkable deliverance from the army of Sennacherib; and to observe its happy results in the augmenting prosperity of the people, and in the complete success of his plans of reformation. ¶ *I shall behold man no more.* I shall see the living no more; I shall die, and go among the dead. He regarded it as a privilege to live, and to enjoy the society of his friends and fellow-worshippers in the temple—a privilege from which he felt that he was about to be cut off. ¶ *With the inhabitants of the world.* Or rather, 'amongst the inhabitants of the land of stillness;' that is, of the land of shades—*sheol.* He would not there see man as he saw him on earth, living and active, but would be a shade in the land of shades; himself still, in a world of stillness. 'I shall be associated with them there, and of course be cut off from the privileges of the society of living men.' [See Supplementary Note on ch. xiv. 9.] The Hebrew word rendered 'world' (חֶדֶל), is from חָדַל, *to cease*, to leave off, to desist; to become languid, flaccid, pendulous. It then conveys the idea of leaving off, of resting, of being still (Judg. v. 6; Job iii. 17; xiv. 6; Isa. ii. 22). Hence the idea of *frailty* (Ps. xxxix. 5); and hence the word here denotes probably the place of rest, the region of the dead, and is synonymous with the land of *silence*, such as the grave and the region of the dead are in contradistinction from the hurry and bustle of this world. Our translation seems to have been made as if the word was חֶלֶד, *life, lifetime*; hence the world (Ps. xvii. 14; xlix. 2). The Vulgate renders it, '*Habitatorem quietis.*' The LXX. simply, 'I shall behold man no more.'

12. *Mine age.* The word which is here used (דּוֹר) means properly the revolving period or circle of human life. The parallelism seems to demand, however, that it should be used in the sense of *dwelling* or habitation, so as to correspond with the 'shepherd's tent.' Accordingly, Lowth and Noyes render it, 'Habitation.' So also do Gesenius and Rosenmüller. The Arabic word has this signification; and the Hebrew verb דור also means *to dwell, to remain*, as in the Chaldee. Here the word means a dwelling, or habitation; that is, a tent, as the habitations of the Orientals were mostly tents. ¶ *Is departed* (נִסַּע). The idea here is, that his dwelling was to be transferred from one place to another, as when a tent or encampment was broken up; that is, he was about to cease to dwell on the earth, and to dwell in the land of silence, or among the dead. ¶ *From me as a shepherd's tent.* As suddenly as the tent of a shepherd is taken down, folded up, and transferred to another place. There is doubtless the idea here that he would continue to *exist*, but in another place, as the shepherd would pitch his tent or dwell in another place. He was to be cut off from the earth, but he expected to dwell among the dead. The whole passage conveys the idea that he expected to dwell in another state—as the shepherd dwells in another place when he strikes his tent, and it is removed. ¶ *I have cut off like a weaver my life.* This is another image designed to express substantially the same idea. The sense is, as a weaver takes his web from the loom by cutting the warp, or

13 I reckoned till morning, *that*,
as a lion, so will he break all my
bones: from day *even* to night wilt
thou make an end of me.
14 Like a crane *or* a swallow,
so did I chatter; I did mourn [a] as
a dove: mine eyes fail *with looking*
upward: O LORD, I am oppressed;
undertake for [1] me.

a ch.59.11. 1 or, *ease me*.

the threads which bind it to the beam, and thus *loosens* it and takes it away, so his life was to be cut off. When it is said, 'I cut off' (קִפַּדְתִּי), the idea is, doubtless, I *am* cut off; or my life is cut off. Hezekiah here speaks of himself as the agent, because he might have felt that his sins and unworthiness were the cause. Life is often spoken of as a web that is woven, because an advance is constantly made in filling up the web, and because it is soon finished, and is then cut off. ¶ *He will cut me off*. God was about to cut me off. ¶ *With pining sickness*. Marg. 'From the thrum.' Lowth, 'From the loom.' The word דַּלָּה means properly something hanging down or pendulous; anything pliant or slender. Hence it denotes *hair* or locks (Cant. vii. 6). Here it seems to denote the *threads* or *thrums* which tied the web to the weaver's beam. The image here denotes the cutting off of life as the weaver cuts his web out of the loom, or as he cuts off thrums. The word never means sickness. ¶ *From day* even *to night*. That is, in the space of a single day, or between morning and night—as a weaver with a short web accomplishes it in a single day. The disease of Hezekiah was doubtless the pestilence; and the idea is, that God would cut him off speedily, as it were in a single day. ¶ *Wilt thou make an end of me*. Heb. 'Wilt thou perfect' or 'finish' me; that is, wilt thou take my life.

13. *I reckoned*. There has been considerable variety in interpreting this expression. The LXX. render it, 'I was given up in the morning as to a lion.' The Vulgate renders it, 'I hoped until morning;' and in his commentary, Jerome says it means, that as Job in his trouble and anguish (ch. vii. 4) sustained himself at night expecting the day, and in the daytime waiting for the night, expecting a change for the better, so Hezekiah waited during the night expecting relief in the morning. He knew, says he, that the violence of a burning fever would very soon subside, and he thus composed himself, and calmly waited. So Vitringa renders it, 'I composed my mind until the morning.' Others suppose that the word here used (שִׁוִּיתִי), means, 'I made myself *like* a lion,' that is, in roaring. But the more probable and generally adopted interpretation is, 'I looked to God, hoping that the disease would soon subside, *but* as a lion he crushed my bones. The disease increased in violence, and became past endurance. *Then* I chattered like a swallow, and mourned like a dove, over the certainty that I must die.'—Our translators, by inserting the word 'that,' have greatly marred the sense, as if he had *reckoned* or calculated through the night that God *would* break his bones, or increase the violence of the disease, whereas the reverse was true. He hoped and expected that it would be otherwise, and with that view he composed his mind. ¶ *As a lion so will he break all my bones*. This should be in the past tense. 'He [God] *did* crush all my bones. The connection requires this construction. The idea is, that as a lion crushes the bones of his prey, producing great pain and sudden death, so it was with God in producing great pain and the prospect of sudden death. ¶ *From day* even *to night*, &c. (see Note on ver. 12.) Between morning and night. That is, his pain so resembled the crushing of all the bones of an animal by the lion, that he could not hope to survive the day.

14. *Like a crane*. The word used here (סוּס) denotes usually a *horse*. The Rabbins render it here 'a crane.' Gesenius translates it 'a swallow;' and in his Lexicon interprets the word which is translated 'a swallow' (עָגוּר) to mean *circling*, making gyrations; and the whole phrase, 'as the circling swallow.' The Syriac renders this, 'As the chattering swallow.' The Vulgate, 'As the young of the swallow.' The LXX.

15 What shall I say? he hath both spoken unto me, and himself hath done *it:* I shall go softly all my years in the bitterness of my soul.

---

simply 'As the swallow.' That two birds are intended here, or that some fowl is denoted by the word עָגוּר, is manifest from Jer. viii. 7, where it is mentioned as distinct from the כוּס (the crane) וְכוּס וְעָגוּר. On the meaning of the words Bochart may be consulted (*Hieroz.* i. 2. p. 602). It is probable that the swallow and the crane are intended. The swallow is well known, and is remarkable for its twittering. The crane is also a well-known bird with long limbs made to go in the water. Its noise may be expressive of grief. ¶ *So did I chatter.* Peep, or twitter (see Note on ch. viii. 19). The idea here is doubtless that of pain that was expressed in sounds resembling that made by birds—a broken, unmeaning, unintelligible sighing; or quick breathing, and moaning. ¶ *I did mourn as a dove.* The dove, from its plaintive sound, is an emblem of grief. It is so used in ch. lix. 11. The idea is that of the *lonely* or *solitary* dove that is lamenting or mourning for its companion:

> 'Just as the lonely dove laments its mate.'

¶ *Mine eyes fail.* The word here used (דָּלַל) means properly *to hang down,* to swing like the branches of the willow; then to be languid, feeble, weak. Applied to the eye, it means that it languishes and becomes weak. ¶ With looking *upward.* To God, for relief and comfort. He had looked so long and so intensely toward heaven for aid, that his eyes became weak and feeble. ¶ *O* Lord, *I am oppressed.* This was his language in his affliction. He was so oppressed and borne down, that he cried to God for relief. ¶ *Undertake for me.* Marg. 'Ease me.' The word (עָרַב) more properly means, to become surety for him. See it explained in the Note on ch. xxxvi. 8. Here it means, be surety for my life; give assurance that I shall be restored; take me under thy protection (see Ps. cxix. 122): 'Be surety for thy servant for good.'

15. *What shall I say?* This language seems to denote surprise and gratitude at unexpected deliverance. It is the language of a heart that is overflowing, and that wants words to express its deep emotions. In the previous verse he had described his pain, anguish, and despair. In this he records the sudden and surprising deliverance which God had granted; which was so great that no words could express his sense of it. Nothing could be more natural than this language; nothing would more appropriately express the feelings of a man who had been suddenly restored to health from dangerous sickness, and brought from the borders of the grave. ¶ *He hath both spoken unto me.* That is, he has *promised.* So the word is often used (Deut. xxvi. 17; Jer. iii. 19). He had made the promise by the instrumentality of Isaiah (ver. 5, 6). The promise related to his recovery, to the length of his days, and to his entire deliverance from the hands of the Assyrians. ¶ *And himself hath done* it. He himself has restored me according to his promise, when no one else could have done it. ¶ *I shall go softly.* Lowth renders this, in accordance with the Vulgate, 'Will I reflect.' But the Hebrew will not bear this construction. The word here used (דָּדָה) occurs in but one other place in the Bible (Ps. xlii. 4): 'I *went* with them to the house of God;' *i.e.*, I went with them in a sacred procession to the house of God; I went with a solemn, calm, slow pace. The idea here is, 'I will go humbly, submissively, all my life; I will walk in a serious manner, remembering that I am travelling to the grave; I will avoid pride, pomp, and display; I will suffer the remembrance of my sickness, and of God's mercy to produce a calm, serious, thoughtful demeanour all my life.' This is the *proper* effect of sickness on a pious mind, and it is its *usual* effect. And probably, one design of God was to keep Hezekiah from the ostentatious parade usually attendant on his lofty station; from being elated with his deliverance from the Assyrian; from improper celebrations of that deliverance by revelry and pomp; and to keep him in remembrance, that though he

16 O LORD, by these *things men*
live, [a] and in all these *things is* the
life of my spirit: so wilt thou recover me, and make me to live.
17 Behold, [1] for peace I had great
bitterness; but thou hast [2] in love
to my soul *delivered it* from the pit
of [b] corruption: for thou hast cast
all my sins behind thy back.
18 For the grave [c] cannot praise
thee, death cannot celebrate thee:
they that go down into the pit cannot hope for thy truth.

a Mat.4.4. 1 or, *on my peace* came. 2 *loved my soul from the pit.* b Ps.10.2. c Ps.6.5.

was a monarch, yet he was a mortal man, and that he held his life at the disposal of God. ¶ *In the bitterness of my soul.* I will remember the deep distress, the bitter sorrows of my sickness, and my surprising recovery; and will allow the remembrance of that to diffuse seriousness and gratitude over all my life.

16. *O LORD, by these* things men *live.* The design of this and the following verses is evidently to set forth the goodness of God, and to celebrate his praise for what he had done. The phrase 'these things,' refers evidently to the *promises* of God and their *fulfilment;* and the idea is, that men are sustained in the land of the living only by such gracious interpositions as he had experienced. It was not because men had any power of preserving their own lives, but because God interposed in time of trouble, and restored to health when there was no human prospect that they could recover. ¶ *And in all these* things. In these promises, and in the Divine interposition. ¶ Is *the life of my spirit.* I am alive in virtue only of these things. ¶ *So wilt thou recover me.* Or so *hast* thou recovered me; that is, thou hast restored me to health.

17. *Behold, for peace.* That is, instead of the health, happiness, and prosperity which I had enjoyed, and which I hope still to enjoy. ¶ *I had great bitterness.* Heb. 'Bitterness to me, bitterness;' an emphatic expression, denoting intense sorrow. ¶ *But thou hast in love to my soul.* Marg. 'Loved my soul from the pit.' The word which occurs here (חָשַׁקְתָּ) denotes properly *to join* or *fasten together;* then to be attached to any one; to be united tenderly; to embrace. Here it means that God had loved him, and had thus delivered his soul from death. ¶ Delivered it *from the pit of corruption.* The word rendered corruption (בְּלִי), denotes consumption, destruction, perdition. It may be applied to the grave, or to the deep and dark abode of departed spirits; and the phrase here is evidently synonymous with *sheol* or *hades.* The grave, or the place for the dead, is often represented as *a pit*—deep and dark—to which the living descend (Job xvii. 16; xxxiii. 18, 24, 28, 30; Ps. xxviii. 1; xxx. 3; lv. 23; lxix. 15; lxxxviii. 4; comp. Note on Isa. xiv. 15, 19). ¶ *For thou hast cast all my sins behind thy back.* Thou hast forgiven them; hast ceased to punish me on account of them. This shows that Hezekiah, in accordance with the sentiment everywhere felt and expressed in the Bible, regarded his suffering as the fruit of sin.

18. *For the grave cannot praise thee.* The Hebrew word here is *sheol.* It is put by metonymy here for those who are *in* the grave, *i.e.*, for the dead. The word 'praise' here refers evidently to the public and solemn celebration of the goodness of God. It is clear, I think, that Hezekiah had a belief in a future state, or that he expected to dwell with 'the inhabitants of the land of silence' (ver. 11) when he died. But he did not regard that state as one adapted to the celebration of the public praises of God. It was a land of darkness; an abode of silence and stillness; a place where there was no temple, and no public praise such as he had been accustomed to. A similar sentiment is expressed by David in Ps. vi. 5:

For in death there is no remembrance of thee;
In the grave who shall give thee thanks?

In regard to the Jewish conceptions of the state of the dead, see Notes on ch. xiv. 15, 19.

[See the Supplementary Note on ch. xiv. 9; also the Prefatory Remarks by the Editor on the Author's exposition of Job. The ideas entertained by the Author on the state of knowledge

19 The living, the living, he shall
praise thee, as I *do* this day: the
father [a] to the children shall make
known thy truth.
20 The LORD *was ready* to save
me: therefore we will sing my songs
to the stringed instruments all the
days of our life in the house of the
LORD.
21 For Isaiah had said, Let them
take a lump of figs, and lay *it* for
a plaster upon the boil, and he
shall recover.
22 Hezekiah also had said, What

[a] Ps.78.3,4.

among the ancient saints regarding a future world, cannot but be regarded as peculiarly unfortunate. After the fashion of some German critics, the Old Testament worthies are reduced to the same level with the heroes of Homer and Virgil, as far as this matter is concerned at least.]

¶ *Cannot hope for thy truth.* They are shut out from all the means by which thy truth is brought to the mind, and the offers of salvation are presented. Their probation is at an end; their privileges are closed; their destiny is sealed up. The idea is, it is a privilege to live, because this is a world where the offers of salvation are made, and where those who are conscious of guilt may hope in the mercy of God.

19. *The living, the living.* An emphatic or intensive form of expression, as in ver. 11, 17. Nothing would express his idea but a repetition of the word, as if the heart was full of it. ¶ *The father to the children.* One generation of the living to another. The father shall have so deep a sense of the goodness of God that he shall desire to make it known to his children, and to perpetuate the memory of it in the earth.

20. *The* LORD was ready *to save me.* He was prompt, quick to save me. He did not hesitate or delay. ¶ *Therefore we will sing my songs.* That is, my family and nation. The song of Hezekiah was designed evidently not as a mere *record*, but to be used in celebrating the praises of God, and probably in a public manner in the temple. The restoration of the monarch was a fit occasion for public rejoicing; and it is probable that this ode was composed to be used by the company of singers that were employed constantly in the temple. ¶ *To the stringed instruments.* We will set it to music, and will use it publicly (see Notes on ch. v. 12).

21. *For Isaiah had said.* In the parallel place in Kings the statement in these two verses is introduced *before* the account of the miracle on the sun-dial, and before the account of his recovery (2 Kings xx. 7, 8). The order in which it is introduced, however, is not material. ¶ *Let them take a lump of figs.* The word here used (דְּבֵלָה) denotes *a round cake* of dried figs pressed together in a mass (1 Sam. xxv. 18). Figs were thus pressed together for preservation, and for convenience of conveyance. ¶ *And lay* it *for a plaster.* The word here used (מָרַח) denotes properly *to rub*, bruise, crush by rubbing; then to rub, in, to anoint, to soften. Here it means they were to take dried figs and lay them softened on the ulcer. ¶ *Upon the boil* (הַשְּׁחִין). This word means a burning sore or an inflamed ulcer (Ex. ix. 9, 11; Lev. xiii. 18–20). The verb in Arabic means to be hot, inflamed; to ulcerate. The noun is used to denote a species of black leprosy in Egypt, called Elephantiasis, distinguished by the black scales with which the skin is covered, and by the swelling of the legs. Here it probably denotes a pestilential boil; an eruption, or inflamed ulceration produced by the plague, that threatened immediate death. Jerome says that the plaster of figs was medicinal, and adapted to reduce the inflammation and restore health. There is no improbability in the supposition; nor does any thing in the narrative prohibit us from supposing that natural means might have been used to restore him. The miracle consisted in the arrest of the shade on the sun-dial, and in the announcement of Isaiah that he would recover. That *figs*, when dried, were used in the Materia Medica of the ancients, is asserted by both Pliny and Celsus (see Pliny, *Nat. Hist.* xxiii. 7; Celsus, v. 2, quoted by Lowth.)

22. *Hezekiah also had said.* What

is the sign that I shall also go up to the house [a] of the LORD?

CHAPTER XXXIX.

ANALYSIS.

THIS short chapter completes the historical part of Isaiah. The same record occurs with some slight changes in 2 Kings xx. 12–21. Comp. the Introduction to ch. xxxvi. The chapter is composed of the following parts:—1. The statement that the king of Babylon sent an embassage to Hezekiah to congratulate him on his recovery (1). This embassage contemplated also an inquiry into the truth of the report in regard to the miracle on the sun-dial (2 Chron. xxxii. 31). 2. Hezekiah showed them all his treasures in an ostentatious and improper manner (2). This was permitted, in order that he might be tried, and might know all that was in his own heart, and not be lifted up with pride, and with the conviction of his own righteousness (2 Chron. xxxii. 31). 3. Isaiah is sent with a message to Hezekiah to inquire what he had done, and who those ambassadors were (3–5). 4. He is directed to deliver the solemn message of God that Jerusalem should be taken, and that all its inhabitants and all its treasures should be carried to Babylon—the place whence those ambassadors came (5–7). 5. Hezekiah expresses submission to the just sentence and purpose of God, and gratitude that it should not occur in his days (8).

AT [b] that time Merodach-baladan, the son of Baladan, king of Babylon, sent letters and a present to Hezekiah: for he had heard that he had been sick, and was recovered.

a Ps.84.2. b 2 Ki.20.12,&c.

evidence or proof have I that I shall be restored, and permitted to go to the temple? The miracle on the sun-dial was wrought in answer to this request, and as a demonstration that he should yet be permitted to visit the temple of God (see Note on ver. 7).

CHAPTER XXXIX.

1. *At that time.* That is, soon after his recovery; or after he had amassed great wealth, and was surrounded with the evidences of prosperity (2 Chron. xxxii. 27–31). ¶ *Merodach-baladan, the son of Baladan, king of Babylon* In the parallel place in 2 Kings xx. 12, this name is written Berodach-baladan, by a change of a single letter. Probably the name was written and pronounced both ways. Merodach was an idol of the Babylonians (Jer. l. 2): 'Babylon is taken, Bel is confounded, Merodach is confounded.' This idol, according to Gesenius, was probably the planet *Mars*, or Mars the god of war. To this god, as well as to Saturn, the ancient Semitic nations offered human sacrifices (see Gesenius's *Lex.* and *Comm. in loc.*) The word 'Baladan' is also a compound word, and means 'Bel is his lord.' The name of this idol, *Merodach*, was often incorporated into the proper names of kings, and of others. Thus we have the names Evil-Merodach, Messi-Mordachus, Sisimordachus, Mardocentes, &c. In regard to the statement of Isaiah in this verse, no small degree of difficulty has been felt by commentators, and it is not until quite recently that the difficulty has been removed, and it has been done in a manner to furnish an additional and most striking demonstration of the entire and minute accuracy of the sacred narrative. The difficulty arose from several circumstances—1. This king of Babylon is nowhere else mentioned in sacred history. 2. The kingdom of Assyria was yet flourishing, and Babylon was one of its dependencies. For, only nine years before, Salmanassar the Assyrian monarch is said to have transported the inhabitants of Babylon to other parts (2 Kings xvii. 24), and Manasseh, not many years after, was carried captive to Babylon by the king of Assyria (2 Chron. xxxiii. 11). These instances incontestably prove that at the time of Hezekiah, Babylon was dependent on the Assyrian kings. Who, then, it is asked, was this Merodach-baladan, king of Babylon? If he was governor of that city, how could he send an embassy of congratulation to the Jewish sovereign, then at war with his liege lord? The canon of Ptolemy gives us no king of this name, nor does his chronology appear reconcilable with sacred history.

'In this darkness and doubt,' says Dr. Wiseman, 'we must have continued, and the apparent contradiction of this text to other passages would have remaimed inexplicable, had not the progress of modern Oriental study brought

2 And Hezekiah was glad of them and shewed them the house of his [1]precious things, the silver, and the gold, and the spices, and the precious ointment, and all the house of his [2]armour, and all that was found in his treasures: there was nothing in his house, nor in all his dominion, that Hezekiah shewed them not.

1 or, *spicery*.

2 *vessels*, or, *instruments*, or, *jewels*.

---

to light a document of the most venerable antiquity. This is nothing less than a fragment of Berosus, preserved in the chronicle of Eusebius. This interesting fragment informs us, that after Sennacherib's brother had governed Babylon, as Assyrian viceroy, Acises unjustly possessed himself of the supreme command. After thirty days he was murdered by Merodach-baladan, who usurped the sovereignty for six months, when he was in turn killed, and was succeeded by Elibus. But after three years, Sennacherib collected an army, gave the usurper battle, conquered, and took him prisoner. Having once more reduced Babylon to his obedience, he left his son Assordan, the Esarhaddon of Scripture, as governor of the city.'

The only objection to this statement, or to the entire consistency of this fragment with the Scripture narrative is, that Isaiah relates the murder of Sennacherib, and the succession of Esarhaddon before Merodach-baladan's embassy to Jerusalem. But to this Gesenius has well replied, that this arrangement is followed by the prophet in order to conclude the history of the Assyrian monarch, which has no further connection with the subject, so as not to return to it again.

By this order, also, the prophecy of his murder is more closely connected with the history of its fulfilment (ch. xxxvii. 7; comp. ver. 38). And this solution, which supposes some interval to have elapsed between Sennacherib's return to Nineveh, and his death, is rendered probable by the words of the text itself. 'He went and returned, *and dwelt in Nineveh;* and it came to pass,' &c. (ch. xxxvii. 37, 38.)

Thus we have it certainly explained how there was a king, or rather a usurper in Babylon at the time when it was really a provincial city of the Assyrian empire. Nothing was more probable than that Merodach-baladan, having seized the throne, should endeavour to unite himself in league and amity with the enemies of his master, against whom he had revolted. Hezekiah, who, no less than himself, had thrown off the Assyrian yoke, and was in powerful alliance with the king of Egypt, would be his first resource. No embassy, on the other hand, could be more welcome to the Jewish monarch who had the common enemy in his neighbourhood, and who would be glad to see a division made in his favour by a rebellion in the very heart of that enemy's kingdom. Hence arose that excessive attention which he paid to the envoys of the usurper, and which so offended Isaiah, or rather God, who, as a consequence, threatened the Babylonian captivity (see Dr. Wiseman's *Lectures on Science and Revealed Religion*, pp. 369–371. Ed. And. 1837). ¶ *Sent letters.* The LXX. add, καὶ πρέσβεις—'and ambassadors.' ¶ *And a present.* It was customary among the Orientals, as it is now, to send a valuable present when one prince sent an embassage for any purpose to another. It is stated in 2 Chron. xxxii. 31, that one object of their coming was to make inquiry 'of the wonder that was done in the land;' that is, of the miracle in regard to the retrocession of the shadow on the sun-dial of Ahaz. It is well known that, from the earliest periods, the Babylonians and Chaldeans were distinguished for their attention to astronomy. Indeed, as a science, astronomy was first cultivated on the plains of Chaldea; and there the knowledge of that science was scarcely surpassed by any of the ancient nations. The report which they had heard of this miracle would, therefore, be to them a matter of deep interest as an astronomical fact, and they came to make inquiry into the exact truth of the report.

2. *And Hezekiah was glad of them.* Possibly he regarded himself as flattered by an embassage from so great a distance, and so celebrated a place as Babylon. It is certain that he erred

3 Then came Isaiah the prophet unto king Hezekiah, and said unto him, What said these men? and from whence came they unto thee? And Hezekiah said, They are come from a far country unto me, *even* from Babylon.

---

in some way in regard to the manner in which he received them, and especially in the ostentatious display which he made of his treasures (2 Chron. xxxii. 31). ¶ *And showed them the house of his precious things.* The LXX. render this, Νεχωθᾶ—'The house of Nechotha,' retaining the Hebrew word. The Marg. 'Spicery.' The Hebrew word (נְכֹת) properly means, according to Gesenius, *a contusion,* a breaking to pieces; hence *aromatic powder,* or spices reduced to powder, and then any kind of aromatics. Hence the word here may mean 'the house of his spices,' as Aquila, Symmachus, and the Vulgate translate it; or 'a treasury,' 'a storehouse,' as the Chaldee and the Syriac here render it. It was undoubtedly a treasure or storehouse; but it may have taken its name from the fact, that it was mainly employed as a place in which to keep spices, unguents, and the various kinds of aromatics which were used either in public worship, or for the purposes of luxury. ¶ *The silver and the gold.* Possibly Hezekiah may have obtained no small quantity of silver and gold from what was left in the camp of the Assyrians. It is certain that after he was delivered from danger he was signally prospered, and became one of the most wealthy and magnificent monarchs of the east; 2 Chron. xxxii. 27, 28: 'And Hezekiah had exceeding much riches and honour; and he made himself treasuries for silver and for gold, and for precious stones, and for spices, and for shields, and for all manner of pleasant jewels; storehouses also for the increase of corn, and wine, and oil; and stalls for all manner of beasts, and cotes for flocks.' A considerable part of this wealth arose from presents which were made to him, and from gifts which were made for the service of the temple (2 Chron. xxxii. 23). ¶ *And the precious ointment.* Used for anointing kings and priests. Or more probably the ointment here referred to was that which was in more common use, to anoint the body after bathing, or when they were to appear in public. ¶ *And all the house of his armour.* Marg. 'Vessels,' or 'instruments,' or 'jewels.' The word כְּלִי denotes *any* article of furniture, utensil, or vessel; any trapping, instrument, or tool; and any implement of war, weapon, or arms. Probably it here refers to the latter, and denotes shields, swords, spears, such as were used in war, and such as Hezekiah had prepared for defence. The phrase is equivalent to our word *arsenal* (comp. 2 Chron. xxxii. 27). Solomon had an extensive arsenal of this description (1 Kings x. 16, 17), and it is probable that these were regarded as a part of the necessary defence of the kingdom. ¶ *Nor in all his dominion.* Everything that contributed to the defence, the wealth, or the magnificence of his kingdom he showed to them. The purpose for which Hezekiah thus showed them all that he had, was evidently display. In 2 Chron. xxxii. 25, it is stated that 'Hezekiah rendered not again according to the benefit done unto him, for his heart was lifted up;' and in ver. 31, it is said, that in regard to this transaction, 'God left him, to try him, that he might know all that was in his heart.' The result showed how much God hates pride, and how certainly he will punish all forms of ostentation.

3. *Then came Isaiah.* Isaiah was accustomed to declare the will of God most freely to monarchs (see ch. vii.) ¶ *What said these men?* What proposition have they made? What is the design of their coming? It is *implied* in the question that there had been some improper communication from them. To this question Hezekiah returned no answer. ¶ *And from whence came they?* It was doubtless known in Jerusalem that ambassadors had come, but it would not be likely to be known from what country they had come. ¶ *From a far country.* Probably this was said in order to palliate and excuse his conduct, by

4 Then said he, What have they seen in thine house? And Hezekiah answered, All that *is* in mine house have they seen: there is nothing among my [a] treasures that I have not shewed them.

5 Then said Isaiah to Hezekiah, Hear the word of the LORD of hosts:

6 Behold, the days [b] come, that all that *is* in thine house, and *that* which thy fathers have laid up in store until this day, shall be carried to [c] Babylon: nothing shall be left, saith the LORD.

a Prov.23.5. b Jer.20.5. c 2 Ki.25.6,&c.

intimating to the prophet that it was proper to show respectful attention to foreigners, and that he had done nothing more than was demanded by the laws of hospitality and kindness.

4. *What have they seen?* It is probable that the fact that Hezekiah had showed them the treasures of his kingdom was known in Jerusalem. Such a fact would be likely to attract attention, and to produce inquiry among the people into the cause. ¶ *All that is in mine house.* Here was the confessions of a frank, an honest, and a pious man. There was no concealment; no disguise. Hezekiah knew that he was dealing with a man of God—a man too to whom he had been under great obligations. He knew that Isaiah had come commissioned by God, and that it would be in vain to attempt to conceal anything. Nor does he seem to have wished to make any concealment. If he was conscious that what he had done had been improper, he was willing to confess it; and at any rate he was willing that the exact truth should be known. Had Hezekiah been like Ahaz, he might have spurned Isaiah from his presence as presenting improper inquiries. But Hezekiah was accustomed to regard with respect the messengers of God, and he was therefore willing to submit his whole conduct to the Divine adjudication and reproof. Piety makes a man willing that all that he has done should be known. It saves him from double-dealing and subterfuges, and a disposition to make vain excuses; and it inclines him to fear God, to respect his ambassadors, and to listen to the voice of eternal truth.

5. *Hear the word of the* LORD *of hosts.* Hear what the mighty God that rules in heaven says of this. This is an instance of great fidelity on the part of the prophet. He felt himself sent from God in a solemn manner to rebuke sin in a monarch, and a pious monarch. It is an instance that strikingly resembles the boldness and faithfulness of Nathan when he went to David, and said, 'Thou art the man' (2 Sam. xii. 7).

6. *Behold, the days come.* The captivity of the Jews in Babylon commenced about one hundred and twenty years after this prediction (comp. Jer. xx. 5). ¶ *That all that* is *in thine house.* That is, all the treasures that are in the treasure-house (ver. 2). ¶ *And* that *which thy fathers have laid up in store.* In 2 Kings xviii. 15, 16, we are told that Hezekiah, in order to meet the demands of the king of Assyria, had cut off even the ornaments of the temple, and taken all the treasures which were in 'the king's house.' It is *possible,* however, that there might have been other treasures which had been accumulated by the kings before him which he had not touched. ¶ *Nothing shall be left.* This was literally fulfilled (see 2 Chron. xxxvi. 18). It is remarkable, says Vitringa, that this is the first intimation that the Jews would be carried to Babylon—the first designation of the *place* where they would be so long punished and oppressed. Micah (iv. 10), a contemporary of Isaiah, declares the same thing, but probably this was not before the declaration here made by Isaiah. Moses had declared repeatedly, that, if they were a rebellious people, they should be removed from their own to a foreign land; but he had not designated the country (Lev. xxvi. 33, 34; Deut. xxviii. 64–67; xxx. 3). Ahijah, in the time of Jeroboam (1 Kings xiv. 15), had predicted that they should be carried 'beyond the river,' *i.e.*, the Euphrates; and Amos (v. 27) had said that God would carry them 'into captivity beyond Damascus.' But all these predictions were now concentrated on Babylon;

7 And of thy sons that shall issue from thee, which thou shalt beget, shall they take away; and [a] they shall be eunuchs in the palace of the king of Babylon.

8 Then said Hezekiah to Isaiah, Good [b] *is* the word of the LORD which thou hast spoken. He said moreover, For there shall be peace and truth in my days.

[a] Fulfilled, Dan.1.2-7.

[b] 1 Sam.3.18.

and it was for the first time distinctly announced by Isaiah that that was to be the land where they were to suffer so long and so painful a captivity.

7. *And of thy sons.* Thy posterity (see Note on Matt. i. 1). ¶ *That shall issue from thee.* Of the royal family. The captivity at Babylon occurred more than a hundred years after this, and of course those who were carried there were somewhat remote descendants of Hezekiah. ¶ *And they shall be eunuchs.* The word here used (סָרִיסִים *sârîsîm*) denotes properly and strictly eunuchs, or such persons as were accustomed to attend on the harems of Oriental monarchs (Est. ii. 3, 14, 15). These persons were also employed often in various offices of the court (Est. i. 10, 12, 15), and hence the word often means a minister of court, a court-officer, though not literally an eunuch (Gen. xxxvii. 6; xxxix. 1). It is not easy, however, to tell when the word is to be understood literally, and when not. The Targum understands it of those who should be *nurtured*, or become great in the kingdom of Babylon. That the Jews were advanced to some offices of trust and power in Babylon, is evident from the case of Daniel (i. 2–7). It is by no means improbable, also, that the king of Babylon would have a pride in having among the attendants at his court, or even over the harem, the descendants of the once magnificent monarchs of the Jews.

8. *Good* is *the word of the* LORD. The sense of this is, 'I acquiesce in this; I perceive that it is right; I see in it evidence of benevolence and goodness.' The grounds of his acquiescence seem to have been—1. The fact that he saw that it was just. He felt that he had sinned, and that he had made an improper display of his treasures, and deserved to be punished. 2. He felt that the sentence was mild and merciful. It was less than he deserved, and less than he had reason to expect. 3. It was merciful to *him*, and to his kingdom *at that time*. God was not coming forth to cut him off, or to involve him in any more calamity. 4. His own reign and life were to be full of mercy still. He had abundant cause of gratitude, therefore, that God was dealing with *him* in so much kindness. It cannot be shown that Hezekiah was regardless of his posterity, or unconcerned at the calamity which would come upon them. All that the passage fairly implies is, that he saw that it was right; and that it was proof of great mercy in God that the punishment was deferred, and was not, as in the case of David (2 Sam. 13, 14, *sq.*), to be inflicted in his own time. The nature of the crime of Hezekiah is more fully stated in the parallel passage in 2 Chron. xxxii. 25, 26, 30, 31. ¶ *For there shall be peace.* My kingdom shall not be disturbed during my reign with a foreign invasion. ¶ *And truth.* The truth of God shall be maintained; his worship shall be kept up; his name shall be honoured. ¶ *In my days.* During my reign. He inferred this because Isaiah had said (ver. 7) that *his posterity* would be carried to Babylon. He was assured, therefore, that these calamities would not come in his own time. We may learn from this—1. That we should submit to God when he punishes us. If we have right feelings we shall always see that we deserve all that we are called to suffer. 2. In the midst of severest judgments we may find *some* evidence of mercy. There are *some* considerations on which the mind may fix that will console it with the evidence of the compassion of God, and that will not only make it submissive, but fill it with gratitude. 3. We should accustom ourselves to such views of the Divine dealings, and should *desire* to find in them the evidence of goodness and mercy, and not the evidence of wrath and severity. It is of infinite import-

ance that we should cherish right views of God; and should believe that he is holy, good, and merciful. To do this, we should feel that we deserve *all* that we suffer; we should look at what we *might* have endured; we should look at the mercies *spared* to us, as well as at those which are *taken away;* and we should hold to the belief, as an unwavering principle from which we are never to depart, that God is *good,* SUPREMELY AND WHOLLY GOOD. Then our minds will have peace. Then with Hezekiah we may say, 'Good is the word of JEHOVAH.' Then with the suffering Redeemer of the world we may always say, 'Not my will, but THINE BE DONE' (Luke xxii. 42).

GENERAL INTRODUCTION TO CHAPTERS XL.-LXVI.

It is admitted, on all hands, that the second part of Isaiah, comprising the prophecies which commence at the fortieth chapter, and which continue to the end of the book, is to be regarded as the most sublime, and to us the most important part of the Old Testament. In the previous portions of his prophecies there was much that was local and temporary. Indeed all, or nearly all, that occurs from ch. i. to ch. xxxix. had direct and immediate reference to the times in which the prophet lived, or was suggested by the events which occurred in those times. Not unfrequently, indeed, there were prophecies respecting the Messiah's coming (ch. ii., iv., vii., ix., xi., xxxv.), but the primary reference was to events that were then occurring, or which were soon to occur, and which were local in their character. And though the mind of the prophet is carried forward by the laws of prophetic suggestion (see Introd. § 7, III. (3), and he describes the times of the Messiah, yet the immediate and primary reference of those prophecies is to Judea, or to the kingdoms and countries in the vicinity of Judea, with which the Jews were in various ways connected.

In this portion of the prophecy, however, there is little that is local and temporary. It is occupied with a prophetic statement of events which were to occur long after the time of the prophet; and which would be of interest not only to the Jewish nation, but to the whole human family. It is a beautiful and glowing description of occurrences, in which men of the present and of all subsequent times will have as deep an interest as they who have lived at any former period. Indeed it is not improbable that as the world advances in age, the interest in this portion of Isaiah will increase; and that as the gospel is carried around the globe, the beauty and accuracy of these descriptions will be more clearly seen and highly appreciated; and that nations will yet derive their highest consolations, and see the clearest proof of the inspiration of the Sacred Volume, from the entire correspondence between this portion of Isaiah and the events which are yet to gladden the world. There is no portion of the Old Testament where there is so graphic and clear a description of the times of the Messiah, None of the other prophets linger so long, and with such apparent delight, on the promised coming of the Prince of Peace; or his character and work; on the nature of his instructions, and the manner of his reception; on the trials of his life, and the painful circumstances of his death; on the dignity of his nature, and on his lowly and humble character; on the prevalence of his religion, and on its transforming and happy effects; on the consolations which he would furnish, and on the fact that his religion would bear light and joy around the world.

Lowth supposes that this prophecy was uttered in the latter part of the reign of Hezekiah. A more probable supposition is that of Hengstenberg, that it was uttered in the time of Manasseh. I have endeavoured to show (Introd. § 2) that Isaiah lived some time during the reign of Manasseh. According to this supposition, there was probably an interval of some twelve or fourteen years between the close of the predictions in the first part, and those which occupy this portion of the book. Manasseh was a cruel prince; and his reign was cruel (see Introd. § 3). It was a time of the prevalence of idolatry and sin. In this state of things, it is probable that Isaiah, who was then of great age, withdrew almost entirely from the public functions of the prophetic work, and sought personal consolation, and endeavoured to furnish comfort for the pious portion of the nation, in the contemplation of the future. In this period, I suppose, this portion of the prophecy was conceived and penned. Isaiah, in the close of the previous part of the prophecies (ch. xxxix. 7), had distinctly announced that the nation would be carried to Babylon. He saw that the crimes of the monarch and of the nation were such as would certainly hasten this result. He had retired from the public functions of the prophetic office, and given himself up to the contemplation of happier and purer times. He, therefore, devoted himself to the task of furnishing consolation for the pious portion of the nation, and especially of recording prophetic descriptions which would comfort the Jews when they should be held in long captivity in Babylon. We have seen (Notes on ch. xiii. and xiv.) that Isaiah had before this laid the foundations for these consolations by the assurance that Babylon and its mighty power would be entirely destroyed, and, of course, that the Jewish people could not be held *always* in bondage there. In this part of the prophecy (ch. xl.–lxvi.) his object is to give more full and specific consolations. He therefore places himself, in vision (see Introd. § 7, I. (4), in the midst of the future scenes which he describes, and states distinctly and fully the grounds of consolation. These topics of consolation would arise from two sources—both of which he presents at great length and with great beauty. The first is, that the nation would be delivered from its long and painful captivity. This was the *primary* thing to be done, and this was needful in order to furnish to them consolation. He places himself in that future time. He sees his own nation borne to a distant land, according to his own predictions; sees them sighing in their hard bondage; and sees the city and the temple where they once worshipped the God of their fathers laid in ruins, and all their pleasant things laid waste (ch. lxiv. 11), and the people dispirited and sad in their long and painful captivity. He predicts the close of that captivity, and speaks of it as present to his view. He consoles the people by the assurance that it was coming to an end; names the monarch—Cyrus—by whom their oppressors were to be punished, and by whom they were to be restored to their own land; and describes, in the most beautiful and glowing imagery, their certain return. The second source of consolation is that which relates to the coming of a far more important deliverer than Cyrus, and to a far more important redemption than that from the captivity at Babylon. By the laws of prophetic suggestion, and in accordance with the usual manner of Isaiah, his mind is carried forward to much more momentous events. The descriptions of the prophet insensibly change from the immediate subject under contemplation to the far more important events connected with the coming and work of the Messiah. This was the common rule by which the mind of Isaiah acted; and it is no wonder, therefore, that an event so strikingly resembling the deliverance of man from the bondage of sin by the Messiah as was the deliverance from the captivity of Babylon, should have been suggested by that, and that his thoughts should pass rapidly from one to the other, and the one be forgotten in the other. The eye of the prophet, therefore, glances rapidly from the object more immediately in view in the future, to the object more remote; and he regards the return from the Babylonish captivity as introductory to a far more important deliverance. In the contemplation of that more distant event, therefore, he becomes wholly absorbed; and from this he derives his main topics of consolation. He sees the author of redemption in various scenes—now as a sufferer, humble, poor, and persecuted; and now the more distant glories of the Messiah's kingdom rise to view. He sees him raised up from the dead; his empire extend and spread among the Gentiles; kings and princes from all lands coming to lay their offerings at his feet; the distant tribes of men come bending before him, and his religion of peace and joy diffusing its blessings around the world. In the contemplation of these future glories, he desires to furnish consolation for his afflicted countrymen in Babylon, and at the same time a demonstration of the truth of the oracles of God, and of the certain prevalence of the true religion, which should impart happiness and peace in all future times.

The character of the period when this portion of the prophecy was delivered, and the circumstances under which it was uttered, as well as the object which the prophet had in view, may account for some remarkable features in it which cannot fail to strike the attentive reader—1. The *name* of the prophet does not occur. It may have been designed that the consolation should be furnished rather by the *nature* of the truth, than by the name or authority of the man. When addressing monarchs, and when denouncing the vices and crimes of the age, his name is mentioned (comp. ch. vii. and xxxviii.); the authority under which he acted is stated; and he utters his warnings in the name of JEHOVAH. Here he presents simple truth, in a case where it is to be presumed that his prophetic authority and character were already sufficiently established. 2. There is less of fire and impetuosity, less of severity and abruptness of manner, in this than in the former prophecies. Isaiah was now an old man, and his style, and manner of thinking and of utterance would be naturally mellowed by age. His object, also, was not reproof so much as consolation; it was not, as formerly, to denounce judgment, but to speak of comfort. It was not to rebuke kings and nobles for their crimes, and to rouse the nation to a sense of its danger; it was to mitigate the woes of those in bondage, and to furnish topics of support to those who were groaning in captivity far from the temple of their

God, and from the sepulchres of their fathers. The language of the second part is more gentle and flowing; more tender and mild. There is exquisite beauty and finish, and occasionally there are bursts of the highest sublimity; but there is not the compression of thought, and the struggling as it were for utterance, which there often is in the former part. There, the prophetic impulse is like waters pent up between projecting rocks and hills, it struggles and bursts forth impetuously and irresistibly; in this portion of the prophecy, it is like the placid stream—the full-flowing, majestic river—calm, pure, deep, and sublime. There are, indeed, characteristics of the same style, and of the same author, but it is in different circumstances, and with a different object in view. Homer in the Odyssey has been compared to the sun when setting with full orb, but with diminished brightness; in the Iliad to the sun in his meridian. Isaiah, in this part of his prophecies, resembles the sun shining with steady and pure effulgence without a cloud; in the former part, he resembles the sun when it bursts through clouds in the darkened heavens—the light struggling through the openings in the sky, and amidst the thunders that roll and echo along the hills and vales. 3. The portion which follows (ch. xl.–lxvi.) is a *single* prophecy, apparently uttered at one time, and having one great design. The former part consists of a number of independent and separate predictions, some of them very brief, and having no immediate connection with each other. Here, all is connected, and the same design is kept steadily and constantly in view. His beautiful descriptions roll on, to use one of his own images, 'like a river,' or the 'waves of the sea.' 4. Almost everything which occurs in the prophecy relates to that which was to be fulfilled long after the time of Isaiah. Occasionally there is a slight allusion to the prevalence of idolatry in his own time, but there is no express mention of the events which were then occurring. He does not mention his own circumstances; he does not allude to the name of the monarch who lived when he wrote. He seems to have forgotten the present, and to live and act in the scenes of the distant future. He, therefore, speaks *as if* he were among the exiled Jews in Babylon when their long captivity was about to come to an end; he exhorts, rebukes, administers, comforts, as if they were present, and as if he were directly addressing them. He speaks of the life, sufferings, and death of the Messiah also, as events which he *saw*, and seeks personal consolation and support amidst the prevailing crimes and calamities of his own times, in the contemplation of future scenes.

It will be seen, from what has been said, and from the examination of the prophecy itself, that it possesses a decidedly evangelical character. Indeed, this is so clear and apparent, that many have maintained that the primary reference is to the Messiah, and that it had no relation to the return from the captivity at Babylon. Such was the opinion of the learned Vitringa. Even Grotius, of whom it has been said, that while Cocceius found 'Christ everywhere, he found him nowhere,' admits that the prophecy has an obvious reference to the Messiah. His words are, 'Cum autem omnia Dei beneficia umbram in se contineant eorum quæ Christus præstitit, tum præcipue ista omnia quæ deinceps ab Esaia prænunciabuntur, verbis sæpissime a Deo sic directis, *ut simplicius limpidiusque in res Christi, quam in illas, quas primo significare*

Esaias voluit, convenirent.' Indeed, it is impossible to read this portion of the prophecy without believing that it had reference to the Messiah, and that it was designed to furnish consolation from the contemplation of his glorious reign. That there was a primary reference to the return from the captivity at Babylon, I shall endeavour to show as we advance in the interpretation of the prophecy. But it will also be seen that though the prophet *begins* with that, he *ends* usually with a contemplation of the Redeemer; that these events seem to have lain so near each other in the beautiful field of prophetic vision, that the one naturally suggested the other; and that the description passes from the former object to the latter, so that the contemplation of the person and work of the Messiah, and of the triumphs of his gospel, become the absorbing theme of his glowing language (see Introd. § 7).

CHAPTER XL.

ANALYSIS.

I. The subject of the whole prophecy (ch. xl.–lxvi.) is introduced in ver. 1, 2. The general design is, to comfort the afflicted and oppressed people of God. They are contemplated as in Babylon, and as *near* the close of the exile. Jerusalem is regarded as in ruins (comp. ch. xliv. 26–28; li. 3; lii. 9; lviii. 12); the land is waste and desolate (lxiii. 18); the city and the temple are destroyed (lxiv. 10, 11). Their captivity is about to end, and the people about to be restored to their own land (ch. xliv. 28; lviii. 12; lx. 10; lxv. 9). In this situation, the prophet is directed to address words of consolation to the oppressed and long-captive Jews, and to assure them that their calamities are about to close. Jerusalem —now in ruins—was to be assured that the end of her desolation was near, for that an ample punishment had been taken for all her sins.

II. The prophet next represents the deliverance under an image taken from the march of earthly kings (3–8). The voice of a herald is heard in the wilderness making proclamation, that every obstacle should be removed, that Jehovah might return to Zion conducting his people. As he had conducted them from the land of Egypt, so he was about to conduct them from Babylon, and to appear again in Jerusalem and in the temple. Between Babylon and Jerusalem there was an immense tract of country which was a pathless desert. Through this land the people would naturally be conducted, and the voice of the herald is heard demanding that a highway should be made—in the manner of a herald who preceded an army, and who required valleys to be filled, and roads to be constructed, over which the monarch and his army might pass with ease and safety. It is to be observed that the *main* thing here is not that *the people* should return, and a way be made for *them*, but that Jehovah was about to return to Jerusalem, and that the pathway should be made for *him*. *He* was to be their leader and guide, and this was the principal source of comfort in their return. In this, the Holy Spirit, who directed and inspired the prophet, *purposely* suggests language that would be applicable to a far more important event, when the herald of the Messiah should announce *his* coming. The main thing which the voice was to cry is represented in ver. 6–8. That was, that Jehovah was faithful to his promises, and that his predictions would be certainly fulfilled. Everything else would fade away—the grass would wither, the flower would fail, and the people would die —but the word of Jehovah would be unfailing, and this would be manifest alike in the release of the people from Babylon, and in the coming of the Messiah.

III. The messenger that brought these glad tidings to Jerusalem, is exhorted to announce the happy news to the remaining cities of Judah —to go to an eminence—to lift up the voice— and to proclaim that their God had come (9).

IV. In ver. 10, 11, the assurance is given that he would come 'with a strong hand'—almighty and able to save; he would come as a tender and gentle shepherd, regarding especially the weak and feeble of his people—language alike applicable to God, who should conduct the people from exile to their own land, and to the Messiah; though more strikingly and completely fulfilled in the latter.

V. The mention of the *omnipotence* of JEHOVAH, who was about to conduct his people to their own land, leads the prophet into a most sublime description of his power, majesty, and glory, the object of which seems to be to induce them to put entire confidence in him (12–17). God measures the waters in the hollow of his hand; he metes out the heavens with a span; he measures the dust of the earth, and weighs the mountains (12). None has counselled, or can counsel him;—his understanding is superior to that of all creatures (13, 14). The nations before him are as a drop of a bucket, and as the small dust of the balance, and as nothing (15, 17). All the vast forests of Lebanon, and all the beasts that roam there, would not be sufficient to constitute a burnt-offering that should be a proper expression of his majesty and glory (16).

VI. From this statement of the majesty and glory of God, the prophet shows the absurdity of attempting to form an image or likeness of God, and the certainty that all who trusted in idols should be destroyed, as the stubble is swept away by the whirlwind (18–25).

VII. It follows also, if God is so great and glorious, that the people should put confidence in him. They should believe that he was able to save them; they should wait on him who alone could renew their strength (26–31). The entire scope and design of the chapter, therefore, is, to induce them to put their reliance in God, who was about to come to vindicate his people, and who would assuredly accomplish all his predictions and promises. The argument is a most beautiful one; and the language is unsurpassed in sublimity.

COMFORT [a] ye, comfort ye my people, saith your God.

a Heb 6.17,18.

CHAPTER XL.

1. *Comfort ye, comfort ye my people*. This is the exordium, or the general subject of this and the following chapters. The commencement is abrupt, as often happens in Isaiah and the other prophets. The *scene* where this vision is laid is in Babylon; the *time* near the close of the captivity. The *topic*, or main subject of the consolation, is stated in the following verse—that that captivity was about to end, and that brighter and happier days were to succeed their calamities and their exile. The exhortation to 'comfort' the people is to be understood as a command of God to those in Babylon whose office or duty it would be to address them—that is, to the ministers of religion, or to the prophets. The Targum of Jonathan thus renders it: 'Ye prophets, prophesy consolations concerning my people.' The LXX. render it, 'Comfort ye, comfort ye my people, saith God. O priests, speak to the heart of Jerusalem; comfort her.' The design of Isaiah is doubtless to furnish that which should be to them a source of consolation when amidst the deep distress of their long captivity; to furnish an assurance that the captivity was about to end, and that brighter and happier times were to ensue. The exhortation or command is *repeated*, to give intensity or emphasis to it, in the usual manner in Hebrew, where emphasis is denoted by the *repetition* of a word. The word rendered 'comfort' (from נָחַם *nâhhăm*) means properly *to draw the breath forcibly*, to sigh, pant, groan; then to lament, or grieve (Ps. xc. 13; Jer. xv. 6); then to comfort or console *one's-self* (Gen. xxxviii. 12); then to take vengeance (comp. Note on ch. i. 24). All the forms of the word, and all the significations, indicate *deep emotion*, and the *obtaining of relief* either by repenting, or by taking vengeance, or by administering the proper topics of consolation. Here the topic of consolation is, that their calamities were about to come to an end, *in accordance with the unchanging promises of a faithful God* (ver. 8), and is thus in accordance with what is said in Heb. vi. 17, 18. ¶ *My people.* The people of God. He regarded those in Babylon as his people; and he designed also to adduce such topics of consolation as would be adapted to comfort *all* his people in all ages. ¶ *Saith your God.* The God of those whom he addressed—the God of the prophets or ministers of religion whose office was to comfort the people. We may remark here, that it is an important part of the ministerial office to administer consolation to the people of God in affliction; to exhibit to them his promises; to urge

2 Speak ye [1] comfortably to Jerusalem, and cry unto her that her warfare [2] is accomplished, that her iniquity is pardoned; for she hath received of the LORD's hand double for [a] all her sins.

1 *to the heart.* 2 or, *appointed time.*

a ch.61.7.

the topics of religion which are adapted to sustain them; and especially to uphold and cheer them with the assurance that their trials will soon come to an end, and will all terminate in complete deliverance from sorrow and calamity in heaven.

2. *Speak ye comfortably.* Heb. עַל־לֵב as in the margin, 'To the heart.' The *heart* is the seat of the affections. It is there that sorrow and joy are felt. We are oppressed there with grief, and we speak familiarly of being pained at the heart, and of being of a glad or merry heart. To speak 'to the heart,' is to speak in such a way as to remove the troubles of the heart; to furnish consolation and joy. It means that they were not merely to urge such topics as should convince the understanding, but such also as should be adopted to minister consolation to the heart. So the word is used in Gen. xxxiv. 3: 'And his soul clave unto Dinah—and he loved the damsel, and spake kindly (Heb. to the heart) of the damsel;' Gen. l. 21: 'And he comforted them, and spake kindly unto them' (Heb. to their hearts); see also 2 Chron. xxxii. 6. ¶ *To Jerusalem.* The direction is not merely to speak to the people in Babylon, but also to comfort Jerusalem itself lying in ruins. The general direction is, therefore, that the entire series of topics of consolation should be adduced—the people were to return from their bondage, and Jerusalem was to be rebuilt, and the worship of God to be restored. ¶ *And cry unto her.* In the manner of a crier; or one making public and loud proclamation (comp. ver. 3, 9). Jerusalem is here personified. She is addressed as in ruins, and as about to be rebuilt, and as capable of consolation from this promise. ¶ *That her warfare is accomplished.* LXX. 'That her humiliation (ταπείνωσις) is accomplished.' The Hebrew word (צָבָא, 'warfare') properly means *an army* or *host* (comp. Note on ch. i. 9), and is usually applied to an army going forth to war, or marshalled for battle (2 Sam. viii. 16; x. 7). It is then used to denote an appointed time of service; the discharge of a duty similar to an enlistment, and is applied to the services of the Levites in the tabernacle (Num. iv. 23): 'All that enter in to perform the service (Heb. to war the warfare), to do the work in the tabernacle of the congregation.' Compare Num. viii. 24, 25. Hence it is applied to human life contemplated as a warfare, or enlistment, involving hard service and calamity; an enlistment from which there is to be a discharge by death.

> Is there not a set time [Heb. a warfare] to man
> upon earth?
> Are not his days as the days of an hireling?
> Job vii. 1.

> But if a man die—shall he indeed live again?
> All the days of my appointed time [Heb. my
> warfare] will I wait,
> Till my change come. Job xiv. 14.

Compare Dan. x. 1. The word then means hard service, such as soldiers endure; an appointed time which they are to serve; an enlistment involving hardships, toil, privation, danger, calamity. In this sense it is applied here to Jerusalem—to the trials, calamities, desolations to which she was subjected for her sins, and which were to endure *a definite and fixed time*—like the enlistment of an army. That time was now coming to an end, and to be succeeded by a release, or discharge. Vitringa, who supposes that this refers primarily and solely to the times of the Messiah, regards this as meaning that the definite time of the legal economy, a time of toil, and of vexatious and troublesome ceremonies, was about to end by the coming of the Messiah. But the more correct interpretation is, probably, that which supposes that there was a primary reference to the long and painful captivity of the Jews in Babylon. ¶ *That her iniquity.* The iniquity or sin here referred to, is that long series of acts of rebellion, corruption, and idolatry, with which the Jewish people had been chargeable, and which had rendered their captivity necessary. As a nation, that sin was now expiated, or removed by their protracted punishment in Babylon. It was a sufficient expression of the Divine displeasure at the national offences, and God was *satisfied* (נִרְצָה) with it, and could consistently restore them to their land, and to their former privileges. The whole language here has respect to *national*, and not to individual offences. ¶ *Is pardoned.* Vulg. *Dimissa est iniquitas illius.* LXX. Λέλυται αὐτῆς ἡ ἁμαρτία—'Her sin is loosed,' dissolved, remitted. The word 'pardon' does not quite express the meaning of the word in the original (נִרְצָה). The word רָצָה (*râtzâ*) properly means *to delight in any person or thing;* to take pleasure in; then to receive graciously or favourably; to delight in sacrifices and offerings (Job xxxiii. 26; Ps. li. 18; Ezek. xx. 40); and, in the Hiphil conjugation, to satisfy, or pay off, *i.e.*, to cause to be satisfied, or pleased; and then in Hophal, to be satisfied, to be paid off, to be pleased or satisfied with an expiation, or with an atonement for sins, so as to *delight* in the person who makes it. Here it means not strictly *to pardon*, but it means that they had endured the national punishment which God saw to be necessary; they had *served out* the long and painful enlistment which he had appointed, and now he was *satisfied*, and took delight in restoring them to their own land. It does not refer to the pardon of men in consequence of the atonement made by the Lord Jesus; but it may be used as an *illustration* of that, when God is satisfied with that atonement; and when he has *pleasure* or *delight* in setting the soul free from the bondage of sin, and admitting the sinner to his favour—as he had delight here in restoring his people to their own land. ¶ *For she hath received.* Jerusalem had now been desolate for almost seventy years, on the supposition that this relates to the period near the close of the exile, and that was regarded as an ample or full expression of what she *ought* to suffer for her national offences. ¶ *Of the Lord's hand.* From the hand, or by the agency of JEHOVAH. Whoever were the instruments, her sufferings were to be regarded as his appointment. ¶ *Double for all her sins.* The word rendered 'double' (כִּפְלַיִם) is the dual form from כֶּפֶל, 'a doubling,' and occurs in Job xli. 13:

> Who will rip up the covering of his armour?
> Against *the doubling* of his nostrils who will advance? *Good.*

And in xi. 6:

> And that he would unfold to them the secrets of wisdom.
> That they are *double* to that which is;

that is, there are *double-folds* to God's wisdom, or the wisdom of of God is complicated, inexplicable (Gesenius). The word in Job means 'conduplications, folds, complications, mazes, intricacies' (Good). Here the word has doubtless its usual and proper meaning, and denotes *double, twice as much;* and the expression may denote that God had inflicted on them *double* that which had been usually inflicted on rebellious nations, or on the nation before for its sins. Or the word may be used to denote *abundance*, and the prophet may design to teach that they had been *amply*, or *abundantly* punished for their crimes. 'That is,' says Grotius, 'as much as God judged to be sufficient.' '*Double*, here,' says Calvin, 'is to be received for large and abundant.' Some have supposed (see Rosenmüller, who approves of this interpretation) that the word 'sins' here means the punishment of sins, and that the word 'double' refers to the mercies or favours which they were about to receive, or which God had purposed to confer on them. So Lowth understands it; and renders the word לָקְחָה 'shall receive' (in the future):

> That she shall receive at the hand of JEHOVAH
> [Blessings] double to the punishment of all her sins.

But though it was true that their favours on their return, in the hope of the Messiah, and in their renovated privileges, would be far more numerous than their sufferings had been, yet this does not so well suit the connection, where the prophet is giving *a reason* why they should be released from their bondage, and restored to the privileges of their own land. That reason manifestly is, that they had suffered what was regarded by JEHOVAH as an *ample* expression of his displeasure for their national offences. It does not refer to

3 The [a] voice of him that crieth in the wilderness, Prepare [b] ye the way of the LORD, make straight in the desert a highway for our God.

[a] Mat.3.3. [b] Mal.3.1.

individual sinners; nor to any power which they have to make atonement for their sins; nor does it refer to the atonement made by the Messiah. But it may be remarked, by the way, that in the sufferings of the Redeemer there has been *ample* satisfaction for the sins of his people. The Chaldee interpreter understands this as Rosenmüller does, that the word 'double' refers to the mercies which they had received: 'Because she has received a cup of consolation from the presence of the Lord, *as if* (כְּאִלּוּ) she had been smitten twofold for all her sins.'

3. *The voice of him that crieth.* Lowth and Noyes render this, 'A voice crieth,' and annex the phrase 'in the wilderness' to the latter part of the sentence:

> A voice crieth, 'In the wilderness prepare ye the way of JEHOVAH.'

The Hebrew (קוֹל קוֹרֵא) will bear this construction, though the Vulgate and the LXX. render it as in our common version. The sense is not essentially different, though the parallelism seems to require the translation proposed by Lowth. The design is to state the source of consolation referred to in the previous verses. The time of the exile at Babylon was about to be completed. JEHOVAH was about to conduct his people again to their own country through the pathless wilderness, as he had formerly conducted them from Egypt to the land of promise. The prophet, therefore, represents himself as hearing the voice of a herald, or a forerunner in the pathless waste, giving direction that a way should be made for the return of the people. The whole scene is represented as a march, or return of JEHOVAH at the head of his people to the land of Judea. The idea is taken from the practice of Eastern monarchs, who, whenever they entered on a journey or an expedition, especially through a barren and unfrequented or inhospitable country, sent harbingers or heralds before them to prepare the way. To do this, it was necessary for them to provide supplies, and make bridges, or find fording places over the streams; to level hills, and construct causeways over valleys, or fill them up; and to make a way through the forest which might lie in their intended line of march. This was necessary, because these contemplated expeditions often involved the necessity of marching through countries where there were no public highways that would afford facilities for the passage of an army. Thus Arrian (*Hist.* liv. 30) says of Alexander, 'He now proceeded to the river Indus, the army' *i.e.*, ἡ στρατιά, a *part* of the army, or an army sufficient for the purpose, 'going before, which made a way for him, for otherwise there would have been no mode of passing through that region.' 'When a great prince in the East,' says Paxton, 'sets out on a journey, it is usual to send a party of men before him to clear the way. The state of those countries in every age, where roads are almost unknown, and, from want of cultivation, in many places overgrown with brambles and other thorny plants, which renders travelling, especially with a large retinue, incommodious, requires this precaution. The Emperor of Hindoostan, in his progress through his dominions, as described in the narrative of Sir Thomas Roe's embassy to the court of Delhi, was preceded by a very great company, sent before him to cut up the trees and bushes, to level and smooth the road, and prepare their place of encampment. We shall be able, perhaps, to form a more clear and precise idea from the account which Diodorus gives of the marches of Semiramis, the celebrated Queen of Babylon, into Media and Persia. "In her march to Ecbatana," says the historian, "she came to the Zarcean mountain, which, extending many furlongs, and being full of craggy precipices and deep hollows, could not be passed without taking a great compass. Being therefore desirous of leaving an everlasting memorial of herself, as well as of shortening the way, she ordered the precipices to be digged down, and the hollows to be filled up; and at a great expense she made a shorter and more expeditious road; which to this day is called from her the road of Semiramis. Afterward she went into Persia, and all the other countries of Asia subjected to her dominion, and wherever she went, she ordered the mountains and precipices to be levelled, raised causeways in the plain country, and, at a great expense, made the ways passable."' The writer of the apocryphal Book of Baruch, refers to the same subject by the same images: 'For God hath appointed that every high hill, and banks of long continuance, should be cast down, and valleys filled up, to make even the ground, that Israel may go safely in the glory of God' (ch. v. 7). It is evident that the primary reference of this passage was to the exiles in Babylon, and to their return from their long captivity, to the land of their fathers. The imagery, the circumstances, the design of the prophecy, all seem to demand such an interpretation. At the same time it is as clear, I apprehend, that the prophet was inspired to use language, of design, which should appropriately express a more important event, the coming of the forerunner of the Messiah, and the work which he should perform as preparatory to his advent. There was such a striking *similarity* in the two events, that they could be grouped together in the same part of the prophetic vision or picture; the mind would naturally, by the laws of prophetic suggestion (Introd. § 7, III. (3), glance from one to the other, and the same language would appropriately and accurately express both. Both could be described as the coming of Jehovah to bless and save his people; both occurred after a long state of desolation and bondage—the one a bondage in Babylon, the other in sin and national declension. The pathless desert was literally to be passed through in the one instance; in the other, the condition of the Jews was that which was not unaptly likened to a desert—a condition in regard to real piety not unlike the state of a vast desert in comparison with fruitful fields. 'It was,' says Lowth, 'in this desert country, destitute at that time of all religious cultivation, in true piety and works unfruitful, that John was sent to prepare the way of the Lord by preaching repentance. That this passage *has* a reference to John as the forerunner of the Messiah, is evident from Matt. iii. 3, where it is applied to him, and introduced by this remark: 'For this is he that was spoken of by the prophet Esaias, saying, The voice,' &c. (see also John i. 23.) The events were so similar, in their main features, that the same language would describe both. John was nurtured in the desert, and passed his early life there, until he entered on his public work (Luke ii. 80). He began to preach in a mountainous country, lying east of Jerusalem, and sparsely inhabited, and which was usually spoken of as a desert or wilderness (Matt. iii. 1); and it was here that his voice was heard announcing the coming of the Messiah, and that he pointed him to his own followers (John i. 28, 29). ¶ *In the wilderness.* Babylon was separated from Judea by an immense tract of country, which was one continued desert. A large part of Arabia, called Arabia Deserta, was situated in this region. To pass in a direct line, therefore, from Babylon to Jerusalem, it was necessary to go through this desolate country. It was here that the prophet speaks of hearing a voice commanding the hills to be levelled, and the valleys filled up, that there might be a convenient highway for the people to return (comp. Notes on ch. xxxv. 8–10). ¶ *Prepare ye the way.* This was in the form of the usual proclamation of a monarch commanding the people to make a way for him to pass. Applied to the return of the exile Jews, it means that the command of God had gone forth that all obstacles should be removed. Applied to John, it means that the people were to prepare for the reception of the Messiah; that they were to remove all in their opinions and conduct which would tend to hinder his cordial reception, or which would prevent his success among them. ¶ *Of the* Lord. Of Jehovah. Jehovah was the leader of his people, and was about to conduct them to their own land. The march, therefore, was regarded as that of Jehovah, as a monarch or king, at the head of his people,

4 Every valley shall be exalted,
and every mountain and hill shall
be made low: and the crooked [a] shall
be made [1] straight, and the rough
places [2] plain.

a ch.45.2. 1 or, *a straight place.* 2 or, *a plain place.*

conducting them to their own country; and to prepare the way of JEHOVAH was, therefore, to prepare for his march at the head of his people. Applied to the Messiah, it means that God was about to come to his people to redeem them. This language naturally and obviously implies, that he whose way was thus to be prepared was JEHOVAH, the true God. So it was undoubtedly in regard to him who was to be the leader of the exile Jews to their own land, since none but JEHOVAH could thus conduct them. And if it be admitted that the language has also a reference to the Messiah, then it demonstrates that he was appropriately called JEHOVAH. That John the Baptist had such a view of him, is apparent from what is said of him. Thus, John i. 15, he says of him that, 'he was before' him—which was not true unless he had an existence previous to his birth; he calls him, ver. 18, 'the only-begotten Son, which *is* in the bosom of the Father;' and in ver. 34, he calls him 'the Son of God' (comp. John x. 30, 33, 36). In ch. iii. 31, he says of him, 'he that cometh from above is ABOVE ALL; he that cometh from heaven is ABOVE ALL.' Though this is not one of the most direct and certain proof-texts of the divinity of the Messiah, yet it is one which may be applied to him when that divinity is demonstrated from other places. It is not one that can be used with absolute certainty in an *argument* on the subject, to convince those who deny that divinity—since, even on the supposition that it refers to the Messiah, it may be said plausibly, and with some force, that it may mean that JEHOVAH was about to manifest himself by means of the Messiah; yet it is a passage which those who are convinced of the divinity of Christ from other sources, will apply without hesitation to him as descriptive of his rank, and confirmatory of his divinity. ¶ *Make straight.* Make a straight or *direct* road; one that should conduct at once to their land. The Chaldee renders this verse, 'Prepare a way before the people of JEHOVAH; make in the plain ways before the congregation of our God.' ¶ *A highway* (see Note on ch. xxxv. 8).

4. *Every valley shall be exalted.* That is, every valley, or low piece of ground, shall be filled up so as to make a level highway, as was done in order to facilitate the march of armies. This verse is evidently designed to explain what is intended in ver. 3, by preparing the way for JEHOVAH. Applied to the return of the Jews from Babylon, it means simply that the impassable valleys were to be filled up so as to make a level road for their journey. If applied to the work of John, the forerunner of the Messiah, it means that the nation was to be called on to put itself in a state of preparation for his coming, and for the success of his labours among them. Vitringa, and others, have endeavoured to specify what particular moral qualities in the nation are meant by the 'valley,' by the 'mountain and hill,' and by the 'crooked' and 'rough places.' But the illustrations are such as cannot be demonstrated to be referred to by the prophet. The *general* sense is plain. The *language*, as we have seen, is taken from the march of a monarch at the head of his army. The general idea is, that all obstructions were to be removed, so that the march would be without embarrassment. As applicable to the work of John also, the language means in general, that whatever there was in the opinions, habits, conduct, in the pride, self confidence, and irreligion of the nation that would prevent his cordial reception, was to be removed. ¶ *Every mountain and hill.* They shall be dug down so as to make the journey easy. All obstructions were to be removed. ¶ *And the crooked.* The word here used (עָקֹב) is usually rendered 'crooked;' but perhaps not by any good authority. The verb עָקַב usually denotes *to be behind;* to come from behind; or, as Gesenius supposes, to be elevated like a mound, arched like a hill or tumulus, and is hence applied to the *heel* from the figure (see Gen. xxv. 26;

5 And the glory of the Lord shall be revealed, and all flesh shall see *it* together: for the mouth of the Lord hath spoken *it*.

6 The voice said, Cry. And he said, What shall I cry? All [a] flesh *is* grass, and all the goodliness thereof *is* as the flower of the field.

a Ps.10.15; Ja.1.10,11.

Hos. xii. 4). According to this, the word would denote properly a hill, mound, or acclivity, which would *put back* those who attempted to ascend. ¶ *Shall be made straight.* Marg. 'A straight place.' The Hebrew word (מִישׁוֹר) denotes properly *evenness*, a level region, a plain. The hilly places would be reduced to a level. ¶ *And the rough places.* Those which are hard, *bound up*, stony, difficult to pass. Such as abounded with rocks and precipices, and which presented obstructions to a journey. Such places abounded in the region lying between Palestine and Babylon. ¶ *Plain.* Marg. 'A plain place.' A smooth, level plain.

5. *And the glory of the* Lord. The phrase here means evidently the majesty, power, or honour of Jehovah. He would display his power, and show himself to be a covenant-keeping God, by delivering his people from their bondage, and reconducting them to their own land. This glory and faithfulness would be shown in his delivering them from their captivity in Babylon; and it would be still more illustriously shown in his sending the Messiah to accomplish the deliverance of his people in later days. ¶ *And all flesh.* All men. The word 'flesh' is often used to denote human nature, or mankind in general (Gen. vi. 12; Ps. lxv. 3; cxlv. 21). The idea is, that the deliverance of his people would be such a display of the Divine interposition, so that all nations would discern the evidences of his power and glory. But there is a fulness and a richness in the language which shows that it is not to be confined to that event. It is more strikingly applicable to the advent of the Messiah—and to the fact that through him the glory of Jehovah would be manifest to all nations. Rosenmüller supposes that this should be translated,

> And all flesh shall see together
> That the mouth of Jehovah hath spoken it.

The Hebrew will bear this construction, but there is no necessity for departing from the translation in the common version. The LXX. *add* here the words 'salvation of God,' so as to read it, 'and all flesh shall see the salvation of God,' and this reading has been adopted in Luke iii. 6; or it may be more probable that Luke (iii. 4–6) has quoted from *different parts* of Isaiah, and that he intended to quote that part, not from the version of the LXX., but from Isa. lii. 10. Lowth, on the authority of the LXX., proposes to restore these words to the Hebrew text. But the authority is insufficient. The Vulgate, the Chaldee, the Syriac, and the Hebrew MSS. concur in the reading of the present Hebrew text, and the authority of the Septuagint is altogether insufficient to justify a change. ¶ *For the mouth of the* Lord. The strongest possible confirmation that it would be fulfilled (see Note on ch. xxxiv. 16). The idea is, that God had certainly promised their deliverance from bondage; and that his interposition, in a manner which should attract the attention of all nations, was certainly purposed by him. Few events have ever more impressively manifested the glory of God than the redemption of his people from Babylon; none has occurred, or will ever occur, that will more impressively demonstrate his glory, wisdom, and faithfulness, than the redemption of the world by the Messiah.

6. *The voice said.* Or rather '*a* voice.' Isaiah represents himself here again as hearing a voice. The word 'the' introduced in our translation, mars the sense, inasmuch as it leads to the supposition that it was the voice of the same person or crier referred to in ver. 3. But it is different. *That* was the voice of a *crier* or herald, proclaiming that a way was to be open in the desert. *This* is introduced for a different purpose. It is to proclaim distinctly that while everything else was fading and transitory, the promise of God was firm and secure. Isaiah therefore,

represents himself as hearing *a* voice requiring the prophets (so the Chaldee) *to make a proclamation.* An inquiry was at once made, What should be the nature of the proclamation? The answer was, that all flesh was grass, &c. He had (ver. 3–5) introduced a herald announcing that the way was to be prepared for their return. He now introduces *another* voice with a distinct message to the people, that God was faithful, and that his promises would not fail. A voice, a command is heard, requiring those whose duty it was, to make proclamation. The voice of God; the Spirit speaking to the prophets, commanded them to cry. ¶ *And he said.* Lowth and Noyes read this, 'And I said.' The LXX. and the Vulgate read it also in this manner, in the first person. Two manuscripts examined by Kennicott also read it in the first person. Houbigant, Hensler, and Döderlin adopt this reading. But the authority is not sufficient to justify a change in the Hebrew text. The Syriac and Chaldee read it as it is in the present Hebrew text, in the third person. The sense is, that the person, or prophet to whom the command came to make proclamation, made answer, 'What shall be the nature of my proclamation?' It is equivalent to saying, 'It was answered;' or if Isaiah is the person to whom the voice is represented as coming, it means that *he* answered; and is, therefore, equivalent to the reading in the LXX. and Vulgate, and adopted by Lowth. This is the probable supposition, that Isaiah represents himself as hearing the voice, and as expressing a willingness to make proclamation, but as waiting to know *what* he was to proclaim. ¶ *All flesh.* This is the answer; or this is what he was to proclaim. The general design or scope of the answer was, that he was to proclaim that the promise of Jehovah was secure and firm (ver. 8), and that therefore God would certainly come to deliver them. To make this more impressive by way of contrast, he states that all men are weak and feeble like the grass that is soon withered.—The expression does not refer particularly to the Jews in Babylon, or to any single nation or class of people, but to all men, in all places, and at all times. All princes, nobles, and monarchs; all armies and magistrates are like grass, and will soon pass away. On the one hand, *they* would be unable to accomplish what was needful to be done in the deliverance of the people; and on the other, their oppressors had no power to continue their bondage, since *they* were like grass, and must soon pass away. But Jehovah was ever-enduring, and was able to fulfil all his purposes. ¶ Is *grass.* It is *as* feeble, weak, and as easily consumed as the grass of the field. A similar sentiment is found in Ps. ciii. 15, 16:

> As for man, his days are as grass;
> As a flower of the field so he flourisheth;
> For the wind passeth over it, and it is gone,
> And the place thereof shall know it no more.

See also James i. 10, 11. The passage in Isaiah is evidently quoted by Peter, 1 Ep. i. 24, 25: 'All flesh is as grass, and all the glory of man as the flower of grass. The grass withereth, and the flower thereof falleth away: but the word of the Lord endureth for ever; *and this is the word which by the gospel is preached unto you*'—a passage which proves that Isaiah had reference to the times of the Messiah in the place before us. ¶ *And all the goodliness thereof.* The word rendered 'goodliness' (חֶסֶד) denotes properly, *kindness,* love, goodwill, mercy, favour. Here it is evidently used in the sense of elegance, comeliness, beauty. The LXX. render it δόξα, and so does Peter (1 Ep. i. 24). Applied to *grass,* or to herbs, it denotes the flower, the beauty, the comeliness. Applied to man, it means that which makes him comely and vigorous—health, energy, beauty, talent, wisdom. His vigour is soon gone; his beauty fades; his wisdom ceases; and he falls, like the flower, to the dust. The idea is, that the plans of man must be temporary; that all that appears great in him must be like the flower of the field; but that Jehovah endures, and his plans reach from age to age, and will certainly be accomplished. This important truth was to be proclaimed, that the people might be induced not to trust in man, but put their confidence in the arm of God.

7 The grass withereth, the flower fadeth, because the spirit of the LORD bloweth upon it: surely the people *is* grass.

8 The [a]grass withereth, the flower fadeth: but the word [b]of our God shall stand for ever.

a 1 Pe.1.24,25. b Mark 13.31.

7. *The grass withereth.* Soon withers. Its beauty is soon gone. ¶ *The flower fadeth.* Soon fades; or fades when the wind of JEHOVAH passes over it. So it is also with man. He loses his vigour, and dies at once when JEHOVAH takes away his strength and beauty. ¶ *Because the spirit of the* LORD *bloweth upon it.* This should be rendered, undoubtedly, 'When the *wind* of JEHOVAH bloweth upon it.' The word 'spirit' here does not suit the connection, and does not express the idea of the prophet. The word רוּחַ (*rūăhh*) means, properly, *breath*—a breathing, or blowing; and is often used indeed to denote spirit, soul, life. But it *often* means a breath of wind; a breeze; air in motion (Job xli. 8; Jer. ii. 24; xiv. 6). It is applied to the cool breeze which springs up in the evening (Gen. iii. 8; comp. Cant. ii. 17; iv. 6). It sometimes means a strong and violent wind (Gen. viii. 1; Isa. vii. 2; xli. 16); and also a tempest, or hurricane (Job i. 19; xxx. 15; Isa. xxvii. 8). The 'wind of JEHOVAH' means that which JEHOVAH sends, or causes; and the expression here refers, doubtless, to the hot or poisonous east winds which blow in Oriental countries, and which wither and dry up everything before them (comp. Jonah iv. 8). ¶ *Surely the people* is *grass.* Lowth reads this, 'this people;' referring to the Jewish nation. So the Syriac. Perhaps it refers to the people of Babylon (so Rosenmüller), and means *that* mighty people would fade away like grass. But the more probable interpretation is that which regards it as referring to ALL people, and of course including the Jews and the Babylonians. The sense, according to this view, is, 'all nations shall fade away. All human power shall cease. But the promise of JEHOVAH shall survive. It shall be unchanging amidst all revolutions; it shall survive all the fluctuations which shall take place among men. It may, therefore, be trusted with unwavering reliance.' To *produce* that reliance was the object of the proclamation. On this passage, descriptive of the state of man, the reader will at once be reminded of the beautiful language of Shakspeare:

This is the state of man! To-day he puts forth
The tender leaves of hope: to-morrow blossoms,
And bears his blushing honours thick upon him;
The third day comes a frost, a killing frost,
And when he thinks, good easy man, full surely
His greatness is a-ripening, nips his root,
And then he falls——
——never to hope again.
Hen. VIII., Act. ii. Sc. 2.

In the following passage from Tasso, the same image is adopted:

The gentle budding rose (quoth he) behold,
That first scant peeping forth with virgin beams,
Half ope, half shut, her beauties doth up-fold
In their dear leaves, and less seen fairer seems,
And after spreads them forth more broad and bold,
Then languishes and dies in last extremes.
So in the passing of a day doth pass
The bud and blossom of the life of man,
Nor e'er doth flourish more, but, like the grass
Cut down, becometh withered, pale, and wan.
Fairfax, Edit. Windsor, 1817.

8. *The grass withereth,* &c. This is repeated from the former verse for the sake of emphasis, or strong confirmation. ¶ *But the word of our God.* The phrase 'word of our God,' refers either to his promise to be the protector and deliverer of his people in their captivity, or, in general, means that *all* his promises shall be firm and unchanging. ¶ *Shall stand for ever.* Amidst all revolutions among men, his promise shall be firm. It shall not only live amidst the changes of dynasties, and the revolutions of empires, but it shall *continue* for ever and ever. This is designed for support to an afflicted and oppressed people; and it must have been to them, in their bondage, the source of high consolation. But it is equally so now. Amidst all the changes on earth; the revolutions of empires; the vanishing of kingdoms, God is the same, and his promises are unfailing. We see the grass wither at the return of autumn, or in the drought: we see the flower of the field lose its beauty, and decay; we see

9 O [1]Zion, that bringest good
tidings, get thee up into the high
mountain; O [2]Jerusalem, that
bringest good tidings, lift up thy
voice with strength; lift *it* up, be
not afraid; say unto the cities of
Judah, Behold your God!

1 or, *thou that tellest good tidings to Zion.*
2 or, *thou that tellest good tidings to Jerusalem.*

---

man rejoicing in his vigour and his health, cut down in an instant; we see cities fall, and kingdoms lose their power and vanish from among nations, but God changes not. He presides in all these revolutions, and sits calm and unmoved amidst all these changes. Not one of his promises shall fail; and at the end of all the changes which human things shall undergo, JEHOVAH, the God of his people, will be the same.

9. *O Zion, that bringest good tidings.* This is evidently the continuance of what the 'voice' said, or of the annunciation which was to give joy to an afflicted and oppressed people. There has been, however, much diversity of opinion in regard to the meaning of the passage. The margin renders it, 'Thou that tellest good tidings to Zion,' making Zion the receiver, and not the publisher of the message that was to convey joy. The Vulgate, in a similar way, renders it, 'Ascend a high mountain, thou who bringest good tidings to Zion' (*qui evangelizas Zion*). So the Chaldee, understanding this as an address to the prophet, as in ver. 1, 'Ascend a high mountain, ye prophets, who bring glad tidings to Zion.' So Lowth, Noyes, Gesenius, Grotius, and others. The word מְבַשֶּׂרֶת, from בָּשַׂר (*bâsăr*), means *cheering with good tidings;* announcing good news; bearing joyful intelligence. It is a participle in the feminine gender; and is appropriately applicable to some one that bears good tidings *to* Zion, and not to Zion as appointed to bear glad tidings. Lowth supposes that it is applicable to some female whose office it was to announce glad tidings, and says that it was the common practice for females to engage in the office of proclaiming good news. On an occasion of a public victory or rejoicing, it was customary, says he, for females to assemble together, and to celebrate it with songs, and dances, and rejoicings; and he appeals to the instance of Miriam and the chorus of women (Ex. xv. 20, 21), and to the instance where, after the victory of David over Goliath, 'all the women came out of the cities of Israel singing and dancing to meet Saul' (1 Sam. xviii. 7). But there are objections to this interpretation; first, if this was the sense, the word would have been in the *plural* number, since there is no instance in which a female is employed alone in this service; and, secondly, it was not, according to this, the office of the female to *announce* good tidings, or to communicate a joyful message, but to *celebrate* some occasion of triumph or victory. Grotius supposes that the word is 'feminine in its sound, but common in its signification;' and thus denotes *any* whose office it was to communicate glad tidings. Gesenius (*Comm. in loc.*) says, that the feminine form here is used in a collective sense for מְבַשְּׂרִים in the plural; and supposes that it thus refers to the prophets, or others who were to announce the glad tidings to Zion. Vitringa coincides with our translation, and supposes that the sense is, that Zion was to make proclamation to the other cities of Judah of the deliverance; that the news was first to be communicated to Jerusalem, and that Jerusalem was intrusted with the office of announcing this to the other cities of the land; and that the meaning is, that the gospel was to be preached first *at* Jerusalem, and then from Jerusalem as a centre to the other cities of the land, agreeably to Luke xxiv. 49. In this view, also, Hengstenberg coincides (*Christol.* vol. i. p. 424). But that the former interpretation, which regards Zion as the *receiver*, and not the *promulgator*, of the intelligence, is the true one, is apparent, I think, from the following considerations—1. It is that which is the obvious and most correct construction of the Hebrew. 2. It is that which is found in the ancient versions. 3. It accords with the design of the passage. The main scope of the passage is not to call upon Jerusalem to make known the glad tidings, but it is to convey the good news *to* Jerusalem; to announce to her, lying

10 Behold, the Lord God will come [1] with strong *hand*, and his arm shall rule for him; behold, his reward [a] *is* with him, and [2] his work before him.

1 or, *against the strong*. a Rev.22.12.
2 or, *recompence for his works*.

desolate and waste, that her hard service was at an end, and that she was to be blessed with the return of happier and better times (see ver. 2). It would be a departure from this, to suppose that the subject was diverted in order to give Jerusalem a command to make the proclamation to the other cities of the land—to say nothing of the impropriety of calling on *a city* to go up into a high mountain, and to lift up its voice. On the meaning of the word 'Zion,' see Note on ch. i. 8. ¶ *Get thee up into a high mountain.* You who make this proclamation to Zion. It was not uncommon in ancient times, when a multitude were to be addressed, or a proclamation to be made, for the crier to go into a mountain, where he could be seen and heard. Thus Jotham, addressing the men of Shechem, is said to have gone and 'stood on the top of mount Gerizim, and lifted up his voice' (Judg. ix. 7; comp. Matt. v. 1). The sense is, that the messengers of the joyful news to Zion were to make themselves distinctly heard by all the inhabitants of the city, and of the land. ¶ *Lift up thy voice.* As with a glad and important message. Do not deliver the message as if you were afraid that it should be heard. It is one of joy; and it should be delivered in a clear, decided, animated manner, as if it were important that it should be heard. ¶ *With strength.* Aloud; with effort; with power (comp. ch. xxxv. 3,4). ¶ *Lift* it *up.* Lift up the voice. The command is repeated, to denote emphasis. The mind is full of the subject, and the prophet repeats the command, as a man often does when his mind is full of an idea. The command to deliver the message of God with animation, earnestness, and zeal is one that is not unusual in Isaiah. It should be delivered as if it were true, and as if it were believed to be true. This will not justify, however, boisterous preaching, or a loud and unnatural tone of voice—alike offensive to good taste, injurious to the health, and destructive of the life of the preacher. It is to be remarked, also, that *this* command to lift up the voice, appertains to the glad tidings of the gospel, and not to the terrors of wrath; to the proclamation of mercy, and not to the denunciation of woe. The glad tidings of salvation should be delivered in an animated and ardent manner; the future punishment of the wicked in a tone serious, solemn, subdued. ¶ *Say unto the cities of Judah.* Not to Jerusalem only, but to all the cities of the land. They were alike to be blessed on the return from the captivity—alike in the preaching of the gospel. ¶ *Behold your God!* Lo! your God returns to the city, the temple, and the land! Lo! he comes (Note, ver. 3), conducting his people as a king to their land! Lo! he will come—under the Messiah in future times—to redeem and save! What a glad announcement was this to the desolate and forsaken cities of Judah! What a glad announcement to the wide world, 'Lo! God has come to redeem and save; and the desolate world shall be visited with his salvation and smile, in his mercy through the Messiah!'

10. *Behold, the Lord* God *will come* (see Note on ver. 3). Applied to the condition of the Jews in exile, this means that God would come to deliver them. Applied to the times of the Messiah, it means that God would manifest himself in a powerful manner as mighty to save. ¶ *With strong* hand (בְּחָזָק). Marg. 'Against the strong.' So Vitringa and others understand it; and regard it as referring to the mighty enemies of the people of God, or, as Vitringa particularly supposes, to the great foe of God and his people—the prince of darkness—the devil. Lowth also translates it in this manner, 'Against the strong one.' The LXX. render it, Μετὰ ἰσχύος—'With strength.' This is the more probable meaning—that the Lord would come with the manifestation of strength and power, able to subdue and vanquish all the enemies of his people, and to effect their complete and final salvation. ¶ *And his arm.* The *arm* is a symbol

11 He shall feed his flock like a shepherd; [a] he shall gather the lambs with his arm, and carry *them* in his bosom, *and* shall gently lead those that [1] are with young.

a Ps.23.1; Jn.10.11. 1 or, *give suck*.

of strength, because it is by that that we accomplish our purposes; by that a conqueror slays his enemies in battle, &c. Thus, 'Break thou the arm of the wicked;' *i.e.*, diminish or destroy his power (Ps. x. 15). 'I have broken the arm of Pharaoh king of Egypt' (Ezek. xxx. 21; comp. Jer. xlviii. 25). Thus it is said of God, 'Thou hast a mighty arm' (Ps. lxxxix. 13), and, 'His holy arm hath gotten him the victory' (Ps. xcviii. 1; comp. Ex. vi. 6). The metaphor is taken from the act of stretching out the arm to fight in battle, where the *arm* is the effective instrument in subduing an enemy. ¶ *Shall rule for him.* Lowth renders the phrase, לוֹ (*lō*), 'for him,' 'over him:'—'And his arm shall prevail over him;' *i.e.*, over the strong and mighty foe. The LXX. render it, Μετά κυρίας—'With dominion.' But the meaning seems to be, 'God is mighty by himself; his power resides in his own arm; he is not dependent on others; he will accomplish the deliverance in such a manner that it shall be seen that he did it alone; and he shall rule for himself, without any aid, and so that it shall be manifest that he is the sovereign.' In the deliverance of his people from their captivity, he so directed it, that it was manifest that he was their deliverer and sovereign; and in the redemption of man, the same thing is apparent, that the arm of God effects the deliverance, and that it is his own power that establishes the dominion. ¶ *Behold, his reward is with him.* He will be ready to confer the appropriate reward on his own people. The idea seems to be taken from the custom of a conqueror, who distributes rewards among his followers and soldiers after a signal victory. This was always done in ancient wars, apparently because it seemed to be an act of justice that those who had gained the victory should share also in the result, and this participation of the booty was a stimulus to future effort, as well as a compensation for their valour. The rewards distributed consisted generally of that which was taken from the conquered; gold, and silver, and raiment, as well as captives or slaves (see Gen. xlix. 7; Ex. xv. 9; 1 Sam. xxx. 26; and particularly Judges v. 30):

Have they not sped?
Have they not divided the prey;
To every man a damsel or two;
To Sisera a prey of divers colours,
A prey of divers colours of needle-work,
Of divers colours of needle-work on both sides,
Meet for the necks of them that take the spoil.

The idea here is—1. That JEHOVAH would bestow appropriate rewards on his people. 2. That they would be conferred on his coming, and not be delayed. 3. That it should be done by the hand of God himself. This language was applicable to the interposition of God to save his people from their long exile, and the 'reward' would be ample in the restoration to their own land, and the re-establishment of his worship. It is applicable in a higher sense to the coming of the Messiah to bless the world. His reward was with him. He blessed his faithful followers on earth; he will bless them more abundantly in heaven. It will be assuredly applicable to him when he shall come to gather his people to himself in the great and last day, and the language before us is used with reference to that: 'And behold, I come quickly; and my reward is with me, to give every man according as his work shall be' (Rev. xxii. 12). ¶ *And his work.* Marg. 'Recompense for his work.' The margin here is the correct rendering. The Hebrew word strictly indeed denotes work, labour, business; but it also denotes the *wages* for work (Lev. xix. 13; Ps. cix. 20).

11. *He shall feed his flock.* In the previous verse, the fact had been asserted that God would come to subdue his foes, and to reward his people. In this verse, the mild and gentle character of his government over his people is predicted. It would not be that of a conqueror over vanquished subjects; but it would be mild and tender, like that of a shepherd who carries the lambs, which are unable to walk, in his own arms, and gently leads along the feeble and the delicate. The word translated 'shall

feed' (יִרְעֶה), denotes more than our word *feed* at present. It refers to all the care of a shepherd over his flock; and means to tend, to guard, to govern, to provide pasture, to defend from danger, as a shepherd does his flock. It is often applied in the Scriptures to God, represented as the tender shepherd, and especially to the Redeemer (Ps. xxiii. 1; Ezek. xxxiv. 23; John x. 14; Heb. xiii. 20; 1 Pet. ii. 25; v. 4). It is often applied to a leader or a ruler of a people (2 Sam. v. 2; vii. 7; Jer. xxxii. 2). Thus Homer often uses the phrase, ποιμὴν λαῶν—'shepherds of the people,' to denote a ruler, or monarch. Here it denotes that God would evince towards his people the same tender care, guardianship and protection, which a shepherd shows for his flock. ¶ *He shall gather the lambs with his arm.* This is a most beautiful expression, denoting the care of God the Saviour for the feeblest and weakest of his people, and for the young and feeble in years and piety. A similar thing is often done by a shepherd. The tender lamb, unable to keep up with the flock, becomes weary and exhausted; and the shepherd naturally takes it in his arms and carries it. Such a shepherd as this Virgil beautifully describes:

En, ipse capellas
Protenus æger argo; hanc etiam vix, Tityre, duco;
Hic inter densas corylos modo namque gemellos,
Spem gregis, Ah! silice in nuda connixa reliquet.
Eclog. i. 12.

Lo! I my goats urge fainting o'er the mead;
This, feebler than the rest, with pains I lead.
Yean'd mid yon herds upon the flinty plain,
Her dying twins, my flock's late hope, remain.
Wrangham.

¶ And *shall gently lead*, &c. Marg. 'Give suck.' This is the more correct translation. It denotes the dams of the flock that would be easily exhausted by being overdriven, and of which there was, therefore, especial care necessary. Thus Jacob says to his brother Esau, Gen. xxxiii. 13: 'The flocks and the herds giving suck to their young are with me, and if they should be overdriven all the flock will die.' Of the necessity of such care and attention there is abundant evidence, and indeed it is manifest at a glance. Dr. Shaw, speaking of the exposure of the flocks in Syria, says: 'The greatest skill and vigilance, and even tender care, are required in the management of such immense flocks as wander on the Syrian plains. Their prodigious numbers compel the keepers to remove them too frequently in search of fresh pastures, which proves very destructive to the young that have not strength to follow.' The following extract from Anderson's *Tour through Greece* will also serve to illustrate this passage: 'One of the great delights in travelling through a pastoral country, is to see and feel the force of the beautiful imagery in the Scriptures, borrowed from pastoral life. All day long the shepherd attends his flock, leading them into "green pastures," near fountains of water, and chooses a convenient place for them to "rest at noon." At night he drives them near his tent; and, if there is danger, encloses them in the fold. They know his voice, and follow him. When travelling, he tenderly watches over them, *and carries such as are exhausted in his arms.* Such a shepherd is the Lord Jesus Christ.' No description could more beautifully describe the character of the Redeemer. In the New Testament, he is often described as a kind and tender shepherd, and regarding the welfare of all his flock, and as ready to give his life for them (John x. 7, 9–11, 14, 15; Heb. xiii. 20; 1 Pet. ii. 25; v. 4). We are here also strikingly reminded of the solemn command which he gave to Peter, evincing his tender regard for his flock, 'Feed my lambs:' 'Feed my sheep' (John xvi. 15–17). It proves in regard to the Redeemer—1. That his nature is mild, and gentle, and tender. 2. That he has a kind regard for all his flock, and will consult the real interest of all, as a shepherd does of his flock. 3. That he has a special solicitude for the feeble and infirm, and that they will be the objects of his tender care. 4. That he feels a particular solicitude for the young. He knows their feebleness; he is acquainted with their temptations; he sees the importance of their being trained up with care; and he looks with deep interest, therefore, on all the efforts made to guard them from the ways of sin, and to train them up for his service (comp. Note on ch. xlii. 3).

12. *Who hath measured.* The ob-

12 Who hath measured the waters in the hollow of his hand, and meted out heaven with a span, and comprehended the dust of the earth in a [1] measure, and weighed the mountains in scales, and the hills in a balance?

1 *tierce.*

ject in this and the following verses to ver. 26, is to show the greatness, power, and majesty of God, by strong contrast with his creatures, and more especially with idols. Perhaps the prophet designed to meet and answer an implied objection: that the work of deliverance was so great that it could not be accomplished. The answer was, that God had made all things; that he was infinitely great; that he had entire control over all the nations; and that he could, therefore, remove all obstacles out of the way, and accomplish his great and gracious purposes. By man it could not be done; nor had idol-gods any power to do it; but the Creator and upholder of all could effect this purpose with infinite ease. At the same time that the *argument* here is one that is entirely conclusive, the passage, regarded as a description of the power and majesty of God, is one of vast sublimity and grandeur; nor is there any portion of the Sacred Volume that is more fitted to impress the mind with a sense of the majesty and glory of Jehovah. The question, 'who hath measured,' is designed to imply that the thing referred to here was that which had never been done, and could never be done by man; and the *argument* is, that although that which the prophet predicted was a work which surpassed human power, yet it could be done by that God who had measured the waters in the hollow of his hand. The word 'waters' here refers evidently to the vast collection of waters in the deep—the mighty ocean, together with *all* the waters in the running streams, and in the clouds. See Gen. i. 6, where the firmament is said to have been made to divide the waters from the waters. A reference to the waters *above* the heavens occurs in Ps. cxlviii. 4:

> Praise him, ye heavens of heavens,
> And ye waters that be above the heavens.

And in Prov. xxx. 4, a similar description of the power and majesty of God occurs:

> Who hath gathered the wind in his fists?
> Who hath bound the waters in a garment?
> Who hath established all the ends of the earth?

And in Job xxvi. 8:

> He bindeth up the waters in his thick clouds;
> And the cloud is not rent under them.

The word 'waters' here, therefore, may include *all* the water on the earth, and in the sky. The words, 'the hollow of his hand,' mean properly the hand as it is closed, forming a hollow or a cavity by which water can be taken up. The idea is, that God can take up the vast oceans, and all the waters in the lakes, streams, and clouds, in the palm of his hand, as we take up the smallest quantity in ours. ¶ *And meted out heaven.* The word rendered 'meted,' *i.e.*, measured (כּוּן), means properly *to stand erect,* to set up, or make erect; to found, fit, adjust, dispose, form, create. It usually has the idea of *fitting* or disposing. The word 'span' (זֶרֶת) denotes the space from the end of the thumb to the end of the middle finger, when extended—usually about nine inches. The idea is, that Jehovah was able to compass or grasp the heavens, though so vast, as one can compass or measure a small object with the span. What an illustration of the vastness and illimitable nature of God! ¶ *And comprehended.* And measured (כָּל from כּוּל, *to hold* or *contain*); 'Lo, the heavens, and the heaven of heavens cannot *contain* thee' (1 Kings viii. 27). ¶ *The dust of the earth.* All the earth; all the dust that composes the globe. ¶ *In a measure* (בַּשָּׁלִשׁ). Properly *three;* and then the third part of anything. Jerome supposes that it means *the three fingers,* and that the sense is, that God takes up all the dust of the earth in the first three fingers of the hand. But the more probable signification is, that the word denotes that which was *the third part* of some other measure, as of an ephah, or bath. In Ps. lxxx. 5, the word is used to denote a large measure:

> Thou feedest them with the bread of tears,
> And givest them tears to drink in great measure (שָׁלִישׁ).

13 Who [a] hath directed the Spirit of the LORD, or *being* [1] his counsellor hath taught him?

14 With whom took he counsel, and *who* [2] instructed him, and taught him in the path of judgment, and taught him knowledge, and showed to him the way of understanding? [3]

15 Behold, the nations *are* as a

a Ro.11.34. 1 *man of his counsel.* 2 *made him understand.* 3 *understandings.*

The idea is, that God is so great that he can measure all the dust of the earth as easily as we can measure a small quantity of grain with a measure. ¶ *And weighed the mountains in scales.* The idea here is substantially the same. It is, that God is so mighty that he can weigh the lofty mountains, as we weigh a light object in scales, or in a balance; and perhaps, also, that he has disposed them on the earth *as if* he had weighed them out, and adapted them to their proper places and situations. Throughout this entire passage, there is not only the idea of majesty and power in God, but there is also the idea that he has *fitted* or adjusted everything by his wisdom and power, and adapted it to the condition and wants of his creatures.

13. *Who hath directed.* This passage is quoted by Paul in Rom. xi. 34, and referred to by him in 1 Cor. ii. 16. The word rendered 'directed' here (תִּכֵּן) is the same which is used in the previous verse, 'and *meted out* heaven.' The idea here is, 'Who has fitted, or disposed the mind or spirit of JEHOVAH? What superior being has ordered, instructed, or disposed his understanding? Who has *qualified* him for the exercise of his wisdom, or for the formation and execution of his plans?' The sense is, God is supreme. No one has instructed or guided him, but his plans are his own, and have all been formed by himself alone. And as those plans are infinitely wise, and as he is not dependent on any one for their formation or execution, his people may have confidence in him, and believe that he will be able to execute his purposes. ¶ *The Spirit.* The word '*spirit*' is used in the Bible in a greater variety of senses than almost any other word (see Note on ver. 7). It seems here to be used in the sense of mind, and to refer to God himself. There is no evidence that it refers to the Holy Spirit particularly. 'The word *spirit,* he uses,' says Calvin, 'for reason, judgment. He borrows the similitude from the nature of men, in order that he may more accommodate himself to them; nor, as it seems to me, does he here speak of the essential Spirit of God' (*Comm. in loco*). The design of the prophet is not to refer to the distinction in the Divine nature, or to illustrate the peculiar characteristics of the different persons of the Godhead; but it is to set forth the wisdom of JEHOVAH HIMSELF, the one infinite God, as contradistinguished from idols, and as qualified to guide, govern, and deliver his people. The passage should not be used, therefore, as a proof-text in regard to the existence and wisdom of the Holy Spirit, but is fitted to demonstrate only that God is *untaught;* and that he is independent and infinite in his wisdom. ¶ *Or* being *his counsellor.* Marg., as in Heb. 'Man of his counsel.' He is not dependent for counsel on men or angels. He is supreme, independent, and infinite. None is qualified to instruct him; and all, therefore, should confide in his wisdom and knowledge.

14. *With whom took he counsel.* The sentiment of the former verse is repeated here, in order, probably, to make it more emphatic. ¶ *In the path of judgment.* The way of judging correctly and wisely; or the way of administering justice. It denotes here his boundless wisdom as it is seen in the various arrangements of his creation and providence, by which all things keep their places, and accomplish his vast designs.

15. *Behold, the nations.* All the nations of the earth. This is designed to show the greatness of God, in comparison with that which strikes man as great—a mighty nation; and the main object seems to be, to show that God could accomplish his purposes without their aid, and that they could not resist him in the execution of his plans. If they were as nothing in comparison with him, how easily could he execute his

drop of a bucket, and are counted
as the small dust of the balance:
behold, he taketh up the isles as a
very little thing.
16 And Lebanon *is* not sufficient
to burn, nor the beasts thereof
sufficient for a burnt-offering.
17 All nations before him are
nothing;[a] and they are counted

a Da.4.35.

purposes! If they were as nothing, how little could they resist the execution of his plans! ¶ Are *as a drop of a bucket.* In comparison with him; or are so esteemed by him. The drop that falls from the bucket in drawing water is a trifle. It has no power, and compared with the waters of the ocean it is as nothing. So small is the power of the nations in comparison with God. ¶ *And are counted.* Are thought of, regarded, esteemed by him, or in comparison with him. ¶ *As the small dust of the balance.* The small, fine dust which collects on the best finished and most accurate balance or scales, and which has no effect in making the scales uneven, or making either side preponderate. Nothing can be a more striking representation of the fact that the nations are regarded as nothing in comparison with God. ¶ *Behold, he taketh up the isles.* Or he is able to do it; he could remove the isles as the fine dust is driven before the whirlwind. A more literal translation of this passage would be, 'Lo, the isles are as the dust which is taken up,' or which one takes up; *i.e.*, which is taken up, and carried away by the wind. There is something unusual in the expression that God takes up the isles, and the idea is rather that the isles in his sight are regarded as the fine dust which the wind sweeps away. So the Chaldee renders it, 'Lo, the isles are like ashes which the wind drives away.' The word 'isles,' Vitringa and Jerome regard as denoting not the small portions of land in the sea that are surrounded by water, but lands which are encompassed and enclosed by rivers, like Mesopotamia. But there is no reason why it should not be taken here in its usual signification, as denoting the islands of the sea. They would serve well to be used in connection with mountains and hills in setting forth the vast power of God. ¶ *As a very little thing* (כַּדַּק). The word דַּק (*dăq*) means *that which is beaten small, or fine;* and then fine dust, chaff, or any light thing which the wind easily sweeps away.

16. *And Lebanon.* The expression here refers to the trees or the cedars of Lebanon. Thus it is rendered by the Chaldee: 'And the trees of Lebanon.' For a description of Lebanon, see Note on ch. x. 34. It is probable that the word *Lebanon* here is not used in the limited sense in which it is sometimes employed, to denote a single mountain, or a single range of mountains, but includes the entire ranges lying north of Palestine, and which were comprehended under the general name of Libanus. The idea here is, that all these ranges of mountains, abounding in magnificent trees and forests, would not furnish fuel sufficient to burn the sacrifices which would be an appropriate offering to the majesty and glory of God. ¶ *To burn.* To burn for the purpose of consuming the sacrifice. ¶ *Nor the beasts thereof for a burnt-offering.* As the mountains of Lebanon were extensive forests, they would abound with wild animals. The idea is, that all those animals, if offered in sacrifice, would not be an appropriate expression of what was due to God. It may be remarked here, if all the vast forests of Lebanon on fire, and all its animals consumed as an offering to God, were not sufficient to show forth his glory, how little can our praises express the proper sense of his majesty and honour! How profound should be our reverence for God! With what awful veneration should we come before him! The image employed here by Isaiah is one of great poetic beauty; and nothing, perhaps, could give a deeper impression of the majesty and honour of the great Jehovah.

17. *Are as nothing.* This expresses literally what had been expressed by the beautiful and striking imagery above. ¶ *Less than nothing.* A strong hyperbolic expression denoting the utter insignificance of the nations as compared with God. Such expressions are com-

to him less than [a]nothing and
vanity.
18 To whom then will ye liken
God? or what likeness [b] will ye
compare unto him?
19 The workman [c]melteth a
graven image, and the goldsmith
spreadeth it over with gold, and
casteth silver chains.
20 He that [1]is so impoverished,
that he hath no oblation, chooseth
a tree *that* will not rot; he seeketh
unto him a cunning workman to
prepare a graven image, *that* shall
not be moved.

a Ps.62.9. b 2 Ki.25.6,&c. c ch.41.6,7; 44.12,&c. 1 is *poor of oblation*.

mon in the Scriptures. ¶ *And vanity.* Heb. תֹּהוּ (*thōhū*)—'Emptiness;' the word which in Gen. i. 2 is rendered 'without form.'

18. *To whom then will ye liken God?* Since he is so great, what can resemble him? What form can be made like him? The main idea here intended to be conveyed by the prophet evidently is, that God is great and glorious, and worthy of the confidence of his people. This idea he illustrates by a reference to the attempts which had been made to make a representation of him, and by showing how vain those efforts were. He therefore states the mode in which the images of idols were usually formed, and shows how absurd it was to suppose that they could be any real representation of the true God. It is possible that this was composed in the time of Manasseh, when idolatry prevailed to a great extent in Judah, and that the prophet intended in this manner incidentally to show the folly and absurdity of it.

19. *The workman.* The Hebrew word denotes an artificer of any kind, and is applied to one who engraved on wood or stone (Ex. xxviii. 2); to a workman in iron, brass, stone, wood (Ex. xxxv. 35; Deut. xxvii. 15); or an artizan, or artificer in general. It here refers manifestly to a man who worked in the metals of which idols were commonly made. Those idols were sometimes made of wood, sometimes of clay, but more frequently, as they are at present in India, of metal. It became, undoubtedly, a regular trade or business thus to make idol-gods. ¶ *Melteth.* Casts or founds. ¶ *A graven image* (פֶּסֶל). This word commonly denotes an image carved or graven from wood (Ex. xx. 4; Judg. xvii. 3; Isa. xliv. 15, 17); but it is also frequently applied to a *molten* image, or one that is cast from metals (Jer. x. 14; li. 17). It is used in this sense here; as there is an incongruity in the idea of *casting*, or melting a *graven* image. ¶ *And the goldsmith spreadeth it over with gold.* Idols were frequently overlaid with gold or silver. Those which were in the temples of the gods were probably commonly made in this way, and probably those also which were made for private use, as far as it could be afforded. The word here rendered 'goldsmith,' however, does not of necessity mean a worker in gold, but a smith in general, or a worker in any kind of metals. ¶ *And casteth silver chains.* For the idol. These were not to fasten it, but for the purpose of ornament. The general principle seems to have been to decorate their idols with that which was regarded as the highest ornament among the people; and as chains were used in abundance as a part of their personal ornaments among the Orientals (see Notes on ch. iii. 23), so they made use of the same kind of ornaments for their idols. The idols of the Hindoos now are lavishly decorated in this manner.

20. *He that is so impoverished.* So poor. So it is generally supposed that the word here used is to be understood, though interpreters have not been entirely agreed in regard to its signification. The LXX. render the phrase, 'The carpenter chooseth a sound piece of wood.' The Chaldee, 'He cuts down an ash, a tree which will not rot.' Vulg. 'Perhaps he chooses a tree which is incorruptible.' Jarchi renders it, 'He who is accustomed to examine, and to judge between the wood which is durable, and other wood.' But the signification of the word (from סָכַן *sākhăn, to dwell,* to be familiar with any one) given to it by our translators, is probably the correct one, that of being too poor to make a costly oblation. This notion of poverty,

21 Have [a]ye not known? have ye not heard? hath it not been told you [b]from the beginning? have ye not understood from the foundations of the earth?

[a] Ps.19.1; Ac.14.17; Ro.1.19,20. [b] Ro.3.1,2.

Gesenius supposes, is derived from the notion of *being seated;* and thence of sinking down from languor or debility; and hence from poverty or want. ¶ *That he hath no oblation.* No offering; no sacrifice; no rich gift. He is too poor to make such an offering to his god as would be implied in an idol of brass or other metal, richly overlaid with plates of gold, and decorated with silver chains. In ver. 19, the design seems to have been to describe the more rich and costly idols that were made; in this, to describe those that were made by the poor who were unable to offer such as were made of brass and gold. The word 'oblation,' therefore, *i.e.*, *offering*, in this place, does not denote an offering made to the true God, but an offering made to an idol, such as an image was regarded to be. He could not afford a rich offering, and was constrained to make one of wood. ¶ *Chooseth a tree* that *will not rot.* Wood that will be durable and permanent. Perhaps the idea is, that as he could not afford one of metal, he would choose that which would be the most valuable which he could make—a piece of wood that was durable, and that would thus show his regard for the god that he worshipped. Or possibly the sense may be, that he designed it should not be moved; that he expressed a fixed and settled determination to adhere to the worship of the idol; and that as he had no idea of changing his religion, the permanency and durability of the wood would be regarded as a somewhat more acceptable expression of his worship. ¶ *A cunning workman.* Heb. 'A wise artificer;' a man skilled in the art of carving, and of making images. ¶ *A graven image.* An image engraved or cut from wood, in contradistinction from one that is molten or made from metals. ¶ That *shall not be moved.* That shall stand long, as the expression of his devotion to the service of the idol. The wood that was commonly employed for this purpose as being most durable, as we learn from ch. xliv. 14, was the cedar, the cypress, or the oak (see the Note in that place). The phrase, 'shall not be moved,' does not refer so much to its being fixed in one place, as to its durability and permanency.

21. *Have ye not known?* This is evidently an address to the worshippers of idols, and either designed to be addressed to the Jews themselves in the times of Manasseh, when idolatry abounded, or to *all* idolaters. The prophet had in the previous verses shown the manner in which the idols were made, and the folly of regarding them as objects of worship. He now turns and addresses the worshippers of these idols, as being without excuse. They might have known that these were not the true God. They had had abundant opportunity of learning his existence and of becoming acquainted with his majesty and glory. Tradition had informed them of this, and the creation of the earth demonstrated his greatness and power. The prophet, therefore, asks them whether they had not known this? Whether their conduct was the result of ignorance? And the question implies emphatically that they *had* known, or had abundant opportunity to know of the existence and majesty of God. This was emphatically true of the Jews, and yet they were constantly falling into idolatrous worship. ¶ *From the beginning.* Heb. 'From the head,' *i.e.*, from the very commencement of the world. Has it not been communicated by tradition, from age to age, that there is one God, and that he is the Creator and upholder of all things? This was particularly the case with the Jews, who had had this knowledge from the very commencement of their history, and they were, therefore, entirely without excuse in their tendencies to idolatry. ¶ *From the foundations of the earth.* Have you not learned the existence and greatness of God from the fact that the world has been made, and that it demonstrates the existence and perfection of God? The sacred writers often speak of the earth as resting on a foundation, as upheld, &c.:

For he hath founded it upon the seas,
And established it upon the floods.

22 *It is* [1]he that sitteth upon the circle of the earth, and the inhabitants thereof *are* as grasshoppers; [a]that stretcheth out the heavens as a curtain, and spreadeth them out as a tent to dwell in;

1 or, *Him that sitteth.*

a Job 9.8.

(Ps. xxiv. 2; see also Prov. viii. 29.) Perhaps here, however, the word 'foundation' refers rather to the *time* than to the *manner* in which the earth is made, and corresponds to the phrase 'from the beginning;' and the sense may be, 'Has it not been understood ever since the earth was founded? Has not the tradition of the existence and perfections of God been unbroken and constant?' The argument is, that the existence and greatness of God were fully known by tradition and by his works; and that it was absurd to attempt to form an image of that God who had laid the foundations of the world.

22. It is *he that sitteth.* Marg. 'Him that sitteth,' *i.e.*, have you not known him? The Hebrew literally means 'the sitter, or he sitting on the circle of the earth;' and it may be connected either with ver. 21, 'Have ye not known him sitting on the circle of the earth?' or with ver. 18, 'What likeness will ye compare to him that sitteth on the circle of the earth?' In either case the phrase is designed to show the majesty and glory of God. The word 'sitteth' refers to God as a sovereign or monarch, making the circle of the earth his throne. ¶ *The circle of the earth.* Or rather, *above* (עַל *ăl*) the circle of the earth. The word rendered 'circle' (חוּג) denotes *a circle, sphere,* or *arch;* and is applied to the arch or vault of the heavens, in Prov. viii. 27; Job xxii. 14. The phrase 'circle,' or 'circuit of the earth,' here seems to be used in the same sense as the phrase *orbis terrarum* by the Latins; not as denoting a *sphere,* or not as implying that the earth was a globe, but that it was an extended plain surrounded by oceans and mighty waters. The globular form of the earth was then unknown; and the idea is, that God sat *above* this extended circuit, or circle; and that the vast earth was beneath his feet. ¶ *And the inhabitants thereof* are *like grasshoppers.* Or rather, like locusts, for so the Hebrew word properly means. This is designed to show that the inhabitants of the earth, numerous and mighty as they are, are as nothing compared with God. The *idea* is that God is so exalted, that, as he looks down from that elevated station, all the inhabitants of the world appear to him as locusts—a busy, agitated, moving, impatient multitude, spread over the vast circle of the earth beneath him—as locusts spread in almost interminable bands over the plains in the East. What a striking illustration of the insignificance of man as he is viewed from the heavens! What an impressive description of the nothingness of his mighty plans, and of the vanity of his mightiest works! ¶ *That stretcheth out the heavens.* Referring to the firmament above, as that which seems to be stretched out, or expanded over our heads. The heavens above are often thus compared to an expanse —either solid (Gen. i. 7), or to a curtain, or tent (comp. Note on ch. xxxiv. 4). ¶ *As a curtain.* The word here used (דֹּק) denotes properly *fineness, thinness;* and then a fine or thin cloth, or curtain. Here it means a thin canopy that is stretched over us. The same expression occurs in Ps. civ. 2 (comp. Job ix. 8; Isa. xliv. 24). Probably the reference here is to the veil, curtain, or awning which the Orientals are accustomed to draw over the *court* in their houses. Their houses are constructed with an open court in the centre, with the rooms ranged round it. In that court or open square there are usually fountains, if the situation is so that they can be constructed; and they are cool and refreshing places for the family to sit in the heat of the summer. In hot or rainy weather, a curtain or awning is drawn over this area. According to the image of the prophet here, the heavens are spread out over our heads as such an awning. ¶ *And spreadeth them out as a tent.* As a tent that is made for a habitation. Perhaps the idea is, that the heavens are extended like a tent in order to furnish a dwelling-place for God. Thus

23 That bringeth the princes to nothing:[a] he maketh the judges of the earth as vanity.

24 Yea, they shall not be planted; yea, they shall not be sown; yea, their stock shall not take root in the earth; and he shall also blow upon them, and they shall wither, and the whirlwind shall take them away as stubble.

[a] Job 12.21; Ps.107.40.

the Chaldee renders it. If so, it proves that the universe, so vast, was fitted up to be the dwelling-place of the High and Holy One, and is a most impressive representation of his immensity.

23. *That bringeth the princes to nothing.* That is, all princes and kings. No matter how great their power, their wealth, and their dignity, they are, by his hand, reduced to nothing before him. The design of this passage is to contrast the majesty of God with that of princes and nobles, and to show how far he excels them all. The general truth is therefore stated, that *all* monarchs are by him removed from their thrones, and consigned to nothing. The same idea is expressed in Job xii. 21:

> He poureth contempt upon princes,
> And weakeneth the strength of the mighty.

And in Ps. cvii. 40:

> He poureth contempt upon princes,
> And causeth them to wander in the wilderness
> where there is no way.

The *particular* idea here, as appears from the next verse, is, that the princes and rulers who are opposed to God constitute no real resistance to the execution of his purposes. He can strip off their honours and glory, and obliterate even their names. ¶ *He maketh the judges of the earth.* Kings and princes often executed judgment *personally,* and hence the words judges and kings seem to be synonymous as they are used here, and in Ps. ii. 10:

> Be wise now, therefore, O ye kings;
> Be instructed, ye judges of the earth.

24. *Yea, they shall not be planted.* The kings and rulers—especially they who oppose God in the execution of his purposes. The idea in this verse is, that their name and family should become extinct in the same way as a tree does from which no shoot starts up. Although they were great and mighty, like the tree that sends out far-spreading branches, and strikes its roots deep, yet God would so utterly destroy them that they should have no posterity, and their family become extinct. Princes and kings are often compared to lofty and majestic trees of the forest (comp. Ps. xxxvii. 35; Dan. iv. 7, *sq.*) Vitringa supposes that wicked rulers are particularly intended here, and that the idea is, that the wicked princes that persecuted his people should be entirely extinct on the earth. He refers particularly to Pharaoh, Antiochus Epiphanes, Nero, Domitian, Decius, Gallus, Galerius, Maxenus, Maximus, and some others, as instances of this kind, whose families soon became extinct. It may be remarked, in general, that the families of monarchs and princes become extinct usually much sooner than others. The fact may be owing in part to the usual luxury and vice in the families of the great, and in part to the direct arrangements of God, by which he designs that power shall not be for ever perpetuated in one family, or line. The *general* idea in the passage is, that earthly princes and rulers are as nothing when compared with God, and that he can easily destroy their families and their name. But there is no improbability in the supposition of Vitringa, that the prophet refers particularly to the *enemies* of God and his cause, and that he intends specifically to affirm that none of these enemies could prevent or embarrass the execution of his purposes—since with infinite ease he could entirely destroy their name. ¶ *They shall not be sown.* The same idea under another figure. The former referred to princes under the image of a tree; this refers to them under the image of grain that is sown. The idea is, that their family and name should be annihilated, and should not spring up in a future generation. The same image occurs in Nahum (i. 14), in respect to the king of Assyria: 'The LORD hath given commandment concerning thee, that no more of

thy name be sown;' that is, that thy name and family should become entirely extinct. ¶ *Yea, their stock.* Their stem—referring to the stump or stock of a tree. When a tree is cut down, the roots often still live, and send up shoots, or suckers, that grow into trees. Posterity is often, in the Scriptures, compared to such suckers or shoots from old and decayed trees (see Notes on ch. xi. 1). The meaning here is, that as when a tree falls and dies without sending up any shoots, so princes should die. They should have no descendants; no one of their family should sit on their thrones. ¶ *Shall blow upon them.* As God sends a tempest upon the forest, and uproots the loftiest trees, so he will sweep away the families of princes. Or rather, perhaps, the idea here is, that God sends a strong and burning east wind, and withers up everything before it (see this wind described in the Notes on ch. xxxvii. 26). ¶ *And they shall wither.* Trees, and shrubs, and plants are dried up before that poisonous and fiery wind—the simoom—and so it would be with the princes before the blast of JEHOVAH. ¶ *And the whirlwind shall take them away as stubble.* This, in its literal signification, means that the whirlwind bears away the trees of the forest, and with the same ease God would sweep away the families of the kings and princes that opposed him and oppressed his people. It may illustrate this to observe, that the effects of whirlwinds in the East are often much more violent than they are with us, and that they often bear away to a great distance the branches of trees, and even the trees themselves. The following description of a whirlwind observed by Mr. Bruce, may serve to illustrate this passage, as well as the passage in Ps. lxxxiii. 13:

> O my God, make them like a wheel;
> As the stubble before the wind,

referring to the rotary action of the whirlwind, which often impels straw like a wheel set in rapid motion. 'Mr. Bruce, in his journey through the desert of Senaar, had the singular felicity to contemplate this wonderful phenomenon in all its terrific majesty, without injury, although with considerable danger and alarm. In that vast expanse of desert, from west and to north-west of him, he saw a number of prodigious pillars of sand at different distances, moving, at times, with great celerity, at others, stalking on with majestic slowness; at intervals he thought they were coming, in a very few minutes, to overwhelm him and his companion. Again, they would retreat so as to be almost out of sight, their tops reaching to the very clouds. There, the tops often separated from the bodies; and these, once disjoined, dispersed in the air, and appeared no more. Sometimes they were broken near the middle, as if struck with a large cannon-shot. About noon, they began to advance with considerable swiftness upon them, the wind being very strong at north. Eleven of these awful visitors ranged alongside of them, about the distance of three miles. The greatest diameter of the largest appeared to him, at that distance, as if it would measure ten feet. They retired from them with a wind at south-east, leaving an impression upon the mind of our intrepid traveller, to which he could give no name, though he candidly admits that one ingredient in it was fear, with a considerable deal of wonder and astonishment. He declares it was in vain to think of flying; the swiftest horse, or fastest sailing ship, could be of no use to carry them out of this danger; and the full persuasion of this riveted him to the spot where he stood. Next day, they were gratified with a similar display of moving pillars, in form and disposition like those already described, only they seemed to be more in number and less in size. They came, several times, in a direction close upon them; that is, according to Mr. Bruce's computation, within less than two miles. They became, immediately after sunrise, like a thick wood, and almost darkened the sun; his rays shining through them for near an hour, gave them an appearance of pillars of fire. At another time, they were terrified by an army (as it seemed) of these sand pillars, whose march was constantly south, a number of which seemed once to be coming directly upon them; and though they were little nearer than two miles, a considerable quantity of sand fell around them. On the 21st of November, about

25 To whom[a] then will ye liken
me, or shall I be equal? saith the
Holy One.
26 Lift up your eyes on high,
and behold who hath created these
things, that bringeth out their hosts
by number: he calleth [b]them all
by names, by the greatness of his
might, for that *he is* strong in
power; not one faileth.

[a] De.4.23,&c. [b] Ps.147.4.

eight in the morning, he had a view of the desert to the westward, as before, and the sands had already begun to rise in immense twisted pillars, which darkened the heavens, and moved over the desert with more magnificence than ever. The sun, shining through the pillars, which were thicker, and contained more sand, apparently, than on any of the preceding days, seemed to give those nearest them an appearance as if spotted with stars of gold.'—(Paxton.)

25. *To whom then will ye liken me?* (see ver. 18.) The prophet having thus set forth the majesty and glory of God, asks now with great emphasis, what *could be* an adequate and proper representation of such a God. And if God was such a Being, how great was the folly of idolatry, and how vain all their confidence in the gods which their own hands had made.

26. *Lift up your eyes on high.* Direct your eyes towards heaven, and in the contemplation of the wonders of the starry world, and of God's power there, learn the evidence of his ability to destroy his foes and to save his friends. Lowth connects this verse with the former, and renders it:

> 'Saith the Holy One,
> Lift up your eyes on high.'

The words 'on high' here are evidently synonymous with heaven, and refer to the starry worlds. The design of the passage is to convince them of the folly of idolatry, and of the power and majesty of the true God. It is proof of man's elevated nature that he *can* thus look upward, and trace the evidences of the power and wisdom of God in the heavens; that he can raise his eyes and thoughts above the earth, and fix his attention on the works of God in distant worlds; and in the number, the order, the greatness, and the harmony of the heavenly bodies, trace the proofs of the infinite greatness and wisdom of God. This thought was most beautifully expressed by one of the ancient poets.

> Pronaque cum spectent animalia cætera terram;
> Os homini sublime dedit: cœlumque tueri,
> Jussit et erectos ad sidera tollere vultus.
> Ovid, *Met.* i. 84–86.

In the Scriptures, God not unfrequently appeals to the starry heavens in proof of his existence and perfections, and as the most sublime exhibition of his greatness and power (see Ps. xix. 1–6). And it may be remarked, that this argument is one that increases in strength, in the view of men, from age to age, just in proportion to the advances which are made in the science of astronomy. It is now far more striking than it was in the times of Isaiah; and, indeed, the discoveries in astronomical science in modern times have given a beauty and power to this argument which could have been but imperfectly understood in the times of the prophets. The argument is one that accumulates with every new discovery in astronomy; but is one —such is the vastness and beauty of the system of the universe—which can be contemplated in its full power only amidst the more sublime contemplations of eternity. Those who are disposed to contemplate this argument more fully, may find it presented with great eloquence and beauty in Dr. Chalmers's *Astronomical Discourses*, and in Dick's *Christian Philosopher*. ¶ *Who hath created these* things. These heavens. This is the first evidence of the power of God in the contemplation of the heavens, that God is their *Creator*. The other demonstrations referred to are the fact, that he brings out their armies as if they were a marshalled host, and understands and calls all their names. ¶ *That bringeth out their hosts.* Their *armies*, for so the word 'hosts' means (see Note on ch. i. 9). The word here alludes to the fact that the heavenly bodies seem to be mar-

27 Why sayest thou, O Jacob, and speakest, O Israel, My [a] way is hid from the LORD, and my

a Ps.77.7,&c.

shalled, or regularly arrayed as an army; that they keep their place, preserve their order, and are *apparently led on* from the east to the west, like a vast army under a mighty leader:

> Canst thou *bring forth* Mazzaroth in his season?
> Or canst thou *guide* Arcturus with his sons?
> Job xxxviii. 32.

¶ *By number.* As if he had numbered, or named them; as a military commander would call forth his armies in their proper order, and have them so *numbered* and *enrolled* in the various divisions, that he can command them with ease. ¶ *He calleth them all by names.* This idea is also taken from a military leader, who would know the names of the individuals that composed his army. In smaller divisions of an army, this could of course be done; but the idea is, that God is intimately acquainted with *all* the hosts of stars; that though their numbers appear to us so great, yet he is acquainted with each one individually, and has that knowledge of it which we have of a person or object which we recognize by a *name.* It is said of Cyrus, that he was acquainted by name with every individual that composed his vast army. The practice of giving names to the stars of heaven was early, and is known to have been originated by the Chaldeans. Intimations of this custom we have not unfrequently in the Scriptures, as far back as the time of Job:

> Which maketh Arcturus, and Orion, and Pleiades,
> And the chambers of the south.
> Job ix. 9.

> Canst thou bind the sweet influences of Pleiades?
> Or loose the bands of Orion?
> Canst thou bring forth Mazzaroth in his season?
> Or canst thou guide Arcturus with his sons?
> Job xxxviii. 31, 32.

This power of giving names to all the stars, is beautifully ascribed to God in Ps. cxlvii. 4:

> He telleth the number of the stars,
> He calleth them all by their names.

This view of the greatness of God is more striking now than it was in the times of David or Isaiah. Little then, comparatively, was known of the number of the stars. But since the invention of the telescope the view of the heavenly world has been enlarged almost to immensity; and though the expression 'he calleth them all by their names,' had great sublimity as used in the time of Isaiah, yet it raises in us far higher conceptions of the power and greatness of God when applied to what *we* know now of the heavens. Yet doubtless our view of the heavens is much further beneath the sublime reality than were the prevalent views in the time of the prophet beneath those which we now have. As an illustration of this we may remark, that the milky way which stretches across the heavens, is now ascertained to receive its white appearance from the mingling together of the light of an innumerable number of stars, too remote to be seen by the naked eye. Dr. Herschell examined a portion of the milky way about fifteen degrees long, and two broad, and found that it contained no fewer than fifty thousand stars, large enough to be distinctly counted, and he suspected that that portion contained twice as many more, which, for the want of sufficient light in his telescope, he saw only now and then. It is to be remembered, also, that the galaxy, or milky way, which we see with the naked eye, is only one of a *large number* of nebulæ of similar construction which are arranged apparently in *strata,* and which extend to great length in the heavens. According to this, and on every correct supposition in regard to the heavens, the number of the stars surpasses all our powers of computation. Yet God is said to lead them all forth as *marshalled armies*—how beautiful a description when applied to the *nebulæ!*—and to call all their names. ¶ *By the greatness of his might.* It is his single and unassisted arm that conducts them; his own hand alone that sustains them. ¶ *Not one faileth.* Not one is wanting; not one of the immense host is out of its place, or unnoticed. All are arranged in infinite wisdom; all observe the proper order, and the proper times. How strikingly true is this, on the slightest inspection of the heavens. How im-

judgment is passed over from my God?

28 Hast thou not known, hast thou not heard, *that* the everlasting God, the LORD, the Creator of the ends of the earth, fainteth not, neither [a]is weary? *there* [b]*is* no searching of his understanding.

a ch.59.1. b Ps.147.5.

pressive and grand is it in the higher developments of the discoveries of astronomy!

27. *Why sayest thou?* This verse is designed to reprove the people for their want of confidence in God. The idea is, 'If God is so great; if he arranges the hosts of heaven with such unerring skill, causing all the stars to observe their proper place and their exact times, the interests of his people are safe in his hands.' Piety may always find security in the assurance that He who preserves the unbroken order of the heavens will not fail to keep and save his people.—The language in this verse is to be understood as addressed to the Jews sighing for deliverance in their long and painful captivity in Babylon. Their city and temple had laid waste for many years; their captivity had been long and wearisome, and doubtless many would be ready to say, that it would never end. To furnish an argument to meet this state of despondency, the prophet sets before them this sublime description of the faithfulness and the power of God. ¶ *O Jacob.* A name often given to the Jews as the descendants of Jacob. ¶ *O Israel.* Denoting the same. The name Israel was given to Jacob because he had power to prevail as a prince with God (Gen. xxxii. 28); and it became the common name by which his descendants were known. ¶ *My way is hid from the* LORD. That is, is not seen, or noticed. The word 'way' here denotes evidently the state or condition; the manner of life, or the calamities which they experienced. The term is often thus employed to denote the lot, condition, or manner in which one lives or acts (Ps. xxxvii. 5; Isa. x. 24; Jer. xii. 1). The phrase, 'is hid,' means that God is ignorant of it, or that he does not attend to it; and the complaint here is, that God had not regarded them in their calamities, and would not interpose to save them. ¶ *And my judgment.* My cause. The word here refers to their condition among the people where they were captive, and by whom they were oppressed. They are represented as being deprived of their liberty; and they here complain that God disregarded their cause, and that he did not come forth to deliver them from their oppressions and their trials.

28. *Hast thou not known?* This is the language of the prophet reproving them for complaining of being forsaken, and assuring them that God was faithful to his promises. This argument of the prophet, which continues to the close of the chapter, comprises the main scope of the chapter, which is to induce them to put confidence in God, and to believe that he was able and willing to deliver them. The phrase, 'Hast thou not known?' refers to the fact that the Jewish people had had an abundant opportunity of learning, in their history, and from their fathers, the true character of God, and his entire ability to save them. No people had had so much light on this subject, and now that they were in trial, they ought to recall their former knowledge of his character, and remember his dealings of faithfulness with them and their fathers. It is well for the people of God in times of calamity and trial to recall to their recollection his former dealings with his church. That history will furnish abundant sources of consolation, and abundant assurances that their interests are safe in his hands. ¶ *Hast thou not heard?* From the traditions of the fathers; the instruction which you have received from ancient times. A large part of the knowledge of the Jews was traditionary; and these attributes of God, as a faithful God, had, no doubt, constituted an important part of the knowledge which had thus been communicated to them. ¶ *The everlasting God.* The God who has existed from eternity, unlike the idols of the heathen. If he was from eternity, he would be unchangeable, and his purposes could not fail. ¶ *The Creator of the ends of the earth.* The phrase, 'the

29 He [a] giveth power to the faint;
and to *them that have* no might he
increaseth strength.
30 Even the youths shall faint
and be weary, and the young men
shall utterly fall.
31 But they [b] that wait upon the

a 2 Co.12.9. b Ps.84.7; 92.1,13.

ends of the earth,' means the same as the earth itself. The earth is sometimes spoken of as a vast plain having limits or boundaries (see ver. 22). It is probable that this was the prevailing idea among the ancients (comp. Deut. xxxiii. 17; 1 Sam. ii. 10; Ps. xix. 6; xxii. 27; xlviii. 10; lxv. 5; lxvii. 7; xcviii. 3; Isa. xliii. 6; xlv. 22; lii. 10). The argument here is, that he who has formed the earth could not be exhausted or weary in so small a work as that of protecting his people. ¶ *Fainteth not.* Is not fatigued or exhausted. That God, who has formed and sustained all things, is not exhausted in his powers, but is able still to defend and guard his people. ¶ There is *no searching of his understanding.* The God who made all things must be infinitely wise. There is proof of boundless skill in the works of his hands, and it is impossible for finite mind fully and adequately to search out *all* the proofs of his wisdom and skill. Man can see only a part—a small part, while the vast ocean, the boundless deep of his wisdom, lies still unexplored. This thought is beautifully expressed by Zophar in Job xi. 7-9:—

Canst thou by searching find out God?
Canst thou find out the Almighty unto perfection?
It is as high as heaven;
What canst thou do?
Deeper than hell;
What canst thou know:
The measure thereof is longer than the earth,
And broader than the sea.

The *argument* here is, that that God who has made all things, *must* be intimately acquainted with the wants of his people. They had, therefore, no reason to complain that their way was hidden from the Lord, and their cause passed over by him.—*Perhaps*, also, it is implied, that as his understanding was vast, they ought not to expect to be able to comprehend the reason of all his doings; but should expect that there would be much that was mysterious and unsearchable. The *reasons* of his doings are often hid from his people; and their consolation is to be found in the assurance that he *is* infinitely wise, and that he who rules over the universe *must* know what is best, and CANNOT ERR.

29. *He giveth power to the faint.* To his weak and feeble people. This is one of his attributes; and his people, therefore, should put their trust in him, and look to him for aid (comp. 2 Cor. xii. 9). The design of this verse is to give consolation to the afflicted and down-trodden people in Babylon, by recalling to their minds the truth that it was one of the characteristics of God that he ministered strength to those who were conscious of their own feebleness, and who looked to him for support. It is a truth, however, as applicable to us as to them—a truth inestimably precious to those who feel that they are weak and feeble, and who look to God for aid.

30. *Even the youths shall faint.* The most vigorous young men, those in whom we expect manly strength, and who are best fitted to endure hardy toil. They become weary by labour. Their powers are soon exhausted. The *design* here is, to contrast the most vigorous of the human race with God, and to show that while all *their* powers fail, the power of God is unexhausted and inexhaustible. ¶ *And the young men.* The word here used denotes properly *those who are chosen* or selected (בַּחוּרִים, Gr. ἐκλεκτοί), and may be applied to those who were *selected* or chosen for any hazardous enterprise, or dangerous achievement in war; those who would be selected for vigour or activity. The meaning is, that the most *chosen* or select of the human family—the most vigorous and manly, must be worn down by fatigue, or paralyzed by sickness or death; but that the powers of God never grow weary, and that those who trust in him should never become faint.

31. *But they that wait upon the* LORD. The word rendered 'wait upon' here (from קָוָה), denotes properly *to wait*, in the sense of *expecting*. The phrase, 'to wait on JEHOVAH,' means to wait for his help; that is, to trust in him, to put

LORD shall [1] renew [a] their strength: they shall mount up with wings as eagles; they shall run [b] and not be weary, *and* they shall walk [c] and not faint.

1 *change.* a Ps.103.5. b He.12.1. c Mi.4.5.

---

our hope or confidence in him. It is applicable to those who are in circumstances of danger or want, and who look to him for his merciful interposition. *Here* it properly refers to those who were suffering a long and grievous captivity in Babylon, and who had no prospect of deliverance but in him. The phrase is applicable also to *all* who feel that they are weak, feeble, guilty, and helpless, and who, in view of this, put their trust in JEHOVAH. The promise or assurance here is general in its nature, and is as applicable to his people now as it was in the times of the captivity in Babylon. Religion is often expressed in the Scriptures by 'waiting on JEHOVAH,' *i.e.*, by looking to him for help, expecting deliverance through his aid, putting trust in him (see Ps. xxv. 3, 5, 21; xxvii. 14; xxxvii. 7, 9, 34; lxix. 3; comp. Note on Isa. viii. 17; xxx. 18). It does not *imply* inactivity, or want of personal exertion; it implies merely that our hope of aid and salvation is in him—a feeling that is *as* consistent with the most strenuous endeavours to secure the object, as it is with a state of inactivity and indolence. Indeed, no man can *wait* on God in a proper manner who does not use the means which he has appointed for conveying to us his blessing. To *wait* on him without using any means to obtain his aid, is to tempt him; to expect miraculous interposition is unauthorized, and must meet with disappointment. And they only wait on him in a proper manner who expect his blessing in the common modes in which he imparts it to men—in the use of those means and efforts which he has appointed, and which he is accustomed to bless. The farmer who should *wait* for God to plough and sow his fields, would not only be disappointed, but would be guilty of provoking Him. And so the man who waits for God to do what *he* ought to do; to save him without using any of the means of grace, will not only be disappointed, but will provoke his displeasure. ¶ *Shall renew their strength.* Marg. 'Change.' The Hebrew word commonly means *to change, to alter;* and then to revive, to renew, to cause to flourish again, as, *e.g.*, a tree that has decayed and fallen down (see Note on ch. ix. 10; comp. Job xiv. 7). Here it is evidently used in the sense of renewing, or causing to revive; to increase, and to restore that which is decayed. It means that the people of God who trust in him shall become strong in faith; able to contend with their spiritual foes, to gain the victory over their sins, and to discharge aright the duties, and to meet aright the trials of life. God gives them strength, if they seek him in the way of his appointment—a promise which has been verified in the experience of his people in every age. ¶ *They shall mount up with wings as eagles.* Lowth translates this, 'They shall put forth fresh feathers like the moulting eagle;' and in his note on the passage remarks, that 'it has been a common and popular opinion that the eagle lives and retains his vigour to a great age; and that, beyond the common lot of other birds, he moults in his old age, and renews his feathers, and with them his youth.' He supposes that the passage in Ps. ciii. 5, 'So that thy youth is renewed like the eagles,' refers to this fact. That this was a common and popular opinion among the ancients, is clearly proved by Bochart (*Hieroz*. ii. 2. 1. pp. 165–169). The opinion was, that at stated times the eagle plunged itself in the sea and cast off its old feathers, and that new feathers started forth, and that thus it lived often to the hundredth year, and then threw itself in the sea and died. In accordance with this opinion, the LXX. render this passage, 'They shall put forth fresh feathers (πτεροφυήσουσιν) like eagles.' Vulg. *Assument pennas sicut aquilæ.* The Chaldee renders it, 'They who trust in the Lord shall be gathered from the captivity, and shall increase their strength, and renew their youth as a germ which grows up; upon wings of eagles shall they run and not be fatigued.'—But whatever may be the truth in regard to the eagle, there is no reason

CHAPTER XLI.

ANALYSIS.

THE design of this chapter is the same as that of the preceding, and it is to be regarded as the continuation of the argument commenced there. Its object is to lead those who were addressed, to put confidence in God. In the introduction to ch. xl. it was remarked, that this is to be considered as addressed to the exile Jews in Babylon, near the close of their captivity. Their country, city, and temple had been laid waste. The prophet represents himself as bringing consolation to them in this situation; particularly by the assurance that their long captivity was about to end; that they were about to be restored to their own land, and that their trials were to be succeeded by brighter and happier times. In the previous chapter there were general reasons given why they should put their confidence in God—arising from the firmness of his promises, the fact that he had created all things; that he had all power, &c. In this chapter there is a more definite view given, and a clearer light thrown on the mode in which deliverance would be brought to them. The prophet specifies that God would raise up a deliverer, and that that deliverer would be able to subdue all their enemies. The chapter may be conveniently divided into the following parts:—

I. God calls the distant nations to a public investigation of his ability to aid his people; to an *argument* whether he was able to deliver them; and to the statement of the reasons why they should confide in him (1).

II. He specifies that he will raise up a man from the east—who should be able to overcome the enemies of the Jews, and to effect their deliverance (2–4).

III. The consternation of the nations at the approach of Cyrus, and their excited and agitated fleeing to their idols is described (5–7).

IV. God gives to his people the assurance of his protection, and friendship (8–14). This is shown—1. Because they were the children of Abraham, his friend, and he was bound in covenant faithfulness to protect them (8, 9). 2. By direct assurance that he would aid and protect them; that though they were feeble, yet he was strong enough to deliver them (10–14).

V. He says that he will enable them to overcome and scatter their foes, as the chaff is driven away on the mountains by the whirlwind (15, 16).

VI. He gives to his people the special promise of assistance and comfort. He will meet them in their desolate condition, and will give them consolation *as if* fountains were opened in deserts, and trees producing grateful shade and fruit were planted in the wilderness (17–20).

VII. He appeals directly to the enemies of the Jews, to the worshippers of idols. He challenges them to give any evidence of the power or the divinity of their idols; and appeals to the fact that he had foretold future events; that he had raised up a deliverer for his people in proof of *his* divinity, and *his* power to save (21–29).

The *argument* of the whole is, that the idol-gods were unable to defend the nations which trusted in them; that God would raise up a mighty prince who should be able to deliver the Jews from their long and painful calamity, and

---

to believe that Isaiah here had any reference to the fact that it *moults* in its old age. The translation of Lowth was derived from the Septuagint, and not from the Hebrew text. The meaning of the Hebrew is simply, 'they shall ascend on wings as eagles,' or 'they shall lift up the wings as eagles;' and the image is derived from the fact that the eagle rises on the most vigorous wing of any bird, and ascends apparently further towards the sun. The figure, therefore, denotes strength and vigour of purpose; strong and manly piety; an elevation above the world; communion with God, and a nearness to his throne —as the eagle ascends towards the sun. ¶ *They shall run and not be weary.* This passage, also, is but another mode of expressing the same idea—that they who trust in God would be vigorous, elevated, unwearied; that he would sustain and uphold them; and that in his service they would never faint.—This was at first designed to be applied to the Jews in captivity in Babylon to induce them to put their trust in God. But it is as true now as it was at that time. It has been found in the experience of thousands and tens of thousands, that by waiting on the Lord the heart has been invigorated; the faith has been confirmed; and the affections have been raised above the world. Strength has been given to bear trial without murmuring, to engage in arduous duty without fainting, to pursue the perilous and toilsome journey of life without exhaustion, and to rise above the world in hope and peace on the bed of death.

that they, therefore, should put their trust in JEHOVAH.

KEEP silence [a]before me, O
islands; and let the people
renew *their* strength: let them
come near; then let them speak:
let us come near together to judgment.

2 Who raised up [1]the righteous
man from the east, called [b]him to
his foot, gave [c]the nations before
him, and made *him* rule over kings?
he gave *them* as the dust to his
sword, *and* as driven stubble to his
bow.

[a] Zec.2.13. [1] *righteousness.* [b] ch.46.11. [c] Ezr.1.2.

CHAPTER XLI.

1. *Keep silence before me* (comp. Zech. ii. 13). The idea is, that the heathen nations were to be silent while God should speak, or with a view of entering into an argument with him respecting the comparative power of himself and of idols to defend their respective worshippers. The argument is stated in the following verses, and preparatory to the statement of that argument, the people are exhorted to be silent. This is probably to evince a proper awe and reverence for JEHOVAH, before whom the argument was to be conducted, and a proper sense of the magnitude and sacredness of the inquiry (comp. ver. 21). And it may be remarked here, that the same reasons will apply to *all* approaches which are made to God. When we are about to come before him in prayer or praise; to confess our sins and to plead for pardon; when we engage an argument respecting his being, plans, or perfections; or when we draw near to him in the closet, the family, or the sanctuary, the mind should be filled with awe and reverence. It is well, it is proper, to pause and think of what our emotions should be, and of what we should say, before God (comp. Gen. xxviii. 16, 17). ¶ *O islands* (אִיִּים). This word properly means *islands,* and is so translated here by the Vulgate, the LXX., the Chaldee, the Syriac, and the Arabic. But the word also is used to denote maritime countries; countries that were situated on sea-coasts, or the regions beyond sea (see Note on ch. xx. 6). The word is applied, therefore, to the islands of the Mediterranean; to the maritime coasts; and then, also, it comes to be used in the sense of *any* lands or coasts far remote, or beyond sea (see Ps. lxx. 10; Isa. xxiv. 15; Notes on ch. xl. 15; xli. 5; xlii. 4, 10, 12; xlix. 1; Jer. xxv. 22; Dan. xi. 18). Here it is evidently used in the sense of distant nations or lands; the people who were remote from Palestine, and who were the worshippers of idols. The argument is represented as being *with* them, and they are invited to prepare their minds by suitable reverence for God for the argument which was to be presented. ¶ *And let the people renew* their *strength.* On the word 'renew,' see Note on ch. xl. 31. Here it means, 'Let them make themselves strong; let them prepare the argument; let them be ready to urge as strong reasons as possible; let them fit themselves to enter into the controversy about the power and glory of JEHOVAH' (see ver. 21). ¶ *Let us come near together to judgment.* The word 'judgment' here means evidently controversy, argumentation, debate. Thus it is used in Job ix. 32. The language is that which is used of two parties who come together to try a cause, or to engage in debate; and the sense is, that God proposes to enter into an argumentation with the entire heathen world, in regard to his ability to save his people; that is, he proposes to show the *reasons* why they should trust in him, rather than dread those under whose power they then were, and by whom they had been oppressed. Lowth renders it, correctly expressing the sense, 'Let us enter into solemn debate together.'

2. *Who raised up.* This word (הֵעִיר) is usually applied to the act of arousing one from sleep (Cant. ii. 7; iii. 5; viii. 4; Zec. iv. 1); then to awake, arouse, or stir up to any enterprise. Here it means, that God had caused the man here referred to, to arouse for the overthrow of their enemies; it was by his agency that he had been led to form the plans which should result in their de-

liverance. This is the *first* argument which God urges to induce his people to put confidence in him, and to hope for deliverance; and the fact that he had raised up and qualified such a man for the work, he urges as a proof that he would certainly protect and guard his people. ¶ *The righteous* man *from the east.* Heb. צֶדֶק *tzĕdhĕq*—'Righteousness.' The LXX. render it literally, Δικαιοσύνην—'Righteousness.' The Vulgate renders it, 'The just;' the Syriac as the LXX. The word here evidently means, as in our translation, the just or righteous man. It is common in the Hebrew, as in other languages, to put the abstract for the concrete. In regard to the *person* here referred to, there have been three principal opinions, which it may be proper briefly to notice. 1. The first is, that which refers it to Abraham. This is the interpretation of the Chaldee Paraphrast, who renders it, 'Who has publicly led from the east Abraham, the chosen of the just;' and this interpretation has been adopted by Jarchi, Kimchi, Abarbanel, and by the Jewish writers generally. They say that it means that God had called Abraham from the east; that he conducted him to the land of Canaan, and enabled him to vanquish the people who resided there, and particularly that he vanquished the kings of Sodom and Gomorrah, and delivered Lot from their hands (Gen. xiv.); and that this is designed by God to show them that he who had thus raised up Abraham would raise up *them* also *in* the east. There are, however, objections to this interpretation which seem to be insuperable, a few of which may be referred to. (*a.*) The country from which Abraham came, the land of Chaldea or Mesopotamia, is not commonly in the Scriptures called 'the east,' but the *north* (see Jer. i. 13–15; iv. 6; vi. 1; xxiii. 8; xxv. 9, 26; xxxi. 8; xlvi. 10; l. 3; Dan. xi. 6, 8, 11. This country was situated to the north-east of Palestine, and it is believed is nowhere in the Scriptures called the country of the east. (*b.*) The description which is here given of what was accomplished by him who was raised up from the east, is not one that applies to Abraham. It supposes more important achievements than any that signalized the father of the faithful. There were no acts in the life of Abraham that can be regarded as subduing the 'nations' before him; as ruling over 'kings;' or as scattering them like the dust or the stubble. Indeed, he appears to have been engaged but in one military adventure—the rescue of Lot—and that was of so slight and unimportant a character as not to form the peculiarity of his public life. Had Abraham been referred to here, it would have been for some other trait than that of a conqueror or military chieftain. (*c.*) We shall see that the description and the connection require us to understand it of another—of Cyrus. 2. A second opinion is, that it refers directly and entirely to the Messiah. Many of the fathers, as Jerome, Cyril, Eusebius, Theodoret, Procopius, held this opinion. But the objections to this are insuperable. (*a.*) It is not true that the Messiah was raised up from the east. He was born in the land of Judea, and always lived in that land. (*b.*) The description here is by no means one that applies to him. It is the description of a warrior and a conqueror; of one who subdued nations, and scattered them before him. (*c.*) The connection and design of the passage does not admit of the interpretation. That design is, to lead the Jews in exile to put confidence in God, and to hope for a speedy rescue. In order to this, the prophet directs them to the fact that a king appeared in the east, and that he scattered the nations; and *from these facts* they were to infer that they would themselves be delivered, and that God would be their protector. But how would this design be accomplished by a reference to so remote an event as the coming of the Messiah? 3. The third opinion, therefore, remains, that this refers to Cyrus, the Persian monarch, by whom Babylon was taken, and by whom the Jews were restored to their own land. In support of this interpretation, a few considerations may be adverted to. (*a.*) It agrees with the fact in regard to the country from which Cyrus came for purposes of conquest. He came from the land which is everywhere in the Scriptures called the East. (*b.*) It agrees with the specifications which Isaiah elsewhere makes, where Cyrus is mentioned by name, and where there can be no danger of error in regard to the interpretation (see ch. xliv. 28; xlv. 1–4, 13). Thus in ch. xlvi. 11, it is said of Cyrus, 'Calling a ravenous bird *from the east*, the man that executeth my commandments from a far country. (*c.*) The entire description here is one that applies in a remarkable manner to Cyrus, as will be shown more fully in the Notes on the particular expressions which occur. (*d.*) This supposition accords with the design of the prophet. It was to be an assurance to them not only that God *would* raise up such a man, but that they should be delivered; and as this was intended to comfort them in Babylon, it was intended that *when* they were apprised of the conquests of Cyrus, they were to be *assured* of the fact that God was their protector; and those conquests, therefore, were to be regarded by them as a proof that God would deliver them. This opinion is held by Vitringa, Rosenmüller, and probably by a large majority of the most intelligent commentators. The only objection of weight to it is that suggested by Lowth, that the character of 'a righteous man' does not apply to Cyrus. But to this it may be replied, that the word may be used not to denote one that is *pious*, or a true worshipper of God, but one who was disposed to do justly, or who was not a tyrant; and especially it may be applied to him on account of his delivering the Jews from their hard and oppressive bondage in Babylon, and restoring them to their own land. That was an act of eminent public justice; and the favours which he showed them in enabling them to rebuild their city and temple, were such as to render it not improper that this appellation should be given to him. It may be added also that Cyrus was a prince eminently distinguished for justice and equity, and for a mild and kind administration over his own subjects. Xenophon, who has described his character at length, has proposed him as an example of a just monarch, and his government as an example of an equitable administration. All the ancient writers celebrate his humanity and benevolence (comp. Diod. xiii. 342, and the *Cyropedia* of Xenophon everywhere). As there will be frequent occasion to refer to Cyrus in the Notes on the chapters which follow, it may be proper here to give a very brief outline of his public actions, that his agency in the deliverance of the Jews may be more fully appreciated. Cyrus was the son of Cambyses, the Persian, and of Mandane, the daughter of Astyages, king of the Medes. Astyages is in Scripture called Ahasuerus. Cambyses was, according to Xenophon (*Cyr.* i.), king of Persia, or, according to Herodotus (i. 107), he was a nobleman. If he was the king of Persia, of course Cyrus was the heir of the throne. Cyrus was born in his father's court, A.M. 3405, or B.C. 595, and was educated with great care. At the age of twelve years, his grandfather, Astyages, sent for him and his mother Mandane to court, and he was treated, of course, with great attention. Astyages, or Ahasuerus, had a son by the name of Cyaxares, who was born about a year before Cyrus, and who was heir to the throne of Media. Some time after this, the son of the king of Assyria having invaded Media, Astyages, with his son Cyaxares, and his grandson Cyrus, marched against him. Cyrus defeated the Assyrians, but was soon after recalled by his father Cambyses to Persia, that he might be near him. At the age of sixteen, indeed, and when at the court of his grandfather, Cyrus signalized himself for his valour in a war with the king of Babylon. Evil-Merodach, the son of Nebuchadnezzar, king of Babylon, had invaded the territories of Media, but was repelled with great loss, and Cyrus pursued him with great slaughter to his own borders. This invasion of Evil-Merodach laid the foundation of the hostility between Babylon and Media, which was not terminated until Babylon was taken and destroyed by the united armies of Media and Persia. When Astyages died, after a reign of thirty-five years, he was succeeded by his son Cyaxares, the uncle of Cyrus. He was still involved in a war with the Babylonians. Cyrus was made general of the Persian troops, and at the head of an army of 30,000 men was sent to assist Cyaxares, whom the Babylonians were preparing to attack. The Babylonian monarch at this time was Neriglissar, who had murdered Evil-Merodach, and who had usurped the crown of Babylon. Cyaxares and Cyrus carried on the war against Babylon during the reigns of Neriglissar and his son Laborosoarchod, and of Nabonadius. The Babylonians were defeated, and Cyrus carried his arms into the countries to the west beyond the river Halys—a river running north into the Euxine Sea—and subdued Cappadocia, and conquered Crœsus, the rich king of Lydia, and subdued almost all Asia Minor. Having conquered this country, he returned again, re-crossed the Euphrates, turned his arms against the Assyrians, and then laid siege to Babylon, and took it (see Notes on ch. xiii., xiv.), and subdued that mighty kingdom. During the life of Cyaxares his uncle, he acted in conjunction with him. On the death of this king of Media, Cyrus married his daughter, and thus united the crowns of Media and Persia. After this marriage, he subdued all the nations between Syria and the Red Sea, and died at the age of seventy, after a reign of thirty years. Cyaxares, the uncle of Cyrus, is in the Scripture called Darius the Mede (Dan. v. 31), and it is said there, that it was by him that Babylon was taken. But Babylon was taken by the valour of Cyrus, though acting in connection with, and under Cyaxares; and it is said to have been taken by Cyaxares, or Darius, though it was done by the personal valour of Cyrus. Josephus (*Ant.* xii. 13) says, that Darius with his ally, Cyrus, destroyed the kingdom of Babylon. Jerome assigns three reasons why Babylon is said in the Scriptures to have been taken by Darius or Cyaxares; first, because he was the elder of the two; secondly, because the Medes were at that time more famous than the Persians; and thirdly, because the uncle ought to be preferred to the nephew. The Greek writers say that Babylon was taken by Cyrus, without mentioning Cyaxares or Darius, doubtless because it was done solely by his valour. For a full account of the reign of Cyrus, see Xen. *Cyr.*, Herodotus, and the ancient part of the *Universal History*, vol. iv. Ed. Lond. 1779, 8vo. ¶ *Called him to his foot.* Lowth renders this, 'Hath called him to attend his steps.' Noyes renders it, 'Him whom victory meeteth in his march.' Grotius, 'Called him that he should follow him,' and he refers to Gen. xii. 1; Josh. xxiv. 3; Heb. xi. 8. Rosenmüller renders it, 'Who hath called from the East that man to whom righteousness occurs at his feet,' *i.e.*, attends him. But the idea seems to be, that God had influenced him to follow him as one follows a guide at his feet, or close to him. ¶ *Gave the nations before him.* That is, subdued nations before him. This is justly descriptive of the victorious career of Cyrus. Among the nations whom he subdued, were the Armenians, the Cappadocians, the Lydians, the Phrygians, the Assyrians, the Babylonians, comprising a very large portion of the world, known at that time. Cyrus subdued, according to Xenophon, all the nations lying between the Euxine and Caspian seas on the north, to the Red Sea on the south, and even Egypt, so that his own proclamation was true: 'JEHOVAH, God of heaven, hath given me all the kingdoms of the earth' (Ezra i. 2). ¶ *And made him rule over kings.* As the kings of Babylon, of Lydia, of Cappadocia, who were brought into subjection under him, and acknowledged their dependence on him. ¶ *He hath given them as the dust to his sword.* He has scattered, or destroyed them by his sword, as the dust is driven before the wind. A similar remark is made by David (Ps. xviii. 42)—

Then did I beat them small as the dust before the wind,
I did cast them out as the dirt in the streets.

¶ *And as driven stubble.* The allusion here is to the process of fanning grain. The grain was thrown by a shovel or fan in the air, and the stubble or chaff was driven away. So it is said of the nations before Cyrus, implying that they were utterly scattered. ¶ *To his bow.* The bow was one of the common weapons of war, and the inhabitants of the East were distinguished for its use. The idea in this verse is very beautiful, and is one that is often employed in the Sacred Scriptures, and by Isaiah himself (see Job xxi. 18; Ps. i. 4; xxxv. 5;

3 He pursued them, *and* passed
safely: [1] *even* by the way *that* he
had not gone with his feet.
4 Who hath wrought and done
it, calling the generations from the
beginning? I the LORD, the [a] first,
and with the last; I *am* he.
5 The isles saw *it*, and feared;
the ends of the earth were afraid,
drew near, and came.

1 *in peace.*

a Re.1.17; 22.13.

Notes on ch. xvii. 13; xxix. 5; comp. Hos. xiii. 3).

3. *He pursued them.* When they were driven away. He followed on, and devoted them to discomfiture and ruin. ¶ And *passed safely.* Marg. as Heb. 'In peace.' That is, he followed them uninjured; they had no power to rally, he was not led into ambush, and he was safe as far as he chose to pursue them. ¶ Even *by the way* that *he had not gone with his feet.* By a way that he had not been accustomed to march; in an unusual journey; in a land of strangers. Cyrus had passed his early years on the east of the Euphrates. In his conquests he crossed that river, and extended his march beyond even the river Halys to the western extremity of Asia, and even to Egypt and the Red Sea. The idea here is, that he had not travelled in these regions until he did it for purposes of conquest—an idea which is strictly in accordance with the truth of history.

4. *Who hath wrought and done* it? By whom has all this been accomplished? Has it been by the arm of Cyrus? Has it been by human skill and power? The design of this question is obvious. It is to direct attention to the fact that all this had been done by God, and that he who had raised up such a man, and had accomplished all this by means of him, had power to deliver his people. ¶ *Calling the generations from the beginning.* The idea here seems to be, that all the nations that dwell on the earth in every place owed their origin to God (comp. Acts xvii. 26). The word 'calling' here, seems to be used in the sense of commanding, directing, or ordering them; and the truth taught is, that all the nations were under his control, and had been from the beginning. It was not only true of Cyrus, and of those who were subdued before him, but it was true of all nations and generations. The object seems to be, to lift up the thoughts from the conquests of Cyrus to God's universal dominion over all kingdoms from the beginning of the world. ¶ *I the* LORD, *the first.* Before any creature was made; existing before any other being. The description that God here gives of himself as 'the first and the last,' is one that is often applied to him in the Scriptures, and is one that properly expresses eternity (see ch. xliv. 6; xlviii. 12). It is remarkable also that this expression, which so obviously implies proper eternity, is applied to the Lord Jesus in Rev. i. 17, and xxii. 13. ¶ *And with the last.* The usual form in which this is expressed is simply 'the last' (ch. xliv. 6; xlviii. 12). The idea here seems to be, 'and with the last, I am the same;' *i.e.*, I am unchanging and eternal. None will subsist *after* me; since *with* the last of all created objects I shall be the same that I was in the beginning. Nothing would survive God; or in other words, he would exist for ever and ever. The argument here is, that to this unchanging and eternal God, who had thus raised up and directed Cyrus, and who had control over *all* nations, they might commit themselves with unwavering confidence, and be assured that he was able to protect and deliver them.

5. *The isles saw* it. The distant nations (see Note on ver. 1). They saw what was done in the conquests of the man whom God in this remarkable manner had raised up; and they had had demonstration, therefore, of the mighty power of JEHOVAH above the power of idols. ¶ *And feared.* Were alarmed, and trembled. All were apprehensive that *they* would be subdued, and driven away as with the tempest. ¶ *The ends of the earth.* Distant nations occupying the extremities of the globe (see Note on ch. xl. 28). ¶ *Drew near, and came.* Came together for the purpose of mutual alliance, and self-defence. The prophet evidently

6 They helped every one his neighbour; and *every one* said to his brother, Be [1] of good courage.
7 So [a] the carpenter encouraged the [2] goldsmith, *and* he that smootheth *with* the hammer [3] him that smote the anvil, [4] saying, It *is* ready for the sodering: and he fastened it with nails, *that* it should not be moved.

1 *strong*. a ch.40.19. 2 or, *the founder*. 3 or, *the smiting*. 4 or, *saying of the soder, It* is *good*.

refers to what he says in the following verses, that they formed treaties; endeavoured to prepare for self-defence; looked to their idol-gods, and encouraged each other in their attempts to offer a successful resistance to the victorious arms of Cyrus.

6. *They helped every one his neighbour.* The idolatrous nations. The idea is, that they formed confederations to strengthen each other, and to oppose him whom God had raised up to subdue them. The prophet describes a state of general consternation existing among them, when they supposed that all was in danger, and that their security consisted only in confederation; in increased attention to their religion; in repairing their idols and making new ones, and in conciliating the favour and securing the aid of their gods. It was natural for them to suppose that the calamities which were coming upon them by the invasion of Cyrus were the judgments of their gods, for some neglect, or some prevailing crimes, and that their favour could be secured only by a more diligent attention to their service, and by forming new images and establishing them in the proper places of worship. The prophet, therefore, describes in a graphic manner, the consternation, the alarm, and the haste, everywhere apparent among them, in attempting to conciliate the favour of their idols, and to encourage each other. Nothing is more common, than for men, when they are in danger, to give great attention to religion, though they may greatly neglect or despise it when they are in safety. Men fly *to* temples and churches and altars in the times of plague and the pestilence; and as regularly flee *from* them when the calamity is overpast. ¶ *Be of good courage.* Marg. as Heb. 'Be strong.' The sense is, Do not be alarmed at the invasion of Cyrus. Make new images, set them up in the temples, show unusual zeal in religion, and the favour of the gods may be secured, and the dangers be averted. This is to be understood as the language of the idolatrous nations, among whom Cyrus, under the direction of JEHOVAH, was carrying his conquests and spreading desolation.

7. *So the carpenter* (see Note on ch. xl. 19). ¶ *Encouraged the goldsmith.* Marg. 'The founder' (see Note on ch. xl. 19). The word properly means *one who melts or smelts metals of any kind;* and may be applied either to one who works in gold, silver, or brass. The image here is that of haste, anxiety, solicitude. One workman in the manufacture of idols encouraged another, in order that the idols might be finished as soon as possible, and that thus the favour of the gods might be propitiated, and the impending danger averted. ¶ *He that smootheth* with *the hammer.* That is, he encourages or strengthens him that smites on the anvil. The idol was commonly *cast* or founded, and of course was in a rough state. This required to be *smoothed*, or polished, and this was in part done doubtless by a small hammer. ¶ *Him that smote the anvil.* The workman whose office it was to work on the anvil—forming parts of the idol, or perhaps chain. ¶ *It is ready for the sodering.* The parts are ready to be welded, or soldered together. All this is descriptive of haste and anxiety to have the work done; and the object of the prophet is evidently to ridicule their vain solicitude to defend themselves against the plans and purposes of God by efforts of this kind. ¶ *And he fastened it with nails.* He fixed it to its place in the temple, or in the dwelling; and thus showed a purpose that the worship of the idol should be permanent, and fixed. Hooks, or nails, were necessary to keep it in its place, and secure it from falling down. When the idol was thus fixed, they supposed that their kingdoms were safe. They judged that the gods would interpose to protect and defend them from

8 But thou, Israel, *art* my servant, Jacob whom I have [a] chosen, the seed of Abraham my [b] friend.
9 *Thou* whom I have taken from the ends of the earth, and called thee from the chief men thereof, and said unto thee, Thou *art* my servant, I have chosen thee, and not cast thee away.

a Ps.135.4. b 2 Ch.20.7; Ja.2.23.

their foes.—This is a beautiful description of the anxiety, and pains, and consternation of sinners when calamity is coming upon them, and of the nature of their reliances. What could these dumb idols—these masses of brass, or silver, or stone, do to protect them? And in like manner what can all the refuges of sinners do when God comes to judge them, and when the calamities connected with death and the judgment shall overtake them? They are just as full of consternation as were the heathen who are here described; and all their refuges will be just as little to be relied on as were the senseless images which the heathen had made for their defence.

8. *But thou, Israel,* art *my servant.* This is an address directly to the Jews, and is designed to shew them, in view of the truths which had just been urged, that God was their protector and friend. Those who relied on idols were trusting to that which could not aid them. But those who trusted in him were safe. For their protection he had raised up Cyrus, for this purpose he had subdued the nations before him. God now expresses to them the assurance that though the nations should be destroyed, yet that he had chosen *them,* and would remember them, and his promise made to Abraham, their illustrious ancestor. The word 'servant' here is used in a mild and gentle sense, not to denote bondage or slavery, but to denote that they had been engaged in his *service,* and that he regarded them as subject to his laws, and as under his protection. ¶ *Jacob whom I have chosen.* The descendants of Jacob, whom I have selected to be my people. *Abraham my friend.* Heb. 'Loving me,' my lover. Abraham was regarded as the friend of God (see 2 Chron. xx. 7). 'And he was called the Friend of God' (James ii. 23). This most honourable appellation he deserved by a life of devoted piety, and by habitually submitting himself to the will of God. The idea in this verse is, that as they were the descendants of *his friend,* God deemed himself bound to protect and deliver them according to his gracious promises; and this is one of the many instances where the Divine favour is manifested to descendants in consequence of the piety and prayers of their ancestors.

9. Thou *whom I have taken from the ends of the earth.* From Chaldea—regarded by the Jews as the remote part of the earth. Thus in ch. xiii. 5, it is said of the Medes that they came 'from a far country, from the end of heaven' (see Note on that place). Abraham was called from Ur of the Chaldees—a city still remaining on the east of the river Euphrates. It is probably the same place as the Persian fortress *Ur,* between Nesibis and the Tigris. It was visited by Mr. Wolfe, Mr. Buckingham, and by others. ¶ *And called thee from the chief men thereof.* Or rather, from the *extremities* of the earth. The word אֲצִיל means properly *a side;* and when applied to the earth, means the sides ends, or extremities of it. In Ex. xxiv. 11, it is rendered 'nobles,' from an Arabic word signifying to be deep-rooted, and hence those who are sprung from an ancient stock (Gesenius). In this place it is evidently used in the same sense as the word (אֵצֶל) meaning *side,* in the sense of *extremity,* or *end.* The parallelism requires us to give this interpretation to the word. So Jerome renders it, *à longinquis ejus* (sc. *terræ*). The LXX. render it, Ἐκ τῶν σκοπιῶν—'From the speculations of the earth' (Thompson), or rather perhaps meaning from the extremity of *vision;* from the countries lying in the distant horizon; or from the elevated places which offered an extensive range of vision. The Chaldee renders it, 'From the kingdoms I have selected thee.' Symmachus renders it, Ἀπὸ τῶν ἀγκώνων αὐτῆς—from its angles, its corners, its extremities. Some have supposed that this refers to the deliverance from Egypt,

10 Fear [a] thou not; for I *am* with
thee;[b] be not dismayed, for I *am*
thy God: I will [c] strengthen thee;
yea, I will help thee: yea, I will
uphold thee with the right hand of
my righteousness.
11 Behold, all they that were
incensed against thee shall be
ashamed[d] and confounded: they
shall be as nothing; and they [1] that
strive with thee shall perish.
12 Thou shalt seek them, and
shalt not find them, *even* [2] them that
contended with thee: [3] they that
war against thee shall be as nothing,
and as a thing of nought.
13 For I the LORD thy God will
hold thy [e] right hand, saying unto
thee, Fear not; I will help thee.
14 Fear not, thou worm Jacob,
and ye [4] men of Israel; I will help
thee, saith the LORD, and thy Redeemer,
the Holy One of Israel.

a ver. 13,14; ch.43.5. b De.31.6,8. c ch.40.29. d ch.45.24; Zc.12.3. 1 *the men of thy strife.* 2 *the men of thy contention.* 3 *the men of thy war.* e De.33.26,29. 4 or, *few men.*

but the more probable interpretation is that which refers it to the call of Abraham from Chaldea; and the idea is, that as God had called him from that distant land, and had made him his friend, he would preserve and guard his posterity. *Perhaps* it may be implied that he would be favourable to them in that same country from whence he had called their illustrious progenitor, and would in like manner conduct them to the land of promise, *i.e.*, to their own land.

10. *Fear thou not.* This verse is plain in its meaning, and is full of consolation. It is to be regarded as addressed primarily to the exiled Jews during their long and painful captivity in Babylon; and the idea is, that they who had been selected by God to be his peculiar people had nothing to fear. But the promise is one that may be regarded as addressed to all his people in similar circumstances, and it is as true now as it was then, that those whom God has chosen have nothing to fear. ¶ *For I* am *with thee.* This is a reason why they should not be afraid. God was their protector, and of whom should they be afraid. 'If God be for us, who can be against us?' What higher consolation can man desire than the assurance that he is with him to protect him? ¶ *Be not dismayed.* The word here rendered 'dismayed' (תִּשְׁתָּע) is derived from שָׁעָה, *to see, to look;* and then to look about as one does in a state of alarm, or danger. The sense here is, that they should be calm, and under no apprehension from their foes. ¶ *For I* am *thy God.* I am able to preserve and strengthen thee. The God of heaven was their God; and as he had all power, and that power was pledged for their protection, they had nothing to fear. ¶ *I will uphold thee.* I will enable you to bear all your trials. ¶ *With the right hand of my righteousness.* With my faithful right hand. The phrase is a Hebrew mode of expression, meaning that God's hand was faithful, that it might be relied on, and would secure them.

11. *All they that were incensed against thee.* They who were enraged against thee, *i.e.*, the Chaldeans who made war upon you, and reduced you to bondage. ¶ *Shall be ashamed and confounded.* To be ashamed and confounded is often used as synonymous with being overcome and destroyed. ¶ *They that strive with thee.* Marg. as Heb. 'The men of thy strife.' The expression refers to their enemies, the Babylonians.

12. *Thou shalt seek them.* This denotes that it would be impossible to find them, for they should cease to exist. The whole verse, with the verse following, is emphatic, repeating in varied terms what was said before, and meaning that their foes should be entirely destroyed.

14. *Fear not* (see Note on ver. 10). ¶ *Thou worm.* This word is properly applied as it is with us, to denote a worm, such as is generated in putrid substances (Ex. xvi. 20; Isa. xiv. 11; lxvi. 24); or such as destroy plants (Jonah iv. 7; Deut. xxviii. 39). It is used also to describe a person that is poor, afflicted, and an object of insignificance (Job xxv. 5, 6)—

Behold even to the moon, and it shineth not;
Yea, the stars are not pure in his sight.

15 Behold, I will make thee a new sharp threshing instrument having [1]teeth: thou shalt thresh the [a]mountains, and beat *them* small, and shalt make the hills as chaff.

1 *mouths.*

a Mi.4.13.

How much less man, that is a worm;
And the son of man which is a worm?

And in Ps. xxii. 6—

But I am a worm, and no man;
A reproach of men, and despised of the people.

In the passage before us, it is applied to the Jews in Babylon as poor and afflicted, and as objects of contempt in view of their enemies. It implies that in themselves they were unable to defend or deliver themselves, and in this state of helplessness, God offers to aid them, and assures them that they have nothing to fear. ¶ And *ye men of Israel* (מְתֵי יִשְׂרָאֵל *mĕthē Isrâēl.*) Marg. 'Few men.' There has been a great variety in the explanation of this phrase. Aquila renders it, Τεθνεῶτες, and Theodotion, Νεκροὶ, 'dead.' So the Vulgate, *Qui mortui estis ex Israel.* The LXX. render it, 'Fear not, Jacob, O diminutive Israel' (ὀλιγοστὸς Ἰσραὴλ). Chaldee, 'Fear not, O tribe of the house of Jacob, ye seed of Israel.' Lowth renders it, 'Ye mortals of Israel.' The Hebrew denotes properly, as in our translation, 'men of Israel;' but there is evidently included the idea of fewness or feebleness. The parallelism requires us so to understand it; and the word men, or *mortal* men, may well express the idea of feebleness. ¶ *And thy Redeemer.* On the meaning of this word, see Notes on ch. xxxv. 9; xliii. 1, 3. It is applied here to the rescue from the captivity of Babylon, and is used in the general sense of deliverer. God would deliver, or rescue them as he had done in times past. He had done it so often, that this might be regarded as his *appropriate appellation*, that he was THE REDEEMER of his people. ¶ *The Holy One of Israel.* The Holy Being whom the Israelites adored, and who was *their* protector, and their friend (see Note on ch. ii. 4). This appellation is often given to God (see ch. v. 19, 24; x. 20; xii. 6; xvii. 7; xxix. 19; xxx. 11, 12). We may remark in view of these verses—1. That the people of God are in themselves feeble and defenceless. They have no strength on which they can rely. They are often so encompassed with difficulties which they feel they have no strength to overcome, that they are disposed to apply to themselves the appellation of 'worm,' and by others they are looked on as objects of contempt, and are despised. 2. They have nothing to fear. Though they are feeble, their God and Redeemer is strong. He is *their* Redeemer, and *their* friend, and they may put their trust in him. Their enemies cannot ultimately triumph over them, but they will be scattered and become as nothing. 3. In times of trial, want, and persecution, the friends of God should put their trust alone in him. It is often the plan of God so to afflict and humble his people, that they shall feel their utter helplessness and dependence, and be led to him as the only source of strength.

15. *Behold, I will make thee,* &c. The object of the illustration in this verse and the following is, to show that God would clothe them with power, and that all difficulties in their way would vanish. To express this idea, the prophet uses an image derived from the mode of threshing in the East, where the heavy wain or sledge was made to pass over a large pile of sheaves, and to bruise out the grain, and separate the chaff, so that the wind would drive it away. The phrase, 'I will make thee,' means, 'I will constitute, or appoint thee,' *i.e.*, thou shalt be such a threshing instrument. It is not that God would make such a sledge or wain *for* them, but that they should *be* such themselves; they should beat down and remove the obstacles in the way as the threshing wain crushed the pile of grain. ¶ *A new sharp threshing instrument.* A threshing wain, or a corn-drag. For a description of this, comp. Notes on ch. xxviii. 27, 28. ¶ *Having teeth.* Or, with double edges. The Hebrew word is applied to a sword, and means a two-edged sword (Ps. cxlix. 6). The instrument here referred to was serrated, or so made as to cut up the straw and separate the grain from the chaff. The

following descriptions from Lowth and Niebuhr, may serve still further to illustrate the nature of the instrument here referred to. 'The drag consisted of a sort of frame of strong planks made rough at the bottom with hard stones or iron; it was drawn by horses or oxen over the corn-sheaves spread on the floor, the driver sitting upon it. The wain was much like the drag, but had wheels of iron teeth, or edges like a saw. The axle was armed with iron teeth or serrated wheels throughout: it moved upon three rollers armed with iron teeth or wheels, to cut the straw. In Syria, they make use of the drag, constructed in the very same manner as above described. This not only forced out the

THRESHING WITH THE DRAG.—From Description de l' Egypte.

grain, but cut the straw in pieces, for fodder for the cattle, for in the eastern countries they have no hay. The last method is well known from the law of Moses, which forbids the ox to be muzzled, when he treadeth out the corn (Deut. xxv. 4).'—(Lowth.) 'In threshing their corn, the Arabians lay the sheaves down in a certain order, and then lead over them two oxen, dragging a large stone. This mode of separating the ears from the straw is not unlike that of Egypt. They use oxen, as the ancients did, to beat out their corn, by trampling upon the sheaves, and dragging after them a clumsy machine. This machine is not, as in Arabia, a stone cylinder, nor a plank with sharp stones, as in Syria, but a sort of sledge, consisting of three rollers, fitted with irons, which turn upon axles. A farmer chooses out a level spot in his fields, and has his corn carried thither in sheaves, upon asses or dromedaries. Two oxen are then yoked in a sledge, a driver gets upon it, and drives them backwards and forwards upon the sheaves, and fresh oxen succeed in the yoke from time to time. By this operation, the chaff is very much cut down; the whole is then winnowed, and the pure grain thus separated. This mode of threshing out the corn is tedious and inconvenient; it destroys the chaff, and injures the quality of grain.'—(Niebuhr.) In another place Niebuhr tells us that two parcels or layers of corn are threshed out in a day; and they move each of them as many as eight times, with a wooden fork of five prongs, which they call *meddre*. Afterwards, they throw the straw into the middle of the ring, where it forms a heap, which grows bigger and bigger; when the first layer is threshed, they replace the straw in the ring, and thresh it as before. Thus, the straw becomes every time smaller, till at last it resembles chopped straw. After this, with the fork just described, they cast the whole some yards from thence, and against the wind, which, driving back the straw, the corn and the ears not threshed out fall apart from it and make another heap. A man collects the clods of dirt, and

16 Thou shalt fan [a] them, and the wind shall carry them away, and the whirlwind shall scatter them: and thou shalt rejoice in [b] the LORD, *and* shalt glory [c] in the Holy One of Israel.

17 *When* the poor and needy seek water, and *there is* none, *and* their tongue faileth for thirst, I the LORD will hear them, *I* the God of Israel will not forsake them.

18 I will open rivers [d] in high

[a] Mat.3.12. [b] Ro.5.11. [c] ch.45.25. [d] Ps.105.41.

other impurities, to which any corn adheres, and throws them into a sieve. They afterwards place in a ring the heaps, in which a good many entire ears are still found, and drive over them, for four or five hours together, a dozen couples of oxen, joined two and two, till, by absolute trampling, they have separated the grains, which they throw into the air with a shovel to cleanse them. ¶ *Thou shalt thresh the mountains.* The words 'mountains' and 'hills' in this verse seem designed to denote the kingdoms greater and smaller that should be opposed to the Jews, and that should become subject to them (Rosenmüller). Grotius supposes that the prophet refers particularly to the Medes and Babylonians. But perhaps the words are used to denote simply difficulties or obstacles in their way, and the expression may mean that they would be able to overcome all those obstacles, and to subdue all that opposed them, *as if* in a march they should crush all the mountains, and dissipate all the hills by an exertion of power.

16. *Thou shalt fan them.* Keeping up the figure commenced in the previous verse. To fan here means to winnow, an operation which was performed by throwing the threshed grain up with a shovel into the air, so that the wind drove the chaff away. So all their enemies, and all the obstacles which were in their way should be scattered. ¶ *And the whirlwind shall scatter them.* The ancients believed that men might be swept away by a storm or whirlwind. See Job xxvii.—

The east wind carrieth him away and he departeth;
And as a storm hurleth him out of his place.

Comp. Homer, *Odys.* xx. 63, *sq.*, thus rendered by Pope:

Snatch me, ye whirlwinds! far from human race,
Tost through the void illimitable space;
Or if dismounted from the rapid cloud,
Me with his whelming wave let ocean shroud!

See Notes on Job xxx. 22. ¶ *And thou shalt rejoice in the* LORD. In view of the aid which he has vouchsafed, and the deliverance which he has wrought for you. ¶ *Shalt glory.* Shalt boast, or shalt exult. You will regard God as the author of your deliverance, and joy in the proofs of his interposition, and of his gracious protection and care.

17. When *the poor and needy seek water.* Water is often used in the Scriptures as an emblem of the provisions of Divine mercy. Bursting fountains in a desert, and flowing streams unexpectedly met with in a dry and thirsty land, are often also employed to denote the comfort and refreshment which the gospel furnishes to sinful and suffering man in his journey through this world. The 'poor and needy' here, doubtless refer primarily to the afflicted captives in Babylon. But the expression of the prophet is general, and the description is as applicable to his people at all times in similar circumstances as it was to them. The image here is derived from their anticipated return from Babylon to Judea. The journey lay through a vast pathless desert (see Notes on ch. xl. 3). In that journey when they were weary, faint and thirsty, God would meet and refresh them as if he should open fountains in their way, and plant trees with far-reaching boughs and thick foliage along the road to produce a grateful shade, and make the whole journey through a pleasant grove. As he met their fathers in their journey from Egypt to the land of Canaan, and had brought water from the flinty rock in the desert (Ex. xv. 22, *sq.*), so in their journey through the sands of Arabia Deserta, he would again meet them, and provide for all their want.

18. *I will open rivers.* That is, I will cause rivers to flow (see Note on ch. xxxv. 7). The allusion here is doubtless to the miraculous supply of water in the

places, and fountains in the midst
of the valleys: I will make the wilderness [a] a pool of water, and the
dry land springs of water.
19 I [b] will plant in the wilderness
the cedar, the shittah-tree, and the
myrtle, and the oil-tree; I will set
in the desert the fir-tree, *and* the
pine, and the box-tree together;

a Ps.107.35. b ch.55.13.

desert when the Israelites had come out of Egypt. God then supplied their wants; and in a similar manner he would always meet his people, and would supply their wants *as if* rivers of pure water were made to flow from dry and barren hills. ¶ *In high places.* The word here used denotes properly barrenness or nakedness (Job xxxiii. 21); and then a hill that is bare, or destitute of trees. It is applied usually to hills in a desert (Jer. iii. 2, 21; iv. 71; vii. 29; xiv. 6). Such hills, without trees, and in a dry and lonely desert, were of course usually without water. The idea is, that God would refresh them *as if* rivers were made to flow from such hills; and it may not improperly be regarded as a promise that God would meet and bless his people in situations, and from sources where they least expected refreshment and comfort. ¶ *And fountains in the midst of the valleys* (see Note on ch. xxx. 25; xxxv. 6). ¶ *I will make the wilderness* (see Note on ch. xxxv. 7).

19. *I will plant in the wilderness.* The image in this verse is one that is frequent in Isaiah. It is designed to show that God would furnish for his people abundant consolations, and that he would furnish unanticipated sources of comfort, and would remove from them their anticipated trials and calamities. The image refers to the return of the exiles to their own land. That journey lay through Arabia Deserta—a vast desert—where they would naturally expect to meet with nothing but barren hills, naked rocks, parched plains, and burning sands. God says that he would bless them in the same manner *as if* in that desolate wilderness he should plant the cedar, the acacia, the myrtle, and the fir-tree, and should make the whole distance a grove, where fountains would bubble along their way, and streams burst forth from the hills (comp. Notes on ch. xxxii. 15). ¶ *The cedar.* The large and beautiful cedar, with lofty height, and extended branches, such as grew on Lebanon (comp. Note on ch. ix. 10; xxxvii. 24). ¶ *The shittah-tree.* This is the Hebrew name without change, שִׁטָּה (*shittâh*). The Vulgate is *spinam.* The LXX. render it, Πύξον—'The box.' Lowth renders it, 'The acacia.' Probably the *acacia*, or the *spina Ægyptiaca*—the Egyptian thorn of the ancients—is intended by it. It is a large tree, growing abundantly in Egypt and Arabia, and is the tree from which the gum-arabic is obtained. It is covered

ACACIA TREE (*Acacia vera*).

with large black thorns, and the wood is hard, and, when old, resembles ebony.

MYRTLE (*Myrtus communis*).

¶ *And the myrtle.* The myrtle is a tree which rises with a shrubby upright stem,

20 That they may see and know,
and consider, and understand together, that the hand of the LORD
hath done this, and the Holy One
of Israel hath created it.
21 Produce [1]your cause, saith

1 *cause to come near.*

eight or ten feet high. Its branches form a dense, full head, closely garnished with oval lanceolate leaves. It has numerous small pale flowers from the axillas, singly on each footstalk (*Encyc.*) There are several species of the myrtle, and they are especially distinguished for their forming a dense and close top, and thus constituting a valuable tree for shade. It is a tree that grows with great rapidity. ¶ *And the oil-tree.* Heb. 'Tree of oil;' *i.e.*, producing oil. Doubtless the *olive* is intended here, from whose fruit *oil* was obtained in abundance. This was a common tree in Palestine, and was one

OLIVE (*Olea Europea*).

of the most valued that grew. ¶ *The fir-tree.* The word here used (בְּרוֹשׁ *berōsh*) is commonly rendered, in our version, 'fir-tree' (Isa. lx. 13; lv. 13; Zech. xi. 2; Hos. xiv. 8, 9; 2 Sam. vi. 5; 1 Kings v. 8, 10; vi. 15, 34; Nah. ii. 3, and in other places). Our translators understood it evidently as referring to the cedar. It is often joined, however, with the cedar (see Note on Isa. xiv. 8; comp. ch. xxxvii. 54; Zech. xi. 1, 2), and evidently denotes another tree, probably of the same class. It is probable that the word usually denotes the *cypress.* There are various kinds of cypress. Some are evergreen, and some are deciduous, as the American white cedar. The wood of these trees is remarkable for its durability. Among the ancients, coffins were made of it, and the tree itself was an emblem of mourning. It is here mentioned because its extended branches and dense foliage would produce a grateful shade. ¶ And *the pine.* The LXX. render this, Λεύκην—'The white poplar.' The Vulgate renders it, 'The elm.' Gesenius supposes that a species of hard oak, *holm* or *ilex*, is intended. It is not easy, however, to determine what species of tree is meant. ¶ *The box-tree.* Gesenius supposes that by this word is denoted some tall tree—a species of cedar growing on mount Lebanon that was distinguished by the smallness of its cones, and the upward direction of its branches. With us the word *box* denotes a shrub used for bordering flower-beds. But the word here denotes *a tree*—such as was sufficient to constitute a shade.

20. *That they.* The Jews, the people who shall be rescued from their long captivity, and restored again to their own land. So rich and unexpected would be the blessings—as if in a pathless desert the most beautiful and refreshing trees and fountains should suddenly spring up—that they would have the fullest demonstration that they came from God. ¶ *Hath created it.* That is, all this is to be traced to him. In the apocryphal book of Baruch there is an expression respecting the return from Babylon remarkably similar to that which is used here by Isaiah: 'Even the woods and every sweet-smelling tree shall overshadow Israel by the commandment of God' (ch. v. 8).

21. *Produce your cause.* This address is made to the same persons who are referred to in ver. 1—the worshippers of idols; and the prophet here returns to the subject with reference to a further argument on the comparative power of JEHOVAH and idols. In the former part of the chapter, God had urged his claims to confidence from the fact that he had raised up Cyrus; that the idols were weak and feeble

the LORD: bring forth your strong *reasons,* saith the King of Jacob.

22 Let them [a]bring *them* forth, and show us what shall happen: let them show the former things what they *be,* that we may [1]consider them, and know the latter end of them; or declare us things for to come.

23 Show the things that are to come hereafter, that we may know

a Jn.13.19. 1 set our heart upon.

compared with him; and from the fact that it was his fixed purpose to defend his people, and to meet and refresh them when faint and weary. In the verses which follow the 21st, he urges his claims to confidence from the fact that he alone was able *to predict future events,* and calls on the worshippers of idols to show their claims in the same manner. This is the 'cause' which is now to be tried. ¶ *Bring forth your strong* reasons. Adduce the arguments which you deem to be of the greatest strength and power (comp. Notes on ver. 1). The object is, to call on them to bring forward the most convincing demonstration on which they relied, of their power and their ability to save. The argument to which God appeals is, that he had foretold future events. He calls on them to show that they had given, or could give, equal demonstration of their divinity. Lowth regards this as a call on the idol-gods to come forth in person and show their strength. But the interpretation which supposes that it refers to their reasons, or arguments, accords better with the parallelism, and with the connection.

22. *Let them bring* them *forth.* Let the idols, or the worshippers of idols, bring forth the evidences of their divine nature and power. Or more probably it means, 'let them draw near or approach.' ¶ *And show us what shall happen.* None but the true God can discern the future, and predict what is to occur. To be able to do this, is therefore a proof of divinity to which God often appeals as a demonstration of his own Divine character (see ch. xliv. 7, 8; xlv. 3–7; xlvi. 9, 10). This idea, that none but the true God can know all things, and can with certainty foretell future events, is one that was admitted even by the heathen (see Xen. *Cyr.* i.—'The immortal gods know all things, both the past, the present, and those things which shall proceed from each thing. It was on this belief also that the worshippers of idols endeavoured to sustain the credit of their idol-gods; and accordingly, nearly all the reputation which the oracle at Delphi, and other shrines, obtained, arose from the remarkable sagacity which was evinced in predicting future events, or the skilful ambiguity in which they so couched their responses as to be able to preserve their influence whatever might be the result. ¶ *Let them show the former things what they* be. The idea in this passage seems to be, 'Let them foretell the *entire series* of events; let them predict in their order, the things which shall *first* occur, as well as those which shall finally happen. Let them not select merely an isolated and unconnected event in futurity, but let them declare those which shall have a mutual relation and dependency, and whose causes are now hid.' The argument in the passage is, that it required a far more profound knowledge to predict the *series* of events as they should actually occur; to foretell their *order* of occurrence, than it did to foretell one single isolated occurrence. The latter, the false prophets of the heathen often undertook to do; and undoubtedly they often evinced great sagacity in it. But they never undertook to detail minutely a *series* of occurrences, and to state the *order* in which they would happen. In the Scriptures, it is the common way to foretell the *order* of events, or a *series* of transactions pertaining often to many individuals or nations, and stretching far into futurity. And it is perfectly manifest that none could do this but God (comp. ch. xlvi. 10). ¶ *Or declare us things for to come.* Declare *any* event that is to occur; anything in the future. If they cannot predict the *order* of things, or a *series* of events, let them clearly foretell *any* single event in futurity.

23. *That we may know that ye* are

that ye *are* gods: yea, do good, or
do evil, that we may be dismayed,
and behold *it* together.
24 Behold, ye *are* [1] of nothing,
and your work [2] of nought: an abomination *is he that* chooseth you.
25 I [a] have raised up *one* from the
north, and he shall come: from the
rising of the sun shall he call upon
my name; and he shall come upon
princes as *upon* mortar, and as the
potter treadeth clay.

1 or, worse *than nothing*. 2 or, worse *than of a viper*. a ver. 2.

---

gods. The prediction of future events is the highest evidence of omniscience, and of course of divinity. In this passage it is *admitted* that if they could do it, it would prove that they were worthy of adoration; and it is *demanded*, that *if* they were gods they should be able to make such a prediction as would demonstrate that they were invested with a Divine nature. ¶ *Yea, do good, or do evil. Do something;* show that you have some power; either defend your friends, or prostrate your foes; accomplish *something*—anything, good or bad, that shall prove that you have power. This is said in opposition to the character which is usually given to idols in the Scriptures—that they were dumb, deaf, dead, inactive, powerless (see Ps. cxv.) The command here to 'do evil,' means to punish their enemies, or to inflict vengeance on their foes; and the idea is, that they had no power to do anything; either to do good to their worshippers, or harm to their enemies; and that thus they showed that they were no gods. The same idea is expressed in Jer. x. 3–5: 'They [idols] are upright as the palm-tree, but speak not; they must needs be borne, because they cannot go. Be not afraid of them, for they cannot do evil, neither also is it in them to do good.' ¶ *That we may be dismayed* (see Note on ver. 10). The word 'we' here refers to those who were the friends and worshippers of JEHOVAH. 'That I, JEHOVAH, and my friends and worshippers, may be alarmed, and afraid of what idols may be able to do.' God and his people were regarded as the foes of idols, and God here calls on them to prove that there is any reason why he and his people should be afraid of their power. ¶ *And behold it together.* That we may *all* see it; that I and my people may have full demonstration of your power.

24. *Behold, ye* are *of nothing.* Marg. 'Worse than nothing.' This refers to idols; and the idea is, that they were utterly vain and powerless; they were as unable to render aid to their worshippers as *absolute nothingness* would be, and all their confidence in them was vain and foolish. ¶ *And your work.* All that you do, or all that it is pretended that you do. ¶ *Of nought.* Marg. 'Worse than a viper.' The word used here in the common Hebrew text (אֶפַע) occurs in no other place. Gesenius supposes that this is a corrupt reading for אֶפֶס (*nothing*), and so our translators have regarded it, and in this opinion most expositors agree. Hahn has adopted this reading in his Hebrew Bible. The Jewish Rabbins suppose generally that the word אֶפַע is the same word as אֶפְעֶה, *a viper*, according to the reading in the margin. But this interpretation is contrary to the connection, as well as the ancient versions. The Vulgate and Chaldee render it, 'Of nought.' The Syriac renders it, 'Your works are of the sword.' This is probably one of the few instances in which there has been a corruption of the Hebrew text (comp. ch. xl. 17; xli. 12, 19). ¶ *An abomination* is he that *chooseth you.* They who select idols as the object of worship, and offer to them homage, are regarded as abominable by God.

25. *I have raised up* one. In the previous verses God had shown that the idols had no power of predicting future events. He stakes, so to speak, the question of his divinity on that point, and the whole controversy between him and them is to be decided by the inquiry whether they had the power of foretelling what would come to pass. He here urges *his* claims to divinity on this ground, that he had power to foretell future events. In illustration of this, he appeals to the fact that he had raised up, *i.e.*, *in purpose*, or *would* afterwards raise up Cyrus, in accordance with his

26 Who hath declared from the
beginning, that we may know? and
beforetime, that we may say, *He
is* righteous? yea, *there is* none that
showeth; yea, *there is* none that
declareth; yea, *there is* none that
heareth your words.

---

predictions, and in such a way that it would be distinctly seen that he had this power of foretelling future events. To see the force of this argument, it must be remembered that the Jews are contemplated as in Babylon, and near the close of their captivity; that God by the prophets, and especially by Isaiah, distinctly foretold the fact that he would raise up Cyrus to be their deliverer; that these predictions were uttered at least a hundred and fifty years before the time of their fulfilment; and that they would *then* have abundant evidence that they were accomplished. To these recorded predictions and to their fulfilment, God here appeals, and designs that in that future time when they should be in exile, his people should have evidence that He was worthy of their entire confidence, and that even the heathen should see that JEHOVAH was the true God, and that the idols were nothing. The personage referred to here is undoubtedly Cyrus (see Notes on ver. 2; comp. ch. xlv. 1). ¶ *From the north.* In ver. 2, he is said to have been raised up 'from the east.' Both were true. Cyrus was born in Persia, in the country called in the Scriptures 'the east,' but he early went to Media, and came from Media under the direction of his uncle, Cyaxares, when he attacked and subdued Babylon. Media was situated on the north and north-east of Babylon. ¶ *From the rising of the sun.* The east—the land of the birth of Cyrus. ¶ *Shall he call upon my name.* This expression means, probably, that he should acknowledge JEHOVAH to be the true God, and recognize him as the source of all his success. This he did in his proclamation respecting the restoration of the Jews to their own land: 'Thus saith Cyrus, king of Persia, JEHOVAH, God of heaven, hath given me all the kingdoms of the earth' (Ezra i. 2). There is no decided evidence that Cyrus regarded himself as a worshipper of JEHOVAH, or that he was a pious man, but he was brought to make a public recognition of him as the true God, and to feel that he owed the success of his arms to him. ¶ *And he shall come upon princes.* Upon the kings of the nations against whom he shall make war (see ver. 2, 3). The word here rendered 'princes' (from סֶגֶן or סָגָן), denotes properly *a deputy, a prefect, a governor,* or one under another, and is usually applied to the governors of provinces, or the Babylonian princes, or magistrates (Jer. li. 23, 28, 57; Ezek. xxiii. 6, 12, 33; Dan. iii. 2, 27; vi. 8). It is sometimes applied, however, to the chiefs and rulers in Jerusalem in the times of Ezra and Nehemiah (Ezra ix. 2; Neh. ii. 16; iv. 8, 13; v. 7). Here it is used as a general term; and the sense is, that he would tread down and subdue the kings and princes of the nations that he invaded. ¶ *As upon mortar* (see Note on ch. x. 6).

26. *Who hath declared from the beginning.* The meaning of this passage is, 'there is no one among the soothsayers, and the worshippers of idols, who has predicted the birth, the character, and the conquests of Cyrus. There is among the heathen no recorded prediction on the subject, as there is among the Jews, that when he shall have come, it may be said that a prediction is accomplished.' ¶ *And beforetime.* Formerly; before the event occurred. ¶ *That we may say.* That it may be said; that there may be evidence, or reason for the affirmation. ¶ He is *righteous.* The words 'he is' are not in the Hebrew. The original is simply 'righteous' (צַדִּיק *tzăddīq*), *just, i.e.*, it is just, or true; the prediction is fulfilled. It does not refer to the character of God, but to the certainty of the fulfilment of the prediction. ¶ There is *none that showeth.* There is no one among the worshippers of false gods, the soothsayers and necromancers, that has predicted these events. ¶ *None that heareth your words.* There is no one that has heard such a prediction among you.

27 The first *shall say* to Zion,
Behold, behold them: and I will
give to Jerusalem one [a] that bringeth
good [b] tidings.
28 For I beheld, and *there was*
no man; even among them, and
there was no counsellor, that, when
I asked of them, could [1] answer a
word.
29 Behold, they *are* all vanity;
their works *are* nothing; their
molten images *are* wind and confusion.

[a] ch.40.9. [b] Lu 2.10,11. [1] *return.*

27. *The first* shall say *to Zion.* This translation is unhappy. It does not convey any clear meaning, nor is it possible from the translation to conjecture what the word 'first' refers to. The correct rendering undoubtedly is, '*I* first said to Zion;' and the sense is, 'I, JEHOVAH, first gave to Zion the announcement of these things. I predicted the restoration of the Jews to their own land, and the raising up of the man who should deliver them; and I only have uttered the prophecies respecting the time and circumstances in which these events would occur.' The LXX. render it, 'I will first give notice to Zion, and I will comfort Jerusalem in the way.' The Chaldee renders it, 'The words of consolation which the prophets have uttered respecting Zion in the beginning, lo, they are about to come to pass.' The sense of the passage is, that no one of the idol-gods, or their prophets, had predicted these events. The first intimation of them had been by JEHOVAH, and this had been made to Zion, and designed for its consolation. ¶ *Behold, behold them.* Lo, these events are about to come to pass. Zion, or Jerusalem, was to behold them, for they were intended to effect its deliverance, and secure its welfare. The words 'Zion' and 'Jerusalem' here seem intended to denote the Jewish people in general, or to refer to Jerusalem as the capital of the Jewish nation. The intimation had been given in the capital of the nation, and thence to the entire people. ¶ *And I will give.* Or rather, I give, or I have given. The passage means, that the bearer of the good tidings of the raising up of a deliverer should be sent to the Jewish people. To them the joyful news was announced long before the event; the news of the raising up of such a man—an event of so much interest to them—was made to them long before the heathen had any intimation of it; and it would occur as the fulfilment of an ancient prophecy recorded among the Jews. The prophet refers here, doubtless, in the main, to his own prophecies uttered so long before the event would occur, and which would be distinctly known when they would be in exile in Babylon.

28. *For I beheld.* I looked upon the heathen world, among all the pretended prophets, and the priests of pagan idolatry. ¶ *And* there was *no man.* No man among them who could predict these future events. ¶ *No counsellor.* No one qualified to give counsel, or that could anticipate by his sagacity what would take place. ¶ *That, when I asked of them.* In the manner referred to in this chapter. There is no one of whom it could be inquired what would take place in future times. ¶ *Could answer a word.* They were unable to discern what would come to pass, or to predict the events which are referred to here.

29. *Behold, they* are *all vanity.* They are unable to predict future events; they are unable to defend their friends, or to injure their enemies. This is the conclusion of the trial or debate (Notes, ver. 1), and that conclusion is, that they were utterly destitute of strength, and that they were entirely unworthy of confidence and regard. ¶ *Their molten images* (see Note on ch. xl. 19). ¶ Are *wind.* Have no solidity or power. The doctrine of the whole chapter is, that confidence should be reposed in God, and in him alone. He is the friend of his people, and he is able to protect them. He will deliver them from the hand of all their enemies; and he will be always their God, protector, and guide. The idols of the heathen have no power; and it is folly, as well as sin, to trust in them, or to suppose that they can aid their friends.

CHAPTER XLII.

ANALYSIS.

THIS chapter is a continuation of the same general subject which was presented in the two previous chapters. It is to be regarded (see the analysis of ch. xl.) as addressed to the exile Jews in Babylon, and near the close of their captivity, and the general object is to induce them to repose confidence in God, and to assure them of deliverance. The primary purpose of these chapters, therefore, is, to direct the attention to him who was to be raised up from the east, to rescue them from their bondage, that is, Cyrus. But in doing this, the mind of the prophet, by the laws of prophetic suggestion (see Introd. to Isaiah, § 7, III. 3), is also led to a far greater deliverer, and so entirely, and intently at times, as to lose sight altogether of Cyrus; and the restoration of the Jews to their own land is forgotten in the sublimer contemplation of the redemption of the world. In the previous chapters, the attention of the prophet had been particularly directed to Cyrus, with an occasional reference to the Messiah. In the commencement of this chapter, he seems to have lost sight of Cyrus altogether, and to have fixed the attention wholly on the future Messiah (see Notes on ver. 1). The chapter is, as I apprehend, occupied mainly, or entirely, with a description of the character and work of the Messiah. The evidence of this will be adduced in the Notes on the chapter itself. The *design* for which the Messiah is introduced is to convince the Jews that God was their protector, and that it was his purpose that the long-promised Prince and Saviour should yet arise from their restored and recovered nation. Of course, if this *was* to occur, their national existence would be preserved. There is, therefore, in the chapter, a reference to their return to their own land, though the main scope relates to the Messiah.

The chapter may be regarded as divided into two portions. In the *first* (ver. 1–9), the prophet describes the Messiah. JEHOVAH is introduced as speaking, and in ver. 1–4 he describes his character. He is the servant of JEHOVAH, endowed with the fulness of the Divine Spirit; meek, and lowly, and gentle, and kind; unobtrusive and noiseless in his movements, and yet securing the conquest of truth. JEHOVAH then (5–7), addresses the Messiah himself directly, and states the object for which he had appointed him, to be a light to the Gentiles, to open the eyes of the blind, and to be the pledge of the covenant between him and his people. In ver. 8, 9, JEHOVAH turns to the people for whom the prophecy was given, and awakens their attention to the subject, reminds them of the predictions which had been made, and says that the fulfilment of this prophecy, like all former predictions, would demonstrate his superiority over idols, and show that he was the true God.

The *second* part of the chapter (10–25), consists mainly of a call on the world, and especially on the exile Jews, to rejoice in view of the truth here announced. This general call contains the following portions or parts:—

(1.) In the exordium (10–12) JEHOVAH calls on the inhabitants of all the earth to praise and glorify his name, and makes his appeal to those who are upon the sea, to the inhabitants of the isles, to the wilderness and solitary places, to the villages and the inhabitants of the rock, as all having occasion to rejoice on account of this glorious event.

(2.) In ver. 13–17, JEHOVAH speaks particularly of the deliverance of his people, and of the certainty of its being accomplished. He had long delayed to interpose; but now he would come forth in his strength, and annihilate his foes and redeem his people, and make darkness light before them, while all the worshippers of idols should be left without defence or aid.

(3.) The people of Israel are next addressed directly, and their character and duty presented (18–25). They are addressed as a people blind and deaf, and are admonished to rouse themselves, and to strive to attain to true knowledge. Notwithstanding all that God had done for them, and all his gracious interposition, they had hardened their hearts, and shut their eyes, and had steeled themselves against every good impression. For this God had punished them. He had given them as a spoil to their enemies, and overwhelmed them in grievous and long-continued calamities. They were now called on to attend to his instructions and promises, and henceforward be an obedient people.

It may be added, also, that it is equally vain to trust in *any* being for salvation but God. He only is able to protect and defend us; and it is a source of unspeakable consolation now, as it was in times past, that he is the friend of his people; and that, in times of deepest darkness and distress, he can raise up deliverers, as he did Cyrus, and will in his own way and time rescue his people from all their calamities.

BEHOLD my servant, whom I uphold, mine [a] elect, *in whom* my soul [b] delighteth; I have put my Spirit upon him: he shall bring forth judgment to the Gentiles.

[a] Eph.1.4. [b] Mat.17.5.

CHAPTER XLII.

1. *Behold.* This word is designed to call attention to the person that is immediately referred to. It is an intimation that the subject is of importance, and should command their regard. ¶ *My servant.* This phrase denotes properly any one who acknowledges or worships God; any one who is regarded as serving or obeying him. It is a term which may be applied to any one who is esteemed to be a pious man, or who is obedient to the commands of God, and is often applied to the people of God (Gen. l. 17; 1 Chron. vi. 49; 2 Chron. xxiv. 9; Dan. vi. 20; ix. 2; Titus i. 1; James i. 1; 1 Pet. ii. 16; Rev. vii. 3; xv. 3). The word 'servant' may be applied either to Isaiah, Cyrus, or the Messiah; and the question to whom it refers here is to be decided, not by the mere use of the term, but by the connection, and by the characteristics which are ascribed to him who is here designated as the 'servant' of JEHOVAH. There have been no less than five different views in regard to the personage here referred to; and as in the interpretation of the whole prophecy in this chapter, everything depends on this question, it is of importance briefly to examine the opinions which have been entertained. I. One has been that it refers to the Jewish people. The translators of the Septuagint evidently so regarded it. They render it, Ἰακὼβ ὁ παῖς μου, κ.τ.λ.—'Jacob is my servant, I will uphold him; Israel is my chosen one, my soul hath embraced him.' Jarchi also so interprets the passage, but so modifies it as to understand by it 'the righteous in Israel;' and among the moderns, Rosenmüller, Paulus, and some others adopt this interpretation. The principal reason alleged for this interpretation is, that the phrase 'servant of JEHOVAH,' is elsewhere used in a collective sense, and applied to the Jewish people. Rosenmüller appeals particularly to ch. xli. 8, 9; to ver. 19 of this chapter, and to ch. xliv. 21; xlv. 4; xlviii. 20; and argues that it is to be presumed that the prophet used the phrase in a uniform manner, and must therefore be supposed here also to refer to the Jewish people. But the objections are insuperable. 1. In ver. 6, the servant of JEHOVAH here referred to, is plainly distinguished *from* the people, where God says, 'I will give *thee* for a covenant of [with] the people.' 2. The description which the prophet gives here of the character of the 'servant' of JEHOVAH, as meek, mild, gentle, quiet, and humble (ver. 2, 3), is remarkably *unlike* the character which the prophet elsewhere gives of the people, and is as remarkably *like* the character which is everywhere given of the Messiah. 3. It was not true of the Jewish people that they were appointed, as is here said of the 'servant' of God (ver. 7), to 'open the blind eyes, and to bring the prisoners out of prison.' This is evidently applicable only to a teacher, a deliverer, or a guide; and in no sense *can* it be applied to the collected Jewish people. II. A second opinion has been, that by the 'servant of JEHOVAH' Cyrus was intended. Many of the Jewish interpreters have adopted this view, and not a few of the German critics. The principal argument for this opinion is, that what precedes, and what follows, relates particularly to Cyrus; and an appeal is made particularly to ch. xlv. 1, where he is called the Anointed, and to ch. xliv. 28, where he is called the Shepherd. But to this view also, the objections are obvious. 1. The name 'servant of JEHOVAH,' is, it is believed, nowhere given to Cyrus. 2. The description here by no means agrees with Cyrus. That he was distinguished for justice and equity is admitted (see Note on ch. xli. 2), but the expressions here used, that God would 'put his Spirit upon him, that he should not cry, nor lift up his voice, so that it should be heard in the streets,' is one that is by no means applicable to a man whose life was spent mainly in the tumults of war, and in the pomp and carnage of battle and conquest. How *can* this description be applied to a man

who trod down nations, and subdued kings, and who shed rivers of blood? III. Others suppose that the prophet refers to himself. Among the Jews, Aben Ezra, and among others, *Grotius* and *Döderlin* held this opinion. The only reason for this is, that in ch. xx. 3, the name 'servant' of JEHOVAH is given to Isaiah. But the objections to this are plain, and insuperable. 1. Nothing can be urged, as we have seen, from the mere use of the word 'servant.' 2. It is inconceivable that a humble prophet like Isaiah should have applied to himself a description expressive of so much importance as is here attributed to the servant of God. How could the establishment of a new covenant with the people of God, and the conversion of the heathen nations (ver. 6, 7), be ascribed to Isaiah? And in what sense is it true that *he* was appointed to open the eyes of the blind, and to lead the prisoners from the prison? IV. A fourth opinion, which it may be proper just to notice, is that which is advocated by Gesenius, that the phrase here refers to the prophets taken *collectively*. But this opinion is one that scarce deserves a serious refutation. For, 1. The name 'SERVANT of JEHOVAH,' is never given to any *collection* of the prophets. 2. Any such *collection* of the prophets is a mere creature of the fancy. When did they exist? Who composed the collection? And how could the name 'SERVANT' designate them? 3. Of what *collection* of men could it be imagined that the description here given could be applied, that such a collection should not strive, nor cry; that it should be a covenant of the people, and that it should be the means of the conversion of the Gentile world? V. The fifth opinion, therefore, is, that it refers to the Messiah; and the direct arguments in favour of this, independent of the fact that it is applicable to no other one, are so strong as to put it beyond debate. A few of them may be referred to. 1. This is the interpretation of the Chaldee Paraphrase, which has retained the exposition of the ancient and early Jews. 'Behold my servant, the MESSIAH (עַבְדִּי מְשִׁיחָא) I will cause him to come near; my chosen.' 2. There are such applications of the passage in the New Testament to the Lord Jesus, as to leave no room to doubt that, in view of the sacred writers, the passage had this reference. Thus, in Luke ii. 32, he is spoken of as 'a light to lighten the Gentiles' (comp. ver. 6 of the chapter before us). In Acts xxvi. 18, Paul speaks of him as given to the Gentiles, 'to open their eyes, and to turn them from darkness to light' (comp. ch. xlii. 7). In Matt. iii. 17, God says of the Redeemer, 'This is my beloved Son, in whom I am well pleased,'—language remarkably similar to the passage before us (ver. 1), where he says, 'mine elect, in whom my soul delighteth.' And the whole inquiry is put to rest by the fact that Matthew (xii. 17–21) expressly and directly applies the passage to the Lord Jesus, and says that it was fulfilled in him. 3. It may be added, that the entire description is one that is exactly and entirely applicable to the Lord Jesus. It is *as* applicable as if it had been made *after* he had appeared among men, and as if it were the language of biography, and not of prophecy. It is an exceedingly beautiful and tender description of the Son of God; nor *can* there be any objection to its application to him, except what arises from a general purpose not to apply *any* part of the Old Testament to him, if it can be avoided. I shall regard the passage, therefore, as applicable to him, and him alone; and suppose that the design of the Spirit here in introducing this reference to the Messiah is, to comfort the hearts of the exile Jews with the assurance that they *must* be restored to their own land, *because* it was from them that the Messiah was to proceed, and from them that the true religion was to be spread around the world. ¶ *Whom I uphold.* Whom I sustain, or protect; *i.e.*, who is the object of my affection and care. In Matt. iii. 17, the expression is, 'in whom I am well pleased.' And so in Matt. xii. 18, it is rendered, 'my servant, whom I have chosen.' ¶ *Mine elect.* My chosen one; or the one whom I have *selected* to accomplish my great purposes. It implies that God had designated or appointed him for the purpose. In Matt. xii. 18, it is ren-

2 He shall not cry, nor lift up,
nor cause his voice to be heard in
the street.
3 A bruised reed shall he not
break, and the [1] smoking flax shall
he not [2] quench: he shall bring
forth judgment unto truth.

1 or, *dimly burning.* 2 *quench it.*

dered 'my beloved.' It implies that he was the object of the Divine favour, and that God had chosen or appointed him to perform the work of a Messiah. ¶ In whom *my soul delighteth.* This language is applied to the Lord Jesus in Matt. iii. 17; xii. 18. God regarded him as qualified for his work; he approved of what he did; he was well pleased with all his words, and thoughts, and plans. The word 'soul' here, is equivalent to *I* myself—in whom *I* delight. ¶ *I have put my Spirit upon him* (comp. John iii. 34): 'For God giveth not the Spirit by measure unto him.' The Lord Jesus was Divine, yet as Mediator he is everywhere represented as 'the anointed' of God, or as endowed with the influences of the Holy Spirit (comp. Note on ch. xi. 2). See also ch. lxi. 1, where the Messiah says of himself, 'The Spirit of the LORD God is upon me, because he hath anointed me' (comp. Luke iv. 18). Before he entered upon his public ministry, the Spirit of God descended on him at his baptism (Matt. iii. 17), and in all his work he showed that he was endowed abundantly with that Spirit. ¶ *He shall bring forth judgment.* The word 'judgment' (מִשְׁפָּט) is used in a great variety of significations. It properly means *judgment, i.e.,* the act of judging (Lev. xix. 15); the place of judgment (Eccl. iii. 16); a cause, or suit before a judge (Num. xxviii. 5); a sentence of a judge (1 Kings iii. 28); and thence guilt or crime, for which one is judged (Jer. li. 9). It also means right, rectitude, justice; a law, or statute; a claim, privilege, or due; also manner, custom, or fashion; or an ordinance, or institution. Here it is used, probably, in the sense of the order or institution that would be introduced under the Messiah; and it means that he would set up or establish the true religion among the Gentiles. ¶ *To the Gentiles.* This is one of the many declarations which occur in Isaiah, that the Messiah would extend the true religion to pagan nations, and that they should be brought to participate in its privileges.

2. *He shall not cry.* He will not make a clamour or noise; he will not be boisterous, in the manner of a man of strife and contention. ¶ *Nor lift up.* That is, his voice. ¶ *Nor cause his voice to be heard in the street.* He shall not use loud and angry words, as they do who are engaged in conflict, but all his teaching shall be gentle, humble, and mild. How well this agrees with the character of the Lord Jesus it is not necessary to pause to show. He was uniformly unostentatious, modest, and retiring. He did not even desire that his deeds should be blazoned abroad, but sought to be withdrawn from the world, and to pursue his humble path in perfect peace.

3. *A bruised reed.* The word 'reed' means the cane or calamus which grows up in marshy or wet places (ch. xxxvi. 6; see Note on ch. xliii. 24). The word, therefore, literally denotes *that which is fragile,* weak, easily waved by the wind, or broken down; and stands in contrast with a lofty and firm tree (comp. Matt. xi. 7): 'What went ye out into the wilderness to see? A reed shaken with

REEDS (*Calamus aromaticus*).

4 He shall not fail nor be [1] discouraged, till he have set judgment in the earth: and the isles shall wait for his [a] law.

1 *broken.* a Ge.49.10.

the wind?' The word here, therefore, may be applied to men that are conscious of feebleness and sin; that are moved and broken by calamity; that feel that they have no strength to bear up against the ills of life. The word 'bruised' (רָצוּץ *râtzūtz*) means that which is broken or crushed, but not entirely broken off. As used here, it may denote those who are in themselves naturally feeble, and who have been crushed or broken down by a sense of sin, by calamity, or by affliction. We speak familiarly of *crushing* or breaking down by trials; and the phrase here is intensive and emphatic, denoting those who are *at best* like a reed—feeble and fragile; and who, in addition to that, have been broken and oppressed by a sense of their sins, or by calamity. ¶ *Shall he not break.* Shall he not *break off.* He will not carry on the work of destruction, and entirely crush or break it. And the idea is, that he will not make those already broken down with a sense of sin and with calamity, more wretched. He will not deepen their afflictions, or augment their trials, or multiply their sorrows. The sense is, that he will have an affectionate regard for the broken-hearted, the humble, the penitent, and the afflicted. Luther has well expressed this: 'He does not cast away, nor crush, nor condemn the wounded in conscience, those who are terrified in view of their sins; the weak in faith and practice, but watches over and cherishes them, makes them whole, and affectionately embraces them.' The expression is parallel to that which occurs in ch. lxi. 1, where it is said of the Messiah, 'He hath sent me to bind up the broken-hearted;' and to the declaration in ch. l. 4, where it is said, 'that I should know how to speak a word in season to him that is weary.' ¶ *The smoking flax.* The word here used denotes *flax,* and then a *wick* that is made of it. The word rendered 'smoking' (כֵּהָה) means *that which is weak,* small, thin, feeble; then that which is just ready to go out, or to be extinguished; and the phrase refers literally to the expiring wick of a lamp, when the oil is almost consumed, and when it shines with a feeble and dying lustre. It may denote here the condition of one who is feeble and disheartened, and whose love to God seems almost ready to expire. And the promise that he will not extinguish or quench that, means that he would cherish, feed, and cultivate it; he would supply it with grace, as with oil to cherish the dying flame, and cause it to be enkindled, and to rise with a high and steady brilliancy. The whole passage is descriptive of the Redeemer, who nourishes the most feeble piety in the hearts of his people, and who will not suffer true religion in the soul ever to become wholly extinct. It may seem as if the slightest breath of misfortune or opposition would extinguish it for ever; it may be like the dying flame that hangs on the point of the wick, but if there be true religion it will not be extinguished, but will be enkindled to a pure and glowing flame, and it will yet rise high, and burn brightly. ¶ *He shall bring forth judgment* (see ver. 1). The word 'judgment' here evidently denotes the true religion; the laws, institutions, and appointments of God. ¶ *Unto truth.* Matthew (xii. 20) renders this, 'unto victory.' The meaning in Isaiah is, that he shall establish his religion according to truth; he shall faithfully announce the true precepts of religion, and secure their ascendency among men. It shall overcome all falsehood, and all idolatry, and shall obtain a final triumph in all nations. Thus explained, it is clear that Matthew has retained the general idea of the passage, though he has not quoted it literally.

4. *He shall not fail.* He shall not be weak, feeble, or disheartened. However much there may be that shall tend to discourage, yet his purpose is fixed, and he will pursue it with steadiness and ardour until the great work shall be fully accomplished. There *may* be an allusion in the Hebrew word here (יִכְהֶה *yĭkhhê*) to that which is applied to the flax (כֵּהָה *khēhâ*); and the idea *may be* that he shall not become in *his* purposes like

5 Thus saith God the LORD, he that created the heavens, and stretched them out; he that spread forth the earth, and that which cometh out of it; he that giveth breath unto the people upon it, and spirit to them that walk therein:

---

the smoking, flickering, dying flame of a lamp. There shall never be *any* indication, even amidst all embarrassments, that it is his intention to abandon his plan of extending the true religion through all the world. Such also *should* be the fixed and determined purposes of his people. Their zeal should never fail; their ardour should never grow languid. ¶ *Nor be discouraged.* Marg. 'Broken.' The Hebrew word יָרוּץ (*yârūtz*) may be derived either from רָצַץ (*râtzătz*), *to break*, to break in pieces; or from רוּץ (*rūtz*) *to run*, to move hastily, to rush upon any one. Our translators have adopted the former. Gesenius also supposes that this is the true interpretation of the word, and that it means, that he would not be broken, *i.e.*, checked in his zeal, or discouraged by any opposition. The latter interpretation is preferred by Vitringa, Rosenmüller, Hengstenberg, and others. The Chaldee renders it, 'Shall not labour,' *i.e.*, shall not be fatigued, or discouraged. The LXX. render it, 'He shall shine out, and not be broken.' The connection seems to require the sense which our translators have given to it, and according to this, the meaning is, 'he shall not become broken in spirit, or discouraged; he shall persevere amidst all opposition and embarrassment, until he shall accomplish his purposes.' We have a similar phraseology when we speak of a man's being *heart-broken.* ¶ *Till he have set judgment.* Till he has secured the prevalence of the true religion in all the world. ¶ *And the isles.* Distant nations (see Note on ch. xli. 1); the heathen nations. The expression is equivalent to saying that the Gentiles would be desirous of receiving the religion of the Messiah, and would wait for it (see Notes on ch. ii. 3). ¶ *Shall wait.* They shall be dissatisfied with their own religions, and see that their idol-gods are unable to aid them; and they shall be in a posture of *waiting* for some new religion that shall meet their wants. It cannot mean that they shall wait for it, in the sense of their already having a knowledge of it, but that their being sensible that their own religions cannot save them may be represented as a condition of waiting for some better system. It has been true, as in the Sandwich Islands, that the heathen have been so dissatisfied with their own religion as to cast away their idols, and to be without *any* religion, and thus to be in a waiting posture for some new and better system. And it may be true yet that the heathen shall become extensively dissatisfied with their idolatry; that they shall be convinced that some better system is necessary, and that they may thus be prepared to welcome the gospel when it shall be proposed to them. It may be that in this manner God intends to remove the now apparently insuperable obstacles to the spread of the gospel in the heathen world. The LXX. render this, 'And in his name shall the Gentiles trust,' which form has been retained by Matthew (xii. 21). ¶ *His law.* His commands, the institutions of his religion. The word 'law' is often used in the Scriptures to denote the whole of religion.

5. *Thus saith God the* LORD. This verse commences a new form of discourse. It is still JEHOVAH who speaks; but in the previous verses he had spoken *of* the Messiah in the third person; here he is introduced as speaking *to* him directly. He introduces the discourse by showing that he is the Creator and Lord of all things. The *object* of his dwelling on this seems to have been, to show that he had *power* to sustain the Messiah in the work to which he had called him; and to secure for him respect as having been commissioned by him who had formed the heavens and the earth, and who ruled over all. He shows that he had power to accomplish all that he had promised: and he seeks thus to elevate and confirm the hopes of the people with the assurance of their deliverance and salvation. ¶ *And stretched them out.* The heavens are often represented as stretched out as a veil (Gen. i. 6, Heb.)

6 I the LORD have called thee in righteousness, and will hold thine hand, and will keep thee, and give thee for a covenant of the people, for a light [a] of the Gentiles.

a Lu.2.32; Ac.13.47.

or as an expanse that can be rolled up (see Note on ch. xxxiv. 4), or as a tent for the appropriate dwelling-place of God (see Note on ch. xl. 22). His great power and glory are indicated by the fact that he has stretched out what to us appears a vast expanse over our heads. On the grammatical construction of the word which occurs here in the Hebrew, *see* Rosenmüller *in loc.* ¶ *He that spread forth the earth.* He stretched it out as a plain—retaining the idea which was so common among the ancients that the earth was a vast plain, reaching from one end of the heavens to the other. The *words*, however, which are here used are not inconsistent with the idea that the earth is a sphere, since it may still be represented as stretched out, or expanded to a vast extent. The *main* idea in the passage is not to teach the *form* in which the earth is made, but to show that it has been made by God. ¶ *And that which cometh out of it.* The productions of the earth—the trees, shrubs, grain, &c. As the verb *to stretch out* cannot be applied to these, some verb must be understood; as he *produced*, or *caused to grow.* ¶ *He that giveth breath and spirit to them.* This refers, doubtless, to beasts as well as to men; and the idea is, that God is the source of life to all the creatures that live and move on the earth. The argument in the passage is, that as God is the creator and upholder of all; as he has given life to all, and has the universe entirely under his control, he has a right to appoint whom he will to be the medium of his favours to men, and to demand that suitable respect shall be shown to the Messiah whom he has designated for this work.

6. *I the* LORD *have called thee in righteousness.* The phrase 'in righteousness' has been very differently understood by different expositors (see Note on ch. xli. 10). The most probable meaning may be, 'I have done it as a righteous and just God, or in the accomplishment of my righteous purposes. I am the just moral governor of the universe, and to accomplish my purposes of justice and fidelity, I have designated thee to this work.' Lowth has well rendered it, 'For a righteous purpose.' In this work *all* was righteousness. God was righteous, who appointed him; it was *because* he was righteous, and could not save without a mediator and an atonement, that he sent him into the world; he selected one who was eminently righteous to accomplish his purpose; and he came that he might establish righteousness on the earth, and confirm the just government of God (see ver. 21). ¶ *And will hold thine hand.* I will take thee by the hand, as one does who guides and leads another. The phrase denotes the same as to guard, or keep—as we protect a child by taking him by the hand. ¶ *And give thee for a covenant.* This is evidently an abbreviated form of expression, and the meaning is, 'I will give or appoint thee as the medium, or means by which a covenant shall be made with the people; or a mediator of the new covenant which God is about to establish with men' (see ch. xlix. 8). A similar expression occurs in Micah v. 5, where it is said of the Messiah, 'and this *man* shall be the peace;' that is, he shall be the source of peace, or peace shall be established and maintained by him. So in Eph. ii. 14, it is said of him, 'he is our peace.' ¶ *Of the people.* It has been doubted whether this means the Jewish people, or the Gentiles. Grotius, Hengstenberg, Vitringa, and others understand it of the Jews; Rosenmüller and others, of the Gentiles. It is not easy to determine which is the correct interpretation. But the meaning, as I apprehend, is, not that he would confirm the ancient covenant with the descendants of Abraham, as Hengstenberg and Vitringa suppose, but that his covenant would be established with ALL, with both Jews and Gentiles. According to this, it will refer to the Jews, not *as* Jews, or as already interested in the covenant, but as constituting one portion of the world; and the whole expression will mean, that his religion will be extended to Jews and Gentiles: *i.e.*, to the whole

7 To open the blind eyes, to bring
out [a] the prisoners from the prison,
and them that sit in darkness [b] out
of the prison-house.
8 I *am* the LORD; that *is* my
name: and [d] my glory will I not
give to another, neither my praise
to graven images.
9 Behold, the former things are
come to pass, and new things do I
declare; before [e] they spring forth
I tell you of them.

a 2Ti.2.26. b 1 Pe.2.9. c Ps.83.18. d ch.40.11. e Ac.15.18.

world. ¶ *For a light of the Gentiles* (see Luke ii. 32). 'Light' is the emblem of knowledge, instruction, and of the true religion. The Messiah is often called 'light,' and the 'light of the world' (see Matt. iv. 16; comp. Note on Isa. ix. 2; John i. 4, 7, 9; iii. 19; viii. 12; ix. 5; xii. 35, 46; Rev. xxi. 23). This is one of the numerous declarations which occur in Isaiah, that the religion of the Messiah would be extended to the heathen world; and that they, as well as the Jews, would be brought to partake of its privileges.

7. *To open the blind eyes.* This is equivalent to saying that he would impart instruction to those who were ignorant. It relates to the Jews as well as to the Gentiles. He would acquaint them with God, and with the way of salvation. The condition of the world is often represented as one of darkness and blindness. Men see not their true character; they see not their real condition; they are ignorant of God, and of the truths pertaining to their future existence; and they need, therefore, some one who shall enlighten, and sanctify, and save them. ¶ *To bring out the prisoners from the prison* (comp. ch. lxi. 1, 2). This evidently refers to a spiritual deliverance, though the language is derived from deliverance from a prison. It denotes that he would rescue those who were confined in mental darkness by sin; and that their deliverance from the thraldom and darkness of sin would be as wonderful *as if* a prisoner should be delivered suddenly from a dark cell, and be permitted to go forth and breathe the pure air of freedom. Such is the freedom which the gospel imparts; nor can there be a more striking description of its happy effects on the minds and hearts of darkened and wretched men (comp. 1 Pet. ii. 9).

8. *I* am *the* LORD. I am JEHOVAH. Here is also a change in the address. In the previous verses, God had addressed the Messiah. Here he turns to the people, and assures them that he is the only true God, and that he will not suffer the praise that is due to him to be given to any other, or to any graven image. The name JEHOVAH signifies *being*, or *essential existence* (see Note on ch. i. 9). It is a name which is given to none but the true God, and which is everywhere in the Scriptures used to distinguish him from all others. ¶ *That* is *my name.* That is the name which I have chosen by which to distinguish myself from all idols, and which I regard as appropriately expressive of my existence and perfections. Thus it is used in Ps. lxxxiii. 18 (comp. Ps. xcvi. 5). ¶ *And my glory.* The glory, honour, or praise that is due to me. ¶ *Will I not give.* I will not allow it to ascribed to another; I will not allow another to assume or receive the honour which is due to me. ¶ *To another.* To *any* other; whether it be man, or whether it be an idol. God claims that all appropriate honours should be rendered to him, and that men should cherish no opinions, maintain no doctrines, indulge in no feelings, that would be derogatory to the honour of his name. This declaration is designed to counteract the propensity everywhere manifest to attribute to man that which belongs to God, or to ascribe to our own wisdom, skill, or power, that which he alone can accomplish. ¶ *Neither my praise.* The praise which is due to me. He would not permit graven images to receive the praise of having done that which he himself had accomplished.

9. *Behold, the former things are come to pass.* That is, the former things which he had foretold. This is the evidence to which he appeals in proof that he alone was God, and this is the basis on which he calls upon them to believe that what he had predicted in regard to future things would also come to pass. He had by his prophets foretold events

10 Sing unto the LORD a new
song, [a] *and* his praise from the end
of the earth, ye that go down to the
sea, and [1] all that is therein; the
isles, and the inhabitants thereof.
11 Let the wilderness and the
cities thereof lift up *their voice*, the
villages *that* Kedar doth inhabit:
let the inhabitants of the rock sing,
let them shout from the top of the
mountains.

a Re.5.9. 1 *the fulness thereof.*

---

which had now been fulfilled, and this should lead them to confide in him alone as the true God. ¶ *And new things do I declare.* Things pertaining to future events, relating to the coming of the Messiah, and to the universal prevalence of his religion in the world. ¶ *Before they spring forth.* There is here a beautiful image. The metaphor is taken from plants and flowers, the word צָמַח (*tzâmăhh*) properly referring to the springing up of plants, or to their sending out shoots, buds, or flowers. The phrase literally means, 'before they begin to germinate,' *i.e.*, before there are any indications of life, or growth in the plant. The sense is, that God predicted the future events before there was anything by which it might be inferred that such occurrences would take place. It was not done by mere sagacity—as men like Burke and Canning may sometimes predict future events with great probability by marking certain political indications or developments. God did this when there were no such indications, and when it must have been done by mere omniscience. In this respect, all his predictions differ from the *conjectures* of man, and from all the reasonings which are founded on mere sagacity.

10. *Sing unto the* LORD *a new song.* It is common, as we have seen, to celebrate the goodness of God in a hymn of praise on the manifestation of any peculiar act of mercy (see Notes on ch. xii., xxv., xxvi.) Here the prophet calls upon all people to celebrate the Divine mercy in a song of praise in view of his goodness in providing a Redeemer. The sentiment is, that God's goodness in providing a Saviour demands the thanksgiving of all the world. ¶ *A new song.* A song hitherto unsung; one that shall be expressive of the goodness of God in this *new* manifestation of his mercy. None of the hymns of praise that had been employed to express his former acts of goodness would appropriately express this. The mercy was so great that it demanded a song expressly made for the occasion. ¶ And *his praise from the end of the earth.* From all parts of the earth. Let the most distant nations who are to be interested in this great and glorious plan, join in the glad celebration. On the meaning of the phrase, 'end of the earth,' see Note on ch. xl. 28. ¶ *Ye that go down to the sea.* That is, traders, navigators, merchants, seamen; such as do business in the great waters. The sense is, that they would be interested in the plan of mercy through a Redeemer; and hence they are called on to celebrate the goodness of God (comp. Notes on ch. lx. 5). This is referred to by the prophet, first, because of the great multitude who thus go down to the sea; and, secondly, because their conversion will have so important an influence in diffusing the true religion to distant nations. ¶ *And all that is therein.* Marg. as Heb. 'The fulness thereof.' All that fill it; that is, either in ships, or by dwelling on the islands and coasts. The meaning is, that *all* who were upon the sea—the *completeness*, the *wholeness* of the maritime population, being equally interested with all others in the great salvation, should join in celebrating the goodness of God. ¶ *The isles.* A large portion of the inhabitants of the world are dwellers upon islands. In modern times, some of the most signal displays of the Divine mercy, and some of the most remarkable conversions to Christianity, have been there. In the Sandwich Islands, and in Ceylon, God has poured out his Spirit, and their inhabitants have been among the first in the heathen world to embrace the gospel.

11. *Let the wilderness* (see Note on ch. xxxv. 1). The word here denotes the most uncultivated countries, intimating that even the most rude and barbarous people would have occasion to rejoice, and would be interested in the mercy

12 Let [a]them give glory unto
the LORD, and declare his praise
in the islands.
13 The LORD shall go forth
as a mighty man, he shall stir up
jealousy like a [b]man of war: he
shall cry, yea, roar; he [1]shall
prevail against his enemies.

[a] Ps.117.1. [b] Ex.15.3.

[1] or, *behave himself mightily.*

---

of God. ¶ *And the cities thereof.* To us there seems to be something incongruous in speaking of the '*cities*' in a 'wilderness.' But we are to remember that the Hebrews gave the name wilderness or desert to those regions that were mostly uncultivated, or sparsely inhabited. They were places that were chiefly devoted to pasturage, and not cultivated by the plough, or regions of vast plains of sand and far-extended barrenness, with here and there an *oasis* on which a city might be built. Josephus, speaking of the desert or wilderness lying between Jerusalem and Jericho, enumerates several villages or towns in it, showing that though it was mainly a waste, yet that it was not wholly without towns or inhabitants. We are to remember also that large towns or cities for commercial purposes, or thoroughfares, were often built in the few fertile or advantageous places which were found in the midst of desert wastes. Thus we are told of Solomon (2 Chron. viii. 4), that 'he built Tadmor *in the wilderness;*' and we know that Palmyra, and Bozrah, and Sela, were large cities that were built in the midst of regions that were generally to be regarded as deserts, or wastes. ¶ *The villages that Kedar doth inhabit.* Where the inhabitants of Kedar dwell. Kedar was a son of Ishmael (Gen. xxv. 13), the father of the Kedarenians or Cedrei, mentioned by Pliny (*Nat. Hist.* v. 2), who dwell in the vicinity of the Nabathæans in Arabia Deserta. They often changed their place, though it would seem that they usually dwelt in the neighbourhood of Petra, or Sela. The name Kedar is often given to Arabia Deserta, and the word may in some instances denote Arabia in general. The inhabitants of those countries usually dwell in tents, and lead a nomadic and wandering life. ¶ *Let the inhabitants of the rock sing.* It is uncertain whether the word 'rock' here (Heb. סֶלַע *Sĕlă*, Gr. Πέτραν, 'Petra' or 'rock') is to be regarded as a proper name, or to denote in a general sense those who dwell in the rocky part of Arabia. Sela, or Petra, was the name of the celebrated city that was the capital of Idumea (see Notes on ch. xvi. 1); and the connection here would rather lead us to suppose that this city was intended here, and that the inhabitants of the capital were called upon to join with the dwellers in the surrounding cities and villages in celebrating the goodness of God. But it may denote in general those who inhabited the desolate and stony region of Arabia Petrea, or whose home was among the cliffs of the rocks. If so, it is a call upon Arabia in general to rejoice in the mercy of God, and to give glory to him for providing a plan of redemption—an intimation that to the descendants of Ishmael the blessings of the gospel would be extended. ¶ *Let them shout from the top of the mountains.* They who had taken refuge there, or who had made their permanent abode there. Vitringa supposes that the mountains of Paran are meant, which are situated on the north of Mount Sinai. The idea in the verse is, that all the dwellers in Arabia would celebrate the goodness of God, and join in praising him for his mercy in giving a deliverer. They were yet to partake of the benefits of his coming, and to have occasion of joy at his advent. It is possible that Cowper may have had this passage in his eye in the following description of the final and universal prevalence of the gospel:—

> The dwellers in the vales and on the rocks,
> Shout to each other, aad the mountain-tops,
> From distant mountains catch the flying joy:
> Till nation after nation taught the strain,
> Earth rolls the rapturous hosannas round.
>
> *Task.*

12. *Let them give glory—in the islands* (see Note on ch. xli. 1). Let the distant regions praise God.

13. *The Lord shall go forth.* This and the following verses give the reasons why they should praise JEHOVAH. He would go forth in his might to over-

14 I have long time holden my
peace; I have been still, *and* refrained myself: *now* [a] will I cry
like a travailing woman; I will
destroy and [1] devour at once.
15 I will make waste mountains

[a] Job 32.18-20.

[1] *swallow*, or, *sup up*.

come and subdue his foes, and to deliver his people. In his conquests, and in the establishment of his kingdom, all people would have occasion to rejoice and be glad. ¶ *As a mighty man.* As a hero, as a warrior. JEHOVAH is often in the Scriptures represented as a hero, or a man of war:

> JEHOVAH is a man of war:
> JEHOVAH is his name.—Ex. xv. 3.

> Who is this King of glory?
> JEHOVAH, strong and mighty;
> JEHOVAH mighty in battle.—Ps. xxiv. 8.

Comp. Ps. xlv. 3; Isa. xxvii. 1; xxx. 30. ¶ *He shall stir up jealousy.* He shall rouse his vengeance, or his indignation. The word קִנְאָה means *vengeance*, or indignation, as well as jealousy. The image here is that of a warrior who rushes on impetuously to take vengeance on his foes. ¶ *He shall cry.* He shall give a shout, or a loud clamour. Warriors usually entered a battle with a loud shout, designed to stimulate their own courage, and to intimidate their foes. All this language is taken from such an entrance on an engagement, and denotes the fixed determination of God to overthrow all his enemies.

14. *I have long time holden my peace.* This is the language of JEHOVAH, and it means that he had for a long time been patient and forbearing; but that now he would go forth as a warrior to overpower and destroy his foes. ¶ *I will destroy.* The word here used (from נָשַׁם *nâshăm*) denotes properly *to breathe hard*, to pant, as a woman in travail; and then to breathe hard in any manner. It here denotes the hard breathing which is indicative of anger, or a purpose to execute vengeance. ¶ *And devour at once.* Marg. 'Swallow,' or 'Sup up.' The word שָׁאַף means rather *to breathe hard*, to pant, to blow, as in anger, or in the haste of pursuit. The idea in the verse is, that JEHOVAH had for a long time restrained his anger against his foes, and had refrained from executing vengeance on them. But now he would rouse his righteous indignation, and go forth to accomplish his purposes in their destruction. All this language is descriptive of a hero or warrior; and is, of course, not to be regarded as applicable literally to God. He often uses the language of men, and speaks of his purposes under the image of human passions. But we are not to infer that the language is literally applicable to him, nor is it to be interpreted too strictly. It means, in general, that God would go forth with a fixed and settled purpose to destroy his foes.

15. *I will make waste mountains.* This verse denotes the utter desolation which God would bring upon his foes in his anger. The meaning of this part of the verse is, that he would spread desolation over the hills and mountains that were well watered and laid out in gardens and orchards. It was common to plant vineyards on the sides of hills and mountains; and indeed most of the mountains of Palestine and adjacent regions were cultivated nearly to the top. They were favourable to the culture of the vine and the olive; and by making terraces, the greater portion of the hills were thus rescued for purposes of agriculture. Yet an enemy or warrior marching through a land would seek to spread desolation through all its cultivated parts, and lay waste all its fields. God, therefore, represents himself as a conqueror, laying waste the cultivated portions of the country of his foes. ¶ *And dry up all their herbs.* He would destroy all the grain and fruits on which they were depending for support. ¶ *And I will make the rivers islands.* Or rather, dry land, or deserts. I will, in the heat of my anger, dry up the streams, so that the bottoms of those streams shall be dry land. The word here rendered 'islands,' from אִי, properly denotes *dry land*, habitable ground, as opposed to water, the sea, rivers, &c., and the signification 'islands' is a secondary signification. ¶ *And I will dry up the pools.* The pools on which they have been dependent for water for

and [a] hills, and dry up all their
herbs; and I will make the rivers
islands, and I will dry up the pools.
16 And [b] I will bring the blind
by [c] a way *that* they knew not;
I will lead them in paths [d] *that* they
have not known: I will make darkness light before them, and crooked
things [1] straight. These things
will I do [e] unto them, and not [f] forsake them.
17 They [g] shall be turned back,

a ch.49.11. b Ho.2.14. c Ep.5.8. d Ho.2.6.
1 *into straightness.* e Eze.14.23. f He.13.5. g Ps.97.7.

their flocks and herds. The sense of the whole passage is, I will bring to desolation those who worship idols, and the idols themselves. I will produce an entire change among them, *as great* as if I were to spread desolation over their cultivated hills, and to dry up all their streams. The reference is probably to the great changes which God would make in the heathen world. All that flourished on Pagan ground; all that was nurtured by idolatry; all their temples, fanes, altars, shrines, should be overturned and demolished; and in all these things great and permanent changes would be produced. The time would have come when God could no longer bear with the growing abominations of the pagan nations, and when he would go forth as a conqueror to subdue all to himself.

16. *And I will lead the blind.* Having said in the previous verses what he would do to his enemies, God now speaks of his people. He would conduct them to their own land, as a blind people that needed a guide, and would remove whatever obstacle there was in their way. By the 'blind' here, he refers doubtless to his own people. The term is applied originally to his people in captivity, as being ignorant, after their seventy years' exile, of the way of return to their own land. It is *possible* that it may have a reference to the fact, so often charged on them, that they were characteristically a stupid and spiritually blind people. But it is more probable that it is the language of *tenderness* rather than that of objurgation; and denotes their ignorance of the way of return, and their need of a guide, rather than their guilt, and hardness of heart. If applied to the people of God under the New Testament—as the entire strain of the prophecy seems to lead us to conclude—then it denotes that Christians will feel their need of a leader, counsellor, and guide; and that JEHOVAH, as a military leader, will conduct them all in a way which they did not know, and remove all obstacles from their path. ¶ *By a way* that *they knew not.* When they were ignorant what course to take; or in a path which they did not contemplate or design. It is true of all the friends of God that they *have been led* in a way which they knew not. They did not mark out this course for themselves; they did not at first form the plans of life which they came ultimately to pursue; they have been led, by the providence of God, in a different path, and by the Spirit of God they have been inclined to a course which they themselves would never have chosen (comp. Note on ch. xxx. 21). ¶ *I will make darkness light before them.* Darkness, in the Scriptures, is the emblem of ignorance, sin, adversity, and calamity. Here it seems to be the emblem of adverse and opposing events; of calamities, persecutions, and trials. The meaning is, that God would make those events which seemed to be adverse and calamitous, the means of furthering his cause, and promoting the spirit of the true religion, and the happiness of his people. This has been eminently the case with the persecutions which the church has endured. The events which have been apparently most adverse, have been ultimately overruled to the best interests of the true religion. Such was the case with the persecutions under the Roman emperors, and in general such has been the case in all the persecutions which the church has been called to suffer. ¶ *And crooked things straight.* Things which seem to be adverse and opposing—the persecutions and trials which the people of God would be called to endure. ¶ *And not forsake them* (see Notes on ch. xli. 10, 13, 14).

17. *They shall be turned back.* The phrases, to be turned back, and to be suffused with shame, are frequently used

they shall be greatly ashamed,
that trust in graven images, that
say to the molten images, Ye *are*
our gods.
18 Hear, [a] ye deaf; and look, ye
blind, [b] that ye may see.
19 Who *is* blind, but my servant? or deaf, as my messenger
that I sent? who *is* blind as *he*
that is perfect, and blind as the
LORD's servant?

[a] ch.6.10. [b] Jn.9.39.

in the Scriptures to denote a state of disappointment in regard to an object of trust or confidence, and especially of those who had trusted in idols (see Ps. xxxv. 4; lxx. 3; xcvii. 7; comp. Notes on ch. i. 29; xix. 9; xxxvii. 27; see also Ezek. xvi. 52; liv. 63). The sense here is, that they should find no such protection in their idol-gods as they had hoped, and that they should be covered with conscious guilt for ever, having trusted in them and given to them the homage which was due to the true God.

18. *Hear, ye deaf.* This is evidently an address to the Jews, and probably to the Jews of the time of the prophet. He had been predicting the coming of the Messiah, and the influence of his religion on the Gentile world. He had said that God would go forth to destroy the idolatry of the heathen nations, and to convince them of the folly of the worship of images, and to confound them for putting their trust in them. He seems here to have recollected that this was the easily-besetting sin of his own countrymen, and perhaps especially of the times when he penned this portion of the prophecy—under the reign of Manasseh; that that generation was stupid, blind, deaf to the calls of God, and sunk in the deepest debasement of idolatry. In view of this, and of the great truths which he had uttered, he calls on them to hear, to be alarmed, to return to God, and assures them that for these sins they exposed themselves to, and must experience, his sore displeasure. The statement of these truths, and the denouncing of these judgments, occupy the remainder of this chapter. A similar instance occurs in ch. ii., where the prophet, having foretold the coming of the Messiah, and the fact that his religion would be extended among the Gentiles, turns and reproves the Jews for *their* idolatry and crimes (see Notes on that chapter). The Jewish people are often described as 'deaf' to the voice of God, and 'blind' to their duty and their interests (see ch. xxix. 18; xlii. 8). ¶ *And look—that ye may see.* This phrase denotes an attentive, careful, and anxious search, in order that there may be a clear view of the object. The prophet calls them to an attentive contemplation of the object, that they might have a clear and distinct view of it. They had hitherto looked at the subject of religion in a careless, inattentive, and thoughtless manner.

19. *Who is blind, but my servant?* Some of the Jewish expositors suppose that by 'servant' here, the prophet himself is intended, who, they suppose is here called blind and deaf by the impious Jews who rejected his message. But it is evident, that by 'servant' here, the Jewish people themselves are intended, the singular being used for the plural, in a sense similar to that where they are so often called 'Jacob' and 'Israel.' The phrase 'servants of God' is often given to his people, and is used to denote true worshippers. The word is here used to denote those who *professed* to be the true worshippers of JEHOVAH. The prophet had, in the previous verses, spoken of the blindness and stupidity of the Gentile world. He here turns to his own countrymen, and addresses them as more blind, and deaf, and stupid than they. 'Who,' he asks, 'is as blind as they are?' Where are any of the heathen nations so insensible to the appeals of God, and so hard-hearted? The idea of the prophet is, that the Jews had had far greater advantages, and yet they were so sunk in sin that it might be said that comparatively none were blind but they. Even the degradation of the heathen nations, under the circumstances of the case, could not be compared with theirs. ¶ *As my messenger* that *I sent.* Lowth renders this, 'And deaf, as he to whom I have sent

20 Seeing many things, but thou
observest not; opening the ears,
but he heareth not.
21 The LORD is well pleased for
his [a]righteousness' sake: he will
magnify [b]the law, and make [1]*it*
honourable.

[a] Ps.71.16,19; Ro.10.3,4; Phi.3.9. [b] Mat.5.17. [1] or, *him.*

my messengers.' The LXX. render it, 'And deaf but those that rule over them;' by a slight change in the Hebrew text. The Vulgate reads it as Lowth has rendered it. The Chaldee renders it, 'If the wicked are converted, shall they not be called my servants? And the sinners to whom I sent my prophets?' But the sense seems to be this:—The Jewish people were regarded as a people selected and preserved by God for the purpose of preserving and extending the true religion. They might be spoken of as sent for the great purpose of enlightening the world, as God's messengers in the midst of the deep darkness of benighted nations, and as appointed to be the agents by which the true religion was to be perpetuated and propagated on earth. Or perhaps, the word 'messenger' here may denote collectively the Jewish leaders, teachers, and priests, who had been sent as the messengers of God to that people, and who were, with the people, sunk in deep debasement and sin. ¶ *As he that is perfect* (כִּמְשֻׁלָּם). A great variety of interpretations has been offered on this word—arising from the difficulty of giving the appellation 'perfect' to a people so corrupt as were the Jews in the time of Isaiah. Jerome renders it, *Qui venundatus est*—'He that is sold.' The Syriac renders it, 'Who is blind as the prince?' Symmachus renders it, Ὡς ὁ τέλειος; and Kimchi in a similar manner by תָּמִים (*tâmīm*)—'perfect.' The verb שָׁלַם means properly *to be whole, sound, safe;* to be completed, finished, ended: and then, to be at peace or friendship with any one. And it may be applied to the Jews, to whom it undoubtedly refers here, in one of the following senses; either (1.) *ironically*, as claiming to be perfect; or (2.) as those who *professed* to be perfect; or (3.) as being favoured with rites and laws, and a civil and sacred constitution that were complete (Vitringa); or (4.) as being in *friendship* with God, as Grotius and Gesenius suppose. It most probably refers to the fact that they were richly endowed by JEHOVAH with complete and happy institutions adapted to their entire welfare, and such as, in comparison with other nations, were fitted to make them perfect. ¶ *As the* LORD's *servant.* The Jewish people, professing to serve and obey God.

20. *Seeing many things.* That is, the people, the Jews, spoken of here as the servants of God. They had had an opportunity of observing many things pertaining to the law, the government, and the dealing of JEHOVAH. They had often witnessed his interposition in the days of calamity, and he often rescued them from peril. These things they could not but have observed, much as they had chosen to disregard the lessons which they were calculated to convey. ¶ *But thou observest not.* Thou dost not *keep* them (תִשְׁמֹר); thou dost not regard them. ¶ *Opening the ears.* Thou hast thine ears open. They heard the words of the law, and the instructions conveyed by tradition from their fathers, but they did not lay them to heart, or give heed to them (see Note on ch. vi. 10).

21. *The* LORD *is well pleased for his righteousness' sake.* There is great variety in the translation and interpretation of this verse. Lowth renders it:

> Yet JEHOVAH was gracious unto him for his truth's sake;
> He hath exalted his own praise, and made it glorious.

Noyes renders it:

> It pleased JEHOVAH for his goodness' sake
> To give him a law great and glorious;
> And yet it is a robbed and plundered people.

The LXX. render it, 'The Lord God determined that he should be justified, and magnify his praise.' The Chaldee renders it, 'JEHOVAH willed that Israel should be justified; he magnified the doers of his law, and comforted them.' The Syriac, 'The Lord willed on account of his righteousness to magnify his law, and to commend it.' Vitringa explains it, 'God has embraced the Jewish people in his love and favour,

22 But this *is* a people robbed and [a] spoiled; *they* [1] *are* all of them snared in holes, and they are hid in prison-houses: they are for a

[a] ch.18.2.

[1] or, *insnaring all the young men of them.*

---

and regards them as acceptable to himself, not indeed on account of any merit of theirs, or on account of any external advantages, but on account of his own truth, fidelity, and equity, that he might fulfil the promises which he made to their fathers.' This seems to express the sense of the passage. According to this, it refers solely to the Jewish people, and not, as is often supposed, to the Messiah. The phrase, 'is well pleased,' means that JEHOVAH takes delight in his people, or looks upon them with an eye of tenderness and affection. He finds pleasure in contemplating them as *his* people, and in regarding and treating them as such. ¶ *For his righteousness' sake.* Not for the righteousness of his people, but on account of his *own* righteousness; *i.e.*, his own goodness, clemency, mercy, and forbearance. It is not because he sees in them anything that should win his love, or excite his favour; for he says (ver. 22) that they are robbed, and plundered, and hid, and bound in prison. But JEHOVAH had selected their fathers as his own people. He had made them precious promises. He had designs of mercy towards them. He had given them a holy law. He had promised to be their protector and their God. *On this account* he was pleased with them still; and it was on account of his own fidelity and plighted protection, that he was delighted in them as his people. The word 'righteousness,' therefore (צֶדֶק), is used to denote God's purpose *to do right; i.e.*, to adhere to his promises, and to maintain a character of fidelity and integrity. He would not fail, or violate his own pledges to his people. ¶ *He will magnify the law.* The word 'law' here is used to denote the entire series of statutes, or legislative acts of God, in regard to the Jewish people—including all his promises and pledges to them. And the meaning is, that he would so deal with them as to make that law important in their view; so as to show that *he* regarded it as of infinite moment. He would adhere strictly himself to all his own covenant pledges in that law, so as to show that *he* regarded it as sacred and of binding obligation; and all his dealings with them *under* that law would be such as to magnify its importance and purity in their view. The Hebrew is, 'he will make the law great;' that is, he will make it of great importance. ¶ *And make* it *honourable.* Or, make it glorious, by himself showing a constant regard for it, and by so dealing with them that they should be brought to see and feel its importance. According to this, which is the obvious interpretation, the passage has no reference particularly to the Messiah. It *is* true, however, that the *language* here used is such as would appropriately describe the work of the Redeemer; and that a large part of what he did in his public ministry, and by his atonement, was 'to magnify the law and make it honourable;'—to vindicate its equity—to urge its binding obligation—to sustain its claims—to show that it could not be violated with impunity—and to demonstrate that its penalty was just. The whole effect of the Redeemer's work is to do honour to the law of God, nor has anything occurred in the history of our world that has done so much to maintain its authority and binding obligation, as his death on the cross, in the place of sinners.

22. *But this* is *a people robbed and spoiled.* The Jewish people, though highly favoured, have been so unmindful of the goodness of God to them, that he has given them into the hand of their enemies to plunder them. This is to be conceived as spoken *after* the captivity, and while the Jews were in exile. Their being robbed and spoiled, therefore, refers to the invasion of the Chaldeans, and is to be regarded as spoken prophetically of the exiled and oppressed Jews while in Babylon. ¶ They are *all of them snared in holes.* This passage has been variously rendered. Lowth renders it, 'All their chosen youth are taken in the toils;' following in this the translation of Je-

prey, and none delivereth; for a
spoil, [1] and none saith, Restore.
23 Who among you will give ear
to this? *who* will hearken and hear
for [2] the time to come?
24 Who gave Jacob for a spoil,
and Israel to the robbers? did not
the LORD, he [a] against whom we
have sinned? for they would not
walk in his ways, neither were
they obedient unto his law.
25 Therefore he hath poured
upon him the fury of his anger,
and the strength of battle: and
it hath set him on fire [b] round
about, yet [c] he knew not; and it
burned him, yet he laid *it* not to
heart.

1 *treading.* 2 *after time.*

a Ju.2.14; Ne.9.26,27. b De.32.22. c Ho.7.9.

rome, and rendering it as Le Clerc and Houbigant do. The LXX. read it, 'And I saw, and the people were plundered and scattered, and the snare was in all their private chambers, and in their houses where they hid themselves;'—meaning, evidently, that they had been taken by their invaders from the places where they had secreted themselves in their own city and country. The Chaldee renders it, 'All their youth were covered with confusion, and shut up in prison.' The Syriac, 'All their youth are snared, and they have hid them bound in their houses.' This variety of interpretation has arisen in part, because the Hebrew which is rendered in our version, 'in holes' (בַּחוּרִים), may be either the plural form of the word בָּחוּר (*chosen, selected*); and thence *youths*—selected for their beauty or strength; or it may be the plural form of the word חוּר, *a hole* or *cavern*, with the preposition בְּ prefixed. Our translation prefers the latter; and this is probably the correct interpretation, as the *parallel* expression, 'they are hid in prison-houses,' seems to demand this. The literal interpretation of the passage is, therefore, that they were snared, or secured in the caverns, holes, or places of refuge where they sought security. ¶ *And they are hid in prison-houses.* They were concealed in their houses as in prisons, so that they could not go out with safety, or without exposing themselves to the danger of being taken captive. The land was filled with their enemies, and they were obliged to conceal themselves, if possible, from their foes. ¶ *And none saith, Restore.* There is no deliverer—no one who can interpose, and compel the foe to give up his captives. The sense is, the Jewish captives were so strictly confined in Babylon, and under a government so powerful, that there was no one who could rescue them, or that they were so much the object of contempt, that there were none who would feel so much interest in them as to demand them from their foes.

23. *Who among you will give ear to this?* Who is there in the nation that will be so warned by the judgments of God, that he will attend to the lessons which he designs to teach, and reform his life, and return to him? It is implied by these questions that such *ought* to be the effect; it is implied also that they were so sunken and abandoned that they *would* not do it. These judgments were a loud call on the nation to turn to God, and, in time to come, to avoid the sins which had made it necessary for him to interpose in this manner, and give them to spoil.

24. *Who gave Jacob for a spoil?* Who gave up the Jewish people to be plundered? The object of this verse is, to bring distinctly before them the fact that it was JEHOVAH, the God of their fathers, and of their nation, who had brought this calamity upon them. It was not the work of chance, but it was the immediate and direct act of God on account of their sins. Probably, as a people, they were not disposed to believe this; and the prophet, therefore, takes occasion to call their attention particularly to this fact.

25. *Therefore he hath poured upon him the fury of his anger.* His righteous indignation in the overturning of their nation, the destruction of their temple and city, and in carrying them captive into a distant land. ¶ *And it hath set him on fire.* That is, the fury of JEHOVAH kindled the flame of war all around the Jewish nation, and spread

CHAPTER XLIII.

ANALYSIS.

This chapter is evidently a continuation of the subject discussed in the previous chapters, and refers mainly to the promised deliverance from Babylon. The people of God are still contemplated by the prophet as suffering the evils of their long and painful captivity, and his object is to comfort them with the assurances of deliverance. The chapter may be regard as composed of *a succession of arguments*, all tending to show them that God would be their protector, and that their deliverance would be certain. These arguments are not distinguished by any very clear marks of transition, and all divisions of the chapter must be in a measure arbitrary. But perhaps the following arrangement will comprise the considerations which the prophet designed to suggest.

I. In the previous chapter he had severely rebuked the Jews, as being deaf, and blind, and had showed them that it was on account of their sins that these calamities had come upon them. Yet he now turns and says, that they are the people whom he had redeemed, and whom it was his purpose to deliver, and repeats the solemn assurance that they would be rescued (1–7). This assurance consists of many *items* or considerations, showing that they would be recovered, however far they were driven from their own land. 1. God had formed and redeemed them (1). It followed from this that a God of covenant faithfulness would be with them in their trials (2). 2. They had been so precious to him and valuable, that he had given entire nations for their ransom (3). It followed from this, that he would continue to give more, if necessary, for their ransom (4). 3. It was the fixed purpose of God to gather them again, wherever they might be scattered, and they had, therefore, nothing to fear (5–7).

II. God asserts his superiority to all idol-gods. He makes a solemn appeal, as he had done in ch. xli., to show that the idols had no power; and refers to all that he had predicted and to its fulfilment in proof that he was the only true God, and had been faithful to his people (8–13). In doing this, he says—1. That none of the idols had been able to predict future events (8, 9). 2. That the Jewish people were his witnesses that he was the true God, and the only Saviour (10–12). 3. That he had existed for ever, and that none could thwart his designs (13).

III. God asserts his purpose to destroy the power of Babylon (14, 17). He says—1. That he had sent to Babylon [by Cyrus] to bring down their power, and prostrate their nobles (14, 15); and, 2. Appeals to what he had formerly done; refers to the deliverance from Egypt, and asserts it to be his characteristic that he made a way in the sea, and led forth the chariot, the horse, the army, and the power (16, 17).

IV. Yet he tells them (18–21), that all his former wonderful interpositions would be surpassed; that he would do a new thing—so strange, so wonderful, and marvellous, that all that he had formerly done should be forgotten. 1. They are commanded not to remember the former things (18). 2. He would do a new thing —a thing which in all his former interpositions had not been done (19). 3. The characteristics of the future wonder would be, that he would make a way in the wilderness, and rivers in the desert (19); and that even the wild beasts of the desert should be made to honour him (20). 4. He had formed that people for himself, and they should show forth his praise (21).

V. From these promises of protection and assistance, and these assurances of favour, God turns to remind them of their sins, and assures them that it was by no merit of theirs that he would thus interpose to deliver them. 1. He reminds them of their having neglected, as a people, to honour him, and having withheld what was his due (22–24); yet, 2. He would blot out their sins, but it was by no merit of theirs, but by his mere mercy (25, 26). 3. They had been a sinful people, and he had, therefore, humbled their power, and given the nation to reproach, and a curse (27, 28). The same subject is resumed and prosecuted in the next chapter, and they should be read together without any interruption.

BUT [a] now thus saith the LORD that created thee, O Jacob, and he that formed thee, O Israel, Fear not: for I have redeemed

a Je.33.24.26.

desolation everywhere. ¶ *Yet he knew not.* They refused to attend to it, and lay it to heart. They pursued their ways of wickedness, regardless of the threatening judgments, and the impending wrath of God. They did not consider that these evils were inflicted for their crimes, nor did they turn from their sins when they were thus threatened with the wrath of God.

CHAPTER XLIII.

1. *But now.* This expression shows that this chapter is connected with the preceding. The sense is, 'Though God

thee, I have called *thee* by thy
name; thou *art* mine.
2 When [a] thou passest through
the waters, [b] I *will be* with thee;
and through the rivers, they shall
not overflow thee: when thou
walkest through the [c] fire, thou
shalt not be burned; neither shall
the flame kindle upon thee.

a Ps.66.12. *b* Ac.27.20,25. *c* Da.3.25,27.

has punished the nation, and showed them his displeasure (ch. xlii. 24, 25), yet *now* he will have mercy, and will deliver them.' ¶ *That created thee.* The word 'thee' is here used evidently in a collective sense as denoting the Jewish people. It is used because the names 'Jacob' and 'Israel' in the singular number are applied to the people. The word 'created' is here used to denote the idea that, as the peculiar people of God, they owed their origin to him, as the universe owed its origin to his creative power. It means that, as a people, their institutions, laws, customs, and privileges, and whatever they had that was valuable, were all to be traced to him. The same word occurs in verse 7, and again in verse 15, 'I am JEHOVAH—the Creator of Israel, your king' (see also ch. xliv. 1; comp. Ps. c. 3). ¶ *Fear not.* This is to be understood as addressed to them when suffering the evils of the captivity of Babylon. Though they were captives, and had suffered long, yet they had nothing to fear in regard to their final extinction as a people. They should be redeemed from captivity, and restored again to the land of their fathers. The *argument* here is, that they were the chosen people of God; that he had organized them as his people for great and important purposes, and that those purposes must be accomplished. It would follow from that, that they *must* be redeemed from their captivity, and be restored again to their land. ¶ *For I have redeemed thee.* The word גָּאַל (*gâăl*) means properly *to redeem*, to ransom by means of a price, or a valuable consideration, as of captives taken in war; or to redeem a farm that was sold, by paying back the price. It is sometimes used, however, to denote deliverance from danger or bondage without specifying any price that was paid as a ransom. Thus the deliverance of the Jews from Egyptian bondage is sometimes spoken of as a redemption (Ex. vi. 6; xv. 13; comp. Gen. xviii. 16; Isa. xxix. 22; xliv. 23; Jer. xxxi. 11; see Note on ch. i. 27). It is not improbable, however, that wherever *redemption* is spoken of in the Scriptures, even in the most general manner, and as denoting deliverance from danger, oppression, or captivity, there is still retained the idea of *a ransom* in some form; a price paid; a valuable consideration; or *something that was given in the place of that which was redeemed*, and which answered the purpose of a valuable consideration, or a public reason of the deliverance. Thus, in regard to the deliverance from Egypt,—Egypt, Ethiopia, and Seba are mentioned as the ransom (see Note on ver. 3); and so in the deliverance from the captivity, Babylon was given in the place of the ransomed captives, or was destroyed in order that they might be redeemed. So in all notions of redemption; as, *e.g.*, God destroyed the life of the great Redeemer, or caused him to be put to death, in order that his chosen people might be saved. ¶ *I have called* thee *by thy name.* 'To call by name' denotes intimacy of friendship. Here it means that God had *particularly* designated them to be his people. His call had not been general, addressed to the nations at large, but had been addressed to them in particular. Compare Ex. xxxi. 2, where God says that he had designated 'by name' Bezaleel to the work of constructing the tabernacle. ¶ *Thou* art *mine.* They were his, because he had formed them as a people, and had originated their institutions; because he had redeemed them, and because he had particularly designated them as his. The same thing may be said of his church now; and in a still more important sense, that church is his. He has organized it; he has appointed its peculiar institutions; he has redeemed it with precious blood; and he has called his people by name, and designated them as his own.

2. *When thou passest through the*

3 For I *am* the LORD thy God, the Holy One of Israel, thy Saviour: I gave [a] Egypt *for* thy ransom, Ethiopia and Seba for thee.

[a] Prov.21.18.

---

waters. This is a *general* promise, and means that whenever and wherever they should pass through water or fire, he would protect them. It had been true in their past history as a people; and the assurance is here given in order that they might be comforted in view of the calamities which they were then suffering in Babylon. Fire and water are often used in the Scriptures to denote calamity—the latter because it overwhelms; the former because it consumes; see Ps. lxix. 1—'The waters are come into my soul;' also Ps. lxxiii. 10; cxxiv. 4, 5; lxvi. 12—'We went through fire and through water.' ¶ *I* will be *with thee* (comp. Note on ch. xli. 10). ¶ *And through the rivers.* Also expressive of calamity and danger —like attempting to ford deep and rapid streams. ¶ *They shall not overflow thee.* As was the case with the Jordan when they crossed it under the guidance of Joshua, and a pathway was made for the armies of Israel. ¶ *When thou walkest through the fire.* This is expressive of calamity and danger in general *like* passing through fire. Yet it had a literal fulfilment in the case of the three pious Jews who were cast by Nebuchadnezzar into the burning furnace (Dan. iii. 25, 27). ¶ *Neither shall the flame kindle upon thee.* It shall not only not consume thee, but it shall not even burn, or injure thee (see Dan. iii. 27). The Chaldee Paraphrase refers this verse to the passage through the Red Sea, and to the protection which God gave his people there. It is rendered, 'In the beginning, when you passed through the Red Sea, my word was your aid. Pharaoh and Egypt, who were mighty like the waters of a river, were not able to prevail against you. And when thou didst go among a people who were formidable like fire, they could not prevail against you, and the kingdoms which were strong like flame could not consume you.' It is, however, to be understood rather as a promise pertaining to the future; though the *language* is mainly derived, undoubtedly, from God's protecting them in their perils in former times.

3. *For I* am *the* LORD *thy God.* This verse continues the statement of the reasons why he would protect them. He was JEHOVAH *their* God. He was not only the true God, but he was the God who had entered into solemn covenant with *them,* and who would therefore protect and defend them. ¶ *The Holy One of Israel.* It was one of his characteristics that he was the God of Israel. Other nations worshipped other gods. He was THE God of Israel; and as it was presumed that a god would protect his own people, so he bound himself to deliver them. ¶ *Thy Saviour.* This was another characteristic. He *had* saved them in days of peril; and he had assumed towards them the relation of a Saviour; and he would maintain that character. ¶ *I gave Egypt* for *thy ransom.* This is a very important passage in regard to the meaning of the word 'ransom.' The word נָתַתִּי (*năthăttī*)—'I gave' is rendered by Gesenius (*Comm. in loc.*), and by Noyes, in the future, 'I will give.' Gesenius supposes that it refers to the fact that the countries specified *would* be made desolate, in order to effect the deliverance of the Jews. He observes that although Cyrus did not conquer them, yet that it was done by his successors. In particular, he refers to the fact that Cambyses invaded and subdued Egypt (Herod. iii. 15); and that he then entered into, and subdued Ethiopia and Meroë (Strabo xvii.; Jos. *Ant.* ii. 10. 2). But the word properly refers to the past time, and the scope of the passage requires us to understand it of past events. For God is giving a *reason* why his people might expect protection, and the reason here is, that he *had* been their deliverer, and that his purpose to protect them was so fixed and determined, that he had even brought ruin on nations more mighty and numerous than themselves, in order to effect their deliverance. The *argument* is, that *if* he had suffered Egypt, Ethiopia, and Seba to be desolated and

ruined *instead of them*, or in order to effect their deliverance, they had nothing to fear from Babylon or any other hostile nation, but that he would effect their deliverance even at the expense of the overthrow of the most mighty kingdoms. The word rendered 'ransom' here is כֹּפֶר (*kōphĕr*). It is derived from כָּפַר (*kâphăr*)—whence the Latin *cooperio;* the Italian *coprire*, the French *couvrir;* the Norman *coverer*, and *converer;* and the English *cover*, and means literally to cover; to cover over; to overlay with anything, as pitch, as in Gen. vi. 14. Hence to cover over sins; to overlook; to forgive; and hence to make an expiation for sins, or to atone for transgression so that it may be forgiven (Gen. xxxii. 21; Ex. xxx. 15; Lev. iv. 20; v. 26; xi. 24; xvi. 6; Ps. lxv. 4; lxxviii. 38; Prov. xvi. 14; Jer. xviii. 25; Ezek. xlv. 20; Dan. ix. 24). The noun (כֹּפֶר) means—1. A *village* or *hamlet*, as being a *cover* or shelter to the inhabitants (1 Sam. vi. 18; comp. the word כָּפָר in 1 Chron. xxvii. 25; Neh. vi. 2; Cant. vi. 12). 2. *Pitch*, as a material for overlaying (Gen. vi. 14). 3. The *cypress-flower*, the *alhenna* of the Arabs, so called because the powder of the leaves was used to *cover over* or besmear the nails in order to produce the reddish colour which Oriental females regarded as an ornament (Simonis; Cant. i. 14; iv. 13, marg.) 4. A *ransom;* a price of redemption, or an expiation; so called because by it sins were covered over, concealed, or removed (Ex. xxix. 36; xxx. 10, 16). In such an expiation, that which was offered as the ransom was supposed to take the place of that for which the expiation was made, and this idea is distinctly retained in the versions of this passage. Thus the LXX., Ἐποίησα ἄλλαγμά σου Αἴγυπτον, κ.τ.λ.—'I made Egypt, &c., thy *ἄλλαγμα*—a commutation for thee; a change for thee; I put it in thy place, and it was destroyed instead of thee.' So the Chaldee, 'I gave the Egyptians as a commutation for thee' (חֲלִיפָךְ). So the Syriac, 'I gave Egypt *in thy place*' (ܚܠܦܝܟ). The true interpretation, therefore, is, that Egypt was regarded as having been given up to desolation and destruction *instead* of the Israelites. One of them must perish; and God chose that Egypt, though so much more mighty and powerful, should be reduced to desolation *in order* to deliver his people. They took their place, and were destroyed *instead* of the Hebrews, in order that they might be delivered from the bondage under which they groaned. This may be used as a striking *illustration* of the atonement made for sin, when the Lord Jesus, the expiatory offering, was made to suffer in the stead—*ἄλλαγμα*—of his people, and in order that sinners might live. And if God's giving up the Egyptians to destruction—themselves so guilty and deserving of death—in order to save his people, was a proof of his love for them, how much greater is the demonstration of his love when he gives his own holy Son to the bitter pains of death on a cross, in order that his church may be redeemed! There has been much variety, as has already been intimated, in the interpretation of this, and in regard to the time and events referred to. It has, by many, been supposed to refer to the invasion by Sennacherib, who, when he was about to fall upon Jerusalem, turned his arms against the Egyptians and their allies, by which means Jerusalem was saved by devoting those nations to desolation. Vitringa explains it of Shalmaneser's design upon the kingdom of Judah, after he had destroyed that of Samaria, from which he was diverted by carrying the war against the Egyptians, Cusheans, and Sabeans. But of this, Lowth says, there is no clear proof in history. Secker supposes that it refers to the fact that Cyrus overcame those nations, and that they were given him for releasing the Jews. Lowth says, 'perhaps it may mean, generally, that God had often saved his people at the expense of other nations, whom he had as it were in their stead given up to destruction.' The exact historical facts in the case cannot be clearly made out; nor is this to be wondered at, that many things of this nature should remain obscure for want of the light of history, which in regard to those times is extremely deficient. In regard to Egypt, however, I think the case is clear. Nothing is more manifest than that the prophet refers to that

4 Since thou wast precious in
my sight, thou hast been honourable, and I have loved thee: therefore will I give men for thee, and
people for thy [1] life.
5 Fear not; for I *am* with thee:

[1] or, *person.*

great and wonderful fact—the common-place illustration of the sacred writers—that the Egyptians were destroyed in order to effect the deliverance of the Jews, and were thus given as a ransom for them. ¶ *Ethiopia.* Heb. 'Cush.' In regard to this country, see Note on ch. xviii. 1. It is not improbable that the prophet here refers to the facts referred to in that chapter, and the destruction which it is there said would come upon that land. ¶ *And Seba.* This was the name of a people descended from Cush (Gen. x. 7); and hence the name of the country which they occupied. According to Josephus (*Ant.* ii. 10. 2), it seems to have been *Meroë*, a province of Ethiopia, distinguished for its wealth and commerce, surrounded by the two arms or branches of the Nile. There still remain the ruins of a metropolis of the same name, not far from the town of Shandy (Keppel's *Travels in Nubia and Arabia*, 1829). Meroë is a great island or peninsula in the north of Ethiopia, and is formed by the Nile, and the Astaboras, which unites with the Nile. It was probably anciently called *Seba*, and was conquered by Cambyses, the successor of Cyrus, and by him called *Meroë*, after his sister. That it was near to Ethiopia is apparent from the fact that it is mentioned in connection with it (comp. Ps. lxx. 10; Isa. xlv. 14;—Herod. iii. 20). They would naturally ally themselves to the Ethiopians, and share the same fate.

4. *Since thou wast precious in my sight.* This verse contains another reason why God would defend and deliver them. That reason was, that he had loved them as his people; and he was willing, therefore, that other people should be overcome in order that they might be saved. ¶ *Thou hast been honourable.* This does not refer so much to their personal character, as to the fact that they had been honoured by him with being the depository of the precious truths of his religion. It means that *he* had made them honourable by the favours bestowed on them; not that they were honourable in reference to their own personal character and worth. ¶ *Therefore will I give men for thee.* As in the case of Egypt, Ethiopia, and Seba (ver. 3). He would cause other nations to be destroyed, if it were necessary, in order to effect their deliverance, and to restore them to their own land. We learn here—1. That nations and armies are in the hand of God, and at his disposal. 2. That his people are dear to his heart, and that it is his purpose to defend them. 3. That the revolutions among nations, the rise of one empire, and the fall of another, are often in order to promote the welfare of his church, to defend it in danger, and deliver it in time of calamity. 4. That his people should put the utmost confidence in God as being able to defend them, and as having formed a purpose to preserve and save them. Expressions similar to those used in this verse occur frequently among the Arabians (see Rosenmüller *in loco*). ¶ *For thy life.* Marg. 'Person.' Heb. 'For thy soul;' that is, on account of thee; or in thy place (see Notes on ver. 3).

5. *Fear not* (see Note on ch. xli. 10, 14; comp. ch. xliii. 1). ¶ *I will bring thy seed.* Thy children; thy descendants. The sense is, I will re-collect my scattered people from all parts of the world. The passage appears to have been taken from Deut. xxx. 3, where God promises to gather his people together again if they should be scattered among the nations, and should then repent. Vitringa understands this of the *spiritual* descendants of the Jews, or of those who should believe on the Messiah among the Gentiles, and who should *become* the people of God. But the more natural interpretation is, to refer it to the Jews who were scattered abroad during the exile at Babylon, and as a promise to re-collect them again in their own land. ¶ *From the east,* &c. From all parts of the earth; from all lands where they were scattered. That they were driven to other places than Babylon on the invasion of their land by the Chaldeans, is abundantly manifest in

I will bring thy seed from the east,
and gather thee from the west;
6 I will say to the north, Give
up; and to the south, Keep not
back: bring [a] my sons from far,
and my daughters from the ends
of the earth:
7 *Even* every one that is called
by [b] my name: for I have created
him for my glory, I have formed
him; yea, I have made [c] him.
8 Bring forth the blind [d] people
that have eyes, and the deaf that
have ears.
9 Let all the nations be gathered together, and let the people
be assembled: who among them
can declare this, and show us former things? let them bring forth
their witnesses that they may be
justified: or let them hear, and
say, *It is* truth.

a ch.18.7. b Ja.2.7. c Ep.2.10. d Eze.12.2.

the historical records (Jer. ix. 16; Eze. v. 12; xvii. 21; Amos ix. 9; Zech. ii. 6).

6. *I will say to the north, Give up.* Give up my people, or restore them to their own land. ¶ *Bring my sons,* &c. Bring all my people from the distant lands where they have been driven in their dispersion. This is a beautiful passage. As if all lands were under the control of God, and he could at once command and they would obey, he calls on them to yield up his people to their own country. He issues a commandment which is heard in all quarters of the globe, and the scattered people of God come flocking again to their own land.

7. *Every one that is called by my name.* To be called by the name of any one, is synonymous with being regarded as his son, since a son bears the name of his father (see ch. xliv. 5; xlviii. 1). The expression, therefore, means here, all who were regarded as the children of God; and the promise is, that all such should be re-gathered to their own land. ¶ *For I have created him* (see Note on ver. 1). ¶ *For my glory.* In order to show forth, and illustrate my glory. They shall be, therefore, defended and protected; and my glory shall be shown in their recovery and salvation.

8. *Bring forth the blind people.* Many have understood this of the Jews. So Vitringa, Rosenmüller, Grotius, and others understand it. But Lowth, more correctly, regards it as referring to the Gentiles. It is designed as an argument to show the superiority of God over all idols, and to demonstrate that he was able to deliver his people from captivity and exile. He appeals, therefore (ver. 9), to his own people in proof of his divinity and power. None of the heathen (ver. 8) had been able to predict future events, none of the heathen gods, therefore, could save; but JEHOVAH, who had so often foretold events that were fulfilled, *was* able to deliver, and of that fact his own people had had abundant evidence. ¶ *That have eyes.* They had natural faculties to see and know God (comp. Rom. i. 20), but they had not improved them, and they had, therefore, run into the sin and folly of idolatry. The phrase 'bring forth,' implies a solemn appeal made by God to them to enter into an argument on the subject (comp. Note on ch. xli. 1).

9. *Let all the nations be gathered together.* Let them be assembled to give evidence, or to adduce proofs that their idols are worthy of confidence (ch. xli. 1). ¶ *Who among them can declare this?* Who among them *hath* predicted this state of things? Who has foretold the events which are now occurring? It is implied here, that JEHOVAH *had* done this, but none of the heathen gods had done it (see Note on ch. xli. 21). ¶ *And show us former things* (see Note on ch. xli. 22). The *order* of events, the manner in which one event shall succeed another. Not merely, who can declare *one single event,* but who can declare the *succession,* the *order* in which many events shall follow each other—a far more difficult thing than to declare one single future event. Neither had been done by the heathen; both had been done by God. ¶ *That they may be justified.* That it may be demonstrated that they are what they pretend to be, and that they are worthy of the confi-

10 Ye [a] *are* my witnesses, saith
the LORD, and my servant [b] whom
I have chosen: that ye may know
and believe me, and understand
that I *am* he: before me [c] there was
no [1] God formed, neither shall there
be after me.

11 I, *even* I, *am* the LORD; and
beside me *there* is no [d] Saviour.

12 I have declared and have
saved, and I have showed, when
there was no strange *god* among
you: therefore ye *are* my witnesses,
saith the LORD, that I *am* God.

a ch.44.8. b Ph.2.7. c Col.1.17. 1 or, *nothing formed of God.* d Ho.13.4; Ac.4.12.

dence of men. The word 'justified' here, is used in the sense of being *right*, or *true*;—let them in this manner show that their claims are just, and well founded. ¶ *Or let them hear, and say,* It is *truth* (see Note on ch. xli. 26).

10. *Ye* are *my witnesses.* They were his witnesses, because, first, he had given to them predictions of future events which had been literally fulfilled: secondly, by his power of delivering them so often manifested, he had shown that he was a God able to save. Neither of these had been done by the idol-gods (comp. ch. xliv. 8). ¶ *And believe me.* Or rather, confide in me. ¶ *Before me there was no God formed.* I am the only true, the eternal God. In this expression, JEHOVAH says that he was the *first* being. He derived his existence from no one. Perhaps the Hebrew will bear a little more emphasis than is conveyed by our translation. 'Before me, God was not formed,' implying that *he* was God, and that he existed anterior to all other beings. It was an opinion among the Greeks, that the same gods had not always reigned, but that the more ancient divinities had been expelled by the more modern. It is possible that some such opinion may have prevailed in the oriental idolatry, and that God here means to say, in opposition to that, that he had not *succeeded* any other God in his kingdom. His dominion was original, underived, and independent. ¶ *Neither shall there be after me.* He would never cease to live; he would never vacate his throne for another. This expression is equivalent to that which occurs in the Book of Revelation, 'I am Alpha and Omega, the first and the last' (Rev. i. 11); and it is remarkable that this language, which obviously implies eternity, and which in Isaiah is used expressly to prove the divinity of JEHOVAH, is, in the passage referred to in the Book of Revelation, applied no less unequivocally to the Lord Jesus Christ.

11. *I,* even *I,* am *the* LORD. The repetition of the pronoun 'I' makes it emphatic. The design is, to affirm that there was no other being to whom the name 'JEHOVAH' appertained. There was no other one who had the attributes which the name involved; there was, therefore, no other God. On the meaning of the word JEHOVAH, see Note on ch. i. 2. ¶ *And beside me* there *is no Saviour.* There is no one who can deliver from oppression, and captivity, and exile, such as the Jews suffered in Babylon; there is no one but he who can save from sin, and from hell. All salvation, therefore, must come from God; and if we obtain deliverance from temporal ills, or from eternal death, we must seek it from him.

12. *I have declared.* I have announced or predicted future events; I have warned of danger; I have marked out the path of safety. He had thus shown that he was the true God (see Note on ch. xli. 22, 23). ¶ *And have saved.* I have delivered the nation in former times of danger, and have thus shown that I would protect them. ¶ *And have showed.* Heb. 'Caused to hear.' I have made known future events, and have thus showed that I was God. ¶ *When* there was *no strange* god *among you.* Before the time when there was any idol in the nation, and when, therefore, it could not be pretended that deliverance was to be traced to any one but to JEHOVAH. The word 'god' here is not in the original, but is properly supplied. The word זָר is evidently used instead of אֵל זָר, as in Ps. xliv. 20; lxxxi. 9. It denotes a god that is worshipped by foreigners. The sense is, that their former deliverance

13 Yea, before the day *was*, I
am he; and *there is* none that can
deliver out of my hand: I will work,
and who [a]shall [1]let it?
14 Thus saith the LORD, your
Redeemer, the Holy One of Israel;
For your sake I have sent to Babylon, and have brought down all their
nobles,[2] and the Chaldeans, whose
cry *is* in the ships.

a ch.46.10. 1 turn it back. 2 bars.

could in no sense be traced to any such foreign god. ¶ *Therefore, ye* are *my witnesses.* You who have so often been defended; you who have the predictions respecting future events, can be appealed to as evidence that I am the only true God, able to deliver. The doctrine taught in this passage is, that God may appeal to his dealings with his people as a demonstration that he is the true God, and that he is faithful and able to deliver—an appeal which may be made to his church at large in view of its trials, persecutions, and deliverances; and to every one who is his true friend and worshipper.

13. *Yea, before the day* was. Before the first day, or before the beginning of time; from eternity. The LXX. render it correctly, 'Απ' ἀρχῆς, and the Vulgate (*Ab initio*), 'From the beginning.' ¶ *I* am *he.* I am the same (ver. 10). ¶ *I will work.* I will accomplish my designs. ¶ *And who shall let it?* Marg. as Heb. 'Turn it back.' The meaning is, 'Who can hinder it?' And the doctrine taught here is—1. That God is from everlasting; for if he was before *time,* he must have been eternal. 2. That he is unchangeably the same—a doctrine which is, as it is here designed to be used, the only sure foundation for the security of his people—for who can trust a being who is fickle, changing, vacillating? 3. That he can deliver his people always, no matter what are their circumstances. 4. That he will accomplish all his plans; no matter whether to save his people, or to destroy his foes. 5. That no one—man or devil—can hinder him. How can the feeble arm of a creature resist God? 6. That opposition to him is as fruitless as it is wicked. If men wish for happiness, they must *fall in* with his plans, and aid in the furtherance of his designs.

14. *Thus saith the* LORD *your Redeemer.* This verse commences another argument for the safety of his people. It is the assurance to the Jews in Babylon that he had sent to them a deliverer, and would bring down the pride of the Chaldeans, and demolish their city. ¶ *Your Redeemer* (see Note on ver. 1). ¶ *I have sent to Babylon.* That is, the Persians and Medes, under the command of Cyrus (comp. Note on ch. xiii. 3). This implies that God had command over all their armies and had the power of sending them where he pleased (comp. Notes on ch. x. 5, 6). This is to be understood as seen by the prophet in vision. He sees the armies of Cyrus encompass Babylon and the haughty city fall, and then says that God had sent or directed them there. ¶ *And have brought down all their nobles.* Marg. 'Bars.' But the word in this place probably means neither, but rather *fugitives* (comp. Notes on ch. xxvii. 1). The word used (בָּרִיחַ, *bâriăhh*) means sometimes *bar, cross-bar,* that which passed from one side of the tabernacle to the other through rings, in order to carry it; then a bar, or bolt of any kind (Judg. xvi. 3; Neh. iii. 3). But the word may also denote one who flies; a fugitive; and is properly used in that sense here. The verb בָּרַח, from which the word is derived, means often *to break away, to flee* (Gen. xvi. 8; xxxv. 1, 7; 1 Sam. xix. 12; Job xxvii. 22; Jonah i. 3). Here it means those who endeavoured to escape from the impending calamity and destruction; or it *may* refer to those who had taken refuge in Babylon from other lands, as Babylon was doubtless composed in part of those who had sought a refuge there from other nations—a conflux of strangers. But the former is the more probable interpretation; and the idea seems to be, that JEHOVAH had brought them down to their ships, or had led them to take refuge in their ships from the impending judgments. Jerome, however, understands it of removing the strong bars with which the prisoners of the exile Jews were protected, so that they

15 I *am* the LORD, your Holy One, the Creator of Israel, your King.

16 Thus saith the LORD, which maketh [a] a way in the sea, and a path in the mighty waters:

a Ex.14.16,22; Ps.77.19.

---

would be permitted to go forth in peace and safety. Lowth renders it, 'I will bring down all her strong bars.' The LXX. render it, Φεύγοντες πάντας—'All that fly.' So the Syriac. ¶ *And the Chaldeans.* The inhabitants of Babylon. ¶ *Whose cry* is *in the ships.* Lowth renders this, 'Exulting in their ships.' Noyes, 'Ships of their delight.' The Vulgate, 'Glorying in their ships.' The LXX. 'The Chaldeans shall be bound (δεθήσονται) in ships.' The Syriac, 'Who glory in their ships.' The sense is, probably, that the Chaldeans, when their city was taken, would seek to take refuge in their ships in which they would raise a shout (Rosenmüller). Or it may be, as Lowth supposes, that it was one of the characteristics of the Chaldeans, that they boasted of their ships, and of their commerce. Babylon was, as he remarks, favourably situated to be a commercial and naval power. It was on the large river Euphrates, and hence had access to the Persian Gulf and the ocean; and there can be no doubt that it was engaged, in the height of its power, in commercial enterprises. On the north of the city, the Euphrates was united to the Tigris by the canal called Nahar Malca or the Royal River, and thus a large part of the produce of the northern countries, as far as the Euxine and Caspian seas, naturally descended to Babylon (Herod. i. 194). Semiramis, the founder of Babylon, is said to have had a fleet of three thousand galleys. After the taking of the city by Cyrus, we hear indeed little of the commerce of Babylon. The Euphrates was diverted from its course, and spread over the adjacent country; and the Persian monarchs, in order to prevent the danger of invasion from that quarter, purposely obstructed the navigation, by making dams across both the Tigris and the Euphrates (Strabo xvi.) It is not to be deemed remarkable, therefore, that, in the times of its prosperity, the city of Babylon should be noted for its commerce; or as a city exulting in its shipping, or raising the sailor's cry—a cry such as is heard in any port now where shipping abounds. The word rendered 'cry' (רִנָּה) denotes properly *a shout of rejoicing* or joy (1 Kings xxii. 36; Ps. xxxi. 6; xlii. 5); and then also a mournful cry, an outcry, wailing (Ps. xvii. 1; lxi. 2). Here it may mean the joyful cry of commerce; the shout of the mariner as he leaves the port, or as he returns to his home—the shout, the clamour, which is heard at the wharfs of a commercial city. Such a cry is alluded to by Virgil in the naval games which Æneas celebrated:—

—— ferit athera clamor
Nauticus. *Æneid*, v. 140, 1.

The sense here is, that God had sent to bring down that exulting city, and to destroy all the indications of its commercial importance and prosperity.

15. *I* am *the* LORD. I am JEHOVAH—proved to be such, as the connection demands that we should interpret this, by sending to Babylon and bringing down your oppressors. This interposition in destroying Babylon would be a demonstration that he was JEHOVAH, the only true God, and their God. ¶ *The Creator of Israel* (see Note on ver. 1). ¶ *Your King.* Ruling over you, and showing the right to do it by delivering you from your foes.

16. *Thus saith the* LORD. This verse contains a reference to the deliverance from Egyptian servitude—the great storehouse of argument and illustration with the sacred writers; the standing demonstration of God's merciful interposition in behalf of their nation, and proof that he was their God. ¶ *Which maketh.* Whose characteristic it is to open a path of safety for his people even when deep and rapid floods are before them. The standing proof of this, which undoubtedly the prophet had in his eye, was the deliverance from Egypt. Still, I think, he did not mean to refer to that alone, but to that as an illustration of what God was, and had ever been to his people. ¶ *A way in the sea.* Referring to the path made through the waters

17 Which bringeth forth the
chariot and horse, the army, and
the power; they shall lie down
together, they shall not rise: they
are extinct, they are quenched as
tow.
18 Remember ye not the former
things, neither consider the things
of old.
19 Behold, I will do a new thing:
now it shall spring forth; shall ye
not know it? I will even make a
way in the wilderness, *and* rivers
in the desert.
20 The beast of the field shall
honour me, the dragons and the
owls:[1] because I gave waters in
the wilderness, *and* rivers in the
desert, to give drink to my people,
my chosen.

1 *daughters of the owl*, or, *ostriches*.

of the Red Sea when the children of Israel were permitted to go on dry ground.

17. *Which bringeth forth the chariot and horse.* The reference here is, undoubtedly, to the occurrences which are recorded in Ex. xiv. 4, *sq.*, when Pharaoh and his host are said to have followed the Israelites, but were all submerged in the sea. God is said to have brought them forth in accordance with the general statement so often made, that he controls and directs princes and nations (see Notes on ch. x. 5, 6). ¶ *They shall lie down together.* They shall sink together to death, as Pharaoh and his army sunk together in a watery grave.

> Thou didst blow with thy wind, the sea covered them:
> They sank as lead in the mighty waters.
> Ex. xv. 10.

> The depths have covered them:
> They sank into the bottom as a stone.
> Ex. xv. 5.

¶ *They are extinct.* They are destroyed, as the wick of a lamp is quenched suddenly when immersed in water. This is a striking figure, to denote the suddenness with which it was done, and the completeness of their destruction. As a flame is entirely put out when plunged beneath the water, so the whole host of the Egyptians were suddenly and completely destroyed in the Red Sea. The sentiment in this verse is, that God has power over the nations to control them; that it is one of his characteristics to lead on the enemies of his people to destruction; and that they are suddenly destroyed, and their hopes, and joys, and triumphs put out for ever. If it was so in regard to the Egyptians, it will be also in regard to all his foes. And if this took place in regard to a nation, it shall also in regard to individual sinners who oppose themselves to God.

> How oft is the candle of the wicked put out?
> And how oft cometh their destruction upon them?
> God distributeth sorrows in his anger.
> They are as stubble before the wind,
> And as chaff that the storm carrieth away.
> Job xxi. 17, 18.

18. *Remember ye not, &c.* So great and wonderful shall be God's future interpositions in your behalf, that what he has done, great as that was, shall be comparatively forgotten. ¶ *The former things.* The deliverance from Egypt, and the overthrow of his enemies there. ¶ *The things of old.* The things that were formerly done.

19. *I will do a new thing.* Something that has not hitherto occurred, some unheard of and wonderful event, that shall far surpass all that he had formerly done (see Note on ch. xlii. 9). ¶ *Now it shall spring forth* (see Note on ch. xlii. 9). It shall spring up as the grass does from the earth; or it shall *bud forth* like the opening leaves and flowers—a beautiful figure, denoting the manner in which the events of Divine Providence come to pass. ¶ *I will even make a way in the wilderness.* In this part of the verse, the prophet describes the anxious care which God would show in protecting his people, and providing for them in conducting them to their native land. See the expressions fully explained in the Notes on ch. xli. 17–19.

20. *The beast of the field shall honour me.* The sense of this passage is plain, and the image is highly poetical and beautiful. God would pour such copious floods of waters through the waste sandy deserts to supply his people, that even the wild beasts would be sensible of his

21 This people have I formed
for myself; they shall [a] show forth
my praise.
22 But thou hast not called upon
me, O Jacob; but thou hast been
weary [b] of me, O Israel.
23 Thou hast not brought me the
small [1] cattle of thy burnt-offerings;
neither hast thou honoured me with
thy sacrifices: I have not caused
thee to [c] serve with an offering, nor
wearied thee with incense.

a Ep.1.6,12. b Mal.1.13. 1 lambs, or, kids. c Mat. 11.30.

abundant goodness, and would break forth into thanksgiving and praise for the unusual supply. ¶ *The dragons* (see Note on ch. xiii. 22). The LXX. render the word here used (תַּנִּים *tănnīm*), by σειρῆνες—'sirens'—among the ancients a marine monster that was fabled to use sweet and alluring tones of music. It is probable, however, that the LXX. understood here some species of wild-fowl which responded to one another. The Syriac translator here interprets it as denoting some wild animal of the canine species—a wood-dog. ¶ *And the owls.* Marg. as Heb. 'Daughters of the owl, or ostrich' (see Note on ch. xiii. 21).

21. *This people have I formed for myself.* To preserve the remembrance of my name; to transmit the knowledge of the true God to future times, and to celebrate my praise (see Notes on ver. 1). ¶ *They shall show forth my praise.* They shall celebrate my goodness; or, by their restoration to their own land, they shall show manifestly that they are my people.

22. *But thou hast not called upon me.* The design of this and the following verses, is to show them that they were indebted to the Divine mercy alone for their deliverance from bondage. It was not because they had been either meritorious or faithful; it was not because they had deserved these favours at his hand; for they had been a people that had been distinguished for neglecting their God. On that account, these calamities had come upon them, and their deliverance, therefore, was to be an act of mere unmerited favour. ¶ *Thou hast been weary.* As a people, you have been weary of my service. They had accounted his laws grievous and oppressive; and they had groaned under what they regarded as burdensome rites and ceremonies (see Amos viii. 5, 6; Mal. i. 13). God here refers, doubtless, to the times before the captivity, and is stating what was the general characteristic of the people.

23. *Thou hast not brought me.* As a people you have withheld from me the sacrifices which were commanded. They had not maintained and observed his worship as he had required. ¶ *The small cattle.* Marg. 'Lambs,' or 'kids.' The Hebrew word (שֶׂה) denotes properly one of a flock—a sheep or a goat. It should have been so rendered here. These animals were used for burnt-offerings, and the Jews were required to offer them daily to God. ¶ *Of thy burnt-offerings* (comp. Ex. xxix. 38; Num. xxviii. 3). The burnt-offering was wholly consumed on the altar. ¶ *With thy sacrifices.* Bloody offerings. There is little difference between this word and that rendered 'burnt-offerings.' If there is any, it is that the word rendered 'sacrifice' (זֶבַח) is of wider signification, and expresses sacrifice in general; the word rendered 'burnt-offering' (עֹלָה), denotes that which is consumed, or which *ascends* as an offering. The holocaust refers to its being burned; the sacrifice to the offering, however made. ¶ *I have not caused thee to serve with an offering.* 'I have not made *a slave* of thee; I have not exacted such a service as would be oppressive and intolerable—such as is imposed on a slave.' The word here used (עָבַד), is often used in such a sense, and with such a reference (Lev. xxv. 39); 'Thou shalt not compel him to serve the service of a bondman' (Ex. i. 14; Jer. xxii. 13; xxv. 14; xxx. 8). The sense is, that the laws of God on the subject, were not grievous and oppressive. ¶ *With an offering.* The word here used (מִנְחָה *mĭnhhâ*) denotes properly a *bloodless* oblation, and is thus distinguished from those mentioned before. It consisted of flour mingled with salt, oil, and incense; or of the fruits of

24 Thou hast bought me no sweet cane with money, neither hast thou [1] filled me with the fat of thy sacrifices: but thou hast made me to serve with thy sins, thou hast wearied [a] me with thine iniquities.

1 *made me drunk*, or, *abundantly moistened*.
a Mal.1.17.

the earth, &c. (see Notes on ch. i. 11; comp. Lev. ii. 2; Num. xxviii. 5.) ¶ *Nor wearied thee.* By exacting incense. I have not so exacted it as to make it burdensome and wearisome to you. ¶ *With incense* (see Note on ch. i. 13). The word לְבוֹנָה (Gr. λίβανος) denotes properly *frankincense*, a substance so called from its white colour, from לָבַן, *to be white.* It is found in Arabia (Isa. lx. 6; Jer. vi. 20), and in Palestine (Cant. iv. 6, 14), and was obtained by making incisions in the bark of trees. It was much used in worship among the Jews as well as by other nations. It was *burned* in order to produce an agreeable fragrance (Ex. xxx. 8; xxxvii. 29; Lev. xvi. 13).

24. *Thou hast bought me.* You have not purchased this—implying that it was not produced in Palestine, but was an article of commerce. It was to be obtained only from abroad. This is expressly affirmed in Jer. vi. 20: 'To what purpose cometh there to me incense from Sheba, *and the sweet cane from a far country?*' That it was an article of commerce is also apparent from Ezek. xxvii. 19: 'Dan also and Javan going to and fro occupied in thy fairs (*i.e.* Tyre): bright iron, cassia, and calamus (קָנֶה), were in thy market.' ¶ *Sweet cane.* The word here used (קָנֶה), denotes properly *cane, reed, calamus* (Gr. κάννα and κάννη, Latin *canna*, whence the English *cane*, Fr. *canne*, It. *canna*). It usually refers to a reed growing in wet or marshy ground. It denotes also sweet cane, *calamus aromaticus.* It is sometimes joined with the word בֹּשֶׂם (*bōsĕm*), aromatic, odour, fragrance, spice, as in Ex. xxx. 23; see also Jer. vi. 20. According to Pliny (xii. 22) it grew in Arabia, Syria, and India; according to Theophrastus, in the vales of Lebanon (*Hist. Plant.* ix. 7). It was used among the Hebrews in compounding the sacred perfumes (Ex. xxx. 23). It is a knotty root, of a reddish colour, and contains a soft white pith—in resemblance probably not unlike the calamus so well known in this country. Strabo and Diodorus Siculus say that it grew in Saba. Hasselquist says that it is common in the deserts of the two Arabias. It is gathered near Jambo, a port town of Arabia Petrea, from whence it is brought into Egypt. The Venetians purchase it, and use it in the composition of their *theriaca.* It is much esteemed among the Arabs on account of its fragrance. *See* Calmet (Art. *Cane*), and Gesenius (*Lex.* and *Comm. in loco*). It was not probably used in the worship of God anywhere except among the Hebrews. The heathens made use of incense, but I do not know that they used the calamus. ¶ *Neither hast thou filled me.* Marg. 'Made me drunk,' or 'abundantly moistened.' The word here used (רָוָה *râvâ*), means properly *to drink to the full*, to be satisfied, sated with drink. See it explained in the Notes on ch. xxxiv. 6. It is applied to water which is drank, or to *fat* which is sucked in or drank rather than eaten (Ps. xxxvi. 9); or to a sword as drinking up blood. Here it means to satiate, or to satisfy. They had not offered the fat of sacrifices so as to satiate God. Probably this passage does not mean that the Jews had wholly neglected the public worship of God; they had not worshipped him with a proper spirit, and had thus served him with their sins, and wearied him with their transgressions. It is true, also, that while they were abundant in external rites and ceremonies, they frequently made oblations to idols, rather than to the true God. Perhaps, therefore, an emphasis is to be placed on the word 'me' in this passage, meaning, that however diligent and regular they had been in the performance of the external rites and duties of religion, yet that *God* had been neglected. ¶ *Thou hast made me to serve with thy sins.* You have made it oppressive, burdensome, wearisome for me, like the hard and onerous service of a

25 I, *even* I, *am* he that blotteth out [a]thy transgressions for mine own [b]sake, and will not remember thy [c]sins.

26 Put me in remembrance: let us plead together: declare thou, that thou mayest be [d]justified.

a Je.50.20. b Eze 36.22,32. c Je.31.34. d Ro.8.33.

slave (see Note on ver. 23; comp. Note on ch. i. 14).

25. *I,* even *I,* am *he.* This verse contains a gracious assurance that their sins would be blotted out, and the reason why it would be done. The pronoun 'I' is repeated to make it emphatic, as in ver. 11. Perhaps also God designs to show them the evil of the sins which are mentioned in the previous verses, by the assurance that they were committed against him who alone could forgive, and who had promised them pardon. The passage also reminds them, that it was God alone who *could* pardon the sins of which, as a nation, they had been guilty. ¶ *That blotteth out thy transgressions.* This metaphor is taken from the custom of keeping accounts, where, when a debt is paid, the charge is blotted or cancelled. Thus God says he blotted out the sins of the Jews. He cancelled them. He forgave them. Of course, when forgiven, punishment could not be exacted, and he would treat them as pardoned; *i.e.*, as his friends. ¶ *For mine own sake.* Not because you deserve it, or have any claim, or that it would not be right to punish you. Not even primarily to promote your happiness and salvation, but for *my* sake; 1. To show the benevolence of my character; 2. To promote my glory by your forgiveness and salvation (see Ezek. xxxvi. 22). ¶ *And will not remember thy sins.* They shall be forgiven. Hezekiah (xxxviii. 17) expresses the same idea by saying 'thou hast cast all my sins behind thy back.' We may learn from this verse—1. That it is God only who can pardon sin. How vain, then, is it for man to attempt it! How wicked for man to claim the prerogative! And yet it is an essential part of the papal system that the Pope and his priests have the power of remitting the penalty of transgression. 2. That this is done by God *solely* for his own sake. It is not (*a.*) because we have any *claim* to it; for then it would not be pardon, but justice. It is not (*b.*) because we have any power to compel God to forgive; for who can contend with him, and how could mere *power* procure pardon? It is not (*c.*) because we have any *merit*; for *then* also it would be justice, and we *have* no merit. Nor is it (*d.*) primarily in order that we may be happy; for our happiness is a matter not worthy to be named, compared with the honour of God. But it is solely for his own sake—to promote his glory—to show his perfections—to evince the greatness of his mercy and compassion—and to show his boundless and eternal love. 3. They who *are* pardoned should live to his glory, and not to themselves. For *that* they were forgiven, and it should be the grand purpose of their lives so to live as to show forth the goodness, compassion, and love of that merciful Being who has blotted out their sins. 4. If men are ever pardoned, they must come to God—and to God alone. They must come, not to *justify* themselves, but to confess their crimes. And they must come with a willingness that God should pardon them on just such terms as he pleases; at just such a time as he pleases; *and solely with a view to the promotion of his own glory.* Unless they have this feeling, they never *can* be forgiven, nor *should* they be forgiven.

26. *Put me in remembrance.* That is, urge all the arguments in your own defence which you can urge. State everything in self-vindication which can be stated. The language here is taken from the practice of courts when a cause is on trial; and God urges them on *their* side, to urge all in self-vindication which they can urge. On *his* part, he alleged that the princes and rulers of the nation had sinned (ver. 27); that the whole nation had transgressed (ver. 23, 24), and that for this they were justly punished (ver. 28). He here urges them to advance all in self-defence which they could—if they could pretend that He had forgotten anything; that they had merits which he had not considered; or that he had charged them with crime

27 Thy first father hath sinned, and thy [1]teachers have transgressed against me.

[1] interpreters.

with undue severity. ¶ *Let us plead together*. Heb. 'Let us be judged together' (see Note on ch. xli. 1). ¶ *Declare thou, that thou mayest be justified*. That you may show that you are just, or righteous; that you may demonstrate that you are unjustly accused of crime, and punished with undue severity.

27. *Thy first father hath sinned*. This is the argument on the side of God, to show that they were neither unjustly punished, nor punished with undue severity. The argument is, that their rulers and teachers had been guilty of crime, and that therefore it was right to bring all this vengeance upon the nation. Various interpretations have been given of the phrase 'thy first father.' A slight notice of them will lead to the correct exposition. 1. Many have supposed that *Adam* is here referred to. Thus Piscator, Calovius, and most of the fathers, understand it; and, among the Jews, Kimchi. But the objections to this are plain. (*a*.) Adam was not peculiarly the first father or ancestor of the Jews, but of the whole human race. (*b*.) The Jews never boasted, or gloried in him as the founder of their nation, but they always referred to Abraham under this appellation (Mat. iii. 9; John viii. 33, 39). (*c*.) It would have been irrelevant to the design of the prophet to have referred to the sin of Adam in this case. God was vindicating his own cause and conduct in destroying their capital and temple, and in sending them as captives to a distant land. How would it prove that he was right in this, to say that Adam was a transgressor? How would it demonstrate his justice *in these peculiar inflictions* of his anger to refer to the apostacy of the ancestor of the whole human race? 2. Others refer it to Abraham. This was the sentiment of Jerome, and of some others; and by those who maintain this opinion, it is supposed to refer to his doubting the truth of the promise (Gen. xv. 8); or to the denial of his wife, and his sin in inducing her to say that she was his sister (Gen. xii. 11; xx. 2); or to the fact that when young he was an idolater. But the obvious objection to this is, that Abraham is everywhere in the Scriptures proposed as an example of one eminently devoted to God; nor could it be said that these calamities had come upon them in consequence of his unfaithfulness, and his sins. 3. Others refer it to the rulers and princes individually. Thus Grotius refers it to Manasseh; Aben Ezra to Jeroboam, &c. 4. Others, as Vitringa, refer it to the high priest, and particularly to Uriah, who lived in the time of Ahaz, and particularly to the fact, that, in obedience to the command of Ahaz, he constructed an altar in Jerusalem like the one which he had seen and admired in Damascus (2 Kings xvi. 10–16). The objection to this interpretation is, that no reason can be given for selecting *this* particular act from a number of similar abominations on the part of the priests and rulers, as the cause of the national calamities. It was only one instance out of many of the crimes which brought the national judgments upon them. 5. Others, as Gesenius, suppose that the word is to be taken *collectively*, not as referring to any particular individual, but to the high priests in general. It is not uncommon to give the name 'father' thus to a principal man among a people, and especially to one eminent in religious authority. The word 'first' here does not refer to *time*, but to *rank;* not the ancestor of the people, but the one having appropriately the title of father, who had the priority also in rank. The LXX. render it, Οἱ πατέρες ὑμῶν πρῶτοι. It refers therefore, probably, to the character of the presiding officers in religion, and means that the priests, supreme in rank, and whose example was so important, had sinned; that there was irreligion at the very foundation of influence and authority; and that therefore it was necessary to bring these heavy judgments on the nation. No one acquainted with the history of the Jewish people in the times immediately preceding the captivity, can doubt that this was the character of the high priesthood.

[Gesenius and some others give the words a

28 Therefore I have profaned the princes[1] of the sanctuary, and have given Jacob to the curse, and Israel to reproaches.

1 or, *holy princes.*

collective sense, as signifying either the succession of priests or ancestors in general. The interpretation which understands the phrase of Abraham, is supposed by some to be at variance with the uniform mention of that patriarch in terms of commendation. But these terms are perfectly consistent with the proposition that *he was a sinner*, which may here be the exact sense of חֹטֵא. To the application of the phrase to Adam, it has been objected, that he was not peculiarly the father of the Jews. To this it may be answered, that if the guilt of the national progenitor would prove the point in question, much more would it be established by the fact of their belonging to a guilty race. At the same time it may be considered as implied, that all their fathers, who had since lived, shared in the original depravity; and thus the same sense is obtained that would have been expressed by the collective explanation of *first father*, while the latter is still taken in its strict and full sense, as denoting the progenitor of all mankind.—Alexander.]

¶ *And thy teachers.* Marg. 'Interpreters.' The word here used (מְלִצֶיךָ) is derived from לוּץ. This word means *to stammer*, to speak unintelligibly; and then to speak in a foreign and barbarous language, and then to interpret, from the idea of speaking a foreign tongue. Hence it may be used in the sense of an *internuncius*, or a messenger (2 Chron. xxxii. 31; comp. Notes on Job xxxiii. 23). That it refers here to the priests, there can be no doubt, and is properly applied to them because they sustained the office of *interpreting* his will to the people, and generally of acting as *internuncii* or messengers between God and them. The LXX. render it, Ἄρχοντες —'Rulers.'

28. *Therefore I have profaned.* The princes of the sanctuary, *i.e.*, the priests, were by their office regarded as sacred, or set apart to the service of God. To depose them from that office, to subject them to punishment, and to send them into captivity, was, therefore, regarded as *profaning* them. They were stripped of their office, and robes, and honours, and reduced to the same condition, and compelled to meet with the same treatment, as the common people. The sense is, that he *had made them common* (for so the word חָלַל is used in Ex. xxxi. 14; xix. 22; Lev. xix. 8; xxi. 9; Mal. i. 12; ii. 2); he did not regard their office; he used them all alike. ¶ *The princes of the sanctuary.* Marg. 'Holy princes.' It means, either those who presided over and directed the services of the sanctuary, called in 1 Chron. xxiv. 5, 'governors of the sanctuary;' or those who were holy in office. The LXX. render it, Οἱ ἄρχοντες τὰ ἅγια μου —'Who preside over my holy things,' or my sanctuary. Vulg. *Principes sanctos*—'Holy princes.' The Syriac, 'Thy princes have profaned the sanctuary.' The sense is, that God had disregarded the official character of those who were set apart to the sacred office, and had punished them in common with the people at large for their sins. ¶ *And have given Jacob to the curse.* The LXX. render it, 'I have given Jacob to be destroyed' (ἀπωλέσαι). The Hebrew word here (חֵרֶם *hhērĕm*), is that which is commonly used to denote a solemn *anathema*, excommunication, or devotion to destruction (see Note on ch. xxxiv. 5). ¶ *To reproaches.* The reproach, contempt, and scorn which they met with in their captivity, and in a land of strangers (comp. Ps. cxxxvii. 3, 4).

Thus far God states the reasons why he had punished the nation. It had been on account of the national irreligion and sins, and the destruction had come upon all, but pre-eminently on the priests and the rulers. In the arbitrary division which is made in the Bible into chapters, a very improper separation has been made by making the chapter close here. The sense of the whole passage is materially injured by this division, and the scope of the whole argument is forgotten. The design of the entire argument is, to show that God would not leave his people; that though he punished them, he would not utterly destroy them; and that he would appear again for their rescue, and restore them to their own land. This argument is prosecuted in the

CHAPTER XLIV.

ANALYSIS.

It has already been observed (Note on ch. xliii. 28), that the commencement of this chapter is properly a continuation and completion of the argument commenced there; and that the division should have been made at what is now the close of the fifth verse of this chapter. This chapter may be divided into the following parts:—

I. The assurance that though they had sinned (ch. xliii. 23–28) God would have mercy on them, and would restore them to his favour, and to their land (1–5). They had nothing to fear (1, 2): God would bless their offspring, and they should grow and flourish like willows by the waters (3–5), and there should be among them a general turning to the LORD, and devotion to his service (5).

II. An argument to show that JEHOVAH was the true God; and a severe and most sarcastic reproof of idolatry—designed to reprove idolaters, and to lead the people to put their confidence in JEHOVAH (6–20). This argument consists of the following parts—1. A solemn assertion of JEHOVAH himself, that there was no other God (6). 2. An appeal to the fact that he only had foretold future events, and that he only could do it (7, 8). 3. A sarcastic statement of the manner in which idols were made, and of course, the folly of worshipping them (9–20).

III. The assurance that JEHOVAH would deliver his people from all their calamities and oppressions (21–28). This part contains—1. The *assurance* that he would do it, and that their sins were blotted out (21, 22). 2. A calling upon the heavens and the earth to rejoice over so great and glorious an event (23). 3. An appeal to what JEHOVAH *had* done, and *could* do, as an evidence that he could deliver his people, to wit: he had formed the heavens—he had made the earth without aid—he made diviners mad—he frustrated the plans of the wise, and he had confirmed the promises which he had made by his servants (24–26); he said to Jerusalem that it should be inhabited, and the cities of Judah that they should be rebuilt; he had dried up the rivers; and he had raised up Cyrus for the express purpose of delivering his people (26–28); and by all this, it should be known that he would visit, and vindicate, and restore them.

YET now hear, O Jacob, my servant; and Israel, whom I have chosen:

2 Thus saith the LORD that made thee, and formed thee from the womb, *which* will help [a] thee; Fear not, O Jacob, my servant; and thou, [b] Jeshurun, [c] whom I have chosen.

a Ps.46.5; He.4.16. *b* De.32.15. *c* Ro.8.30.

following chapter; and in the commencement of that chapter the thought is pursued, that though God had thus punished them, yet he would appear and save them. The beginning of that chapter is properly the continuation and completion of the argument urged here, and *this* chapter should have closed at what is now the fifth verse of chapter xliv.

CHAPTER XLIV.

1. *Yet now hear.* This should be read in immediate connection with the previous chapter. 'Notwithstanding you have sinned, *yet* now hear the gracious promise which is made in regard to your deliverance.'

2. *Thus saith the* LORD *that made thee* (see Note on ch. xliii. 1). ¶ *And formed thee from the womb.* This is equivalent to the declaration that he was their Maker, or Creator. It means, that from the very beginning of their history as a people, he had formed and moulded all their institutions, and directed all things in regard to them—as much as he is the former of the body from the commencement of its existence. It may be observed that the words, 'from the womb,' are joined by some interpreters with the phrase, 'that formed thee,' meaning, that he had been the originator of all their customs, privileges, and laws, from the beginning of their history; and by others with the phrase, 'will help thee,' meaning, that from the commencement of their existence as a nation, he had been their helper. According to the Masoretic marks of distinction, the former is the true sense. So the LXX., Aben Ezra, Kimchi, Lowth, &c.; but Jerome, Luther, and some others, prefer the latter mode. ¶ *Fear not* (see Note on ch. xli. 10). Though you have sinned as a people (ch. xliii. 23, 24, 27), and though all these heavy judgments have

3 For [a] I will pour water upon
him that is thirsty, and floods upon
the dry ground; I will pour my
Spirit upon thy seed, [b] and my
blessing upon thine offspring.

a Jn.7.38. b ch.59.21.

---

come upon you (ch. xliii. 28), yet you have no reason to fear that God will finally abandon and destroy you. ¶ *And thou Jeshurun* (וִישֻׁרוּן). This word occurs but four times in the Bible, as a poetical name for the people of Israel, apparently expressing affection and tenderness (Deut. xxxii. 15; xxxiii. 5, 26; and in this place). It is, says Gesenius (*Comm. in loc.*), 'a flattering appellation (*schmeichelwort*) for Israel,' and is probably a diminutive from יָשׁוּר = יָשָׁר *yâshŭr=yâshŏr*, the passive form in an intransitive verb with an active signification. The ending וּן *ôn*, he adds, is *terminatio charitiva*—a termination indicating affection, or kindness. In his *Lexicon*, he observes, however (as translated by Robinson), that 'it seems not improbable that it was a diminutive form of the name יִשְׂרָאֵל (*Israel*), which was current in common life for the fuller form יִשְׂרָאֵלוּן (*Israelun*), a title of affection for Israel, but, like other common words of this sort, contracted, and more freely inflected, so as at the same time to imply an allusion to the signification of *right* or *uprightness*, contained in the root יָשַׁר.' Jerome renders it, *Rectissime*—'Most upright.' The LXX. render it, Ἠγαπημένος Ἰσραὴλ—'Beloved Israel.' The Syriac renders it, 'Israel.' So also the Chaldee. It is, doubtless, a title of affection, and probably includes the notion of uprightness, or integrity.

3. *For I will pour water.* Floods, rivers, streams, and waters, are often used in the Scriptures, and especially in Isaiah, to denote plenteous Divine blessings, particularly the abundant influences of the Holy Spirit (see Note on ch. xxxv. 6, 7). That it here refers to the Holy Spirit and his influences, is proved by the parallel expressions in the subsequent part of the verse. ¶ *Upon him that is thirsty.* Or rather, 'on the thirsty land.' The word צָמֵא refers here rather to land, and the *figure* is taken from a burning sandy desert, where waters would be made to burst out in copious streams (see ch. xxxv. 6, 7). The sense is, that God would bestow blessings upon them as signal and marvellous, as if floods of waters were made to descend on the dry, parched, and desolated earth. ¶ *And floods.* The word נוֹזְלִים, from נָזַל, *to flow*, to run as liquids, means properly *flowings*, and is used for streams and rivers (Ex. xv. 8; Ps. lxxviii. 16; Prov. v. 15; Jer. xviii.) It means here that the spiritual influences which would descend on the afflicted, desolate, comfortless, and exiled people, would be like torrents of rain poured on the thirsty earth. This beautiful figure is common in the Scriptures:

> He shall come down like rain upon the grass,
> And as showers that water the earth.
> Ps. lxxii. 6.

> My doctrine shall drop as the rain
> My speech shall distil as the dew,
> As the small rain upon the tender herb,
> And as the showers upon the grass.
> Deut. xxxii. 2.

¶ *I will pour my Spirit upon thy seed* (see ch. lix. 21). This is in accordance with the promises everywhere made in the Bible to the people of God (see Gen. xii. 7; xiii. 15; xv. 18; xvii. 7, 8; Ex. xx. 6; Deut. vii. 9; Ps. lxxxix. 4; Isa. xliii. 5). It may be regarded, first, as a promise of the richest blessings to them as parents—since there is to a parent's heart no prospect so consoling as that which relates to his offspring; and, secondly, as an assurance of the perpetuity of their religion; of their return from captivity, and their restoration to their own land.

4. *And they shall spring up.* The idea is, that as plants and trees planted by water-courses, and in well-watered fields, grow and flourish, so should their children grow in virtue, hope, piety, and zeal. ¶ As *among the grass.* They shall spring up and flourish as the grass does when abundantly watered from heaven. On the meaning of the unusual form of the word בְּבֵין, in the Hebrew (*in among*), see Vitringa and Rosenmüller. The ב here is undoubtedly an

4 And they shall spring up [a] *as*
among the grass, as willows by the
water-courses.
5 One [b] shall say, I am the
LORD'S; and another shall call
himself by the name of Jacob;
and another shall subscribe *with*
his hand unto the LORD, and surname *himself* by the name of
Israel.

a Ac.2 41.

b Je.50.5; 2 Co.8.5.

---

error of the transcriber for כ (*as*)—an error which, from the similarity of the letters, might be readily made. The LXX. read it, 'Ὡς—'As.' The Chaldee reads it, כ (*as*). ¶ *As willows by the water-courses.* Willows are usually planted in such places, and grow rapidly and luxuriantly. It denotes here, abundant increase, vigour and beauty; and means that their posterity would be greatly blessed of God. A similar figure to denote the prosperity and happiness of the righteous occurs in Ps. i. 3:

And he shall be like a tree planted by the rivers
of water,
That bringeth forth his fruit in his season;
His leaf also shall not wither.

These two verses teach us—1. That God will pour his blessings on the children of his people—a promise which in all ages, when parents are faithful, is abundantly fulfilled. 2. That one of the richest blessings which can be imparted to a people is, that God's Spirit should descend on their children. 3. That the Spirit of God alone is the source of true happiness and prosperity to our children. All else—property, learning, accomplishment, beauty, vigour, will be vain. It is by his blessing only —by the influence of piety—that they will spring forth as among the grass, and like willows by the streams of water. 4. Parents should pray earnestly for a revival of religion. No better description can be given of a revival than that given here—the Spirit of God descending like streams and floods on the young; and their springing forth in the graces of piety as among the grass, and growing in love to God and love to men like willows by the water-courses. Who would not pray for such a work of grace? What family, what congregation, what people can be happy without it?

5. *One shall say.* It shall be common to say this, or a profession of religion shall be common. The various expressions in this verse mean substantially the same thing—that there should prevail among the people a disposition to make a profession of attachment to JEHOVAH in every proper public manner. It is in immediate connection with what is said in the previous verses, that he would pour his Spirit upon them, and especially on their children. The effect would be, that many would make a public profession of religion. This refers, doubtless, in the main, to the period after their return from the captivity, and to the general prevalence of religion then. But it is also true of the people of God at all times—especially under the Messiah. God pours his Spirit like gentle dews, or rains, on the families of his people; and the effect is, that many publicly profess attachment to him. ¶ *I am the* LORD'S. I belong to JEHOVAH; I devote myself to him. This expresses the true nature of a profession of religion—a feeling that we are not our own, but that we belong to God. It is, that we not only feel that we are bound to worship him, but that we actually *belong* to him; that our bodies and spirits, and all that we have and are, are to be sacredly employed in his service (see 1 Cor. vi. 20; 2 Cor. vii. 5; v. 14, 15). Nothing, in few words, can more appropriately describe the true nature of a profession of religion than the expression here used (לַיהוָה אָנִי) 'For JEHOVAH am I' —'I am wholly, and entirely, and for ever for JEHOVAH, to obey him; to do his will; to suffer patiently all that he appoints; to live where he directs; to die when, where, and how he pleases; to moulder in the grave according to his will; to be raised up by his power; and to serve him for ever in a better world.' ¶ *And another shall call* himself *by the name of Jacob.* The Chaldee renders this, 'He shall pray in the name of Jacob.' The idea seems to be, that he should call himself *a friend*

of Jacob—an Israelite. He should regard himself as belonging to the same family and the same religion, as Jacob; as worshipping the same God; and as maintaining the same belief. To call one's self by the same name as another, is indicative of friendship and affection; and is expressive of a purpose to be united to him, and to identify our interest with his. The idea is that which one would express by saying, that he cast in his interest with the people of God, or he became identified with them; as we now say, a man calls himself by the name of Christ, *i.e.*, a Christian. Jerome renders this, 'He shall call by the name of Jacob,' *i.e.*, sinners to repentance (comp. Note on ch. xliii. 7; xlviii. 1; Ps. xxiv. 6). ¶ *And another shall subscribe* with *his hand unto the* Lord. The LXX. render this, 'And another shall write with his hand (χειρί), I am of God.' Lowth, 'On his hand,' Aquila and Symmachus, Χειρά. Lowth supposes that the allusion here is to the marks which were made indelible by puncture with ink on the hand or on other parts of the body. He supposes that the mark thus indelibly impressed was the name of the person, or the name of the master if he was a slave, or some indication by which it might be known to whom he belonged. In this way, the soldier marked himself with the name of his commander; the idolater, with the name of his god; and in this way, Procopius says, that the early Christians marked themselves. On this passage he says, 'Because many marked their wrists or their arms with the sign of the cross, or with the name of Christ' (see Rev. xx. 4; Spencer, *De Leg. Heb.* ii. 20). But all this is too refined, and is evidently a departure from the true sense of the passage. The mark, or writing, was not *on* the hand, but *with* it—literally, 'and this shall write his hand to Jehovah;' and the figure is evidently taken from the mode of making a contract or bargain, where the name is subscribed to the instrument. It was a solemn compact or covenant, by which they enrolled themselves among the worshippers of God, and pledged themselves to his service. The *manner* of a contract among the Hebrews is described in Jer. xxxii. 10, 12, 44. A public, solemn, and recorded covenant, to which the names of princes, Levites, and priests, were subscribed, and which was sealed, by which they bound themselves to the service of God, is mentioned in Neh. ix. 38. Here it denotes the solemn manner in which they would profess to be worshippers of the true God; and it is expressive of the true nature of a profession of religion. The *name* is given in to God. It is enrolled by the voluntary desire of him who makes the profession among his friends. It is done, after the manner of solemn compacts among men, in the presence of witnesses (Heb. xii. 1). Among Christians, it is sealed in a solemn manner by baptism, and the Lord's supper It has, therefore, all the binding force and obligation of a solemn compact; and every professor of religion should regard his covenant with God as the most sacred of all compacts, and as having a more solemn obligation than any other. And yet, how many professors are there who would shrink back with horror from the idea of breaking a compact with man, who have no alarm at the idea of having proved unfaithful to their solemn pledge that they would belong wholly to God, and would live to him alone! Let every professor of religion remember that his profession has all the force of a solemn compact; that he has voluntarily subscribed his name, and enrolled himself among the friends of God; and that there is no agreement of a more binding nature than that which unites him in public profession to the cause and the kingdom of the Saviour. ¶ *And surname himself by the name of Israel.* Shall call himself an Israelite, and shall be a worshipper of the same God. The word rendered 'shall surname' (כָּנָה *kânâ*, not used in Kal, in Piel כִּנָּה *k'innâ*), means to address in a friendly and soothing manner; to speak kindly to any one. Gesenius renders it, 'And kindly, soothingly names the name of Israel.' But the idea is probably that expressed in our translation. The word sometimes denotes a giving of flattering titles to any one, by way of compliment (Job xxxii. 21, 22):

6 Thus saith the LORD the King
of Israel, and his Redeemer the
LORD [a] of hosts; I [b] *am* the first,
and I *am* the last; and besides [c] me
there is no God.

7 And [d] who, as I, shall call,
and shall declare it, and set it in
order for me, since I appointed the
ancient people? and the things
that are coming, and shall come,
let them show unto them.

a ch.43.14. b Re.1.8,17. c De.4.35; 32.39. d ch.46.9,10.

Let me not, I pray you, accept any man's person;
Neither let me *give flattering titles* unto man.
For I know not *to give flattering titles;*
In so doing my Maker would soon take me away.

In Isa. xlv. 4, it is rendered, 'I have surnamed thee [Cyrus], though thou hast not known me.' The word does not occur elsewhere. It conveys the idea of *an honourable title;* and means here, I think, that he would call himself by the *honourable appellation* of Israel—or an Israelite—a worshipper of the God of Jacob. It implies that a profession of the true religion *is* honourable, and that it is and should be esteemed so by him who makes it. It is observable, also, that this verse contains an instance of the parallelism in the Hebrew writings where the alternate members correspond to each other. Here the first and third members, and the second and the fourth correspond to each other (see Introd. § 8).

6. *Thus saith the* LORD. This commences, as I suppose (see Analysis), the argument to prove that JEHOVAH is the only true God, and that the idols were vanity. The object is, to show to the Jews, that he who had made to them such promises of protection and deliverance was able to perform what he had pledged himself to do. ¶ *The King of Israel* (see Notes on ch. xli. 21). ¶ *And his Redeemer* (see Notes on ch. xliii. 1). ¶ *The* LORD *of hosts* (see Notes on ch. i. 9). ¶ *I* am *the first* (see Notes on ch. xli. 4). ¶ *And I* am *the last.* In ch. xli. 4, this is expressed '*with* the last;' in Rev. i. 8, 'I am Alpha and Omega.' The sense is, that God existed before all things, and will exist for ever. ¶ *And besides me* there is *no God.* This is repeatedly declared (Deut. iv. 35, 39; see Note on ch. xliii. 10–12). This great truth it was God's purpose to keep steadily before the minds of the Jews; and to keep it in the world, and ultimately to diffuse it abroad among the nations, was one of the leading reasons why he selected them as a peculiar people, and separated them from the rest of mankind.

7. *And who, as I.* This verse contains an *argument* to prove that he is God. In proof of this, he appeals to the fact that he alone can predict future events, and certainly declare the *order*, and the *time* in which they will come to pass (see Notes on ch. xli. 21–23; xliv. 9, 10). ¶ *Shall call.* That is, call forth the event, or command that to happen which he wills—one of the highest possible exhibitions of power. See a similar use of the word *call* in ch. xlvi. 2; xlviii. 15. ¶ *And shall declare it.* Declare, or announce with certainty the future event. ¶ *And set it in order.* Arrange it; secure the proper succession and place (see Notes on ch. xli. 22). The word here used (עָרַךְ) denotes properly *to place in a row;* set in order; arrange. It is of the same signification as the Greek τάσσω or τάττω, and is applied to placing the wood upon the altar in a proper manner (Gen. xxii. 9); or to placing the shew-bread in proper order on the table (Lev. xxiv. 8); and especially to setting an army in order, or putting it in battle array (Gen. xiv. 8; Judg. xx. 20, 22; 1 Sam. xvii. 2). Here it means, that God would arrange the events in a proper order—as an army is marshalled and arrayed for battle. There should be no improper sequences of events; no chance; no hap-hazard; no confusion. The events which take place under his government, occur in proper order and time, and so as best to subserve his plans. ¶ *For me.* In order to execute my plans, and to promote my glory. The events on earth are FOR GOD. They are such as he chooses to ordain, and are arranged in the manner which he chooses. ¶ *Since I appointed the ancient people.* 'From my constituting the people of old;' that is, God had given them intimations of future events from the very period when he in times long past, had selected and

8 Fear [a]ye not, neither be
afraid: have not I told thee from
that time, and have declared *it?*
ye *are* even my [b]witnesses. Is
there a God besides me? yea,
there is no [1]God; I know not *any*.
9 They [c]that make a graven
image *are* all of them vanity: and
their [2]delectable things shall not
profit: and they *are* their own witnesses;
they see not, nor know, that
they may be ashamed.
10 Who hath formed a god, or
molten a graven image *that* is
profitable [d]for nothing?

a Prov.3.25,26. b 1 Jn.5.10. 1 *rock*. c ch.41.24,29. 2 *desirable*. d Hab.2.18; 1 Co.8.4.

appointed them as his people. They were, therefore, qualified to be his witnesses (8). ¶ *And the things that are coming, let them show* (see Notes on ch. xli. 22, 23).

8. *Fear ye not, neither be afraid* (see Notes on ch. xli. 10). The word here rendered 'be afraid,' occurs nowhere else in the Bible. There can be no doubt, however, in regard to its meaning. The LXX. render it, Μηδὲ πλανᾶσθε—'Neither be deceived.' All the other ancient versions express the sense to fear, to be afraid (Gesenius, *Lex.* on the word רָהָה). ¶ *Have not I told thee from that time.* Have I not fully declared from the very commencement of your history as a people, in the main what shall occur? ¶ *Ye* are *even my witnesses* (see Notes on ch. xliii. 12). ¶ *Is there a God besides me?* This is a strong mode of affirming that there is no God besides JEHOVAH (see Note on ver. 6). ¶ *Yea*, there is *no God*. Marg. 'Rock' (צוּר, *tzūr*). The word *rock* is often applied to God (see Note on ch. xxx. 29; comp. Deut. xxxii. 4, 30, 31; Ps. xix. 14; xxxi. 2, 3; xlii. 9; *et sæpe al.* The idea is taken from the fact that a lofty rock or fastness was inaccessible by an enemy, and that those who fled there were safe.

9. *They that make a graven image.* A graven image is one that is cut, or sculptured out of wood or stone, in contradistinction from one that is molten, which is made by being cast. Here it is used to denote an image, or an idol-god in general. God had asserted in the previous verses his own divinity, and he now proceeds to show, at length, the vanity of idols, and of idol-worship. This same topic was introduced in ch. xl. 18–20 (see Notes on that passage), but it is here pursued at greater length, and in a tone and manner far more sarcastic and severe. *Perhaps* the prophet had two immediate objects in view; first, to reprove the idolatrous spirit in his own time, which prevailed especially in the early part of the reign of Manasseh; and secondly, to show to the exile Jews in Babylon that the gods of the Babylonians could not protect their city, and that JEHOVAH could rescue his own people. He *begins*, therefore, by saying, that the *makers* of the idols were all of them vanity. Of course, the idols themselves could have no more power than their makers, and must be vanity also. ¶ Are *all of them vanity* (see Note on ch. xli. 29). ¶ *And their delectable things.* Marg. 'Desirable.' The sense is, their valued works, their idol-gods, on which they have lavished so much expense, and which they prize so highly. ¶ *Shall not profit.* Shall not be able to aid or protect them; shall be of no advantage to them (see Hab. ii. 18). ¶ *And they* are *their own witnesses.* They can foretell nothing; they can furnish no aid; they cannot defend in times of danger. This may refer either to the worshippers, or to the idols themselves—and was alike true of both. ¶ *They see not.* They have no power of discerning anything. How can they then foresee future events? ¶ *That they may be ashamed.* The same sentiment is repeated in ver. 11, and in ch. xlv. 16. The sense is, that shame and confusion *must* await all who put their trust in an idol-god.

10. *Who hath formed a god.* The LXX. read this verse in connection with the close of the previous verse, 'But they shall be ashamed who make a god, and all who sculpture unprofitable things.' This interpretation also, Lowth, by a change in the Hebrew text on the authority of a MS. in the Bodleian library, has adopted. This change is

11 Behold, all his fellows shall
be [a]ashamed; and the workmen,
they *are* of men: let them all be
gathered together, let them stand
up; *yet* they shall fear, *and* they
shall be ashamed together.
12 The smith [b]with the [1]tongs
both worketh in the coals, and
fashioneth it with hammers, and
worketh it with the strength of
his arms: yea, he is hungry, and
his strength faileth: he drinketh
no water, and is faint.

a Ps.97.7. *b* ch.40.19,&c. 1 or, *an axe.*

made by reading כִּי (*kī*) instead of מִי (*mī*) in the beginning of the verse. But the authority of the change, being that of a single MS. and the Septuagint, is not sufficient. Nor is it necessary. The question is designed to be ironical and sarcastic: 'Who is there,' says the prophet, 'that has done this? Who are they that are engaged in this stupid work? Do they give marks of a sound mind? What is, and must be the character of a man that has formed *a god*, and that has made an unprofitable graven image?

11. *Behold, all his fellows.* All that are joined in making, and in worshipping it, are regarded as the fellows, or the companions (חֲבֵרָיו) of the idol-god (see Hos. iv. 17—'Ephraim *is joined* to idols'). They and the idols constitute one company or fellowship, intimately allied to each other. ¶ *Shall be ashamed.* Shall be confounded when they find that their idols cannot aid them. ¶ *And the workmen.* The allusion to the workmen is to show that what they made could not be worthy of the confidence of men as an object of worship. ¶ *They* are *of men.* They are mortal men; they must themselves soon die. It is ridiculous, therefore, for them to attempt to make a god that can defend or save, or that should be adored. ¶ *Let them all be gathered together.* For purposes of trial, or to urge their claims to the power of making an object that should be adored (see Note on ch. xli. 1). ¶ *Let them stand up.* As in a court of justice, to defend their cause (see Note on ch. xli. 21). ¶ *They shall fear.* They shall be alarmed when danger comes. They shall find that their idol-gods cannot defend them.

12. *The smith with the tongs.* The prophet proceeds here to show the folly and absurdity of idolatry; and in order to this he goes into an extended statement (ver. 12–19) of the manner in which idols were usually made. Lowth remarks, 'The sacred writers are generally large and eloquent on the subject of idolatry; they treat it with great severity, and set forth the absurdity of it in the strongest light. But this passage of Isaiah far exceeds anything that was ever written on the subject, in force of argument, energy of expression, and elegance of composition. One or two of the Apocryphal writers have attempted to imitate the prophet, but with very ill success (Wisd. xiii. 11–19; xv. 7, &c.; Baruch vi.)' Horace, however, has given a description of the making of idols, which, for severity of satire, and pungency of sarcasm, has a strong resemblance to this description in Isaiah:—

Olim truncus eram ficulnus, inutile lignum;
Cum faber, incertus scamnum faceretne Priapum
Maluit esse Deum.

Sat. I. viii. 1–3.

Lowth renders the phrase 'the smith with the tongs,' 'The smith cutteth off a portion of iron.' Noyes, 'The smith prepareth an axe.' The LXX. 'The carpenter sharpeneth (ὤξυνε) iron' (σίδηρον), *i.e.*, an axe. So also the Syriac. Gesenius renders it, 'The smith makes an axe.' Many other renderings of the passage have been proposed. The idea in this verse is, I think, that the prophet describes *the commencement of the process of making a graven image.* For that purpose, he goes back even to the making of the instruments by which it is manufactured, and in this verse he describes the process of making an axe, with a view to the cutting down of the tree, and forming a god. That he does not here refer to the making of the idol itself is apparent from the fact that the process here described is that of working *in iron;* but idols were not made of iron, and that here described especially (ver. 11, *sq.*) is one made of wood. The phrase here used, therefore, refers to the pro-

13 The carpenter stretcheth out *his* rule, he marketh it out with a line, he fitteth it with planes, and he marketh it out with the compass, and maketh it after the figure of a man, according to the beauty of a man; that it may remain in the house.

---

cess of axe-making with a view to cutting down a tree to make a god; and the prophet describes the ardour and activity with which it is done, to show how much haste they were in to complete it. The literal translation of this phrase is, 'The workman (חָרַשׁ, st. const. for חָרָשׁ) of iron [maketh] an axe.' ¶ *Both worketh in the coals.* And he works the piece of iron of which he is making an axe in the coals. He blows the coals in order to produce an intense heat (see ch. liv. 16)—'Behold, I have created the smith that bloweth the coals in the fire.' ¶ *And fashioneth it with hammers.* Forms the mass of iron into an axe. Axes were not *cast*, but *wrought.* ¶ *And worketh it with the strength of his arms.* Or, he works it with his strong arms—referring to the fact that the arm of the smith, by constant usage, becomes exceedingly strong. A description remarkably similar to this occurs in Virgil when he is describing the Cyclops:

> Illi inter sese magna vi brachia tollunt
> In numerum; versantque tenaci forcipe ferrum.
> *Georg.* iv. 174, 175.

> Heaved with vast strength their arms in order rise,
> And blow to blow in measured chime replies;
> While with firm tongs they turn the sparkling ore,
> And Etna's caves with ponderous anvils roar.
> SOTHEBY.

¶ *Yea, he is hungry.* He exhausts himself by his hard labour. The idea is, that he is so anxious to have it done, so engaged, so diligent, that he does not even stop to take necessary refreshment. ¶ *And his strength faileth.* He works till he is completely exhausted. ¶ *He drinketh no water.* He does not intermit his work even long enough to take a draught of water, so hurried is he. While the iron is hot, he works with intense ardour, lest it should grow cool, and his work be retarded—a very graphic description of what all have seen in a blacksmith's shop. The Rev. J. Williams states that when the South Sea islanders made an idol, they strictly abstained from food; and although they might be, and were sometimes, three days about the work, no water, and he believes no food, passed their lips all the time. This fact would convey a satisfactory elucidation of an allusion not otherwise easily explained (*Pictorial Bible*).

13. *The carpenter.* The axe is made (ver. 12), and the carpenter now proceeds to the construction of the god. ¶ *Stretcheth out* his *rule.* For the purpose of laying out his work, or measuring it. The word here rendered 'rule,'

ANCIENT EGYPTIAN SCULPTORS
Blocking out stone for the formation of an Idol.
From Rosellini.

however (קַו), means properly *a line;* and should be so rendered here. The carpenter *stretches out* a line, but not a rule. ¶ *He marketh it out with a line.* He marks out the shape; the length, and breadth, and thickness of the body, in the rough and unhewn piece of wood He has an idea in his mind of the proper *shape* of a god, and he goes to work to make one of that form. The expression 'to mark out with a line,' is, however, not congruous. The word which is here used, and which is rendered 'line' (שֶׂרֶד) occurs nowhere else in the Bible. Lowth and Kimchi render it, 'Red ochre.' According to this the reference is to the chalk, red clay, or crayon, which a carpenter uses on a line to mark out his work. But according to Gesenius, the word means an *awl*, or a *stylus*, or *engraver*, with which the

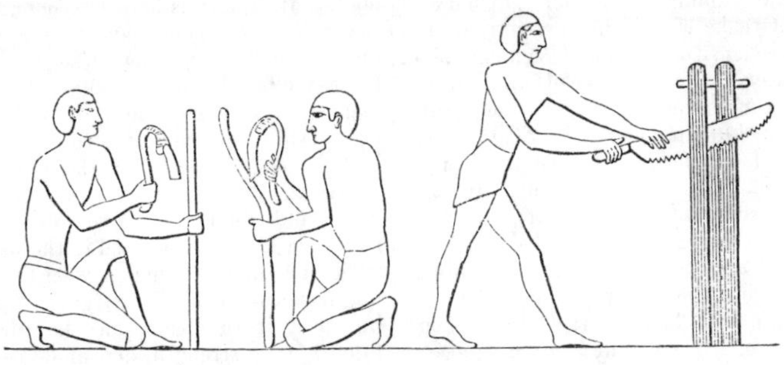

ANCIENT EGYPTIAN CARPENTERS WITH THE ADZE AND SAW.—From Rosellini.

artist sketches the outlines of the figure to be sculptured. A carpenter always uses such an instrument in laying out and marking his work. ¶ *He fitteth it with planes.* Or rather with *chisels*, or carving-tools, with which wooden images were carved. Planes are rather adapted to a smooth surface; carving is performed with chisels. The word

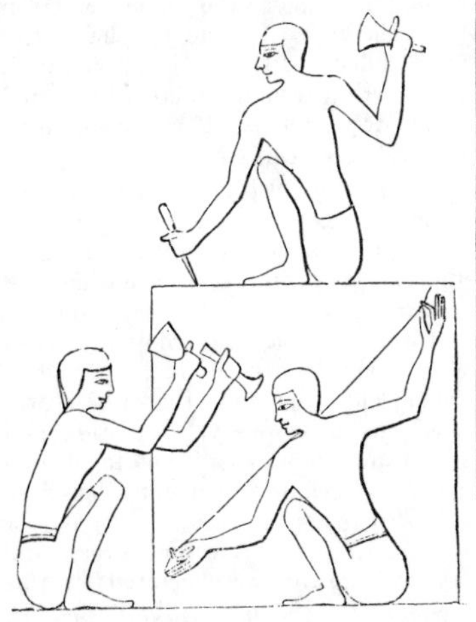

CARVING AN IDOL.—From Rosellini.

is derived from קָצַע, *to cut off*. The Chaldee renders it, אִזְמֵל—'A knife.' The LXX. render this, 'Framed it by rule, and glued the parts together.'

¶ *Marketh it out with the compass.* From חוּג (*hhūg*), *to make a circle*, to revolve, as compasses do. By a compass he accurately designates the parts, and marks out the symmetry of the form. ¶ *According to the beauty of a man.* Perhaps there may be a little sarcasm here in the thought that *a god* should be made in the shape of a man.

PAINTING AN IDOL.—From Rosellini.

It was true, however, that the statues of the gods among the ancients were made after the most perfect conceptions

14 He heweth him down cedars, and taketh the cypress and the oak, which he [1]strengtheneth for himself among the trees of the forest: he planteth an ash, and the rain doth nourish *it*.

[1] or, *taketh courage.*

of the human form. The statuary of the Greeks was of this description, and the images of Apollo, of Venus, and of Jupiter, have been celebrated everywhere as the most perfect representations of the human form. ¶ *That it may remain in the house.* To dwell in a temple. Such statues were usually made to decorate a temple; or rather perhaps temples were reared to be dwelling-places of the gods. It *may* be implied here, that the idol was of no use but to remain in a house. It could not hear, or save. It was like a useless piece of furniture, and had none of the attributes of God.

14. *He heweth him down cedars.* In the previous verses, the prophet had described the formation of an axe with which the work was to be done (ver. 12), and the laying out, and carving of the idol (ver. 13). In this verse he proceeds to describe the *material* of which the idol was made, and the different purposes (ver. 15–17) to which that material was applied. The *object* is to show the amazing stupidity of those who should worship a god made of the same material from which they made a fire to warm themselves, or to cook their food. For a description of cedars, see Notes on ch. ix. 10. ¶ *And taketh.* Takes to himself; that is, makes use of. ¶ *The cypress* (תִּרְזָה *tirzâ*). This word occurs nowhere else in the Bible. It is probably derived from a root (תָּרַז *târăz*), signifying *to be hard*, or *firm*. Hence it probably means some species of wood that derived its name from its hardness or firmness. Jerome translates it, *Ilex* (a species of oak)—'the holm-oak.' It was an evergreen. This species of evergreen, Gesenius says, was abundant in Palestine. ¶ *And the oak.* The oak was commonly used for this purpose on account of its hardness and durability. ¶ *Which he strengtheneth for himself.* Marg. 'Taketh courage.' The word אִמֵּץ means properly *to strengthen*, to make strong, to repair, to replace, to harden. Rosenmüller and Gesenius suppose that it means here *to choose, i.e.*, to set fast, or appoint; and they appeal to Ps. lxxx. 15, 17, 'thou *madest strong* for thyself.' Kimchi supposes that it means, that he gave himself with the utmost diligence and care to select the best kinds of wood for the purpose. Vitringa, that he was intent on his work, and did not leave the place, but refreshed himself with food in the woods without returning home, in order that he might accomplish his design. Others interpret it to mean that he girded himself with strength, and made use of his most intense efforts in felling the trees of the forest. Lowth renders it, 'Layeth in good store of the trees of the forest.' It may mean that he gave himself with great diligence to the work; or may it not mean that he *planted* such trees, and took great pains in watering and cultivating them for this purpose? ¶ *He planteth an ash* (אֹרֶן). The Septuagint renders it, Πίτυν—'Pine.' Jerome also renders it, *Pinum.* Gesenius supposes the name was given from the fact that the tree had a tall and slender top, which, when it vibrated, gave forth a tremulous, creaking sound (from רָנַן *rânăn*). This derivation is, however, somewhat fanciful. Most interpreters regard it as the *ash*—a well-known tree. In idolatrous countries, where it is common to have idols in almost every family, the business of *idol-making* is a very important manufacture. Of course, large quantities of wood would be needed; and it would be an object to procure that which was most pure, or as we say, 'clear stuff,' and which would work easily, and to advantage. It became important, therefore, to *cultivate* that wood, as we do for shipbuilding, or for cabinet-work, and doubtless groves were planted for this purpose. ¶ *And the rain doth nourish* it. These circumstances are mentioned to show the folly of worshipping a god that was formed in this manner. *Perhaps* also the prophet means to intimate that though the man planted the tree,

15 Then shall it be for a man
to burn: for he will take thereof and
warm himself; yea, he kindleth *it*,
and baketh bread; yea, he maketh
a god, and worshippeth *it:* he maketh it a graven image, and falleth
down thereto.
16 He burneth part thereof in
the fire: with part thereof he eateth flesh; he roasteth roast, and is
satisfied, yea, he warmeth *himself*,
and saith, Aha, I am warm, I have
seen the fire:
17 And the residue thereof he
maketh a god, *even* his graven
image: he falleth down unto it, and
worshippeth *it*, and prayeth unto it,
and saith, Deliver me, for thou *art*
my god.
18 They [a]have not known nor
understood: for [b]he hath [1]shut
their eyes, that they cannot see;
and their hearts, that they cannot
understand.

[a] ch.45.20. [b] ch.6.9,10. [1] *daubed.*

yet that he could not make it grow. He was dependent on the rains of heaven; and even in making an idol-god he was indebted to the providential care of the true God. Men, even in their schemes of wickedness, are dependent on God. Even in forming and executing plans to oppose and resist him, they can do nothing without his aid. He preserves them, feeds them, clothes them; and the instruments which they use against him are those which he has nurtured. On the rain of heaven; on the sunbeam and the dew; on the teeming earth, and on the elements which he has made, and which he controls, they are dependent; and they can do nothing in their wicked plans without abusing the bounties of his Providence, and the expressions of his tender mercy.

15. *Then shall it be for a man to burn.* It will afford materials for a fire. The design of this verse and the following is, to ridicule the idea of a man's using parts of the same tree to make a fire to cook his victuals, to warm himself, and to shape a god. Nothing could be more stupid than the conduct here referred to, and yet it is common all over the heathen world. It shows the utter debasement of the race, that they thus of the same tree make a fire, cook their food, and construct their gods.

16. *With part thereof he eateth flesh.* That is, he prepares flesh to eat, or prepares his food. ¶ *He roasteth roast.* He roasts meat.

18. *They have not known nor understood.* They are stupid, ignorant, and blind. Nothing could more strikingly show their ignorance and stupidity than this idol worship. ¶ *He hath shut their eyes.* God hath closed their eyes. Marg. 'Daubed.' The word here used, טַח from טוּחַ denotes properly *to spread over;* to besmear; to plaster; as, *e.g.*, a wall with mortar (Lev. xiv. 42; 1 Chron. xxix. 4; Ezek. xiii. 10, 22, 28). Here it means to cover over the eyes so as to prevent vision; and hence, metaphorically, to make them stupid, ignorant, dull. It is attributed to God in accordance with the common statement of the Scriptures, that he does what he permits to be done (see Notes on ch. vi. 9, 10). It does not mean that God had done it by any physical, or direct agency, but that it had occurred under the administration of his Providence. It is also true that the Hebrew writers sometimes employ an active verb when the signification is passive, and when the main idea is, that anything was *in fact* done. Here the main point is not the *agent* by which this was done, but *the fact* that their eyes were blinded—and perhaps all the force of the verb טַח used here would be expressed if it was rendered in an impersonal, or in a passive form, 'it is covered as to their eyes,' *i.e.*, their eyes are shut, without suggesting that it was done by God. So the LXX. render it, Ἀπημαυρώθησαν—'They are blind,' or involved in darkness. So the Chaldee, מְטַמְטְמָן (also in the plural)—'Their eyes are obscured' or blind. It cannot be proved from this text that God is, by direct agency, the author by whom it was done. It was not uncommon to shut up, or seal up the eyes for various purposes in the East, and unquestionably the prophet alludes

19 And none [1]considereth [a]in
his heart, neither *is there* knowledge nor understanding to say,
I have burnt part of it in the fire;
yea, also I have baked bread upon
the coals thereof; I have roasted
flesh, and eaten *it;* and shall I make
the residue thereof an abomination?
shall I fall down to [2]the stock of a
tree?
20 He feedeth on ashes: a deceived heart [b]hath turned him
aside, that he cannot deliver his
soul, nor say, *Is there* not a lie in
my right hand?

1 *setteth to.* a Ho.7.2. 2 *that which comes of.* b Ho.4.12; Ro.1.21; 2 Th.2.11.

---

to some such custom. 'It is one of the solemnities at a Jewish wedding at Aleppo, according to Dr. Russell, who mentions it as the most remarkable thing in their ceremonies at that time. It is done by fastening the eyelids together with a gum, and the bridegroom is the person, he says, if he remembered right, that opens the bride's eyes at the appointed time. It is also used as a punishment in those countries. So Sir Thomas Roe's chaplain, in his account of his voyages to East India, tells us of a son of the Great Mogul, whom he had seen, and with whom Sir Thomas had conversed, that had before that time been cast into prison by his father, where his eyes were sealed up, by something put before them, which might not be taken off for three years; after which time the seal was taken away, that he might with freedom enjoy the light, though not his liberty.'—(Harmer's *Obs.* vol. iii., pp. 507, 508. Ed. Lond. 8vo, 1808.)

19. *And none considereth in his heart.* Marg. 'Setteth to.' He does not place the subject near his heart or mind; he does not think of it. A similar phrase occurs in ch. xlvi. 8: 'Bring it again to mind.' It is a phrase drawn from the act of placing an object near us, in order to examine it closely; and we express the same idea by the phrase 'looking at a thing,' or 'looking at it closely.' The sense is, they had not attentively and carefully thought on the folly of what they were doing—a sentiment which is as true of all sinners as it was of stupid idolaters. ¶ *An abomination.* A name that is often given to an idol (2 Kings xi. 5, 7; xxiii. 13). The meaning is, that an idol was abominable and detestable in the sight of a holy God. It was that which he could not endure. ¶ *Shall I fall down to the stock of a tree?* Marg. 'That which comes of.' The word בּוּל means properly *produce, increase,* and here evidently a stock or trunk of wood. So it is in the Chaldee.

20. *He feedeth on ashes.* There have been various interpretations of this. Jerome renders it, 'A part of it is ashes;' the Chaldee, 'Lo! half of the god is reduced to ashes;' the Septuagint, 'Know thou that their heart is ashes.' The word here rendered 'feedeth' (רֹעֶה) means properly *to feed,* graze, pasture; and then, figuratively, to delight, or take pleasure in any person or thing (Prov. xiii. 20; xv. 14; xxviii. 7; xxix. 3). In Hos. xii. 1, 'Ephraim *feedeth* on wind,' it means to strive after something vain or unprofitable; to seek that which will prove to be vain and unsatisfactory. So here it means, that in their idol-service they would not obtain that which they sought. It would be like a man who sought for food, and found it to be dust or ashes; and the service of an idol compared with what man needed, or compared with the true religion, would be like ashes compared with nutritious and wholesome diet. This graphic description of the effect of idolatry is just as true of the ways of sin, and of the pursuits of the world now. It is true of the gay and the fashionable; of those who seek happiness in riches and honours; of all those who make this world their portion, that they are feeding on ashes—they seek that which is vain, unsubstantial, unsatisfactory, and which will yet fill the soul itself with disgust and loathing. ¶ *A deceived heart hath turned him aside.* This is the true source of the difficulty; this is the fountain of all idolatry and sin. The *heart* is first wrong, and then the understanding, and the whole conduct is turned aside from the path of truth and duty (comp. Rom. i. 28). ¶ *A lie in my right hand.* The right hand is the instrument of action.

21 Remember these, O Jacob
and Israel; for thou *art* my servant: I have formed thee; thou *art* my servant: O Israel, thou shalt not be [a] forgotten of me.
22 I have blotted out, [b] as a
thick cloud, thy transgressions, and, as a cloud, thy sins: return unto me; for I have [c] redeemed thee.
23 [d] Sing, O ye heavens; for
the LORD hath done *it*: shout, ye lower parts of the earth, break forth into singing, ye mountains, O [e] forest, and every tree therein: for the LORD hath redeemed Jacob, and glorified [f] himself in Israel.

a ch.49.14,15. *b* ch.1.18; Ps.103.12. *c* 1 Co.6.20; 1 Pe.1.18; Re.5.9.
d Ps.96.11,12; Re.18.20. *e* Eze.36.1,8. *f* ch.55.13.

A lie is a name often given to an idol as being false and delusive. The sense is, that that which they had been making, and on which they were depending, was deceitful and vain. The work of their right hand—the fruit of their skill and toil, was deceptive, and could not save them. The doctrine is, that that which sinners rely on to save their souls; that which has cost their highest efforts as a scheme to save them, is false and delusive. All schemes of religion of human origin are of this description; and all will be alike deceptive and ruinous to the soul.

21. *Remember these.* Remember these things which are now said about the folly of idolatry, and the vanity of worshipping idols. The object of the argument is, to turn their attention to God, and to lead them to put their trust in him. ¶ *Thou* art *my servant* (see Notes on ch. xlii. 19; xliii. 1).

22. *I have blotted out.* The word here used (מָחָה), means properly *to wipe away,* and is often applied to sins, as if the account was wiped off, or as we express it, blotted out (Ps. li. 3, 11; see Note on ch. xliii. 25). The phrase, 'to blot out sins like a cloud,' however, is unusual, and the idea not very obvious. The true idea would be expressed by rendering it, 'I have made them to vanish as a thick cloud;' and the sense is, as the wind drives away a thick cloud, however dark and frowning it may be, so that the sky is clear and serene, so God had caused their sins to disappear, and had removed the storm of his anger. Nothing can more strikingly represent *sin* in its nature and consequences, than a dense, dark, frowning cloud that comes over the heavens, and shuts out the sun, and fills the air with gloom; and nothing can more beautifully represent the nature and effect of pardon than the idea of removing such a cloud, and leaving the sky pure, the air calm and serene, and the sun pouring down his beams of warmth and light on the earth. So the soul of the sinner is enveloped and overshadowed with a dense cloud; but pardon dissipates that cloud, and it is calm, and joyful, and serene. ¶ *And as a cloud.* The Chaldee render this, 'As a flying cloud.' The difference between the two words here rendered 'thick cloud,' and 'cloud' (עָב and עָנָן) is, that the former is expressive of a cloud as *dense,* thick, compact; and the latter as *covering* or veiling the heavens. Lowth renders the latter word 'Vapour;' Noyes, 'Mist.' Both words, however, usually denote a cloud. A passage similar to this is found in Demosthenes, as quoted by Lowth: 'This decree made the danger then hanging over the city pass away like a cloud.' ¶ *Return unto me.* Since your sins are pardoned, and such mercy has been shown, return now, and serve me. The *argument* here is derived from the mercy of God in forgiving them, and the *doctrine* is, that the fact that God has forgiven us imposes the strongest obligations to devote ourselves to his service. The fact that we are redeemed and pardoned is the highest argument why we should consecrate all our powers to him who has purchased and forgiven us.

23. *Sing, O ye heavens* (see ch. xlii. 10). It is common in the sacred writings to call on the heavens, the earth, and all created things, to join in the praise of God on any great and glorious event (see Ps. xcvi. 1, 11, 12; cxlviii.) The *occasion* of the joy here was the fact that God had redeemed his people—a fact, in the joy of which the heavens and earth were called to participate. An

24 Thus [a]saith the LORD, thy Redeemer, and he that formed thee from [b]the womb, I *am* the LORD that maketh all *things;* that stretcheth [c]forth the heavens alone: that spreadeth abroad the earth by myself;

25 That [d]frustrateth the tokens of the liars, and maketh diviners mad; that turneth wise *men* backward, and maketh their knowledge foolish.

[a] ver.6. [b] Ga.1.15. [c] Ps.104.2. [d] 2 Ch.18.11,34; Je.50.36; 1 Co.3.19.

apostrophe such as the prophet here uses is common in all writings, where inanimate objects are addressed as having life, and as capable of sharing in the emotions of the speaker. Vitringa has endeavoured to show that the various objects here enumerated are emblematic, and that by the heavens are meant the angels which are in heaven; by the lower parts of the earth, the more humble and obscure republics of the heathen; by the mountains, the greater and more mighty kingdoms; by the forest, and the trees, large and spacious cities, with their nobles. So Grotius also interprets the passage. But the passage is a highly-wrought expression of elevated feeling; the language of poetry, where the prophet calls on all objects to exult;—an apostrophe to the highest heavens and the lowest part of the earth—the mountains and the forests—the most sublime objects in nature—to exult in the fact that the Jewish people were delivered from their long and painful captivity, and restored again to their own land. ¶ *The* LORD *hath done* it. Has delivered his people from their captivity in Babylon. There is, however, no impropriety in supposing that the eye of the prophet also rested on the glorious deliverance of his people by the Messiah; and that he regarded one event as emblematic of, and introductory to the other. The *language* here used will certainly appropriately express the feelings which should be manifested in view of the plan of redemption under the Messiah. ¶ *Shout, ye lower parts of the earth.* The foundations of the earth; the parts remote from the high heavens. Let the highest and the lowest objects shout; the highest heavens, and the depths of the earth. The LXX. render it, Τὰ θεμέλια τῆς γῆς—'The foundations of the earth.' So the Chaldee. ¶ *Ye mountains.* So in Psalm cxlviii. 9, 13: 'Mountains and all hills; fruitful trees and all cedars—let them praise the name of the LORD.' ¶ *O forest,* and *every tree therein.* Referring either to Lebanon, as being the most magnificent forest known to the prophet; or to any forest as a great and sublime object.

24. *Thy Redeemer* (see Note on ch. xliii. 1). ¶ *And he that formed thee from thee womb* (see Note on ver. 2). ¶ *That stretcheth forth the heavens* (see Note on ch. xl. 22). ¶ *That spreadeth abroad the earth.* Representing the earth, as is often done in the Scriptures, as a plain. God here appeals to the fact that he alone had made the heavens and the earth, as the demonstration that he is able to accomplish what is here said of the deliverance of his people. The same God that made the heavens is the Redeemer and Protector of the church, and THEREFORE the church is safe.

25. *That frustrateth.* Heb. 'Breaking:' *i.e.,* destroying, rendering vain. The idea is, that that which necromancers and diviners relied on as certain demonstration that what they predicted would be fulfilled, God makes vain and inefficacious. The event which they predicted did not follow, and all their alleged proofs that they were endowed with Divine or miraculous power he rendered vain. ¶ *The tokens.* Heb. אֹתוֹת—'Signs.' This word is usually applied to miracles, or to signs of the Divine interposition and presence. Here it means the things on which diviners and soothsayers relied; the tricks of cunning and sleight-of-hand which they adduced as miracles, or as demonstrations that they were under a divine influence. See the word more fully explained in the Notes on ch. vii. 2. ¶ *The liars.* Deceivers, boasters—meaning conjurers, or false prophets (comp. Jer. l. 36; see also Note on Isa. xvi. 6). ¶ *And maketh diviners mad.* That is, makes them foolish, or deprives

26 That confirmeth [a]the word of his servant, and performeth the counsel of his messengers; that saith to Jerusalem, Thou shalt be inhabited; and to the cities of Judah, Ye shall be built; and I will raise up the [1]decayed places thereof:

27 That saith to the deep, Be dry, and I will dry up thy rivers:

[a] Zec.1.6; 2 Pe.1.19.

[1] *wastes.*

them of wisdom. They pretend to foretell future events, but the event does not correspond with the prediction. God orders it otherwise, and thus they are shown to be foolish, or unwise. ¶ *That turneth wise men backward.* Lowth renders this, 'Who reverseth the devices of the sages.' The sense is, he puts them to shame. The idea seems to be derived from the fact that when one is ashamed, or disappointed, or fails of performing what he promised, he turns away his face (see 1 Kings ii. 16, *marg.*) The 'wise men,' here denote the sages; the diviners, the soothsayers; and the sense is, that they were not able to predict future events, and that when their prediction failed, they would be suffused with shame. ¶ *And maketh their knowledge foolish.* He makes them appear to be fools. It is well known that soothsayers and diviners abounded in the East; and it is not improbable that the prophet here means that when Babylon was attacked by Cyrus, the diviners and soothsayers would predict his defeat, and the overthrow of his army, but that the result would show that they were utterly incapable of predicting a future event. The whole passage here has reference to the taking of Babylon by Cyrus, and should be interpreted accordingly.

26. *That confirmeth the word of his servant.* Probably the word 'servant' here is to be taken in a *collective* sense, as referring to the prophets in general who had foretold the return of the Jews to their own land, and the rebuilding of Jerusalem. Or it may be, that the prophet refers more particularly to himself as having made a full prediction of this event. The parallel expression, 'his messengers,' however, is in the plural number, and thus it is rendered probable that the word here refers to the prophets collectively. The idea is, that it was a characteristic of God to establish the words of his servants the prophets, and that their predictions in regard to the return from the captivity in a special manner would be fulfilled. ¶ *The counsel of his messengers.* The prophets whom he had sent to announce future events, and to give counsel and consolation to the nation. ¶ *That saith to Jerusalem.* Jerusalem is here supposed to be lying in ruins, and the people to be in captivity in Babylon. In this situation, God is represented as addressing desolate Jerusalem, and saying, that it should be again inhabited, and that the cities of Judah should be rebuilt. ¶ *The decayed places.* Marg. 'Wastes.' No land, probably, was ever more completely desolated than the land of Judea when its inhabitants were carried to Babylon.

27. *That saith to the deep, Be dry.* Lowth supposes, that this refers to the fact that Cyrus took Babylon by diverting from their course the waters of the river Euphrates, and thus leaving the bed of the river dry, so that he could march his army under the walls of the city (see Notes on ch. xiii., xiv.) With this interpretation, also, Vitringa, J. H. Michaelis, Grotius, Rosenmüller, and some others, accord. Gesenius supposes that it is a description of the power of God in general; and some others have referred it to the dividing of the waters of the Red Sea when the Hebrews came out of Egypt, as in ch. xliii. 16, 17. The most obvious interpretation is that of Lowth, Vitringa, &c., by which it is supposed that it refers to the drying up of the Euphrates and the streams about Babylon, when Cyrus took the city. The principal *reasons* for this interpretation are, first, that the entire statement in these verses has reference to the events connected with the taking of Babylon; secondly, that it is strikingly descriptive of the manner in which the city was taken by Cyrus; and thirdly, that Cyrus is expressly mentioned (ver.

28 That saith of Cyrus, *He is* my shepherd, and shall perform all my pleasure: even saying to Jerusalem, Thou shalt be [a]built; and to the temple, Thy foundation shall be laid.

[a] Ezr.1.1,&c.

28), as being concerned in the transaction here referred to. The word rendered 'deep' (צוּלָה) denotes properly *anything sunk;* the depth of the sea; an abyss. But it may be applied to a deep river, and especially to the Euphrates, as a deep and mighty stream. In Jer. li. 36, the word 'sea' is applied to the Euphrates:

'I will dry up her sea,
And make her springs dry.'

Cyrus took the city of Babylon, after having besieged it a long time in vain, by turning the waters of the river into a vast lake, forty miles square, which had been constructed in order to carry off the superfluous waters in a time of inundation. By doing this, he laid the channel of the river almost dry, and was thus enabled to enter the city above and below, under the walls, and to take it by surprise. The LXX. render the word 'deep' here by Ἀβύσσῳ—'Abyss.' The Chaldee, 'Who says to Babylon, Be desolate, and I will dry up your streams.' ¶ *I will dry up thy rivers.* Referring doubtless to the numerous canals or artificial streams by which Babylon and the adjacent country were watered. These were supplied from the Euphrates, and when that was diverted from its usual bed, of course they became dry.

28. *That saith of Cyrus.* This is the first time in which Cyrus is expressly named by Isaiah, though he is often referred to. He is mentioned by him only in one other place expressly by name (ch. xlv. 1). He is several times mentioned elsewhere in the Old Testament (2 Chron. xxvi. 22, 23; Ezra i. 1, 2, 7; iii. 7; iv. 3; v. 13, 17; Dan. i. 21; vi. 28; x. 1). He began his reign about B.C. 550, and this prophecy was therefore delivered not far from a hundred and fifty years before he ascended the throne. None but God himself, or he whom God inspired, could have mentioned so long before, *the name* of him who should deliver the Jewish people from bondage; and if this was delivered, therefore, by Isaiah, it proves that he was under Divine inspiration. The name of Cyrus (כּוֹרֶשׁ, *Korĕsh;* Gr. Κῦρος), the Greek writers say, means 'the sun.' It is contracted from the Persian word *khorschid,* which in that language has this signification. Cyrus was the celebrated king of the Medes and Persians, and was the son of Cambyses the Persian, and of Mandane, daughter of Astyages, king of the Medes. For an account of his character and reign, see the Notes on ch. xli. 2, where I have anticipated all that is needful to be said here. ¶ He is *my shepherd.* A shepherd is one who leads and guides a flock, and then the word denotes, by a natural and easy metaphor, a ruler, or leader of a people. Thus the name is given to Moses in Isa. xliii. 2; comp. Ps. lxxvii. 20, and Ezek. xxxiv. 23. The name here is given to Cyrus because God would employ him to conduct his people again to their own land. The word 'my' implies, that he was under the direction of God, and was employed in his service. ¶ *And shall perform all my pleasure.* In destroying the city and kingdom of Babylon; in delivering the Jewish captives; and in rebuilding Jerusalem, and the temple. ¶ *Even saying to Jerusalem.* That is, I say to Jerusalem. The Vulgate and the LXX. render this as meaning God, and not Cyrus, and doubtless this is the true construction. It was one of the things which God would do, to say to Jerusalem that it should be rebuilt. ¶ *And to the temple.* Though now desolate and in ruins, yet it shall be reconstructed, and its foundation shall be firmly laid. The phrase 'to Jerusalem,' and 'to the temple,' should be rendered 'of,' in accordance with a common signification of the preposition לְ, and as it is rendered in the former part of the verse when speaking of Cyrus (comp. Gen. xx. 13; Judg. ix. 54). It was indeed under the direction of Cyrus that the city of Jerusalem was rebuilt, and the temple reconstructed (Ezra i. 1); but still it was to be traced to God, who raised him up

CHAPTER XLV.

ANALYSIS.

The subject which was introduced in the previous chapter (ver. 28) constitutes the main topic of this. God had there introduced the name of Cyrus as he who was to deliver his people from their captivity, and to restore them to their own land. This chapter is almost entirely occupied with a statement of the deliverance which would be effected through him—with an occasional reference to the more important deliverance which would be effected under the Messiah. The general subject of the chapter is the overthrow of Babylon, the deliverance of the Jews by Cyrus, and the events consequent on that, adapted to give consolation to the friends of God, particularly the future conversion of the Gentiles to the true religion.

I. An apostrophe to Cyrus, stating the design for which God had raised him up, and what he would do for him (1–8). This statement also comprises several items:—1. God would subdue nations before him, open brazen gates, and give him the treasures of kings (1–3). 2. The design for which God would do this would be, that he might deliver his people, and that the world might know that Jehovah was the true and only God (4–7). 3. The joyful consequences of this event—so great that the heavens are represented as dropping down righteousness, and the earth as bringing forth salvation in consequence of it (8).

II. Those who strive with their Maker are reproved and rebuked (9, 10). This is probably designed to apply to the people of Babylon, or to complainers in general in regard to the government of God.

III. God vindicates himself against the calumnies and objections of his enemies, and states the evidence that he is God, and the consequence of his interposition in raising up Cyrus. 1. He condescends to reason with men, and is willing to be inquired of respecting future events (11). 2. He had made the earth and all things, and he had raised up Cyrus for the purpose of delivering his people (12, 13). 3. He states the consequence of his raising up Cyrus, and their deliverance, for the purpose of comforting his people (14). 4. All the worshippers of idols should be ashamed and confounded (15, 16) 5. They who put their trust in God should never be confounded (17).

IV. God vindicates his own character; and calls on the nations of idolaters to come and compare the claims of idols with him, and especially appeals, in proof that he is God, to his power of predicting future events (18–21).

V. The chapter closes by a call on all nations to trust in him in view of the fact that he is the only true God; and with an assurance that all *should* yet trust in him, and that the true religion should yet spread over the world (22–25). This is designed further to comfort the people of God in their exile, and is a striking prophecy of the final universal prevalence of the gospel.

THUS saith the Lord to his anointed, to Cyrus, whose right hand I [1] have holden, to subdue nations before him; and I will loose [a] the loins of kings, to open before him the two-leaved gates; and the gates shall not be shut:

1 or, *strengthened.* a Dan.5.6,30.

for this purpose. That this passage was seen by Cyrus is the testimony of Josephus, and is morally certain from the nature of the case, since, otherwise, it is incredible that he should have aided the Jews in returning to their own land, and in rebuilding their city and temple (see Introd. § 2). This is one of the numerous instances in the Bible, in which God claims control and jurisdiction even over heathen princes and monarchs, and in which he says that their plans are under his direction, and made subservient to his will. It is *one* of the proofs that God presides over all, and that he makes the voluntary purposes of men subservient to him, and a part of the means of executing his glorious designs in relation to his people. Indeed, all the proud monarchs and conquerors of the earth have been in some sense instruments in his hand of executing his pleasure.

CHAPTER XLV.

1. *Thus saith the* Lord *to his anointed.* This is a direct apostrophe to Cyrus, though it was uttered not less than one hundred and fifty years before Babylon was taken by him. The word 'anointed' is that which is usually rendered *Messiah* (מָשִׁיחַ), and here is rendered by the LXX. Τῷ χριστῷ μου Κύρῳ—'To Cyrus, my Christ,' *i.e.*, my anointed. It properly means *the anointed*, and was a title which was commonly given to the kings of Israel, because they were set apart to their office by the ceremony of anointing, who hence

were called οἱ χριστοὶ Κυρίου—'The anointed of the Lord' (1 Sam. ii. 10, 35; xii. 3, 5; xvi. 6; xxiv. 7, 11; xxvi. 9, 11, 23; 2 Sam. i. 14, 16; xix. 22, 23). There is no evidence that the Persian kings were inaugurated or consecrated by oil, but this is an appellation which was common among the Jews, and is applied to Cyrus in accordance with their usual mode of designating kings. It means here that God had solemnly set apart Cyrus to perform an important public service in his cause. It does not mean that Cyrus was a man of piety, or a worshipper of the true God, of which there is no certain evidence, but that his appointment as king was owing to the arrangement of God's providence, and that he was to be employed in accomplishing his purposes. The title does not designate holiness of character, but appointment to an office. ¶ *Whose right hand I have holden.* Marg. 'Strengthened.' Lowth, 'Whom I hold fast by the right hand.' The idea seems to be, that God had upheld, sustained, strengthened him—as we do one who is feeble, by taking his right hand (see Notes on ch. xli. 13; xlii. 6). ¶ *To subdue nations before him.* For a general account of the conquests of Cyrus, see Notes on ch. xli. 2. It may be added here, that 'besides his native subjects, the nations which Cyrus subdued, and over which he reigned, were the Cilicians, Syrians, Paphlagonians, Cappadocians, Phrygians, Lydians, Carians, Phenicians, Arabians, Babylonians, Assyrians, Bactrians, Sacæ, and Maryandines. Xenophon describes his empire as extending from the Mediterranean and Egypt to the Indian Ocean, and from Ethiopia to the Euxine Sea, and conveys a physical idea of its extent by observing that the extremities were difficult to inhabit, from opposite causes—some from excess of heat, and others from excess of cold; some from a scarcity of water, and others from too great abundance.'—(*Pictorial Bible.*) ¶ *And I will loose the loins of kings.* The ancients dressed in a large, loose, flowing robe thrown over an under-garment or tunic, which was shaped to the body. The outer robe was girded with a sash when they toiled, or laboured, or went to war, or ran. Hence, 'to gird up the loins' is indicative of preparation for a journey, for labour, or for war To *unloose* the girdle, or the loins, was indicative of a state of rest, repose, or feebleness; and the phrase here means that God would so order it in his providence that the kings would be unprepared to meet him, or so feeble that they would not be able to resist him (comp. Job xxxviii. 3; Jer. i. 17). See also Job xii. 21:

> He poureth contempt upon princes,
> And weakeneth the strength of the mighty;

Marg. more correctly, 'Looseth the girdle of the strong.' There was a *literal* fulfilment of this in regard to Belshazzar, king of Babylon, when the city was taken by Cyrus. When the hand came forth on the walls of his palace, and the mysterious finger wrote his condemnation, it is said, 'Then the king's countenance was changed, and his thoughts troubled him, *so that the joints of his loins were loosed*, and his knees smote one against the other' (Dan. v. 6). The Vulgate renders this, 'I will turn the backs of kings.' ¶ *To open before him the two-leaved gates, and the gates shall not be shut.* The folding gates of a city, or a palace. It so happened in the scene of revelry which prevailed in Babylon when Cyrus took it, that the gates within the city which led from the streets to the river were left open. The city was not only *enclosed* with walls, but there were walls within the city on each side of the river Euphrates with gates, by which the inhabitants had access to the water of the river. Had not these gates been left open on that occasion, contrary to the usual custom, the Persians would have been shut up in the bed of the river, and could all have been destroyed. It also happened in the revelry of that night, that the gates of the palace were left open, so that there was access to every part of the city. Herodotus (i. 191) says, 'If the besieged had been aware of the designs of Cyrus, or had discovered the project before its actual accomplishment, they might have effected the total destruction of these troops. They had only to secure the little gates which led to the river, and to have manned the embankments on either side, and they might have in-

2 I will go before thee, and
make the crooked places straight:
I will break [a] in pieces the gates of
brass, and cut in sunder the bars
of iron:
3 And I will give thee the trea-

a Ps.107.17.

closed the Persians in a net from which they could never have escaped; as it happened they were taken by surprise; and such is the extent of that city, that, as the inhabitants themselves affirm, they who lived in the extremities were made prisoners before the alarm was communicated to the centre of the palace.' None but an omniscient Being could have predicted, a hundred and fifty years before it occurred, that such an event would take place; and this is one of the many prophecies which demonstrate in the most particular manner that Isaiah was inspired.

2. *I will go before thee.* To prepare the way for conquest, a proof that it is by the providence of God that the proud conquerors of the earth are enabled to triumph. The idea is, I will take away everything that would retard or oppose your victorious march. ¶ *And make the crooked paths straight* (see Note on ch. xl. 4). The Chaldee renders this, 'My word shall go before thee, and I will prostrate the walls.' Lowth renders it, 'Make the mountains plain.' Noyes, 'Make the high places plain.' The LXX. render it, Ὄρη ὁμαλιῶ—'Level mountains.' Vulg. *Gloriosos terræ humiliabo*—'The high places of the earth I will bring down.' The word הֲדוּרִים (*hădhūrīm*) is from הָדַר (*hādhăr*), *to be large*, ample, swollen, tumid; and probably means the swollen, tumid places, *i.e.*, the hills or elevated places; and the idea is, that God would make them level, or would remove all obstructions out of his way. ¶ *I will break in pieces the gates of brass.* Ancient cities were surrounded by walls, and secured by strong gates, which were not unfrequently made of brass. To Babylon there were one hundred gates, twenty-five on each side of the city, which, with their posts, were made of brass. 'In the circumference of the walls,' says Herodotus (i. 179), 'at different distances, were a hundred massy gates of brass, whose hinges and frames were of the same metal.' It was to this, doubtless, that the passage before us refers. ¶ *The bars of iron.* With which the gates of the city were fastened. 'One method of securing the gates of fortified places among the ancients, was to cover them with thick plates of iron—a custom which is still used in the East, and seems to be of great antiquity, We learn from Pitts, that Algiers has five gates, and some of these have two, some three other gates within them, and some of them plated all over with iron. Pococke, speaking of a bridge near Antioch, called the iron bridge, says, that there are two towers belonging to it, the gates of which are covered with iron plates. Some of these gates are plated over with brass; such are the enormous gates of the principal mosque at Damascus, formerly the church of John the Baptist' (Paxton). The general idea in these passages is, that Cyrus would owe his success to Divine interposition; and that that interposition would be so striking that it would be *manifest* that he owed his success to the favour of Heaven. This was so clear in the history of Cyrus, that it is recognized by himself, and was also recognized even by the heathen who witnessed the success of his arms. Thus Cyrus says (Ezra i. 2), 'JEHOVAH, God of heaven, hath given me all the kingdoms of the earth.' Thus Herodotus (i. 124) records the fact that Harpagus said in a letter to Cyrus, 'Son of Cambyses, Heaven evidently favours you, or you could never have thus risen superior to fortune.' So Herodotus (i. 205) says that Cyrus regarded himself as endowed with powers more than human: 'When he considered the peculiar circumstances of his birth, he believed himself more than human. He reflected also on the prosperity of his arms, and that wherever he had extended his excursions, he had been followed by success and victory.'

3. *And I will give thee the treasures of darkness.* The treasures which kings have amassed, and which they have laid up in dark and secure places. The word 'darkness,' here, means that which was

sures of darkness, and the hidden riches of secret places, that thou mayest know that I the LORD, which [a]call *thee* by thy name, *am* the God of Israel.

[a] ch 48.15.

hidden, unknown, secret (comp. Job xii. 22). The treasures of the kings of the East were usually hidden in some obscure and strong place, and were not to be touched except in cases of pressing necessity. Alexander found vast quantities of treasure thus hidden among the Persians; and it was by taking such treasures that the rapacity of the soldiers who followed a conqueror was satisfied, and in fact by a division of the spoils thus taken that they were paid. There can be no doubt that large quantities of treasure in this manner would be found in Babylon. The following observations from Harmer (*Obs.* pp. 111, 511–513), will show that it was common to conceal treasures in this manner in the East; 'We are told by travellers in the East, that they have met with great difficulties, very often from a notion universally disseminated among them, that all Europeans are magicians, and that their visits to those eastern countries are not to satisfy curiosity, but to find out, and get possession of those vast treasures they believe to be buried there in great quantities. These representations are very common; but Sir J. Chardin gives us a more particular and amusing account of affairs of this kind: "It is common in the Indies, for those sorcerers that accompany conquerors, everywhere to point out the place where treasures are hid. Thus, at Surat, when Siragi came thither, there were people who, with a stick striking on the ground or against walls, found out those that had been hollowed or dug up, and ordered such places to be opened." He then intimates that something of this nature had happened to him in Mingrelia. Among the various contradictions that agitate the human breast, this appears to be a remarkable one; they firmly believe the power of magicians to discover hidden treasures, and yet they continue to hide them. Dr. Perry has given us an account of some mighty treasures hidden in the ground by some of the principal people of the Turkish empire, which, upon a revolution, were discovered by domestics privy to the secret. D'Herbelot has given us accounts of treasures concealed in the same manner, some of them of great princes, discovered by accidents extremely remarkable; but this account of Chardin's, of conquerors pretending to find out hidden treasures by means of sorcerers, is very extraordinary. As, however, people of this cast have made great pretences to mighty things, in all ages, and were not unfrequently confided in by princes, there is reason to believe they pretended sometimes, by their art, to discover treasures, anciently, to princes, of which they had gained intelligence by other methods; and, as God opposed his prophets, at various times, to pretended sorcerers, it is not unlikely that the prophet Isaiah points at some such prophetic discoveries, in those remarkable words (Isa. xlv. 3): "And I will give thee the treasures of darkness, and hidden riches of secret places, that thou mayest know that I the LORD, which call thee by thy name, am the God of Israel." I will give them, by enabling some prophet of mine to tell thee where they are concealed. Such a supposition throws a great energy into those words.' The belief that the ruins of cities abound with treasures that were deposited there long since, prevails in the East, and the inhabitants of those countries regard all travellers who come there, Burckhardt informs us, as coming to find treasures, and as having power to remove them by enchantment. 'It is very unfortunate,' says he, 'for European travellers, that the idea of treasures being hidden in ancient edifices is so strongly rooted in the minds of the Arabs and Turks; they believe that it is sufficient for a true magician to have seen and observed the spot where treasures are hidden (of which he is supposed to be already informed by the old books of the infidels who lived on the spot), in order to be able afterwards at his ease to command the guardian of the treasure to set the whole before him. It was of no avail to tell them to follow me and see whether I searched for money. Their reply was, "Of course you will not dare to take it out before us, but we know that if you are a skilful magician you will order it to follow you through the air to whatever place you please." If the traveller takes the dimensions of a building or a column, they are persuaded it is a magical proceeding.'—(*Travels in Syria*, pp. 428, 429. Ed. Lond. 4to, 1822.) Laborde, in his account of a visit to Petra, or Sela, has given an account of a splendid temple cut in the solid rock, which is called the Khasné, or 'treasury of Pharaoh.' It is sculptured out of an enormous block of freestone, and is one of the most splendid remains of antiquity. It is believed by the Arabs to have been the place where Pharaoh, supposed to have been the founder of the costly edifices of Petra, had deposited his wealth. 'After having searched in vain,' says Laborde, 'all the coffins and funeral monuments, to find his wealth, they supposed it must be in the urn which surmounted the Khasné. But, unhappily, being out of their reach, it has only served the more to kindle their desires. Hence whenever they pass through the ravine, they stop for a moment, charge their guns, aim at the urn, and endeavour by firing at it, to break off some fragments, with a view to demolish it altogether, and get at the treasure which it is supposed to contain.'—(Laborde's *Sinai and Petra*, p. 170. Ed. Lond. 1836.) The treasures which Cyrus obtained in his conquests are known to have been immense. Sardis, the capital of Crœsus, king of Lydia, the most wealthy monarch of his time, was, according to Herodotus (i. 84), given up to be plundered; and his hoarded wealth became the spoil of the victor (see also Xen. *Cyr.* vii.) That Babylon abounded in treasures is expressly declared by Jeremiah (ch. li. 13): 'O thou that dwellest upon many waters, abundant in treasures.' These treasures also, according to Jeremiah (ch. l. 37), became the spoil of the conqueror of the city. Pliny also has given a description of the wealth which Cyrus obtained in his conquests, which strikingly confirms what Isaiah here declares: 'Cyrus, in the conquest of Asia, obtained thirty-four thousand pounds weight of gold, besides golden vases, and gold that was wrought with leaves, and the palm-tree, and the vine. In which victory also he obtained five hundred thousand talents of silver, and the goblet of Semiramis, which weighed fifteen talents.'—(*Nat. Hist.* 33. 3.) Brerewood has estimated that this gold and silver amounted to one hundred and twenty-six millions, and two hundred and twenty-four thousand pounds sterling.—(*De Pon. et Men.* 10.) Babylon was the centre of an immense traffic that was carried on between the eastern parts of Asia and the western parts of Asia and Europe. For a description of this commerce, see an article in the *Bib. Rep.* vol. vii. pp. 364–390. Babylonian garments, it will be remembered, of great value, had made their way to Palestine in the time of Joshua (vii. 21). Tapestries embroidered with figures of griffons and other monsters of eastern imagination were articles of export (Isaac Vossius, *Observatio*). Carpets were wrought there of the finest materials and workmanship, and formed an article of extensive exportation. They were of high repute in the times of Cyrus; whose tomb at Pasargada was adorned with them (Arrian, *Exped. Alex.* vi. 29). Great quantities of gold were used in Babylon. The vast image of gold erected by Nebuchadnezzar in the plain of Dura is proof enough of this fact. The image was sixty cubits high and six broad (Dan. iii. 1). Herodotus (i. 183) informs us that the Chaldeans used a thousand talents of frankincense annually in the temple of Jupiter. ¶ *That thou mayest know.* That from these signal successes, and these favours of heaven, you may learn that JEHOVAH is the true God. This he would learn because he would see that he owed it to Heaven (see Note on ver. 2); and because the prediction which God had made of his success would convince him that he was the true and only God. That it had this effect on Cyrus is apparent from his own proclamation (see Ezra i. 2). God took this method of making himself known to the monarch of the most mighty kingdom of the earth, in order, as he repeatedly declares, that through his dealings with kingdoms and men he may be acknowledged. ¶ *Which call* thee *by thy name* (see Notes on ch. xliii. 1). That thou mayest know that I, who so long before desig-

4 For Jacob my servant's sake, and Israel mine elect, I have even called thee by thy name: I have surnamed thee, though thou hast not known me.
5 I [a] *am* the LORD, and [b] *there is* no God besides me: I girded thee, [c] though thou hast not known me:
6 That [d] they may know from the rising of the sun, and from the west, that *there is* none besides me: I *am* the LORD, and *there is* none else.

a De.4.35,39. *b* ver.14,18,22. *c* Ps.18.32,39. *d* ch.37.20; Mal.1.11.

nated thee by name, am the true God. The argument is, that none but God could have foretold *the name* of him who should be the deliverer of his people. ¶ *Am the God of Israel.* That the God of Israel was the true and only God. The point to be made known was not that he was the God of Israel, but that the God of Israel was JEHOVAH the true God.

4. *For Jacob my servant's sake* (see Note on ch. xlii. 19). The statement here is, that God had raised up Cyrus on account of his own people. The sentiment is common in the Bible, that kings and nations are in the hand of God; and that he overrules and directs their actions for the accomplishment of his own purposes, and especially to protect, defend, and deliver his people (see Note on ch. x. 5; comp. ch. xlvii. 6). ¶ *I have surnamed thee.* On the meaning of the word 'surname,' see Notes on ch. xliv. 5. The reference here is to the fact that he had appointed him to accomplish important purposes, and had designated him as his 'shepherd' (ch. xliv. 28), and his 'anointed' (ch. xlv. 1). ¶ *Though thou hast not known me.* Before he was called to accomplish these important services, he was a stranger to JEHOVAH, and it was only when he should have been so signally favoured of Heaven, and should be made acquainted with the Divine will in regard to the deliverance of his people and the rebuilding of the temple (Ezra i. 1–3), that he would be acquainted with the true God.

5. *I* am *the* LORD, &c. (see Notes on ch. xlii. 8; xliii. 2; xliv. 8; and ver. 14, 18, 22, of this chapter). ¶ *I girded thee,* &c. (see Note on ver. 1). The sense is, I girded thee with the girdle—the military belt; I prepared thee, and strengthened thee for war and conquest. Even men who are strangers to the true God are sustained by him, and are unable to accomplish anything without his providential aid.

6. *That they may know from the rising of the sun, and from the west.* This phrase is evidently here used to designate the whole world. Kimchi says, that the reason why the north and the south are not mentioned here is, that the earth from the east to the west is perfectly inhabitable, but not so from the north to the south. That this was accomplished, see Ezra i. 1, *sq.* Cyrus made public proclamation that JEHOVAH had given him all the kingdoms of the earth, and had commanded him to rebuild the temple in Jerusalem. The purpose of all this arrangement was, to secure the acknowledgment of the truth that JEHOVAH was the only true God, as extensively as possible. Nothing could be better adapted to this than the actual course of events. For, 1. The conquest of Jerusalem by Nebuchadnezzar was an event which would be extensively known throughout all nations. 2. Babylon was then the magnificent capital of the heathen world, and the kingdom of which it was the centre was the most mighty kingdom of the earth. 3. The fact of the conquest of Babylon, and the manner in which it was done, would be known all over that empire, and would attract universal attention. Nothing had ever occurred more remarkable; nothing more fitted to excite the wonder of mankind. 4. The hand of JEHOVAH was so manifest in this, and the prophecies which had been uttered were so distinctly fulfilled, that Cyrus himself acknowledged that it was of JEHOVAH. The existence, the name, and the truth of JEHOVAH became known as far as the name and exploits of Cyrus; and there was a public recognition of the true God by him who had conquered the most mighty capital of the world, and whose

7 I [a]form the light, and create
darkness; I make peace, [b]and create [c]evil. I the LORD do all these
things.

a Ge.1 4. b Ps.29.11. c Am.5.6.

opinions and laws were to enter into the constitution of the Medo-Persian empire that was to succeed.

7. *I form the light, and create darkness.* Light, in the Bible, is the emblem of knowledge, innocence, pure religion, and of prosperity in general; and darkness is the emblem of the opposite. Light here seems to be the emblem of peace and prosperity, and darkness the emblem of adversity; and the sentiment of the verse is, that all things prosperous and adverse are under the providential control and direction of God. Of *light,* it is literally true that God made it; and emblematically true that he is the source of knowledge, prosperity, happiness, and pure religion. Of *darkness,* it is literally true also that the night is formed by him; that he withdraws the light of the sun, and leaves the earth enveloped in gloomy shades. It is emblematically true also that calamity, ignorance, disappointment, and want of success are ordered by him; and not less true that all the moral darkness, or evil, that prevails on earth, is under the direction and ordering of his Providence. There is no reason to think, however, that the words 'darkness' and 'evil' are to be understood as referring to moral darkness; that is, *sin.* A strict regard should be had to the connection in the interpretation of such passages; and the connection here does not demand such an interpretation. The main subject is, *the prosperity which would attend the arms of Cyrus, the consequent reverses and calamities of the nations whom he would subdue, and the proof thence furnished that* JEHOVAH *was the true God;* and the passage should be limited in the interpretation to this design. The statement is, that all this was under his direction. It was not the work of chance or hap-hazard. It was not accomplished or caused by idols. It was not originated by any inferior or subordinate cause. It was to be traced entirely to God. The successes of arms, and the blessings of peace were to be traced to him; and the reverses of arms, and the calamities of war to him also. This is all that the connection of the passage demands; and this is in accordance with the interpretation of Kimchi, Jerome, Rosenmüller, Gesenius, Calvin, and Grotius. The comment of Grotius is, 'Giving safety to the people, as the Persians; sending calamities upon the people, as upon the Medes and Babylonians.' Lowth, Jerome, Vitringa, Jahn, and some others, suppose that there is reference here to the prevalent doctrine among the Persians, and the followers of the Magian religion in general, which prevailed all over the East, and in which Cyrus was probably educated, that there are two supreme, independent, co-existent and eternal causes always acting in opposition to each other—the one the author of all good, and the other of all evil; and that these principles or causes are constantly struggling with each other. The good being or principle, they call light; and the evil, darkness; the one, Oromasden, and the other Ahrimanen. It was further the doctrine of the Magians that when the good principle had the ascendency, happiness prevailed; and when the evil principle prevailed, misery abounded. Lowth supposes, that God here means to assert his complete and absolute superiority over all other things or principles; and that all those powers whom the Persians supposed to be the original authors of good and evil to mankind were subordinate, and must be subject to him; and that there is no power that is not subservient to him, and under his control. That these opinions prevailed in very early times, and perhaps as early as Isaiah, there seems no good reason to doubt (Hyde, *de Relig. Veter.* Persar, xxii.) But there is no good evidence that Isaiah here referred to those opinions. Good and evil, prosperity and adversity, abound in the world at all times; and all that is required in order to a correct understanding of this passage is the general statement that all these things are under providential direction. ¶ *I make peace.* I hush the contending passions of men; I dispose to peace, and prevent wars when I choose—a passage

8 Drop [a] down, ye heavens, from
above, and let the skies pour down
righteousness; let the earth open,
and let them bring forth salvation,
and [b] let righteousness spring up
together. I the LORD have created
it.

a Ps.85.11. b Ps.72.3.

which proves that the most violent passions are under his control. No passions are more uncontrollable than those which lead to wars; and nowhere is there a more striking display of the Omnipotence of God than in his power to repress the pride, ambition, and spirit of revenge of conquerors and kings:

> Which stilleth the noise of the seas,
> The noise of their waves,
> And the tumult of the people.
> Ps. lxv. 7.

¶ *And create evil.* The parallelism here shows that this is not to be understood in the sense of *all* evil, but of that which is the opposite of peace and prosperity. That is, God directs judgments, disappointments, trials, and calamities; he has power to suffer the mad passions of men to rage, and to afflict nations with war; he presides over adverse as well as prosperous events. The passage does not prove that God is the author of moral evil, or sin, and such a sentiment is abhorrent to the general strain of the Bible, and to all just views of the character of a holy God.

8. *Drop down, ye heavens, from above.* That is, as a result of the benefits that shall follow from the rescue of the people from their captivity and exile. The mind of the prophet is carried forward to future times, and he sees effects from that interposition, as striking as if the heavens should distil righteousness; and sees the prevalence of piety and happiness as if they should spring out of the earth. It may be designed primarily to denote the happy results of their return to their own land, and the peace and prosperity which would ensue. But there is a beauty and elevation in the language which is better applicable to the remote and distant consequences of their return—the coming and reign of the Messiah. The figure is that of the rain and dew descending from heaven, and watering the earth, and producing fertility and beauty; and the idea is, that piety and peace would prevail in a manner resembling the verdure of the fields under such rains and dews. A figure remarkably similar to this is employed by the Psalmist (lxxxv. 11, 12):

> Truth shall spring out of the earth;
> And righteousness shall look down from heaven.
> Yea, the LORD shall give that which is good;
> And our land shall yield her increase.

The phrase, 'drop down, ye heavens, from above,' means, pour forth, or distil, as the clouds distil, or drop down the rain or dew (Ps. xlv. 12, 13). It is appropriately applied to rain or dew, and here means that righteousness would be as abundant as if poured down like dews or showers from heaven. The LXX. however, render it, 'Let the heavens above be glad,' but evidently erroneously. ¶ *And let the skies.* The word here used (שְׁחָקִים) is derived from the verb שָׁחַק, *to rub*, pound fine, or beat in pieces; and is then applied to dust (see ch. xl. 15); to a thin cloud; a cloud of dust; and then to clouds in general (Job xxxvi. 28; xxxvii. 18; xxxviii. 37). The sense here is, that righteousness should be poured down like rain from the clouds of heaven; that is, it should be abundant, and should prevail on the earth. ¶ *Pour down righteousness.* The result of the deliverance from the captivity shall be, that righteousness shall be abundant. During the captivity they had been far away from their native land; the temple was destroyed; the fire had ceased to burn on the altars; the praises of God had ceased to be celebrated in his courts; and all the means by which piety had been nourished had been withdrawn. This state of things was strikingly similar to the earth when the rain is withheld, and all verdure droops and dies. But after the return from the exile, righteousness would abound under the re-establishment of the temple service and the means of grace. Nor can there be any doubt, I think, that the mind of the prophet was also fixed on the prevalence of religion which would yet take place under the Messiah, whose coming, though re-

9 Wo unto him that striveth with his Maker! *Let the* [a] potsherd *strive* with the potsherds of the earth. Shall the clay say to him that fashioneth it, What makest thou? or thy work, He hath no hands?

[a] Je.18.6.

motely, would be one of the results of the return from the exile, and of whose advent, that return would be so strikingly emblematic. ¶ *Let the earth open.* As it does when the showers descend and render it mellow, and when it brings forth grass and plants and fruits. ¶ *And let them bring forth salvation.* The Chaldee renders this, 'Let the earth open, and the dead revive, and righteousness be revealed at the same time.' The idea is, let the earth and the heavens produce righteousness, or become fruitful in producing salvation. Salvation shall abound *as if* it descended like showers and dews, and as if the fertile earth everywhere produced it. Vitringa supposes that it means that the hearts of men would be opened and prepared for repentance and the reception of the truth by the Holy Spirit, as the earth is made mellow and adapted to the reception of seed by the rain and dew. ¶ *And let righteousness spring up together.* Let it at the same time *germinate* as a plant does. It shall spring forth like green grass, and like flowers and plants in the well-watered earth. The language in the verse is figurative, and very beautiful. The idea is, that peace, prosperity, and righteousness start up like the fruits of the earth when it is well watered with the dews and rains of heaven; that the land and world would be clothed in moral loveliness; and that the fruits of salvation would be abundant everywhere. That there was a *partial* fulfilment of this on the return to the land of Canaan, there can be no doubt. The Jews were, for a time at least, much more distinguished for piety than they had been before. Idolatry ceased; the temple was rebuilt; the worship of God was re-established; and the nation enjoyed unwonted prosperity. But there is a richness and fulness in the language which is not met by anything that occurred in the return from the exile; and it doubtless receives its entire fulfilment only under that more important deliverance of which the return from Babylon was but the emblem. As referred to the Messiah, and to his reign, may we not regard it as descriptive of the following things? 1. The prevalence and diffusion of the knowledge of salvation under his own preaching and that of the apostles. Religion was revived throughout Judea, and spread with vast rapidity throughout almost the whole of the known world. It seemed as if the very heavens shed down righteousness on all lands, and the earth, so long barren and sterile, brought forth the fruits of salvation. Every country partook of the benefits of the descending showers of grace, and the moral world put on a new aspect—like the earth after descending dews and rains. 2. It is beautifully descriptive of a revival of religion like that on the day of Pentecost. In such scenes, it seems as if the very heavens 'poured down' righteousness. A church smiles under its influence like parched and barren fields under rains and dews, and society puts on an aspect of loveliness like the earth after copious showers. Salvation seems to start forth with the beauty of the green grass, or of the unfolding buds, producing leaves and flowers and abundant fruits. There cannot be found anywhere a more beautiful description of a genuine revival of pure religion than in this verse. 3. It is descriptive, doubtless, of what is *yet* to take place in the better days which are to succeed the present, when the knowledge of the Lord shall fill the earth. All the earth shall be blessed, as if descending showers should produce universal fertility, and every land, now desolate, barren, sterile, and horrid by sin, shall become 'like a well-watered garden' in reference to salvation.

9. *Wo unto him that striveth with his Maker!* This verse commences a new subject. Its connection with the preceding is not very obvious. It may be designed to prevent the objections and cavils of the unbelieving Jews who were disposed to murmur against God,

and to arraign the wisdom of his dispensations in regard to them, in permitting them to be oppressed by their enemies, and in promising them deliverance instead of preventing their captivity. So Lowth understands it. Rosenmüller regards it as designed to meet a cavil, because God chose to deliver them by Cyrus, a foreign prince, and a stranger to the true religion, rather than by one of their own nation. Kimchi, and some others, suppose that it is designed to repress the pride of the Babylonians, who designed to keep the Jews in bondage, and who would thus contend with God. But perhaps the idea is of a more general nature. It may be designed to refer to the fact that *any* interposition of God, any mode of manifesting himself to men, meets with enemies, and with those who are disposed to contend with him, and *especially* any display of his mercy and grace in a great revival of religion. In the previous verse the prophet had spoken of the revival of religion. Perhaps he here adverts to the fact that *such* a manifestation of his mercy would meet with opposition. So it was when the Saviour came, and when Christianity spread around the world; so it is in every revival now; and so it will be, perhaps, in the spreading of the gospel throughout the world in the time that shall usher in the millennium. Men thus contend with their Maker; resist the influences of his Spirit; strive against the appeals made to them; *oppose his sovereignty;* are enraged at the preaching of the gospel, and often combine to oppose him. That this is the meaning of this passage, seems to be the sentiment of the apostle Paul, who has borrowed this image, and has applied it in a similar manner: 'Nay but, O man, who art thou that repliest against God? Shall the thing formed say to him that formed it, Why hast thou made me thus? Hath not the potter power over the clay, of the same lump to make one vessel unto honour, and another unto dishonour?' (Rom. ix. 20, 21.) It is *implied* that men are opposed to the ways which God takes to govern the world; it is *affirmed* that calamity shall follow all the resistance which men shall make. This we shall follow, because, first, God has all power, and all who contend with him must be defeated and overthrown; and, secondly, because God is *right,* and the sinner who opposes him is wrong, and must and will be punished for his resistance. ¶ Let the *potsherd* strive *with the potsherds of the earth.* Lowth renders this,

> Woe unto him that contendeth with the power that formed him;
> The potsherd with the moulder of the clay.

The word rendered 'potsherd' (חֶרֶשׂ) means properly *a shard,* or *sherd, i.e.,* a fragment of an earthen vessel (Deut. vi. 21; xi. 33; Job ii. 8; xli. 22; Ps. xxii. 16). It is then put proverbially for anything frail and mean. Here it is undoubtedly put for man, regarded as weak and contemptible in his efforts against God. Our translation would seem to denote that it was *appropriate* for man to contend with equals, but not with one so much his superior as God; or that he might have some hope of success in contending with his fellow-men, but none in contending with his Maker. But this sense does not well suit the connection. The idea in the mind of the prophet is not that such contentions are either proper or appropriate among men, but it is the supreme folly and sin of contending with God; and the thought in illustration of this is not that men may appropriately contend with each other, but it is the superlative weakness and fragility of man. The translation proposed, therefore, by Jerome, 'Wo to him who contends with his Maker—*testa de samiis terræ*—a potsherd among the earthen pots [made of the earth of Samos] of the earth'—and which is found in the Syriac, and adopted by Rosenmüller, Gesenius, and Noyes, is doubtless the true rendering. According to Gesenius, the particle אֶת here means *by* or *among;* and the idea is, that man is a potsherd among the potsherds of the earth; a weak fragile creature among others equally so—and yet *presuming* impiously to contend with the God that made him. The LXX. render this, 'Is anything endowed with excellence? I fashioned it like the clay of a potter. Will the ploughman plough the ground all the day long? Will the clay say to the potter,' &c.

10 Wo unto him that saith unto *his* father, What begettest thou? or to the woman, What hast thou brought forth?

11 Thus saith the LORD, the Holy One of Israel, and his Maker, Ask me of things to come concerning my sons; [a]and concerning the work of mine hands command [b]ye me.

a Je.31.1; Ga.3.26. b Jn.16.23.

¶ *Shall the clay,* &c. It would be absurd for the clay to complain to him that moulds it, of the form which he chooses to give it. Not *less* absurd is it for man, made of clay, and moulded by the hand of God, to complain of the fashion in which he has made him; of the rank which he has assigned him in the scale of being; and of the purposes which he designs to accomplish by him. ¶ *He hath no hands.* He has no skill, no wisdom, no power. It is by the *hand* chiefly that pottery is moulded; and the hands here stand for the skill or wisdom which is evinced in making it. The Syriac renders it, 'Neither am I the work of thy hands.'

10. *Wo unto him that saith unto* his *father,* &c. It is wicked and foolish for a son to complain of his father or mother in regard to his birth, or of his rank and condition of life. Probably the idea is, that if a child is by his birth placed in circumstances less advantageous than others, he would have no right to complain of his parents, or to regard them as having acted improperly in having entered into the marriage relation. In like manner it would be *not less* improper, certainly, to complain of God who has brought us into existence by his own power, and who acts as a sovereign in the various allotments of our lives. The design is to rebuke the spirit of complaining against the allotments of Providence—a spirit which perhaps prevailed among the Jews, and which in fact is found everywhere among men; and to show that God, as a sovereign, has a right to dispose of his creatures in the manner which he shall judge to be best. The passage proves—1. That man is formed by God, and that all his affairs are ordered by him as really as the work of the potter is moulded by the hands of the workman. 2. That God had a *design* in making man, and in ordering and arranging his circumstances in life. 3. That man is little qualified to judge of that design, and not at all qualified to pronounce it unwise, any more than the clay could charge him that worked it into a vessel with want of wisdom; and, 4. That God is a sovereign, and does as he pleases. He has formed man as he chose, as really as the potter moulds the clay into any shape which he pleases. He has given him his rank in creation; given him such a body—strong, vigorous, and comely; or feeble, deformed, and sickly, as he pleased; he has given him such an intellect—vigorous, manly, and powerful; or weak, feeble, and timid, as he pleased; he has determined his circumstances in life—whether riches, poverty, an elevated rank, or a depressed condition, just as he saw fit; and he is a sovereign also in the dispensation of his grace—having a right to pardon whom he will; nor has man any right to complain. This passage, however, should not be adduced to prove that God, *in all respects,* moulds the character and destiny of men as the potter does the clay. Regard should be had in the interpretation to the fact that God is just, and good, and wise, as well as a sovereign; and that man is himself a moral agent, and subject to the laws of moral agency which God has appointed. God does nothing wrong. He does not compel man to sin, and then condemn him for it. He does not *make* him a transgressor by physical power, as the potter moulds the clay, and then doom him for it to destruction. He does his pleasure according to the eternal laws of equity; and man has no right to call in question the rectitude of his sovereign dispensations.

11. *Thus saith the* LORD. This verse is designed still further to illustrate the general subject referred to in this chapter, and especially to show them, that instead of complaining of his designs, or of finding fault with his sovereignty, it was their privilege to

12 I [a] have made the earth, and
created man upon it: I, *even* my
hands, have stretched out the heavens, and all their host have I commanded.
13 I have raised him up in righ-

a Ps.102.25; He.11.3.

inquire respecting his dealings, and even to 'command' him. He was willing to be inquired of, and to instruct them in regard to the events which were occurring. ¶ *And his Maker* (see Note on ch. xliii. 1). ¶ *Ask me of things to come.* 'I alone can direct and order future events; and it is your duty and privilege to make inquiry respecting those events. Lowth renders this as a question, 'Do ye question me concerning my children?' But the more correct rendering is doubtless that in our translation, where it is represented as a duty to make inquiry respecting future events from God. The idea is—1. That God alone could direct future events, and give information respecting them. 2. That instead of complaining of his allotments, they should humbly inquire of him in regard to their design, and the proper manner of meeting them; and 3. That if they were made the subject of humble, fervent, believing prayer, he would order them so as to promote their welfare, and would furnish them grace to meet them in a proper manner. ¶ *Concerning my sons.* Those who are my adopted children. It is implied that God loved them as his children, and that they had the privilege of pleading for his favour and regard, with the assurance that he would be propitious to their cry, and would order events so as to promote their welfare. ¶ *And concerning the work of my hands.* In regard to what I do. This is also read as a question by Lowth; 'And do ye give me directions concerning the work of my hands?' According to this interpretation, God would reprove them for presuming to give him direction about what he should do, in accordance with the sentiment in ver. 9, 10. This interpretation also is adopted by Vitringa, Jarchi, Aben Ezra, and some others. Grotius renders it, 'Hinder, if you can, my doing what I will with them. Thus you will show what you can do, and what I can do.' Rosenmüller supposes it to mean, 'Commit my sons, and the work of my hands to me; suffer me to do with my own what I will.' It seems to me, however, that the word 'command' is here to be taken rather as indicating the privilege of his people to present their desires in the language of fervent and respectful petition; and that God here indicates that he would, so to speak, allow them to *direct* him; that he would hear their prayers, and would conform the events of his administration to their wishes and their welfare. This is the most obvious interpretation; and this will perhaps suit the connection as well as any other. Instead of complaining, and opposing his administration (ver. 9, 10), it was their privilege to come before him and spread out their wants, and even to *give direction* in regard to future events, so far as the events of his administration would bear on them, and he would meet their desires. Thus interpreted, it accords with the numerous passages of the Bible which command us to pray; and with the promises of God that he will lend a listening ear to our cries.

12. *I have made the earth.* God here asserts that he had made all things, doubtless with a view to show that he was able to hear their cry, and to grant an answer to their requests. His agency was visible everywhere, alike in forming and sustaining all things, and in raising up for them a deliverer. They might, therefore, go before him with confidence, and spread out all their wants. ¶ *Have stretched out the heavens* (see Notes on ch. xl. 26). ¶ *And all their host.* The stars (see Notes on ch. xl. 26). ¶ *Have I commanded.* All are under my direction and control. What more can be needed by his people than the friendship and protection of him who made the heavens and the earth, and who leads on the stars!

13. *I have raised him up.* That is. Cyrus (see Notes on ch. xli. 2). ¶ *In righteousness.* In ch. xli. 2, he is called 'the righteous man.' He had raised him up to accomplish his own righteous plans. It does not necessarily mean

teousness, and I will [1] direct all his ways: he shall build [a] my city, and he shall let go my captives, not for price [b] nor reward, saith the LORD of hosts.

14 Thus saith the LORD, The labour of Egypt, and merchandise of Ethiopia and of the Sabeans, men of stature, shall come over unto [c] thee, and they shall be thine: they shall come after thee; in chains [d] they shall come over, and they shall fall down unto thee, they shall make supplication unto thee, *saying*, Surely [e] God *is* in thee; and *there is* none else, *there is* no God.

1 or, *make straight.* a 2 Ch.36.22; Ezr.1.1,&c.

b ch.52.3. c Ps.68.31; 72.10,11; ch.49.23; 60.9-16. d Ps.149.8. e 1 Co.14.25.

that Cyrus was a righteous man (see Notes on ch. xli. 2). ¶ *And I will direct all his ways.* Marg. 'Make straight.' This is the meaning of the Hebrew word (see Notes on ch. xl. 4). The sense here is, I will make his paths all smooth and level, *i.e.*, whatever obstacles are in his way I will remove, and give him eminent success. ¶ *He shall build my city.* Jerusalem. See Ezra i. 2, where, in his proclamation, Cyrus says, 'JEHOVAH, God of heaven, hath given me all the kingdoms of the earth; and he hath charged me to build him an house at Jerusalem, which is in Judah.' It is very probable that Cyrus was made acquainted with these predictions of Isaiah. Nothing would be more natural than that the Jews in Babylon, when he should become master of the city, knowing that he was the monarch to whom Isaiah referred, and that he had been raised up for their deliverance, should acquaint him with these remarkable prophecies, and show him that God had long before designated him to accomplish this great work (comp. Notes on ch. xliv. 28). ¶ *And he shall let go my captives.* Heb. 'My captivity,' or 'my migration;' *i.e.*, those of his people who were in captivity. ¶ *Not for price.* They shall not be purchased of him as slaves, nor shall they be required to purchase their own freedom. They shall be sent away as freemen, and no price shall be exacted for their ransom (comp. ch. lii. 3). The Jews in Babylon were regarded as captives in war, and therefore as slaves. ¶ *Nor for reward.* The Hebrew word here used (שֹׁחַד) denotes properly that which is given to conciliate the favour of others, and hence often a *bribe.* Here it means, that nothing should be given to Cyrus for their purchase, or to induce him to set them at liberty. He should do it of his own accord. It was a fact that he not only released them, but that he endowed them with rich and valuable gifts, to enable them to restore their temple and city (Ezra i. 7-11).

14. *Thus saith the* LORD. This verse is designed to denote the favours which in subsequent times would be conferred on Jerusalem, the city which (ver. 13) was to be rebuilt. It has reference, according to Lowth, to the conversion of the Gentiles, and their admission into the church of God. Grotius, however, understands it as addressed to Cyrus, and as meaning that because he had released the Jews without reward, therefore God would give him the wealth of Egypt, Ethiopia, Sabæa, and that those nations should be subject to him. But in this opinion probably he stands alone, and the objections to it are so obvious that they need not be specified. Some of the Jewish interpreters suppose that it refers to the same events as those recorded in ch. xliii. 3, and that it relates to the fact that God *had formerly* given those nations for the deliverance and protection of his people. They suppose that particular reference is had to the slaughter and destruction of the army of Sennacherib. Vitringa regards it as referring to the fact that proselytes should be made from all these nations to the true religion, and finds, as he supposes, a fulfilment of it in the times of the Saviour and the apostles. In regard to the true meaning of the passage, we may observe—1. That it refers to the times that would *succeed* their return from their exile; and not to events that were then past. This is apparent on the face of the passage. 2. It relates to Jerusalem, or to the people

of God, and not to Cyrus. This is evident, because it was not true that these nations became subject to *Cyrus* after his taking Babylon, for it was not Cyrus, but his son Cambyses that invaded and subdued Egypt, and because the whole phraseology has reference to a conversion to religion, and not to the subjection involved in the conquests of war. 3. It appropriately relates to a conversion to the true God, and an embracing of the true religion. This is implied in the language in the close of the verse, 'saying, Surely God is in thee; and there is none else, there is no God.' 4. The passage, therefore, means, that subsequent to their return from Babylon, there would be the conversion of those nations; or that they—perhaps here mentioned as the representatives of great and mighty nations in general—would be converted to the true faith, and that their wealth and power would be consecrated to the cause of JEHOVAH. The *time* when this was to be, is not fixed in the prophecy itself. It is only determined that it was to be *subsequent* to the return from the exile, and to be one of the consequences of that return. The fulfilment, therefore, may be sought either under the first preaching of the gospel, or in times still more remote. A more full explanation will occur in the examination of the different parts of the verse. ¶ *The labour of Egypt.* That is, the fruit, or result of the labour of Egypt; the wealth of Egypt (see the word thus used in Job x. 3; Ps. lxxviii. 46; Isa. lv. 2; Jer. iii. 24; xx. 5; Ezek. xxiii. 9). The idea is, that Egypt would be converted to the true religion, and its wealth consecrated to the service of the true God. The conversion of Egypt is not unfrequently foretold (Ps. lxviii. 31):

> Princes shall come out of Egypt.
> Ethiopia shall soon stretch out her hands unto
> God.

See Notes on ch. xix. 18–22—where the conversion of Egypt is introduced and discussed at length. ¶ *And merchandise of Ethiopia.* On the situation of Ethiopia, see Notes on ch xviii. 1. The word 'merchandise' here means the same as wealth, since their wealth consisted in their traffic. That Cush or Ethiopia would be converted to the true religion and be united to the people of God, is declared in the passage above quoted from Ps. lxviii. 31; and also in various other places. Thus in Ps. lxvii. 4: 'Behold Philistia, and Tyre, with Ethiopia; this man was born there;' Zeph. iii. 10: 'From beyond the ruins of Ethiopia, my suppliants, even the daughters of my dispersed, shall bring mine offering.' ¶ *And of the Sabeans, men of stature* (סְבָאִים) The inhabitants of Seba (סְבָא *Sebâ*, not שְׁבָא *Shebâ*). Sheba, and the Sabeans of that name were a country and people of Arabia Felix—comprising a considerable part of the country now known as *Yemen*, lying in the south-west part of Arabia (Joel iv. 8; Job i. 15). That country abounded in frankincense, myrrh, spices, gold, and precious stones (1 Kings x. 1; Isa. lx. 6; Jer. vi. 20). *Seba*, here referred to, was a different country. It was inhabited by a descendant of Cush (Gen. x. 7), and was probably the same as Meroë in Upper Egypt (see Notes on ch. xliii. 3). That this people was distinguished for height of stature is expressly affirmed by Herodotus (iii. 20), who says of the Ethiopians, among whom the Sabeans are to be reckoned, that they were 'the tallest of men' (λέγονται εἶναι μέγιστοι ἀνθρώπων); and Solinus affirms that the Ethiopians are 'twelve feet high.' Agatharchides, an ancient Greek poet, quoted by Bochart (*Phaleg.* ii. 26), says of the Sabeans, τὰ σώματά ἐστι τῶν κατοικούντων ἀξιολογωτερα—'the bodies of those who dwell there are worthy of special remark.' This shows at least a coincidence between the accounts of Scripture and of profane writers. This country is alluded to by Solomon in Psal. lxxii. 10:

> The kings of Tarshish and of the isles shall bring
> presents;
> The kings of Sheba and Seba shall offer gifts.

They are connected here with the Egyptians, and with the inhabitants of Ethiopia or Cush; and their conversion to the true religion would occur probably about the same time. Doubtless the Christian religion was early introduced into these countries, for among those converted on the day of Pentecost, were foreigners from Egypt, and the adjacent countries (Acts ii. 10, 11), who would carry the gospel with them on their return. See also the case of the eunuch of Ethiopia (Acts viii. 26–39), by whom, undoubtedly, the gospel was conveyed to that region. The first Bishop of Ethiopia was Frumentius, who was made bishop of that country about A.D. 330. There is a current tradition among the Ethiopians that the Queen of Sheba, who visited Solomon, was called *Maqueda*, and that she was not from Arabia, but was a queen of their own country. They say that she adopted the Jewish religion, and introduced it among her people; and the eunuch, who was treasurer under Queen Candace, was probably a Jew by religion if not by birth. Yet there will be in future times a more signal fulfilment of this prophecy, when the inhabitants of these countries, and the people of all other nations, shall be converted to the true religion, and shall give themselves to God (comp. Notes on ch. lx. 3–14). That prophecy has a remarkable similarity to this, and indeed is little more than a beautiful expansion of it. ¶ *Shall come over unto thee.* To thy religion; or shall be united to thee in the worship of the true God. It denotes a change not of place, but of character, and of religion. ¶ *And they shall be thine.* A part of thy people; united to thee. The whole *language* of this description, however, is taken from the custom in the conquests of war, where one nation is made subject to another, and is led along in chains. It is here figurative, denoting that the true religion would make rapid and extensive *conquests* among the heathen; that is, that the true religion would everywhere triumph over all others. The phrase 'shall come over,' denotes that their subjection would be voluntary, and that they should freely abandon their own systems; while the phrases 'shall be thine,' 'in chains,' denote the triumphant and mighty power of the truth. ¶ *They shall come after thee.* You shall precede them in the honour of having conveyed to them the true religion, and in that priority of rank which always belongs to those who are first blessed with intelligence, and with the revelation of God. ¶ *In chains shall they come over.* Language taken from conquests, when subjugated nations are led along as captives; and here denoting the *power* of that truth which would subdue their false systems, and bring them into complete and entire *subjection* to the true religion. This does not mean that it would be against their will, or that they could not have resisted it; but merely that they would be in fact as entirely subject to the true religion as are prisoners of war, in chains, to the will of their conquerors (see Notes on ch. xiv. 1, 2). ¶ *And they shall fall down unto thee.* Recognizing thee as having the knowledge of the true God. To fall down is indicative of reverence; and it means here that Jerusalem would be honoured as being the source whence the true religion should emanate (comp. Luke xxiv. 47). An expression similar to that here used occurs in Isa. xlix. 23: 'And kings—and queens—shall bow down to thee with their face toward the earth, and lick up the dust of thy feet.' ¶ *They shall make supplication unto thee.* Lowth renders this, 'And in suppliant guise address thee.' The Hebrew properly means, they shall pray unto thee; but the idea is, that they should come as suppliants to Jerusalem, confessing that there was the knowledge of the only true God, and praying her inhabitants to impart to them an acquaintance with the true religion (see Notes on ch. ii. 3). The idea indicated by this is, that there would be a condition of anxious solicitude among heathen nations on the subject of the true religion, and that they would seek counsel and direction from those who were in possession of it. Such a state has already existed to some extent among the heathen; and the Scriptures, I think, lead us to suppose that the final spread and triumph of the gospel will be preceded by such an inquiry prevailing extensively in the heathen world. God will show them the folly of idolatry; he will raise up reformers among themselves; the extension of commercial intercourse will acquaint them with the comparative happiness and prosperity of Christian nations; and the growing consciousness of their own inferiority will lead them to desire that which has conferred so extensive benefits on other

15 Verily, thou *art* a God [a] that hidest thyself, O God of Israel, the Saviour.

16 They shall be ashamed, and also confounded, all of them: they shall go to confusion [b] together, *that are* makers of idols.

17 *But* Israel [c] shall be saved in the LORD with an everlasting salvation; [d] ye shall not be ashamed nor [e] confounded [f] world without end.

a Ps.44.24; ch.8.17. *b* Ps.97.7. *c* Ro.2.28,29; 11.26. *d* Je 31.3. *e* Ps.25.2,3. *f* 1 Pe.2.6.

lands, and lead them to come as suppliants, and ask that teachers and the ministers of religion may be sent to them. One of the most remarkable characteristics of the present time is, that heathen nations are becoming increasingly sensible of their ignorance and comparative degradation; that they welcome the ministers and teachers sent out from Christian lands; and the increased commerce of the world is thus preparing the world for the final spread of the gospel. ¶ *God* is *in thee.* In Jerusalem; or thou art in possession of the only true system of religion, and art the worshipper of the only true God (see ch. xlix. 7; lx. 14).

15. *Verily thou* art *a God that hidest thyself.* That is, that hidest thy counsels and plans. The idea is, that the ways of God seems to be dark until the distant event discloses his purpose; that a long series of mysterious events seem to succeed each other, trying to the faith of his people, and where the reason of his doings cannot be seen. The remark here seems to be made by the prophet, in view of the fact, that the dealings of God with his people in their long and painful exile would be to them inscrutable, but that a future glorious manifestation would disclose the nature of his designs, and make his purposes known (see ch. lv. 8, 9): 'My thoughts are not your thoughts, neither are your ways my ways' (comp. Ps. xliv. 24; Notes on Isa. viii. 17). ¶ *The Saviour.* Still the Saviour of his people, though his ways are mysterious and the reasons of his dealings are unknown. The LXX. render this, 'For thou art God, though we did not know it, O God of Israel the Saviour.'—This verse teaches us that we should not repine or murmur under the mysterious allotments of Providence. They may be dark now. But in due time they will be disclosed, and we shall be permitted to see his design, and to witness results so glorious, as shall satisfy us that his ways are all just, and his dealings right.

16. *They shall be ashamed and confounded.* That is, they shall find all their hopes fail, and shall be suffused with shame that they were ever so senseless as to trust in blocks of wood and stone (see Notes on ch. i. 29; xx. 5; xxx. 5; xliii. 17). ¶ *They shall go to confusion.* They shall all retire in shame and disgrace. That is, when they have gone to supplicate their idols, they shall find them unable to render them any aid, and they shall retire with shame.

17. But *Israel shall be saved.* Referring primarily to the Jews in Babylon, but affirming the universal truth that the true Israel (comp. Rom. ii. 28, 29), that is, the people of God, shall be saved from all their trials, and shall be brought to his everlasting kingdom. ¶ *In the* LORD. By JEHOVAH—בַּיהוָֹה; LXX. Ἀπὸ κυρίου. It shall be done by the power of JEHOVAH, and shall be traced to him alone. No mere human power could have saved them from their captivity in Babylon; no human power can save the soul from hell. ¶ *With an everlasting salvation.* It shall not be a temporary deliverance; but it shall be perpetual. In heaven his people shall meet no more foes; they shall suffer no more calamity; they shall be driven into no exile; they shall never die. ¶ *Ye shall not be ashamed nor confounded.* This means—1. That they should never find God *to fail, i.e.*, to be either unable or unwilling to befriend and rescue them (Ps. xlvi. 1). 2. That they should never be *ashamed, i.e.*, have cause to regret that they had put their trust in him. The idea is, that they who become his friends never regret it; never are ashamed of it. The time never can come, when any one who has become a true friend of God

18 For thus saith the LORD that created the heavens, God himself that formed the earth and made it, he hath established it, he created it not in vain, he formed it to be inhabited; I *am* the LORD, and *there is* none else.

19 I have not spoken in secret, in a [a]dark place of the earth: I said not unto the seed of Jacob, Seek ye me in [b]vain. I the LORD speak righteousness, I declare things that are right.

[a] De.29.29; 30.11,&c. [b] Ps.9.10; 69.32.

will regret it. In prosperity or adversity; in sickness or health; at home or abroad; in safety or in danger; in life or in death: there will be no situation in which they will be ashamed that they gave their hearts to God. There never have been any *true* Christians who regretted that they became the friends of the Redeemer. Their religion may have exposed them to persecution; their names may have been cast out as evil; they may have been stripped of their property; they may have been thrown into dungeons, laid on the rack, or led to the stake; but they have not regretted that they became the friends of God. Nor will they *ever* regret it. No man on a dying bed regrets that he is a friend of God. No man at the judgment bar will be ashamed to be a Christian. And in all the interminable duration of the world to come, the period never will, never *can* arrive, when any one will ever be ashamed that he gave his heart *early*, and *entirely* to the Redeemer. Why then should not all become his friends? Why will not men pursue that course which they know they never *can* regret, rather than the ways of sin and folly, which they *know* must cover them with shame and confusion hereafter?

18. *For thus saith the* LORD. This verse is designed to induce them to put unwavering confidence in the true God. For this purpose, the prophet enumerates the great things which God had done in proof that he alone was Almighty, and was worthy of trust. ¶ *He hath established it.* That is, the earth. The language here is derived from the supposition that the earth is laid upon a foundation, and is made firm. The LXX. render this, 'God who displayed the earth to view, and who, having made it, divided it' (διώρισεν αὐτὴν); that is, parcelled it out to be inhabited. This accords well with the scope of the passage. ¶ *He created it not in vain.* He did not form it to remain a vast desert without inhabitants. ¶ *He formed it to be inhabited.* By man, and the various tribes of animals. He makes it a convenient habitation for them; adapts its climates, its soil, and its productions, to their nature; and makes it yield abundance for their support. The main idea, I think, in the statement of this general truth, is, that God designed that the earth at large should be inhabited; and that, therefore, he intended that Judea—then lying waste while the captives were in Babylon—should be re-peopled, and again become the happy abode of the returning exiles. So Grotius interprets it. The Jews, from this passage, infer, that the earth shall be inhabited after the resurrection—an idea which has every probability, since there will not be fewer reasons why the earth shall be inhabited *then* than there are now; nor can there be any reasons why the earth should *then* exist in vain any more than now. ¶ *And* there is *none else* (see Note on ver. 6).

19. *I have not spoken in secret.* The word rendered 'secret' (סֵתֶר) denotes *a hiding*, or *covering*; and the phrase here means secretly, privately. He did not imitate the heathen oracles by uttering his predictions from dark and deep caverns, and encompassed with the circumstances of awful mystery, and with designed obscurity. ¶ *In a dark place of the earth.* From a cave, or dark recess, in the manner of the heathen oracles. The heathen responses were usually given from some dark cavern or recess, doubtless the better to impress with awe the minds of those who consulted the oracles, and to make them more ready to credit the revelations of the fancied god. Such was the seat of the Sybil, mentioned by Virgil, *Æn.* vi. 4:—

Excisum Euboicæ latus ingens rupis in antrum

20 Assemble yourselves and come; draw near together, ye *that are* escaped of the nations: [a] they have no knowledge that set up the wood of their graven image, and pray unto a god *that* cannot save.

a Ep.2.12-16.

Such also was the famous oracle at Delphi. Strabo (ix.) says, 'The oracle is said to be a hollow cavern of considerable depth, with an opening not very wide.' Diodorus, giving an account of this oracle, says, 'that there was in that place a great chasm, or cleft in the earth; in which very place is now situated what is called the Adytum of the temple.' In contradistinction from all this, God says that he had spoken openly, and without these circumstances of designed obscurity and darkness. In the *language* here, there is a remarkable resemblance to what the Saviour said of himself, and it is not improbable that he had this passage in his mind: 'I spake openly to the world; I ever taught in the synagogue, and in the temple, whither the Jews always resort; and in secret have I said nothing' (John xviii. 20). A similar declaration occurs in Deut. xxx. 11: 'This commandment which I command thee this day, it is not hidden from thee, neither is it far off.' ¶ *I said not to the seed of Jacob.* The seed, or the race of Jacob, here means his people: and the idea is, that he had not commanded them to call upon him without his being ready to answer them. ¶ *Seek ye me in vain.* The phrase, 'seek ye,' may refer to worship in general; or more properly to their calling upon him in times of calamity and trial. The sense is, that it had not been a vain or useless thing for them to serve him; that he had been their protector, and their friend; and that they had not gone to him, and spread out their wants for nought. It is still true, that God does not command his people to seek him in vain (comp. Deut. xxxii. 47). His service is always attended with a rich blessing to them; and they are his witnesses that he confers on them inexpressibly great and valuable rewards. It follows from this—first, that his people have abundant encouragement to go to him in all times of trial, persecution, and affliction; secondly, that they have encouragement to go to him in a low state of religion, to confess their sins, to supplicate his mercy, and to pray for the influences of his Holy Spirit, and the revival of his work; and, thirdly, that the service of God is always attended with rich reward. Idols do not benefit those who serve them. The pursuit of pleasure, gain, and ambition, is often attended with *no* reward, and is *never* attended with any benefits that satisfy the wants of the undying mind; but the service of God meets all the wants of the soul, fills all its desires, and confers permanent and eternal rewards. ¶ *I the* LORD *speak righteousness.* This stands in opposition to the heathen oracles, which often gave false, delusive, and unjust responses. But not so with God. He had not spoken, as they did, from deep and dark places—fit emblems of the obscurity of their answers; he had not, as they had, commanded a service that was unprofitable and vain; and he had not, as they had, uttered oracles which were untrue and fitted to delude. ¶ *I declare things that are right.* Lowth renders this, 'Who give direct answers;' and supposes it refers to the fact, that the heathen oracles often give ambiguous and deceitful responses. God never deceived. His responses were always true and unambiguous.

20. *Assemble yourselves, and come.* This, like the passage in ch. xli. 1, *sq.*, is a solemn appeal to the worshippers of idols, to come and produce the evidences of their being endowed with omniscience, and with almighty power, and of their having claims to the homage of their worshippers. ¶ *Ye* that are *escaped of the nations.* This phrase has been very variously interpreted. Kimchi supposes that it means those who were *distinguished* among the nations, their chiefs, and rulers; Aben Ezra, that the Babylonians are meant especially; Vitringa, that the phrase denotes *proselytes,* as those who have escaped from the idolatry of the heathen, and have embraced the true religion; Grotius, that it denotes those who survived the

21 Tell ye, and bring *them* near;
yea, let them take counsel together:
who hath declared this from ancient
time? *who* hath told it from that
time? *have* not I the LORD? and
there is no God else beside me; a
just [a] God and a Saviour: *there is*
none beside me.

a Ro.3.26.

slaughter which Cyrus inflicted on the nations. Rosenmüller coincides in opinion with Vitringa. The word here used (פָּלִיט) denotes properly one who has escaped by flight from battle, danger, or slaughter (Gen. xiv. 13; Josh. viii. 32). It is not used anywhere in the sense of a proselyte; and the idea here is, I think, that those who escaped from the slaughter which Cyrus would bring on the nations, were invited to come and declare what benefit they had derived from trusting in idol-gods. In ver. 16, God had said they should all be ashamed and confounded who thus put their trust in idols; and he here calls on them as living witnesses that it was so. Those who had put their confidence in idols, and who had seen Cyrus carry his arms over nations notwithstanding their vain confidence, could now testify that no reliance was to be placed on them, and could be adduced as witnesses to show the importance of putting their trust in JEHOVAH. ¶ *That set up the wood.* The word 'wood' is used here to show the folly of worshipping an image thus made, and to show how utterly unable it was to save.

21. *Tell ye, and bring* them *near.* That is, announce, and bring forward your strongest arguments (see Notes on ch. xli. 1). ¶ *Who hath declared this from ancient time?* Who has clearly announced the events respecting Cyrus, and the conquest of Babylon, and the deliverance from the captivity? The argument is an appeal to the fact that God had clearly foretold these events long before, and that therefore he was the true God. To this argument he often appeals in proof that he alone is God (see Note on ch. xli. 22, 23). ¶ *And* there is *no God else beside me* (see ver. 5). ¶ *A just God.* A God whose attribute it is always to do right; whose word is true; whose promises are fulfilled; whose threatenings are executed; and who always does that which, under the circumstances of the case, *ought to be done.* This does not refer *particularly* to the fact that he will punish the guilty, but, in the connection here, rather seems to mean that his course would be one of equity. ¶ *And a Saviour.* Saving his people. It was a characteristic of him, that he saved or preserved his people; and his equity, or truth, or justice, was seen in his doing that. His being 'a just God' and 'a Saviour' are not set here in contrast or contradiction, as if there was any incongruity in them, or as if they needed to be reconciled; but they refer to the same thing, and mean that he was just and true *in saving* his people; it was a characteristic of him that he was *so* true to his promises, and so equitable in his government, that he *would* save them. There is here no peculiar and special reference to the work of the atonement. But the *language* is such as will accurately express the great leading fact in regard to the salvation of sinners. It is in the cross of the Redeemer that God has shown himself eminently to be just, and yet a Saviour; true, and merciful; expressing his abhorrence of sin, and yet pardoning it; maintaining the honour of his violated law, and yet remitting its penalty and forgiving the offender. It is here, in the beautiful language of the Psalmist (lxxxv. 10), that

Mercy and truth are met together,
Righteousness and peace have kissed each other.

The same idea is expressed in Rom. iii. 26: 'That he might be just, and the justifier of him that believeth in Jesus.' It is the glory of the character of God that he *can* be thus just and merciful at the same time; that he can maintain the honour of his law, secure the stability of his government, and yet extend pardon to any extent. No human administration can do this. Pardon under a human government *always* does much to weaken the authority of the government, and to set aside the majesty of the law. If *never* exercised, indeed, government

22 Look [a] unto me, and be ye saved, all the ends of the earth; for I *am* God, and *there is* none else.

a Ps.22.27; Jn.3 14,15.

assumes the form of tyranny; if *often*, the law loses its terrors, and crime will walk fearless through the earth. But in the Divine administration, through the atonement, pardon may be extended to any extent, and yet the honour of the law be maintained, for the substituted sufferings of the innocent in the place of the guilty, will *in fact* do more to restrain from transgression than where the guilty themselves suffer. Of no human administration can it be said that it is at the same time just, and yet forgiving; evincing hatred of the violation of the law, and yet extending mercy to any extent to the violators of the laws. The blending together of these apparently inconsistent attributes belongs only to God, and is manifested only in the plan of salvation through the atonement.

22. *Look unto me, and be ye saved.* This is said in view of the declaration made in the previous verse, that he is a just God and a Saviour. It is *because* he sustains this character that all are invited to look to him; and the doctrine is, that the fact that God is at the same time just and yet a Saviour, or can save consistently *with* his justice, is an argument why they should look to him, and confide in him. If he is at the same time just—true to his promises; righteous in his dealings; maintaining the honour of his law and government, and showing his hatred of sin; and also merciful, kind, and forgiving, it is a ground of confidence in him, and we should rejoice in the privilege of looking to him for salvation. The phrase 'look unto me' means the same as, direct the attention to, as we do to one from whom we expect aid. It denotes a conviction on our part of helplessness—as when a man is drowning, he casts an imploring eye to one on the shore who can help him; or when a man is dying, he casts an imploring eye on a physician for assistance. Thus the direction to look to God for salvation implies a deep conviction of helplessness and of sin; and a deep conviction that he only can save. At the same time it shows the ease of salvation. What is more easy than to *look* to one for help? What more easy than to cast the eyes towards God the Saviour? What more reasonable than that he should require us to do it? And what more just than that God, if men *will not* LOOK to him in order that they may be saved, should cast them off for ever? Assuredly, if a dying, ruined, and helpless sinner will not do so simple a thing as *to look* to God for salvation, he *ought* to be excluded from heaven, and the universe will acquiesce in the decision which consigns him to despair. ¶ *All the ends of the earth.* For the meaning of this phrase, see Note on ch. xl. 28. The invitation here proves—1. That the offers of the gospel are universal. None are excluded. The ends of the earth, the remotest parts of the world, are invited to embrace salvation, and all those portions of the world might, under this invitation, come and accept the offers of life. 2. That God is willing to save all; since he would not give an invitation at all unless he was *willing* to save them. 3. That there is ample provision for their salvation; since God could not invite them to accept of what was not provided for them, nor could he ask them to partake of salvation which had no existence. 4. That it is his serious and settled purpose that all the ends of the earth *shall be* invited to embrace the offers of life. The invitation has gone from his lips, and the command has gone forth that it should be carried to every creature (Mark xvi. 15), and now it appertains to his church to bear the glad news of salvation around the world. God intends that it shall be done, and on his church rests the responsibility of seeing it speedily executed. ¶ *For I am God.* This is a *reason* why they should look to him to be saved. It is clear that none but the true God can save the soul. No one else but he can pronounce sin forgiven; no one but he can rescue from a deserved hell. No idol, no man, no angel can save; and if, therefore, the sinner is saved, he must come to the true God, and depend on

23 I have sworn [a]by myself, the
word is gone out of my mouth *in*
righteousness, and shall not return,
That unto me [b]every knee shall
bow, every tongue shall [c]swear.

a Ge 22.16; He.6.13. b Phi.2.10. c De.6.13.

him. That he *may* thus come, whatever may have been his character, is abundantly proved by this passage. This verse contains truth enough, if properly understood and applied, to save the world; and on the ground of this, all men, of all ages, nations, climes, ranks, and character, might come and obtain eternal salvation.

23. *I have sworn by myself.* This verse contains a fuller statement of the truth intimated in the previous verse, that the benefits of salvation should yet be extended to all the world. It is the expression of God's solemn purpose that all nations should yet be brought to acknowledge him, and partake of the benefits of the true religion. The expression, 'I have sworn by myself,' denotes a purpose formed in the most solemn manner, and ratified in the most sacred form. God could swear by no greater (Heb. vi. 13, 16); and this, therefore, is the most solemn assurance that could be possibly given that the purpose which he had formed should be executed. To swear by himself is the same as to swear by his life, or to affirm solemnly that the event shall as certainly occur as that he exists. The same idea is often expressed by the phrase, 'as I live.' See a parallel declaration in Num. xiv. 21: 'But as truly as I live, all the earth shall be filled with the glory of the LORD' (comp. Num. xiv. 28; Isa. xlix. 18; Jer. xxii. 24; Ezek. v. 11; xiv. 16, 18, 20; Zeph. ii. 9; Rom. xiv. 11). This passage is quoted by Paul in Rom. xiv. 11, where the phrase, 'I have sworn by myself' is rendered, 'as I live, saith the Lord,' showing that they are equivalent expressions. ¶ *The word is gone out of my mouth.* The LXX. render this, 'Righteousness shall proceed from my mouth, my words shall not return.' Lowth renders it, 'Truth is gone forth from my mouth; the word, and it shall not be revoked.' Jerome, 'The word of righteousness has gone forth from my mouth, and shall not return.' Rosenmüller accords with the interpretation of Lowth. Probably the correct translation is 'righteousness (*i.e.*, the righteous sentence, or purpose, where the word צְדָקָה is used in the sense of *truth*, see ver. 19), has gone out of my mouth, the word (*i.e.*, the promise), and it shall not return.' In this construction the וְ before לֹא (*lō*) has the force of a relative pronoun, and is to be referred to דָּבָר (*dhâbhâr*), 'the word.' The sense is, that God had spoken it, and that all which he has spoken shall certainly be fulfilled. The fact that the declaration has once passed his lips, is full proof that the purpose shall be accomplished. This is not to be understood of any promise which he had made before, but it is a solemn declaration which he now makes by the prophet. ¶ *That unto me every knee shall bow.* To bow or bend the knee, is indicative of homage or adoration; and the idea is, that all should yet acknowledge him to be God (see Note on Rom. xiv. 11). The ancient mode of offering adoration, or of paying homage, was to place the knee on the ground, and then slowly to incline the body until the head touched the earth. This is practised now in eastern countries (comp. Gen. xli. 43; 1 Kings xix. 18; 2 Chron. vi. 13; Matt. xxvii. 29; Rom. xi. 4; Phil. ii. 10; Eph. iii. 14). The obvious and proper signification of this is, that the time would come when God would be everywhere acknowledged as the true God. It refers therefore to the future period of glory on the earth, when all men shall have embraced the true religion, and when idolatry shall have come to an end. ¶ *Every tongue shall swear.* This expression is evidently taken from the practice of taking an oath of allegiance to a sovereign, and here means that all would solemnly acknowledge him to be the true God, and submit themselves to his government and will. See the phrase explained in the Note on ch. xix. 18. That this refers to the Messiah and his times, is apparent from the fact that it is twice referred to by the apostle Paul, and applied by him to the

24 Surely, [1] shall *one* say, In the
LORD have I [2] righteousness [a] and
strength : [b] *even* to him [c] shall *men*
come ; and all that are incensed
against him shall be ashamed.

25 In the LORD shall all the seed
of Israel be justified, [d] and shall
glory.

1 or, *he shall say of me, In the LORD is all righteousness and strength.* 2 *righteousnesses.*
a Je.23.6; 1 Co.1.30,31. *b* Ze.10.6,12; Ep.6.10. *c* Jn.12.32. *d* Ro.5.1.

Lord Jesus and his religion (Rom. xiv. 11; Phil. ii. 10). It is a glorious promise which remains yet to be fulfilled, and there is no promise in the Bible more certain than that this earth shall yet be filled with the knowledge of the true God.

24. *Surely, shall* one *say.* Marg. 'He shall say of me, In the LORD is all righteousness and strength.' The design of the verse is, to set forth more fully the effect of the prevalence of the true religion; and the main thought is, that there shall be an universal acknowledgment that salvation and strength were in JEHOVAH alone. Idols and men could not save; and salvation was to be traced to JEHOVAH only. A literal translation of the passage would be, 'Truly in JEHOVAH, he said unto me,' or it is said unto me, *i.e.*, I heard it said, 'is righteousness and strength,' that is, this would be everywhere the prevailing sentiment that righteousness and strength were to be found in JEHOVAH alone. The sense is, first, that it was by him alone that they could be pardoned and justified; and, secondly, that it was by him alone that they could obtain *strength* to meet their enemies, to overcome their sins, to discharge their duties, to encounter temptations, to bear afflictions, and to support them in death. These two things, righteousness and strength, are all that man needs. The whole of religion consists essentially in the feeling that righteousness and strength are to be found in God our Saviour. The LXX. render this, 'Every tongue shall swear to God, saying, Righteousness and glory shall come unto him, and all those who make distinctions among them shall be ashamed.' ¶ Even *to him shall* men *come.* For the purpose of being saved (see Notes on ch. ii. 3). ¶ *And all that are incensed against him.* All that are opposed to his government and laws. ¶ *Shall be ashamed* (see Note on ver. 16). The enemies of God shall see their own feebleness and folly; and they shall be ashamed that they have endeavoured to oppose one so mighty and so glorious as the living God. The multitudes that have in various ways resisted him shall see the folly of their course, and be overwhelmed with shame that they have dared to lift the hand against the God that made the heavens. Jarchi renders this, 'All who have opposed themselves to God, shall come to him, led by penitence on account of the things which they have done, and shall be ashamed.'

25. *In the* LORD. It shall be only in JEHOVAH that they shall find justification, and this must mean, that it is by his mercy and grace. The entire passage here, I suppose, has reference to the times of the Redeemer (see Notes on ver. 21–24). If so, it means that justification can be obtained only by the mercy of God through a Redeemer. The great truth is, therefore, here brought into view, which constitutes the sum of the New Testament, that men are not justified by their own works, but by the mercy and grace of God. ¶ *All the seed of Israel.* All the spiritual seed or descendants of Jacob. It cannot mean that every individual shall be justified and saved, for the Bible abundantly teaches the contrary (see Matt. viii. 11, 12; Rom. xi.) But it must mean that all who have a character resembling that of Israel, or Jacob; all who are the true children and friends of God (see Rom. ii. 28, 29; iv. 9–13). ¶ *Be justified.* Be regarded and treated as righteous. Their sins shall be pardoned, and they shall be acknowledged and treated as the children of God (see Notes on Rom. iii. 24, 25). *To justify*, here, is not to pronounce them innocent, or to regard them as deserving of his favour; but it is to receive them into favour, and to resolve to treat them *as if* they had not sinned; that is, to treat them as if they were righteous. All this is by the mere mercy and grace of God, and is through the

CHAPTER XLVI.

ANALYSIS.

This chapter is a continuation of the argument before commenced to show the folly of idolatry, and to induce the captive and exile Jews to put their trust in Jehovah. The argument consists of the following particulars:—

I. The idols of Babylon should be overthrown (1, 2). The prophet sees those idols removed from their places, laid on beasts of burden, and borne away. They were unable to deliver their city from the arm of the conqueror, but were themselves carried into captivity. The exiles, therefore, had the certain prospect of deliverance.

II. God appeals to the fact, that he had always protected the Jewish people; that he had dealt with them as a parent in the infancy and youth of their nation, and he solemnly assures them that he would not leave them in their old age and their trials (3, 4).

III. He shows them the folly of idolatry, and the vanity of idols (5–7). They could not aid or defend in the day of trial; and, therefore, the people should put their trust in the true God.

IV. He appeals to them by the recollection of former events, and reminds them of his merciful interposition (8, 9).

V. He appeals to them by the fact that he had predicted future events, and especially by the fact that he had raised up a distinguished conqueror—Cyrus—who would accomplish all his pleasure (10, 11).

VI. He assures them that his righteous purpose was near to be accomplished, and that he would restore Zion to its former splendour, and that his salvation should be made known to his people (12, 13).

The *scene* of this prophecy is laid in Babylon, and at the time when the city was about to be taken by Cyrus, and the Jews about to be delivered from captivity. The idols of the Chaldeans, unable to defend their city, are borne in haste away for safety, and Cyrus is at the gates. The *design* is to give to the exiles there an assurance that when they should see these things, they should conclude that their deliverance drew near; and to furnish them thus with ample demonstration that Jehovah was the true God, and that he was their protector and friend. In their long and painful captivity also, they would have these promises to comfort them; and when they surveyed the splendour of the idol worship in Babylon, and their hearts were pained with the prevalent idolatry, they would have also the assurance that those idols were to be removed, and that that idolatry would come to an end.

BEL [a] boweth down, Nebo [b] stoopeth; their idols were upon the beasts; [c] and upon the cattle: your carriages *were* heavy loaden; *they are* a burden to the weary *beast*.

[a] Je.50.51. [b] Je.48.1,&c. [c] Je.10.5.

merits of the Redeemer, who died in their place. ¶ *And shall glory.* Or rather, shall praise and celebrate his goodness. The word here used (הָלַל *hâlăl*) means, in Piel, *to sing*, to chant, to celebrate the praises of any one (1 Chron. xvi. 36; Ps. xliv. 9; cxvii. 1; cxlv. 2), and is the word of which the word *hallelujah* is in part composed. Here it means, that the effect of their being justified by Jehovah would be, that they would be filled with joy, and would celebrate the goodness of God. This effect of being justified, is more fully stated in Rom. v. 1–5. It is a result which always follows; and a disposition to praise and magnify the name of God in view of his boundless mercy in providing a way by which sinners may be justified, is one of the first promptings of a renewed heart, and one of the evidences that a soul is born again.

CHAPTER XLVI.

1. *Bel boweth down.* Bel or Belus (בֵּל *Bēl*, from בְּעֵל *Bĕēl*, the same as בַּעַל *Băăl*) was the chief domestic god of the Babylonians, and was worshipped in the celebrated tower of Babylon (comp. Jer. l. 2; li. 44). It was usual to compound names of the titles of the divinities that were worshipped, and hence we often meet with this name, as in Bel-shazzar, Bel-teshazzar, Baal-Peor, Baal-zebub, Baal-Gad, Baal-Berith. The Greek and Roman writers compare Bel with Jupiter, and the common name which they give to this idol is *Jupiter Belus* (Pliny, *Nat. Hist.* xxxvii. 10; Cic. *De Nat. Deor.* iii. 16; Diod. ii. 8, 9). Herodotus (i. 181–183) says, that in the centre of each division of the city of Babylon (for the Euphrates divided the city into two parts) there is a circular space surrounded by a wall. In one

of these stands the royal palace, which fills a large and strongly defended space. The temple of Jupiter Belus, says he, occupies the other, whose huge gates of brass may still be seen. It is a square building, each side of which is of the length of two furlongs. In the midst, a tower rises of the solid depth and height of one furlong; on which, resting as a base, seven other turrets are built in regular succession. The ascent on the outside, winding from the ground, is continued to the highest tower; and in the middle of the whole structure there is a convenient resting-place. In this temple there is a small chapel, which contains a figure of Jupiter in a sitting posture, with a large table before him; these, with the base of the table, and the seat of the throne, are all of the purest gold. There was formerly in this temple a statue of solid gold, twelve cubits high. This was seized, says Herodotus, by Xerxes, who put the priest to death who endeavoured to prevent its removal. The upper room of this tower was occupied as an observatory. The idol *Baal*, or *Bel*, was peculiarly the god of the Phenicians, of the Canaanites, of the Chaldeans, of the Moabites, and of some of the surrounding nations. The most common opinion has been, that the idol was the *sun* (see Notes on ch. xvii. 8, 9), and that, under this name, this luminary received divine honours. But Gesenius supposes that by the name *Jupiter Belus* was not denoted Jupiter, 'the father of the gods,' but the planet Jupiter, *Stella Jovis*, which was regarded, together with Venus, as the giver of all good fortune; and which forms with Venus the most fortunate of all constellations under which sovereigns can be born. The planet Jupiter, therefore, he supposes to have been worshipped under the name *Bel*, and the planet Venus under the name of Astarte, or Astareth (see Gesenius, *Comm. zu Isaiah*, ii. 333, *sq.*, and Robinson's *Calmet, Art.* BAAL). The phrase 'boweth down,' means here, probably, that the idol sunk down, fell, or was removed. It was unable to defend the city, and was taken captive, and carried away. Jerome renders it, *Confractus est Bel*—'Bel is broken.' The LXX. Ἔπεσε Βὴλ—'Bel has fallen.' Perhaps in the *language* there is allusion to the fact that Dagon *fell* before the ark of God (1 Sam. v. 2, 3, 7). The sense is, that even the object of worship—that which was regarded as the most sacred among the Chaldeans—would be removed. ¶ *Nebo stoopeth.* This was an idol-god of the Chaldeans. In the astrological mythology of the Babylonians, according to Gesenius (*Comm. zu Isaiah* ii. 333, *sq.*), this idol was the planet Mercury. He is regarded as the scribe of the heavens, who records the succession of the celestial and terrestrial events; and is related to the Egyptian Hermes and Anubis. The extensive worship of this idol among the Chaldeans and Assyrians is evident from the many compound proper names occurring in the Scriptures, of which this word forms a part, as Neb-uchadnezzar, Neb-uzaradan: and also in the classics, as Nab-onad, Nab-onassar. Nebo was, therefore, regarded as an attendant on Bel, or as his scribe. The exact form of the idol is, however, unknown. The word 'stoopeth,' means that it had fallen down, as when one is struck dead he falls suddenly to the earth; and the language denotes *conquest*, where even the idols so long worshipped would be thrown down. The scene is in Babylon, and the image in the mind of the prophet is that of the city taken, and the idols that were worshipped thrown down by the conqueror, and carried away in triumph. ¶ *Their idols were upon the beasts.* That is, they are laid upon the beasts to be borne away in triumph. It was customary for conquerors to carry away all that was splendid and valuable, to grace their triumph on their return; and nothing would be a more certain indication of victory, or a more splendid accompaniment to a triumph, than the gods whom the vanquished nations had adored. Thus in Jer. xlviii. 7, it is said, 'And Chemosh shall go forth into captivity, with his priests and his princes together' (comp. Jer. xlix. 3, marg.) ¶ *Your carriages.* That is, they were laden with the idols that were thus borne off in triumph. ¶ They are *a burden.* They are so numerous; so heavy; and to be borne so far. This is a very striking and impressive manner of foretelling that the city of Babylon would be destroyed. Instead of employing the

2 They stoop, they bow down together, they could not deliver the burden, but [1] themselves are gone into captivity.
3 Hearken unto me, O house of Jacob, and all the remnant of the house of Israel, which are borne by [a] *me* from the belly, which are carried from the womb.
4 And *even* to *your* old age [b] I *am* he; and *even* to hoar hairs will I carry *you*: I have made, and I will bear; even I will carry, and will deliver *you*.

1 *their soul.*

a Ex.19.4; Ps.71.6,18. b Ps.92.14.

direct language of prophecy, the prophet represents himself as *seeing* the heavy laden animals and waggons moving along slowly, pressed down under the weight of the captured gods to be borne into the distant country of the conqueror. They move forth from Babylon, and the caravan laden with the idols, the spoils of victory, is seen slowly moving forward to a distant land.

2. *They stoop.* Bel, and Nebo, and all the Babylonian gods (see ver. 1). ¶ *They could not deliver the burden.* The word 'burden' here, probably means the *load* of metal, wood, and stone, of which the idols were composed. The gods whom the Babylonians worshipped had not even power to protect the images which were made to represent them, and which had now become a heavy burden to the animals and wains which were carrying them away. They could not rescue them from the hands of the conqueror; and how unable were they, therefore, to defend those who put their trust in them. The Vulgate renders this, 'They could not deliver him that bare them.' The LXX. 'You are carrying them like a burden bound on the weary, faint, and hungry; who are all without strength, and unable to escape from battle; and as for them, they are carried away captives!' ¶ *But themselves.* Marg. as Heb. 'Their soul.' The sense is, that the gods thus worshipped, so far from being able to defend those who worshipped them, had themselves become captive, and were borne to a distant land.

3. *Hearken unto me.* From this view of the captive gods, the address is now turned to the Jews. The utter vanity of the idols had been set before them; and in view of that, God now addresses his own people, and entreats them to put their trust in him. The address he commences with words of great tenderness and endearment, designed to lead them to confide in him as their Father and friend. ¶ *And all the remnant.* All who were left from slaughter, and all who were borne into captivity to Babylon. The language here is all full of tenderness, and is fitted to inspire them with confidence in God. The idols of the heathen, so far from being able to protect their worshippers, were themselves carried away into ignoble bondage, but JEHOVAH was himself able to carry his people, and to sustain them. ¶ *Which are borne* by me. Like an indulgent father, or a tender nurse, he had carried them from the very infancy of their nation. The same image occurs in Deut. i. 31: 'And in the wilderness, where thou hast seen how that the LORD thy God bare thee, as a man doth bear his son, in all the way that ye went, until ye came into this place.' A similar figure occurs in Ex. xix. 4: 'Ye have seen, how I bare you on eagles' wings, and brought you unto myself' (so Deut. xxxii. 11, 12; comp. Num. xi. 12; Isa. lxiii. 9). All this here stands opposed to the idols of the Babylonians. They were unable to protect their people. They were themselves made captive. But God had shown the part of a father and a protector to his people in all times. He had sustained and guided them; he had never forsaken them; he had never, like the idol-gods, been *compelled* to leave them in the power of their enemies. From the fact that he had always, even from the infancy of their nation, thus protected them, they are called on to put their trust in him.

4. *And* even *to* your *old age, I* am *he.* Or rather, I am the same. I remain, unchangeably, with the same tenderness, the same affection, the same care. In this the care of God for his people surpasses that of the most tender parent, and the most kind nourisher of the

5 To whom will ye liken me, and
make *me* equal, and compare me,
that we may be like?
6 They [a]lavish gold out of the
bag, and weigh silver in the balance,
and hire a goldsmith; and he
maketh it a god: they fall down;
yea, they worship.
7 They bear him upon the
shoulder, they carry him, and set
him in his place, and he standeth;
from his place shall he not remove:
yea, *one* shall cry unto him, yet
can he not answer, nor save him
out of his trouble.

a ch.41.7,&c.

---

young. The care of the parent naturally dies away as the child reaches manhood, and he is usually removed by death before the son or daughter that excited so much solicitude in infancy and childhood, reaches old age. But not so with God. His people are always the objects of his tender solicitude. Age does not make them less dependent, and experience only teaches them more and more their need of his sustaining grace. The *argument* here is, that he who had watched over the infancy of his people with so much solicitude, would not leave them in the exposures, and infirmities, and trials of the advanced years of their history. The *doctrine* is, first, that his people *always* need his protection and care; secondly, that he will never leave nor forsake them; thirdly, that he who is the God of infancy and childhood will be the God of age, and that he will not leave or forsake his people, who have been the objects of his care and affection in childhood, when they become old. For though this passage refers primarily to a *people*, or a community as such, yet I see no reason why the principle should not be regarded as applicable to those who are literally aged. They *need* the care of God no less than childhood does; and if they have walked in his ways in the vigour and strength of their life, he will not cast them off 'when they are old and gray-headed.' Hoary hairs, therefore, if 'found in the way of righteousness,' may trust in God; and the 'second childhood' of man may find him no less certainly a protector than the first.

5. *To whom will ye liken me* (see Notes on ch. xl. 18, 25). The design of this and the following verses is to show the folly of idolatry, and the vanity of trusting in idols. This is a subject that the prophet often dwells on. The argument here is derived from the fact that the idols of Babylon were unable to defend the city, and were themselves carried away in triumph (ver. 1, 2). If so, how vain was it to rely on them! how foolish to suppose that the living and true God could resemble such weak and defenceless blocks!

6. *They lavish gold.* The word here used means properly to shake out; and then to pour out abundantly, or in a lavish manner. It is used in connection with the idea of *squandering* in Deut. xxi. 20; Prov. xxiii. 21; xxviii. 7. Here the idea is, that they spared no expense; they poured out gold as if it were vile and worthless, in order to make an idol. The design of this verse is, to show the superstition of those who were idolaters; and, particularly, how much they were willing to devote in order to maintain idol-worship. ¶ *Out of the bag.* They pour their gold out of the bag, or purse, where they have kept it; that is, they lavish it freely. ¶ *And weigh silver in the balance.* Perhaps the idea is here, that they used silver so lavishly that they did not wait to count it, but weighed it as they would the grosser metals. The word here used and translated 'balance' (קָנֶה), means properly *cane, reed, calamus;* then a measuring reed or rod (Ezek. xl. 3, 5); then a rod, or beam of a balance, or scales (Gr. ζυγὸς). ¶ *And hire a goldsmith* (see Notes on ch. xl. 19, 20). ¶ *And he maketh it a god.* The goldsmith manufactures the gold and the silver into an image. The object of the prophet is to deride the custom of offering divine homage to a god formed in this manner (see Notes on ch. xliv. 9–19).

7. *They bear him upon the shoulder.* They carry the idol which they have made on their shoulder to the temple, or place where it is to be fixed. This cir-

8 Remember this, and show yourselves men: bring *it* again to mind,
O ye transgressors.
9 Remember the former things
of old; for I *am* God, and *there is*
none else; *I am* God, and *there is*
none like me;
10 Declaring the end from the
beginning, and from ancient times
the things that are not *yet* done,

---

cumstance, with the others, is doubtless introduced to show how ridiculous and absurd it was to offer divine homage to a god whom they could thus carry about on the shoulder. ¶ *And set him in his place.* Fix the idol on its basis or pedestal, in its proper niche, or place in the temple. The whole design of this verse is to contrast the idol with JEHOVAH. JEHOVAH is uncreated and eternal; the idol, on the contrary, is made by men, is borne about, is fixed in its place, has no power to move, remains there until it is taken down, and has no ability either to hear or save those who worship it.

8. *Remember this.* Bear in mind what is now said of the manner in which idols are made. This is addressed, doubtless, to the Jews, and is designed to keep them from idolatry. ¶ *And show yourselves men.* Act as men; throw away the childish trifles of idolaters. The word here used (הִתְאֹשָׁשׁוּ) occurs nowhere else in the Bible. It is, according to Gesenius, derived from אִישׁ, *a man*, and means to act *as a man*. A similar word is used in 1 Cor. xvi. 13 (ἀνδρίζεσθε, from ἀνήρ, *a man*), and is correctly rendered there, 'quit you like men.' This Greek word often occurs in the Septuagint. It is used as a translation of אָמֵץ, in Josh. i. 6, 7, 9, 18; 1 Chron. xxviii. 20; 2 Chron. xxxii. 7; Neh. ii. 1; of גָּדַל, in Ruth i. 12; of חָזַק, in Deut. xxxi. 6, 7, 23; Josh. x. 25; 2 Kings x. 12; xiii. 28; Ps. xxvi. 20, and in several other places. Jerome renders the Hebrew word here, 'Be confounded;' the LXX. Στενάξατε—'Groan;' the Syriac, 'Consider,' or understand. The meaning is, that they were to act as became men—not as children; as became those endowed with an immortal mind, and not as the brutes. So Kimchi renders it: 'Be men, and not brutes, which neither consider nor understand.' ¶ *O ye transgressors.* Ye who have violated the laws of God by the worship of idols. In the time of Manasseh, the Israelites were much addicted to idolatry, and probably this is to be regarded as addressed to them, and as designed to recall them from it to the worship of the true God.

9. *Remember the former things,* &c. Bear in mind the repeated and constant proofs that have been given that JEHOVAH is the true God—the proofs derived from the prediction of future events, and from the frequent interpositions of his providence in your behalf as a nation. ¶ *For I am God* (see Notes on ch. xliv. 6).

10. *Declaring the end from the beginning.* Foretelling accurately the course of future events. This is an argument to which God often appeals in proof that he is the only true God (see ch. xli. 22, 23; xliii. 12; xliv. 26). ¶ *My counsel shall stand.* My purpose, my design, my will. The phrase 'shall stand' means that it shall be stable, settled, fixed, established. This proves—1. That God has a *purpose* or *plan* in regard to human affairs. If he had not, he could not predict future events, since a contingent event cannot be foreknown and predicted; that is, it cannot be foretold that an event shall certainly occur in one way, when by the very supposition of its being *contingent* it may happen either that way, or some other way, or not at all. 2. That God's plan will not be frustrated. He has *power* enough to secure the execution of his designs, and he will exert that power in order that all his plans may be accomplished. —We may observe, also, that it is a matter of unspeakable joy that God *has* a plan, and that it will be executed. For (1.) If there were *no plan* in relation to human things, the mind could find no rest. If there was no evidence that One Mind presided over human affairs; that an infinitely wise plan had been formed, and that all things had been adjusted so as best to secure the ultimate accomplishment of that plan, everything would have the appearance of chaos, and the mind must be filled

saying, My counsel shall stand,
and I will do all my pleasure:
11 Calling a ravenous bird from
the east, the man [1] that executeth
my counsel from a far country;
yea, I have spoken *it*, I will also
bring it to pass; I have purposed
it, I will also do it.
12 Hearken unto me, ye [a] stout-hearted,
that *are* far from righteousness:

1 *of my.* [a] Ac.7.51.

with doubts and distractions. But our anxieties vanish in regard to the apparent irregularities and disorders of the universe, when we feel that all things are under the direction of an Infinite Mind, and will be made to accomplish his plans, and further his great designs. (2.) If his plans were *not accomplished*, there would be occasion of equal doubt and dismay. If there was any power that could defeat the purposes of God; if there was any stubbornness of matter, or any inflexible perverseness in the nature of mind; if there were any unexpected and unforeseen extraneous causes that could interpose to thwart his plans, then the mind must be full of agitation and distress. But the moment it can fasten on the conviction that God has formed a plan that embraces all things, and that all things which occur will be in some way made tributary to that plan, that moment the mind can be calm in resignation to his holy will. ¶ *And I will do all my pleasure.* I will accomplish all my wish, or effect all my desire. The word here rendered 'pleasure' (חֵפֶץ) means properly *delight* or *pleasure* (1 Sam. xv. 22; Ps. i. 2; xvi. 3; Eccl. v. 4; xii. 10); then desire, wish, will (Job xxxi. 16); and then business, cause, affairs (Isa. liii. 10). Here it means that God would accomplish everything which was to him an object of desire; everything which he wished, or willed. And why should he not? Who has power to hinder or prevent him (Rom. ix. 19)? And why should not we rejoice that he will do all that is pleasing to him? What better evidence have we that it is desirable that anything should be done, than that it is agreeable, or pleasing to God? What better security can we have that it is right, than that he wills it? What more substantial and permanent ground of rejoicing is there in regard to anything, than that it is such as God prefers, loves, and wills?

11. *Calling a ravenous bird from the east.* There can be no doubt that Cyrus is intended here (see Notes on ch. xli. 2, 25). The *east* here means Persia. The word rendered 'ravenous bird' (עַיִט) is rendered *fowl* in Job xxviii. 7; *bird* or *birds* in Jer. xii. 9; *fowls* in Gen. xv. 11; Isa. xviii. 6; and *ravenous birds* in Ezek. xxxix. 4. It does not occur elsewhere in the Bible. It is here used as an emblem of a warlike king, and the emblem may either denote the rapidity of his movements—moving with the flight of an eagle; or it may denote the devastation which he would spread—an emblem in either sense peculiarly applicable to Cyrus. It is not uncommon in the Bible to compare a warlike prince to an eagle (Jer. xlix. 22; Ezek. xvii. 3); and the idea here is, probably, that Cyrus would come with great power and velocity upon nations, like the king of birds, and would pounce suddenly and unexpectedly upon his prey. Perhaps also there may be here allusion to the standard or banner of Cyrus. Xenophon (*Cyrop.* vii.) says that it was a golden eagle affixed to a long spear; and it is well remarked by Lowth, that Xenophon has used the very word which the prophet uses here, as near as could be, expressing it in Greek letters. The word of the prophet is עַיִט (*āyīt*); the Greek word used by Xenophon is ἀετὸς (*aetos*). The Chaldee has, however, given a different rendering to this passage: 'I, who say that I will gather my captivity from the east, and will lead publicly like a swift bird from a distant land the sons of Abraham, my friend.' ¶ *The man that executeth my counsel.* Marg. as Heb. 'Of my counsel.' It may either mean the man whom he had designated by his counsel; or it may mean the man who should execute his purpose. ¶ *Yea, I have spoken.* He spake it by the prophets; and the idea is, that all that he had spoken should be certainly accomplished.

12. *Hearken unto me.* This is de-

13 I bring near my righteousness; [a] it shall not be far off, and my salvation shall not tarry: [b] and I will place salvation in Zion for Israel [c] my glory.

a Ro.1.17. b Ps.46.1,5; Ha.2.3. c Ps.14.7.

CHAPTER XLVII.

ANALYSIS.

In the closing verse of the previous chapter, God had given the assurance that his people should certainly be delivered from their captivity in Babylon, and restored to their own land. In this chapter, he describes the vengeance which he would take on Babylon, and the entire chapter is occupied in portraying, under various images, the prostration and humiliation of that proud and oppressive seat of magnificence and of empire. Babylon is described under the image of a lady, carefully nourished and decorated; and all the images of her destruction are drawn from those circumstances which would tend to humble a gay and proud female that had been accustomed to luxury, and unused to scenes of humiliation, poverty, and bereavement. The *scope* of the chapter is, to state the crimes for which she would be humbled and punished, and the manner in which it would be done. These are intermingled, but they may be contemplated separately. The chapter may, therefore, be regarded as consisting of the following items:—

I. Babylon is addressed, by an apostrophe to her, as the seat of empire, and her humiliation is directly predicted under the image of a gay, and delicately reared female, suddenly reduced to circumstances of great humiliation and disgrace (1–5). She is commanded to sit down in the dust; she should no longer be treated as tender and delicate (1); she would be reduced to the most abject condition—like a delicate and tender female from elevated life compel'ed to perform the most menial offices, and stripped of all her gay attire (2, 3); she was to sit in darkness, or obscurity; her honour was to be taken away, and she was no more to be called the lady of kingdoms (5); and all this was to be done by Jehovah, to take vengeance on the oppressors of his people (3, 4).

II. God states the reasons why he would thus humble and punish her (6, 7). It was because she had shown no mercy to his people, and had laid a heavy yoke on an ancient nation (6); and because she had vainly calculated that her power and magnificence would continue for ever, notwithstanding the manner in which she had oppressed the people whom God had given into her hand (7).

III. The nature of the punishment which should come upon her for this is more distinctly and fully predicted, intermingled with further statements of the *causes* why she should be punished and humbled (8, 9). The *causes* were, that luxury and effeminacy abounded; that she was proud, and did not apprehend that it was possible that she should be reduced from her state of magnificence and grandeur; and that she had cherished sorcerers and enchantments.

signed to call the attention of the sceptical and unbelieving Jews to the important truth which he was delivering. Many among them might be disposed to say that the fulfilment was delayed, and he therefore calls upon them to attend particularly to his solemn declarations. ¶ *Ye stout-hearted.* The phrase 'stout-hearted' would naturally denote those who were bold and courageous. But here it evidently means those whose hearts were *strong against God;* who nerved themselves to resist and oppose his plans and government; who were *stubborn* and rebellious.

13. *I bring near my righteousness.* The word 'righteousness' here evidently denotes his *truth;* the fulfilment of his promises. His righteous and true character would be manifested to them so plainly and clearly, that they would be able no longer to doubt. It would not be remote in time, or in place, but it would be so near that they could see it, and so plain that they could no longer doubt or misunderstand it. ¶ *And my salvation shall not tarry.* The people shall be delivered from their bondage at the exact time which has been predicted. ¶ *I will place salvation in Zion.* Zion or Jerusalem shall be rebuilt, and salvation shall emanate from that as from a centre to the whole world. ¶ *Israel my glory.* The people whom he had chosen, and who reflected his glory. God's honour and glory on earth are seen in, and by the church, and he designs that the church shall be the means of making his glory known among men. Or it may mean, I will give my glory to Israel. I will show to them my perfections, and will make their nation the place of the manifestations of my glorious attributes.

The *punishment* was, that she should be reduced in a moment to the condition of a widow, and to the state of one who had been suddenly bereft of all her children.

IV. The crime and the punishment of the city are further stated (10, 11). The *crime* was, that she had supposed no avenging God saw her; and that she had become proud and vain of her wisdom and knowledge. The *punishment* would be, that evil would come upon her from a quarter where she little expected it, and in a manner which she could not prevent.

V. Babylon is sarcastically called on to invoke to her aid those in whom she had trusted—the astrologers, the star-gazers, and those who practised sorcery and enchantments (12, 13).

VI. The chapter concludes with a statement of the utter vanity of the sorcerers, and the absolute folly of trusting in them (14, 15). Even the flame would pass over them; and so far were they from having any power to deliver those who trusted in them, that they had no power to preserve themselves from ruin.

This chapter, therefore, contains many very particular statements about the manner in which Babylon was to be destroyed, statements which will be found to have been fulfilled with surprising accuracy. They are statements, moreover, which could not have been the result of conjecture, or mere political sagacity, for political conjecture and sagacity do not descend to minute particulars and details. It is to be borne in remembrance that this prophecy was uttered a hundred and fifty years before its fulfilment, and that there were no circumstances existing in the time of Isaiah which could have laid the foundation for conjecture in regard to the events predicted here. The temple was then standing; the city of Jerusalem was strongly fortified; the kingdom of Judah was powerful; Babylon was just rising into magnificence; the power which ultimately overthrew it had scarcely begun to start into being: and none of the causes which ultimately led Cyrus to attack and destroy it, had as yet an existence. And if these things were so, then the conclusion is inevitable that Isaiah was under the influence of Divine inspiration. It is the *particularity* of the description in the prophets long before the events occurred, which, more than anything else, distinguishes them from mere political conjecture; and *if* the particular descriptions here and elsewhere recorded of the overthrow of Babylon, and of other future events, were actually made *before* the events occurred, then the conclusion is irresistible that they were inspired by God.

COME [a]down, and sit in the dust, O virgin daughter of Babylon; sit on the ground: *there is* no throne, O daughter of the Chaldeans; for thou shalt no more be called tender and delicate.

[a] Ps.18.27; Je.48.18.

CHAPTER XLVII.

1. *Come down.* Descend from the throne; or from the seat of magnificence and power. The design of this verse has already been stated in the analysis. It is to foretell that Babylon would be humbled, and that she would be reduced from her magnificence and pride to a condition of abject wretchedness. She is therefore represented as a proud female accustomed to luxury and ease, suddenly brought to the lowest condition, and compelled to perform the most menial services. ¶ *And sit in the dust.* To sit on the ground, and to cast dust on the head, is a condition often referred to in the Scriptures as expressive of humiliation and of mourning (Josh. viii. 6; Job ii. 12; x. 9; Ps. xxii. 15; Lam. iii. 29). In this manner also, on the medals which were struck by Titus and Vespasian to commemorate the capture of Jerusalem, Jerusalem is represented under the image of a female sitting on the ground under a palm-tree, with the inscription *Judæa capta* (see Notes on ch. iii. 26). The design here is, to represent Babylon as reduced to the lowest condition, and as having great occasion of grief. ¶ *O virgin daughter of Babylon.* It is common in the Scriptures to speak of cities under the image of a virgin, a daughter, or a beautiful woman (see Notes on ch. i. 8; xxxvii. 22; comp. Lam. i. 15; Jer. xxxi. 21; xlvi. 11). Kimchi supposes that the term 'virgin' is here given to Babylon, because it had remained to that time uncaptured by any foreign power; but the main purpose is doubtless to refer to Babylon as a beautiful and splendid city, and as being distinguished for delicacy, and the prevalence of what was regarded as ornamental. Gesenius supposes that the words 'virgin daughter of Babylon,' denote not Babylon itself, but Chaldea, and that the whole land or nation is personified. But the common inter-

2 Take the millstones, and grind meal: uncover thy locks, make bare the leg, uncover the thigh, pass over the rivers.

---

pretation, and one evidently more in accordance with the Scripture usage, is to refer it to the city itself. ¶ *There is no throne.* Thou shalt be reduced from the throne; or the throne shall be taken away. That is, Babylon shall be no longer the seat of empire, or the capital of kingdoms. How truly this was fulfilled, needs not to be told to those who are familiar with the history of Babylon. Its power was broken when Cyrus conquered it; its walls were reduced by Darius; Seleucia rose in its stead, and took away its trade and a large portion of its inhabitants, until it was completely destroyed, so that it became for a long time a question where it had formerly stood (see Notes on ch. xiii., xvi.) ¶ *Thou shalt no more be called tender and delicate.* A place to which luxuries flow, and where they abound. The allusion is to a female that had been delicately and tenderly brought up, and that would be reduced to the lowest condition of servitude, and even of disgrace. It is *possible* that there may be an allusion here to the effeminacy and the consequent corruption of morals which prevailed in Babylon, and which made it a place sought with greediness by those who wished to spend their time in licentious pleasures. The corruption of Babylon, consequent on its wealth and magnificence, was almost proverbial, and was unsurpassed by any city of ancient times. The following extract from Curtius (v. 1), which it would not be proper to translate, will give some idea of the prevailing state of morals :—'Nihil urbis ejus corruptius moribus, nihil ad irritandas illiciendasque immodicas voluptates instructius. Liberos conjugesque cum hospitibus stupro coire, modo pretium flagitii detur, parentes maritique patiuntur. Babylonii maxime in vinum, et quæ ebrietatem sequuntur effusi sunt. Fœminarum conviva ineuntium, in principio modestus est habitus, dein summa quæque amicula exuunt paulatimque pudorem profanant; ad ultimum (horror auribus est) ima corporum velamenta projiciunt. Nec meretricum hoc dedecus est, sed matronarum virginumque apud quas comitas habetur vulgati corporis vilitas.' See also the description of a loathsome, disgusting, and abominable custom which prevailed nowhere else, even in the corrupt nations of antiquity, except Babylon, in Herod. i. 199. I cannot transcribe this passage. The description is too loathsome, and would do little good. Its *substance* is expressed in a single sentence, πασᾶν γυναῖκα ἐπιχωρίην .... μιχθῆναι ἀνδρὶ ξείνῳ. It adds to the abomination of this custom that it was connected with the rites of religion, and was a part of the worship of the gods!! Strabo, speaking of this custom (iii. 348), says, Ἔθος κατά τι λόγιον ξένῳ μίγνυσθαι. See also Baruch vi. 43, where the same custom is alluded to. For an extended description of the wealth and commerce of Babylon, see an article in the *Amer. Bib. Rep.* vol. vii. pp. 364–390.

2. *Take the millstones, and grind meal.* The design of this is plain. Babylon, that had been regarded as a delicately-trained female, was to be reduced to the lowest condition of poverty and wretchedness—represented here by being compelled to perform the most menial and laborious offices, and submitting to the deepest disgrace and ignominy. There is an allusion here to the custom of grinding in the East. The mills which were there commonly used, and which are also extensively used to this day, consisted of two stones, of which the lower one was convex on the upper side, and the upper one was concave on the lower side, so that they fitted into each other. The hole for receiving the grain was in the centre of the upper stone, and in the process of grinding the lower one was fixed, and the upper one was turned round, usually by two women (see Matt. xxiv. 41), with considerable velocity by means of a handle. Watermills were not invented till a little before the time of Augustus Cæsar; and windmills long after. The custom of using handmills is the primitive custom everywhere, and they are still in use in some parts of Scotland, and generally in

the East.—(See Mr. Pennant's *Tour to the Hebrides*, and the Oriental travellers

ANCIENT HANDMILL USED IN SCOTLAND.

generally. Grinding was usually performed by the women, though it was often regarded as the work of slaves. It was often inflicted on slaves as a punishment.

> Molendum in pistrino; vapulandum; habendæ compedes.
>
> Terent. *Phormio* ii. 1. 19.

In the East it was the usual work of female slaves (see Ex. xi. 5, in the LXX.) 'Women alone are employed to grind their corn.'—(Shaw, *Algiers and Tunis*, p. 297.) 'They are the female slaves that are generally employed in the East at those handmills. It is extremely laborious, and esteemed the lowest employment in the house.'—(Sir J. Chardin, Harmer's *Obs.* i. 153.) Compare Lowth, and Gesen. *Comm. über Isaiah.* This idea of its being a low employment is expressed by Job xxxi. 10: 'Let my wife grind unto another.' The idea of its being a most humble and laborious employment was long since exhibited by Homer:

> A woman next, then labouring at the mill,
> Hard by, where all his numerous mills he kept,
> Gave him the sign propitious from within.
> Twelve damsels toiled to turn them, day by day
> Meal grinding, some of barley, some of wheat,
> Marrow of man. The rest (their portion ground)
> All slept, one only from her task as yet
> Ceased not, for she was feeblest of them all;
> She rested on her mill, and thus pronounced:
> 'Jove, Father, Governor, of heaven and earth!
> 'O grant the prayer
> Of *a poor bond-woman.* Appoint their feast,
> This day the last, that in Ulysses' house,
> The suitors shall enjoy, for whom I drudge,
> Grinding, to weariness of heart and limb,
> Meal for their use.'
>
> Cowper.

The sense here is, that Babylon should be reduced to the lowest state, like that

MODERN EGYPTIAN MILL FOR GRINDING CORN.

of reducing a female delicately and tenderly reared, to the hard and laborious condition of working the handmill—the usual work of slaves. ¶ *Uncover thy locks.* Gesenius renders this, 'Raise thy veil.' The word here used (צַמָּה) is rendered 'locks,' in Cant. iv. 1, 3; vi. 7, as well as here. It occurs nowhere else in the Bible. Gesenius derives it from צָמַם (*tzâmăm*), *to braid, to plaid,* and then to bind fast, as a veil; to veil. Jerome renders it, *Denuda turpetudinem tuam.* The LXX. render it, Τὸ κατακάλυμμα σου—'Thy veil.' The Syriac also renders it, 'Thy veil.' The Chaldee has paraphrased the whole verse thus: 'Go into servitude; reveal the glory of thy kingdom. Broken are thy princes; dispersed are the people of thy host; they have gone into captivity like the waters of a river.' Jarchi says, that the word here used (צַמָּה) denotes whatever is bound up, or tied together. Kimchi says that it means the hair, which a woman disposes around her temples over her face, and which she covers with a veil, deeming it an ornament; but that when a female goes into captivity this is removed, as a sign of an abject condition. It properly means that which is plaited, or gathered together; and it *may* refer either to the hair so plaited as an ornament, or a covering for the head and face (comp. Note on 1 Cor. xi. 15); or it may denote a veil. To remove either would be regarded as disgraceful. It is known that oriental females pay great attention to their hair, and also that it is a universal custom to wear a close veil. To remove either, and to leave the head bare, or the face exposed, was deemed highly humiliating and dishonourable (see Notes on ch. iii. 24). 'The head,' says the Editor of the *Pictorial Bible,* 'is the seat of female modesty in the East; and no woman allows her head to be seen bare. In our travelling experience, we saw the *faces* of very many women, but never the bare head of any except one—a female servant, whose *face* we were in the constant habit of seeing, and whom we accidentally surprised while dressing her hair. The perfect consternation, and deep sense of humiliation which she expressed on that occasion, could not easily be forgotten, and furnish a most striking illustration of the present text.' ¶ *Make bare the leg.* In the interpretation of this, also, commentators vary. Jerome renders it, *Discoopteri humerum*—'Uncover the shoulder.' The LXX. Ἀνακάλυψαι τὰς πολιάς—'Uncover thy gray locks.' The Syriac, 'Cut off thy hoary hairs.' Jarchi and Kimchi suppose it means, 'Remove the waters from the paths, so that they might pass over them.' The word here used (שֹׁבֶל *shōbhĕl*), is derived from שָׁבַל *shâbhăl, to go;* to go up, to rise; to grow; to flow copiously. Hence the noun in its various forms means a path (Ps. lxxvii. 19; Jer. xviii. 15); ears of corn, *shibboleth* (Gen. xli. 5, Judg. xii. 6; Ruth ii. 2; Job xxiv. 24; Isa. xvii. 5); floods (Ps. lxix. 15); branches (Zech. iv. 12). In no place has it the certain signification of *a leg;* but it rather refers to that which *flows:* flows copiously; and probably here means the train of a robe (Gesenius, and Rosenmüller): and the expression means 'uncover, or make bare the train;' that is, lift it up, as would be necessary in passing through a stream, so that the leg would be made bare. The Orientals, as is well known, wore a long, loose, flowing robe, and in passing through waters, it would be necessary to lift, or gather it up, so that the legs would be bare. The idea is, that she who had sat as a queen, and who had been clad in the rich, loose, and flowing robe which those usually wore who were in the most elevated ranks of life, would now be compelled to leave the seat of magnificence, and in such a manner as to be subject to the deepest shame and disgrace. ¶ *Uncover the thigh.* By collecting, and gathering up the train of the robe, so as to pass through the streams ¶ *Pass over the rivers.* Heb. 'Pass the rivers;' that is, by wading, or fording them. This image is taken from the fact that Babylon was surrounded by many artificial rivers or streams, and that one in passing from it would be compelled to ford many of them. It does not mean that the *population* of Babylon would be removed into captivity by the conquerors—for there is no evidence that this was done; but the image is that of Babylon, represented as a delicately-reared and magnificently attired female, compelled to ford the streams. The idea is, that the power and magnificence of the city would be

3 Thy nakedness shall be [a] uncovered, yea, thy shame shall be seen : I will take vengeance, and I will not meet *thee as* a man.

4 *As for* our [b] Redeemer, the LORD of hosts *is* his name, the Holy One of Israel.

a Je.13.22,26; Na.3.5. b Je.50.34.

transferred to other places. Rosenmüller remarks that it is common in the countries bordering on the Tigris and the Euphrates, for females of humble rank to ford the streams, or even to swim across them.

3. *Thy nakedness.* This denotes the abject condition to which the city would be reduced. All its pride would be taken away; and it would be brought to such a state as to fill its inhabitants with the deepest mortification and shame. Vitringa supposes that it means, that all the imbecility and weakness; the vileness; the real poverty; the cruelty and injustice of Babylon, would be exposed. But it more probably means, that it would be reduced to the deepest ignominy. No language could more forcibly express the depths of its shame and disgrace than that which the prophet here uses. ¶ *I will take vengeance.* This expresses *literally* what had been before expressed in a figurative manner. The whole purpose of God was to inflict vengeance on her for her pride, her luxury, and oppression, and especially for her want of kindness towards his people (see ver. 6). ¶ *And I will not meet* thee as *a man.* This phrase has been very variously interpreted. Jerome renders it, 'And man shall not resist me.' The LXX. render it, 'I will take that which is just of thee, and will no more deliver thee up to men.' The Syriac, 'I will not suffer man to meet thee.' Grotius, 'I will not suffer any man to be an intercessor.' So Lowth, 'Neither will I suffer man to intercede with me.' Noyes, 'I will make peace with none.' So Gesenius (*Lex.* by Robinson) renders it, 'I will take vengeance, and will not make peace with man; *i.e.*, will make peace with none before all are destroyed.' The word here used (אֶפְגַּע) is derived from פָּגַע, which means, *to strike upon* or *against:* to impinge upon any one, or anything; to fall upon in a hostile manner (1 Sam. xxii. 17); to kill, to slay (Judg. viii. 21; xv. 12); to *assail* with petitions, to urge, entreat any one (Ruth i. 16; Jer. vii. 16); to light upon, or meet with any one (Gen. xxviii. 11), and then, according to Gesenius, to *strike* a league with any one, to make peace with him. Jarchi renders it, 'I will not solicit any man that he should take vengeance;' *i.e.*, I will do it myself. Aben Ezra, 'I will not admit the intercession of any man.' Vitringa renders it, 'I will take vengeance, and will not have a man to concur with me; that is, although I should not have a man to concur with me who should execute the vengeance which I meditate; on which account I have raised up Cyrus from Persia, of whom no one thought.' In my view, the meaning which best accords with the usual sense of the word, is that proposed by Lowth, that no one should be allowed to interpose, or intercede for them. *All* the interpretations concur in the same general signification, that Babylon should be totally destroyed; and that no man, whether, as Jerome supposes, by resistance, or as Lowth, by intercession, should be allowed to oppose the execution of the Divine purpose of vengeance.

4. As for *our Redeemer.* This verse stands absolutely, and is not connected with the preceding or the following. It seems to be an expression of admiration, or of grateful surprise, by which the prophet saw JEHOVAH as the Redeemer of his people. He saw, in vision, Babylon humbled, and, full of the subject, he breaks out into an expression of grateful surprise and rejoicing. 'O! our Redeemer! it is the work of *our Saviour*, the Holy One of Israel! How great is his power! How faithful is he! How manifestly is he revealed! Babylon is destroyed. Her idols could not save her. Her destruction has been accomplished by him who is the Redeemer of his people, and the Holy One of Israel.' Lowth regards this verse as the language of a *chorus* that breaks in upon the midst of the subject, celebrating the praises of God. The subject is resumed in the next verse.

5 Sit thou silent, and get thee into darkness, O daughter of the Chaldeans: for thou shalt no more be called The lady of kingdoms.
6 I [a] was wroth with my people; I have polluted mine inheritance, and given them into thine hand: thou [b] didst show them no mercy; upon the ancient hast thou very heavily laid the yoke.

a 2 Ch.28.9; Ze.1.15. b Ob.10.16.

5. *Sit thou silent.* The same general sentiment is expressed here as in the preceding verses, though the figure is changed. In ver. 1–3, Babylon is represented under the image of a gay and delicately-reared female, suddenly reduced from her exalted station, and compelled to engage in the most menial and laborious employment. Here she is represented as in a posture of mourning. To sit in silence is emblematic of deep sorrow, or affliction (see Lam. ii. 10): 'The elders of the daughter of Zion sit upon the ground and keep silence, they have cast up dust upon their heads;'—see Note on Isa. iii. 26: 'And she (Jerusalem) being desolate shall sit upon the ground;' Job ii. 13: 'So they (the three friends of Job) sat down with him upon the ground seven days and seven nights, and none spake a word unto him, for they saw that his grief was very great.' Compare Ezra ix. 4. ¶ *Get thee into darkness.* That is, into a place of mourning. Persons greatly afflicted, almost as a matter of course, shut out the light from their dwellings, as emblematic of their feelings. This is common even in this country—and particularly in the city in which I write—where the universal custom prevails of making a house dark during the time of mourning. Nature prompts to this; for there is an obvious similarity between darkness and sorrow. That this custom also prevailed in the East is apparent (see Lam. iii. 2): 'He hath led me, and brought me into darkness, and not into light;' Mic. viii. 8: 'When I sit in darkness, the LORD shall be a light unto me.' The idea is, that Babylon would be brought to desolation, and have occasion of sorrow, like a delicately-trained female suddenly deprived of children (ver. 9), and that she would seek a place of darkness and silence where she might fully indulge her grief. ¶ *O daughter of the Chaldeans* (see Notes on ver. 1). ¶ *For thou shalt no more be called The lady of kingdoms.* The magnificence, splendour, beauty, and power, which have given occasion to this appellation, and which have led the nations by common consent to give it to thee, shall be entirely and for ever removed. The appellation, 'lady of kingdoms,' is equivalent to that so often used of Rome, as 'the mistress of the world;' and the idea is, that Babylon sustained by its power and splendour the relation of mistress, and that all other cities were regarded as servants, or as subordinate.

6. *I was wroth with my people.* In this verse and the following, a reason is assigned why God would deal so severely with her. One of the reasons was, that in executing the punishment which *he* had designed on the Jewish people, she had done it with pride, ambition, and severity; so that though God intended *they* should be punished, yet the feelings of Babylon in doing it, were such also as to deserve his decided rebuke and wrath. ¶ *I have polluted mine inheritance.* Jerusalem and the land of Judea (see Notes on ch. xliii. 28). He had stripped it of its glory; caused the temple and city to be destroyed; and spread desolation over the land. Though it had been done by the Chaldeans, yet it had been in accordance with his purpose, and under his direction (Deut. iv. 20; Ps. xxviii. 9). ¶ *Thou didst show them no mercy.* Though God had given up his people to be punished for their sins, yet this did not justify the spirit with which the Chaldeans had done it, or make proper the cruelty which they had evinced towards them. It is true that some of the Jewish captives, as, *e.g.*, Daniel, were honoured and favoured in Babylon. It is not improbable that the circumstances of many of them were comparatively easy while there, and that they acquired possessions and formed attachments there which made them unwilling to leave that land when Cyrus permitted them to return to their own country. But it is also true, that Ne-

7 And thou saidst, I [a] shall be a lady for ever; *so* that thou didst not lay these *things* to thy heart, neither didst remember the latter end of it.

8 Therefore hear now this, thou *that art* given to pleasures, that dwellest [b] carelessly; that sayest in thine heart, I *am*, and none else besides me; I shall not sit *as* a widow, neither shall I know the loss of children:

[a] Re.18.7. [b] Zep.2.15.

buchadnezzar showed them no compassion when he destroyed the temple and city, that the mass of them were treated with great indignity and cruelty in Babylon. See Ps. cxxxvii. 1–3, where they pathetically and beautifully record their sufferings:

By the rivers of Babylon there we sat down,
Yea, we wept when we remembered Zion.
For there they that carried us away captive
required of us a song;
And they that wasted us required of us mirth.
Saying, Sing us one of the songs of Zion.

Thus also Jeremiah (i. 17) describes the cruelty of their conquerors: 'Israel is a scattered sheep—the lions have driven him away; this Nebuchadnezzar hath broken his bones' (see also 2 Kings xxv. 5, 6–36; Jer. li. 34; Lam. iv. 16; v. 11–14). ¶ *Upon the ancient.* That is, upon the old man. The idea is, that they had oppressed, and reduced to hard servitude, those who were venerable by years, and by experience. To treat the aged with veneration is everywhere in the Scriptures regarded as an important and sacred duty (Lev. xix. 32; Job xxxii. 4–6); and to disregard age, and pour contempt on hoary hairs, is everywhere spoken of as a crime of an aggravated nature (comp. 2 Kings ii. 23–25; Prov. xxx. 17). That the Chaldeans had thus disregarded age and rank, is a frequent subject of complaint among the sacred writers:

They respected not the persons of the priests,
They favoured not the elders.
Lam. iv. 16.

Princes are hanged up by their hand.
The faces of elders were not honoured.
Lam. v. 12.

¶ *Laid the yoke.* The yoke in the Bible is an emblem of slavery or bondage (Lev. xxvi. 13; Deut. xxxiii. 48); of afflictions and crosses (Lam. iii. 27); of punishment for sin (Lam. i. 14); of God's commandments (Matt. xi. 29, 30). Here it refers to the bondage and affliction which they experienced in Babylon.

7. *And thou saidst, I shall be a lady for ever.* This passage describes the pride and self-confidence of Babylon. She was confident in her wealth; the strength of her gates and walls; and in her abundant resources to resist an enemy, or to sustain a siege. Babylon was ten miles square; and it was supposed to contain provisions enough to maintain a siege for many years. There were, moreover, no symptoms of internal decay; there were no apparent external reasons why her prosperity should not continue; there were no causes at work, which human sagacity could detect, which would prevent her continuing to any indefinite period of time. ¶ *Thou didst not lay these* things *to thy heart.* Thou didst not consider what, under the government of a holy and just God, must be the effect of treating a captured and oppressed people in this manner. Babylon supposed, that notwithstanding her pride, and haughtiness, and oppressions, she would be able to stand for ever. ¶ *Neither didst remember the latter end of it.* The end of pride, arrogance, and cruelty. The sense is, that Babylon might have learned from the fate of other kingdoms that had been, like her, arrogant and cruel, what must inevitably be her own destiny. But she refused to learn a lesson from their doom. So common is it for nations to disregard the lessons which history teaches; so common for individuals to neglect the warnings furnished by the destruction of the wicked.

8. *Therefore hear now this.* The prophet proceeds, in this verse and the following, to detail more particularly the sins of Babylon, and to state the certainty of the punishment which would come upon her. In the previous verses, the denunciation of punishment had been figurative. It had been represented under the image of a lady deli-

9 But these two *things* shall come to thee in a moment, in one day, the loss of children, and widowhood: they shall come upon thee in their perfection, for the multitude of thy sorceries, *and* for the great abundance of thine enchantments.

---

cately trained and nurtured, doomed to the lowest condition of life, and compelled to stoop to the most menial offices. Here the prophet uses language without figure, and states directly her crimes, and her doom. ¶ That art *given to pleasures*. Devoted to dissipation, and to the effeminate pleasures which luxury engenders (see Notes on ver. 1). Curtius, in his *History of Babylon as it was in the times of Alexander* (v. 5. 36), Herodotus (i. 198), and Strabo *Georg.* xvi.), have given a description of it, all representing it as corrupt, licentious, and dissipated in the extreme. Curtius, in the passage quoted on ver. 1, says, among other things, that no city was more corrupt in its morals; nowhere were there so many excitements to licentious and guilty pleasures. ¶ *That dwellest carelessly.* In vain security; without any consciousness of danger, and without alarm (comp. Zeph. ii. 15). ¶ *I* am, *and none else besides me.* The language of pride. She regarded herself as the principal city of the world, and all others as unworthy to be named in comparison with her (comp. Note on ch. xlv. 6). Language remarkably similar to this occurs in Martial's description of Rome (xii. 8):

> Terrarum dea gentiumque, Roma,
> Cui par est nihil, et nihil secundum—

Rome, goddess of the earth and of nations, to whom nothing is equal, nothing second.' ¶ *I shall not sit* as *a widow.* On the word 'sit,' see Note on ver. 1. The sense is, that she would never be lonely, sad, and afflicted, like a wife deprived of her husband, and a mother of her children. The figure is changed from ver. 1, where she is represented as a virgin; but the same idea is presented under another form (comp. Note on ch. xxiii. 4).

9. *In a moment, in one day.* This is designed, undoubtedly, to describe the suddenness with which Babylon would be destroyed. It would not decay slowly, and by natural causes, but it would be suddenly and unexpectedly destroyed. How strikingly this was fulfilled, it is not needful to pause to state (see Notes on ch. xiii., xiv.) In the single night in which Babylon was taken by Cyrus, a death-blow was given to all her greatness and power, and at that moment a train of causes was originated which did not cease to operate until it became a pile of ruins. ¶ *The loss of children, and widowhood.* Babylon would be in the situation of a wife and a mother who is instantaneously deprived of her husband, and bereft of all her children. ¶ *They shall come upon thee in their perfection.* In full measure; completely; entirely. You shall know all that is meant by this condition. The state referred to is that of a wife who is suddenly deprived of her husband, and who, at the same time, and by the same stroke, is bereft of all her children. And the sense is, that Babylon would know *all* that was meant by such a condition, and would experience the utmost extremity of grief which such a condition involved. ¶ *For the multitude of thy sorceries.* This was one of the reasons why God would thus destroy her, that sorceries and enchantments abounded there. Lowth, however, renders this, 'Notwithstanding the multitude of thy sorceries.' So Noyes, 'In spite of thy sorceries.' The Hebrew is, '*In* the multitude (בְּרֹב) of thy sorceries.' Jerome renders it, 'On account of (*propter*) the multitude of thy sorceries.' The LXX. 'In (ἐν) thy sorcery.' Perhaps the idea is, that sorcery and enchantment abounded, and that these calamities would come notwithstanding all that they could do. They would come *in the very midst* of the abounding necromancy and enchantments, while the people practised these arts, and while they depended on them. That this trust in sorcery was one cause why these judgments would come upon them, is apparent from ver. 10, 11. And that they would not be able to protect the city, or that these judgments would come in spite of all their efforts, is ap-

10 For thou hast trusted in thy wickedness: [a]thou hast said, None seeth [b]me. Thy wisdom and thy knowledge it hath [1]perverted thee; and thou hast said in thine heart, I *am*, and none else besides me.
11 Therefore shall evil come upon thee; thou shalt not know [2]from whence it riseth: and mischief shall fall upon thee; thou shalt not be able to [3]put it off: and desolation shall come upon thee suddenly, *which* [c]thou shalt not know.

a Ec.8.8. *b* Ps.94.7.

1 or, *caused thee to turn away.* 2 *the morning thereof.* 3 *expiate.* *c* 1 Th.5.3.

parent from ver. 13. The idea is exactly expressed by a literal translation of the Hebrew. They would come upon her IN, *i.e.*, *in the very midst* of the multitude of sorceries and enchantments. The word here rendered 'sorceries,' means *magic*, incantation, and is applied to the work of magicians (2 Kings ix. 22; Neh. iii. 4; Micah v. 11; comp. Ex. vii. 2; Deut. xviii. 10; Dan. ii. 2; Mal. iii. 5). Magic, it is well known, abounded in the East, and indeed this may be regarded as the birthplace of the art (see Note on ch. ii. 6). ¶ And *for the great abundance of thine enchantments.* Heb. 'And in the strength;' that is, in the full vigour of thine enchantments. While they would abound, and while they would exert their utmost power to preserve the city. The word rendered 'enchantments,' means properly *society*, company, community—from being *associated*, or *bound together;* and then spells, or enchantments, from the notion that they *bound* or confined the object that was the subject of the charm. The idea was that of controlling, binding, or restraining any one whom they pleased, by the power of a spell.

10. *For thou hast trusted in thy wickedness.* The word 'wickedness' here refers doubtless to the pride, arrogance, ambition, and oppressions of Babylon. It means, that she had supposed that she was able by these to maintain the ascendancy over other nations, and perpetuate her dominion. She supposed that by her great power, her natural advantages, and her wealth, she could resist the causes which had operated to destroy other nations. Men often confide in their own wickedness—their cunning, their artifices, their frauds, their acts of oppression and cruelty, and suppose that they are secure against the judgments of God. ¶ *None seeth me.* Compare Ps. x. 11: 'He said in his heart, God hath forgotten; he hideth his face; he will never see it.' See also Ps. xciv. 7. ¶ *Thy wisdom.* Probably the wisdom here referred to, was that for which Babylon was distinguished, the supposed science of astrology, and the arts of divination and of incantation. It may, however, refer to the purposes of the kings and princes of Babylon; and the meaning may be, that it had been perverted and ruined by relying on their counsels. But it more probably refers to the confidence in the wisdom and science which prevailed there. ¶ *Hath perverted thee.* Marg. 'Caused thee to turn away.' That is, hath turned thee away from the path of virtue, truth, and safety. It has been the cause of thy downfall. ¶ *I* am, &c. (see ver. 8.)

11. *Therefore shall evil come upon thee.* In consequence of thy pride and self-confidence; of the prevalence of corruption, licentiousness, and sin; of the prevalence of the arts of magic and of divination abounding there; and of the cruel and unfeeling oppression of the people of God;—for all these crimes ruin shall come certainly and suddenly upon thee. ¶ *Thou shalt not know from whence it cometh.* Marg. 'The morning thereof.' The margin expresses the true sense of the phrase. The word here used (שַׁחַר *shâhhăr*) means *the aurora*, the dawn, the morning (see Notes on ch. xiv. 12). Lowth has strangely rendered it, 'Evil shall come upon thee, which thou shalt not know how to deprecate.' But the word properly means the dawning of the morning, the aurora; and the sense is, that calamity should befall them whose rising or dawning they did not see, or anticipate. It would come unexpectedly and suddenly, like the first rays of the morning. It would spring up as if from no antecedent cause

12 Stand now with thy enchantments, and with the multitude of thy sorceries, wherein thou hast laboured from thy youth; if so be thou shalt be able to profit, if so be thou mayest prevail.

13 Thou art wearied [a] in the multitude of thy counsels. Let now the astrologers,[1] [b] the star-gazers, the monthly [2] prognosticators, stand up and save thee from *these things* that shall come upon thee.

[a] Eze.24.12. 1 *viewers of the heavens.* [b] Da.2.2. 2 *that give knowledge concerning the months.*

which would seem to lead to it, as the light comes suddenly out of the darkness. ¶ *And mischief.* Destruction; ruin. ¶ *Thou shalt not be able to put it off.* Marg. 'Expiate.' This is the sense of the Hebrew (see Notes on ch. xliii. 3). The meaning is, that they could not then avert these calamities by any sacrifices, deprecations, or prayers. Ruin would suddenly and certainly come; and they had nothing which they could offer to God as an expiation by which it could then be prevented. We need not say how strikingly descriptive this is of the destruction of Babylon. Her ruin came silently and suddenly upon her, as the first rays of morning light steal upon the world, and in such a way that she could not meet it, or turn it away.

12. *Stand now with thy enchantments* (see Notes on ver. 9). This is evidently sarcastic and ironical. It is a call on those who practised the arts of magic to stand forth, and to show whether they were able to defend the city, and to save the nation. ¶ *Wherein thou hast laboured.* Or in practising which thou hast been diligently employed. ¶ *From thy youth.* From the very commencement of thy national existence. Babylon was always distinguished for these arts. Now was a time when their value was to be put to the test, and when it was to be seen whether they were able to save the nation. ¶ *If so be.* Or, perhaps, or possibly, they may be able to profit thee—the language of irony. Perhaps by the aid of these arts you may be able to repel your foes.

13. *Thou art wearied.* Thou hast practised so many arts, and practised them so long, that thou art exhausted in them. The 'counsels' here referred to, are those which the astrologers and diviners would take in examining the prognostications, and the supposed indications of future events. ¶ *Let now the astrologers.* Call in now the aid of the various classes of diviners on whom thou hast relied to save thee from the impending calamity and ruin. The words here rendered 'astrologers' (הֹבְרֵי שָׁמַיִם) mean properly *the dividers of the heavens;* those who divided, or cut up the heavens for the purpose of augury, or to take a horoscope (Gesenius). What this art was is not certainly known. It is probable that it referred to their designating certain stars, or constellations, or conjunctions of the planets in certain parts of the heavens, as being fortunate and propitious, and certain others as unfortunate and unpropitious. At first, astrology was synonymous with astronomy. But in process of time, it came to denote the science which professes to discover certain connections between the position and movements of the heavenly bodies, and the events which occur on the earth. It was supposed that the rising and setting, the conjunction and opposition of the planets, exerted a powerful influence over the fates of men; over the health of their bodies, the character of their minds, and the vicissitudes of their lives. Some regarded, it would seem, the positions of the stars as mere *signs* of the events which were to follow; and others, and probably by far the larger portion, supposed that those positions had a *positive influence* in directing and controlling the affairs of this lower world. The origin of this science is involved in great obscurity. Aristotle ascribes the invention to the Babylonians and Egyptians. Ptolemy concurs in this opinion, and Cicero traces it to the same origin. Lucian says that both these nations, as well as the Lybians, borrowed it from the Ethiopians, and that the Greeks owed their knowledge of this pretended science to the poet Orpheus. The science prevailed, it is probable, however, much more early in India; and in China it appears to be co-

14 Behold they shall be as stubble; [a] the fire shall burn them; they shall not deliver [1] themselves from the power of the flame: *there shall* not *be* a coal to warm at, *nor* fire to sit before it.

15 Thus shall they be unto thee with whom thou hast laboured, *even* thy merchants from thy youth: they shall wander every one to his quarter; [b] none shall save thee.

a Na.1.10. 1 *their souls.* b ch.56.11.

eval with their history. The Arabians have been distinguished for their attachment to it; and even Tycho Brahe was a zealous defender of astrology, and Kepler believed that the conjunctions of the planets were capable of producing great effects on human affairs. It is also a remarkable fact that Lord Bacon thought that the science required to be purified from errors rather than altogether rejected. Those who wish to inquire into the various systems of astrology, and the arts by which this absurd science has maintained an influence in the world, may consult the *Edin. Encyclopedia*, Art. *Astrology*, and the authorities enumerated there. The thing referred to in the passage before us, and which was practised in Babylon, was, probably, that of *forecasting* future events, or telling what would occur by the observation of the positions of the heavenly bodies. ¶ *The star-gazers.* Those who endeavour to tell what will occur by the contemplation of the relative positions of the stars. ¶ *The monthly prognosticators.* Marg. 'That give knowledge concerning the months.' That is, at the commencement of the months they give knowledge of what events might be expected to occur during the month;—perhaps from the dip of the moon, or its riding high or low, &c. Something of this kind is still retained by those persons who speak of a dry or wet moon; or who expect a change of weather at the change of the moon—all of which is just as wise as were the old systems of astrology among the Chaldeans. This whole passage would have been more literally and better translated by preserving the order of the Hebrew. 'Let them stand up now and save thee, who are astrologers; who gaze upon the stars, and who make known at the new moons what things will come upon thee.'

14. *Behold, they shall be as stubble.* They shall be no more able to resist the judgments which are coming upon the city, than dry stubble can resist the action of the fire. A similar figure is used in ch. i. 31 (see Notes on that verse). Compare also ch. xxix. 6; xxx. 30, where fire is a symbol of the devouring judgments of God. ¶ *They shall not deliver themselves.* Marg. as Heb. 'Their souls.' The meaning is, that they would be unable to protect themselves from the calamities which would come upon them and the city. ¶ There shall *not* be *a coal to warm at.* The meaning is, that they would be entirely consumed—so completely, that not even a coal or spark would be left, as when stubble, or a piece of wood, is entirely burned up. According to this interpretation, the sense is, that the judgments of God would come upon them and the city, so that entire destruction would ensue. Rosenmüller, however, Cocceius, and some others, suppose this should be rendered, 'there shall not remain a coal so that bread could be baked by it.' But the more common, and more correct interpretation, is that suggested above. Compare Gesenius and Rosenmüller on the place.

15. *With whom thou hast laboured.* The multitude of diviners, astrologers, and merchants, with whom thou hast been connected and employed. The idea is, that Babylon had been the mart where all of them had been assembled. ¶ Even *thy merchants from thy youth.* Babylon was favourably situated for traffic; and was distinguished for it. Foreigners and strangers had resorted there, and it was filled with those who had come there for purposes of trade. The sense here is, that the same destruction which would come upon the diviners, would come on all who had been engaged there in traffic and merchandise. It does not mean that the *individuals* who were thus engaged would be destroyed, but that destruction would come *upon the business;* it

would come *in spite* of all the efforts of the astrologers, and *in spite* of all the mercantile advantages of the place. The destruction would be as entire *as if* a fire should pass over stubble, and leave not a coal or a spark. What a striking description of the total ruin of the commercial advantages of Babylon! ¶ *From thy youth.* From the very foundation of the city. ¶ *They shall wander every one to his own quarter.* All shall leave Babylon, and it shall be utterly forsaken as a place of commerce, and all who have been engaged in mercantile transactions there shall go to other places. The phrase, 'his own quarter' (לְעֶבְרוֹ), means, *to his own way;* they shall be driven from Babylon, and wander to other places. They shall flee from the danger; and if they practise their arts, or engage in commerce, it shall be done in other places besides Babylon. ¶ *None shall save thee.* How truly this was fulfilled need not here be stated. All its arts of astrology, its wealth, its mercantile advantages, the strength of its walls and gates, were insufficient to save it, and now it lies a wide waste—

SITE OF BABYLON DURING AN INUNDATION OF THE EUPHRATES.

a scene of vast and doleful ruin (see Notes on ch. xiii., xiv.) So certainly will all the predictions of God be accomplished; so vain are the arts and devices of man, the strength of fortifications, and the advantages for commerce, when God purposes to inflict his vengeance on a guilty nation. The skill of astrology, the advantages of science, accumulated treasures, brazen gates and massive walls, and commercial advantages, the influx of foreigners, and a fertile soil, cannot save it. All these things are in the hands of God; and he can withdraw them when he pleases. Babylon once had advantages for commerce equal to most of the celebrated marts now of Europe and America. So had Palmyra, and Tyre, and Baalbec, and Petra, and Alexandria, and Antioch. Babylon was in the midst of a country as fertile by nature as most parts of the United States. She had as little prospect of losing the commerce of the world, and of ceasing to be a place of wealth and power, as Paris, or London,

CHAPTER XLVIII.

ANALYSIS.

THIS chapter contains renewed assurances of the deliverance of the exile Jews from Babylon. It is designed, in the main, to state the causes for which the captivity would occur, and to furnish the assurance also that, notwithstanding the judgment that should come upon them, God would deliver them from bondage. It contains lamentations that there was a necessity for bringing these calamities upon them; assurances that God had loved them; appeals to themselves in proof that all that they had suffered had been predicted; and a solemn command to go forth out of Babylon. It is to be regarded as addressed to the exile Jews *in* Babylon, though it is not improbable that the prophet designed it to have a bearing on the Jews of his own time, as given to idolatry, and that he intended that the former part of the chapter should be an indirect rebuke to them by showing them the consequences of their proneness to idolatry. The chapter is exceedingly tender, and full of love, and is an expression of the kindness which God has for his own people.

It is not very susceptible of division, or of easy analysis, but the following topics present probably the main points of the chapter.

I. A reproof of the Jews for their idolatrous tendencies, reminding them that this was the characteristic of the nation, and indirectly intimating that all their calamities would come upon them on account of that (1-8). This part contains—1. An address to the Jews, as those who professed to worship God, though in insincerity and hypocrisy (1, 2). 2. A solemn declaration of God that he had foretold all these events, and that they could not be traced in any manner to the power of idols, and that he, therefore, was God (3-7). 3. Their character had been that of rebellion and treachery, from the very commencement of their history (8).

II. Promises of deliverance from the evils which their sins had brought upon them, with expressions of regret that their conduct had been such as to make such judgments necessary (9-19). 1. God says that he would restrain his anger, and would not wholly cut them off (9). 2. The purpose of the calamities brought upon them was to refine and purify them, as in a furnace (10). 3. All his dealings with them had been for his own glory, and so as to promote his own honour (11). 4. An assertion of his power, and his ability to accomplish what he had purposed (12, 13). 5. He had solemnly purposed to destroy Babylon, and the Chaldeans (14). 6. He had raised up for that purpose one who should accomplish his designs (15, 16). 7. He expresses his deep regret that their conduct had been such as to make it necessary to bring these heavy judgments on them, and states what would have been the result if they had observed his commandments. Their peace would have been as a river, their righteousness as the waves of the sea, and their offspring as the sand (17-19).

III. A command to go forth from Babylon, implying the highest assurance that they should be delivered from their long and painful captivity (20-22). 1. They should go out with singing and triumph; and the ends of the earth

---

or Liverpool, or New York. Yet how easy was it for God, in the accomplishment of his plans, to turn away the tide of her prosperity, and reduce her to ruins. How easy, in the arrangements of his providence, to spread desolation over all the once fertile plains of Chaldea, and to make those plains pools of water. And so with equal ease, if he pleases, and by causes as little known as were those which destroyed Babylon, can he take away the commercial advantages of any city now on earth. Tyre has lost all its commercial importance; the richly-laden caravan has ceased to pause at Petra; Tadmor lies waste. Baalbec is known only by the far-strewed ruins, and Nineveh and Babylon are stripped of all that ever *made* them great, and *can* rise no more. God has taken away the importance and the power of Rome, once, like Babylon, the mistress of the world, by suffering the *malaria* to desolate all the region in her vicinity; and so with equal truth, all that contributes to the commercial importance of New York, Philadelphia, Boston, London, or Paris, are under the control of God. By some secret causes he could make these cities a wide scene of ruins; and they *may be*, if they are *like* Babylon and Tyre and Tadmor in their character, yet *like* them in their doom. They should feel that the sources of their prosperity and their preservation are not in themselves, but in the favour and protection of God. Virtue, justice, and piety, will better preserve them than wealth; and without these they *must be*, in spite of their commercial advantages, what the once celebrated cities of antiquity now are.

should see it (20). 2. God would provide for them in the deserts, and cause the waters to flow for them in their journey through the pathless wilderness (21).

The chapter concludes with a general declaration that the wicked have no peace, implying that they only have peace and security who put their trust in God (22).

HEAR ye this, O house of Jacob,
which are called by the name
of Israel, and are come forth out of
the waters [a] of Judah; which swear
by the name of the LORD, and make
mention of the God of Israel, *but* not
in [b] truth, nor in righteousness.
2 For they call themselves of the
holy city, [c] and stay [d] themselves
upon the God of Israel; The LORD
of hosts *is* his name.

a Ps.68.26. *b* De.5.28,29; Je.5.2; Jn.4.21. *c* ch.52.1. *d* Mi.3.11.

CHAPTER XLVIII.

1. *Hear ye this.* This is an address to the Jews regarded as *in* Babylon, and is designed to remind them of their origin, and of their privileges as the descendants of Jacob, and having the name of Israel (comp. Notes on ch. xliii. 1). ¶ *And are come forth out of the waters of Judah.* This metaphor is taken from a fountain which sends forth its streams of water, and the idea is, that they owed their origin to Judah, as the streams flowed from a fountain. A similar figure is used by Balaam in describing the vast increase of the Jews: (Num. xxxiv.) 'He shall pour the waters out of his buckets, and his seed shall be in many waters.' So in Deut. xxxiii. 28: 'The fountain of Jacob shall be upon a land of corn and wine.' So Ps. lxviii. 26:

Bless ye God in the congregations,
JEHOVAH, ye that are of the fountain of Israel.
Marg.

The idea is, that *Judah* was the fountain, or origin of the people who were then exiled in Babylon. The ten tribes had revolted, and had been carried away, and the name of Benjamin had been absorbed in that of Judah, and this had become the common name of the nation. Perhaps *Judah* is here mentioned with honour as the fountain of the nation, because it was from him that the Messiah was to descend (Gen. xlix. 10); and this mention of his name would serve to bring that promise to view, and would be an assurance that the nation would not be destroyed, nor the power finally depart until He should come. ¶ *Which swear by the name.* Who worship JEHOVAH, and acknowledge him as the only true God (see Notes on ch. xix. 18; xlv. 23; comp. ch. xlviii. 1; lxv. 16). ¶ *And make mention.* That is, in your prayers and praises. You acknowledge him, and profess to worship him. ¶ But *not in truth.* In a hypocritical manner; not in sincerity. Compare Jer. v. 2: 'And though they say, The Lord liveth, surely they swear falsely.'

2. *For they call themselves of the holy city.* Of Jerusalem (see ch. lii. 1; Neh. xi. 1; Matt. iv. 5; xxvii. 53; Rev. xxi. 2–27). The word rendered 'for' here, (כִּי *kī*) means, as it often does, *although;* and the sense is, although they call themselves of the holy city, they do not worship God in sincerity and truth. Jerusalem was called 'the holy city,' because the temple, the ark, and the symbol of the Divine presence were there, and it was the place where God was worshipped. It was deemed sacred by the Jews, and they regarded it as sufficient proof of goodness, it would seem, that they had dwelt there. Even in Babylon they would pride themselves on this, and suppose, perhaps, that it entitled them to Divine protection and favour. ¶ *And stay themselves upon the God of Israel.* In time of danger and trial they profess to seek him, and to commit their cause to him. ¶ *The* LORD *of hosts is his name* (see Notes on ch. i. 9). The object of the prophet in here mentioning his holy name is, probably, to show them the guilt of their conduct. He was JEHOVAH, the source of all existence. He was the God of all the hosts of heaven, and all the armies on earth. How wicked, therefore, it was to come before him in a false and hypocritical manner, and while they were professedly worshipping him, to be really offering their hearts to idols, and to be char-

3 I have declared the former
things from the beginning; and
they went forth out of my mouth,
and I showed them; I did *them*
suddenly, and they came to pass.
4 Because I knew that thou *art*
obstinate, [1] and thy neck [a] *is* an iron
sinew, and thy brow brass;
5 I have even from the beginning
declared *it* to thee; before it came
to pass I showed *it* thee: lest thou
shouldest say, Mine idol hath done

1 *hard.*

a De.31.27.

---

acteristically inclined to relapse into idolatry!

3. *I have declared the former things.* That is, in former times I have predicted future events by the prophets, which have come to pass as they were foretold. Though the fulfilment might have appeared to be long delayed, yet it came to pass at the very time, showing it to be an exact fulfilment of the prophecy. The design of thus referring to the former predictions is, to remind them of their proneness to disregard his declarations, and to recall to their attention the fact that all that he said would be certainly accomplished. As a people, they had been prone to disbelieve his word. He saw that the same thing would take place in Babylon, and that there also they would disbelieve his prophecies about raising up Cyrus, and restoring them to their own land. He therefore endeavours to anticipate this, by reminding them of their former unbelief, and of the fact that all that he *had* foretold in former times had come to pass. ¶ *From the beginning.* In regard to this, and the meaning of the phrase, 'the former things,' see Notes on ch. xli. 22; xliii. 9. The phrase, 'former things,' refers to the things which *precede* others; the series, or order of events. ¶ *I did* them *suddenly.* They came to pass at an unexpected time; when you were not looking for them, and when perhaps you were doubting whether they would occur, or were calling in question the Divine veracity. The idea is, that God in like manner would, certainly, and suddenly, accomplish his predictions about Babylon, and their release from their captivity.

4. *Because I knew that thou* art *obstinate.* I made these frequent predictions, and fulfilled them in this striking manner, because I knew that as a people, you were prone to unbelief, and in order that you might have the most full and undoubted demonstration of the truth of what was declared. As they were disinclined to credit his promises, and as he saw that in their long captivity they would be prone to disbelieve what he had said respecting their deliverance under Cyrus, he had, therefore, given them these numerous evidences of the certainty of the fulfilment of all his prophecies, in order that their minds might credit what he said about their return to their own land. ¶ *That thou* art *obstinate.* Marg. as Heb. 'Hard,' The sense is, that they were obstinate and intractable—an expression probably taken from a bullock which refuses to receive the yoke. The word *hard*, as expressive of obstinacy, is often combined with others. Thus, in Ex. xxxii. 9; xxxiv. 9, 'hard of neck,' *i.e.*, stiff-necked, stubborn; 'hard of face' (Ezek. ii. 4); 'hard of heart' (Ezek. iii. 7). The idea is, that they were, as a people, obstinate, rebellious, and indisposed to submit to the laws of God—a charge which is often brought against them by the sacred writers, and which is abundantly verified by all their history as a people (comp. Ex. xxxii. 9; xxxiii. 3–5; xxxiv. 9; Deut. ix. 6–13; xxxi. 27; 2 Chron. xxx. 8; Ezek. ii. 4; Acts vii. 51). ¶ *Thy neck* is *an iron sinew.* The word גִּיד (*ghīdh*) means properly *a cord, thong*, or *band;* then a nerve, sinew, muscle, or tendon. The metaphor is taken from oxen when they make their neck stiff, and refuse to submit it to the yoke. ¶ *And thy brow brass.* Thy forehead is hard and insensible as brass. The phrase is applied to the shameless brow of a harlot (Jer. iii. 3; Ezek. iii. 7), where there is an utter want of modesty, and consummate impudence. A brow of brass is an image of insensibility, or obstinacy (so in Jer. vi. 28).

5. *I have even from the beginning*

them; and my graven image, and
my molten image, hath commanded
them.
6 Thou hast heard, see all this;
and will not ye declare *it?* I have
showed thee new things from this
time, even hidden things, [a] and thou
didst not know them.
7 They are created now, and not
from the beginning; even before the
day when thou heardest them not;
lest thou shouldest say, Behold, I
knew them.

[a] 1 Co.2.9,10.

declared it *to thee.* He had foretold future events, so that they had abundant demonstration that he was the true God, and so that they could not be under a mistake in regard to the source of their deliverances from danger. ¶ *Mine idol hath done them.* The idols and molten images had not foretold these events, and when they came to pass, it could not, therefore, be pretended that they had been produced by idols. By predicting them, JEHOVAH kept up the proof that he was the true God, and demonstrated that he alone was worthy of their confidence and regard.

6. *Thou hast heard.* You are witnesses that the prediction was uttered long before it was fulfilled. ¶ *See all this.* Behold how it is all fulfilled. Bear witness that the event is as it was predicted. ¶ *And will ye not declare it?* Will you not bear witness to the entire fulfilment of the prophecy? God appeals to them as qualified to testify that what he had declared had come to pass, and calls on them to make this known as a demonstration that he alone was God (see Notes on ch. xliv. 8). ¶ *I have showed thee new things from this time.* From this time I make known a thing which has not before occurred, that you may have a similar demonstration that JEHOVAH is God. The 'new thing' here referred to, is, doubtless, the prediction of the deliverance from the captivity at Babylon—a new thing, in contradistinction from those which had been before predicted, and which were already fulfilled (see Notes on ch. xlii. 9; xliii. 19). ¶ *Even hidden things.* Events which are so concealed that they could not be conjectured by any political sagacity, or by any contemplation of mere natural causes. They are, as it were, laid up in dark treasure-houses (comp. ch. xlv. 3), and they can be known only by him to whom 'the darkness shineth as the day,' and to whom the night and the day are both alike (Ps. cxxxix. 12).

7. *They are created now.* The LXX. render this, Νῦν γίνεται—'Done now;' and many expositors interpret it in the sense that they are now brought into light, as if they were created. Aben Ezra renders it, 'They are decreed and determined by me.' Rosenmüller supposes that it refers to the revelation, or making known those things. Lowth renders it, 'They are produced now, and not of old.' Noyes, 'It is revealed now, and not long ago.' But the sense is probably this: God is saying that they did not foresee them, nor were they able to conjecture them by the contemplation of any natural causes. There were no natural causes in operation at the time the predictions were made, respecting the destruction of Babylon, by which it could be conjectured that that event would take place; and when the event occurred, it was as if it had been *created* anew. It was the result of Almighty power and energy, and was to be traced to him alone. The sense is, that it could no more be predicted, at the time when the prophecy was uttered, from the operation of any natural causes, than *an act of creation* could be predicted, which depended on the exercise of the Divine will alone. It was a case which God only could understand, in the same way as he alone could understand the purposes and the time of his own act of creating the world. ¶ *And not from the beginning.* The events have not been so formed from the beginning that they could be predicted by the operation of natural causes, and by political sagacity. ¶ *Even before the day when thou heardest them not.* The sense of this is probably, 'and before this day thou hast not heard of them;' that is, these predictions pertain to new events, and are not to be found in antecedent prophecies.

8 Yea, thou heardest not; yea, thou knewest not; yea, from that time *that* thine ear was not opened: for I knew [a] that thou wouldest deal very treacherously, [b] and wast called a transgressor from the [c] womb.

9 For [d] my name's sake will I defer mine anger, and for my praise will I refrain for thee, that I cut thee not off.

a Ps.139.1-4. *b* Je.5.11; Ho.5.7; 6.7. *c* Ps.51.5. *d* Ps.79.9; 106.8.

The prophet did not speak now of the deliverance from Egypt, and of the blessings of the promised land, which had constituted the burden of many of the former prophecies, but he spoke of a *new* thing; of the deliverance from Babylon, and of events which they could by no natural sagacity anticipate, so that they could claim that they knew them. ¶ *Lest thou shouldest say, Behold, I knew them.* The taking of Babylon by Cyrus, and the deliverance of the exiles from their bondage, are events which can be foreseen only by God. Yet the prophet says that he had declared these events, which thus lay entirely beyond the power of human conjecture, long before they occurred, so that they could not *possibly* pretend that they knew them by any natural sagacity, or that an idol had effected this.

8. *Yea, thou heardest not.* This verse is designed to show not only that these events could not have been foreseen by them, but that when they were actually made known to them, they were stupid, dull, and incredulous. It is not only re-affirming what had been said in the previous verses, but is designed to show that they were characteristically and constantly a perverse, hardened, and insensible people. The phrase, 'thou heardest not,' therefore means that they did not attend to these things when they *were* uttered, and were prone to disregard God, and all his predictions and promises. ¶ *Yea, from that time that thine ear was not opened.* The word 'that' which is here supplied by our translators, greatly obscures the sense. The meaning is, 'from the first, thine ear was not open to receive them' (Lowth); that is, they were stupid, insensible, and uniformly prone to disregard the messages of God. To open the ear, denotes a prompt and ready attention to what God says (see ch. l. 5), and to close the ear denotes an unwillingness to listen to what is spoken by him. ¶ *For I knew that thou wouldest deal very treacherously.* I knew that, as a people, you are characteristically false and perfidious. This does not refer to their conduct towards other nations, but to their conduct towards God. They were false and unfaithful to him, and the sense is, that *if* God had not foretold the destruction of Babylon and their deliverance from it so clearly that there could have been no misunderstanding of it, and no perversion, they would have also perverted this, and ascribed it to something else than to him. *Perhaps* they might, as their forefathers did, when they came out of Egypt (Ex. xxxii. 4), have ascribed it to idols (comp. ver. 5), and the result might have been a relapse into that very sin, to cure which was the design of removing them to Babylon. ¶ *And wast called.* This was thy appropriate appellation. ¶ *From the womb.* From the very commencement of your national history; from the very time when the nation was first organized (see Notes on ch. xliv. 2).

9. *For my name's sake* (see Notes on ch. xliii. 25; comp. ch. lxvi. 5). It is possible that the design of this verse may be, to answer an objection. 'If the character of the nation is such, it might be said, 'why should God *desire* to restore them again to their own land? If their sins have been so great as to make these heavy judgments proper, why not suffer them to remain under the infliction of the deserved judgment? Why should God interpose? why raise up Cyrus? why overthrow Babylon? why conduct them across a pathless wilderness, and provide for them in a sandy desert?' To this the answer is, that it was not on *their* account. It was not because they were deserving of his favour, nor was it primarily and mainly in order that they might be happy. It was *on his own*

10 Behold, I have refined [a] thee,
but not [1] with silver; I have chosen
thee in the furnace [b] of affliction.

a Ps.66 10. 1 or, *for*, Eze.22.20-22. b Zec.13.9; 1 Pe.4.12.

account—in order to show his covenant faithfulness; his fidelity to the promises made to their fathers, his mercy, his compassion, his readiness to pardon, and his unchanging love.—And this is the reason why he 'defers his anger,' in relation to any of the children of men. His own glory, and not their happiness, is the main object in view. And this is right. The glory, the honour, and the happiness of God, are of more importance than the welfare of any of his creatures; because, first, they are *in themselves* of more importance, just in proportion as God is more elevated than any of his creatures; and, secondly, the welfare of *any* or *all* of his creatures depends on the maintaining of the honour of God, and of his government, and on the manifestation of his perfections to the universe (see the treatise of President Edwards on *The end for which God created the world*, in *Works*, vol. iii. New York Ed. 1830). ¶ *Will I defer mine anger.* That is, I will spare you, and restore you again to your own land (see Note on ver. 11). ¶ *And for my praise will I refrain for thee.* Will I refrain my anger in reference to you as a nation. The word here used (חָטַם *hhâtăm*) denotes properly *to muzzle*, and is commonly employed with reference to an animal in order to tame or subdue it. Here it means that God would restrain himself; he would not put forth his anger in order to destroy them. Learn hence—1. That God acts with reference to his own glory, in order to manifest his own perfections, and to secure his praise. 2. That the reason why the wicked are not cut off sooner in their transgressions is, that He may show his forbearance, and secure praise by long-suffering. 3. That the reason why the righteous are kept amidst their frequent failures in duty, their unfaithfulness, and their many imperfections, is, that God may get glory by showing his covenant fidelity. 4. That it is one evidence of piety—and one that is indispensable—that there should be a willingness that God should secure his own glory in his own way, and that there should be a constant desire that *his* praise should be promoted, whatever may befall his creatures.

10. *Behold, I have refined thee.* This refers to the Jews in their afflictions and captivity in Babylon. It states *one* design which he had in view in those afflictions—to purify them. The word here used, and rendered 'refined' (צָרַף *tzârăph*), means properly *to melt;* to smelt metals; to subject them to the action of fire, in order to remove the scoria or dross from them (see Notes on ch. i. 25). Then it means to purify in any manner. Here it means that God had used these afflictions for the same purpose for which fire is used in regard to metals, in order that every impurity in their moral and religious character might be removed. ¶ *But not with silver.* Marg. 'For.' Heb. בְּכֶסֶף (*bhĕkhâsĕph*). Many different interpretations of this have been proposed. Jerome renders it, *Non quasi argentum*—'Not as silver.' The LXX. Οὐχ ἕνεκεν ἀργυρίου—'Not on account of silver.' Grotius explains it, 'I have a long time tried thee by afflictions, but nothing good appears in thee;' that is, I have not found you to be silver, or to be pure, as when a worker in metals applies the usual heat to a mass of ore for the purpose of separating the dross, and obtains no silver. Gesenius explains it to mean, 'I sought to make you better by afflictions, but the end was not reached; you were not as silver which is obtained by melting, but as dross.' Rosenmüller supposes it means, that he had not tried them with that intensity of heat which was necessary to melt and refine silver; and remarks, that those skilled in metals observe that gold is easily liquified, but that silver requires a more intense heat to purify it. Jarchi renders it, 'Not by the fire of Gehenna as silver is melted by the fire.' Kimchi explains it, 'Not as one who is smelting silver, and who removes all the scoria from it, and so consumes it that nothing but pure silver remains. If that had been done, but few of you would have

11 For mine own sake, *even* for mine own sake, will I do *it:* for how [a] should *my name* be polluted? and [b] I will not give my glory unto another.

12 Hearken unto me, O Jacob and

a De.32.26,27.

b ch.42.8.

been left.' Vitringa supposes that it means, that God had sent them to Babylon to be purified, yet it was not to be done *with* silver. It was by the agency of a people who were wicked, sinful, and unbelieving. Amidst this variety of interpretation, it is difficult to determine the sense. Probably it may be, I have melted thee, and found no silver; or the result has not been that you have been shown to be pure by all your trials; and thus it will agree with what is said above, that they were perverse, false, and rebellious as a people. ¶ *I have chosen thee.* Lowth renders this, 'I have tried thee.' The Vulgate and the LXX., however, render it, 'I have chosen thee.' The word here used (from בָּחַר *bâhăr*) means, according to Gesenius—1. *To prove, to try, to examine;* and the primary idea, according to him, is that of *rubbing* with the *lapis* Lydius, or touchstone, or else of cutting in pieces for the purpose of examining. 2. *To approve, choose,* or *select.* This is the most common signification in the Hebrew Bible (Gen. xiii. 11; Ex. xvii. 9; Josh. xxiv. 15; Job ix. 14; xv. 5; xxix. 25). 3. *To delight in* (Gen. vi. 2; Isa. i. 29). Probably the meaning here is, 'I have proved or tried thee in the furnace of affliction.' It was true, however, that God had *chosen* or selected their nation to be his people when they were suffering in the furnace of affliction in Egypt; and it is also true that God *chooses* sinners now, or converts them, as the result of heavy affliction. Possibly this may be the idea, that their affliction had *prepared* them to embrace his offers and to seek consolation in him; and he may design to teach that one effect of affliction is to *prepare* the mind to embrace the offers of mercy. ¶ *In the furnace of affliction.* Referring particularly to their trials in Babylon. Afflictions are often likened to fire—from the fact that fire is used to purify or try metals, and afflictions have the same object in reference to the people of God.

11. *For mine own sake* (see ver. 9). The expression here is repeated to denote emphasis. He had thrown them into the furnace of affliction on his own account, *i.e.*, in order that his own name should not be profaned by their irreligion and idolatry, and that the glory which was due to him should not be given to idols. ¶ *For how should* my name *be polluted?* The sense is, that it would be inconsistent with his perfections to see his name profaned without endeavouring to correct and prevent it; and in order to this, that he brought these afflictions upon them. They had profaned his name by their irreligion and hypocrisy. In order to correct this evil, and to prevent it in future, he had brought these national judgments on them, and removed them to Babylon. The doctrine here taught is, that when the conduct of God's professed people is such as to dishonour God, and to make his name a subject of reproach with the wicked, he will visit them with heavy judgments. He *cannot* indulge them in a course of life which will reflect dishonour on his own name. ¶ *And I will not give my glory unto another* (see Notes on ch. xlii. 8). The sense here is this. The Jews had, as a nation, been prone to ascribe to idols that which was due to God alone. To correct this, and to make an *effectual* reform, he had removed them to Babylon, and doomed them to a long and painful captivity there. It may be added that the punishment *was* effectual, and that their long trial in Babylon served entirely to correct all their idolatrous propensities as a nation.

12. *Hearken unto me.* This is a solemn call on the Jews in Babylon to attend to what he was now about to say. It is the commencement of a new part of the argument, containing the assurance that he would deliver them, and utterly destroy the Chaldeans. He begins, therefore, by asserting that he is the only true God, and that he is able to accomplish all his purposes. ¶ *My called.* The people whom I have chosen, or called. ¶ *I* am *he.* I am the

Israel, my called; I *am* he: I [a] *am*
the first, I also *am* the last.
13 Mine [b] hand also hath laid the
foundation of the earth, and [1] my
right hand hath spanned the heavens: *when* I [c] call unto them, they
stand up together.
14 All ye, assemble yourselves,
and hear; which among them hath
declared these *things?* The LORD
hath loved [d] him; he will [e] do his
pleasure on Babylon, and his arm
shall be on the Chaldeans.
15 I, *even* I, have spoken; yea,
I have called him: I [f] have brought
him, and he shall make his way
prosperous.

a Re.22.18. b Ps.102.25; c ch.40.26. d Mar.10.21. e ch.44.28. f Ezr.1.2.

1 or, *the palm of my right hand hath spread out.*

same; or I am the true and only God. ¶ *I* am *the first* (see Notes on ch. xli. 4; xliv. 6).

13. *Mine hand also hath laid,* &c. I am the Creator of all things, and I have all power, and am abundantly able to deliver you from all your foes. ¶ *And my right hand hath spanned the heavens.* Marg. 'The palm of my right hand hath spread out.' The sense is, that he by his right hand had spanned, or measured the heavens. The phrase is designed to show his greatness and his power (see Notes on ch. xl. 12). ¶ *When I call unto them* (see Note on ch. xl. 26). The sense here is, that he who had power thus to command the hosts of heaven, and to secure their perfect obedience by his word, had power also to defend his people, and to deliver them from their foes, and conduct them in safety to their own land.

14. *All ye, assemble yourselves and hear.* Ye Jews who are in Babylon, gather together, and listen to the assurance that God is able to protect you, and that he will certainly restore you to your own country. ¶ *Which among them.* Who among the heathen? ¶ *Hath declared these* things? The things relating to the destruction of Babylon, and the rescue of his people. This is an appeal similar to that which God has often made, that he alone can predict future events. None of the astrologers, soothsayers, or diviners of Babylon had been able to foretell the expedition and the conquests of Cyrus, and the capture of the city. If they *had* been able to foresee the danger, they might have guarded against it, and the city might have been saved. But God had predicted it a hundred and fifty years before it occurred, and this demonstrated, therefore, that he alone was God. ¶ *The* LORD *hath loved him.* Lowth renders this, 'He whom JEHOVAH hath loved will execute his will on Babylon.' The LXX. render it, 'Loving thee, I will execute thy will against Babylon.' There can be no doubt that it refers to Cyrus, and that the meaning is, that he whom JEHOVAH had loved would accomplish his will on Babylon. It does not necessarily mean that JEHOVAH was pleased with his moral character, or that he was a pious man (comp. Notes on ch. xli. 2); but that he was so well pleased with him as an instrument to accomplish his purposes, that he chose to employ him for that end. ¶ *He will do his pleasure on Babylon.* He will accomplish all his desire on that city; that is, he will take, and subdue it. The word 'his' here, may refer either to Cyrus or to JEHOVAH. Probably it means that Cyrus would do to Babylon what would be pleasing to JEHOVAH. ¶ *And his arm.* The arm is a symbol of strength, and is the instrument by which we execute our purposes.

15. *I,* even *I, have spoken.* The word 'I' is repeated to give emphasis, and to furnish the utmost security that it should be certainly accomplished. It means, that JEHOVAH, and he alone, had declared this, and that it was entirely by his power that Cyrus had been raised up, and had been made prosperous. ¶ *Yea, I have called him* (see Note on ch. xli. 2). ¶ *I have brought him.* I have led him on his way in his conquests. ¶ *And he shall make his way prosperous.* There is a change of person in this verse, from the first to the third, which is quite common in the writings of Isaiah.

16. *Come ye near unto me* (see ver. 14). ¶ *I have not spoken in secret* (see Notes on ch. xlv. 19). The idea here

16 Come ye near unto me, hear ye this; I have not spoken in secret from the beginning; from the time that it was, there *am* I: and now the [a] Lord God and his Spirit hath sent me.

[a] ch.61.11; Zec.2.8,9-11; Lu.4.18-21.

is, that he had foretold the raising up of Cyrus, and his agency in delivering his people, in terms so plain that it could not be pretended that it was *conjectured*, and so clear that there was no ambiguity. ¶ *From the time that it was, there* am *I.* From the moment when the purpose was formed, and when it began to be accomplished, I was present. The meaning is, that everything in regard to raising up Cyrus, and to the delivery of his people from Babylon, had been entirely under his direction. ¶ *And now the Lord* God *and his Spirit hath sent me.* There is evidently a change in the speaker here. In the former part of the verse, it is God who is the speaker. But here it is he who is sent to bear the message. Or, if this should be regarded, as Lowth and many others suppose, as the Messiah who is speaking to the exiled Jews, then it is an assertion that *he* had been sent by the Lord God and his Spirit. There is an ambiguity in the original, which is not retained in our common translation. The Hebrew is, 'And now the Lord Jehovah hath sent me, and his Spirit;' and the meaning may be either, as in our version, that Jehovah *and* his Spirit were united in sending the person referred to; or that Jehovah had sent him, and at the same time had also sent his Spirit to accompany what he said. Grotius renders it, 'The Lord by his Spirit has given me these commands.' Jerome understands the word 'Spirit' as in the nominative case, and as meaning that the Spirit united with Jehovah in sending the person referred to—*Dominus Deus misit me, et spiritus ejus.* The LXX., like the Hebrew, is ambiguous—Νῦν κύριος κύριος ἀπέστειλέ με, καὶ τὸ πνεῦμα αὐτοῦ. The Syriac has the same ambiguity. The Targum of Jonathan renders it, 'And now Jehovah (יְיָ) God hath sent me and his word.' It is perhaps not possible to determine, where there is such ambiguity in the form of the sentence, what is the exact meaning. As it is not common, however, in the Scriptures, to speak of the Spirit of God as sending, or commissioning his servants; and as the object of the speaker here is evidently to conciliate respect for his message as being inspired, it is probably to be regarded as meaning that he had been sent by Jehovah and was accompanied *with* the influences of his Spirit. Many of the reformers, and others since their time, have supposed that this refers to the Messiah, and have endeavoured to derive a demonstration from this verse of the doctrine of the Trinity. The argument which it has been supposed these words furnish on that subject is, that three persons are here spoken of, the person who sends, *i.e.*, God the Father; the person who is sent, *i.e.*, the Messiah; and the Spirit, who concurs in sending him, or by whom he is endowed. But the evidence that this refers to the Messiah is too slight to lay the foundation for such an argument; and nothing is gained to the cause of truth by such forced interpretations. *It would require more time, and toil, and ingenuity to demonstrate that this passage had reference to the Messiah, than it would to demonstrate the doctrine of the Trinity, and the divinity of the Redeemer, from the unequivocal declarations of the New Testament.* The remark of Calvin on this verse, and on this mode of interpretation, is full of good sense: 'This verse interpreters explain in different ways. Many refer it to Christ, but the prophet designs no such thing. *Cavendæ autem sunt nobis violentæ et coactæ interpretationes*—(such forced and violent interpretations are to be avoided).' The *scope* of the passage demands, as it seems to me, that it should be referred to the prophet himself. His object is, to state that he had not come at his own instance, or without being commissioned. He had been sent by God, and was attended by the Spirit of inspiration. He foretold events which the Spirit of God alone could make known to men. It is, therefore, a strong asseveration that his words demanded their attention, and

17 Thus saith the LORD, thy
Redeemer, the Holy One of Israel;
I *am* the LORD thy God which teacheth [a] thee to profit, [b] which leadeth
thee [c] by the way *that* thou shouldest go.

18 O [d] that thou hadst hearkened
to my commandments! then had
thy [e] peace been as a river, and thy
righteousness as the waves of the
sea:

a Mi.4.2. b De.8.17,18. c Ps.32.8; 73.24. d Ps.81.13-16. e Ps.119.165.

that they had every ground of consolation, and every possible evidence that they would be rescued from their bondage. It is a full claim to Divine inspiration, and is one of the many assertions which are found in the Scriptures where the sacred writers claim to have been sent by God, and taught by his Spirit.

17. *Thy Redeemer* (see Notes on ch. xli. 14; xliii. 1). ¶ *Which teacheth thee to profit.* Teaching you what things will most conduce to your welfare. The reference here is chiefly to the afflictions which they suffered in Babylon. ¶ *Which leadeth thee.* I am thy conductor and guide. God taught them, as he does his people now, by his Providence, his revealed word, and his Spirit, the way in which they ought to go. It is one of his characteristics that he is the guide and director of his people.

18. *O that thou hadst hearkened to my commandments!* This expresses the earnest wish and desire of God. He would greatly have *preferred* that they should have kept his law. He had no wish that they should sin, and that these judgments should come upon them. The doctrine taught here is, that God greatly *prefers* that men should keep his laws. He does not desire that they should be sinners, or that they should be punished. It was so with regard to the Jews; and it is so with regard to all. In all cases, at all times, and with reference to all his creatures, he prefers holiness to sin; he sincerely desires that there should be perfect obedience to his commandments. It is to be remarked also that this is not merely prospective, or a declaration in the abstract. It relates to sin which had been actually committed, and proves that even in regard to that, God would have *preferred* that it had not been committed. A declaration remarkably similar to this, occurs in Ps. lxxxi. 13–16:

O that my people had hearkened unto me,
And Israel had walked in my ways;
I should soon have subdued their enemies,
And turned their hand against their adversaries.
The haters of the Lord should have submitted themselves unto him:
But their time should have endured for ever.
He should have fed them also with the finest of the wheat;
And with honey out of the rock should I have satisfied thee.

Compare Deut. xxii. 29; Isa. v. 1–7; Ezek. xviii. 23–32; Matt. xxiii. 37; Luke xix. 21. ¶ *Then had thy peace been as a river.* The word 'peace' here (שָׁלוֹם *shâlôm*) means properly *wholeness, soundness,* and then health, welfare, prosperity, good of every kind. It then denotes peace, as opposed to war, and also concord and friendship. Here it evidently denotes prosperity in general, as opposed to the calamities which actually came upon them. ¶ *As a river.* That is, abundant—like a full, flowing river that fills the banks, and that conveys fertility and blessedness through a land. 'The heathen, in order to represent the universal power and beneficence of Jupiter, used the symbol of a river flowing from his throne; and to this the *Sycophant* in Plautus alludes (*Trium.* Act iv. Sc. 2, v. 98), in his saying that he had been at the head of that river:

Ad caput amnis, quod de cœlo exoritur, sub solio Jovis.

See also Wemyss' *Key to the Symbolical Language of Scripture,* Art. *River*. Rivers are often used by the sacred writers, and particularly by Isaiah, as symbolical of plenty and prosperity (ch. xxxii. 2; xxxiii. 31; xli. 18; xliii. 19). ¶ *And thy righteousness.* The holiness and purity of the nation. Religion, with all its inestimable benefits, would have abounded to the utmost extent. Instead of the prevailing idolatry and corruption, the hypocrisy and insin-

19 Thy seed also had been as the
sand, and the offspring of thy bowels
like the gravel thereof; his name
should not have been cut off nor
destroyed from before me.
20 Go [a] ye forth of Babylon, flee
ye from the Chaldeans, with a voice
of singing declare ye, tell this, utter
it *even* to the end of the earth; say
ye, The LORD hath redeemed [b] his
servant Jacob.

a Je.51.6,45. b 2 Sa.7.23.

cerity which had abounded, and which made it necessary for God to remove them, they would have been distinguished for sincerity, purity, love, and holy living. And this *proves* that God would have *preferred* the prevalence of holiness. ¶ *As the waves of the sea.* What can be a more beautiful or sublime image than this? What can more strikingly represent the *abundance* of the blessings which religion would have conferred on the land? The waves of the sea are an emblem of plenty. They seem to be boundless. They are constantly rolling. And so their righteousness would have been without a limit; and would have rolled unceasingly its rich blessings over the land. Who can doubt that this would have been a better state, a condition to have been *preferred* to that which actually existed?

19. *Thy seed also.* Instead of being reduced to a small number by the calamities incident to war, and being comparatively a small and powerless people sighing in captivity, you would have been a numerous and mighty nation. This is another of the blessings which would have followed from obedience to the commands of God; and it proves that a people who are virtuous and pious will become numerous and mighty. Vice, and the diseases, the wars, and the Divine judgments consequent on vice, tend to depopulate a nation, and to make it feeble. ¶ *As the sand.* This is often used to denote a great and indefinite number (Gen. xxii. 17; xxxii. 12; xli. 49; Josh. xi. 4; Judg. vii. 12; 1 Sam. xiii. 5; 2 Sam. xvii. 11; 1 Kings iv. 20–29; Job xxix. 18; Ps. cxxxix. 18; Note on Isa. x. 22; Hos. i. 10; Rev. xx. 8). ¶ *And the offspring of thy bowels.* On the meaning of the word used here, see Note on ch. xxii. 24. ¶ *Like the gravel thereof.* Literally, 'and the offspring of thy bowels shall be like its bowels,' *i.e.*, like the offspring of the sea. The phrase refers probably rather to the fish of the sea, or the innumerable multitudes of animals that swim in the sea, than to the gravel. There is no place where the word means gravel. Jerome, however, renders it, *Ut lapili ejus*—'As its pebbles.' The LXX. Ὡς ὁ χοῦς τῆς γῆς—'As the dust of the earth.' The Chaldee also renders it, 'As the stones of the sea;' and the Syriac also. The sense is essentially the same—that the number of the people of the nation would have been vast. ¶ *His name should not have been cut off.* This does not imply of necessity that they had ceased to be a nation when they were in Babylon, but the meaning is, that if they had been, and would continue to be, obedient, their national existence would have been perpetuated to the end of time. When they ceased to be a distinct nation, and their name was blotted out among the kingdoms of the earth, it was for national crime and unbelief (Rom. xi. 20).

20. *Go ye forth of Babylon.* The prophet now directly addresses those who were in exile in Babylon, and commands them to depart from it. The design of this is, to furnish the assurance that they should be delivered, and to show them the duty of leaving the place of their long captivity when the opportunity of doing it should occur. It is also designed to show that when it should occur, it would be attended with great joy and rejoicing. ¶ *Flee ye from the Chaldeans with a voice of singing.* With the utmost exultation and joy. They should rejoice that their captivity was ended; they should exult at the prospect of being restored again to their own land. ¶ *Utter it* even *to the end of the earth.* It is an event so great and wonderful that all the nations should be made acquainted with it. ¶ *The* LORD *hath redeemed,* &c. JEHOVAH has rescued from cap-

21 And they thirsted not *when* he led them through the deserts; he caused the waters [a]to flow out of the rock for them; he clave the rock also, and the waters gushed out.

22 *There is* no peace, [b]saith the LORD, unto the wicked.

[a] Ex.17.6. [b] ch.57.21.

tivity his people (see Notes on ch. xliii. 1).

21. *And they thirsted not.* This is a part of that for which they would be called to celebrate his name. It was not merely that he had redeemed them, but that he had abundantly provided for their wants in the desert, and guided them safe through the pathless wilderness to their own land (see Notes on ch. xxxv. 6, 7; xli. 17, 18). ¶ *He caused the waters to flow out of the rock for them.* The allusion here is undoubtedly to the fact that God caused the waters to flow out of the rock that Moses smote in the wilderness (Ex. xvii. 6; Num. xx. 11). This is not to be regarded as literally true that God would, in like manner, smite the rocks and cause waters to flow by miracle on their return from Babylon. There is no record that any such event took place, and it is not necessary so to understand this passage. It is a part of the triumphant song which they are represented as singing after their return to their own land. In that song, they celebrate his gracious interposition in language that was familiar to them, and by illustrations that were well known. They therefore speak of his mercy to them *as if* he had smitten the rock in the desert on their return, and caused the waters to flow; and the sense is, that his mercy to them then was similar to his goodness to their fathers when he led them to the land of promise. He met all their necessities; and his gracious interposition was experienced all the way *as really* as though he had smitten the rock, or caused cool and refreshing fountains to break out in the desert.

22. There is *no peace, saith the* LORD, *unto the wicked.* This verse contains a sentiment whose truth no one can doubt. To the transgressor of the laws of God there can be no permanent peace, enjoyment, or prosperity. The word *peace* is used in the Scriptures in all these senses (see Note on ver. 18 of this chapter). There may be the *appearance* of joy, and there may be temporary prosperity. But there is no abiding, substantial, permanent happiness, such as is enjoyed by those who fear and love God. This sentiment occurs not unfrequently in Isaiah. It is repeated in ch. lvii. 21; and in ch. lvii. 20, he says that 'the wicked are like the troubled sea when it cannot rest, whose waters cast up mire and dirt.' Of the *truth* of the declaration here there can be no doubt; but it is not perfectly apparent why it is introduced here. It is probably a part of the *song* with which they would celebrate their return; and it may have been used for one of the following reasons:—1. As a general maxim, expressed in view of the joy which *they* had in their return to their own land. They had elevated peace and triumph and joy. This was produced by the fact that they had evidence that they were the objects of the Divine favour and protection. How natural was it in view of these blessings to say, that the wicked had no such comfort, and in general, that there was *no* peace to them of any kind, or from any quarter. Or, 2. It may have been uttered in view of the fact that many of their countrymen may have chosen to remain in Babylon when they returned to their own land. They probably formed connections there, amassed wealth, and refused to attend those who returned to Judea to rebuild the temple. And the meaning may be, that they, amidst all the wealth which they might have gained, and amidst the idolatries which prevailed in Babylon, could never enjoy the peace which *they* now had in their return to the land of their fathers. Whatever was the reason why it was here used, it contains a most important truth which demands the attention of all men. The wicked, as a matter of sober truth and verity, *have* no permanent and substantial peace and joy. They have none—1. In the *act* of wickedness. Sin may be attended with the gratifications of bad passions, but in the act of sinning, as such, there can

CHAPTER XLIX.

ANALYSIS.

In the chapters which precede this, the deliverance from Babylon has been the main subject of the prophecy. There has been, indeed, decided reference in many places to the Messiah and his times: but the primary idea has been the restoration from Babylon. In this chapter, it has been commonly supposed that the Messiah is introduced directly and personally, and that there is a primary reference to him and his work. There has been, indeed, great difference of opinion among interpreters on this point; but the common sentiment has been, that the chapter has a direct reference to him. Some of the opinions which have been held may be briefly referred to as introductory to the exposition of the chapter—since the exposition of the whole chapter will be affected by the view which is taken of its primary and main design. This statement will be abridged from Hengstenberg (*Christology*, vol. i.)

1. According to some, the people of Israel are here introduced as speaking. This is the opinion of Paulus, Döderlin, and Rosenmüller. The argument on which Rosenmüller relies is, that in ver. 3, the speaker is expressly called 'Israel.' According to this idea, the whole people are represented as *a prophet* who is here introduced as speaking; who had laboured in vain; and who, though Israel was not to be gathered, was in future times to be the instructor of the whole world (ver. 4–6). Yet this interpretation is forced and unnatural. To say nothing of the impropriety of representing the collected Jewish people as a prophet—an idea not to be found elsewhere; according to this interpretation, the people are represented as labouring in vain, when as yet they had made no effort for the conversion of the heathen, and, in ver. 5, this same people, as a prophet, is represented as 'not gathered,' and then, in ver. 6, turning to the Gentiles in order to be a light to them, and for salvation to the ends of the earth. It should be added, also, that even the ancient Jewish commentators who have applied ch. liii. to the Jewish people, have not ventured on such an interpretation here. The only argument on which Rosenmüller relies in favour of this interpretation—that drawn from the fact that the name 'Israel' is given to the speaker—will be considered in the Notes on ver. 3.

2. According to others, the prophet here refers to himself. This opinion was held by Jarchi, Aben Ezra, Kimchi, Grotius, and, among recent interpreters, by Koppe, Hensler, and Staudlin. But this interpretation has little probability. It is incredible that the prophet should speak of himself as the light of the heathen world. The speaker represents himself as not satisfied (ver. 6) that the Jewish people should be given to him, but as sent for the salvation of the ends of the earth. Before this same individual

---

be no substantial happiness. 2. They have no solid, substantial, elevated peace in the business or the pleasures of life. This world can furnish no such joys as are derived from the hope of a life to come. Pleasures 'pall upon the sense,' riches take wings; disappointment comes; and the highest earthly and sensual pleasure leaves a sad sense of want—a feeling that there is *something* in the capacities and wants of the undying mind which has not been filled. 3. They have no peace of conscience; no deep and abiding conviction that they are right. They are often troubled; and there is nothing which this world can furnish which will give peace to a bosom that is agitated with a sense of the guilt of sin. 4. They have no *peace* on a deathbed. There may be stupidity, callousness, insensibility, freedom from much pain or alarm. But that is not peace, any more than sterility is fruitfulness; or than death is life; or than the frost of winter is the verdure of spring; or than a desert is a fruitful field. 5. There is often in these circumstances the reverse of peace. There is not only no positive peace, but there is the opposite. There is often disappointment, care, anxiety, distress, deep alarm, and the awful apprehension of eternal wrath. There is no situation in life or death, where the sinner can certainly *calculate* on peace, or where he will be sure to find it. There is every probability that his mind will be often filled with alarm, and that his deathbed will be one of despair. 6. There is no peace to the wicked beyond the grave. *A sinner* CAN *have no peace at the judgment bar of God; he* CAN *have no peace in hell.* In all the future world there is no place where he can find repose; and whatever this life may be, even if it be a life of prosperity and external comfort, yet to him there will be no prosperity in the future world, and no external or internal peace there.

who thus speaks, and who is rejected and despised by the Jewish people, kings and princes are represented as prostrating themselves with the deepest reverence (ver. 7). But it is certain that Isaiah never formed any such extravagant expectations for himself. Besides, there is the same objection to applying the name 'Israel' (ver. 3) to the prophet Isaiah which there is to the Messiah.

3. Gesenius supposes that this refers, not to the prophet Isaiah alone, but to the collective body of the prophets, as represented by him. But to this view also there are insuperable objections. (1.) Everything in the statement here proves that the subject is an individual, and not a mere personification. The personal pronouns are used throughout (see ver. 1, 2, 4, &c.), and the whole aspect of the account is that relating to an individual. It would be as proper to regard a statement made anywhere respecting an individual as referring to some collective body, as to interpret this in this manner. (2.) The prophets taken collectively cannot bear the name 'Israel' (ver. 3); and even Gesenius admits this, and in order to evade the force of it, denies the genuineness of the word 'Israel' in the third verse. (3.) The prophets nowhere represent themselves as called to exert an influence on the heathen world, but their representation is, that the heathen would be converted by the Messiah.

4. The only other opinion which has been extensively held, is that which refers the chapter directly to the Messiah. This was the opinion of the Christian fathers generally, and is the opinion of Lowth, Vitringa, Calvin, Hengstenberg, and of most modern interpreters. The particular reasons for this opinion will be more clearly seen in the Notes on the chapter itself, particularly ver. 1–9. In favour of this interpretation it may be observed in general:—(1.) That if the other interpretations which have been referred to are unfounded, it follows as a matter of course that it must have reference to the Messiah. (2.) The accurate agreement of the words and phrases in the prophecy with the character of the Redeemer, as developed in the New Testament, proves the same thing. (3.) It is referred to the times of the Messiah in Acts xiii. 47, and in 2 Cor. vi. 2.

The chapter may be contemplated under the following division of parts, or subjects, viz.:—

I. The Messiah is introduced as himself speaking, and stating the object of his mission, and his rejection by the Jewish nation, and the fact that he would be for a light to the Gentiles (1–6). This portion consists of the following subjects: 1. The exordium, in which he calls the distant nations to hear his voice (1). 2. His call to the office of the Messiah, and his qualifications for the work (1–3). He was called from the womb (1); he was eminently endowed for the work, as a sharp sword, or a polished shaft is for battle (2); he was the selected servant of God, by whom he designed to be glorified (3). 3. The want of success in his work (4). He had laboured in vain, yet he could commit his cause to God with the certainty of entire *future* success, and with the assurance of the Divine approbation. 4. His future success would be glorious (5, 6). He would yet gather in the tribes of Israel, and be for a light to the heathen world, and for salvation to the ends of the earth.

II. A direct promise from JEHOVAH to the Messiah of ultimate success in his work (7–12). 1. Men would indeed despise and reject him. 2. Yet kings and princes would arise and honour him (7). 3. JEHOVAH had heard him, and would yet give him for a covenant to the world; a mediator to recover the earth back to himself (8). 4. He would lead forth the prisoners, and those who sat in darkness (9): he would protect and provide for them so that the sun should not smite them, and so that their wants should be supplied (10): he would remove all obstructions from their path, and would level mountains and exalt valleys (11): and his followers would come from far, from a distant land (12).

III. A song of praise in view of the glorious results of the work of the Messiah (13).

IV. Zion is comforted with the assurance that God had not forgotten her (14–21). 1. Zion had said that JEHOVAH had forgotten her, and left her to suffer alone without pity or compassion (14). 2. God assures her that he could no more forget her than a mother could forget her child (15). 3. He had engraven her name on the palms of his hands (16). 4. All her enemies and destroyers would flee away (17). 5. She would be yet decorated and adorned as a bride, instead of being desolate (18); and would be greatly increased and enlarged by accessions from the Gentile world, so that the place where she dwelt would be too strait for her (19–21).

V. God would extend salvation, with all its blessings, to the Gentiles. Kings and queens would become the patrons of the church of God, and all the foes of himself and his cause be destroyed (22–26).

LISTEN, O isles, unto me; and hearken, ye people from far; The LORD hath called me from the [a] womb; from the bowels of my mother hath he made mention of my name.

[a] Je.1.5; Lu.1.15,31; Ga.1.15.

2 And he hath made my mouth like a sharp sword; [a]in [b]the shadow of his hand hath he hid me, and made me a polished shaft; [c]in his quiver hath he hid me;

a Ho.6.5; He.4.12; Re 1.16. b ch.21.16. c Ps.45.5.

CHAPTER XLIX.

1. *Listen.* This is the exordium, or introduction. According to the interpretation which refers it to the Messiah, it is to be regarded as the voice of the Redeemer calling the distant parts of the earth to give a respectful attention to the statement of his qualifications for his work, and to the assurances that his salvation would be extended to them (comp. ch. xli. 1). The Redeemer here is to be regarded as having already come in the flesh, and as having been rejected and despised by the Jews (see ver. 4, 5), and as now turning to the Gentile world, and proffering salvation to them. The *time* when this is supposed to occur, therefore, as seen by the prophet, is when the Messiah had preached in vain to his own countrymen, and when there was a manifest fitness and propriety in his extending the offer of salvation to the heathen world. ¶ *O isles.* Ye distant lands (see Note on ch. xli. 1). The word is used here, as it is there, in the sense of countries *beyond sea;* distant, unknown regions; the dark, heathen world. ¶ *Ye people from far.* The reason why the Messiah thus addresses them is stated in ver. 6. It is because he was appointed to be a light to them, and because, having been rejected by the Jewish nation, it was resolved to extend the offers and the blessings of salvation to other lands. ¶ *The* LORD *hath called me from the womb.* JEHOVAH hath set me apart to this office from my very birth. The stress here is laid on the *fact* that he was thus called, and not on the particular time when it was done. The idea is, that he had not presumptuously assumed this office; he had not entered on it without being appointed to it; he had been designated to it even before he was born (see ver. 5). A similar expression is used in respect to Jeremiah (i. 5): 'Before I formed thee in the belly, I knew thee; and before thou camest forth out of the womb I sanctified thee; and I ordained thee a prophet unto the nations.' Paul also uses a similar expression respecting himself (Gal. i. 15): 'But when it pleased God, who separated me from my mother's womb.' That this actually occurred in regard to the Redeemer, it is not needful to pause here to show (see Luke i. 31). ¶ *From the bowels of my mother hath he made mention of my name.* This is another form of stating the fact that he had been designated to this office from his very infancy. Many have supposed that the reference here is to the fact that Mary was commanded by the angel, before his birth, to call his name Jesus (Luke i. 31). The same command was also repeated to Joseph in a dream (Matt. i. 21). So Jerome, Vitringa, Michaelis, and some others understand it. By others it has been supposed that the phrase 'he hath made mention of my name' is the same as to call. The Hebrew is literally, 'He has caused my name to be remembered from the bowels of my mother.' The LXX. render it, 'He hath called my name.' Grotius renders it, 'He has given to me a beautiful name, by which salvation is signified as about to come from the Lord.' I see no objection to the supposition that this refers to the fact that his name was actually designated before he was born. The phrase seems obviously to imply more than merely to *call* to an office; and as his name was thus actually designated by God, and as he designed that there should be special significancy and applicability *in* the name, there can be no impropriety in supposing that this refers to that fact. If so, the idea is, that he was not only *appointed* to the work of the Messiah from his birth, but that he actually had a *name* given him by God before he was born, which expressed the fact that he would *save* men, and which constituted a reason why the distant heathen lands should hearken to his voice.

2. *And he hath made my mouth.* The idea here is, that he had qualified him for a convincing and powerful eloquence—for the utterance of words which would penetrate the heart like a sharp sword. The mouth here, by an obvious figure, stands for discourse. The comparison of words that are pungent, penetrating,

powerful, to a sword, is common. Indeed the very terms that I have incidentally used, 'pungent,' 'penetrating,' are instances of the same kind of figure, and are drawn from a *needle*, or anything sharp and pointed, that penetrates. Instances of this occur in the following places in the Scriptures :—'The words of the wise are as goads, and as nails fastened by the masters of assemblies' (Eccl. xii. 11). 'The word of God is quick and powerful, and sharper than any two-edged sword, piercing even to the dividing asunder of soul and spirit, and of the joints and marrow' (Heb. iv. 12). In Rev. i. 16, probably in reference to this passage, the Redeemer is represented as seen by John as having a 'sharp two-edged sword' proceeding out of his mouth. So in ch. xix. 15: 'And out of his mouth goeth a sharp sword.' The bold and striking metaphor of the sword and arrow applied to powerful discourse, has been used also by heathen writers with great elegance and force. In the passages quoted by Lowth, it is said of Pericles by Aristophanes:

> 'His powerful speech
> Pierced the hearer's soul, and left behind
> Deep in his bosom its keen point infixt.'

So Pindar, *Olym.* ii. 160:

> 'Come on! thy brightest shafts prepare,
> And bend, O Muse, thy sounding bow:
> Say, through what paths of liquid air
> Our arrows shall we throw?'
>
> West.

A similar expression occurs in a fragment of Eupolis, in Diod. Sic. xii. 40, when speaking of Pericles:

> —*καὶ μόνος τῶν ῥητόρων*
> *τὸ κέντρον ἐγκατέλειπε τοῖς ἀκροωμένοις.*

A similar metaphor occurs frequently in Arabic poetry. 'As arrows his words enter into the heart.' ¶ *In the shadow of his hand hath he hid me.* This passage has been very variously interpreted. Many have understood it as meaning that the shadow of the hand of God would cover or defend him—as a shade or shadow protects from heat. The word 'shadow' is used for protection in Isa. xxv. 4; Ps. xvii. 8; xxxvi. 8. This is the interpretation which Gesenius adopts. Piscator says that it means that God protected him from the snares of the Scribes and Pharisees. Others suppose that it means that he was hidden or protected, as the sword is in the sheath, which is under the left hand, so that it can be easily drawn by the right hand. But Vitringa remarks that the figure here is that of a drawn sword, and he supposes that the meaning is, that the shadow of the hand of God is what covers and defends it, and serves, as it were, for a scabbard. Hengstenberg coincides with this opinion, and supposes that the image is taken from a dirk which a man carries in his hand, and which he suddenly draws forth in the moment of attack. In the parallel member of the sentence, the Redeemer is represented as an arrow that is laid up in a quiver, ready to be drawn forth at any moment. Here, the image is that of a sword under the Divine protection, and the idea is, that the shadow of the hand of God constitutes the protection, the covering of the sword. He is the defender of the Messiah, and of his words; and his hand shall guard him as the scabbard does the sword, or as the quiver does the arrow. The Messiah, like the sword, and the polished arrow, was fitted for the execution of the plans of God, and was ready at any moment to be engaged in his cause. His words, his doctrines, would be like the sharp sword and polished arrow. They would penetrate the heart of his foes, and by his doctrines, and the truths which he would teach, he would carry his conquests around the world. ¶ *And made me a polished shaft.* The word rendered 'polished' (בָּרוּר *bârûr*), may mean either chosen, or polished. It properly means that which is separated, or severed from others; then select, chosen. Then it may mean anything which is cleansed, or purified, and here may denote an arrow that is *cleansed* from rust; *i.e.*, polished, or made bright. The word 'shaft' (חֵץ *hhētz*), means properly *an arrow;* and the sense here is, that the Messiah pierced the hearts of men like a pointed and polished arrow that is sped from the bow. ¶ *In his quiver.* The word 'quiver' means the covering that was made for arrows, and which was so slung over the shoulder that they could be readily reached by

3 And said unto me, Thou *art* my servant, O Israel, in whom I will be glorified.[a]

[a] ch.43.21; Jn.13.31; 1 Pe.2.9.

the hand as they should be needed. ¶ *Hath he hid me.* 'Before his appearing,' says Hengstenberg, 'the Messiah was concealed with God like a sword kept in its sheath, or like an arrow lying in the quiver.' But perhaps this is too much refined and forced. The meaning is, probably, simply that he had protected him. 'God, by his own power,' says Calvin, 'protected Christ and his doctrine, so that nothing could hinder its course.' Yet there is, undoubtedly, the idea that he was adapted to produce rapid and mighty execution; that he was fitted, like an arrow, to overcome the foes of God; and that he was kept in the 'quiver' for that purpose.

3. *And said unto me.* That is, as I suppose, to the Messiah. God said to him that he was his servant; he by whom he would be particularly glorified and honoured. ¶ *Thou* art *my servant, O Israel.* There has been great variety, as was intimated in the analysis of the chapter, in the interpretation of this verse. The question of difficulty is, to whom does the word 'Israel' refer? And if it refer to the Messiah, why is this name given to him? There is no variety in the ancient versions, or in the MSS. The opinions which have been maintained have been referred to in the analysis, and are briefly these—1. The most obvious interpretation of the verse, if it stood alone, would be to refer it to the Jews as 'the servant of Jehovah,' in accordance with ch. xli. 8, by whom he would be glorified in accordance with the declaration in ch. xliv. 23. This is the opinion of Rosenmüller and of some others. But the objection to this is, that the things which are affirmed of this 'servant,' by no means apply to the Jews. It is evidently an individual that is addressed; and in no conceivable sense can that be true of the Jews at large which is affirmed of this person in ver. 4, *sq.* 2. It has been referred to Isaiah. This was the opinion of Grotius, Dathe, Saadias, Döderlin, and others. Grotius supposes it means, 'thou art my servant for the good of Israel.' So Dathe renders it: 'It is for Israel's benefit that I will glorify myself in thee.' Saadias renders it, 'Thou art my ambassador to Israel.' Aben Ezra says of the passage, 'Thou art my servant, descended from Israel, in whom I will be glorified. Or, the sense is this: Thou who in my eyes art reputed as equal to all Israel.' But, as has been remarked in the analysis, this interpretation is attended with *all* the difficulty of the interpretation which refers it to the Messiah, and is inconsistent with the known character of Isaiah, and with the declarations made of the person referred to in the following verses. There is certainly no more reason why the name 'Israel' should be given to Isaiah, than there is why it should be given to the Messiah; and it is certain that Isaiah never arrogated to himself such high honour as that of being a light to the Gentiles, and a covenant of the people, and as being one before whom kings would rise up, and to whom princes would do homage. 3. Gesenius supposes that the word 'Israel' is not genuine, but has come by error into the text. But for this there is no authority except one manuscript, to which he himself attaches no weight. 4. The only other interpretation, therefore, is that which refers it to the Messiah. This, which has been the common exposition of commentators, most manifestly agrees with the verses which follow, and with the account which occurs in the New Testament. The account in ver. 4–8, is such as can be applied to no other one than he, and is as accurate and beautiful a description of him as if it had been made by one who had witnessed his labours, and heard from him the statement of his own plans. But still, a material question arises, why is this name 'Israel' applied to the Messiah? It is applied to him nowhere else, and it is certainly remarkable that a name should be applied to an individual which is usually applied to an entire people. To this question the following answers, which are, indeed, little more than conjectures, may be returned:—1. Lowth and Vitringa suppose that it is because

4 Then I said, I have laboured in vain, I have spent my strength for nought, and in vain; *yet* surely my judgment *is* with the LORD, and my [1] work with my God.

1 or, *reward*, ch.40.10.

the name, in its full import and signification, can be given only to him; and that there is a reference here to the fact recorded in Gen. xxxii. 28, where Jacob is said to have wrestled with God, and prevailed, and was, in consequence of that, called Israel. The full import of that name, says Lowth, pertains only to the Messiah, 'who contended powerfully with God in behalf of mankind.' 2. It is common in the Scriptures to use the *names* which occurred in the history of the Jews as descriptive of things which were to occur under the times of the Messiah, or as representing *in general* events that might occur at any time. Thus the names, *Moab, Edom, Ashur*, were used to denote the foes of God in general; the name of Elijah was given to John the Baptist (Hengstenberg). 3. In accordance with this, the name David is not unfrequently given to the Messiah, and he is spoken of under this name, as he was to be his descendant and successor. 4. For the same reason, the name *Israel* may be given to him—not as the name of the Jewish people—but the name of the illustrious ancestor of the Jewish race, because he would possess his spirit, and would, like him, wrestle with God. He was to be a prince having power with God (comp. Gen. xxxii. 28), and would prevail. In many respects there would be a resemblance between him and this pious and illustrious ancestor of the Jewish people. ¶ *In whom I will be glorified.* This means that the result of the Redeemer's work would be such as eminently to honour God. He would be glorified by the gift of such a Saviour; by his instructions, his example, the effect of his ministry while on earth, and by his death. The effect of the work of the Messiah as adapted to glorify God, is often referred to in the New Testament (see John xii. 28; xiii. 31, 32; xiv. 13; xvi. 14; xvii. 1–5).

4. *Then I said.* I the Messiah. In the previous verses he speaks of his appointment to the office of Messiah, and of his dignity. The design here is to prepare the way for the announcement of the fact that he would make known his gospel to the heathen, and would be for a light to the Gentiles. For this purpose he speaks of his labours among his own countrymen; he laments the little success which attended his work at the commencement, but consoles himself with the reflection that his cause was with God, and that his labours would not go unrewarded. ¶ *I have laboured in vain.* This is to be regarded as the language of the Messiah when his ministry would be attended with comparatively little success; and when in view of that fact, he would commit himself to God, and resolve to extend his gospel to other nations. The expression here used is not to be taken *absolutely*, as if he had *no* success in his work, but it means that he had *comparatively* no success; he was not received and welcomed by the united people; he was rejected and despised by them as a whole. It is true that the Saviour *had* success in his work, and far more success than is commonly supposed (see Notes on 1 Cor. xv. 6). But it is also true that by the nation at large he was despised and and rejected. The idea here is, that there were not results in his ministry, at all commensurate with the severity of his labours, and the strength of his claims. ¶ *I have spent my strength for nought.* Comparatively for nought. This does not mean that he would not be ultimately as successful as he desired to be (comp. Notes on ch. liii. 11); but it means, that in his personal ministry he had exhausted his strength, and seen comparatively little fruit of his toils. ¶ Yet *surely my judgment* is *with the* LORD. My cause is committed to him, and he will regard it. This expresses the confidence of the speaker, that God approved of his work, and that he would ultimately give such effect to his labours as he had desired. The sense is, 'I know that JEHOVAH approves my work, and that he will grant me the reward of my toils, and my sufferings.' ¶ *And my work with my God.* Marg. 'Reward' (see Notes on ch. xl. 10). The

5 And now, saith the LORD, that formed thee from the womb *to be* his servant, to bring Jacob again to him, [1] Though Israel be not [a] gathered, yet shall I be glorious in the eyes of the LORD, and my God shall be my strength.

1 or, *That Israel may be gathered to him, and I may.*
a Mat.23.37.

idea is, that he knew that God would own and accept his work though it was rejected by men. It indicates perfect confidence in God, and a calm and unwavering assurance of his favour, though his work was comparatively unsuccessful—a spirit which, it is needless to say, was evinced throughout the whole life of the Redeemer. Never did he doubt that God approved his work; never did he become disheartened and desponding, as if God would not ultimately give success to his plans and to the labours of his life. He calmly committed himself to God. He did not attempt to avenge himself for being rejected, or for any of the injuries done him. But he left his name, his character, his reputation, his plans, his labours, all with God, believing that *his* cause was the cause of God, and that *he* would yet be abundantly rewarded for all his toils. This verse teaches—1. That the most faithful labours, the most self-denying toil, and the efforts of the most holy life, may be for a time unsuccessful. If the Redeemer of the world had occasion to say that he had laboured in vain, assuredly his ministers should not be surprised that they have occasion to use the same language. It may be no fault of the ministry that they are unsuccessful. The world may be so sinful, and opposition may be got up so mighty, as to frustrate their plans, and prevent their success. 2. Yet, though at present unsuccessful, faithful labour will ultimately do good, and be blessed. In some way, and at some period, all honest effort in the cause of God may be expected to be crowned with success. 3. They who labour faithfully may commit their cause to God, with the assurance that they and their work will be accepted. The ground of their acceptance is not the success of their labours. They will be acceptable in proportion to the amount of their fidelity and self-denying zeal (see Notes on 2 Cor. ii. 15, 16). 4. The ministers of religion, when their message is rejected, and the world turns away from their ministry, should imitate the example of the Redeemer, and say, 'my judgment is with JEHOVAH. My cause is his cause; and the result of my labours I commit to him.' To do this as he did, they should labour as he did; they should honestly devote all their strength and talent and time to his service; and THEN they can confidently commit all to him, and THEN and THEN ONLY they will find peace, as he did, in the assurance that their work will be ultimately blessed, and that they will find acceptance with him.

5. *And now, saith the* LORD *that formed me.* This verse contains the reason why he cherished the hope that his work would not be unaccepted. The reason is, that JEHOVAH had said to him that he should be glorious in his eyes, and that he would be his strength. He stood so high in his favour, and he had such assurances of that favour, that he could confidently commit himself to his care. ¶ *That formed thee from the womb.* Who appointed me before I was born to the office of a servant to accomplish important purposes (see Notes on ver. 1). ¶ *To bring Jacob again to him.* To recover the Jewish people again to the pure worship of JEHOVAH. To them the Messiah was first to be sent, and when they rejected him, he was to proffer the same salvation to the Gentiles (see ver. 6; comp. Matt. xxi. 33–43). Accordingly the Saviour spent his life in preaching to the Jews, and in endeavouring to bring them back to God, and for this purpose he regarded himself as sent (Matt. xv. 24; see Acts iii. 26). ¶ *Though Israel be not gathered.* This metaphor is taken from a scattered flock which a shepherd endeavours to gather, or collect to himself. There is great variety in the interpretation of this expression. The margin reads it, 'That Israel may be gathered to him, and I may' be glorious. So Lowth, 'That Israel unto him may be gathered.' So Noyes, 'To gather Israel to him.' Jerome renders

6 And he said, [1] It is a light thing
that thou shouldest be my servant,
to raise up the tribes of Jacob, and
to restore the [2] preserved of Israel;
I will also give thee for a light [a] to
the Gentiles, that thou mayest be
my salvation unto the end of the
earth.

1 or, *Art thou lighter than that thou*, &c. 2 or, *desolations*. *a* Ac.13.47.

it, 'Israel shall not be gathered.' The LXX. render it, 'To gather Jacob unto him, and Israel.' The Syriac, 'That I may gather Jacob unto him, and assemble Israel.' This variety has arisen from the different readings in the Hebrew text. The reading in the text is לֹא (*not*); but instead of this the marginal reading, or the Keri of the Masorites is, לוֹ *lō*, (*to him*). 'Five MSS. (two ancient),' says Lowth, 'confirm the Keri, or marginal construction of the Masorites; and so read Aquila, and the Chaldee, LXX., and Arabic.' Gesenius and Rosenmüller adopt this, and suppose that לֹא (*lō*), is only a different form of writing לוֹ. Grotius and Hengstenberg render it as it is in our version. It is impossible to determine the true reading; and the only guide is the context, and the views which shall be entertained of the design of the passage. To me it seems that the parallelism demands that we should adopt the reading of the Keri, the LXX., the Chaldee, and the Syriac, and which has been adopted by Lowth. According to this, it means that he had been appointed to gather in the lost sheep of the house of Israel, and gave his life to it. Other parts of this statement (ver. 4–6) show, that by them he was rejected, and that then salvation was sent to other parts of the world. Luther renders it, 'That Israel be not carried away.' ¶ *Yet shall I be.* Or, *and* (וְ) I shall be glorious. The sense is, that as the result of this appointment he would be *in some way* glorious in the sight of JEHOVAH. Though he would be rejected by the nation, yet he would be honoured by God. He would not only approve his character and work, but would secure his being honoured among men by making him the light of the Gentiles (comp. ch. xliii. 4). ¶ *And my God shall be my strength.* He might be rejected by the people, but in God he would find an unfailing source of support and consolation. It is not needful to say, that this applies most accurately to the character of the Redeemer as exhibited in the New Testament.

6. *And he said.* That is, JEHOVAH said in his promise to the Messiah. ¶ *It is a light thing.* Marg. 'Art thou lighter than that thou,' &c. Lowth renders it, 'It is a small thing.' Hengstenberg, 'It is too little that thou shouldest be my servant to raise up the tribes of Jacob.' The sense is, that God designed to glorify him in an eminent degree, and that it would not be as much honour as he designed to confer on him, to appoint him merely to produce a reformation among the Jews, and to recover them to the spiritual worship of God. He designed him for a far more important work—for the recovery of the Gentile world, and for the spread of the true religion among all nations. The LXX. render this, 'It is a great thing for thee to be called my servant.' The Chaldee proposes it as a question, 'Is it a small thing for you that you are called my servant?' ¶ *My servant* (see ver. 3). ¶ *To raise up the tribes of Jacob.* Heb. (לְהָקִים)—'To establish,' or confirm the tribes of Jacob; that is, to establish them in the worship of God, and in prosperity. This is to be understood in a spiritual sense, since it is to be synonymous with the blessings which he would bestow on the heathen. His work in regard to both, was to be substantially the same. In regard to the Jews, it was to confirm them in the worship of the true God; and in regard to the heathen, it was to bring them to the knowledge of the same God. ¶ *And to restore.* To bring back (לְהָשִׁיב) that is, to recover them from their sin and hypocrisy, and bring them back to the worship of the true and only God. The Chaldee, however, renders this, 'To bring back the captivity of Israel.' But it means, doubtless, to recover the alienated Jewish people to the pure and spiritual worship of God. ¶ *The preserved*

7 Thus saith the LORD, the Redeemer of Israel, *and* his Holy One, to him [1] whom man despiseth, [a] to him whom the [b] nation abhorreth, to a servant of rulers, [c] Kings shall see and arise, princes also shall worship, because of the LORD that is faithful, *and* the Holy One of Israel, and he shall choose thee.

1 or, *that is despised in soul.* a ch.53.3. b Lu.23.18-23. c Ps.72.10,11.

---

of Israel. Lowth renders this, 'To restore the branches of Israel;' as if it were נִצְרֵי (*nĕtzârē*) in the text, instead of נְצוּרֵי (*nĕtzūrē*). The word נֵצֶר (*nētzĕr*) means *branch* (see Notes on ch. xi. 1; xiv. 9), and Lowth supposes that it means the branches of Israel; *i.e.*, the descendants of Israel or Jacob, by a similitude drawn from the branches of a tree which are all derived from the same stem, or root. The Syriac here renders it, 'The branch of Israel.' But the word properly means those who are kept, or preserved (from נָצַר, *to keep, preserve*), and may be applied either *literally* to those who were kept alive, or who survived any battle, captivity, or calamity—as a remnant; or *spiritually*, to those who are preserved for purposes of mercy and grace out of the common mass that is corrupt and unbelieving. It refers here, I suppose, to the latter, and means those whom it was the purpose of God to *preserve* out of the common mass of the Jews that were sunk in hypocrisy and sin. These, it was the design of God to restore to himself, and to do this, was the primary object in the appointment of the Messiah. ¶ *I will also give thee for a light to the Gentiles.* I will appoint thee to the higher office of extending the knowledge of the true religion to the darkened heathen world. The same expression and the same promise occur in ch. xlii. 6 (see Notes on that verse). ¶ *That thou mayest be my salvation unto the end of the earth* (see Note on ch. xlii. 10). The true religion shall be extended to the heathen nations, and all parts of the world shall see the salvation of God. This great work was to be intrusted to the Redeemer, and it was regarded as a high honour that he should thus be made the means of diffusing light and truth among all nations. We may learn hence, first, that God will raise up the tribes of Jacob; that is, that large numbers of the Jews shall yet be 'preserved,' or recovered to himself; secondly, that the gospel shall certainly be extended to the ends of the earth; thirdly, that it is an honour to be made instrumental in extending the true religion. So great is this honour, that it is mentioned as the highest which could be conferred even on the Redeemer in this world. And if *he* deemed it an honour, shall *we* not also regard it as a privilege to engage in the work of Christian missions, and to endeavour to save the world from ruin? There is no higher glory for man than to tread in the footsteps of the Son of God; and he who, by self-denial and charity, and personal toil and prayer, does most for the conversion of this whole world to God, is most like the Redeemer, and will have the most elevated seat in the glories of the heavenly world.

7. *Thus saith the* LORD. This verse contains a promise of the future honour that should await the Redeemer, and of the success which should crown his work. The sense is, that JEHOVAH had promised to him who was despised and rejected, that kings and princes should yet rise up and honour him. ¶ *The Redeemer of Israel* (see Note on ch. xliii. 1). ¶ *To him whom man despiseth.* On the construction of the Hebrew here, see Gesenius, Vitringa, and Hengstenberg. The phrase לִבְזֹה־נֶפֶשׁ (*to the despised of soul*), means evidently one who is despised, rejected, contemned by men. The word 'soul' here (נֶפֶשׁ) means the same as man; *i.e.*, every man. It was a characteristic of him that he was despised and rejected by all; and the prophet, in this verse, has given a summary of all that he has said respecting him in ch. liii. ¶ *To him whom the nation abhorreth.* The word 'nation' here refers doubtless to the Jewish people, as in ch. i. 4; x. 6. The word rendered 'abhorreth' means *for an abomination* (לִמְתָעֵב, Piel participle, from תָּעַב), and the idea is, that he was re-

garded as an abomination by the people. The same idea is more fully expressed in ch. liii. 3, 4, that the Messiah would be rejected and treated with abhorrence by the nation as such—a statement which the slightest acquaintance with the New Testament will lead any one to see has been literally fulfilled. No being ever excited more *abhorrence;* no man was ever regarded with so much abomination by any people as Jesus of Nazareth was, and still is, by the Jewish people. He was condemned by the Sanhedrim; publicly rejected by the nation; and at the instigation and by the desire of the assembled people at Jerusalem, he was executed as a malefactor in the most shameful and ignominious manner then known (see Luke xxiii. 18–23). To this day, his name excites the utmost contempt among Jews, and they turn from him and his claims with the deepest abhorrence. The common name by which he is designated in the Jewish writings is *Tolvi*—'the crucified;' and nothing excites more deep abhorrence and contempt than the doctrine that they, and all others, can be saved only by the merits of 'the crucified.' The Chaldee renders all this in the plural, 'To those who are contemned among the people, to those who have migrated to other kingdoms, to those who serve other lords.' ¶ *To a servant of rulers.* This probably means that the Messiah voluntarily submitted himself to human power, and yielded obedience to human rulers. The idea, if interpreted by the facts as recorded in the New Testament, is, that though he was the ruler of all worlds, yet he voluntarily became subject to human laws, and yielded submission and obedience to human rulers. For this purpose he conformed to the existing institutions of his country at the time when he lived; he paid the customary tax or tribute that was laid for the support of religion (Matt. xvii. 27); he submitted to a trial before the Sanhedrim, and before Pilate, though both were conducted in a manner that violated all the principles of justice; and he submitted to the unjust decree which condemned him to die. He was, therefore, all his life, subject to rulers. He was not only exemplary and strict in obeying the laws of the land; but he became, in a more strict sense, their *servant,* as he was deprived of his liberty, comfort, and life at their caprice. He refrained himself from exerting his Divine power, and voluntarily became subject to the will of others. ¶ *Kings shall see and arise.* That is, kings shall see this, and shall rise up with demonstrations of respect and reverence. They shall see the fulfilment of the Divine promises by which he is destined to be the light of the nations, and they shall render him honour as their teacher and Redeemer. To rise up, or to prostrate themselves, are both marks of respect and veneration. ¶ *Princes also shall worship.* The word here used, (יִשְׁתַּחֲווּ, from שָׁחָה) means *to bow down,* to incline one's self; it then means to prostrate one's self before any one, in order to do him honour or reverence. This was the customary mode of showing respect or reverence in the East. It consisted generally in falling upon the knees, and then touching the forehead to the ground, and is often alluded to in the Bible (see Gen. xlii. 6; xviii. 2; xix. 1; Neh. viii. 6). This honour was paid not only to kings and princes as superior (2 Sam. ix. 8), but also to equals (Gen. xxiii. 7; xxxvii. 7, 9, 10). It was the customary form of religious homage, as it is still in the East, and denoted sometimes religious worship (Gen. xxii. 5; 1 Sam. i. 3); but not necessarily, or always (see Note on Matt. ii. 11; comp. Matt. viii. 2; xiv. 33; xv. 25; xviii. 26; Mark v. 6). Here it does not mean that they would render to him religious homage, but that they would show him honour, or respect. ¶ *Because of the* Lord *that is faithful.* It is because Jehovah is faithful in the fulfilment of his promises, and will certainly bring this to pass. The fact that he shall be thus honoured shall be traced entirely to the faithfulness of a covenant-keeping God. ¶ *And he shall choose thee.* Select thee to accomplish this, and to be thus a light to the heathen world. It is needless to say that this has been fulfilled. Kings and princes *have* bowed before the Redeemer; and the time will yet come when in far greater numbers they shall adore him. It is *as* needless to say, that these ex-

8 Thus saith the LORD, In an acceptable [a] time have I heard thee, and in a day of salvation have I helped thee: and I will preserve thee, and give thee for a covenant of the people, to [1] establish the earth, to cause to inherit the desolate heritages;

a Ps.69.13; 2 Co.6.2; Ep.1.6.

1 or, *raise up*.

pressions can be applied to no other one than the Messiah. It was not true of Isaiah that he was the light of the heathen, or for salvation to the ends of the earth; nor was it true of him that kings arose and honoured him, or that princes prostrated themselves before him, and did him reverence. Of the Messiah, the Lord Jesus alone, was all this true; and the assurance is thus given, that though he was rejected by his own nation, yet the time will come when the kings and princes of all the world shall do him homage.

8. *Thus saith the* LORD. Still an address to the Messiah, and designed to give the assurance that he should extend the true religion, and repair the evils of sin on the earth. The Messiah is represented as having asked for the Divine favour to attend his efforts, and this is the answer, and the assurance that his petition had not been offered in vain. ¶ *In an acceptable time.* Heb. 'In a time of *delight* or *will*,' *i.e.*, a time when JEHOVAH was *willing*, or pleased to hear him. The word רָצוֹן (*râtzōn*) means properly delight, satisfaction, acceptance (Prov. xiv. 35; Isa. lvi. 7); will, or pleasure (Esth. viii. 1; Ps. xl. 9; Dan. viii. 4-11); then also goodwill, favour, grace (Prov. xvi. 15; xix. 12). The LXX. render this, Καιρῷ δεκτῷ—'In an acceptable time.' So Jerome, Gesenius, and Hengstenberg render it, 'In a time of grace or mercy.' The main idea is plain, that JEHOVAH was well pleased to hear him when he called upon him, and would answer his prayers. In a time of favour; in a time that shall be adjudged to be the best fitted to the purposes of salvation, JEHOVAH will be pleased to exalt the Messiah to glory, and to make him the means of salvation to all mankind. ¶ *Have I heard thee.* Have I heard thy petitions, and the desires of thy heart. The giving of the world to the Messiah is represented as in answer to his prayer in Ps. ii. 8:

Ask of me, and I shall give thee the heathen for
thine inheritance,
And the uttermost parts of the earth for thy
possession.

¶ *And in a day of salvation.* In a time when I am disposed to grant salvation; when the period for imparting salvation shall have arrived. ¶ *Have I helped thee.* Have I imparted the assistance which is needful to accomplish the great purpose of salvation to the world. This passage is quoted by Paul in 2 Cor. vi. 2, and is by him applied to the times of the Messiah. It means that the time would come, fixed by the purpose of God, which would be a period in which he would be disposed, *i.e.*, well pleased, to extend salvation to the world through the Messiah; and that *in* that time he would afford all the requisite aid and help by his grace, for the extension of the true religion among the nations. ¶ *I will preserve thee.* That is, the cause of the Redeemer would be dear to the heart of God, and he would preserve that cause from being destroyed on the earth. ¶ *And give thee for a covenant of the people.* The 'people' (עָם) refers doubtless primarily to the Jews—the better portion of the Israelitish people—the true Israel (Rom. ii. 28, 29). To them he was first sent, and his own personal work was with them (see Notes on ver. 6). On the meaning of the phrase 'for a covenant,' see Notes on ch. xlii. 6. ¶ *To establish the earth.* Marg. as Heb. 'To raise up.' The language is derived from restoring the ruins of a land that has been overrun by an enemy, when the cities have been demolished, and the country laid waste. It is to be taken here in a spiritual sense, as meaning that the work of the Messiah would be *like that* which would be accomplished *if* a land lying waste should be restored to its former prosperity. In regard to the spiritual interests of the people, he would accomplish what would be accomplished if there should be such a restora-

9 That thou mayest say to the prisoners, [a] Go forth; to them that *are* in darkness, [b] Show yourselves: they shall feed in the ways, and their pastures *shall be* in all high places.

a Ze.9.12. b 1 Pe.2.9.

tion; that is, he would recover the true Israel from the ravages of sin, and would establish the church on a firm foundation. ¶ *To cause to inherit the desolate heritages.* The image here is taken from the condition of the land of Israel during the Babylonish captivity. It was in ruins. The cities were all desolate. Such, spiritually, would be the condition of the nation when the Messiah should come; and his work would be like restoring the exiles to their own land, and causing them to re-enter on their former possessions. The one would be an appropriate emblem of the other; and the work of the Messiah would be like rebuilding dilapidated towns; restoring fertility to desolate fields; replanting vineyards and olive gardens; and diffusing smiling peace and plenty over a land that had been subjected to the ravages of fire and sword, and that had long been a scene of mournful desolation.

9. *That thou mayest say to the prisoners, Go forth.* This language occurs also in ch. xlii. 7. For an explanation of it, see the Notes on that place. ¶ *To them that* are *in darkness.* Synonymous with being prisoners, as prisoners are usually confined in dark cells. ¶ *Show yourselves.* Heb. 'Reveal,' or manifest yourselves; that is, as those who come out of a dark cell come into light, so do you, who have been confined in the darkness of sin, come forth into the light of the Sun of righteousness, and be manifest as the redeemed. ¶ *They shall feed in the ways.* In the remainder of this verse, and in the following verses, the Messiah is represented under the image of a shepherd, who leads forth his flock to green fields, and who takes care that they shall be guarded from the heat of the sun, and shall not hunger nor thirst. The phrase 'they shall feed in the ways,' means, probably, that in the way in which they were going they should find abundant food. They should not be compelled to turn aside for pasturage, or to go and seek for it in distant places. It is equivalent to the language which so often occurs, that God would provide for the wants of his people, even when passing through a desert, and that he would open before them unexpected sources of supply. ¶ *And their pastures* shall be *in all high places.* This means, that on the hills and mountains, that are naturally barren and unproductive, they should find an abundance of food. To see the force of this, we are to remember that in many parts of the East the hills and mountains are utterly destitute of vegetation. This is the case with the mountainous regions of Horeb and Sinai, and even with the mountains about Jerusalem, and with the hills and mountains in Arabia Deserta. The idea here is, that in *the ways,* or paths that were commonly travelled, and where all verdure would be consumed or trodden down by the caravans, and on the hills that were usually barren and desolate, they would find abundance. God would supply them *as if* he should make the green grass spring up in the hard-trodden way, and on the barren and rocky hills vegetation should start up suddenly in abundance, and all their wants should be supplied. This is an image which we have frequently had in Isaiah, and perhaps the meaning may be, that to his people the Redeemer would open unexpected sources of comfort and joy; that in places and times in which they would scarcely look for a supply of their spiritual wants, he would suddenly meet and satisfy them *as if* green grass for flocks and herds should suddenly start up in the down-trodden way, or luxuriant vegetation burst forth on the sides and the tops of barren, rocky, and desolate hills. Harmer, however, supposes that this whole description refers rather to the custom which prevailed in the East, of making feasts or entertainments by the sides of fountains or rivers. 'To fountains or rivers,' Dr. Chandler tells us in his *Travels,* 'the Turks and the Greeks frequently repair for refreshment; especially the latter, in their fes-

10 They shall not hunger [a] nor thirst; neither shall the heat nor sun smite them; for he that hath mercy on them shall lead [b] them, even by the springs of water shall he guide them.

11 And [c] I will make all my mountains a way, and my highways shall be exalted.

a Re.7.16. b Ps.23.2. c Ps.107.4,7.

tivals, when whole families are seen sitting on the grass, and enjoying their early or evening repast, beneath the trees, by the side of a rill.'—(*Travels in Asia Minor*, p. 21.) Comp. 1 Kings i. 9. Thus Harmer supposes that the purpose of the prophet is, to contrast the state of the Jews when they were shut up in prison in Babylon, secluded from fresh air, and even the light itself, or in unwholesome dungeons, with their state when walking at liberty, enjoying the verdure, and the enlivening air of the country; passing from the tears, the groans, and the apprehensions of such a dismal confinement, to the music, the songs, and the exquisite repasts of Eastern parties of pleasure (*see* Harmer's *Obs.*, vol. ii. pp. 18–25; Ed. Lond. 1808). The interpretation, however, above suggested, seems to me most natural and beautiful.

10. *They shall not hunger nor thirst.* All their wants shall be abundantly provided for, as a shepherd will provide for his flock. In the book of Revelation, this entire passage is applied (ch. vii. 16, 17) to the happiness of the redeemed in heaven, and the use which is made of it there is not foreign to the sense in Isaiah. It means that the Messiah as a shepherd shall abundantly satisfy all the wants of his people; and it may with as much propriety be applied to the joys of heaven, as to the happiness which they will experience on earth. Their longing desires for holiness and salvation; their hungering and thirsting after righteousness (Matt. v. 6), shall be abundantly satisfied. ¶ *Neither shall the heat nor sun smite them.* In Rev. vii. 16, this is, 'Neither shall the sun light on them, nor any heat;' that is, the burning heat of the sun shall not oppress them—an image of refreshment, protection, and joy, as when the traveller in burning sands finds the grateful shade of a rock or of a grove (see Notes on ch. iv. 6; xiv. 3; xxv. 4; xxxii. 2). The word here rendered 'heat' (שָׁרָב *shârâbh*), denotes properly *heat, burning;* and then the heated vapour which in burning deserts produces the phenomenon of the *mirage* (see it explained in the Notes on ch. xxxv. 7). It is equivalent here to intense heat; and means that they shall not be exposed to any suffering like that of the intense heat of the burning sun reflected from sandy wastes. ¶ *For he that hath mercy on them.* That God and Saviour who shall have redeemed them shall be their shepherd and their guide, and they shall have nothing to fear. ¶ *Even by the springs of water.* In Rev. vii. 17, 'Shall lead them unto living fountains of waters' (see Notes on ch. xxxv. 6). The whole figure in this verse is taken from the character of a faithful shepherd who conducts his flock to places where they may feed in plenty; who guards them from the intense heat of a burning sun on sandy plains; and who leads them beside cooling and refreshing streams. It is a most beautiful image of the tender care of the Great Shepherd of his people in a world like this—a world in its main features, in regard to real comforts, not unaptly compared to barren hills, and pathless burning sands.

11. *And I will make all my mountains a way.* I will make all the mountains for a highway; or an even, level way. That is, he would remove all obstructions from their path. The image is taken from the return from Babylon to the land of Palestine, in which God so often promises to make the hills a plain, and the crooked places straight (see Notes on ch. xl. 4). ¶ *And my highways shall be exalted.* That is, the way shall be cast up (see ch. lvii. 14; lxii. 10), as when a road is made over valleys and gulf (see Notes on ch. xl. 4).

12. *Behold, these shall come from far.* That is, one part shall come from a distant land, and another from the north and the west. This is a state-

12 Behold, these shall come from far; and lo, these from the north and from the west; and these from the land of Sinim.

ment of the fulfilment of the promise made to him (ver. 6, 7), that he should be for a light to the Gentiles, and that kings and princes should rise up and honour him. The words 'from far,' denote a distant land, without specifying the particular direction from which they would come. The most distant nations should embrace his religion, and submit to him. Lowth and Secker understand it of Babylon; Grotius of the East, that is, Persia, and the other countries east of Judea. But it more properly denotes *any* distant country; and the sense is, that converts should be made from the most distant lands. ¶ *And lo, these.* Another portion. ¶ *From the north.* The regions north of Palestine. ¶ *And from the west.* Heb. 'From the sea;' that is, the Mediterranean. This word is commonly used to denote the west. The western countries known to the Hebrews were some of the islands of that sea, and a few of the maritime regions. The idea here in general is, that those regions would furnish many who would embrace the true religion. If it be understood as referring to the Messiah, and the accession to his kingdom among the Gentiles, it is needless to say that the prediction has been already strikingly fulfilled. Christianity soon spread to the west of Palestine, and the countries in Europe have been thus far the principal seat of its influence and power. It has since spread still further to the west; and, from a western world unknown to Isaiah, millions have come and acknowledged the Messiah as their Redeemer. ¶ *And these.* Another portion, carrying out the idea that they were to come from every part of the world. ¶ *From the land of Sinim.* There have been many different opinions in regard to the 'land of Sinim.' The name 'Sinim' (סִינִים) occurs nowhere else in the Bible, and of course it is not easy to determine what country is meant. It is evident that it is some *remote* country, and it is remarkable that it is the only land specified here by name. Some, it is said, should come from far, some from the north, others from the west, and another portion from the country here specifically mentioned. Jerome understands it of the south in general—*Isti de terra Australi.* The LXX. understand it as denoting Persia—Ἄλλοι δὲ ἐκ γῆς Περσῶν. The Chaldee also interprets it as Jerome has done, of the south. The Syriac has not translated it, but retained the name *Sinim.* The Arabic coincides with the Septuagint, and renders it, 'From the land of Persia.' Grotius supposes that it means the region of Sinim to the south of Palestine, and Vitringa also coincides with this opinion. Bochart supposes that it means the same as Sin or Syene, *i.e.*, Pelusium, a city of Egypt; and that it is used to denote Egypt, as Pelusium was a principal city in Egypt. In Ezek. xxx. 15, *Sin* or Pelusium (marg.) is mentioned as 'the strength of Egypt.' Gesenius supposes that it refers to the *Chinese*, and that the country here referred to is Sina or China. 'This very ancient and celebrated people,' says he, 'was known to the Arabians and Syrians by the name Sin, Tcin, Tshini; and a Hebrew writer might well have heard of them, especially if sojourning in Babylon, the metropolis as it were of all Asia. This name appears to have been given to the Chinese by the other Asiatics; for the Chinese themselves do not employ it, and seem indeed to be destitute of any ancient domestic name, either adopting the names of the reigning dynasties, or ostentatiously assuming high-sounding titles, as "people of the empire in the centre of the world."' The Rev. Peter Parker, M.D., missionary to China, remarked in an address delivered in Philadelphia, that 'the Chinese have been known from time immemorial by the name *Tschin.* Tschin means a Chinaman.' When they first received this appellation, cannot be determined, nor is the reason of its being given to them now known. As there is remarkable permanency in the *names* as well as in the *customs* of the East, it is possible that they may have had it from the commencement of their history. If so, there is no improbability in supposing that the name was known

13 Sing, O heavens; and be joyful, O earth; and break forth into singing, O mountains; for the LORD hath comforted his people, and will have mercy upon his afflicted.

14 But Zion said, [a] The LORD hath forsaken me, and my Lord hath forgotten me.

15 Can a woman forget her sucking child, [1] that she should not have compassion on the son of her womb? yea, they may forget, yet [b] will I not forget thee.

a Ps.77.9,10.

1 *from having compassion.* b ch.44.21; Mat.7.11.

to the Jews in the time of Isaiah. Solomon had opened a considerable commerce with the East. For this he had built Palmyra, or Tadmor, and caravans passed constantly towards Palestine and Tyre, conveying the rich productions of India. The country of *Tschin* or *Sinim* may be easily supposed to have been often referred to by the foreign merchants as a land of great extent and riches, and it is not impossible that even at that early day a part of the merchandise conveyed to the west might have come from that land. It is not necessary to suppose that the Hebrews in the time of Isaiah had any very extensive or clear views of that country; but all that is necessary to be supposed is, that they conceived of the nation as lying far in the east, and as abounding in wealth, sufficiently so to entitle it to the pre-eminency which it now has in the enumeration of the nations that would be blessed by the gospel. If this be the correct interpretation—and I have on a re-examination come to this opinion, though a different view was given in the first edition of these Notes—then the passage furnishes an interesting prediction respecting the future conversion of the largest kingdom of the world. It may be added, that this is the only place where that country is referred to in the Bible, and there may be some plausibility in the supposition that while so many other nations, far inferior in numbers and importance, are mentioned by name, one so vast as this would not wholly be omitted by the Spirit of Inspiration.

13. *Sing, O heavens.* In view of the glorious truths stated in the previous verses, that kings should rise up, and princes worship; that the Messiah would be for a light to the Gentiles, and that the true religion would be extended to each of the four quarters of the globe. The idea in this verse is, that it was an occasion on which the heavens and the earth would have cause to exult together. It is common in Isaiah thus to interpose a song of praise on the announcement of any great and glorious truth, and to call on the heavens and the earth to rejoice together (see Notes on ch. xii.; xlii. 10, 11; xliv. 23).

14. *But Zion said.* On the word 'Zion,' see Note on ch. i. 8. The language here is that of complaint, and expresses the deep feeling of the people of God amidst many calamities, afflictions, and trials. It may be applicable to the exile Jews in Babylon during their long captivity, as if God had forsaken them; or to those who were waiting for the coming of the Messiah, and who were sighing for the Divine interposition under him to restore the beauty of Zion, and to extend his kingdom; or in general, to the church when wickedness triumphs in a community, and when God seems to have forsaken Zion, and to have forgotten its interests. The *language* here was suggested, doubtless, by a view of the desolations of Jerusalem and Judea, and of the long and painful captivity in Babylon; but it is general, and is applicable to the people of God, in all times of similar oppression and distress. The *object* of the prophet is to furnish the assurance that, whatever might be the trials and the sufferings of his people, God had not forgotten them, and he neither could nor would forsake them. For this purpose, he makes use of two most striking and forcible arguments (ver. 15, 16), to show in the strongest possible manner that the interests of his people were safe.

15. *Can a woman forget her sucking child?* The design of this verse is apparent. It is to show that the love which God has for his people is stronger than that which is produced by the most tender ties created by any natural relation. The love of a mother for her in-

16 Behold, I have graven [a] thee upon the palms of *my* hands; thy walls *are* continually before me.

[a] Ca.8.6.

17 Thy children shall make haste; thy destroyers [b] and they that made thee waste, shall go forth of thee.

[b] Eze.28.24; Mat.13.41,42; Re 22.15.

fant child is the strongest attachment in nature. The question here implies that it was unusual for a mother to be unmindful of that tie, and to forsake the child that she should nourish and love. ¶ *That she should not have compassion.* That she should not pity and succour it in times of sickness and distress; that she should see it suffer without any attempt to relieve it, and turn away, and see it die unpitied and unalleviated. ¶ *Yea, they may forget.* They will sooner forget their child than God will forget his afflicted and suffering people. The phrase 'they may forget,' implies that such a thing may occur. In heathen lands, strong as is the instinct which binds a mother to her offspring, it has not been uncommon for a mother to expose her infant child, and to leave it to die. In illustration of this fact, see Notes on Rom. i. 31.

16. *Behold, I have graven thee upon the palms of* my *hands.* This is another argument in answer to the complaint of Zion in ver. 14. There have been various interpretations of this passage. Grotius supposes that it refers to a custom of placing some mark or sign on the hand, or on one of the fingers when they wished to remember anything, and appeals to Ex. xiii. 9. Lowth supposes that it is an allusion to some practice common among the Jews at that time, of making marks on their hands or arms by means of punctures in the skin with some sign or representation of the city or temple, to show their zeal and affection for it. In illustration of this, he refers to the fact that the pilgrims to the Holy Sepulchre are accustomed to get themselves marked in this manner with what are called the signs of Jerusalem. Vitringa supposes that it alludes to the custom of architects, in which they delineate the size, form, and proportions of an edifice on parchment, before they commence building it—such as we mean by the draft or model of the building; and that the sense here is, that God, in like manner, had delineated or drawn Jerusalem on his hands long before it was founded, and had it constantly before his eyes. According to this, the idea is, that God had *laid out* the plan of Jerusalem long before it was built, and that it was so dear to him that he had even engraven it on his hands. Others have supposed that it refers to a device on a signet, or on a ring worn on the finger or the wrist, and that the plan of Jerusalem was drawn and engraven there. To me, it seems that the view of Lowth is most accordant with probability, and is best sustained by the Oriental customs. The *essential idea* is, that Zion was dear to his heart; and that he had sketched or delineated it as an object in which he felt a deep interest—so deep as even to delineate its outlines on the palms of his hands, where it would be constantly before him. ¶ *Thy walls.* The meaning is, that he constantly looked upon them; that he never forgot them. He had a constant and sacred regard for his people, and amidst all their disasters and trials, still remembered them.

17. *Thy children.* The children of Zion—the true people of God. But there is here considerable variety in the interpretation. The Hebrew of the present text is בָּנַיִךְ (*thy sons*). But Jerome reads it, *Structores tui*—'Thy builders;' as if it were בונין. The LXX. render it, 'Thou shalt be speedily built (ταχὺ οἰκοδομηθήσῃ) by those by whom thou hast been destroyed.' The Chaldee renders it, 'Those that rebuild thy waste places shall hasten.' The Syriac reads it, 'Thy sons;' and the Arabic, 'Thou shalt be rebuilt by those by whom thou hast been destroyed.' But there is no good authority for changing the present Hebrew text, nor is it necessary. The sense probably is, the descendants of those who dwelt in Zion, who are now in exile, shall hasten to rebuild the wastes of the desolate capital, and restore its ruins. And may it not mean, that in the great work under the Messiah, of restoring the nation to the wor-

18 Lift up thine eyes round about,
and behold: all these [a] gather themselves together, *and* come to thee.
As I live, saith the LORD, thou shalt
surely clothe thee with them all as
with an ornament, and bind them *on
thee* as a bride *doth*.
19 For thy waste, and thy desolate places, and the land of thy
destruction, shall even now be too
narrow by reason of the inhabitants,
and they that swallowed thee up
shall be far away.
20 The children which thou shalt
have, after [b] thou hast lost the other,
shall say again in thy ears, The
place *is* too strait for me: give
place for me that I may dwell.

a ch.60.8; Zec.2.4; 10.10.

b Ro.11.11,&c.

---

ship of God, and of spreading the true religion, God would make use of those who dwelt in Zion; that is, of the Jews, as his ambassadors? ¶ *They that made thee waste.* Language drawn from the destruction of Jerusalen. The sense is, that they would seek no longer to retain possession, but would permit its former inhabitants to return, and engage in repairing its ruins.

18. *Lift up thine eyes round about.* That is, see the multitudes that shall be converted to thee; see thy ruined city rise again in its former beauty; see the Gentiles come and yield themselves to the worship of the true God; see kings and princes approach and do thee homage. ¶ *All these gather themselves.* That is, from a far country, from the north, the west, and the south, ver. 12. ¶ As *I live, saith the* LORD. The customary form of an oath when JEHOVAH swears. It is a solemn assurance that the event shall as certainly occur as he has an existence (see Note on ch. xlv. 23; comp. Jer. xxii. 24; Ezek. v. 11; xiv. 16, 18, 20; xvi. 48). ¶ *Thou shalt surely clothe thee with them.* Zion is here represented, as it is often elsewhere, as a female (see Note on ch. i. 8); and the accession of converts from abroad is represented under the figure of bridal ornaments. The accession of converts from the Gentiles should be to her what jewels are to a bride. ¶ *And bind them* on thee *as a bride* doth. The sentence here is manifestly incomplete. It means, as a bride binds on her ornaments. The LXX. have supplied this, and render it, 'As a bride her ornaments' (ὡς κόσμον νύμφη). The sentiment is, that the accession of the large number of converts under the Messiah to the true church of God, would be the real ornament of Zion, and would greatly increase her beauty and loveliness.

19. *For thy waste and thy desolate places.* Thy land over which ruin has been spread, and over which the exile nation mourns. ¶ *And the land of thy destruction.* That is, thy land laid in ruins. The construction is not uncommon where a noun is used to express the sense of an adjective. Thus in Ps. ii. 6, the Hebrew phrase (*marg.*) is correctly rendered 'my holy hill.' Here the sense is, that their entire country had been so laid waste as to be a land of desolation. ¶ *Shall even now be too narrow.* Shall be too limited to contain all who shall become converted to the true God. The contracted territory of Palestine shall be incapable of sustaining all who will acknowledge the true God, and who shall be regarded as his friends. ¶ *And they that swallowed thee up.* The enemies that laid waste thy land, and that *absorbed*, as it were, thy inhabitants, and removed them to a distant land. They shall be all gone, and the land shall smile again in prosperity and in loveliness.

20. *The children which thou shalt have.* The increase of the population shall be so great. ¶ *After thou hast lost the other.* Heb. 'The sons of thy widowhood.' That is, after thou hast lost those that have been killed in the wars, and those that have died in captivity in a distant land, there shall be again a great increase *as if* they were given to a widowed mother. And perhaps the *general* truth is taught here, that the persecution of the people of God will be attended ultimately with a vast increase; and that all the attempts to obliterate the church will only tend finally to enlarge and strengthen it.

21 Then shalt thou say in thine heart, Who hath begotten me these, seeing I have lost my children, and am desolate, a captive, and moving to and fro? and who hath brought up these? Behold, I was left alone; these, where *had* they *been?*

22 Thus saith [a] the Lord God Behold, I will lift up mine hand to the Gentiles, and set up my standard to the people: and they shall bring thy sons in *their* [1] arms, and thy daughters shall be carried upon *their* shoulders.

a ch.66.20.

1 *bosom.*

¶ *Shall say again in thy ears.* Or, shall say to thee. ¶ *The place* is *too strait for me.* There is not room for us all. The entire language here denotes a vast accession to the church of God. It is indicative of such an increase as took place when the gospel was proclaimed by the apostles to the Gentiles, and of such an increase as shall yet more abundantly take place when the whole world shall become converted to God.

21. *Then shalt thou say in thine heart.* Thou shalt wonder at the multitude, and shalt ask with astonishment whence they all come. This verse is designed to describe the great increase of the true people of God under the image of a mother who had been deprived of her children, who should suddenly see herself surrounded with more than had been lost, and should ask in astonishment whence they all came. ¶ *Who hath begotten me these.* The idea here is, that the increase would be from other nations. They would not be the natural increase of Zion or Jerusalem, but they would come in from abroad—as if a family that had been bereaved should be increased by an accession from other families. ¶ *I have lost my children.* Jerusalem had been desolated by wars, and had become like a widow that was bereft of all her sons (comp. Notes on ch. xlvii. 8, 9). ¶ *A captive, and removing to and fro.* A captive in Babylon, and compelled to wander from my own land, and to live in a strange and distant country. ¶ *These, where* had *they* been? The image in this entire verse is one of great beauty. It represents a mother who had been suddenly deprived of all her children, who had been made a widow, and conveyed as a captive from land to land. She had seen ruin spread all around her dwelling, and regarded herself as alone. Suddenly she finds herself restored to her home, and surrounded with a happy family. She sees it increased beyond its former numbers, and herself blessed with more than her former prosperity. She looks with surprise on this accession, and asks with wonder whence all these have come, and where they have been. The *language* in this verse is beautifully expressive of the agitation of such a state of mind, and of the effect which would be thus produced. The idea is plain. Jerusalem had been desolate. Her inhabitants had been carried captive, or had been put to death. But she should be restored, and the church of God would be increased by a vast accession from the Gentile world, so much that the narrow limits which had been formerly occupied—the territory of Palestine—would now be too small for the vast numbers that would be united to those who professed to love and worship God.

22. *Behold, I will lift up mine hand to the Gentiles.* To lift up the hand is a sign of beckoning to, or inviting; and the idea here is, that God would call the Gentiles to partake of the blessings of the true religion, and to embrace the Messiah (see Notes on ch. xi. 11). ¶ *And set up my standard to the people.* To the people of other lands; the word here being synonymous with the word Gentiles. A standard, or an ensign was erected in times of war to rally the forces of a nation around it; and the sense here is, that God would erect an ensign high in the sight of all the nations, and would call them to himself, as a military leader musters his forces for battle; that is, he would call the nations to embrace the true religion. See this phrase explained in the Note on ch. xi. 12. ¶ *They shall bring thy sons in* their *arms.* Marg. 'Bosom.' Jerome renders it, *In ulnis*—'In their

23 And kings shall be thy [1] nursing fathers, and their [2] queens thy nursing mothers: they shall bow down to thee with *their* face toward the earth, and lick [a] up the dust of thy feet; and thou shalt know that I am the LORD: for they shall not be ashamed [b] that wait for thee.

1 *nourishers.* 2 *princesses.*

a Ps.72.9,&c. b Ro 9.33.

---

arms.' The LXX. Ἐν κόλπῳ—'In the bosom.' Aquila, Symmachus, and Theodotion, Ἀγκάλαις—'In their arms.' If it means bosom, as Gesenius renders it, it refers to the bosom of a garment in which things are carried. But it more probably means in the arms, as children are borne; and the idea is, that the distant nations would come and bear with them those who were the children of Zion, that is, those who would become the true friends and worshippers of God. ¶ *And thy daughters shall be carried upon* their *shoulders.* Referring, doubtless, to the manner in which children were carried. In ch. lxvi. 12, the same idea is expressed by their being carried upon the sides, referring to the custom still prevalent in the East, of placing a child when it is nursed astride on the side of the mother. The following quotation will more fully explain the customs here alluded to. 'It is a custom in many parts of the East, to carry their children astride upon the hip, with the arm around the body. In the kingdom of Algiers, where the slaves take the children out, the boys ride upon their shoulders; and in a religious procession, which Symes had an opportunity of seeing at Ava, the capital of the Burman empire, the first personages of rank that passed by were three children borne astride, on men's shoulders. It is evident, from these facts, that the Oriental children are carried sometimes the one way, sometimes the other. Nor was the custom, in reality, different in Judea, though the prophet expresses himself in these terms: "They shall bring thy sons in their arms, and thy daughters shall be carried upon their shoulders;" for, according to Dr. Russel, the children able to support themselves are usually carried astride on the shoulders; but in infancy they are carried in the arms, or awkwardly on one haunch. Dandini tells us that, on horseback, the Asiatics "carry their children upon their shoulders with great dexterity. These children hold by the head of him who carries them, whether he be on horseback or on foot, and do not hinder him from walking or doing what he pleases." This augments the import of the passage in Isaiah, who speaks of the Gentiles bringing children thus; so that distance is no objection to this mode of conveyance, since they may thus be brought on horseback from among the people, however remote.'—(Paxton.) 'Children of both sexes are carried on the shoulders. Thus may be seen the father carrying his son, the little fellow being astride on the shoulder, having, with his hands, hold of his father's head. Girls, however, sit on the shoulder, as if on a chair, their legs hanging in front, while they also, with their hands, lay hold of the head. In going to, or returning from heathen festivals, thousands of parents and their children may be thus seen marching along with joy.'—(Roberts.) The sense is, that converts should come from every land—that the nations should flock to the standard of the Messiah. And why may it not be regarded as a legitimate interpretation of this passage, that those who come should bring their children, their sons and their daughters, with them? That they were borne upon the arm, or upon the shoulder, is indicative of their being young children; and that is no forced interpretation of this passage which regards it as teaching, that the parents who should be converted among the Gentiles should bring their offspring to the Redeemer, and present them publicly to God.

23. *And kings shall be thy nursing fathers.* Marg. 'Nourishers.' That is, they would patronize the church of God; they would protect it by their laws, and foster it by their influence, and become the personal advocates of the cause of Zion. The idea is properly that of guarding, educating, and providing for children; and the sense is, that kings and princes would evince the same tender care for the interests of the people of God which a parent or a nurse

24 Shall the prey be taken from the mighty, [a] or [1] the lawful captive delivered?

25 But thus saith the LORD, Even the [2] captives of the mighty shall be taken away, and the prey of the terrible shall be delivered: for I will contend with him that contendeth with thee, and I will save thy children.

a Mat.12.29. 1 *the captivity of the just.* 2 *captivity.*

does for a child. It is needless to say that this has been already to a considerable extent fulfilled, and that many princes and monarchs have been the patrons of the church, though doubtless it is destined to a more ample fulfilment still in the brighter days of this world's history, when the gospel shall spread everywhere. It is remarkable that, in the Sandwich and South Sea Islands, the Christian religion has been uniformly, almost, taken under the protection of the kings and chiefs since its first introduction there, and has been carried forward and extended under their direct authority. ¶ *They shall bow down to thee with* their *face toward the earth.* A posture indicating the profoundest reverence. This is the common posture of showing great respect in the East. ¶ *And lick up the dust of thy feet.* An act denoting the utmost possible respect and veneration for the church and people of God. ¶ *For they shall not be ashamed that wait for me.* They who worship me shall not be ashamed of the act requiring the deepest self-abasement, to show their reverence for me. Even those of most elevated rank shall be willing to humble themselves with the profoundest expressions of adoration.

24. *Shall the prey be taken from the mighty?* This seems to be the language of Zion. It is not exactly the language of incredulity; it is the language of amazement and wonder God had made great promises. He had promised a restoration of the captive Jews to their own land, and of their complete deliverance from the power of the Chaldeans. He had still further promised that the blessings of the true religion should be extended to the Gentiles, and that kings and queens should come and show the profoundest adoration for God and for his cause. With amazement and wonder at the greatness of these promises, with a full view of the difficulties to be surmounted, Zion asks here how it can be accomplished. It would involve the work of taking the prey from a mighty conqueror, and delivering the captive from the hand of the strong and the terrible—a work which had not been usually done. ¶ *Or the lawful captive delivered?* Marg. 'The captivity of the just.' Lowth reads this, 'Shall the prey seized by the terrible be rescued?' So Noyes. Lowth says of the present Hebrew text, that the reading is a 'palpable mistake;' and that instead of צַדִּיק (*the just*), the meaning should be עָרִיץ (*the terrible*). Jerome so read it, and renders it, *A robusto*—'The prey taken by the strong.' So the Syriac reads it. The LXX. render it, 'If any one is taken captive unjustly (ἀδίκως), shall he be saved?' But there is no authority from the MSS. for changing the present reading of the Hebrew text; and it is not necessary. The word 'just,' here may either refer to the fact that the just were taken captive, and to the difficulty of rescuing them; or perhaps, as Rosenmüller suggests, it may be taken in the sense of *severe*, or *rigid*, standing opposed to benignity or mercy, and thus may be synonymous with severity and harshness; and the meaning may be that it was difficult to rescue a captive from the hands of those who had no clemency or benignity, such as was Babylon. Grotius understands it of those who were taken captive in a just war, or by the rights of war. But the connection rather demands that we should interpret it of those who were made captive by those who were indisposed to clemency, and who were severe and rigid in their treatment of their prisoners. The idea is, that it was difficult or almost impossible to rescue captives from such hands, and that therefore it was a matter of wonder and amazement that that *could* be accomplished which God here promises.

25. *But thus saith the* LORD. The

26 And I will feed them that oppress thee with their own flesh; and
they shall be drunken with [a] their
own blood, as with [2] sweet wine:
and all flesh shall know that I the
LORD *am* thy Saviour and thy Redeemer, the Mighty One of Jacob.

a Re.16.6. 2 or, *new*.

meaning of this verse is, that however difficult or impracticable this might seem to be, yet it should be done. The captives taken by the terrible and the mighty should be rescued, and should be restored to their own land. ¶ *Even the captives of the mighty shall be taken away.* Marg. as Heb. 'The captivity of the mighty.' That which could not have been rescued by any ordinary means. The language here refers undoubtedly to Babylon, and to the captivity of the Jews there. ¶ *The prey of the terrible.* Of a nation formidable, cruel, and not inclined to compassion; in the previous verse described as 'just,' *i.e.*, indisposed to mercy. ¶ *For I will contend with him.* I will punish the nation that has inflicted these wrongs on thee, and will thus rescue thee from bondage.

26. *And I will feed them that oppress thee with their own flesh.* The language here used is that which appropriately describes the distresses resulting from discord and internal strifes. Similar language occurs in ch. ix. 20 (see Note on that verse). Their rage shall be excited against each other; and there shall be anarchy, internal discord, and the desire of mutual revenge. They shall destroy themselves by mutual conflicts, until they are gorged with slaughter, and drunk with blood. ¶ *And they shall be drunken with their own blood.* A similar expression occurs in Rev. xvi. 6: 'For they have shed the blood of the prophets, and thou hast given them blood to drink.' This expression describes a state of internal strife, where blood would be profusely shed, and where it would be, as it were, the drink of those who were contending with each other. Grotius supposes that it refers to the conflicts between the Persians and the Medes, and those of the Medes and Persians with the Babylonians. Vitringa supposes it received its fulfilment in the contests which took place in the Roman empire, particularly during the reign of Diocletian, when so many rivals contended for the sovereignty. Perhaps, however, it is in vain to attempt to refer this to any single conflict, or state of anarchy. The language is general; and it may mean in general that God would guard and protect his people; and that in doing this, he would fill the ranks of his foes with confusion, and suffer them to be torn and distracted with internal strifes; and amidst those strifes, and by means of them, would secure the deliverance and safety of his own people. It has not unfrequently happened that he has suffered or caused discord to spring up among the enemies of his people, and distracted their counsels, and thus secured the safety and welfare of those whom they were opposing and persecuting. ¶ *As with sweet wine.* Marg. 'New.' The Hebrew word (עָסִיס) means *must*, or new wine (Joel i. 5; iv. 18; Amos ix. 13). The LXX. render it, Οἶνον νέον—'New wine.' The *must*, or new wine, was the pure juice which ran first after the grapes had been laid in a heap preparatory to pressure. The ancients had the art of preserving this for a long time, so as to retain its peculiar flavour, and were in the habit of drinking it in the morning (see Hor. *Sat.* ii. 4). This had the intoxicating property very slightly, if at all; and Harmer (*Obs.* vol. ii. p. 151) supposes that the kind here meant was rather such as was used in 'royal palaces for its gratefulness,' which was capable of being kept to a great age. It is possible, I think, that there may be an allusion here to the fact that it required a *large quantity of the must* or new wine to produce intoxication, and that the idea here is that a large quantity of blood would be shed. ¶ *And all flesh.* The effect of all this shall be to diffuse the true religion throughout the world. The result of the contentions that shall be excited among the enemies of the people of God; of their civil wars and mutual slaughter; and of the consequent protection and defence of the

CHAPTER L.

ANALYSIS.

This chapter properly consists of two parts. The first comprises the first three verses, and contains a statement of the reasons why the Jews had been rejected and punished. They are to be regarded as in exile in Babylon. It might be alleged by some of the unbelieving among them, that the calamities which came upon them were proof of caprice in God, or of want of faithfulness, or of power, and not any proof that they were suffering under his righteous displeasure. To meet these implied charges, and to show them the true cause of their suffering, is the design of this portion of the chapter. In this, God says—1. That their sufferings were not the result of mere will, or of caprice, on his part, as a husband often puts away his wife without any good reason (1). 2. There was a reason for their rejection, and that reason was, their sins. They had brought all these calamities upon themselves, and had, in fact, sold themselves. 3. It was not for want of power on the part of God to save them. His hand was not shortened, and he had abundantly shown that he had power to defend his people (2, 3). He was able to dry up the sea, and to make the rivers a desert, and he clothed the heavens with blackness, and he was abundantly able, therefore, to save his people.

II. The second part of the chapter comprises the portion from ver. 4–11. This relates to a different subject; and, in regard to it, there has been considerable variety of interpretation. A speaker is introduced who claims to be eminently qualified for the office to which he was called (4); who has been amply endowed by God for the embassage on which he is sent (5); who meets with opposition, and who yet receives it all with meekness (6); who puts his trust in God, and confides in him alone (7–9); and who calls on all who fear the Lord to hear him (10); and who threatens to inflict punishment on all who do not listen to him (11). This portion of the chapter has been referred, by different interpreters, to different individuals. Grotius, Rosenmüller, and Gesenius, suppose that it refers to the prophet himself. Döderlein, Dathe, Koppe, Augusti, and some others, suppose that it refers either to the prophet himself, or to some other one living in exile at the time of the captivity. Jerome says that this, also, was the prevailing interpretation among the Jews in his time. Paulus supposes that it is not the prophet who speaks, but the better and more pious portion of the Jewish people. But the more common interpretation is that which refers it to the Messiah. In favour of this interpretation, the following considerations may be suggested:—1. The prophet himself is not known to have been in the circumstances here described (6); nor is there any evidence that this can be applied to him. Of any other prophet to whom it would apply we have no knowledge, nor would there be any propriety in so applying the language of Isaiah, if we did know of any such one. 2. The Messianic interpretation has almost universally prevailed in the Christian church—an argument of value only as showing that when so many agree in interpreting any writing, there is presumptive proof that they have not mistaken its meaning. 3. All the characteristics of the servant of God here referred to, apply to the Redeemer, and are descriptive of him and of his work. All that is said of his humiliation and meekness; of the opposition which he encountered, and of his confidence in God, applies eminently to the Lord Jesus, and to no other one. 4. The closing part (ver. 11), where the speaker threatens to

---

people whom they were endeavouring to destroy, shall be to diffuse the true religion among the nations, and to bring all men to acknowledge that he who thus protects his church is the true and only God. It would be easy to show the fulfilment of this prediction from the records of the past, and from the efforts which have been made to destroy the church of God. But that would be foreign to the design of these notes. A very slight acquaintance with the repeated efforts to destroy the ancient people of God in Egypt, in the wilderness, in Babylon, and under Antiochus Epiphanes; with the early persecution of the Christians in Judea; with the successive persecutions in the Roman empire from the time of Nero to Diocletian; with the persecution of the Waldenses in Switzerland; of the Huguenots in France; and of the Reformers in England, will be sufficient to convince any one that God is the protector of the church, and that no weapons formed against her shall prosper. Her enemies shall be distracted in their counsels, and left to anarchy and overthrow; and the church shall rise resplendent from all their persecutions, and shall prosper ultimately just in proportion to their efforts to destroy it.

inflict punishment on his foes, cannot be used with reference to Isaiah or any other prophet, but has a striking applicability to the Messiah. 6. In Luke xviii. 32, the passage (ver. 6) is applied by the Lord Jesus to himself. He says that the prophecies in regard to him must be fulfilled, and, among other things, says that the fact that he should be 'spitted on,' should be a fulfilment of a prophecy—a statement which has an obvious and manifest reference to this passage in Isaiah.

The passage, if it refers to the Messiah, relates particularly to his humiliation and sufferings, and accords with that in ch. liii. It embraces the following points:—1. He was endowed for his work, and especially fitted to comfort the afflicted and weary (4). 2. He was entirely obedient to God, and submitted to all his arrangements with cheerfulness (5). 3. He submitted with meekness to all the injuries inflicted on him by others—even to their deepest expressions of contempt (6). 4. He was sustained in these trials because he put his trust in God, and believed that he could deliver him (7-9). 5. He calls upon all who feared God to put their trust in him, and stay themselves upon their God—an address to the pious portion of the nation (10). 6. He warns those who were trusting to themselves, and who were seeking their own welfare only, that he would himself inflict exemplary punishment upon them, and that they should lie down in sorrow (11).

THUS saith the LORD, Where *is* the bill of your mother's divorcement, [a] whom I have put away? or which of my creditors *is it* to whom I have sold you? Behold, for your iniquities have ye sold yourselves, [b] and for your transgressions is your mother put away.

[a] Je.3.8; Ho.2.2. [b] ch.52.3.

CHAPTER L.

1. *Thus saith the* LORD. To the Jews in Babylon, who were suffering under his hand, and who might be disposed to complain that God had dealt with them with as much caprice and cruelty as a man did with his wife, when he gave her a writing of divorce, and put her away without any just cause. ¶ *Where is the bill of your mother's divorcement?* God here speaks of himself as the *husband* of his people, as having married the church to himself, denoting the tender affection which he had for his people. This figure is frequently used in the Bible. Thus in ch. lxii. 5: 'As the bridegroom rejoiceth over the bride, so shall thy God rejoice over thee;' 'For thy Maker is thy husband' (Isa. liv. 5); 'Turn, O backsliding children, saith the Lord; for I am married unto you' (Jer. iii. 14). Thus in Rev. xxi. 9, the church is called 'the bride, the Lamb's wife.' Compare Ezek. xvi. See Lowth on Hebrew poetry, Lec. xxxi. The phrase, 'bill of divorcement,' refers to the writing or instrument which a husband was by law obliged to give a wife when he chose to put her away. This custom of divorce Moses found probably in existence among the Jews, and also in surrounding nations, and as it was difficult if not impossible at once to remove it, he permitted it on account of the hardness of the hearts of the Jews (Deut. xxiv. 1; comp. Matt. xix. 8). It originated probably from the erroneous views which then prevailed of the nature of the marriage compact. It was extensively regarded as substantially like any other compact, in which the wife became a *purchase* from her father, and of course as she had been purchased, the husband claimed the right of dismissing her when he pleased. Moses nowhere defines the causes for which a man might put away his wife, but left these to be judged of by the people themselves. But he regulated the way in which it might be done. He ordained a law which was designed to operate as a material check on the hasty feelings, the caprice, and the passions of the husband. He designed that it should be with him, if exercised, not a matter of mere excited feeling, but that he should take time to deliberate upon it; and hence he ordained that in all cases a formal instrument of writing should be executed releasing the wife from the marriage tie, and leaving her at liberty to pursue her own inclinations in regard to future marriages (Deut. xxiv. 2). It is evident that this would operate very materially in favour of the wife, and in checking and restraining the excited passions of the husband (see Jahn's *Bib. Antiq.* § 160; Michaelis's *Comm. on the Laws of Moses*, vol. i.

2 Wherefore, when I came, *was there* no man? when I called, *was there* none to answer? Is my hand shortened at all, that it cannot redeem? or have I no power to deliver? behold, at my rebuke I dry up the sea, I make the rivers a wilderness: their fish stinketh, because *there is* no water, and dieth for thirst.

pp. 450–478; ii. 127–40. Ed. Lond. 1814, 8vo.) In the passage before us, God says that he had not rejected his people. He had not been governed by the caprice, sudden passion, or cruelty which husbands often evinced. There was a just cause why he had treated them as he had, and he did not regard them as the children of a divorced wife. The phrase, 'your mother,' here is used to denote the ancestry from whom they were descended. They were not regarded as the children of a disgraced mother. ¶ *Or which of my creditors* is it *to whom I have sold you?* Among the Hebrews, a father had the right, by the law of Moses, if he was oppressed with debt, to sell his children (Ex. xxi. 7; Neh. v. 5). In like manner, if a man had stolen anything, and had nothing to make restitution, he might be sold for the theft (Ex. xxii. 3). If a man also was poor and unable to pay his debts, he might be sold (Lev. xxv. 39; 2 Kings iv. 1; Matt. xviii. 25). On the subject of slavery among the Hebrews, and the Mosaic laws in regard to it, see Michaelis's *Comm. on the Laws of Moses*, vol. ii. pp. 155, *sq.* In this passage, God says that he had not been governed by any such motives in his dealings with his people. He had not dealt with them as a poor parent sometimes felt himself under a necessity of doing, when he sold his children, or as a creditor did when a man was not able to pay him. He had been governed by different motives, and he had punished them only on account of their transgressions. ¶ *Ye have sold yourselves.* That is, you have gone into captivity only on account of your sins. It has been your own act, and you have thus become bondmen to a foreign power only by your own choice. ¶ *Is your mother put away.* Retaining the figure respecting divorce. The nation has been rejected, and suffered to go into exile, only on account of its transgressions.

2. *Wherefore, when I came,* was there *no man?* That is, when I came to call you to repentance, why was there no man of the nation to yield obedience? The sense is, that they had not been punished without warning. He had called them to repentance, but no one heard his voice. The Chaldee renders this, 'Wherefore did I send my prophets, and they did not turn? They prophesied, but they did not attend.' ¶ *When I called,* was there *none to answer?* None obeyed, or regarded my voice. It was not, therefore, by his fault that they had been punished, but it was because they did not listen to the messengers which he had sent unto them. ¶ *Is my hand shortened at all?* The meaning of this is, that it was not because God was unable to save, that they had been thus punished. The hand, in the Scriptures, is an emblem of strength, as it is the instrument by which we accomplish our purposes. To shorten the hand, *i.e.*, to cut it off, is an emblem of diminishing, or destroying our ability to execute any purpose (see ch. lix. 1). So in Ex. xi. 23: 'Is the LORD's hand waxed short?' ¶ *That it cannot redeem?* That it cannot rescue or deliver you. The idea is, that it was not because he was less able to save them than he had been in former times, that they were sold into captivity, and sighed in bondage. ¶ *Behold, at my rebuke.* At my chiding—as a father rebukes a disobedient child, or as a man would rebuke an excited multitude. Similar language is used of the Saviour when he stilled the tempest on the sea of Gennesareth; 'Then he arose and rebuked the winds and the sea, and there was a great calm' (Matt. viii. 26). The reference here is, undoubtedly, to the fact that God dried up the Red Sea, or made a way for the children of Israel to pass through it. The idea is, that he who had power to perform such a stupendous miracle as that, had power also to deliver his people at any time, and that, therefore, it was for no want of power in him that the Jews were suffering in exile. ¶ *I make*

3 I clothe the heavens with blackness, and I make sackcloth their
covering.
4 The Lord GOD hath given me
the tongue of the learned, [a] that I
should know how to speak a word
in season to *him that is* weary: [b] he
wakeneth morning by morning: he
wakeneth mine ear to hear as the
learned.

[a] Mat.13.54.

[b] Mat.11.28.

---

the rivers a wilderness. I dry up streams at pleasure, and have power even to make the bed of rivers, and all the country watered by them, a pathless, and an unfruitful desert. ¶ *Their fish stinketh.* The waters leave them, and the fish die, and putrify. It is not uncommon in the East for large streams and even rivers thus to be dried up by the intense heat of the sun, and by being lost in the sand. Thus the river Barrady which flows through the fertile plain on which Damascus is situated, and which is divided into innumerable streams and canals to water the city and the gardens adjacent to it, after flowing to a short distance from the city is wholly lost—partly absorbed in the sands, and partly dried up by the intense rays of the sun (see Jones's *Excursions to Jerusalem, Egypt, &c.*) The idea here is, that it was God who had power to dry up those streams, and that he who could do that, could save and vindicate his people.

3. *I clothe the heavens with blackness.* With the dark clouds of a tempest—perhaps with an allusion to the remarkable clouds and tempests that encircled the brow of Sinai when he gave the law. Or possibly alluding to the thick darkness which he brought over the land of Egypt (Ex. x. 21; Grotius). In the previous verse, he had stated what he did on the earth, and referred to the exhibitions of his great power there. He here refers to the exhibition of his power in the sky; and the argument is, that he who had thus the power to spread darkness over the face of the sky, had power also to deliver his people. ¶ *I make sackcloth their covering.* Alluding to the clouds. Sackcloth was a coarse and dark cloth which was usually worn as an emblem of mourning (see Note on ch. iii. 24). The same image is used in Rev. vi. 12: 'And I beheld when he had opened the sixth seal, and lo, there was a great earthquake; and the sun became black as sackcloth of hair.' To say, therefore, that the heavens were clothed with sackcloth, is one of the most striking and impressive figures which can be conceived.

4. *The Lord* GOD *hath given me.* This verse commences a new subject, and the deliverer is directly introduced as himself speaking. The reasons why this is supposed to refer to the Messiah, have been given in the analysis to the chapter. Those reasons will be strengthened by the examination of the particular expressions in the passage, and by showing, as we proceed in the exposition, in what way they are applicable to him. It will be assumed that the reference is to the Messiah; and we shall find that it is a most beautiful description of his character, and of some of the principal events of his life. This verse is designed to state how he was fitted for the peculiar work to which he was called. The whole endowment is traced to JEHOVAH. It was he who had called him; he who had given him the tongue of the learned, and he who had carefully and attentively qualified him for his work. ¶ *The tongue of the learned.* Heb. 'The tongue of those who are instructed;' *i.e.*, of the eloquent; or the tongue of instruction (παιδείας, LXX.); that is, he has qualified me to instruct others. It does not mean human science or learning; nor does it mean that any other had been qualified as he was, or that there were any others who were learned like him. But it means that on the subject of religion he was eminently endowed with intelligence, and with eloquence. In regard to the Redeemer's power of instruction, the discourses which he delivered, as recorded in the New Testament, and especially his sermon on the mount, may be referred to. None on the subject of religion ever spake like him; none was ever so well qualified to instruct mankind (comp. Matt. xiii. 54). ¶ *That I should know how to speak a word in season.* The Hebrew here is, 'That I might know how to strengthen with a word the weary;' that is, that

5 The Lord GOD hath opened
mine [a] ear, and I was not [b] rebellious, neither turned away back.
6 [c] I gave my back to the smiters,
and my cheeks to them that plucked
off the hair: I hid not my face from
shame and spitting.

[a] Ps.40.6-8. [b] Mat.26.39; Jn.14.31. [c] Mat.26.67;27.26.

he might sustain, comfort, and refresh them by his promises and his counsels. How eminently he was fitted to alleviate those who were heavy laden with sin, and to comfort those who were burdened with calamities and trials, may be seen by the slightest reference to the New Testament, and the most partial acquaintance with his instructions and his life. The *weary* here are those who are burdened with a sense of guilt; who feel that they have no strength to bear up under the mighty load, and who therefore seek relief (see Matt. xi. 28). ¶ *He wakeneth morning by morning.* That is, he wakens me every morning early. The language is taken from an instructor who awakens his pupils early, in order that they may receive instruction. The idea is, that the Redeemer would be eminently endowed, under the Divine instruction and guidance, for his work. He would be one who was, so to speak, in the school of God; and who would be qualified to impart instruction to others. ¶ *He wakeneth mine ear.* To awaken the ear is to prepare one to receive instruction. The expressions, to open the ear, to uncover the ear, to awaken the ear, often occur in the Scriptures, in the sense of preparing to receive instruction, or of disposing to receive Divine communications. The sense here is plain. The Messiah would be taught of God, and would be inclined to receive all that he imparted. ¶ *To hear as the learned.* Many translate the phrase here 'as disciples,' that is, as those who are learning. So Lowth; 'With the attention of a learner.' So Noyes; 'In the manner of a disciple.' The LXX. render it, 'He has given me an ear to hear.' The idea is, probably, that he was attentive as they are who wish to learn; that is, as docile disciples. The figure is taken from a master who in the morning summons his pupils around him, and imparts instruction to them. And the doctrine which is taught is, that the Messiah would be eminently qualified, by Divine teaching, to be the instructor of mankind. The Chaldee paraphrases this, 'Morning by morning, he anticipates (the dawn), that he may send his prophets, if perhaps they may open the ears of sinners, and receive instruction.'

5. *The Lord* GOD *hath opened mine ear.* This is another expression denoting that he was attentive to the import of the Divine commission (see Ps. xl. 6). ¶ *And I was not rebellious.* I willingly undertook the task of communicating the Divine will to mankind. The statement here is in accordance with all that is said of the Messiah, that he was willing to come and do the will of God, and that whatever trials the work involved he was prepared to meet them (see Ps. xl. 6–8; comp. Heb. x. 4–10).

6. *I gave my back to the smiters.* I submitted willingly to be scourged, or whipped. This is one of the parts of this chapter which can be applied to no other one but the Messiah. There is not the slightest evidence, whatever may be supposed to have been the probability, that Isaiah was subjected to any such trial as this, or that he was scourged in a public manner. Yet it was literally fulfilled in the Lord Jesus Christ (Matt. xxvii. 26; comp. Luke xviii. 33). ¶ *And my cheeks to them that plucked off the hair.* Literally, 'My cheeks to those who pluck, or pull.' The word here used (מָרַט) means properly *to polish*, to sharpen, to make smooth; then to make smooth the head, to make bald; that is, to pluck out the hair, or the beard. To do this was to offer the highest insult that could be imagined among the Orientals. The beard is suffered to grow long, and is regarded as a mark of honour. Nothing is regarded as more infamous than to cut it off (see 2 Sam. x. 4), or to pluck it out; and there is nothing which an Oriental will sooner resent than an insult offered to his beard. 'It is a custom among the Orientals, as well among the Greeks as among other nations, to cultivate the beard with the utmost care and solicitude, so that they regard it as the highest

7 For the Lord GOD will help me; therefore shall I not be confounded: therefore have I set my face like a flint, and I know that I shall not be ashamed.

8 *He is* near that [a]justifieth me; who will contend with me? let us stand together: who *is* [1]mine adversary? [b]let him come near to me.

a Ro.8.32-34. 1 *the master of my cause.* b Ze.3.1,&c.; Re.12.10.

possible insult if a single hair of the beard is taken away by violence.'—(William of Tyre, an eastern archbishop, *Gesta Dei*, p. 802, quoted in Harmer, vol. ii. p. 359.) It is customary to beg by the beard, and to swear by the beard. 'By your beard; by the life of your beard; God preserve your beard; God pour his blessings on your beard,'—are common expressions there. The Mahometans have such a respect for the beard that they think it criminal to shave (Harmer, vol. ii. p. 360). The LXX. render this, 'I gave my cheeks to buffeting' (εἰς ῥαπίσματα); that is, to being smitten with the open hand, which was literally fulfilled in the case of the Redeemer (Matt. xxvi. 67; Mark xiv. 65). The general sense of this expression is, that he would be treated with the highest insult. ¶ *I hid not my face from shame and spitting.* To spit on any one was regarded among the Orientals, as it is everywhere else, as an expression of the highest insult and indignity (Deut. xxv. 9; Num. xii. 14; Job xxx. 10). Among the Orientals also it was regarded as an insult—as it should be everywhere—to spit in the presence of any person. Thus among the Medes, Herodotus (i. 99) says that Deioces ordained that, 'to spit in the king's presence, or in the presence of each other, was an act of indecency.' So also among the Arabians, it is regarded as an offence (Niebuhr's *Travels*, i. 57). Thus Monsieur d'Arvieux tells us (*Voydans la Pal.* p. 140) 'the Arabs are sometimes disposed to think, that when a person spits, it is done out of contempt; and that they never do it before their superiors' (Harmer, iv. 439). This act of the highest indignity was performed in reference to the Redeemer (Matt. xxvi. 67; xxvii. 30); and this expression of their contempt he bore with the utmost meekness. This expression is one of the proofs that this entire passage refers to the Messiah. It is said (Luke xvii. 32) that the prophecies should be fulfilled by his being spit upon, and yet there is no other prophecy of the Old Testament but this which contains such a prediction.

7. *For the Lord* GOD *will help me.* That is, he will sustain me amidst all these expressions of contempt and scorn. ¶ *Shall I not be confounded.* Heb. 'I shall not be ashamed;' that is, I will bear all this with the assurance of his favour and protection, and I will not blush to be thus treated in a cause so glorious, and which must finally triumph and prevail. ¶ *Therefore have I set my face like a flint.* To harden the face, the brow, the forehead, might be used either in a bad or a good sense—in the former as denoting shamelessness or haughtiness (see Note on ch. xlviii. 4); in the latter denoting courage, firmness, resolution. It is used in this sense here; and it means that the Messiah would be firm and resolute amidst all the contempt and scorn which he would meet, and would not shrink from any kind or degree of suffering which should be necessary to accomplish the great work in which he was engaged. A similar expression occurs in Ezek. iii. 8, 9: 'Behold, I have made thy face strong against their faces, and thy forehead strong against their foreheads. As an adamant, harder than a flint, have I made thy forehead; fear them not, neither be dismayed at their looks.'

8. He is *near that justifieth me.* That is, God, who will vindicate my character, and who approves what I do, does not leave nor forsake me, and I can with confidence commit myself and my cause to him (see Note on ch. xlix. 4). The word *justify* here is not used in the sense in which it is often in the Scriptures, to denote the act by which a sinner is justified before God, but in the proper, judicial sense, that he would declare him *to be* righteous; he would vindicate his character, and show him to be innocent. This was done by all the testimonies of God in his favour—by the voice which spake from heaven at his baptism—by

9 Behold, the Lord GOD will help
me; who *is* he *that* shall condemn
me? [a]lo, they all shall wax old as
a garment; the moth [b]shall eat
them up.
10 Who *is* among you that feareth the LORD, that obeyeth the voice
of his servant, that walketh *in* darkness, [c]and hath no light? let him
trust [d]in the name of the LORD, and
stay upon his God.

[a] Job 13.28. [b] ch.51.8. [c] Ps.23.4; Mi.7.8. [d] Job 13.15; Ps.52.3; Na.1.7; He.10.35 37.

---

the miracles which he wrought, showing that he was commissioned and approved by God—by the fact that even Pilate was constrained to declare him innocent—by the wonders that attended his crucifixion, showing that 'he was a righteous man,' even in the view of the Roman centurion (Luke xxiii. 47), and by the fact that he was raised from the dead, and was taken to heaven, and placed at the right hand of the Father—thus showing that his whole work was approved by God, and furnishing the most ample vindication of his character from all the accusations of his foes. ¶ *Who will contend with me?* This question indicates confidence in God, and in the integrity of his own character. The language is taken from transactions in the courts of justice; and it is a solemn call, on any who would dare to oppose him, to enter into a trial, and allege the accusations against him before the tribunal of a holy God. ¶ *Let us stand together.* Before the seat of judgment as in a court (comp. Note on ch. xli. 1). ¶ *Who* is *mine adversary?* Marg. 'Who is the master of my cause?' The Heb. is 'Lord (בַּעַל *băăl*) of judgment.' The expression means not merely one who has a lawsuit, or a cause, but one who is 'lord of the judgment,' *i.e.*, possessor of the cause, or one who has *a claim*, and can demand that the judgment should be in his favour. And the call here is on any who should have such a claim to prefer against the Messiah; who should have any real ground of accusation against him; that is, it is an assertion of innocence. ¶ *Let him come near to me.* Let him come and make his charges, and enter on the trial.

9. *The Lord* GOD *will help me* (see ver. 7). In the Hebrew this is, 'The Lord JEHOVAH,' as it is in ver. 7 also, and these are among the places where our translators have improperly rendered the word יְהוִֹה (JEHOVAH) by the word 'God.' ¶ *Who* is *he* that *shall condemn me?* If JEHOVAH is my advocate and friend, my cause *must* be right. Similar language is used by the apostle Paul: 'If God be for us, who can be against us?' (Rom. viii. 31); and in Ps. cxviii. 6:

> JEHOVAH is on my side; I will not fear:
> What can man do unto me?

¶ *They all shall wax old.* All my enemies shall pass away, as a garment is worn out and cast aside. The idea is, that the Messiah would survive all their attacks; his cause, his truth, and his reputation would live, while all the power, the influence, the reputation of his adversaries, would vanish as a garment that is worn out and then thrown away. The same image respecting his enemies is used again in ch. li. 8. ¶ *The moth shall eat them up.* The moth is a well known insect attached particularly to woollen clothes, and which soon consumes them (see Note on Job iv. 19). In eastern countries, where wealth consisted much in changes of raiment, the depredations of the moth would be particularly to be feared, and hence it is frequently referred to in the Bible. The sense here is, that the adversaries of the Messiah would be wholly destroyed.

10. *Who* is *among you that feareth the* LORD? This whole prophecy is concluded with an address made in this verse to the friends of God, and in the next to his enemies. It is the language of the Messiah, calling on the one class to put their trust in JEHOVAH, and threatening the other with displeasure and wrath. The exhortation in this verse is made in view of what is said in the previous verses. It is the entreaty of the Redeemer to all who love and fear God, and who may be placed in circumstances of trial and darkness as he was, to imitate his example, and not to rely on their own power, but to put their trust in the arm of JEHOVAH. He had done this (ver. 7–9). He had

11 Behold, all ye that kindle a fire, that compass *yourselves* about with sparks; walk [a] in the light of your fire, and in the sparks *that* ye have kindled. This shall ye have of mine hand, ye shall lie down [b] in sorrow.

a Ec.11.9. b Ps.16.4.

been afflicted, persecuted, forsaken, by men (ver. 6), and he had at that time confided in God and committed his cause to him; and he had never left or forsaken him. Encouraged by his example, he exhorts all others to cast themselves on the care of him who would defend a righteous cause. ¶ *That feareth the* LORD. Who are worshippers of JEHOVAH. ¶ *That obeyeth the voice of his servant.* The Messiah (see Note on ch. xlii. 1). This is another characteristic of piety. They who fear the Lord will also obey the voice of the Redeemer (John v. 23). ¶ *That walketh in darkness.* In a manner similar to the Messiah (ver. 6). God's true people experience afflictions like others, and have often trials peculiarly their own. They are sometimes in deep darkness of mind, and see no light. Comfort has forsaken them, and their days and nights are passed in gloom. ¶ *Let him trust in the name of the* LORD. The Messiah had done this (ver. 8, 9), and he exhorts all others to do it. Doing this they would obtain Divine assistance, and would find that he would never leave nor forsake them. ¶ *And stay upon his God.* Lean upon him, as one does on a staff or other support. This may be regarded still as the language of the merciful Redeemer, appealing to his own example, and entreating all who are in like circumstances, to put their trust in God.

11. *Behold, all ye that kindle a fire.* This verse refers to the wicked. In the previous verse, the Messiah had called upon all the pious to put their trust in God, and it is there implied that they would do so. But it would not be so with the wicked. In times of darkness and calamity, instead of trusting in God they would confide in their own resources, and endeavour to kindle a light for themselves in which they might walk. But the result would be, that they would find no comfort, and would ultimately under his hand lie down in sorrow. The figure is continued from the previous verse. The pious who are in darkness wait patiently for the light which JEHOVAH shall kindle for them But not so with the wicked. They attempt to kindle a light for themselves, and to walk in that. The phrase, 'that kindle a fire,' refers to all the plans which men form with reference to their own salvation; all which they rely upon to guide them through the darkness of this world. It may include, therefore, all the schemes of human philosophy, of false religion, of heathenism, of infidelity, deism, and self-righteousness; all dependence on our good works, our charities, and our prayers. All these are false lights which men enkindle, in order to guide themselves when they resolve to cast off God, to renounce his revelation, and to resist his Spirit. It may have had a primary reference to the Jews, who so often rejected the Divine guidance, and who relied so much on themselves; but it also includes all the plans which men devise to conduct themselves to heaven. The confidence of the pious (ver. 10) is in the light of God; that of the wicked is in the light of men. ¶ *That compass* yourselves *about with sparks.* There has been considerable variety in the interpretation of the word here rendered *sparks* (זִיקוֹת). It occurs nowhere else in the Bible, though the word זִקִּים occurs in Prov. xxvi. 18, where it is rendered in the text 'firebrands,' and in the margin 'flames,' or 'sparks.' Gesenius supposes that these are different forms of the same word, and renders the word here, 'burning arrows, fiery darts.' The Vulgate renders it 'flames.' The LXX. φλογὶ—'flame.' In the Syriac the word has the sense of lightning. Vitringa supposes it means 'faggots,' and that the sense is, that they encompass themselves with faggots, in order to make a great conflagration. Lowth renders it, very loosely, 'Who heap the fuel round about.' But it is probable that the common version has given the true sense, and that the reference is to

CHAPTER LI.

ANALYSIS.

This chapter, together with ch. lii. 1–12, is one connected portion, and injury has been done by separating it. It is a part of Isaiah of exquisite beauty, and is a most suitable introduction to the important portion which follows (ch. lii. 13–18; liii.) respecting the Messiah. This is designed chiefly to comfort the Jews in their exile. They are regarded as in Babylon near the close of their captivity, and as earnestly desiring to be rescued. It is somewhat *dramatic* in its character, and is made up of alternate addresses of God and his people—the one urging the strong language of consolation, and the other fervent petitions for deliverance. The following analysis will give a correct view of the chapter:—

I. God addresses them in the language of consolation, and directs them to remember the founder of their nation, and assures them that he is able also to deliver them (1–3). 1. He speaks of them as pious, and as seeking the Lord (1). 2. They were to remember Abraham and Sarah—the *quarry*, so to speak, from which the nation had been hewed; they were to remember how feeble they were, and yet how God had made a great nation of them, and to feel assured that God was equally able to conduct them forth and to multiply them into a great nation (1, 2). 3. A direct promise that God would comfort Zion, and make it like Eden (3).

II. God calls upon his people to hearken to him, with the assurance that he would extend the true religion even to the Gentile world, and that his salvation should be more permanent than were the heavens (4–6). 1. He would make his religion a light to the Jewish people (4). Though now in darkness, yet they should be brought forth into light. 2. He would extend it to the isles—to the heathen world (5). 3. It should be everlasting. The heavens should grow old and vanish, but his salvation should not be abolished (6).

III. God assures them that they have no reason to despond on account of the number and power of their enemies. However mighty they were, yet they should be consumed as the moth eats up a garment, and as the worm consumes wool (7, 8).

IV. The people are introduced as calling upon God, and as beseeching him to interpose as he had done in former times in their behalf (9, 10). In this appeal they refer to what God had done in former periods when he cut Rahab, *i.e.*, Egypt, in pieces, and delivered his people, and they cry to him to interpose in like manner again, and to deliver them.

V. To this petition Jehovah replies (11–16) He assures them—1. That his redeemed shall return with joy and triumph (11). 2. He that had made the heavens was their comforter, and they had nothing to fear from man, or the fury of any oppressor (12, 13). 3. The captive exile was soon to be unloosed, and they hastened that they might be restored; that is, it would soon occur (14). 4. Jehovah, who had divided the

---

human devices, which give no steady and clear light, but which may be compared with a spark struck from a flint. The idea probably is, that all human devices for salvation bear the same resemblance to the true plan proposed by God, which a momentary spark in the dark does to the clear shining of a bright light like that of the sun. If this is the sense, it is a most graphic and striking description of the nature of all the schemes by which the sinner hopes to save himself. ¶ *Walk in the light of your fire.* That is, you will walk in that light. It is not a *command* as if he wished them to do it, but it is a declaration which is intended to direct their attention to the fact that if they did this they would lie down in sorrow. It is language such as we often use, as when we say to a young man, 'go on a little further in a career of dissipation, and you will bring yourself to poverty and shame and death.' Or as if we should say to a man near a precipice, 'go on a little further, and you will fall down and be dashed in pieces.' The essential idea is, that this course would lead to ruin. It is implied that they would walk on in this way, and be destroyed. ¶ *This shall ye have.* As the result of this, you shall lie down in sorrow. Herder renders this:

> One movement of my hand upon you,
> And ye shall lie down in sorrow.

How simple and yet how sublime an expression is this! The Messiah but lifts his hand and the lights are quenched. His foes lie down sad and dejected, in darkness and sorrow. The idea is, that they would receive their doom from his hand, and that it would be as easy for him as is the uplifting or waving of the hand, to quench all their lights, and consign them to grief (comp. Matt. xxv.)

sea, was their protector. He had given them a solemn promise, and he had covered his people with the shadow of his hand, and he would defend them (15, 16).

VI. The chapter closes with a direct address to Jerusalem, and with assurances that it shall be rebuilt, and that it would be no more visited with such calamities (17–23). 1. The calamities of Jerusalem are enumerated. She had drunk the cup of the fury of JEHOVAH; she had been forsaken of those who were qualified to guide her; desolation and destruction had therefore come upon her; her sons had fainted in the streets, and had drunk of the fury of God (17–20). 2. God promises deliverance. She was drunken, but not with wine. God had taken out of her hand the cup of trembling, and she should no more drink it again; he would put that cup into the hand of those who had afflicted her, and they should drink it (21–23).

HEARKEN [a] to me, ye that [b] follow after righteousness, ye that seek the LORD: look unto the rock *whence* ye are hewn, and to the hole of the pit *whence* ye are digged.
2 Look [c] unto Abraham your fa-

[a] ver.7. [b] Ro.9.30,31. [c] He.11.8-12.

CHAPTER LI.

1. *Hearken unto me.* That is, to the God of their fathers, who now addresses them. They are regarded as in exile and bondage, and as desponding in regard to their prospects. In this situation, God, or perhaps more properly the Messiah (comp. Notes on ch. l.), is introduced as addressing them with the assurances of deliverance. ¶ *Ye that follow after righteousness.* This is addressed evidently to those who sought to be righteous, and who truly feared the Lord. There was a portion of the nation that continued faithful to JEHOVAH. They still loved and worshipped him in exile, and they were anxiously looking for deliverance and for a return to their own land. ¶ *Look unto the rock* whence *ye are hewn.* To Abraham the founder of the nation. The figure is taken from the act of quarrying stone for the purposes of building; and the essential idea here is, that God had formed the nation from the beginning, as a mason constructs a building; that he had, so to speak, taken the materials rough and unhewn from the very quarry; that he had shaped, and fitted them, and moulded them into an edifice. The idea is not that their origin was dishonourable or obscure. It is not that Abraham was not an honoured ancestor, or that they should be ashamed of the founder of their nation. But the idea is, that God had had the entire moulding of the nation; that he had taken Abraham and Sarah from a distant land, and had formed them into a great people and nation for his own purpose. The *argument* is, that he who had done this was able to raise them up from captivity, and make them again a great people. Probably allusion is made to this passage by the Saviour in Matt. iii. 9, where he says, 'For I say unto you, that God is able of these stones to raise up children unto Abraham.' ¶ *The hole of the pit.* The word rendered 'hole' means such an excavation as men make who are taking stones from a quarry. It expresses substantially the same idea as the previous member of the verse. This language is sometimes addressed to Christians, with a view to produce humility by reminding them that they have been taken by God from a state of sin, and raised up, as it were, from a deep and dark pit of pollution. But this is not the sense of the passage, nor will it bear such an application. It *may* be used to denote that *God* has taken them, as stone is taken from the quarry; that he found them in their natural state as unhewn blocks of marble are; that he has moulded and formed them by his own agency, and fitted them into his spiritual temple; and that they owe all the beauty and grace of their Christian deportment to him; that this is an argument to prove that he who had done so much for them as to transform them, so to speak, from rough and unsightly blocks to polished stones, fitted for his spiritual temple on earth, is able to keep them still, and to fit them for his temple above. Such is the argument in the passage before us; and such a use of it is, of course, perfectly legitimate and fair.

2. *Look unto Abraham.* What was figuratively expressed in the former verse is here expressed literally. They

ther, and unto Sarah *that* bare you:
for I called [a] him alone, and [b] blessed
him, and increased him.
3 For the LORD shall comfort
Zion: [c] he will comfort all her
waste places, and he will make
her wilderness like Eden, and her
desert like the garden of the LORD;
joy [d] and gladness shall be found
therein, thanksgiving, and the voice
of melody.
4 Hearken unto me, my people,
and give ear unto me, O my nation:
for a law [e] shall proceed from me,
and I will make my judgment to rest
for a light of the people.

a Ge.12.1,2. b Ge.22.17; 24.1,35. c ch.52.9; Ps.85.88. d 1 Pe.1.8. e Ro.8.2.

were directed to remember that God had taken Abraham and Sarah from a distant land, and that from so humble a beginning he had increased them to a great nation. The *argument* is, that he was able to bless and increase the exile Jews, though comparatively feeble and few. ¶ *For I called him alone.* Heb. 'For one I called him;' that is, he was alone; there was but one, and he increased to a mighty nation. So Jerome, *Quia unum vocavi eum.* So the LXX. Ὅτι εἷς ἦν—'For he was one.' The point of the declaration here is, that God had called *one individual*—Abraham—and that he had caused him to increase till a mighty nation had sprung from him, and that he had the same power to increase the little remnant that remained in Babylon until they should again become a mighty people.

3. *For the* LORD *shall comfort Zion.* On the word 'Zion,' see Notes on ch. i. 8. The meaning here is, that he would again restore it from its ruins. The argument is drawn from the statement in the previous verses. If God had raised up so great a nation from so humble an origin, he had power to restore the waste places of Judea to more than their former beauty and prosperity (see Notes on ch. xl. 1). ¶ *And he will make her wilderness.* Judea is here represented as lying waste. It is to be remembered that the time to which the prophet here refers is that of the captivity, and near its close. Of course, as that would have continued seventy years, in so long a period Judea would have become almost an extended wilderness, a wide waste. Any country that was naturally as fertile as Judea, would in that time be overrun with briers, thorns, and underbrush, and even with a wild and luxuriant growth of the trees of the forest. ¶ *Like Eden* (Gen. ii.) Like a cultivated and fertile garden—distinguished not only for its fertility, but for its beauty and order. ¶ *Her desert like the garden of the* LORD. Like the garden which the LORD planted (Gen. ii. 8). LXX. Ὡς παράδεισον κυρίου—'As the paradise of the LORD.' The idea is, that it should be again distinguished for its beauty and fertility. ¶ *Joy and gladness.* The sound of rejoicing and praise shall be again heard there, where are now heard the cries of wild beasts. ¶ *The voice of melody.* Heb. 'A psalm.' The praises of God shall again be celebrated.

4. *Hearken unto me, my people.* Lowth reads this;

> Attend unto me, O ye people,
> And give ear unto me, O ye nations.

The reason why he proposes this change is, that he supposes the address here is made to the Gentiles and not to the Jews, and in favour of the change he observes, that two MSS. read it in this manner. Gesenius (*Comm.*) says that three codices read עַמִּים (*peoples*), instead of עַמִּי (*my people*); and that thirteen read לְאוּמִּים (*nations*), instead of לְאוּמִּי (*my nation*). Noyes also has adopted this reading. But the authority is too slight to justify a change in the text. The Vulgate reads it in accordance with the present Hebrew text, and so substantially do the LXX. They render it, 'Hear me, hear me, my people, and ye kings, give ear unto me.' It is not necessary to suppose any change in the text. The address is to the Jews; and the design is, to comfort them in view of the fact that the heathen would be brought to partake of the privileges and blessings of the true religion. They would not only be restored to their own land, but the true religion would be extended also to the distant nations of the

5 My [a] righteousness *is* near; my
salvation is gone forth, and mine
arms shall judge [b] the people: the
isles [c] shall wait upon me, and on
mine arm shall they trust.
6 Lift up your eyes to the heavens, and look upon the earth beneath; for [d] the heavens shall vanish
away like smoke, and the earth shall
wax old like a garment, and they
that dwell therein shall die in like
manner: but my salvation shall be
for ever, and my righteousness shall
not [e] be abolished.

a ch.56.1. b Ps 98.9. c ch.42.4; 60.9. d He.1.11,12; 2 Pe.3.10,12. e Da.9.24.

earth. In view of this great and glorious truth, JEHOVAH calls on his people to hearken to him, and receive the glad announcement. It was a truth in which they were deeply interested, and to which they should therefore attend. ¶ *For a law shall proceed from me.* The idea here is, that JEHOVAH would give law to the distant nations by the diffusion of the true religion. ¶ *And I will make my judgment to rest for a light.* The word 'judgment' here is equivalent to *law*, or *statute*, or to the institutions of the true religion. The word here rendered 'to rest' (אַרְגִּיעַ from רָגַע), Lowth renders, 'I will cause to break forth.' Noyes renders it, 'I will establish.' The Vulgate, *Requiescet*—'Shall rest.' The LXX. render it simply, 'My judgment for a light of the nation.' The word properly means *to make afraid*, to terrify, to restrain by threats; rendered 'divideth' in Job xxvi. 12; Isa. li. 15; then, to be afraid, to shrink from fear, and hence to be still, or quiet, *as if* cowering down from fear. Here it means that he would *set firmly* his law; he would place it so that it would be established and immovable.

5. *My righteousness* is *near*. The word 'righteousness' is used in a great variety of significations. Here it means, probably, the faithful completion of his promises to his people (Lowth). ¶ *My salvation is gone forth.* The promise of salvation is gone forth, and already the execution of that purpose is commenced. He would soon deliver his people; he would at no distant period extend salvation to all nations. ¶ *And mine arm shall judge the people.* That is, shall dispense judgment to them. The 'arm' here is put for himself, as the arm is the instrument by which we execute our purposes (see Notes on ver. 9). ¶ *The isles shall wait upon me.* The distant nations; the heathen lands (see Note on ch. xli. 1). The idea is, that distant lands would become interested in the true religion, and acknowledge and worship the true God.

6. *Lift up your eyes to the heavens.* The design of directing their attention to the heavens and the earth is, probably, to impress them more deeply with a conviction of the certainty of his salvation in this manner, viz.: the heavens and the earth appear firm and fixed; there is in them no apparent tendency to dissolution and decay. Yet though apparently thus fixed and determined, they will all vanish away, but the promise of God will be unfailing. ¶ *For the heavens shall vanish away.* The word which is here rendered 'shall vanish away' (מָלַח), occurs nowhere else in the Bible. The primary idea, according to Gesenius, is that of smoothness and softness. Then it means to glide away, to disappear. The idea here is, that the heavens would disappear, as smoke is dissipated and disappears in the air. The idea of the vanishing, or the disappearing of the heavens and the earth, is one that often occurs in the Scriptures (see Notes on ch. xxxiv. 4; comp. Ps. cii. 26; Heb. i. 11, 12; 2 Pet. iii. 10–12). ¶ *The earth shall wax old,* &c. Shall decay, and be destroyed (see Ps. cii. 26). ¶ *And they that dwell therein shall die in like manner.* Lowth renders this, 'Like the vilest insect.' Noyes, 'Like flies.' The Vulgate, and the LXX., however, render it as it is in our version. Rosenmüller renders it, 'As flies.' Gesenius renders it, 'Like a gnat.' This variety of interpretation arises from the different explanation of the word כֵּן (*khēn*), which usually means, *as, so, thus, in like manner,* &c. The plural form, however, (כִּנִּים *k'nnīm*), occurs in Ex. viii. 17; Ps. cv. 31, and is rendered by the LXX.

7 Hearken [a]unto me, ye that know righteousness, the people in whose heart [b]*is* my law; fear ye not [c]the reproach of men, neither be ye afraid of their revilings.
8 For the moth shall eat [d]them up like a garment, and the worm shall eat them like wool: but my righteousness shall be for ever, and my salvation from generation to generation.

[a] ver.1. [b] Ps.37.31. [c] Mat.10.28. [d] Job 4.19-21.

σκνῖφες, and by the Vulgate *sciniphes*, a species of small gnats, very troublesome from their sting, which abounds in the marshy regions of Egypt; and according to this the idea is, that the most mighty inhabitants of the earth would die like gnats, or the smallest and vilest insects. This interpretation gives a more impressive sense than our version, but it is doubtful whether it can be justified. The word occurs nowhere else in this sense, and the authority of the ancient versions is against it. The idea as given in the common translation is not feeble, as Gesenius supposes, but is a deeply impressive one, that the heavens, the earth, and all the inhabitants should vanish away together, and alike disappear. ¶ *But my salvation shall be for ever.* It is a glorious truth that the redemption which God shall give his people shall survive the revolutions of kingdoms, and the consummation of all earthly things. It is not improbable that the Saviour had this passage in his eye when he said, 'Heaven and earth shall pass away, but my word shall not pass away' (Matt. xxiv. 35).

7. *Hearken unto me, ye that know righteousness.* My people who are acquainted with my law, and who are to be saved. This is addressed to the pious part of the Jewish nation. ¶ *Fear ye not the reproach of men.* If we have the promise of God, and the assurance of his favour, we shall have no occasion to dread the reproaches and the scoffs of men (comp. Matt. x. 28).

8. *For the moth* (see ch. l. 9). The idea is, that they shall be consumed as the moth eats up a garment; or rather, that the moth itself shall consume them as it does a garment: that is, that they were so weak when compared with Jehovah that even the moth, one of the smallest, and most contemptible of insects, would consume them. An expression remarkably similar to this occurs in Job iv. 18–20:

> Behold in his servants he putteth no confidence,
> And his angels he chargeth with frailty;
> How much more true is this of those who dwell in houses of clay,
> Whose foundation is in the dust!
> They are crushed before the moth-worm!
> Between morning and evening they are destroyed;
> Without any one regarding it, they perish for ever.

Perhaps the following extract from Niebuhr may throw some light on the passage, as showing that man may be crushed by so feeble a thing as a worm. 'A disease very common in Yemen is the attack of the Guiney-worm, or the *Verea-Medinensis*, as it is called by the physicians of Europe. This disease is supposed to be occasioned by the use of the putrid waters, which people are obliged to drink in various parts of Yemen; and for this reason the Arabians always pass water, with the nature of which they are unacquainted, through a linen cloth before using it. When one unfortunately swallows the eggs of this insect, no immediate consequence follows; but after a considerable time the worm begins to show itself through the skin. Our physician, Mr. Cramer, was within a few days of his death attacked by five of these worms at once, although this was more than five months after we left Arabia. In the isle of Karek I saw a French officer named Le Page, who, after a long and difficult journey, performed on foot, and in an Indian dress, between Pondicherry and Surat, through the heat of India, was busy extracting a worm out of his body He supposed he had got it by drinking bad water in the country of the Mahrattas. This disorder is not dangerous if the person who is affected can extract the worm without breaking it. With this view it is rolled on a small bit of wood as it comes out of the skin. It is slender as a thread, and two or three feet long. If unluckily it be broken, it then returns into the body, and the most disagreeable consequences ensue—palsy, a

9 Awake, awake, put on [a]strength, O arm of the LORD; awake, as in the ancient days, in the generations of old. *Art* thou not it that hath cut [b]Rahab, *and* wounded [c]the dragon?

10 *Art* thou not it which [d]hath dried the sea, the waters of the great deep; that hath made the depths of the sea a way for the ransomed to pass over?

a Re.11.7. b Ps.89.10. c ch.27.1; Ps.74.13,14. d Ex.14.21.

gangrene, and sometimes death.' A thought similar to that of Isaiah respecting man, has been beautifully expressed by Gray:

> To contemplation's sober eye,
> Such is the race of man;
> And they that creep, and they that fly,
> Shall end where they began.
>
> Alike the busy and the gay,
> But flutter through life's little day,
> In fortune's varying colours drest;
> Brush'd by the hand of rough mischance,
> Or chill'd by age, their airy dance
> They leave, in dust to rest.

¶ *And the worm shall eat them like wool.* The word rendered 'worm' (סָס), probably means the same as the moth. The Arabic renders it by *moth, weevil.* The LXX. Σής. It is of unfrequent occurrence in the Scriptures.

9. *Awake, awake.* This verse commences a new subject (see the analysis of the chapter). It is the solemn and impassioned entreaty of those who were in exile that God would interpose in their behalf, as he did in behalf of his people when they were suffering in cruel bondage in Egypt. The word 'awake' here, which is addressed to the *arm* of Jehovah, is a petition that it might be roused from its apparent stupor and inactivity, and its power exerted in their behalf. ¶ *O arm of the* LORD. The *arm* is the instrument by which we execute any purpose. It is that by which the warrior engages in battle, and by which he wields the weapon to prostrate his foes. The *arm* of JEHOVAH had seemed to slumber. For seventy years the prophet sees the oppressed and suffering people in bondage, and God had not come forth to rescue them. He hears them now lifting the voice of earnest and tender entreaty, that he would interpose as he had in former times, and save them from the calamities which they were enduring. ¶ *Awake, as in the ancient days.* That is, in the time when the Jews were delivered from their bondage in the land of Egypt.

¶ Art *thou not it.* Art thou not the same arm? Was it not by this arm that the children of Israel were delivered from bondage, and may we not look to it for protection still? ¶ *That hath cut Rahab.* That is, cut it in pieces, or destroyed it. It was that arm which wielded the sword of justice and of vengeance by which Rahab was cut in pieces. The word 'Rahab' here means Egypt. On the meaning of the word, see Notes on ch. xxx. 7; comp. Ps. lxxxviii. 8; lxxxix. 10. ¶ And *wounded the dragon.* The word here rendered dragon (תַּנִּין *tănnīn*) means properly any great fish or sea-monster; a serpent, a dragon (see Notes on ch. xxvii. 1), or a crocodile. Here it means, probably, the crocodile, as emblematic of Egypt, because the Nile abounded in crocodiles, and because a monster so unwieldy and formidable and unsightly, was no unapt representation of the proud and cruel king of Egypt. The king of Egypt is not unfrequently compared with the crocodile (see Ps. xxxiv. 13, 14; Ezek. xxix. 3; xxxii. 2). Here the sense is, that he had sorely wounded, *i.e.*, had greatly weakened the power of that cruel nation, which for strength was not unfitly represented by the crocodile, one of the most mighty of monsters, but which, like a pierced and wounded monster, was greatly enfeebled when God visited it with plagues, and destroyed its hosts in the sea.

10. Art *thou not it.* Art thou not still the same? The ground of the appeal is, that the same arm that dried up the sea, and made a path for the Jewish people, was still able to interpose and rescue them. ¶ *Which hath dried the sea.* The Red Sea when the children of Israel passed over (Ex. xiv. 21). This is the common illustration to which the Hebrew prophets and poets appeal, when they wish to refer to the interposition of God in favour of their nation (comp. Ps. cv.; see Notes on ch. xliii. 16).

11 Therefore [a] the redeemed of
the LORD shall return, and come
with singing unto Zion; and everlasting joy [b] *shall be* upon their head:
they shall obtain gladness and joy;
and sorrow [c] and mourning shall
flee away.
12 I, [d] *even* I, *am* he that comforteth you: who *art* thou, that thou
shouldest be afraid of a man *that*
shall die, and of the son of man
which shall be made *as* grass;
13 And forgettest the LORD thy
Maker, that hath stretched forth
the heavens, and laid the foundations of the earth; and hast feared
continually every day because of the
fury of the oppressor, as if he [1] were
ready to destroy? and [e] where *is* the
fury of the oppressor?

a ch.35.10. b Jude 24. c Re.21.4. d ver.3.

1 or, *made himself ready.* e Job 20.7.

¶ *For the ransomed to pass over.* Those who had been ransomed from Egypt. The word rendered 'ransomed' is that which is commonly rendered 'redeemed.' The argument in this verse is, that he who had overcome all the obstacles in the way of their deliverance from Egypt, was able also to overcome all the obstacles in the way of their deliverance from Babylon; and that he who had thus interposed might be expected again to manifest his mercy, and save them again from oppression. The *principle* involved in the argument is as applicable now as it was then. All God's past interpositions—and especially the great and wonderful interposition when he gave his Son for his church—constitute an argument that he will still continue to regard the interests of his people, and will interpose in their behalf, and save them.

11. *Therefore the redeemed of the* LORD. This is probably the language of JEHOVAH assuring them, in answer to their prayer, that his ransomed people should again return to Zion. ¶ *And everlasting joy* shall be *upon their head.* This entire verse occurs also in ch. xxxv. 10. See it explained in the Note on that verse. The custom of *singing* alluded to here on a journey is now very common in the East. It is practised to relieve the tediousness of a journey over extended plains, as well as to induce the camels in a caravan to move with greater rapidity. The idea here is, that the caravan that should return from Babylon to Jerusalem, across the extended plains, should make the journey amidst general exultation and joy—cheered on their way by songs, and relieving the tedium of their journey by notes of gladness and of praise.

12. *I,* even *I,* am *he that comforteth you.* The word 'I' is repeated here to give emphasis to the passage, and to impress deeply upon them the fact that their consolation came alone from God. The argument is, that since God was their protector and friend, they had no occasion to fear anything that man could do. ¶ *Of a man* that *shall die.* God your comforter will endure for ever. But all men—even the most mighty—must soon die. And if God is our protector, what occasion can we have to fear what a mere mortal can do to us? ¶ *And of the son of man.* This phrase is common in the Hebrew Scriptures, and means the same as man. ¶ *Shall be made* as *grass.* They shall perish as grass does that is cut down at midday (see Notes on ch. xl. 6, 7).

13. *And forgettest the* LORD *thy Maker.* These verses are designed to rebuke that state of the mind—alas! too common, even among the people of God—where they are intimidated by the number and strength of their foes, and forget their dependence on God, and his promises of aid. In such circumstances God reproves them for their want of confidence in him, and calls on them to remember that he has made the heavens, and has all power to save them. ¶ *That hath stretched forth the heavens* (see Notes on ch. xl. 12, 26). ¶ *And hast feared continually every day.* They had continually feared and trembled before their oppressors. ¶ *Because of the fury of the oppressor.* Those who had oppressed them in Babylon. ¶ *As if he were ready to destroy.* Marg. 'Made himself ready.' The idea is, that he was *preparing* to destroy the people—perhaps as a marksman is making ready his bow and

14 The captive exile hasteneth that he may be loosed, and that he should not die in the pit, [a] nor that his bread should fail.

15 But I am the LORD thy God, that divided the sea, whose waves roared: The LORD of hosts *is* his name.

16 And I have put my words [b] in

a Zec.9.11. b Jn.3.34.

arrows. The oppressor had been preparing to crush them in the dust, and they trembled, and did not remember that God was abundantly able to protect them. ¶ *And where is the fury of the oppressor?* What is there to dread? The idea is, that the enemies of the Jews would be cut off, and that they should therefore put their confidence in God, and rely on his promised aid.

14. *The captive exile.* Lowth renders this, evidently very improperly, 'He marcheth on with speed who cometh to set the captive free;' and supposes that it refers to Cyrus, if understood of the temporal redemption from the captivity at Babylon; in the spiritual sense, to the Messiah. But the meaning evidently is, that the exile who had been so long as it were enchained in Babylon, was about to be set free, and that the time was very near when the captivity was to end. The prisoner should not die there, but should be conducted again to his own land. The word here used, and rendered 'captive exile' (צֹעֶה from צָעָה), means properly *that which is turned on one side*, or *inclined*, as, *e.g.*, a vessel for pouring (Jer. xlviii. 12). Then it means that which is inclined, bent, or bowed down as a captive in bonds. The Chaldee renders this, 'Vengeance shall be quickly revealed, and the just shall not die in corruption, and their food shall not fail.' Aben Ezra renders it, 'Bound.' The idea is, that they who were bowed down under bondage and oppression in Babylon, should very soon be released. This is one of the numerous passages which show that the *scene* of the prophetic vision is Babylon, and the *time* near the close of the captivity, and that the design of the prophet is to comfort them there, and to afford them the assurance that they would soon be released. ¶ *And that he should not die in the pit.* That is, in Babylon, represented as a prison, or a pit. The nation would be restored to their own land. Prisoners were often confined in a deep *pit* or cavern, and hence the word is synonymous with prison. The following extract from Paxton will illustrate this. 'The Athenians, and particularly the tribe of Hippothoontis, frequently condemned offenders to the pit. It was a dark, noisome hole, and had sharp spikes at the top, that no criminal might escape; and others at the bottom, to pierce and torment those unhappy persons who were thrown in. Similar to this place was the Lacedemonian Καιαδας, into which Aristomenes the Messenian being cast, made his escape in a very surprising manner.' Comp. also Gen. xxxvii. 20; Num. xvi. 30; Ps. ix. 15; xxviii. 1; xxx. 3, 9; xl. 2; lv. 23; cxix. 85; cxl. 10; Jer. xxxvii. 21; Zec. ix. 11. ¶ *Nor that his bread should fail.* His wants shall be supplied until he is released.

15. *But I am the* LORD *thy God.* In order to show them that he was able to save them, God again refers to the fact that he had divided the sea, and delivered their fathers from bondage and oppression. ¶ *That divided the sea.* The Red Sea. The Chaldee renders this, 'That rebuked the sea.' The LXX. Ὁ ταράσσων—'Who disturbs the sea,' or, who excites a tempest. Lowth renders it, 'Who stilleth at once the sea.' The Hebrew word is the same which occurs in ver. 4, where it is rendered, 'I will make my judgment *to rest*' (רָגַע). Probably the idea here is, that he restrains the raging of the sea *as if* by fear; *i.e.*, makes it tranquil or still by rebuking it. He had this power over all raging seas, and he had shown it in a special manner by his rebuking the Red Sea and making it rest, and causing a way to be made through it, when the children of Israel came out of Egypt. ¶ *The* LORD *of hosts is his name* (see Notes on ch. i. 9; comp. Notes on ch. xlii. 8).

16. *And I have put my words in thy mouth.* That is, he had committed his

thy mouth, and have covered thee
in the shadow [a] of mine hand, that
I may plant the heavens, [b] and lay
the foundations of the earth, and
say unto Zion, Thou *art* my people.
17 Awake, awake, stand up, O
Jerusalem, which hast drunk at the
hand of the LORD the cup of his
fury: [c] thou hast drunken the dregs
of the cup of trembling, *and* wrung
them out.

[a] ch.49.2. [b] 2 Pe.3.13. [c] ver.22; Ps.75.8.

truth to the Jewish people; to Zion. He had intrusted them with his statutes and his laws; he had given them the promise of the Messiah, and through him the assurance that the true religion would be spread to other nations. He would, therefore, preserve them, and restore them again to their own land. ¶ *And have covered thee in the shadow of mine hand.* That is, I have protected thee (see Notes on ch. xlix. 2). ¶ *That I may plant the heavens.* Lowth renders this, 'To stretch out the heavens.' Noyes, 'To establish the heavens.' Jerome, *Ut plantes cœlos*—'That thou mayest plant the heavens.' The LXX. 'Εν ᾗ ἔστησα τὸν οὐρανὸν—'By which I have established heaven.' The Chaldee renders it, 'In the shadow of my power have I protected thee, that I might raise up the people of whom it was said, that they should be multiplied as the stars of heaven.' But the language here is evidently entirely figurative. It refers to the restoration of the Jews to their own land; to the re-establishment of religion there; to the introduction of the new economy under the Messiah, and to all the great changes which would be consequent on that. This is compared with the work of forming the heavens, and laying the foundation of the earth. It would require almighty power; and it would produce so great changes, that it might be compared to the work of creating the universe out of nothing. Probably also the idea is included here that *stability* would be given to the true religion by what God was about to do—a permanency that might be compared with the firmness and duration of the heavens and the earth. ¶ *And say unto Zion,* &c. That is, God would restore them to their own land, and acknowledge them as his own.

17. *Awake, awake* (see Notes on ver. 9). This verse commences an address to Jerusalem under a new figure or image. The figure employed is that of a man who has been overcome by the cup of the wrath of JEHOVAH, that had produced the same effect as inebriation. Jerusalem had reeled and fallen prostrate. There had been none to sustain her, and she had sunk to the dust. Calamities of the most appalling kind had come upon her, and she is now called on to arouse from this condition, and to recover her former splendour and power. ¶ *Which hast drunk at the hand of the* LORD. The wrath of JEHOVAH is not unfrequently compared to a cup producing intoxication. The reason is, that it produces a similar effect. It prostrates the strength, and makes the subject of it reel, stagger, and fall. In like manner, all calamities are represented under the image of a cup that is drunk, producing a prostrating effect on the frame. Thus the Saviour says, 'The cup which my Father hath given me, shall I not drink it?' (John xviii. 11; comp. Matt. xx. 22, 23; xxvi. 39, 42). The effects of drinking the cup of God's displeasure are often beautifully set forth. Thus, in Ps. lxxv. 8:

> In the hand of JEHOVAH there is a cup, and the wine is red;
> It is full of a mixed liquor, and he poureth out of the same,
> Verily the dregs thereof all the ungodly of the earth shall wring them out and drink them.

Plato, as referred to by Lowth, has an idea resembling this. 'Suppose,' says he, 'God had given to men a medicating potion inducing fear; so that the more any one should drink of it, so much the more miserable he should find himself at every draught, and become fearful of everything present and future; and at last, though the most courageous of men, should become totally possessed by fear; and afterwards, having slept off the effects of it, should become himself again.' A similar image is used by Homer (*Iliad,* xvi. 527, *sq.*), where he places two vessels at the

18 *There is* none to guide her
among all the sons *whom* she hath
brought forth; neither *is there any*
that taketh her by the hand, of all
the sons *that* she hath brought up.
19 These two *things* [1] are come
unto thee; who shall be sorry for

1 *happened.*

threshold of Jupiter, one of good, the other of evil. He gives to some a mixed potion of each; to others from the evil vessel only, and these are completely miserable:

Two urns by Jove's high throne have ever stood,
The source of evil one, and one of good;
From thence the cup of mortal man he fills,
Blessings to these; to those distributes ills.
To most he mingles both: The wretch decreed
To taste the bad unmix'd, is curs'd indeed;
Pursued by wrongs, by meagre famine driven,
He wanders, outcast by both earth and heaven:
The happiest taste not happiness sincere,
But find the cordial draught is dash'd with care.

But nowhere is this image handled with greater force and sublimity than in this passage of Isaiah. Jerusalem is here represented as staggering under the effects of it; she reels and falls; none assist her from whence she might expect aid; not one of them is able to support her. All her sons had fainted and become powerless (ver. 20); they were lying prostrate at the head of every street, like a bull taken in a net, struggling in vain to rend it, and to extricate himself. Jehovah's wrath had produced complete and total prostration throughout the whole city. ¶ *Thou hast drunken the dregs.* Gesenius renders this, 'The goblet cup.' But the common view taken of the passage is, that it means that the cup had been drunk to the dregs. All the intoxicating liquor had been poured off. They had entirely exhausted the cup of the wrath of God. Similar language occurs in Rev. xiv. 10: 'The same shall drink of the wine of the wrath of God, which is poured out without mixture, into the cup of his indignation.' The idea of the *dregs* is taken from the fact that, among the ancients, various substances, as honey, dates, &c., were put into wine, in order to produce the intoxicating quality in the highest degree. The sediment of course would remain at the bottom of the cask or cup when the wine was poured off. Homer, who lived about a thousand years before Christ, and whose descriptions are always regarded as exact accounts of the customs in his time, frequently mentions potent drugs as being mixed with wines. In the *Odyssey* (iv. 220), he tells us that Helen prepared for Telemachus and his companions a beverage which was highly stupefactive, and soothing to his mind. To produce these qualities, he says that she threw into the wine drugs which were

Νηπενθες τ' ἀλοχον τε κακων ἐπιληθον ἀπαντων—

'Grief-assuaging, rage-allaying, and the oblivious antidote for every species of misfortune.' Such mixtures were common among the Hebrews. It is possible that John (Rev. xiv. 10) refers to such a mixture of the simple juice of the grape with intoxicating drugs when he uses the expression implying a seeming contradiction, κεκερασμένου ἀκράτου —(*mixed, unmixed wine*)—rendered in our version, 'poured out without mixture.' The reference is rather to the pure juice of the grape *mixed*, or mingled with intoxicating drugs. ¶ *The cup of trembling.* The cup producing trembling, or intoxication (comp. Jer. xxv. 15; xlix. 12; li. 7; Lam. iv. 21; Hab. ii. 16; Ezek. xxiii. 31–33). The same figure occurs often in the Arabic poets (see Gesenius *Comm. zu. Isa. in loc.*) ¶ And *wrung* them *out* (מָצִית). This properly means, to suck out; that is, they had as it were sucked off all the liquid from the dregs.

18. There is *none to guide her.* The image here is taken from the condition of one who is under the influence of an intoxicating draught, and who needs some one to sustain and guide him. The idea is, than among all the inhabitants of Jerusalem in the time of the calamity, there was none who could restore to order the agitated and distracted affairs of the nation. All its wisdom was destroyed; its counsels perplexed; its power overcome. ¶ *All the sons* whom *she hath brought forth.* All the inhabitants of Jerusalem.

19. *These two* things *are come unto thee.* Marg. 'Happened.' That is, two sources of calamity have come upon thee;

thee? desolation, and [1]destruction,
and the famine, and the sword: by
whom [a]shall I comfort thee?
20 Thy sons have fainted, they
lie at the head of all the streets, as
a wild bull in a net: they are full
of the fury of the LORD, the rebuke of thy God.

1 *breaking.*

a La.2.11-13; Am.7.2.

to wit, famine and the sword, producing desolation and destruction; or desolation *by* famine, and destruction *by* the sword (see Lowth *on Heb. Poetry*, Lect. xix.) The idea here is, that far-spread destruction had occurred, caused by the two things, famine and the sword. ¶ *Who shall be sorry for thee?* That is, who shall be able so to pity thee as to furnish relief? ¶ *Desolation.* By famine. ¶ *And destruction.* Marg. as Heb. 'Breaking.' It refers to the calamities which would be inflicted by the sword. The land would be desolated, and famine would spread over it. This refers, doubtless, to the series of calamities that would come upon it in connection with the invasion of the Chaldeans. ¶ *By whom shall I comfort thee?* This intimates a desire on the part of JEHOVAH to give them consolation. But the idea is, that the land would be laid waste, and that they who would have been the natural comforters should be destroyed. There would be none left to whom a resort could be had for consolation.

20. *Thy sons.* Jerusalem is here represented as a mother. Her sons, that is, her inhabitants, had become weak and prostrate everywhere, and were unable to afford consolation. ¶ *They lie at the head of all the streets.* The 'head' of the streets is the same which in Lam. ii. 19; iv. 1, is denominated 'the top of the streets.' The head or top of the streets denotes, doubtless, the *beginning* of a way or street; the corner from which other streets diverge. These would be public places, where many would be naturally assembled, and where, in time of a siege, they would be driven together. This is a description of the state produced by famine. Weak, pale, and emaciated, the inhabitants of Jerusalem, in the places of public concourse, would lie prostrate and inefficient, and unable to meet and repel their foes. They would be overpowered with famine, as a wild bull is insnared in a net, and rendered incapable of any effort. This refers undoubtedly to the famine that would be produced during the siege of the Babylonians. The state of things under the siege has been also described by Jeremiah:

Arise, cry out in the night;
In the beginning of the watches pour out thine heart before the Lord;
Lift up thy hands toward him for the life of thy young children,
That faint for hunger at the top of every street.

The young and old lie on the ground in the streets,
My virgins and my young men are fallen by the sword;
Thou hast slain them in the day of thy anger;
Thou hast killed, and not pitied.—Lam. ii. 19–21.

The tongue of the sucking child cleaveth to the roof of his mouth for thirst;
The young children ask bread, and no man breaketh it unto them;
They that did feed delicately are desolate in the streets;
They that were brought up in scarlet embrace dunghills.—Lam. iv. 4, 5.

¶ *As a wild bull in a net.* The word here rendered 'wild bull' is תוֹא. Gesenius supposes it is the same as תְּאוֹ, a species of *gazelle*, so called from its swiftness. Aquila, Symm. and Theod. render it here, Ὄρυξ—'Oryx;' Jerome also renders it, *Oryx*—'A wild goat' or stag. The LXX. render it, Σευτλίον ἡμίεφθον—'A parboiled beet!' The Chaldee, 'As broken bottles.' Bochart (*Hieroz.* i. 3. 28), supposes it means a species of mountain-goat, and demonstrates that it is common in the East to take such animals in a net. Lowth renders it, 'Oryx.' The streets of Hebrew towns, like those of ancient Babylon, and of most modern Oriental cities, had gates which were closed at night, and on some occasions of broil and danger. A person then wishing to escape would be arrested by the closed gate and if he was pursued, would be taken somewhat like a wild bull in a net. It was formerly the custom, as it is now in Oriental countries, to take wild animals in this manner. A space of ground of considerable extent—usually in the vicinity of springs and brooks, where the animals were in the habit of repair-

21 Therefore, hear now this, thou
afflicted, and drunken, [a] but not
with wine:
22 Thus saith thy Lord the LORD,
and thy God *that* pleadeth [b] the
cause of his people, Behold, I have
taken out of thine hand the cup of
trembling, *even* the dregs of the cup
of my fury; thou shalt no more
drink [c] it again.
23 But [d] I will put it into the hand
of them that afflict thee; which have
said to thy soul, Bow down, that we
may go over: and thou hast laid
thy [e] body as the ground, and as
the street, to them that went over.

a La.3.15. b Ps.35.1; Je.50.34; Mi.7.9. c ch.54.7-9. d Je.25.17-29. e Ps.66.11,12.

ing morning and evening—was enclosed by nets into which the animals were driven by horsemen and hounds, and when there enclosed, they were easily taken. Such scenes are still represented in Egyptian paintings (*see* Wilkinson's *Ancient Egyptians*, vol. iii. pp. 2–36), and such a custom prevailed among the Romans. Virgil represents Æneas and Dido as repairing to a wood for the purpose of hunting at break of day, and the attendants as surrounding the grove with nets or toils.

Venatum Æneas, unaque miserrima Dido,
In nemus ire parant, ubi primos crastinus ortus
Extulerit Titan, radusque retexerit orbem.
His ego nigrantem commixta grandine nimbum,
Dum trepidant alæ, *saltusque indagine cingunt*,
Desuper infundam, et tonitru cœlum omne ciebo.
Æn. iv. 117, *sq.*

The idea here is plain. It is, that as a wild animal is secured by the toils of the hunter, and rendered unable to escape, so it was with the inhabitants of Jerusalem suffering under the wrath of God. They were humbled, and prostrate, and powerless, and were, like the stag that was caught, entirely at the disposal of him who had thus insnared them.

21. *And drunken, but not with wine.* Overcome and prostrate, but not under the influence of intoxicating drink. They were prostrate by the wrath of God.

22. *I have taken out of thy hand the cup of trembling* (see Notes on ver. 17). This verse contains a promise that they would be delivered from the effect of the wrath of God, under which they had been suffering so long. ¶ *Thou shalt no more drink it again.* Thou shalt no more be subject to similar trials and calamities (see ch. liv. 7–9). Probably the idea here is, not that Jerusalem would never be again destroyed, which would not be true, for it was afterwards subjected to severer trials under the Romans; but that *the people* who should then return—the pious exiles—should be preserved for ever after from similar sufferings. The object of the prophet is to console *them*, and this he does by the assurance that they should be subjected to such trials no more.

23. *But I will put it into the hand of them that afflict thee.* The nations that have made war upon thee, and that have reduced thee to bondage, particularly the Babylonians. The calamities which the Jews had suffered, God would transfer to their foes. ¶ *Which have said to thy soul, Bow down, that we may go over.* This is a striking description of the pride of eastern conquerors. It was not uncommon for conquerors actually to put their feet on the necks of conquered kings, and tread them in the dust. Thus in Josh. x. 24, 'Joshua called for all the men of Israel, and said unto the captains of the men of war that went with them, Come near, put your feet upon the necks of these kings.' So David says, 'Thou has given me the necks of mine enemies' (Ps. xviii. 40). 'The emperor Valerianus being through treachery taken prisoner by Sapor king of Persia, was treated by him as the basest and most abject slave; for the Persian monarch commanded the unhappy Roman to bow himself down and offer him his back, on which he set his foot in order to mount his chariot, or his horse, whenever he had occasion.' —(Lactantius, as quoted by Lowth.) Mr. Lane (*Modern Egyptians*, vol. i. p. 199) describes an annual ceremony which may serve to illustrate this passage:—'A considerable number of Durweeshes, says he (I am sure there were not less than sixty, but I could not count their number), laid themselves down upon the ground, side by side, as close as possible to each other, having their backs

upwards, having their legs extended, and their arms placed together beneath their foreheads. When the Sheikh approached, his horse hesitated several minutes to step upon the back of the first prostrate man; but being pulled and urged on

CEREMONY OF THE DOSEH OR TREADING.—From Lane's Modern Egyptians.

behind, he at length stepped upon them; and then without apparent fear, ambled with a high pace over them all, led by two persons, who ran over the prostrate men, one sometimes treading on the feet, and the other on the heads. Not one of the men thus trampled on by the horse seemed to be hurt; but each the moment that the animal had passed over him, jumped up and followed the Sheikh. Each of them received two treads from the horse, one from one of his fore-legs, and a second from a hind-leg.' It seems probable that this is a relic of an ancient usage alluded to in the Bible, in which captives were made to lie down on the ground, and the conqueror rode insultingly over them. ¶ *Thou hast laid thy body as the ground.* That is, you were utterly humbled and prostrated (comp. Ps. lxvi. 11, 12). From all this, however, the promise is, that they should be rescued and delivered. The account of their deliverance is contained in the following chapter (ch. lii. 1–12); and the assurance of rescue is there made more cheering and glorious by directing the eye forward to the coming of the Messiah (ch. lii. 13–15; liii. 1–12), and to the glorious results which would follow from his advent (ch. liv. *sq.*) These chapters are all connected, and they should be read continuously. Material injury is done to the sense by the manner in which the division is made, if indeed any division should have been made at all.

CHAPTER LII.

ANALYSIS.

THIS chapter is intimately connected with the preceding, and, with that, constitutes one connected portion (see the analysis of chapter li.) This portion, however, extends only to ver. 13 of this chapter, where there commences a prophecy extending through ch. liii., relating solely to the Messiah, and constituting the most important and interesting part of the Old Testament. In this chapter, the object is to console the pious part of the Jewish community. The general topic is, the promise of a rich blessing, first at the deliverance from the captivity at Babylon, and then, in a more complete sense, at the coming of the Messiah. The chapter comprises the following topics:—

1. Jerusalem, long in bondage, is called on to arise and shake herself from the dust, and to put on her beautiful garments (1, 2). She is addressed in accordance with language that is common in Isaiah, and the other prophets, as a female sitting on the ground, covered with dust, and mourning over her desolations.

2. JEHOVAH expressly promises to deliver his people from their captivity and bondage (3–6). In stating this, he says (3), that they had sold themselves for nothing, and should be redeemed without money; he appeals to the fact that he had delivered them from Egyptian oppression in former years, and that he was as able to deliver them now (4); and he says (5, 6), that he would have compassion on them now that they were suffering under their grievous bondage, and would furnish them with the most ample demonstration that he alone was God.

3. The prophet, in vision, sees the messenger on the mountains that comes to proclaim restoration to Zion (7, 8). He speaks of the beauty of the feet of him who bears the glad message (7); and says that when that messenger is seen bearing the glad tidings, 'the watchman' should join in the exultation (8).

4. Jerusalem, and all the waste and desolate regions of Judea, are called on to break out into singing at the glad and glorious events which would occur when the people of God should be again restored (9, 10).

5. In view of all this, the people are called on to depart from Babylon, and to return to their own land (11, 12). They were to go out pure. They were not to contaminate themselves with the polluted objects of idolatry. They were about to bear back again to Jerusalem the consecrated vessels of the house of JEHOVAH, and they should be clean and holy. They should not go out with haste, as if driven out, but they would go defended by JEHOVAH, and conducted by him to their own land.

6. At ver. 13, the subject and the scene changes. The eye of the prophet becomes fixed on that greater future event to which the deliverance from Babylon was preparatory, and the whole attention becomes absorbed in the person, the manner of life, and the work of the Messiah. This part of the chapter (13–15), is an essential part of the prophecy which is continued through ch. liii., and should by no means have been separated from it. In this portion of the prophecy, all reference to the captivity at Babylon ceases; and the eye of the prophet is fixed, without vacillating, on the person of the Redeemer. In no other portion of the Old Testament is there so clear and sublime a description of the Messiah as is furnished here; and no other portion demands so profoundly and prayerfully the attention of those who would understand the great mystery of redeeming mercy and love.

AWAKE, awake; put on thy strength, O Zion; put on thy beautiful garments, O Jerusalem, the holy [a]city: for [b]henceforth there shall no more come unto thee the uncircumcised and the unclean.

a Ne.11.1; Re.21.2,27. *b* Na.1.15.

CHAPTER LII.

1. *Awake, awake* (see Notes on ch. li. 9). This address to Jerusalem is intimately connected with the closing verses of the preceding chapter. Jerusalem is there represented as down-trodden in the dust before her enemies. Here she is described under the image of a female that had been clad in the habiliments of mourning, and she is now called on to arise from this condition, and to put on the garments that would be indicative of gladness and of joy. The idea is, that the time had come now in which she was to be delivered from her long captivity, and was to be restored to her former prosperity and splendour. ¶ *Put on thy strength.* Heb. 'Clothe thyself with thy strength.' The idea is, exert thyself, be strong, bold, confident; arise from thy dejection, and become courageous as one does when he is about to engage in an enterprise that promises success, and that demands effort. ¶ *Put*

2 Shake [a] thyself from the dust; arise, *and* sit down, O Jerusalem: loose thyself from the bands of thy neck, O captive daughter of Zion.

a Zec.2.7.

on thy beautiful garments. Jerusalem is here addressed, as she often is, as a female (see Note on ch. i. 8). She was to lay aside the garments expressive of grief and of captivity, and deck herself with those which were appropriate to a state of prosperity. ¶ *The uncircumcised and the unclean.* The idea is, that those only should enter Jerusalem and dwell there who would be worshippers of the true God. The uncircumcised are emblems of the impure, the unconverted, and the idolatrous; and the meaning is, that in future times the church would be pure and holy. It cannot mean that *no* uncircumcised man or idolater would ever again enter the city of Jerusalem, for this would not be true. It was a fact that Antiochus and his armies, and Titus and his army entered Jerusalem, and undoubtedly hosts of others did also who were not circumcised. But this refers to the future times, when the church of God would be pure. Its members would, in the main, be possessors of the true religion, and would adorn it. Probably, therefore, the view of the prophet extended to the purer and happier times under the Messiah, when the church should be characteristically and eminently holy, and when, as a great law of that church, none should be admitted, who did not profess that they were converted.

2. *Shake thyself from the dust.* To sit on the ground, to sit in the dust, is an expression descriptive of mourning (Job ii. 13). Jerusalem is here called on to arise and shake off the dust, as indicating that the days of her grief were ended, and that she was about to be restored to her former beauty and splendour. ¶ *Arise* and *sit down.* There is an incongruity in this expression in our translation, which does not occur in the original. The idea in the Hebrew is not that which seems to be implied in this expression to arise and sit down in *the same place*, but it means to arise from the dust, and sit in a more elevated, or honourable place. She had been represented as sitting on the earth, where her loose flowing robes would be supposed to become covered with dust. She is here called on to arise from that humble condition, and to occupy the divan, or a chair of dignity and honour. Lowth renders this, 'Ascend thy lofty seat,' and supposes it means that she was to occupy a throne, or an elevated seat of honour, and he quotes oriental customs to justify this interpretation. Noyes renders it, 'Arise and sit erect.' The Chaldee renders it, 'Rise, sit upon the throne of thy glory.' The following quotation, from Jowett's *Christian Researches*, will explain the custom which is here alluded to: 'It is no uncommon thing to see an individual, or group of persons, even when very well dressed, sitting with their feet drawn under them, upon the bare earth, passing whole hours in idle conversation. Europeans would require a chair, but the natives here prefer the ground. In the heat of summer and autumn, it is pleasant to them to while away their time in this manner, under the shade of a tree. Richly adorned females, as well as men, may often be seen thus amusing themselves. As may naturally be expected, with whatever care they may, at first sitting down, choose their place, yet the flowing dress by degrees gathers up the dust; as this occurs, they, from time to time, arise, adjust themselves, shake off the dust, and then sit down again. The captive daughter of Zion, therefore, brought down to the dust of suffering and oppression, is commanded to arise and shake herself from that dust, and then, with grace, and dignity, and composure, and security, to *sit down;* to take, as it were, again her seat and her rank, amid the company of the nations of the earth, which had before afflicted her, and trampled her to the earth.' ¶ *Loose thyself from the bands of thy neck.* Jerusalem had been a captive, and confined as a prisoner. She is now called on to cast off these chains from her neck, and to be again at liberty. In captivity, chains or bands were attached to various parts of the body. They were usually affixed to the wrists or ankles, but it would seem also that

3 For thus saith the LORD, Ye have
sold [a] yourselves for nought; and ye
shall be redeemed without money.
4 For thus saith the Lord GOD,
My people went down aforetime into
Egypt to sojourn there; and the
Assyrians oppressed them without
cause.

[a] Ro.7.14-25.

sometimes collars were affixed to the neck. The idea is, that the Jews, who had been so long held captive, were about to be released, and restored to their own land.

3. *Ye have sold yourselves for nought.* You became captives and prisoners without any price being paid for you. You *cost* nothing to those who made you prisoners. The idea is, that as they who had made them prisoners had done so without paying any price for them, it was equitable that they should be released in the same manner. When their captors had paid nothing for them, God would suffer nothing to be paid for them in turn; and they should be released, as they had been sold, without a price paid for them. Perhaps God intends here to reproach them for selling themselves in this manner without *any* compensation of any kind, and to show them the folly of it; but, at the same time, he intends to assure them that no price would be paid for their ransom. ¶ *Ye shall be redeemed.* You shall be delivered from your long and painful captivity without any price being paid to the Babylonians. This was to be a remarkable proof of the power of God. Men do not usually give up captives and slaves, in whatever way they may have taken them, without demanding a price or ransom. But here God says that he designs to effect their deliverance without any such price being demanded or paid, and that as they had gone into captivity unpurchased, so they should return unpurchased. Accordingly he so overruled events as completely to effect this. The Babylonians, perhaps, in no way could have been induced to surrender them. God, therefore, designed to raise up Cyrus, a mild, just, and equitable prince; and to dispose him to suffer the exiles to depart, and to aid them in their return to their own land. In this way, they were rescued without money and without price, by the interposition of another.

4. *For thus saith the Lord* GOD. In order to show them that he could redeem them without money, God reminds them of what had been done in former times. The numerous captives in Egypt, whose services were so valuable to the Egyptians, and whom the Egyptians were so unwilling to suffer to depart, he had rescued by his own power, and had delivered for ever from that bondage. The idea here is, that with the same ease he could rescue the captives in Babylon, and restore them to their own land without a price. ¶ *My people went down.* That is, Jacob and his sons. The phrase 'went down,' is applied to a journey to Egypt, because Judea was a mountainous and elevated country compared with Egypt, and a journey there was in fact *a descent* to a more level and lower country. ¶ *To sojourn there.* Not to dwell there permanently, but to remain there only for a time. They went in fact only to remain until the severity of the famine should have passed by, and until they could return with safety to the land of Canaan. ¶ *And the Assyrians oppressed them without cause.* A considerable variety has existed in the interpretation of this passage. The LXX. render it, 'And to the Assyrians they were carried by force.' Some have supposed that this refers to the oppressions that they experienced in Egypt, and that the name 'Assyrian' is here given to Pharaoh. So Forerius and Cajetan understand it. They suppose that the name, 'the Assyrian,' became, in the apprehension of the Jews, the common name of that which was proud, oppressive, and haughty, and might therefore be used to designate Pharaoh. But there are insuperable objections to this. For the name 'the Assyrian' is not elsewhere given to Pharaoh in the Scriptures, nor can it be supposed to be given to him but with great impropriety. It is not true that Pharaoh was an Assyrian; nor is it true that the Israelites were oppressed by the Assyrians while they remained in Egypt. Others have supposed that this refers to Nebuchadnezzar

5 Now, therefore, what have I here, saith the LORD, that my people is taken away for nought? they that rule over them make them to howl, saith the LORD; that my name continually every day [a] *is* blasphemed.

a Ro.2.24.

and the Chaldeans in general, and that the name 'the Assyrian' is given them in a large and general sense, as ruling over that which constituted the empire of Assyria, and that the prophet here refers to the calamities which they were suffering in Babylon. But the objection to this is not the less decisive. It is true that Babylon was formerly a part or province of Assyria, and true also that in the time of the Jewish captivity it was the capital of the kingdom of which the former empire of Assyria became a subject province. But the name Babylonian, in the Scriptures, is kept distinct from that of Assyrian, and they are not used interchangeably. Nor does the connection of the passage require us to understand it in this sense. The whole passage is in a high degree elliptical, and something must be supplied to make out the sense. The general design of it is, to show that God would certainly deliver the Jews from the captivity at Babylon without money. For this purpose, the prophet appeals to the former instances of his interposition when deliverance had been effected in that way. A *paraphrase* of the passage, and a filling up of the parts which are omitted in the brief and abrupt manner of the prophet, will show the sense. 'Ye have been sold for nought, and ye shall be ransomed without price. As a proof that I can do it, and will do it, remember that my people went down formerly to Egypt, and designed to sojourn there for a little time, and that they were there reduced to slavery, and oppressed by Pharaoh, but that I ransomed them without money, and brought them forth by my own power. Remember, further, how often the Assyrian has oppressed them also, without cause. Remember the history of Sennacherib, Tiglath-pileser, and Salmaneser, and how they have laid the land waste, and remember also how I have delivered it from these oppressions. With the same certainty, and the same ease, I can deliver the people from the captivity at Babylon.' The prophet, therefore, refers to different periods and events; and the idea is, that God had delivered them when they had been oppressed *alike* by the Egyptian, and by the Assyrians, and that he who had so often interposed would also rescue them from their oppression in Babylon.

5. *Now, therefore, what have I here?* In Babylon, referring to the captivity of the Jews there. The idea is, that a state of things existed there which demanded his interposition as really as it did when his people had been oppressed by the Egyptians, or by the Assyrian. His people had been taken away for nought; they were subject to cruel oppressions; and his own name was continually blasphemed. In this state of things, it is inferred, that he would certainly come to their rescue, and that his own perfections as well as their welfare demanded that he should interpose to redeem them. The phrase, 'what have I here?' is equivalent to saying, what shall I do? what am I properly called on to do? or what reason is there now in Babylon for my interposition to rescue my people? It is implied, that such was the state of things, that God felt that there was something that demanded his interposition. ¶ *That my people is taken away for nought.* This was one thing existing in Babylon that demanded his interposition. His people had been made captive by the Chaldeans, and were now suffering under their oppressions. This had been done 'for nought;' that is, it had been done without any just claim. It was on their part a mere act of gross and severe oppression, and this demanded the interposition of a righteous God. ¶ *They that rule over them make them to howl.* Lowth renders this, 'They that are lords over them make their boast of it.' Noyes renders it, 'And their tyrants exult.' The LXX. render it, 'My people are taken away for nought: wonder ye, and raise a mournful cry' (ὀλολύζετε). Jerome renders it, 'Their lords act unjustly, and they therefore howl when they are de-

6 Therefore my people shall know my name: therefore *they shall know* in that day that I *am* he that doth speak: behold, *it is* I.

7 How beautiful [a] upon the mountains [b] are the feet of him that bringeth good tidings, that publisheth peace; that bringeth good tidings of [c] good, that publisheth salvation; that saith unto Zion, Thy God reigneth!

a Na.1.15; Ro.10.15. b ch.25.6,7; Ca.2.8. c Lu.2.10,11.

livered to torments.' Aben Ezra supposes that by 'their lords' here, or those who rule over them, are meant the rulers of the Jewish people, and that the idea is, that they lament and howl over the calamities and oppressions of the people. But it is probable, after all, that our translators have given the true sense of the text, and that the idea is, that they were suffering such grievous oppressions in Babylon as to make them lift up the cry of lamentation and of grief. This was a reason why God should interpose as he had done in former times, and bring deliverance. ¶ *And my name continually every day is blasphemed.* That is, in Babylon. The proud and oppressive Babylonians delight to add to the sorrows of the exiles by reproaching the name of their God, and by saying that he was unable to defend them and their city from ruin. This is the third reason why God would interpose to rescue them. The three reasons in this verse are, that they had been taken away for nought; that they were suffering grievous and painful oppression; and that the name of God was reproached. On all these accounts he felt that he *had* something to do in Babylon, and that his interposition was demanded.

6. *Therefore my people shall know my name.* The idea in this verse is, that his people should have such exhibitions of his power as to furnish to them demonstration that he was God.

7. *How beautiful upon the mountains.* This passage is applied by Paul to the ministers of the gospel (see Rom. x. 15). The meaning here seems to be this: Isaiah was describing the certain return of the Jews to their own land. He sees in vision the heralds announcing their return to Jerusalem running on the distant hills. A herald bearing good news is a beautiful object; and he says that his feet are beautiful; *i.e.*, his *running* is beautiful. He came to declare that the long and painful captivity was closed, and that the holy city and its temple were again to rise with splendour, and that peace and plenty and joy were to be spread over the land. Such a messenger coming with haste, the prophet says, would be a beautiful object. Some have supposed (*see* Campbell *on the Gospels*, Diss. v. p. 11, § 3, 4), that the idea here is, that *the feet* of messengers when they travelled in the dust were naturally offensive and disgusting, but that the messenger of peace and prosperity to those who had been oppressed and afflicted by the ravages of war, was so charming as to transform a most disagreeable into a pleasing object. But I cannot see any such allusion here. It is true that the feet of those who had travelled far in dry and dusty roads would present a spectacle offensive to the beholder; and it is true also, as Dr. Campbell suggests, that the consideration that they who were coming were messengers of peace and safety would convert deformity into beauty, and make us behold with delight this indication of their embassy. But it seems to me that this passage has much higher beauty. The idea in the mind of the prophet is not, that the messenger is *so near* that the sordid appearance of his feet could be seen. The beholder is supposed to be standing amidst the ruins of the desolated city, and the messenger is seen *running* on the distant hills. The long anticipated herald announcing that these ruins are to rise, at length appears. Seen on the distant hills, running rapidly, he is a beautiful object. It is his feet, his *running*, his haste, that attracts attention; an indication that he bears a message of joy, and that the nation is about to be restored. Nahum, who is supposed to have lived after Isaiah, has evidently copied from him this beautiful image:—

> Behold upon the mountains the feet of the joyful messenger,
> Of him that announceth peace;

8 Thy watchmen shall lift up the voice; with the voice together shall they sing; for they shall see [a] eye to eye, when the LORD shall bring again Zion.

[a] 1 Cor.13.12.

Celebrate, O Judah, thy festivals: perform thy vows;
For no more shall pass through thee the wicked one;
He is utterly cut off. Nah. i. 15.

¶ *That publisheth peace.* This declaration is *general*, that the coming of such a messenger would be attended with joy. The particular and special idea here is, that it would be a joyful announcement that this captivity was ended, and that Zion was about to be restored. ¶ *That bringeth good tidings of good.* He announces that which is good or which is a joyful message. ¶ *That saith unto Zion, thy God reigneth.* That is, thy God has delivered the people from their captivity, and is about to reign again in Zion. This was applied at first to the return from the captivity. Paul, as has been already observed, applies it to the ministers of the gospel. That is, it is language which will well express the nature of the message which the ministers of the gospel bear to their fellow-men. The sense is here, that the coming of a messenger bringing good tidings is universally agreeable to men. And it the coming of a messenger announcing that peace is made, is pleasant; or if the coming of such a messenger declaring that the captivity at Babylon was ended, was delightful, how much more so should be the coming of the herald announcing that man may be at peace with his Maker?

8. *Thy watchmen.* This language is taken from the custom of placing watchmen on the walls of a city, or on elevated towers, who could see if an enemy approached, and who of course would be the first to discern a messenger at a distance who was coming to announce good news. The idea is, that there would be as great joy at the announcement of the return of the exiles, *as if* they who were stationed on the wall should see the long-expected herald on the distant hills, coming to announce that they were about to return, and that the city and temple were about to be rebuilt. It was originally applicable to the return from Babylon. But it contains also the *general* truth that they who are appointed to watch over Zion and its interests, will rejoice at all the tokens of God's favour to his people, and especially when he comes to bless them after long times of darkness, depression, and calamity. It is by no means, therefore, departing from the spirit of this passage, to apply it to the joy of the ministers of religion in the visits of Divine mercy to a church and people. ¶ *Shall lift up the voice.* That is, with rejoicing. ¶ *With the voice together shall they sing.* They shall mingle their praises and thanksgivings. The idea is, that all who are appointed to guard Zion, should feel a common interest in her welfare, and rejoice when the Lord comes to visit and bless his people. The Hebrew here is more abrupt and emphatic than our common translation would make it. It is literally, 'The voice of thy watchmen! They lift up the voice together; they sing'—as if the prophet suddenly heard a shout. It is the exulting shout of the watchmen of Zion; and it comes as *one* voice, with no discord, no jarring. ¶ *For they shall see eye to eye.* Lowth renders this, 'For face to face shall they see.' Noyes, 'For with their own eyes shall they behold.' Jerome renders it, *Oculo ad oculum*—'Eye to eye.' The LXX. render it, 'Οφθαλμοὶ πρὸς ὀφθαλμοὺς, κ.τ.λ.—'Eyes shall look to eyes when the Lord shall have mercy upon Zion.' Interpreters have been divided in regard to its meaning. The sense may be, either that they shall see face to face, *i.e.*, distinctly, clearly, as when one is near another; or it may mean that they shall be *united*—they shall contemplate the same object, or look steadily at the same thing. Rosenmüller, Gesenius, Forerius, Junius, and some others, understand it in the former sense. So the Chaldee, 'For they shall see with their own eyes the great things which the Lord will do when he shall bring back his own glory to Zion.' The phrase in Hebrew occurs in no other place, except in Num. xiv. 14, which our translators have rendered,

9 Break forth into joy, sing together, ye waste places of Jerusalem: for the LORD hath comforted his people, he hath redeemed Jerusalem.

10 The [a] LORD hath made bare his holy arm in the eyes of all the nations; and all [b] the ends of the earth shall see the salvation of our God.

a Ps.98.2,3.

b Lu.3.6.

'For thou, LORD, art seen *face to face*.' Heb. 'Eye to eye;' that is, near, openly, manifestly, without any veil or interposing medium. The expression, 'face to face,' meaning openly, plainly, manifestly, as one sees who is close to another, occurs frequently in the Bible (see Gen. xxxii. 30; Ex. xxxiii. 11; Deut. v. 4; xxxiv. 10; Judg. vi. 22; Prov. xxvii. 19; Ezek. xxx. 35; Acts xxv. 16; 1 Cor. xiii. 12; 2 John 12; 3 John 14). So the phrase, 'mouth to mouth,' occurs in a similar sense (Num. xii. 8). And there can be but little doubt, it seems to me, that this is the sense here, and that the prophet means to say, that the great and marvellous doings of JEHOVAH would be seen openly and manifestly, and that the watchmen would thence have occasion to rejoice. Another reason for this opinion, besides the fact that it accords with the common usage, is, that the phrase, 'to see eye to eye,' in the sense of being united and harmonious, is not very intelligible. It is not easy to form an image or conception of the watchman in this attitude as denoting harmony. To look into the eyes of each other does not of necessity denote harmony, for men oftentimes do this for other purposes. The idea therefore is, that when JEHOVAH should bring back and bless his people, the watchmen would have a full and glorious exhibition of his mercy and goodness, and the result would be, that they would greatly rejoice, and unitedly celebrate his name. According to this interpretation, it does not mean that the ministers of religion would have the same precise views, or embrace the same doctrines, however true this may be, or however desirable in itself, but that they would have an open, clear, and bright manifestation of the presence of God, and would lift up their voices together with exultation and praise. ¶ *When the Lord shall bring again Zion.* Zion here denotes the people who dwelt in Jerusalem; and the idea is, when the Lord shall again restore them to their own land. It is not a departure from the sense of the passage, however, to apply it in a more general manner, and to use it as demonstrating that any signal interposition of God in favour of his people should be the occasion of joy, and shall lead the ministers of religion to exult in God, and to praise his name.

9. *Break forth into joy.* Jerusalem, at the time here referred to, was lying waste and in ruins. This call on the waste places of Jerusalem to break out into expressions of praise, is in accordance with a style which frequently occurs in Isaiah, and in other sacred writers, by which inanimate objects are called on to manifest their joy (see Notes on ch. xiv. 7, 8; xlii. 11). ¶ *For the* LORD *hath comforted his people.* That is, he *does* comfort his people, and redeem them. This is seen by the prophet in vision, and to his view it is represented as if it were passing before his eyes. ¶ *He hath redeemed Jerusalem.* On the meaning of the word 'redeemed,' see Notes on ch. xliii. 1–3. The idea here is, that JEHOVAH was about to restore his people from their long captivity, and again to cause Jerusalem to be rebuilt.

10. *The* LORD *hath made bare his holy arm.* That is, in delivering his people from bondage. This metaphor is taken from warriors, who made bare the arm for battle; and the sense is, that God had come to the rescue of his people as a warrior, and that his interpositions would be seen and recognized and acknowledged by all the nations. The metaphor is derived from the manner in which the Orientals dressed. The following extract from Jowett's *Christian Researches* will explain the language:—'The loose sleeve of the Arab shirt, as well as that of the outer garment, leaves the arm so completely free, that in an instant the left hand passing up the right arm makes it bare; and this is done when a person, a soldier, for ex-

11 Depart [a] ye, depart ye, go ye out from thence, touch [b] no unclean *thing;* go ye out of the midst of her; be [c] ye clean, that bear the vessels of the LORD.

a Zec.2.6,7; 2Co.6.17; Re.18.4.
b Le.15.5,&c.; Hag.2.13.
c Le.22.2,&c.

ample, about to strike with the sword, intends to give the arm full play. The image represents JEHOVAH as suddenly prepared to inflict some tremendous, yet righteous judgment, so effectual "that all the ends of the earth shall see the salvation of God."' The phrase '*holy* arm,' seems to mean that God would be engaged in a holy and just cause. It would not be an arm of conquest, or of oppression; but it would be made bare in a holy cause, and all its inflictions would be righteous. ¶ *And all the ends of the earth.* For an explanation of the phrase 'the ends of the earth,' see Notes on ch. xl. 28. The meaning here is, that the deliverance of his people referred to would be so remarkable as to be conspicuous to all the world. The most distant nations would see it, and would be constrained to recognize his hand. It was fulfilled in the rescue of the nation from the captivity at Babylon. The conquest of Babylon was an event that was so momentous in its consequences, as to be known to all the kingdoms of the earth; and the proclamation of Cyrus (Ezra i. 1, 2), and the consequent restoration of his people to their own land, were calculated to make the name of JEHOVAH known to all nations.

11. *Depart ye, depart ye.* This is a direct address to the exiles in their captivity. The same command occurs in ch. xlviii. 20 (see Notes on that place). It is *repeated* here for the sake of emphasis; and the urgency of the command implies that there was some delay likely to be apprehended on the part of the exiles themselves. The fact seems to have been, that though the captivity was at first attended with every circumstance fitted to give pain, and though they were subjected to *many* privations and sorrows in Babylon (see Ps. cxxxvii.), yet that many of them became strongly attached to a residence there, and were strongly indisposed to return. They were there seventy years. Most of those who were made captive would have died before the close of the exile. Their children, who constituted the generation to whom the command to return would be addressed, would have known the land of their fathers only by report. It was a distant land; and was to be reached only by a long and perilous journey across a pathless desert. They had been born in Babylon. It was their home; and there were the graves of their parents and kindred. Some had been advanced to posts of office and honour: many, it is probable, had lands, and friends, and property in Babylon. The consequence would, therefore, be, that there would be strong reluctance on their part to leave the country of their exile, and to encounter the perils and trials incident to a return to their own land. It is not improbable, also, that many of them may have formed improper connections and attachments in that distant land, and that they would be unwilling to relinquish them, and return to the land of their fathers. It was necessary, therefore, that the most urgent commands should be addressed to them, and the strongest motives presented to them, to induce them to return to the country of their fathers. And after all, it is evident that but comparatively a small portion of the exile Jews ever were prevailed on to leave Babylon, and to adventure upon the perilous journey of a return to Zion. ¶ *Touch no unclean thing.* Separate yourselves wholly from an idolatrous nation, and preserve yourselves pure. The apostle Paul (2 Cor. vi. 17, 18) has applied this to Christians, and uses it as expressing the obligation to come out from the world, and to be separate from all its influences. Babylon is regarded by the apostle as not an unapt emblem of the world, and the command to come out from her as not an improper expression of the obligation to the friends of the Redeemer to be separate from all that is evil. John (Rev. xviii. 4) has applied this passage also to denote the duty of true Christians to separate themselves from the mystical Babylon—the papal community—and not to be partaker of her sins. The passage is applied in both

12 For ye shall not go out with haste, nor go by flight: for the LORD will go before you; and the God of Israel [1] *will be* your rereward.

1 *gather you up.*

these instances, because Babylon, in Scripture language, is regarded as emblematic of whatever is oppressive, proud, arrogant, persecuting, impure, and abominable. ¶ *That bear the vessels of the* LORD. That bear again to your own land the sacred vessels of the sanctuary. It is to be remembered that when the Jews were taken to Babylon, Nebuchadnezzar carried there all the sacred utensils of the temple, and that they were used in their festivals as common vessels in Babylon (2 Chron. xxxvii. 18; Dan. v. 2–5). These vessels Cyrus commanded to be again restored, when the exiles returned to their own land (Ezra i. 7–11). They whose office it was to carry them, were the priests and Levites (Num. i. 50; iv. 15); and the command here pertains particularly to them. They were required to be holy; to feel the importance of their office, and to be separate from all that is evil. The passage has no original reference to ministers of the gospel, but the *principle* is implied that they who are appointed to serve God as his ministers in any way should be pure and holy.

12. *For ye shall not go out with haste.* As if driven out, or compelled to flee. You shall not go from Babylon as your fathers went from Egypt, in a rapid flight, and in a confused and tumultuous manner (see Deut. xvi. 3). The idea here is, that they should have time to prepare themselves to go out, and to become fit to bear the vessels of the Lord. It was a fact that when they left Babylon they did it with the utmost deliberation, and had ample time to make any preparation that was necessary. ¶ *For the* LORD *will go before you.* JEHOVAH will conduct you, as a general advances at the head of an army. The figure here is taken from the march of an army, and the image is that of JEHOVAH as the leader or head of the host in the march through the desert between Babylon and Jerusalem (see Notes on ch. xl. 3, 4). ¶ *And the God of Israel* will be *your rereward.* Marg. 'Gather you up.' The Hebrew word used here (אָסַף) means properly *to collect*, to gather together, as fruits, &c. It is then applied to the act of bringing up the rear of an army; and means to be a rear-ward, or guard, *agmen claudere*—as collecting, and bringing together the stragglers, and defending the army in its march, from an attack in the rear. The LXX. render it, 'The God of Israel is he who collects you' (ὁ ἐπισυνάγων ὑμᾶς), *i.e.*, brings up the rear. The Chaldee, 'The God of Israel will collect together your captivity.'—Here the chapter should have closed, for here closes the account of the return of the exiles from Babylon. The mind of the prophet seems here to leave the captive Jews on their way to their own land, with JEHOVAH going at their head, and guarding the rear of the returning band, and to have passed to the contemplation of him of whose coming all these events were preliminary and introductory—the Messiah. *Perhaps* the *rationale* of this apparent transition is this. It is undoubtedly the doctrine of the Bible that he who was revealed as the guide of his people in ancient times, and who appeared under various names, as 'the angel of JEHOVAH,' 'the angel of the covenant,' &c., was he who afterwards became incarnate—the Saviour of the world. So the prophet seems to have regarded him; and here fixing his attention on the JEHOVAH who was thus to guide his people and be their defence, by an easy transition the mind is carried forward to the time when he would be incarnate, and would die for men. Leaving, therefore, so to speak, the contemplation of him as conducting his people across the barren wastes which separated Babylon from Judea, the mind is, by no unnatural transition, carried forward to the time when he would become a man of sorrows, and would redeem and save the world. According to this supposition, it is the same glorious Being whom Isaiah sees as the protector of his people, and almost in the same instant as the man of sorrows; and the contemplation of him as the suffering Messiah becomes so absorbing and intense, that he ab-

CHAPTERS LII. 13–15; LIII.

THE most important portion of Isaiah, and of the Old Testament, commences here, and here should have been the beginning of a new chapter. It is the description of the suffering Messiah, and is continued to the close of the next chapter. As the closing verses of this chapter are connected with the following chapter, and as it is of great importance to have just views of the design of this portion of Isaiah, it is proper in this place to give an analysis of this part of the prophecy. And as no other part of the Bible has excited so much the attention of the friends and foes of Christianity; as so various and conflicting views have prevailed in regard to its meaning: and as the proper interpretation of the passage must have an important bearing on the controversy with Jews and infidels, and on the practical views of Christians, I shall be justified in going into an examination of its meaning at considerably greater length than has been deemed necessary in other portions of the prophecy. It may be remarked in general—(1.) That if the common interpretation of the passage, as describing a suffering Saviour, be correct, then it settles the controversy with the *Jews,* and demonstrates that *their* notions of the Messiah are false. (2.) If this was written at the time when it is claimed by Christians to have been written, then it settles the controversy with infidels. The description is so particular and minute; the correspondence with the life, the character, and the death of the Lord Jesus, is so complete, that it *could* not have been the result of conjecture or accident. At the same time, it is a correspondence which could not have been brought about by an impostor who meant to avail himself of this ancient prophecy to promote his designs; for a large portion of the circumstances are such as *did not depend on himself,* but grew out of the feelings and purposes of others. *On the supposition that this had been found as an ancient prophecy, it would have been impossible for any impostor so to have shaped the course of events as to have made his character and life appear to be a fulfilment of it.* And unless the infidel could either make it out that this prophecy was not in existence, or that, being in existence, it was possible for a deceiver *to create* an exact coincidence between it and his life and character and death, then, in all honesty, he should admit that it was given by inspiration, and that the Bible is true. (3.) A correct exposition of this will be of inestimable value in giving to the Christian just views of the atonement, and of the whole doctrine of redemption. Probably in no portion of the Bible of the same length, not even in the New Testament, is there to be found so clear an exhibition of the purpose for which the Saviour died. I shall endeavour, therefore, to prepare the way for an exposition of the passage, by a consideration of several points that are necessary to a correct understanding of it.

§ 1. *Evidence that it was written before the birth of Jesus of Nazareth.*

On this point there will be, and can be, no dispute among Jews and Christians. The general argument to prove this, is the same as that which demonstrates that Isaiah wrote at all before that time. For a view of this, the reader is referred to the Introduction. But this general argument may be presented in a more specific form, and includes the following particulars:—(1.) It is quoted in the New Testament as part of the prophetic writings then well known (see Matt. viii. 17; John xii. 38; Acts viii. 28–35; Rom. x. 16; 1 Pet. ii. 21–25). That the passage was in existence at the time when the New Testament was written, is manifest from these quotations. So far as the argument with the infidel is concerned, it is immaterial whether it was written 700 years before the events took place, or only fifty, or ten. It would still be prophecy, and it would still be incumbent on him to show how it came to be so accurately accomplished. (2.) It is quoted and translated by writers who undoubtedly lived before the Christian era. Thus, it is found in the Septuagint, and in the Chaldee—both of which can be demonstrated to have been made before Christ was born. (3.) There is not the slightest evidence that it has been interpolated or corrupted, or changed so as to adapt it to the Lord Jesus. It is the same in all copies, and in all versions. (4.) It has never

ruptly closes the description of him as the guide of the exiles to their own land. He sees him as a sufferer. He sees the manner and the design of his death. He contemplates the certain result of that humiliation and death in the spread of the true religion, and in the extension of his kingdom among men. Henceforward, therefore, to the end of Isaiah, we meet with no reference, if we except in a very few instances, to the condition of the exiles in Babylon, or to their return to their own land. The mind of the prophet is absorbed in describing the glories of the Messiah, and the certain spread of his gospel around the globe.

even been pretended that it has been introduced for the purpose of furnishing an argument for the truth of Christianity. No infidel has ever pretended that it does not stand on the same footing as any other portion of Isaiah. (5.) It is such a passage as Jews *would* not have forged. It is opposed to all their prevailing notions of the Messiah. They have anticipated a magnificent temporal prince and a conqueror: and one of the main reasons why they have rejected the Lord Jesus has been, that he was obscure in his origin, poor, despised, and put to death; in other words, because he has corresponded so entirely with the description here. No passage of the Old Testament has ever given them greater perplexity than this, and it is morally certain that if the Jews had ever forged a pretended prophecy of the Messiah, it would not have been in the language of this portion of Isaiah. They would have described him as the magnificent successor of David and Solomon; as a mighty prince and a warrior; as the head of universal empire, and would have said that by his victorious arms he would subdue the earth to himself, and would make Jerusalem the capital of the world. They never would have described him as despised and rejected of men, and as making his grave with the wicked in his death. (6.) Christians *could* not have forged and interpolated this. The Jews have always jealously guarded their own Scriptures; and nothing would have so certainly excited their attention as an attempt to interpolate a passage like this, furnishing at once an irrefragable argument against their opinions of the Messiah, and so obviously applicable to Jesus of Nazareth. It is, moreover, true, that no Jewish writer has ever pretended that the passage has either been forged, or changed in any way, so as to accommodate it to the opinions of Christians respecting the Messiah. These remarks may seem to be unnecessary, and this argument useless, to those who have examined the authenticity of the sacred writings. They are of use only in the argument with the enemies of Christianity. For, if this passage was written at the time when it is supposed to have been, and if it had reference to the Lord Jesus, then it demonstrates that Isaiah was inspired, and furnishes an argument for the truth of revelation which is irrefragable. It is incumbent on the unbeliever to destroy all the alleged proofs that it was written by Isaiah, or, as an honest man, he should admit the truth of inspiration and of prophecy, and yield his heart to the influence of the truth of the Bible. In general, it may be observed, that an attempt to destroy the credibility of this portion of Isaiah as having been written several hundred years before the Christian era, would destroy the credibility of all the ancient writings; and that we have *as much* evidence that this is the production of Isaiah, as we have of the credibility or the authenticity of the writings of Homer or Herodotus.

§ 2. *History of the interpretation of the passage by the Jews.*

In order to a clear understanding of the passage, it is proper to give a summary view of the modes of interpretation which have prevailed in regard to it both among Jews and Christians. For this historical view, I am indebted mainly to Hengstenberg, *Chris.* i. p. 484, *sq.* The several opinions which have prevailed among the Jewish expositors are the following:—

There is the fullest evidence that the passage was applied by the early Jews, both before and after the birth of Jesus, to the Messiah, until they were pressed by its application to Jesus of Nazareth, and were compelled in self-defence to adopt some other mode of interpretation; and even after that, it is evident, also, that not a few of the better and more pious portion of the Jewish nation still continued to regard it as descriptive of the Messiah. So obvious is the application to the Messiah, so clear and full is the description, that many of them have adopted the opinion that there would be two Messiahs, one a suffering Messiah, and the other a glorious and triumphant prince and conqueror. The Old Testament plainly foretold that the Messiah would be 'God and man; exalted and debased; master and servant; priest and victim; prince and subject; involved in death, and yet a victor over death; rich and poor; a king, a conqueror, glorious; a man of griefs, exposed to infirmities, unknown, and in a state of abjection and humiliation.'—(Calmet.) All these apparently contradictory qualities had their fulfilment in the person of Jesus of Nazareth; but they were the source of great difficulty to the Jews, and have led to the great variety of opinions which have prevailed among them in regard to him. In the Lord Jesus they harmonize; but when the Jews resolved to reject him, they were at once thrown into endless embarrassment in regard to the character, coming, and work of him whom they had so long expected. The following extract from Calmet (*Dic.*) will explain some of the modern prevailing views of him, and is necessary to a clear understanding of the grounds which have been taken in the interpretation of this prophecy:—'Some of them, as the famous Hillel, who lived, according to the Jews, before Christ, maintain that the Messiah was already come in the person of Hezekiah; others, that the belief of the coming of the Messiah is no article of faith. Buxtorf says, that the greater part of the modern Rabbins believe that the Messiah has been come a good while, but keeps himself concealed in some part of the world or other, and will not manifest himself, because of the sins of the Jews. Jarchi affirms, that the Hebrews believe that the Messiah was born on the day of the last destruction of Jerusalem by the Romans. Some assign him the terrestrial paradise for his habitation; others the city of Rome, where, according to the Talmudists, he keeps himself concealed among the leprous and infirm, at the gate of the city, expecting Elias to come and manifest him. A great number believe that he is yet to come, but they are strangely divided about the time and the circumstances of his coming. Some expect him at the end of 6000 years. Kimchi, who lived in the twelfth century, believed that the coming of the Messiah was very near. Some have fixed the time of the end of their misfortunes to A.D. 1492, others to 1598, others to 1600, others yet later. Last of all, tired out with these uncertainties, they have pronounced an anathema against any who shall pretend to calculate the time of the coming of the Messiah.'

It is capable, however, of clear demonstration, that the ancient Jews, before the birth of Jesus, were not thus embarrassed in the interpretation of their own prophets. The following extracts from their writings will show that the opinion early prevailed that the passage before us had reference to the Messiah, and that they had to some extent right views of him. Even by the later Jewish interpreters who give a different exposition of the prophecy, it is admitted that it was formerly referred to the Messiah. This is admitted by Aben Ezra, Jarchi, Abarbanel, and Moses Nachmanides. Among the testimonies of the ancient Jews are the following:—The Chaldee Paraphrast, Jonathan, expressly refers it to the Messiah. Thus, in ver. 13 of this chapter, he renders the first member, 'Behold, my servant the Messiah shall prosper.' Thus, in the Medrasch Tanchuma (an old commentary on the Pentateuch), on the words 'Behold, my servant shall prosper,' it is remarked, This is the king Messiah, who is high, and lifted up, and very exalted, higher than Abraham, exalted above Moses, higher than the ministering angels.' Similar is the language of Rabbi Moses Haddarschan on Gen. i. 3: 'JEHOVAH spake: Messiah, my righteous one, those who are concealed with thee, will be such that their sins will bring a heavy yoke upon thee. The Messiah answered: Lord of the world, I cheerfully take upon myself those plagues and sorrows. Immediately, therefore, the Messiah took upon himself, out of love, all torments and sufferings, as it is written in Isa. liii., "He was abused and oppressed."' Many other passages may be seen collected by Hengstenberg, *Chris.* i. 485, 486.

But this interpretation was abandoned by the Jewish interpreters when the passage was urged against them by Christians as demonstrating that Jesus of Nazareth was the Messiah, and when they could not reconcile it with their prevailing notions that the Messiah was to be a magnificent temporal prince. Gesenius asserts that 'the later Jews, no doubt, relinquished this interpretation in consequence of their controversy with Christians.' The Jews early formed the opinion that the Messiah was to be a king like David and Solomon, and was to be distinguished as a conqueror. They, therefore, looked exclusively at the passages of the Old Testament which spoke of his exaltation, and they were rendered averse to applying a passage like this to him, which spoke of his poverty, rejection, humiliation, and death. They did not, or would not, understand how passages apparently so contradictory, could be applied to the same individual; and they therefore fixed their attention on those which predicted his exaltation and majesty, and rejected the idea that the Messiah would be a sufferer. So long as they applied this portion of Isaiah to the Messiah, they could not deny that there was a remarkable correspondence between it and Jesus of Nazareth, and they were unable to meet the force of the argument thence derived in favour of his claims to the Messiahship. It became necessary, therefore, for the Jews to seek some other explanation of the passage, and to deny that it had reference to the Messiah. Accordingly, the great effort of the Jewish interpreters has been to ascertain to whom the passage can be made, with any show of probability, to apply. The great mass agree that it is not to be applied to the Messiah, and this is now the prevailing opinion among them.

Among the more modern Jewish expositors who agree that the passage is not to be applied to the Messiah, the following opinions have prevailed:—

1. The most commonly received opinion is, that it refers to the Jewish people. This is the opinion of Jarchi, Aben Ezra, Kimchi, Abarbanel, and Lipmann. According to them, the prophecy describes the condition of the Jews in their present calamity and exile; the firmness with which they endure it for the honour of God, and resist every temptation to forsake his law and worship; and the prosperity, honour, and glory which they shall obtain in the time of their redemption. In

ch. liii. 1-10, the heathen are regarded as speaking, and making an humble and penitential confession that they have hitherto mistaken the people of God, and unjustly despised them on account of their sufferings, since it now appears from their exaltation that those sufferings have not been inflicted on them on account of their sins.

2. Others take the appellation, 'salvation of JEHOVAH,' in the passage, to mean, the *pious* portion of the nation taken collectively, and regarded as making a kind of vicarious satisfaction for the ungodly. This class of interpreters among the Jews, however, has been small. They refer it to those among them who endure much affliction and suffering, but more especially to those who are publicly put to death. They mention particularly Rabbi Akiba as one who suffered martyrdom in this manner. This interpretation retains, indeed, the essential idea of *substitution* which runs through the passage, and it is not improbable that it is on this account that it has found so little favour with the modern Jews, since they reject with abhorrence the whole doctrine of vicarious sufferings as designed to make an atonement for others.

3. A few others among the Jews make the passage refer to an individual. Abarbanel, besides supposing that it refers to the Jewish people in general, suggests also that it may refer particularly to Isaiah. Rabbi Saadias Haggaon explained the whole as referring to Jeremiah. Still the passage is so plain in its general meaning, the reference to the Messiah is so obvious, that the Rabbins have not been able, with all their ingenuity, to propose an interpretation that shall be entirely satisfactory to their nation. It has probably been the means of the conversion of more Jews from the errors of their system to Christianity, than any other portion of their Scriptures. We know that, as it was explained and applied by Philip, it was the means of the conversion of the Ethiopian eunuch (Acts viii. 27–40). And so Jo. Isaac Levita, a learned Jew, says it was the means of first leading him to the Christian religion. 'I frankly confess,' says he, 'that this chapter first conducted me to the Christian faith. For more than a thousand times I read this chapter, and accurately compared it with many translations, I found that it contained a hundred more mysteries respecting Christ, than are found in any version.' Many similar instances occur, says Hengstenberg, in the reports of Missionaries among the Jews.

§ 3. *History of the interpretation of the passage by Christians.*

For seventeen centuries the view which was taken of this passage was uniform. By all the fathers of the Christian church it was regarded as having an indisputable reference to Christ. In their arguments with the Jews, it was quoted as containing a full refutation of their opinions respecting the Messiah, and as demonstrating that Jesus of Nazareth was he who had been so long announced by the prophets as 'he who was to come.' In their arguments with infidels, it was a strong proof to which they appealed of the truth of revelation; and in their homilies and expositions it was referred uniformly to the Lord Jesus. If we except Grotius, who supposed that it referred to Jeremiah, who, he says (Note on ch. lii. 13), was *figura Christi*—the type of the Messiah—it was not till the last quarter of the sixteenth century that this interpretation began to be called in question. The reason why the uniform exposition of the Christian church was abandoned then by any was, that it could *no longer be retained* consistently with the notions which prevailed, especially in Germany, of the Bible. The grand principle which began to prevail in the interpretation of the Bible was, that *all* which is there recorded is to be accounted for on natural principles. But if this passage refers to the Messiah, it harmonizes so exactly with the life and character of the Redeemer, and it is so entirely removed from the possible range of mere conjecture, that it cannot be accounted for except on the supposition of supernatural revelation. Many professed Christian interpreters, therefore, have sought other ways of explaining it, and have diligently inquired to whom it referred. As a *specimen* of the manner in which the exposition of the Bible has been conducted in Germany, we may just refer to the opinions which have prevailed in the interpretation of this, the plainest and most splendid of all the prophecies pertaining to the Messiah.

1. Comparatively the greatest number of the non-Messianic interpreters make the whole Jewish people the subject. A large number of German expositors, whose names may be seen in Hengstenberg's *Christol.* i. 494, have adopted this view. The only difference between this interpretation and that adopted by the later Jews is, that the German critics suppose it refers to the Jews in the Babylonish exile, while the Jews suppose that it refers to their nation suffering in their present exile.

2. It was held by Eckermann that it refers to the Jewish nation in the abstract, in opposition to its individual members. In other words, it seems to have been held that the nation in the abstract was guilty and was suffering, while the individual members were innocent, and escaped suffering and punishment.

3. It has been held that it refers to the pious part of the Jewish people, as contrasted with the ungodly. This opinion was defended by Paulus. His view is the following: The pious part of the Jewish people were carried into captivity with the ungodly, not on account of their own sins, but the sins of the latter. The ungodly inferred that the hope of the pious that JEHOVAH would help them was in vain, but as the exile came to an end, and the pious returned, they saw that they had erred, and that their hope was well-grounded. They deeply lament, therefore, that they have not long ago done penance.

4. One author has maintained that the Jewish priesthood is the subject of the prophecy, but in this he stands alone.

5. It has been maintained by others that the *prophets collectively* are referred to in the passage. This was at first the opinion of Rosenmüller, but was abandoned by him, and was then defended by De Wette, and is maintained by Gesenius.

6. Others have referred it to some individual. Thus Grotius supposes that Jeremiah is meant. Augusti supposed that Uzziah was intended. Others that Hezekiah was meant; and others that Isaiah here referred to himself; and others that it refers to some unknown prophet slain by the Jews in their exile; and others that it refers to the Maccabees!

These strange and absurd opinions are specimens of the unhappy manner of exposition which has prevailed among the German neologists; and they are specimens, too, of the reluctance of the human mind to embrace the truth as it is in Jesus, and of its proneness to the wildest aberrations, where mere human reason is suffered to take the reins in the interpretation of the Bible. Perhaps there is scarcely to be found an instance of *interpretation* that is more fitted to humble us in regard to the proneness of men to err, than in these modes of explaining this beautiful portion of Isaiah. And there is not to be found anywhere a more striking proof of the reluctance of the human mind to contemplate the sufferings and death of the Redeemer of the world, or to embrace the great and glorious truth that men can be saved only by the vicarious sacrifice of the Son of God.

§ 4. *Proof that it refers to the Messiah.*

More ample proof of this will be furnished in the exposition of the passage itself, than can now be given. But still, it may not be improper to refer to a few of the considerations which go to demonstrate that the prophet here refers to the Lord Jesus Christ.

I. He refers to an *individual,* and not to a people, or a nation. It is not either to the collective body of the Jewish people, or to the pious portion of the Jewish people, or to the collective body of the prophets. This is evident on the slightest examination of the passage. The prophet speaks of the 'servant of JEHOVAH;' and the whole representation is that of an individual, and not of any collective body of men. Thus his visage was marred, and his form was disfigured: he was as a tender plant; he was despised; he was rejected; he was smitten, wounded, put to death; he made his grave with the wicked and with the rich. Of what collective body of men could this be said? How absurd to apply this to a *nation,* or to any portion of a nation! It *cannot* be applied (A) *to the whole people.* In ch. liii. 3, the subject is called 'a man,' an appellation which cannot be given to a nation. Nor is there an instance in all the sacred writings where there can be found such an extended allegory as this would be, on the supposition that this refers to the Jewish people. Besides, with what possible propriety can it be said of *a nation* that it has borne the griefs and carried the sorrows of others; that it was stricken for the transgression of the people of God; that it was made an offering for sin; and that it made intercession for the sin of the transgressors? If *this* refers to a nation, then all settled views of interpretation are at an end. The circumstances which are usually supposed to mark individual existence may in all other circumstances in like manner be supposed to mean nations, and we shall have no longer any way-marks in guiding us in the interpretation of the plainest writings. Nor (B) can it refer to the pious portion of the Jewish people taken collectively. For the subject of the prophecy suffers *voluntarily;* he himself *innocent,* bears the sins of others (liii. 4–6, 9); his sufferings are the efficient cause of the righteousness of his people (ver. 11); and he suffers quietly and patiently, without allowing himself to be provoked to bitterness against the authors of his sufferings. Of all these four marks, not one belongs to the people of Israel. For (*a*) they went not voluntarily into the Babylonish exile, but were carried there by violence. (*b*) They did not suffer innocently, but suffered for their sins, (*c*) The sufferings of the Jews can in no sense be represented as the cause of the righteousness of others. (*d*) Nor did the Jews evince that patience and devotedness to the will of God which is here attributed to the subject of this prophecy. How can it be said that they were led like a lamb to the slaughter, that they did not open the mouth to complain, when even the noblest and best of them poured out their sad-

Less in complaints and lamentations? Compare Jer. xx. 7, *sq.;* xv. 10–21; Ps. cxxxvii. 8, 9. Nor (C) can it refer to the prophets taken collectively, as Gesenius supposes. On this it is sufficient to ask, Where did such a collection of the prophets ever exist? When did they suffer together? What evidence is there that they were in exile? Where and when did they take upon themselves the sins of the people, or suffer for them, or make their grave with the wicked and the rich in their death, or see of the travail of the soul, and become the means of the justification of many? All that has been said in favour of this is so entirely the work of conjecture, and is so manifestly designed to evade the obvious reference to the Messiah, that it is necessary to refer to it only as a specimen of the manner of interpretation which has prevailed, and which still prevails in the explanation of the sacred Scriptures. But if the passage does not refer either to the collective Jewish people, or to the pious portion of them, or to the prophets regarded as a collective body, then it must refer *to an individual,* and the only question is whether, it refers to the Messiah, or to some individual of the Jewish nation. As a simple and satisfactory argument that it refers to some individual, an appeal might be made to the common sense of the mass of men. Not one in a million—and he not unless he had some favourite hypothesis to defend—would ever suppose, on reading the passage, that it *could* have any reference to a collection of people of any kind. But the common sense of the mass of men is generally the best criterion of the meaning of any written document, and the best interpreter of the Bible.

II. If it refers to an individual, it must refer to the Messiah. It cannot refer to Isaiah, or Jeremiah, or Uzziah, or Akiba, for the following, among other reasons:—(*a*) The advocates of this theory have not been able to agree on any individual to whom it can be applied. Grotius suggested Jeremiah, some others Uzziah, or Isaiah, and some of the Jews Akiba. But each of these theories has been confined to the single interpreter who suggested it, and has been rejected by all the rest of the world. What better proof could there be that there is not even *plausibility* in the statement? What stronger demonstration that it is a theory *got up* on purpose to avoid the reference to the Messiah? (*b*) None of the individuals named had any claim to the statements here made respecting the individual sufferer. Did kings shut their mouths at them, and stand in awe of them? Did Jeremiah sprinkle many nations? Did Uzziah bear the griefs and the sorrows of men? Did JEHOVAH lay on Isaiah the iniquity of all men? Did either of them make their grave with the wicked and the rich in their death? But if it cannot be shown to have reference to any other individual, then the fair inference is, that it refers to the Messiah.

III. The argument that it refers to the Messiah has all the force of tradition in its favour. We have seen that the Jews, in more ancient times, referred this prophecy to the Messiah. This fact proves that such is the *obvious* reference. When their minds were not prejudiced and blinded by their hatred of Jesus of Nazareth, and their opposition to his claims; when they were looking forward with deep anxiety to the coming of a deliverer, they applied this passage to him. And though there were embarrassments in their minds, and they were not well able to explain how this was consistent with what is elsewhere stated of his exalted nature, yet such was its obvious reference to the Messiah, that they did not dare to call it in question. Such was the fact in the Christian church for seventeen hundred years. It was the unbroken and the unvarying voice of interpretation. Now this proves, not indeed that it is *necessarily* the true interpretation, for that is to be settled on other grounds than mere tradition, but that it is the exposition which the language naturally conveys. The unvarying sense affixed to any written document for seventeen hundred years, is *likely* to be the true sense. And especially is this so, if the document in question has been in the hands of the learned and the unlearned; the high and the low; the rich and the poor; the bond and the free; and if they concur in giving to it the same interpretation, such an interpretation cannot easily or readily be set aside.

IV. The quotations in the New Testament prove that it refers to the Messiah. They go to demonstrate at the same time two points; first, that such was the prevailing mode of interpretation at that time, otherwise the passage would not have been quoted as *proof* that Jesus was the Messiah; and secondly, that such is the correct mode of interpretation. The places where it is quoted are the following:—1. In John xii. 37, 38, 'But though he had done so many miracles before them, yet they believed not on him; that the saying of Esaias the prophet might be fulfilled which he spake, Lord, who hath believed our report? And to whom hath the arm of the Lord been revealed?' In this passage, Isa. liii. 1 is quoted to explain the unbelief of the Jewish people in the time of the Saviour, with the formula ἵνα πληρωθῇ—'that it might be fulfilled,' the usual formula in quoting a passage from the Old Testament which is fulfilled in the New. No one can doubt that John meant to be understood as affirming that the passage in Isaiah had a designed applicability to the person and the times of the Redeemer. The same passage is quoted by Paul in Rom. x. 16: 'But they have not all obeyed the gospel. For Esaias saith, Lord, who hath believed our report?' 2. The passage in Luke xxii. 37 is still more decisive. 'For I say unto you, That this that is written must yet be accomplished in me, And he was reckoned among the transgressors: for the things concerning me have an end,' *i.e.*, a completion, a fulfilment. Here Isa. lii. 12 is expressly and directly applied by the Saviour himself to his own sufferings and death. No one can doubt that he meant to say that it had original reference to him, and would be fulfilled in him. The same passage is applied, and in the same sense, by Mark (ch. xv. 28), to the sufferings and death of the Redeemer. 3. In Acts viii. 35, Isa. liii. 7, 8 is applied by Philip the evangelist to the Redeemer; and is explained as having a reference to him. 4. In Matt. viii. 17, the declaration of Isaiah (liii. 4), 'Himself took our infirmities, and bore our sicknesses,' is applied expressly to the Messiah. These passages, directly quoting Isaiah, and applying them to the Messiah, demonstrate that in view of the writers of the New Testament, and of the Saviour himself, Isaiah had reference to the Messiah. To those who admit the inspiration and the Divine authority of the New Testament, these proofs are sufficient demonstration of the position.

V. This view is enforced by another consideration. It is, that not only is the passage expressly *quoted* in the New Testament, but it is alluded to in connection with the death of the Redeemer as an atoning sacrifice for sin, in such a manner as to show that it was regarded by the sacred writers as having reference to the Messiah. It is sufficient here to refer to the following places:—Mark ix. 12; John iii. 5; Rom. iv. 25; 1 Cor. xv. 3; 2 Cor. v. 21; 1 Pet. i. 19; ii. 21–25. A careful examination of these passages would convince any one, that the writers of the New Testament were accustomed to regard the passage in Isaiah as having undoubted reference to the Messiah, and that this was so universally the interpretation of the passage in their times, as to make it proper simply to *refer* to it without formally quoting it. It may be added here, that it accords with the current and uniform statement in the New Testament about the design of the death of the Redeemer.

VI. One other argument may be here referred to, which I propose to state more at length when the exposition of the fifty-third chapter shall have been made. It arises from the exact correspondence between the passage and the events in the life, the sufferings, and the death of the Redeemer—a correspondence so minute that it cannot be the result of accident; so much depending on external circumstances and on the agency of others, that it could not have been produced by the effort of an impostor; and so peculiar that it can be found in no other person but the Messiah. We shall be better able to appreciate the force of this argument when we have the correct exposition of the passage before us.

To the view which has thus been taken of the design of this portion of Isaiah, there occurs one objection, often made by infidels, which I deem it important here to notice. It is, that the transactions here referred to are represented as *past*, and that it must be supposed to refer to some event which had occurred before the time when this was written. This ground has also been taken by Gesenius in proof that it cannot refer to the Messiah: 'The suffering, contempt, and death,' says he, 'of the servant of God, are here represented throughout as past, since all in ch. liii. 1–10, is in the *præter*. Only the glorification is future, and is represented in the future tense.' In reply to this, we may observe—1. That the transactions referred to are not *all* represented as past. The glorification of the person referred to is described in the future tense, and of course as a future event (ch. lii. 13–15; liii. 11, 12). It may be added also here, that those who will examine the Hebrew, will perceive that not everything in regard to his sufferings is represented as past (see ver. 7, 8, 10). But, 2. The true answer to this objection is to be found in a correct view of the nature of prophecy; and the objection has been supposed to have force only because the true character of prophecy has not been apprehended. It is a feature of the true nature of prophecy that the prophet is placed in vision *in the midst* of the scenes which he describes as future. He describes the events as if they were actually passing before his eyes. See this view of prophecy explained in the Introduction, § 7 According to this, Isaiah is to be regarded as placed in vision amidst the scenes which he describes. He looks on the suffering Redeemer. He describes his humiliation, his rejection, his trial, his death, and the feelings of those who rejected him, as if it actually occurred before his eyes. He sees him *now* rejected by men and put to death; but he also casts his eye into the future and sees him exalted, and his religion spreading into all the world. Though, therefore, the events which he describes were to occur several hundred years afterwards, yet they are portrayed, as his other prophecies are, as passing before his eyes, and as events which he was permitted in vision to see.

ANALYSIS.

IN ch. lii. 13–15, JEHOVAH speaks of his servant the Messiah, and describes the state of his humiliation, and of his subsequent exaltation. These verses contain, in fact, an *epitome* of what is enlarged upon in the next chapter. The sum of it is, that his servant should be, on the whole, prospered and exalted (13); yet he would be subjected to the deepest trial and humiliation (14); but as the result of this, he would redeem the nations of the earth, and their kings and rulers would regard him with profound reverence (15). A display of the Divine perfections would accompany the work of the servant of JEHOVAH such as they had never beheld, and they would be called on to contemplate wonders of which they had not before heard.

Ch. liii. contains a more minute explanation and statement of what is said in general in ch. lii. 13–15. For convenience, it may be regarded as divided into the following portions:—

I. An expression of amazement and lamentation at the fact that so few had embraced the annunciation respecting the Messiah, and had been properly affected by the important statements respecting his sufferings, his death, and his glorification (1).

II. A description of his rejection, his sufferings, his death (2–10). Here the prophet describes the scene as actually passing before his eyes. He speaks as if he himself were one of the Jewish nation who had rejected him, and who had procured his death. He describes the misapprehension under which it was done, and the depth of the sorrow to which the Messiah was subjected, and the design which JEHOVAH had in view in these sufferings. 1. His appearance and rejection are described (2, 3). He is as a shrub that grows in a parched soil without beauty; he is a man of sorrows, instead of being, as they expected, a magnificent prince; he has disappointed their expectations, and there is nothing that corresponded with their anticipations, and nothing, therefore, which should lead them to desire him. 2. The *design* for which he endured his sorrows is stated (4–6). He was thought by the people to be justly put to death, and they judged that God had judicially smitten and afflicted him (4). But this was not the cause. It was because he had borne the sorrows of the nation, and was wounded for their sins (4, 5). They had all gone astray, but JEHOVAH had caused to meet on him the iniquity of all. 3. The *manner* of his sufferings is described (7, 8). He was patient as a lamb; was taken from prison, and cut off. 4. The manner of his *burial* is described (9). It was with the rich. The *reason* why his grave was thus distinguished from that of malefactors was, that in fact he had done no evil. God, therefore, took care that that fact should be marked even in his burial, and though he *died* with malefactors, yet, as the purpose of the atonement did not require ignominy *after* death, he should not be *buried* with them. 5. The *design* for which all this was done is stated (10). It was that his soul might be made an offering for sin, and that it was thus well-pleasing or acceptable to God that he should suffer and die.

III. The result of his sufferings and humiliation is described (10–12). 1. He would see a numerous spiritual posterity, and be abundantly satisfied for all his pains and sorrows (10, 11). 2. By the knowledge of him, a great number would be justified and saved (11). 3. He would be greatly honoured, and proceed to the spiritual conquest of all the world (12).

13 Behold, my servant shall [1] deal prudently, he shall be exalted and extolled, and be very high.

1 or, *prosper;* ch.53.10.

13. *Behold, my servant.* The word 'behold,' indicates here that a new object is pointed out to view, and that it is one that claims attention on account of its importance. It is designed to direct the mind to the Messiah. The point of view which is here taken, is between his humiliation and his glorification. He sees him as having been humbled and rejected (ver. 14, 15; ch. liii. 2–10); about to be exalted and honoured (ver. 13–15; ch. liii. 10–12). The word 'servant' refers to the Messiah. Comp. Notes on ch. xlix. 5, where the word 'servant' is applied also to the Messiah. It means that he would be employed in doing the will of God, and that he would submit to him as a servant does to the law of his master. ¶ *Shall deal prudently.* Marg. 'Prosper.' The word שָׂכַל *sâkhăl,* is used in a twofold signification. It means either *to act wisely,* or *to be prosperous.* In this latter sense it is used in Josh.

14 As many were astonished at thee (his visage was so marred more than any man, and his form more than the sons of men),

---

i. 7, 8; 2 Kings xviii. 7; Jer. x. 21; Prov. xvii. 8. It is not easy to determine what is the meaning here. Jerome renders it, *Intelligent*—'Shall be wise or prudent.' The LXX. render it, Συνήσει ὁ παῖς μου—'My servant shall be intelligent.' The Chaldee renders it, 'Behold my servant the Messiah shall prosper' (יַצְלַח). The Syriac retains the Hebrew word. Jun. and Tremell. render it, 'Shall prosper;' Castellio, 'Shall be wise.' Lowth renders it, 'Shall prosper;' and in this Gesenius and Noyes concur. Hengstenberg proposes to unite the two meanings, and to render it, 'He shall reign well,' as indicative of the prosperous and wise government of the Messiah. It seems to me that the parallelism requires us to understand this not of his personal wisdom and prudence, but of the success of his enterprise. This verse contains a summary statement of what would occur under the Messiah. The general proposition is, that he would be ultimately successful, and to this the prophet comes (ch. liii. 12). He here sees him in affliction, humble, rejected, and despised. But he says that this was not always to be. He would be ultimately exalted. It is on this that he fixes the eye, and it is this which cheers and sustains the prophet in the contemplation of the sufferings of the Messiah. ¶ *He shall be exalted.* In this part of the verse, the prophet combines the verbs which denote elevation or exaltation. The idea is, that he would be exalted to the highest pitch of honour. The word 'exalted,' with us, is often synonymous with *praise;* but here it means, he shall be elevated (נִשָּׂא), or lifted up. The reference here is, undoubtedly, to the fact that the Redeemer would be greatly honoured on earth as the Prince and Saviour of the world (ch. liii. 12), and that in view of the universe he would be elevated to the highest conceivable rank. This is described in the New Testament by his being placed 'at the right hand of God' (Mark xvi. 19); by the fact that 'angels and authorities and powers are made subject unto him' (1 Pet. iii. 22); by the fact that God has 'set him at his own right hand in the heavenly places, far above all principality, and power, and might, and dominion, and every name that is named' (Eph. i. 20–22); and by the fact that he will return in great glory to judge the world (Matt. xxv). The idea is, that as he was the most despised among men, so he would yet be the most honoured; as he had voluntarily assumed the lowest place for the redemption of men, so he would be exalted to the highest place to which human nature could be elevated.

14. *As many were astonished at thee.* This verse is closely connected with the following, and they should be read together. The sense is, 'as many were shocked at him—his form was so disfigured, and his visage so marred—so he shall sprinkle many nations.' That is, the one fact would correspond with the other. The astonishment would be remarkable; the humiliation would be wonderful, and fitted to attract the deepest attention; and so his success and his triumph would correspond with the depth of his humiliation and sufferings. As he had in his humiliation been subjected to the lowest condition, so that all despised him; so hereafter the highest possible reverence would be shown him. Kings and nobles would shut their mouths in his presence, and show him the profoundest veneration. A change of person here occurs which is not uncommon in the Hebrew poets. In ver. 13, Jehovah speaks of the Messiah in the third person; here he changes the form of the address, and speaks of him in the second person. In the following verse the mode of address is again changed, and he speaks of him again in the third person. Lowth, however, proposes to read this in the third person, 'As many were astonished *at him*,' on the authority of two ancient Heb. MSS., and of the Syriac and Chaldee. But the authority is not sufficient to justify a change in the text, nor is it necessary. In the word rendered 'astonished' (שָׁמְמוּ), the

primary idea is that of being struck dumb, or put to silence from sudden astonishment. Whether the astonishment is from admiration or abhorrence is to be determined by the connection. In the latter sense, it is used in ch. xviii. 16; xix. 8. Here it evidently refers to the fact that he was disfigured, and destitute of apparent beauty and attractiveness from his abject condition and his sufferings. They were struck with amazement that one so abject, and that had so little that was attractive, should presume to lay claim to the character of the Messiah. This idea is more fully expressed in the following chapter. Here it is stated *in general* that his appearance was such as to excite universal astonishment, and probably to produce universal disgust. They saw no beauty or comeliness in him (see ch. liii. 2). This expression should also be regarded as standing in contrast with what is added in verse 15. Here it is said they were amazed, astonished, silent, at his appearance of poverty and his humiliation; there it is said, 'kings should shut their mouths at him,' that is, they would be so deeply impressed with his majesty and glory that they would remain in perfect silence—the silence not of contempt, but of profound veneration. ¶ *His visage* (מַרְאֵהוּ). This word denotes properly *sight, seeing, view;* then that which is seen; then appearance, form, *looks* (Ex. xxiv. 17; Ezek. i. 16–28; Dan. x. 18). Here it means, his appearance, his looks. It does not necessarily refer to his face, but to his general appearance. It was so disfigured by distress as to retain scarcely the appearance of a man. ¶ *Was so marred* (מִשְׁחַת). This word properly means *destruction.* Here it means defaced, destroyed, disfigured. There was a disfiguration, or defacement of his aspect, more than that of man. ¶ *More than any man* (מֵאִישׁ). This may either mean, more than any other man, or that he no longer retained the appearance of a man. It probably means the latter—that his visage was so disfigured that it was no longer the aspect of a man. Castellio renders it, *Ut non jam sit homo, non sit unus de humano genere.* ¶ *And his form* (תֹּאֲרוֹ). This word denotes *a form* or *a figure* of the body (1 Sam. xxviii. 14). Here it denotes the figure, or the appearance, referring not to the countenance, but to the general aspect of the body. ¶ *More than the sons of men.* So as to seem not to belong to men, or to be one of the human family. All this evidently refers to the disfiguration which arises from excessive grief and calamity. It means that he was broken down and distressed; that his great sorrows had left their marks on his frame so as to destroy the beautiful symmetry and proportions of the human form. We speak of being crushed with grief; of being borne down with pain; of being laden with sorrow. And we all know the effect of long-continued grief in marring the beauty of the human countenance, and in bowing down the frame. Deep emotion depicts itself on the face, and produces a permanent impression there. The highest beauty fades under long-continued trials, though at first it may seem to be set off to advantage. The rose leaves the cheek, the lustre forsakes the eye, vigour departs from the frame, its erect form is bowed, and the countenance, once brilliant and beautiful, becomes marked with the deep furrows of care and anxiety. Such seems to be the idea here. It is not indeed *said* that the sufferer before this had been distinguished for any extraordinary beauty—though this may not be improperly supposed—but that excessive grief had almost obliterated the traces of intelligence from the face, and destroyed the aspect of man. How well this applies to the Lord Jesus, needs not to be said. We have, indeed, no positive information in regard to his personal appearance. We are not told that he was distinguished for manliness of form, or beauty of countenance. But it is certainly no improbable supposition that when God prepared for him a body (Heb. x. 5) in which the divinity should dwell incarnate, the human form would be rendered as fit as it could be for the indwelling of the celestial inhabitant. And it is no unwarrantable supposition that perfect truth, benevolence, and purity, should depict themselves on the

15 So shall he sprinkle [a]many nations; the kings shall shut their mouths at him: for *that* which had not been told them shall they see, and *that* which they had not heard shall they consider.

[a] Eze.36.25.

countenance of the Redeemer; as they will be manifested in the very aspect wherever they exist—and render him the most beautiful of men—for the expression of these principles and feelings in the countenance constitutes beauty (comp. Notes on ch. liii. 2). Nor is it an improbable supposition, that this beauty was marred by his long-continued and inexpressibly deep sorrows, and that he was so worn down and crushed by the sufferings which he endured as scarcely to have retained the aspect of a man.

15. *So* (כֵּן). This word answers to 'as' (כַּאֲשֶׁר) in the former verse. 'In like manner as many were astonished or shocked at thee—so shall he sprinkle many nations.' The one is to be in some respects commensurate with the other. The comparison seems to consist of two points: 1. *In regard to the numbers.* Many would be shocked: many would be sprinkled by him. Large numbers would be amazed at the fact of his sorrows; and numbers correspondently large would be sprinkled by him. 2. *In the effects.* Many would be struck dumb with amazement at his appearance; and, in like manner, many would be struck dumb with veneration or respect. He would be regarded on the one hand as having scarce the form of a man; on the other, even kings would be silent before him from profound reverence and awe. ¶ *Shall he sprinkle many nations.* The word here rendered 'sprinkle' (יַזֶּה) has been very variously rendered. Jerome renders it, *Asperget*—'Shall sprinkle.' The LXX. 'So shall many nations express admiration (*θαυμάσονται*) at him.' The Chaldee, 'So shall he scatter,' or dissipate (יְבַדַּר) 'many people.' The Syriac renders it, 'Thus shall he purify,' cleanse, make expiation for (ܢܕܟܐ) 'many nations.' The Syriac verb used here means *to purify*, to cleanse, to make holy; and, in *aph.*, to expiate; and the idea of the translator evidently was, that he would purify by making expiation. See the Syriac word used in Luke iii. 17; Acts xi. 9; xxiv. 18; Heb. ix. 22; x. 4. Castellio renders it as Jerome does; and Jun. and Tremell., 'He shall sprinkle many nations with stupor.' Interpreters have also varied in the sense which they have given to this word. Its usual and proper meaning is to *sprinkle*, and so it has been here commonly interpreted. But Martini, Rosenmüller, and Gesenius suppose that it is derived from an Arabic word meaning to leap, to spring, to spring up, to leap for joy, to exult; and that the idea here is, that he should cause many nations to exult, or leap for joy. Parallel places, says Gesenius, occur in ch. xlix. 6, 7; li. 5. Against the common interpretation, 'to sprinkle,' he objects—1. That the verb could not be construed without the accusative, and that if it means that he would sprinkle with blood, the word *blood* would be specified. 2. That the connection is opposed to the idea of sprinkling, and that the antithesis requires some word that shall correspond with שָׁמַם, 'shall be astonished,' and that the phrase 'they shall be joyful,' or 'he shall cause them to exult with joy,' denotes such antithesis. To this it may be replied, that the usual, the universal signification of the word נָזָה (*nâzâ*) in the Old Testament is *to sprinkle.* The word occurs only in the following places, and is in all instances translated 'sprinkle' (Ex. xxix. 21; Lev. v. 9; vi. 6–17, 27; viii. 11, 30; xiv. 7, 16, 27, 51; xvi. 14, 15, 19; Num. viii. 7; xix. 4, 18, 19, 21; 2 Kings ix. 33; Isa. lxiii. 3). It is properly applicable to the act of sprinkling blood, or water; and then comes to be used in the sense of cleansing by the blood that makes expiation for sin, or of cleansing by water as an emblem of purifying. In Ezek. xxxvi. 25, the practice of sprinkling with consecrated water is referred to as synonymous with purifying—though a different word from this is used (זָרַק), 'and I will sprinkle clean water upon you, and ye shall be clean.' If the word used here means

CHAPTER LIII.

WHO hath believed [a] our [1] report? and to whom [b] is the arm of the LORD revealed?

2 For he shall grow up before him as a tender plant, and as a root out of a dry ground; he hath no form nor comeliness; and when we shall see him, *there is* no beauty that we should desire him.

a Jn.1.7,12; Ep.1.18,19. 1 *hearing*, or, *doctrine*. b Jn.12.37; Ro.10.16.

'to sprinkle,' it is used in one of the following significations:—1. To sprinkle *with blood*, in allusion to the Levitical rite of sprinkling the blood of the sacrifice, meaning that in that way sin would be expiated and removed (Lev. xiv. 51; xvi. 14; Heb. ix. 19; x. 22); or, 2. By an allusion to the custom of sprinkling with water as emblematic of purity, or cleansing (Num. viii. 7; xix. 18; Ezek. xxxvi. 25). If used in the former sense, it means, that the Redeemer would make expiation for sin, and that his blood of purifying would be sprinkled on the nations. If in the latter, as is most probable, then it means that he would purify them, as objects were cleansed by the sprinkling of water. If in *either* sense, it means substantially the same thing—that the Redeemer would *purify*, or *cleanse* many nations, *i.e.*, from their sins, and make them holy. Still there is a difficulty in the passage which does not seem to be solved. This difficulty has been thus expressed by Taylor (*Concord.*): 'It seems here to have a peculiar meaning, which is not exactly collected from the other places where this word is used. The *antithesis* points to *regard, esteem, admiration.* "So shall he sprinkle, engage the esteem and admiration of many nations." But how to deduce this from the sense of the word I know not.' It was to meet this difficulty that Martini, Rosenmüller, and Gesenius, propose the sense of leaping, exulting, filling with joy, from the Arabic. But that signification does not accord with the uniform Hebrew usage, and probably the sense of *purifying* is to be retained. It may be remarked that whichever of the above senses is assigned, it furnishes no *argument* for the practice of sprinkling in baptism. It refers to the fact of his purifying or cleansing the nations, and not to the ordinance of Christian baptism; nor should it be used as an argument in reference to the mode in which that should be administered. ¶ *The kings shall shut their mouths at him.* Or rather, kings. It does not refer to any particular kings; but the idea is, that he would be honoured by kings. To shut the mouths here indicates veneration and admiration. See Job xxix. 9, 10, where reverence or respect is indicated in the same way:

The princes refrained talking,
And laid their hand upon their mouth:
The nobles held their peace,
And their tongue cleaved to the roof of their mouth.

See also Micah viii. 16; comp. Job v. 16; Ps. cxlvii. 42. ¶ *For that which had not been told them.* In this part of the verse a reason is given for the veneration which kings would evince. It is, that they should receive intelligence of this wonderful exaltation of the messenger of God which had not before been made known to them as it had been to the Jews. Or, in other words, the great mystery of the incarnation and redemption would contain truths and wonders which they had not contemplated elsewhere. No such events would have occurred within the range of their observation; and the wonders of redemption would stand by themselves as unparalleled in all that they had heard or seen. What is here predicted has been fulfilled. The mystery of the incarnation and the atonement; the sufferings and the death of the Redeemer; his exaltation and his glory, are events which are unparalleled in the history of the world. They are events *fitted* in their nature to excite the profoundest admiration, and to induce kings and nobles to lay their hand on their mouth in token of veneration. No monarch on earth could have evinced such condescension as did the Son of God; none has been elevated to so high a rank in the universe as the Redeemer. That the Son of God should become a man; that his visage should be so disfigured by grief as to have scarcely the aspect of a human being; that he should suffer and die as he did; and that he should be exalted as he is over this whole world, and have the most elevated place in the universe at the right hand of God, are all events fitted to excite the profoundest admiration.

CHAPTER LIII.

1. *Who hath believed our report?* The main design of the prophet in all this portion of his prophecy is, undoubtedly, to state the fact that the Redeemer would be greatly exalted (see ch. lii. 13; liii. 12). But in order to furnish a fair view of his exaltation, it was necessary also to exhibit the depth of his humiliation, and the intensity of his sorrows, and also the fact that he would be rejected by those to whom he was sent. He, therefore, in this verse, to use the language of Calvin, breaks in abruptly upon the order of his discourse, and exclaims that what he had said, and what he was about to say, would be scarcely credited by any one. Preliminary to his exaltation, and to the honours which would be conferred on him, he would be rejected and despised. The word 'report' (שְׁמֻעָה) denotes properly *that which is heard*, tidings, message, news. Marg. 'Hearing,' or 'doctrine.' The LXX. render it, Ἀκοή—'Rumour,' 'message.' It refers to the annunciation, message, or communication which had been made respecting the Messiah. The speaker here is Isaiah, and the word 'our' refers to the fact that the message of Isaiah and of the other prophets had been alike rejected. He groups himself with the other prophets, and says that the annunciation which *they* had made of the Redeemer had been disregarded. The interrogative form is often assumed when it is designed to express a truth with emphasis; and the idea is, therefore, that the message in regard to the Messiah had been rejected, and that almost none had credited and embraced it. ¶ *And to whom is the arm of the* LORD *revealed?* The arm is that by which we execute a purpose, and is often used as the emblem of power (see Notes on ch. xxxiii. 2; xl. 10). Here it denotes the omnipotence or power of God, which would be exhibited through the Messiah. The sense is, 'Who has perceived the power evinced in the work of the Redeemer? To whom is that power manifested which is to be put forth through him, and in connection with his work?' It refers not so much, as it seems to me, to his power in working miracles, as to the omnipotence evinced in rescuing sinners from destruction. In the New Testament, the gospel is not unfrequently called 'the power of God' (Rom. i. 16; 1 Cor. i. 18), for it is that by which God displays his power in saving men. The idea here is, that comparatively few would be brought under that power, and be benefited by it; that is, in the times, and under the preaching of the Messiah. It is to be remembered that the scene of this vision is laid in the midst of the work of the Redeemer. The prophet sees him a sufferer, despised and rejected. He sees that few come to him, and embrace him as their Saviour. He recalls the 'report' and the announcement which he and other prophets had made respecting him; he remembers the record which had been made centuries before respecting the Messiah; and he asks with deep emotion, *as if present* when the Redeemer lived and preached, who had credited what he and the other prophets had said of him. The mass had rejected it all. The passage, therefore, had its fulfilment in the events connected with the ministry of the Redeemer, and in the fact that he was rejected by so many. The Redeemer was more successful in his work as a preacher than is commonly supposed, but still it is true that by the mass of the nation he was despised, and that the announcement which had been made of his true character and work was rejected.

2. *For he shall grow up before him.* In this verse, the prophet describes the humble appearance of the Messiah, and the fact that there was nothing in his personal aspect that corresponded to the expectations that had been formed of him; nothing that should lead them to desire him as their expected deliverer, but everything that could induce them to reject him. He would be of so humble an origin, and with so little that was magnificent in his external appearance, that the nation would despise him. The word rendered 'he shall grow up'

(וַיַּעַל, from עָלָה), means properly, *to go up, to ascend.* Here it evidently applies to the Redeemer as growing up in the manner of a shoot or sucker that springs out of the earth. It means that he would start, as it were, from a decayed stock or stump, as a shoot springs up from a root that is apparently dead. It does not refer to his manner of life before his entrance on the public work of the ministry; not to the mode and style of his education; but to his starting as it were out of a dry and sterile soil where *any* growth could not be expected, or from a stump or stock that was apparently dead (see Notes on ch. xi. 1). The phrase 'before him' (לְפָנָיו), refers to JEHOVAH. He would be seen and observed by him, although unknown to the world. The eyes of men would not regard him as the Messiah while he was growing up, but JEHOVAH would, and his eye would be continually upon him. ¶ *As a tender plant.* The word used here (יוֹנֵק, from יָנַק, *to suck,* Job iii. 12; Cant. viii. 1; Joel ii. 16), may be applied either to a suckling, a sucking child (Deut. xxxii. 25; Ps. viii. 3), or to a sucker, a sprout, a shoot of a tree (Job viii. 16; xiv. 7; xv. 30; Ezek. xvii. 22; Hos. xiv. 7). Jerome here renders it, *Virgultum.* The LXX. render it, Ἀνηγγείλαμεν ὡς παιδίον ἐναντίον αὐτοῦ—'We have made proclamation as a child before him.' But what idea they attached to it, it is impossible now to say; and equally so to determine *how* they came to make such a translation. The Chaldee also, leaving the idea that it refers to the Messiah, renders it, 'And the righteous shall be magnified before him as branches which flourish, and as the tree which sends its roots by the fountains of water; thus shall the holy nation be increased in the land.' The Syriac translates it, 'He shall grow up before him as an infant.' The idea in the passage is plain. It is, that the Messiah would spring up as from an ancient and decayed stock, like a tender shoot or sucker. He would be humble and unpretending in his origin, and would be such that they who had expected a splendid prince would be led to overlook and despise him. ¶ *And as a root* (וְכַשֹּׁרֶשׁ). The word 'root' here is evidently used by synecdoche for the sprout that starts up from a root (see Notes on ch. xi. 10, where the word is used in the same sense). ¶ *Out of a dry ground.* In a barren waste, or where there is no moisture. Such a sprout or shrub is small, puny, and withered up. Such shrubs spring up in deserts, where they are stinted for want of moisture, and they are most striking objects to represent that which is humble and unattractive in its personal appearance. The idea here is, that the Messiah would spring from an ancient family decayed, but in whose root, so to speak, there would be life, as there is remaining life in the stump of a tree that is fallen down; but that there would be nothing in his external appearance that would attract attention, or meet the expectations of the nation. Even then he would not be like a plant of vigorous growth supplied with abundant rains, and growing in a rich and fertile soil, but he would be like the stinted growth of the sands of the desert. Can anything be more strikingly expressive of the actual appearance of the Redeemer, as compared with the expectation of the Jews? Can there be found anywhere a more striking fulfilment of a prophecy than this? And how will the infidel answer the argument thus furnished for the fact that Isaiah was inspired, and that his record was true? ¶ *He hath no form.* That is, no beauty. He has not the beautiful form which was anticipated; the external glory which it was supposed he would assume. On the meaning of the word 'form,' see Notes on ch. lii. 14. It is several times used in the sense of beautiful form or figure (Gen. xxix. 17; xxxix. 6; xli. 18; Deut. xxi. 11; Esth. ii. 17; comp. 1 Sam. xvi. 18). Here it means the same as beautiful form or appearance, and refers to his *state* of abasement rather than to his own personal beauty. There is no evidence that in person he was in any way deformed, or otherwise than beautiful, except as excessive grief may have changed his natural aspect (see Note on ch. lii. 14). ¶ *Nor comeliness* (הָדָר). This word is translated honour, glory, majesty (Deut. xxxiii. 17; Ps. xxix.

4; cxlix. 9; Dan. xi. 20); excellency (Isa. xxxv. 2); beauty (Prov. xx. 29; Ps. cx. 3; 2 Chron. xx. 21). It may be applied to the countenance, to the general aspect, or to the ornaments or apparel of the person. Here it refers to the appearance of the Messiah, as having nothing that was answerable to their expectations. He had no robes of royalty; no diadem sparkling on his brow; no splendid retinue; no gorgeous array. ¶ *And when we shall see him.* This should be connected with the previous words, and should be translated, 'that we should regard him, or attentively look upon him.' The idea is, that there was in his external appearance no such beauty as to lead them to look with interest and attention upon him; nothing that should attract them, as men are attracted by the dazzling and splendid objects of this world. If they saw him, they immediately looked away from him as if he were unworthy of their regard. ¶ There is *no beauty that we should desire him.* He does not appear in the form which we had anticipated. He does not come with the regal pomp and splendour which it was supposed he would assume. He is apparently of humble rank; has few attendants, and has disappointed wholly the expectation of the nation. In regard to the personal appearance of the Redeemer, it is remarkable that the New Testament has given us no information. Not a hint is dropped in reference to his height of stature, or his form; respecting the colour of his hair, his eyes, or his complexion. In all this, on which biographers are usually so full and particular, the evangelists are wholly silent. There was evidently *design* in this; and the purpose was probably to prevent any painting, statuary, or figure of the Redeemer, that would have any claim to being regarded as correct or true. As it stands in the New Testament, there is just the veil of obscurity thrown over this whole subject which is most favourable for the contemplation of the incarnate Deity. We are told that he was a man; we are told also that he was God. The image to the mind's eye is as obscure in the one case as the other; and in both, we are directed to his moral beauty, his holiness, and benevolence, as objects of contemplation, rather than to his external appearance or form. It may be added that there is no authentic information in regard to his appearance that has come down to us by tradition. All the works of sculptors and painters in attempting to depict his form are the mere works of fancy, and are undoubtedly as unlike the glorious reality as they are contrary to the spirit and intention of the Bible. There is, indeed, a letter extant which is claimed by some to have been written by Publius Lentulus, to the Emperor Tiberius, in the time when the Saviour lived, and which gives a description of his personal appearance. As this is the *only* legend of antiquity which even claims to be a description of his person, and as it is often printed, and is regarded as a curiosity, it may not be improper here to present it in a note.* This letter is pronounced by Calmet to be spurious, and it has been abundantly *proved* to be so by Prof. Robinson (see *Bib. Rep.* vol. ii. pp. 367–393). The main arguments against its authenticity, and which entirely settle the question, are —1. The discrepancies and contradictions which exist in the various copies. 2. The fact that in the time of the

* 'There has a man appeared here, who is still living, named Jesus Christ, whose power is extraordinary. He has the title given to him of the great prophet; his disciples call him the Son of God. He raises the dead, and heals all sorts of diseases. He is a tall, well-proportioned man; there is an air of serenity in his countenance, which attracts at once the love and reverence of those who see him. His hair is of the colour of new wine; from the roots to his ears, and from thence to the shoulders, it is curled, and falls down to the lowest part of them. Upon the forehead it parts in two, after the manner of the Nazarenes. His forehead is flat and fair, his face without any defect, and adorned with a very graceful vermilion; his air is majestic and agreeable. His nose and his mouth are very well proportioned; and his beard is thick and forked, of the colour of his hair; his eyes are gray and extremely lively; in his reproofs he is terrible, but in his exhortations and instructions amiable and courteous; there is something wonderfully charming in his face, with a mixture of gravity. He is never seen to laugh, but he has been observed to weep. He is very straight in stature; his hands are large and spreading, and his arms very beautiful. He talks little, but with great gravity, and is the handsomest man in the world.'—(*Bib. Repos.* vol. ii. p. 368.)

3 He is despised and rejected [a] of men; a man of sorrows, and acquainted [b] with grief: and [1] we hid as it were *our* faces from him; he was despised, and we esteemed him not.

a Lu.23.18,&c. *b* He.4.15.

1 *as an hiding of faces from him*, or, *from us*; or, *he hid as it were* his *face from us*.

Saviour, when the epistle purports to have been written, it can be demonstrated that no such man as Publius Lentulus was governor of Judea, or had any such office there, as is claimed for him in the inscriptions to the epistle. 3. That for fifteen hundred years no such epistle is quoted or referred to by any writer—a fact which *could* not have occurred if any such epistle had been in existence. 4. That the style of the epistle is not such as an enlightened Roman would have used, but is such as an ecclesiastic would have employed. 5. That the contents of the epistle are such as a Roman *would* not have used of one who was a Jew. See these arguments presented in detail in the place above referred to. It may be added, that this is the only pretended account which has come down to us respecting the personal appearance of the Saviour, except the *fable* that Christ sent his portrait to Abgar, king of Edessa, in reply to a letter which he had sent requesting him to come and heal him; and the equally fabulous legend, that the impression of his countenance was left upon the handkerchief of the holy Veronica.

3. *He is despised.* This requires no explanation; and it needs no comment to show that it was fulfilled. The Redeemer was eminently the object of contempt and scorn alike by the Pharisees, the Sadducees, and the Romans. In his life on earth it was so; in his death it was still so; and since then, his name and person have been extensively the object of contempt. Nothing is a more striking fulfilment of this than the conduct of the Jews at the present day. The very name of Jesus of Nazareth excites contempt; and they join with their fathers who rejected him in heaping on him every term indicative of scorn. ¶ *Rejected of men.* This phrase is full of meaning, and in three words states the whole history of man in regard to his treatment of the Redeemer. The name 'THE REJECTED OF MEN,' will express all the melancholy history;—rejected by the Jews; by the rich; the great and the learned; by the mass of men of every grade, and age, and rank. No prophecy was ever more strikingly fulfilled; none could condense more significancy into few words. In regard to the exact sense of the phrase, interpreters have varied. Jerome renders it, *Novissimum virorum*—'The last of men;' *i.e.*, the most abject and contemptible of mankind. The LXX. 'His appearance is dishonoured (ἄτιμον) and defective (ἐκλεῖπον) more than the sons of men.' The Chaldee, 'He is indeed despised, but he shall take away the glory of all kings; they are infirm and sad, as if exposed to all calamities and sorrows.' Some render it, 'Most abject of men,' and they refer to Job xix. 14, where the same word is used to denote those friends who forsake the unfortunate. The word חָדֵל, used here, is derived from the verb חָדַל, which means *to cease*, to leave off, to desist; derived, says Gesenius (*Lex.*), from the idea of becoming languid, flaccid; and thence transferred to the act of ceasing from labour. It means usually, to cease, to desist from, to leave, to let alone (see 1 Kings xxii. 6–15; Job vii. 15; x. 20; Isa. ii. 22). According to Gesenius, the word here means *to be left*, to be destitute, or forsaken; and the idea is, that he was forsaken of men. According to Hengstenberg (*Christol.*) it means 'the most abject of men,'—he who *ceases* from men, who ceases to belong to the number of men; *i.e.*, who is the most abject of men. Castellio renders it, *Minus quam homo*—'Less than a man.' Junius and Tremellius, *Abjectissimus virorum*—'The most abject of men.' Grotius, 'Rejected of men.' Symmachus, Ἐλάχιστος ἀνδρῶν—'The least of men.' The idea is, undoubtedly, somehow that of *ceasing* from men, or from being regarded as belonging to men. There was a ceasing, or a withdrawing of that which usually appertains to man, and which belongs to him. And the thought

probably is, that he was not only ‘despised,’ but that there was an advance on that—there was a *ceasing* to treat him *as if* he had human feelings, and was in any way entitled to human fellowship and sympathy. It does not refer, therefore, so much to the *active* means employed to reject him, as to the fact that he was regarded as *cut off from man;* and the idea is not essentially different from this, that he was the most abject and vile of mortals in the estimation of others; so vile as not to be deemed worthy of the treatment due to the *lowest* of men. This idea has been substantially expressed in the Syriac translation. ¶ *A man of sorrows.* What a beautiful expression! A man who was so sad and sorrowful; whose life was so full of sufferings, that it might be said that that was the characteristic of the man. A similar phraseology occurs in Prov. xxix. 1, ‘He that being often reproved,’ in the margin, ‘a man of reproofs;’ in the Heb. ‘A man of chastisements,’ that is, a man who is often chastised. Compare Dan. x. 11: ‘O Daniel, a man greatly beloved,’ Marg. as in Heb. ‘A man of desires;’ *i.e.*, a man greatly desired. Here, the expression means that his life was characterized by sorrows. How remarkably this was fulfilled in the life of the Redeemer, it is not necessary to attempt to show. ¶ *And acquainted with grief.* Heb. וִידוּעַ חֹלִי—‘And knowing grief.’ The word rendered ‘grief,’ means usually sickness, disease (Deut. vii. 15; xxvii. 61; Isa. i. 5); but it also means anxiety, affliction (Eccl. v. 16); and then any evil or calamity (Eccl. vi. 2). Many of the old interpreters explain it as meaning, that he was known or distinguished by disease; that is, affected by it in a remarkable manner. So Symm. Γνωστός νόσῳ. Jerome (Vulg.) renders it, *Scientem infirmitatem.* The LXX. render the whole clause, ‘A man in affliction (ἐν πληγῇ), and knowing to bear languor, or disease’ (εἰδὼς φέρειν μαλακίαν). But if the word here means disease, it is only a figurative designation of severe sufferings both of body and of soul. Hengstenberg, Koppe, and Ammon, suppose that the figure is taken from the leprosy, which was not only one of the most severe of all diseases, but was in a special manner regarded as a Divine judgment. They suppose that many of the expressions which follow may be explained with reference to this (comp. Heb. iv. 15). The idea is, that he was familiar with sorrow and calamity. It does not mean, as it seems to me, that he was to be himself sick and diseased; but that he was to be subject to various kinds of calamity, and that it was to be a characteristic of his life that he was familiar with it. He was intimate with it. He knew it personally; he knew it in others. He lived in the midst of scenes of sorrow, and be became intimately acquainted with its various forms, and with its evils. There is no evidence that the Redeemer was himself sick at any time—which is remarkable—but there is evidence in abundance that he was familiar with all kinds of sorrow, and that his own life was a life of grief. ¶ *And we hid as it were* our *faces from him.* There is here great variety of interpretation and of translation. The margin reads, ‘As an hiding of faces from him,’ or ‘from us,’ or, ‘He hid as it were *his* face from us.’ The Hebrew is literally, ‘And as the hiding of faces from him, or from it;’ and Hengstenberg explains it as meaning, ‘He was as an hiding of the face before it;’ that is, as a thing or person before whom a man covers his face, because he cannot bear the disgusting sight. Jerome (Vulg.) renders it, ‘His face was as it were hidden and despised.’ The LXX. ‘For his countenance was turned away’ (ἀπέστραπται). The Chaldee, ‘And when he took away his countenance of majesty from us, we were despised and reputed as nothing.’ Interpreters have explained it in various ways. 1. ‘He was as one who hides his face before us;’ alluding, as they suppose, to the Mosaic law, which required lepers to cover their faces (Lev. iii. 45), or to the custom of covering the face in mourning, or for shame. 2. Others explain it as meaning, ‘as one before whom is the covering of the face,’ *i.e.*, before whom a man covers the face from shame or disgust. So Gesenius. 3. Others, ‘He was as one causing to conceal the face,’ *i.e.*, he induced others to cover the face before him. His suf-

4 Surely he hath borne our griefs, and carried our sorrows: [a]yet we did esteem him stricken, smitten of God, and afflicted.

a Mat.26.37.

ferings were so terrible as to induce them to turn away. So J. H. Michaelis. The idea seems to be, that he was as one from whom men hide their faces, or turn away. This *might* either arise from a sight of his sufferings, as being so offensive that they would turn away in pain—as in the case of a leper; or it might be, that he was so much an object of contempt, and so unlike what they expected, that they would hide their faces and turn away in scorn. This latter I suppose to be the meaning; and that the idea is, that he was so unlike what they had expected, that they hid their faces in affected or real contempt. ¶ *And we esteemed him not.* That is, we esteemed him as nothing; we set no value on him. In order to give greater energy to a declaration, the Hebrews frequently express a thing positively and then negatively. The prophet had said that they held him in *positive* contempt; he here says that they did not regard him as worthy of their notice. He here speaks in the name of his nation—as one of the Jewish people. 'We, the Jews, the nation to whom he was sent, did not esteem him as the Messiah, or as worthy of our affection or regard.'

4. *Surely.* This is an exceedingly important verse, and is one that is attended with considerable difficulty, from the manner in which it is quoted in the New Testament. The general sense, as it stands in the Hebrew, is not indeed difficult. It is immediately connected in signification with the previous verse. The meaning is, that those who had despised and rejected the Messiah, had greatly erred in contemning him on account of his sufferings and humiliation. 'We turned away from him in horror and contempt. We supposed that he was suffering on account of some great sin of his own. But in this we erred. It was not for *his* sins but for *ours.* It was not that he was smitten of God for his own sins—as if he had been among the worst of mortals—but it was because he had taken *our* sins, and was suffering for *them.* The very thing therefore that gave offence to us, and which made us turn away from him, constituted the most important part of his work, and was really the occasion of highest gratitude.' It is an acknowledgment that they had erred, and a confession of that portion of the nation which would be made sensible of their error, that they had judged improperly of the character of the sufferer. The word rendered 'surely' (אָכֵן, Vulg. *verè*), is sometimes a particle strongly affirming, meaning *truly, of a certain truth* (Gen. xxviii. 16; Ex. ii. 14; Jer. viii. 8). Sometimes it is an adversative particle, meaning *but yet* (Ps. xxxi. 23; Isa. xlix. 24). It is probably used in that sense here, meaning, that though he was despised by them, *yet* he was worthy of their esteem and confidence, for he had borne their griefs. He was not suffering for any sins of his own, but in a cause which, so far from rendering him an object of contempt, made him worthy of their highest regard. ¶ *He hath borne.* Heb. נָשָׂא *nâsâ.* Vulg. *Tulit.* LXX. Φέρει—'He bears.' Chald. 'He prayed (יִבְעֵי) for, or on account of our sins.' Castellio, *Tulit ac toleravit.* In these versions, the sense is that of sustaining, bearing, upholding, carrying, as when one removes a burden from the shoulders of another, and places it on his own. The word נָשָׂא means properly *to take up,* to lift, to raise (Gen. vii. 17), 'The waters increased, and *lifted up* the ark;' (xxix. 1), 'And Jacob *lifted up* his feet (see the margin) and came.' Hence it is applied to lifting up a standard (Jer. iv. 6; l. 2); to lifting up the hand (Deut. xxxii. 40); to lifting up the head (Job x. 15; 2 Kings xxv. 27); to lifting up the eyes (Gen. xiii. 10, *et sæpe*); to lifting up the voice, &c. It then means to bear, to carry, as an infant in the arms (Isa. xlvi. 3); as a tree does its fruit (Ezek. xvii. 8), or as a field its produce (Ps. lxx. 3; Gen. xii. 6). Hence to *endure,* suffer, permit (Job xxi. 3). 'Bear with me, suffer me and I will speak.' Hence to bear the sin of any one, to take upon one's self the suffering which is due to sin (see Notes on ver. 12 of

this chapter; comp. Lev. v. 1, 17; xvii. 16; xx. 19; xxiv. 15; Num. v. 31; ix. 13; xiv. 34; xxx. 16; Ezek. xviii. 19, 20). Hence to bear chastisement, or punishment (Job xxxiv. 31): 'I have borne *chastisement,* I will not offend *any more.*' It is also used in the sense of taking away the sin of any one, expiating, or procuring pardon (Gen. l. 17; Lev. x. 17; Job vii. 21; Ps. xxxiii. 5; lxxxv. 3). In all cases there is the idea of *lifting,* sustaining, taking up, and conveying away, as by *carrying* a burden. It is not simply *removing,* but it is removing somehow by *lifting,* or carrying; that is, either by an act of power, or by so taking them on one's own self as to sustain and carry them. If applied to *sin,* it means that a man must *bear* the burden of the punishment of his own sin, or that the suffering which is due to sin is *taken up* and borne by another. If applied to *diseases,* as in Matt. viii. 17, it must mean that he, as it were, lifted them up and bore them away. It cannot mean that the Saviour literally *took* those sicknesses on himself, and *became sick* in the place of the sick, became a leper in the place of the leper, or was himself possessed with an evil spirit in the place of those who were possessed (Matt. viii. 16), but it must mean that he took them away by his power, and, as it were, lifted them up, and removed them. So when it is said (Isa. liii. 12) that he 'bare the sins of many,' it cannot mean literally that he took those sins on himself in any such sense as that he became a sinner, but only that he so took them upon himself as to *remove* from the sinner the exposure to punishment, and to *bear* himself whatever was necessary as a proper expression of the evil of sin. Peter undoubtedly makes an allusion to this passage (liii. 12) when he says (1 Pet. ii. 24), 'Who his own self bare our sins in his own body on the tree' (see Notes on ver. 12). Matthew (viii. 17) has translated it by ἔλαβε (*he took*), a word which does not differ in signification essentially from that used by Isaiah. It is almost exactly the same word which is used by Symmachus (ἀνέλαβε). ¶ *Our griefs.* The word here used (חֳלִי) means properly *sickness, disease, anxiety, affliction.* It does not refer to *sins,* but to *sufferings.* It is translated 'sickness' (Deut. xxviii. 61; vii. 15; 2 Chron. xxi. 15; 1 Kings xvii. 17); 'disease' (Eccl. vi. 2; 2 Chron. xxi. 18; xvi. 12; Ex. xv. 26); 'grief' (Isa. liii. 3, 4; comp. Jer. xvi. 4). It is never in our version rendered *sin,* and never used to denote sin. 'In ninety-three instances,' says Dr. Magee (*On Atonement and Sacrifice,* p. 229, New York Ed. 1813), 'in which the word here translated (by the LXX.) ἁμαρτίας, or its kindred verb, is found in the Old Testament in any sense that is not entirely foreign from the passage before us, there occurs but this one in which the word is so rendered; it being in all other cases expressed by ἀσθενεία, μαλακία, or some word denoting bodily disease.' 'That the Jews,' he adds, 'considered this passage as referring to bodily diseases, appears from Whitby, and Lightfoot. Hor. Heb. on Matt. viii. 17.' It is rendered in the Vulgate, *Languores*—'Our infirmities.' In the Chaldee, 'He prayed for our sins.' Castellio renders it, *Morbos*—'Diseases;' and so Junius and Tremellius. The LXX. have rendered it, in this place, Ἁμαρτίας—'Sins;' though, from what Dr. Kennicott has advanced in his *Diss. Gen.* § 79, Dr. Magee thinks there can be no doubt that this is a corruption which has crept into the later copies of the Greek. A few Greek MSS. of the Septuagint also read it ἀσθενείας, and one μαλακίας. Matthew (viii. 17) has rendered it, ἀσθενείας—'infirmities,' and intended no doubt to apply it to the fact that the Lord Jesus healed diseases, and there can be no doubt that Matthew has used the passage, not by way of accommodation, but in the true sense in which it is used by Isaiah; and that it means that the Messiah would take upon himself the infirmities of men, and would remove their sources of grief. It does not refer here to the fact that he would take their *sins.* That is stated in other places (ver. 6, 12). But it means that he was so afflicted, that he seemed to have taken upon himself the sicknesses and sorrows of the world; and taking them upon himself he would bear them away. I understand this, therefore, as expressing the twofold idea that he became deeply afflicted for us, and that.

being thus afflicted for us, he was able to carry away our sorrows. In part this would be done by his miraculous power in healing diseases, as mentioned by Matthew; in part by the influence of his religion, in enabling men to bear calamity, and in drying up the fountains of sorrow. Matthew, then, it is believed, has quoted this passage exactly in the sense in which it was used by Isaiah; and if so, it should not be adduced to prove that he bore the *sins* of men—true as is that doctrine, and certainly as it has been affirmed in other parts of this chapter. ¶ *And carried.* Heb. סָבַל *sâbhăl.* This word means properly *to carry,* as a burden; to be laden with, &c. (Isa. xlvi. 4, 7; Gen. xlix. 15.) It is applied to carrying burdens (1 Kings v. 15; 2 Chron. ii. 2; Neh. iv. 10, 17; Eccl. xii. 5). The verb with its derivative noun occurs in twenty-six places in the Old Testament, twenty-three of which relate to carrying burdens, two others relate to sins, and the other (Lam. v. 7) is rendered, 'We *have borne* their iniquities.' The primary idea is undoubtedly that of carrying a burden; lifting it, and bearing it in this manner. ¶ *Our sorrows.* The word used here (מַכְאֹב, from כָּאַב, *to have pain,* sorrow, to grieve, or be sad), means properly *pain, sorrow, grief.* In the Old Testament it is rendered 'sorrow' and 'sorrows' (Eccl. i. 18; Lam. i. 12–18; Isa. lxv. 14; Jer. xlv. 3; xxx. 15); 'grief' (Job xvi. 6; Ps. lxix. 26; 2 Chron. vi. 29); 'pain' (Job xxxiii. 19; Jer. xv. 18; li. 8). Perhaps the proper difference between this word and the word translated *griefs* is, that this refers to pains of the *mind,* that of the *body;* this to anguish, anxiety, or trouble of the soul; that to bodily infirmity and disease. Kennicott affirms that the word here used is to be regarded as applicable to griefs and distresses of the mind. 'It is evidently so interpreted,' says Dr. Magee (p. 220), 'in Ps. xxxii. 10, 'Many SORROWS shall be to the wicked;' and again, Ps. lxix. 29, 'But I am poor and SORROWFUL;' and again, Prov. xiv. 13, 'The heart is SORROWFUL;' and Eccl. i. 18, 'He that increaseth knowledge increaseth SORROW;' and so Eccl. ii. 18; Isa. lxv. 14; Jer. xxx. 15.' Agreeably to this, the word is translated by Lowth, in our common version, and most of the early English versions, 'Sorrows.' The Vulgate renders it, *Dolores;* the LXX. 'For us he is in sorrow' (ὀδυνᾶται), *i.e.,* is deeply grieved, or afflicted. The phrase, therefore, properly seems to mean that he took upon himself the *mental* sorrows of men. He not only took their diseases, and bore them away, but he also took or bore their mental griefs. That is, he subjected himself to the kind of mental sorrow which was needful in order to remove them. The word which is used by Matthew (viii. 17), in the translation of this, is νόσους. This word (νόσος) means properly *sickness,* disease (Matt. iv. 23, 24; ix. 35); but it is also used in a metaphorical sense for pain, sorrow, evil (Rob. *Lex.*) In this sense it is probable that it was designed to be used by Matthew. He refers to the general subject of human ills; to the sicknesses, sorrows, pains, and trials of life; and he evidently means, in accordance with Isaiah, that he took them on himself. He was afflicted for them. He undertook the work of removing them. Part he removed by direct miracle—as sickness;—part he removed by removing the *cause*—by taking away sin by the sacrifice of himself—thus removing the *source* of all ills; and in regard to *all,* he furnished the means of removing them by his own example and instructions, and by the great truths which he revealed as topics of consolation and support. On this important passage, see Magee, *On Atonement and Sacrifice,* pp. 227–262. ¶ *Yet we did esteem him stricken.* Lowth, 'Yet we thought him judicially stricken.' Noyes, 'We esteemed him stricken from above.' Jerome (Vulg.), 'We thought him to be a leper.' The LXX. render it, 'We considered him being in trouble (or in labour, ἐν πόνῳ) and under a stroke (or in a plague or Divine judgment, ἐν πληγῇ), and in affliction.' Chaldee, 'We thought him wounded, smitten from the presence of God, and afflicted.' The general idea is, that they thought he was subjected to great and severe punishment by God for his sins, or regarded him as an object

5 But he *was* wounded [1] for our
transgressions, *he was* bruised for
our iniquities: the chastisement of
our peace *was* upon him; and with
his [2] stripes [a] we are healed.

1 or, *tormented*. 2 *bruise*. a 1 Pe.2.24,25.

of Divine disapprobation. They *inferred* that one who was so abject and so despised; who suffered so much and so long, must have been abandoned by God to judicial sufferings, and that he was experiencing the proper result and effect of his own sins. The word rendered 'stricken,' (נָגוּעַ) means properly *struck*, or *smitten*. It is applied sometimes to the plague, or the leprosy, as an act by which God *smites* suddenly, and destroys men (Gen. xii. 17; Ex. xi. 1; Lev. xiii. 3, 9, 20; 1 Sam. vi. 9; Job xix. 21; Ps. lxxiii. 5), and very often elsewhere. Jerome explains it here by the word *leprous;* and many of the ancient Jews derived from this word the idea that the Messiah would be afflicted with the leprosy. Probably the idea which the word would convey to those who were accustomed to read the Old Testament in Hebrew would be, that he was afflicted or smitten in some way corresponding to the plague or the leprosy; and as these were regarded as special and direct Divine judgments, the idea would be that he would be smitten judicially by God, or be exposed to his displeasure and his curse. It is to be particularly observed here that the prophet does not say that he would thus be *in fact* smitten, accursed, and abandoned by God; but only that he would be thus esteemed, or thought, viz., by the Jews who rejected him and put him to death. It is not here said that he *was* such. Indeed, it is very strongly implied that he was not, since the prophet here is introducing them as confessing their error, and saying that they were mistaken. He was, say they, bearing *our* sorrows, not suffering for his own sins. ¶ *Smitten of God.* Not that he was actually smitten of God, but we esteemed him so. We treated him as one whom we regarded as being under the Divine malediction, and we therefore rejected him. We esteemed him to be smitten *by* God, and we acted as if such an one *should* be rejected and contemned. The word here used (נָכָה) means to *smite*, to strike, and is sometimes employed to denote Divine judgment, as it is here. Thus it means to smite with blindness (Gen. xix. 11); with the pestilence (Num. xiv. 12); with emerods (1 Sam. v. 6); with destruction, spoken of a land (Mal. iii. 24); of the river (Ex. vii. 25) when he turned it into blood. In all such instances, it means that JEHOVAH had inflicted a curse. And this is the idea here. They regarded him as under the judicial inflictions of God, and as suffering what his sins deserved. The foundation of this opinion was laid in the belief so common among the Jews, that great sufferings always argued and supposed great guilt, and were proof of the Divine displeasure. This question constitutes the inquiry in the Book of Job, and was the point in dispute between Job and friends. ¶ *And afflicted.* We esteemed him to be punished by God. In each of these clauses the words, 'For his own sins,' are to be understood. We regarded him as subjected to these calamities on account of his own sins. It did not occur to us that he could be suffering thus for the sins of others. The fact that the Jews attempted to prove that Jesus was a blasphemer, and deserved to die, shows the fulfilment of this, and the estimate which they formed of him (see Luke xxiii. 34; John xvi. 3; Acts iii. 17; 1 Cor. ii. 8).

5. *But he* was *wounded.* Marg. 'Tormented.' Jerome and the LXX. also render this, 'He was wounded.' Junius and Tremellius, 'He was affected with grief.' The Chaldee has given a singular paraphrase of it, showing how confused was the view of the whole passage in the mind of that interpreter. 'And he shall build the house of the sanctuary which was defiled on account of our sins, and which was delivered on account of our iniquities. And in his doctrine, peace shall be multiplied to us. And when we obey his words, our sins shall be remitted to us.' The Syriac renders it in a remarkable manner, 'He is slain on account of our sins,' thus showing

that it was a common belief that the Messiah would be violently put to death. The word rendered 'wounded' (מְחֹלָל), is a participle Pual, from חָלַל (*hhâlăl*), *to bore through*, to perforate, to pierce; hence to wound (1 Sam. xxxi. 3; 1 Chron. x. 3; Ezek. xxviii. 9). There is probably the idea of painful piercing, and it refers to some infliction of positive wounds on the body, and not to mere mental sorrows, or to general humiliation. The obvious idea would be that there would be some act of *piercing*, some penetrating wound that would endanger or take life. Applied to the actual sufferings of the Messiah, it refers undoubtedly to the piercing of his hands, his feet, and his side. The word 'tormented,' in the margin, was added by our translators because the Hebrew word might be regarded as derived from חוּל (*hhûl*), *to writhe*, to be tormented, to be pained—a word not unfrequently applied to the pains of parturition. But it is probable that it is rather to be regarded as derived from חָלַל, *to pierce*, or to wound. ¶ *For our transgressions.* The prophet here places himself among the people for whom the Messiah suffered these things, and says that he was not suffering for his own sins, but on account of theirs. The preposition 'for' (מִן) here answers to the Greek διά, on account of, and denotes the cause for which he suffered, and means, even according to Gesenius (*Lex.*), here, 'the ground or motive on account of, or because of which anything is done.' Compare Deut. vii. 7; Judg. v. 11; Est. v. 9; Ps. lxviii. 30; Cant. iii. 8. It is strikingly parallel to the passage in Rom. iv. 25: 'Who was delivered for (διά) our offences.' Compare 2 Cor. v. 21; Heb. ix. 28; 1 Pet. ii. 24. Here the sense is, that the reason why he thus suffered was, that we were transgressors. All along the prophet keeps up the idea that it was not on account of any sin of which he was guilty that he thus suffered, but it was for the sins of others—an idea which is everywhere exhibited in the New Testament. ¶ *He was bruised.* The word here used (דָּכָא) means properly *to be broken to pieces*, to be bruised, to be crushed (Job vi. 9; Ps. lxxii. 4). Applied to mind, it means to break down or crush by calamities and trials; and by the use of the word here, no doubt, the most severe inward and outward sufferings are designated. The LXX. render it, Μεμαλάκισται—'He was rendered languid,' or feeble. The same idea occurs in the Syriac translation. The meaning is, that he was under such a weight of sorrows on account of our sins, that he was, as it were, crushed to the earth. How true this was of the Lord Jesus it is not necessary here to pause to show. ¶ *The chastisement of our peace.* That is, the chastisement by which our peace is effected or secured was laid upon him; or, he took it upon himself, and bore it, in order that we might have peace. Each word here is exceedingly important, in order to a proper estimate of the nature of the work performed by the Redeemer. The word 'chastisement' (מוּסָר), properly denotes the correction, chastisement, or punishment inflicted by parents on their children, designed to amend their faults (Prov. xxii. 15; xxiii. 13). It is applied also to the discipline and authority of kings (Job xxii. 18); and to the discipline or correction of God (Job v. 17; Hos. v. 2). Sometimes it means admonition or instruction, such as parents give to children, or God to men. It is well rendered by the LXX. by Παιδεία; by Jerome, *Disciplina.* The word does not of necessity denote *punishment*, though it is often used in that sense. It is properly that which *corrects*, whether it be by admonition, counsel, punishment, or suffering. Here it cannot properly mean *punishment*—for there is no punishment where there is no guilt, and the Redeemer had done no sin;—but it means that he took upon himself the sufferings which would secure the peace of those for whom he died—those which, if they could have been endured by themselves, would have effected their peace with God. The word *peace* means evidently their peace with God; reconciliation with their Creator. The work of religion in the soul is often represented as *peace;* and the Redeemer is spoken of as the great agent by whom that is secured. 'For he is our peace' (Eph. ii. 14, 15, 17; comp. Acts x. 36; Rom. v. 1; x. 15). The phrase 'upon him,' means that the burden by which the peace of men was effected was laid upon him, and that he bore it. It is parallel with the expressions which speak of his *bearing* it, *carrying* it, &c. And the sense of the whole is, that he endured the sorrows, whatever they were, which were needful to secure our peace with God. ¶ *And with his stripes.* Marg. 'Bruise.' The word here used in Hebrew (חַבּוּרָה) means properly *stripe, weal, bruise, i.e.*, the mark or print of blows on the skin. Gr. Μώλωπι. Vulg. *Livore.* On the meaning of the Hebrew word, see Notes on ch. i. 6. It occurs in the following places, and is translated by stripe, and stripes (Ex. xxi. 25, *bis*); bruises (Isa. i. 6); hurt (Gen. iv. 23); blueness (Prov. xx. 30); wounds (Ps. xxxviii. 5); and spots, as of a leopard (Jer. xiii. 23). The proper idea is the weal or wound made by bruising; the mark designated by us when we speak of its being 'black and blue.' It is not a flesh wound; it does not draw blood; but the blood and other humours are collected under the skin. The obvious and natural idea conveyed by the word here is, that the individual referred to would be subjected to some treatment that would cause such a weal or stripe; that is, that he would be beaten, or scourged. How literally this was applicable to the Lord Jesus, it is unnecessary to attempt to prove (see Matt. xxvii. 26). It may be remarked here, that this could not be mere conjecture. How could Isaiah, seven hundred years before it occurred, *conjecture* that the Messiah would be *scourged* and *bruised?* It is this *particularity* of prediction, compared with the literal fulfilment, which furnishes the fullest demonstration that the prophet was inspired. In the prediction nothing is *vague* and *general.* All is particular and minute, as if he saw what was done, and the description is as minutely accurate as if he was describing what was actually occurring before his eyes. ¶ *We are healed.* Literally, it is healed to us; or healing has happened to us. The *healing* here referred to, is spiritual healing, or healing from sin. Pardon of sin, and restoration to the favour of God, are not unfrequently represented as an act of *healing.* The figure is derived from the fact that awakened and convicted sinners are often represented as crushed, broken, bruised by the weight of their transgressions, and the removal of the load of sin is represented as an act of healing. 'I said, O LORD, be merciful unto me; heal my soul; for I have sinned againt thee' (Ps. xli. 4). 'Have mercy upon me, O LORD, for I am weak; O LORD, heal me, for my bones are vexed' (Ps. vi. 2). 'Who forgiveth all thine iniquities; who healeth all thy diseases' (Ps. ciii. 3). The idea here is, that the Messiah would be scourged; and that it would be by that scourging that health would be imparted to our souls. It would be in our place, and in our stead; and it would be designed to have the same effect in recovering us, as though it had been inflicted on ourselves. And will it not do it? Is it not a fact that it has such an effect? Is not a man *as* likely to be recovered from a course of sin and folly, who sees another suffer in his place what he ought himself to suffer, as though he was punished himself? Is not a wayward and dissipated son quite as likely to be recovered to a course of virtue by seeing the sufferings which his career of vice causes to a father, a mother, or a sister, as though he himself were subjected to severe punishment? When such a son sees that he is bringing down the gray hairs of his father with sorrow to the grave; when he sees that he is breaking the heart of the mother that bore him; when he sees a sister bathed in tears, or in danger of being reduced to poverty or shame by his course, it will be far more likely to reclaim him than would be personal suffering, or the prospect of poverty, want, and an early death. And it is on this principle that the plan of salvation is founded. We shall be more certainly reclaimed by the voluntary sufferings of the innocent in our behalf, than we should be by being personally punished. Punishment would make no atonement, and would bring back no sinner to God. But the suffering of the Redeemer in behalf of men is adapted to save the world, and will in fact arrest, reclaim, and redeem all who shall ever enter into heaven.

[Sin is not only a crime for which we were

6 All we, like sheep, have gone astray; we have turned every one to his own way; and the LORD hath laid[1] on him the iniquity of us [a] all.

1 *made the iniquities of us all to meet on him.*

a Ro.4.25; 1 Pe.3.18.

condemned to die, and which Christ purchased for us the pardon of, but it is a disease which tends directly to the death of our souls, and which Christ provided for the cure of. *By his stripes, i.e.*, the sufferings he underwent, he purchased for us the Spirit and grace of God, to mortify our corruptions, which are the distempers of our souls; and to put our souls in a good state of health, that they may be fit to serve God, and prepare to enjoy him. And by the doctrine of Christ's cross, and the powerful arguments it furnisheth us with against sin, the dominion of sin is broken in us, and we are fortified against that which feeds the disease.—*Henry.*]

6. *All we, like sheep, have gone astray.* This is the penitent confession of those for whom he suffered. It is an acknowledgment that they were going astray from God; and the reason why the Redeemer suffered was, that the race had wandered away, and that JEHOVAH had laid on him the iniquity of all. Calvin says, 'In order that he might more deeply impress on the minds of men the benefits derived from the death of Christ, he shows how necessary was that healing of which he had just made mention. There is here an elegant antithesis. For in ourselves we were scattered; in Christ we are collected together; by nature we wander, and are driven headlong towards destruction; in Christ we find the way by which we are led to the gate of life.' The condition of the race without a Redeemer is here elegantly compared to a flock without a shepherd, which wanders where it chooses, and which is exposed to all dangers. This image is not unfrequently used to denote estrangement from God (1 Pet. ii. 25): 'For ye were as sheep going astray, but are now returned to the Shepherd and Bishop of your souls.' Compare Num. xxvii. 17; 1 Kings xxii. 17; Ps. cxix. 176; Ezek. xxxiv. 5; Zech. x. 2; Matt. ix. 36. Nothing could more strikingly represent the condition of men. They had wandered from God. They were following their own paths, and pursuing their own pleasures. They were without a protector, and they were exposed on every hand to danger. ¶ *We have turned every one to his own way.* We had all gone in the path which we chose. We were like sheep which have no shepherd, and which wander where they please, with no one to collect, defend, or guide them. One would wander in one direction, and another in another; and, of course, solitary and unprotected, they would be exposed to the more danger. So it was, and is, with man. The bond which should have united him to the Great Shepherd, the Creator, has been broken. We have become lonely wanderers, where each one pursues his own interest, forms his own plans, and seeks to gratify his own pleasures, regardless of the interest of the whole. If we had not sinned, there would have been a common bond to unite us to God, and to each other. But now we, as a race, have become dissocial, selfish, following our own pleasures, and each one living to gratify his own passions. What a true and graphic description of man! How has it been illustrated in all the selfish schemes and purposes of the race! And how is it still illustrated every day in the plans and actions of mortals! ¶ *And the* LORD *hath laid on him.* Lowth renders this, 'JEHOVAH hath made to light on him the iniquity of us all.' Jerome (Vulg.) renders it, *Posuit Dominus in eo*—'The Lord placed on him the iniquity of us all.' The LXX. render it, Κύριος παρέδωκεν αὐτὸν ταῖς ἁμαρτίαις ἡμῶν—'The Lord gave him for our sins.' The Chaldee renders it, 'From the presence of the Lord there was a willingness (רַעֲוָא) to forgive the sins of all of us on account of him.' The Syriac has the same word as the Hebrew. The word here used (פָּגַע) means, properly, *to strike upon* or *against*, to impinge on any one or anything, as the Gr. πηγνύω. It is used in a hostile sense, to denote an act of rushing upon a foe (1 Sam. xxii. 17; to kill, to slay (Judg. viii. 21; xv. 12; 2 Sam. i. 15). It also means to light upon, to meet with any one (Gen. xxviii. 11; xxxii. 2). Hence also to make peace with any one; to strike a league or compact (Isa. lxiv. 4). It is rendered, in our English version, 'reacheth to' (Josh. xix. 11, 22, 26,

7 He was oppressed, and he was afflicted; yet he opened not his mouth: he is brought as a lamb to the slaughter, and as a sheep before her shearers is dumb, so he opened not his mouth.

27, 34); 'came,' (Josh. xvi. 7); 'met' and 'meet' (Gen. xxxii. 1; Ex. xxiii. 4; Num. xxxv. 19; Josh. ii. 16; xviii. 10; Ruth ii. 22; 1 Sam. x. 5; Isa. lxiv. 5; Amos v. 19); 'fall' (Judg. viii. 21; 1 Sam. xxii. 17; 2 Sam. i. 15; 1 Kings ii. 29); 'entreat' (Gen. xviii. 8; Ruth i. 16; Jer. xv. 11); 'make intercession' (Isa. lix. 16; liii. 12; Jer. vii. 16; xxvii. 18; xxxvi. 25); 'he that comes betwixt' (Job xxxvi. 22); and 'occur' (1 Kings v. 4). The radical idea seems to be that of *meeting*, occurring, encountering; and it means here, as Lowth has rendered it, that they were caused to *meet* on him, or perhaps more properly, that JEHOVAH caused them to *rush* upon him, so as to overwhelm him in calamity, as one is overcome or overwhelmed in battle. The sense is, that he was not overcome by his own sins, but that he encountered *ours*, as if they had been made to rush to meet him and to prostrate him. That is, he suffered in our stead; and whatever he was called to endure was in consequence of the fact that he had taken the place of sinners; and having taken their place, he *met* or *encountered* the sufferings which were the proper expressions of God's displeasure, and sunk under the mighty burden of the world's atonement. ¶ *The iniquity of us all* (see Notes on ver. 5). This cannot mean that he became a sinner, or was guilty in the sight of God; for God always regarded him as an innocent being. It can only mean that he suffered *as if* he had been a sinner; or, that he suffered that which, *if* he had been a sinner, would have been a proper expression of the evil of sin. It may be remarked here—1. That it is impossible to find stronger language to denote the fact that his sufferings were intended to make expiation for sin. Of what *martyr* could it be said that JEHOVAH had caused to meet on him the sins of the world? 2. This language is that which naturally expresses the idea that he suffered for *all men*. It is universal in its nature, and naturally conveys the idea that there was no limitation in respect to the number of those for whom he died.*

7. *He was oppressed* (נִגַּשׂ). Lowth renders this, 'It was exacted.' Hengstenberg, 'He was abased.' Jerome (Vulg.), 'He was offered because he was willing.' The LXX. 'He, on account of his affliction, opened not his mouth,'—implying that his silence arose from the extremity of his sorrows. The Chaldee renders it, 'He prayed, and he was heard, and before he opened his mouth he was accepted.' The Syriac, 'He came and humbled himself, neither did he open his mouth.' Kimchi supposes that it means, 'it was exacted;' and that it refers to the fact that taxes were demanded of the exiles, when they were in a foreign land. The word here used (נָגַשׂ) properly means, *to drive*, to impel, to urge; and then to urge a debtor, to exact payment; or to exact tribute, a ransom, &c. (see Deut. xv. 2, 3; 2 Kings xxiii. 35.) Compare Job iii. 18; Zech. ix. 8; x. 4, where one form of the word is rendered 'oppressor;' Job xxxix. 7, the 'driver;' Ex. v. 6, 'taskmasters;' Dan. xi. 20, 'a raiser of taxes.' The idea is that of *urgency*, oppression, vexation, of being hard pressed, and ill treated. It does not refer here necessarily to what was exacted by God, or to sufferings inflicted by him—though it may include those—but it refers to *all* his oppressions, and the severity of his sufferings from all quarters. He was urged, impelled, oppressed, and yet he was patient as a lamb. ¶ *And he was afflicted*. Jahn and Steudel propose to render this, 'He suffered himself to be afflicted.' Hengstenberg renders it, 'He suffered patiently, and opened not his mouth.' Lowth, 'He was made answerable; and he opened not his mouth.' According to this, the idea is, that he had voluntarily taken upon himself the sins of

---

* See the Supplementary Notes on imputation of sin and extent of atonement, under Rom. v. 12, 19; 2 Cor. v. 19; Gal. iii. 13; and 1 Cor. v. 14.

8 He [a] was taken [1] from prison
and from judgment: and who shall
declare his generation? for he [b] was
cut off out of the land of the living;
for the transgression of my people
was he stricken.

a Ac.8.32-35.
1 or, *away by distress and judgment; but who.*
b Da.9.26.

---

men, and that having done so, he was held answerable as a surety. But it is doubtful whether the Hebrew will bear this construction. According to Jerome, the idea is that he voluntarily submitted, and that this was the cause of his sufferings. Hensler renders it, 'God demands the debt, and he the great and righteous one suffers.' It is probable, however, that our translation has retained the correct sense. The word עָנָה, in Niphil, means *to be afflicted*, to suffer, be oppressed or depressed (Ps. cxix. 107), and the idea here is, probably, that he was greatly distressed and afflicted. He was subjected to pains and sorrows which were hard to be borne, and which are usually accompanied with expressions of impatience and lamentation. The fact that *he* did not open his mouth in complaint was therefore the more remarkable, and made the merit of his sufferings the greater. ¶ *Yet he opened not his mouth.* This means that he was perfectly quiet, meek, submissive, patient, He did not open his mouth to complain *of* God on account of the great sorrows which he had appointed to him; nor *to* God on account of his being ill-treated by man. He did not use the language of reviling when he was reviled, nor return on men the evils which they were inflicting on him (comp. Ps. xxxix. 9). How strikingly and literally was this fulfilled in the life of the Lord Jesus! It would seem almost as if it had been written after he lived, and was history rather than prophecy. In no other instance was there ever so striking an example of perfect patience; no other person ever so entirely accorded with the description of the prophet. ¶ *He is brought as a lamb to the slaughter.* This does not mean that he was led to the slaughter as a lamb is, but that as a lamb which is led to be killed is patient and silent, so was he. He made no resistance. He uttered no complaint. He suffered himself to be led quietly along to be put to death. What a striking and beautiful description! How tender and how true! We can almost see here the meek and patient Redeemer led along without resistance; and amidst the clamour of the multitude that were assembled with various feelings to conduct him to death, himself perfectly silent and composed. With all power at his disposal, yet as quiet and gentle as though he had no power; and with a perfect consciousness that he was going to die, as calm and as gentle as though he were ignorant of the design for which they were leading him forth. This image occurs also in Jeremiah, ch. xi. 19, 'But I was like a lamb or an ox that is brought to the slaughter.' ¶ *As a sheep.* As a sheep submits quietly to the operation of shearing. Compare 1 Pet. ii. 23, 'Who when he was reviled, reviled not again.' Jesus never opened his mouth to revile or complain. It was opened only to bless those that cursed him, and to pray for his enemies and murderers.

8. *He was taken from prison.* Marg. 'Away by distress and judgment.' The general idea in this verse is, that the sufferings which he endured for his people were terminated by his being, after some form of trial, cut off out of the land of the living. Lowth renders this, 'By an oppressive judgment he was taken off.' Noyes, 'By oppression and punishment he was taken away.' The LXX. render it, 'In his humiliation (ἐν τῇ ταπεινώσει), his judgment (ἡ κρίσις αὐτοῦ), [his legal trial, *Thomson*], was taken away;' and this translation was followed by Philip when he explained the passage to the eunuch of Ethiopia (Acts viii. 33). The eunuch, a native of Ethiopia, where the Septuagint was commonly used, was reading this portion of Isaiah in that version, and the version was sufficiently accurate to express the general sense of the passage, though it is by no means a literal translation. The Chaldee renders this verse, 'From infirmities and retribution he shall collect our captivity, and the

wonders which shall be done for us in his days who can declare? Because he shall remove the dominion of the people from the land of Israel; the sins which my people have sinned shall come even unto them.' The Hebrew word which is here used (עֹצֶר, from עָצַר, *to shut up, to close*, means properly *a shutting up*, or *closure;* and then constraint, oppression, or vexation. In Ps. cvii. 39, it means violent restraint, or oppression. It does not mean *prison* in the sense in which that word is now used. It refers rather to restraint, and detention; and would be better translated by *confinement*, or by *violent oppression.* The Lord Jesus, moreover, was not confined in prison. He was bound, and placed under a guard, and was thus secured. But neither the word used here, nor the account in the New Testament, leads us to suppose that in fact he was incarcerated. There is a strict and entire conformity between the statement here, and the facts as they occurred on the trial of the Redeemer (see John xviii. 24; comp. Notes on Acts viii. 33). ¶ *And from judgment.* From a judicial decision; or by a judicial sentence. This statement is made in order to make the account of his sufferings more definite. He did not merely suffer affliction; he was not only a man of sorrows in general; he did not suffer in a tumult, or by the excitement of a mob; but he suffered under a form of law, and a sentence was passed in his case (comp. Jer. i. 16; 2 Kings xxv. 6), and in accordance with that he was led forth to death. According to Hengstenberg, the two words here 'by oppression,' and 'by judicial sentence,' are to be taken together as a hendiadys, meaning an oppressive, unrighteous proceeding. So Lowth understands it. It seems to me, however, that they are rather to be taken as denoting separate things—the *detention* or *confinement* preliminary to the trial, and the sentence consequent upon the mock trial. ¶ *And who shall declare his generation?* The word rendered 'declare' means to relate, or announce. 'Who can give a correct statement in regard to it'—implying either that there was some want of willingness or ability to do it. This phrase has been very variously interpreted; and it is by no means easy to fix its exact meaning. Some have supposed that it refers to the fact that when a prisoner was about to be led forth to death, a crier made proclamation calling on any one to come forward and assert his innocence, and declare his manner of life. But there is not sufficient proof that this was done among the Jews, and there is no evidence that it was done in the case of the Lord Jesus. Nor would this interpretation exactly express the sense of the Hebrew. In regard to the meaning of the passage, besides the sense referred to above, we may refer to the following opinions which have been held, and which are arranged by Hengstenberg:—1. Several, as Luther, Calvin, and Vitringa, translate it, 'Who will declare the length of his life?' *i.e.*, who is able to determine the length of his future days—meaning that there would be no end to his existence, and implying that though he would be cut off, yet he would be raised again, and would live for ever. To this, the only material objection is, that the word דּוֹר *dōr* (*generation*), is not elsewhere used in that sense. Calvin, however, does not refer it to the personal life of the Messiah, so to speak, but to his life in the church, or to the perpetuity of his life and principles in the church which he redeemed. His words are: 'Yet we are to remember that the prophet does not speak only of the person of Christ, but embraces the whole body of the church, which ought never to be separated from Christ. We have, therefore, says he, a distinguished testimony respecting the perpetuity of the church. For as Christ lives for ever, so he will not suffer his kingdom to perish.'—(*Comm. in loco.*) 2. Others translate it, 'Who of his contemporaries will consider it,' or 'considered it?' So Storr, Döderlin, Dathe, Rosenmüller and Gesenius render it. According to Gesenius it means, 'Who of his contemporaries considered that he was taken out of the land of the living on account of the sin of my people?' 3. Lowth and some others adopt the interpretation first suggested, and render it, 'His manner of life who would declare?' In support of this, Lowth appeals to the passages from the Mishna and the Gemara of Babylon, where it is said that before any one was punished for a capital crime, proclamation was made before him by a crier in these words, 'Whosoever knows anything about his innocence, let him come and make it known.' On this passage the Gemara of Babylon adds, 'that before the death of Jesus, this proclamation was made forty days; but no defence could be found.' This is certainly false; and there is no sufficient reason to think that the custom prevailed at all in the time of Isaiah, or in the time of the Saviour. 4. Others render it, 'Who can express his posterity, the number of his descendants?' So Hengstenberg renders it. So also Kimchi. 5. Some of the fathers referred it to the humanity of Christ, and to his miraculous conception. This was the belief of Chrysostom. See Calvin *in loco.* So also Morerius and Cajetan understood it. But the word is never used in this sense. The word דּוֹר *dōr* (*generation*), means properly an age, generation of men; the revolving period or circle of human life; from דּוּר *dūr, a circle* (Deut. xxiii. 3, 4, 9; Eccl. i. 4). It then means, also, a dwelling, a habitation (Ps. xlix. 20; Isa. xxxviii. 12). It occurs often in the Old Testament, and is in all other instances translated 'generation,' or 'generations.' Amidst the variety of interpretations which have been proposed, it is perhaps not possible to determine with any considerable degree of certainty what is the true sense of the passage. The only light, it seems to me, which can be thrown on it, is to be derived from the 10th verse, where it is said, 'He shall see his seed, he shall prolong his days;' and this would lead us to suppose that the sense is, that he would have a posterity which no one would be able to enumerate, or declare. According to this, the sense would be, 'He shall be indeed cut off out of the land of the living. But his name, his *race* shall not be extinct. Notwithstanding this, his generation, race, posterity, shall be so numerous that no one shall be able to declare it.' This interpretation is not quite satisfactory, but it has more probabilities in its favour than any other. ¶ *For* (כִּי *ki*). This particle does not here denote the *cause* of what was just stated, but points out the connection (comp. 1 Sam. ii. 21; Ezra x. 1). In these places it denotes the same as 'and.' This seems to be the sense here. Or, if it be here a *causal* particle, it refers not to what immediately goes before, but to the general strain and drift of the discourse. All this would occur to him because he was cut off on account of the transgression of his people. He was taken from confinement, and was dragged to death by a judicial sentence, and he should have a numerous spiritual posterity, *because* he was cut off on account of the sins of the people. ¶ *He was cut off.* This evidently denotes a violent, and not a peaceful death. See Dan. ix. 26: 'And after threescore and two weeks shall the Messiah be cut off, but not for himself.' The LXX. render it, 'For his life is taken away from the earth.' The word here used (גָּזַר), means properly *to cut*, to cut in two, to divide. It is applied to the act of cutting down trees with an axe (see 2 Kings vi. 4). Here the natural and obvious idea is, that he would be violently taken away, as if he was cut down in the midst of his days. The word is never used to denote a peaceful death, or a death in the ordinary course of events; and the idea which would be conveyed by it would be, that the person here spoken of would be cut off in a violent manner in the midst of his life. ¶ *For the transgression of my people.* The meaning of this is not materially different from 'on account of our sins.' 'The speaker here—Isaiah—does not place himself in opposition to the people, but includes himself among them, and speaks of them as his people, *i.e.*, those with whom he was connected.'—(Hengstenberg.) Others, however, suppose that JEHOVAH is here introduced as speaking, and that he says that the Messiah was to be cut off for the sins of *his* people. ¶ *Was he stricken.* Marg. 'The stroke upon him;' *i.e.*, the stroke came upon him. The word rendered in the margin 'stroke' (נֶגַע), denotes properly *a blow* (Deut. xvii. 8

9 And he made his grave with the wicked, and with the rich [a]in his death ;[1] because he had done no violence, neither *was any* deceit in his mouth.

[a] Mat.27.57. [1] *deaths.*

xxi. 5); then a spot, mark, or blemish in the skin, whether produced by the leprosy or any other cause. It is the same word which is used in ver. 4 (see Note on that verse). The Hebrew, which is rendered in the margin 'upon him' (לָמוֹ) has given rise to much discussion. It is properly and usually in the plural form, and it has been seized upon by those who maintain that this whole passage refers not to one individual but to some *collective* body, as of the people, or the prophets (see Analysis prefixed to ch. lii. 13), as decisive of the controversy. To this word Rosenmüller, in his Prolegomena to the chapter, appeals for a decisive termination of the contest, and supposes the prophet to have used this plural form for the express purpose of clearing up any difficulty in regard to his meaning. Gesenius refers to it for the same purpose, to demonstrate that the prophet must have referred to some *collective* body—as the prophets—and not to an individual. Aben Ezra and Abarbanel also maintain the same thing, and defend the position that it can never be applied to an individual. This is not the place to go into an extended examination of this word. The difficulties which have been started in regard to it, have given rise to a thorough critical examination of the use of the particle in the Old Testament, and an inquiry whether it is ever used in the singular number. Those who are disposed to see the process and the result of the investigation, may consult Ewald's *Heb. Grammar*, Leipzig, 1827, p. 365; Wiseman's *Lectures*, pp. 331–333, Andover Edit., 1837; and Hengstenberg's *Christology*, p. 523. In favour of regarding it as here used in the singular number, and as denoting an individual, we may just refer to the following considerations:—1. It is so rendered by Jerome, and in the Syriac version. 2. In some places the suffix מוֹ, attached to nouns, is certainly singular. Thus in Ps. xi. 7, (פָּנֵימוֹ) '*His* face,' speaking of God; Job xxvii. 23, 'Men shall clap their hands at him' (עָלֵימוֹ), where it is certainly singular; Isa. xliv. 15, 'He maketh it a graven image, and falleth down thereto' (לָמוֹ). 3. In Ethiopic the suffix is certainly singular (Wiseman). These considerations show that it is proper to render it in the singular number, and to regard it as referring to an individual. The LXX. render it, Εἰς θάνατον—'Unto death,' and evidently read it as if it were an abbreviation of לָמוּת *lâmŭth*, and they render the whole passage, 'For the transgressions of my people he was led unto death.' This translation is adopted and defended by Lowth, and has also been defended by Dr. Kennicott. The only argument which is urged, however, is, that it was so used by Origen in his controversy with the Jews; that they made no objection to the argument that he urged; and that as Origen and the Jews were both acquainted with the Hebrew text, it is to be presumed that this was then the reading of the original. But this authority is too slight to change the Hebrew text. The single testimony of Origen is too equivocal to determine any question in regard to the reading of the Hebrew text, and too much reliance should not be reposed even on his statements in regard to a matter of fact. This is one of the many instances in which Lowth has ventured to change the Hebrew text with no sufficient authority.

9. *And he made his grave with the wicked.* Jerome renders this, *Et dabit impios pro sepultura et divitem pro morte sua.* The LXX. render it, 'I will give the wicked instead of his burial (ἀντὶ τῆς ταφῆς), and the rich in the place, or instead of his death' (ἀντὶ τοῦ θανάτου). The Chaldee renders it, 'He will deliver the wicked into Gehenna, and the rich in substance who oppress, by a death that is destructive, that the workers of iniquity may no more be established, and that they may no more speak deceit in their mouth.' The Syriac renders it beautifully, 'the wicked gave ܩܒܪܗ a grave,' ܒܡܘܬܗ. Heng-

stenberg renders it, 'They appointed him his grave with the wicked (but he was with a rich man after his death); although he had done nothing unrighteous, and there was no guile in his mouth.' The sense, according to him, is, that not satisfied with his sufferings and death, they sought to insult him even in death, since they wished to bury his corpse among criminals. It is then incidentally remarked, that this object was not accomplished. This whole verse is exceedingly important, and every word in it deserves a serious examination, and attentive consideration. It has been subjected to the closest investigation by critics, and different interpretations have been given to it. They may be seen at length in Rosenmüller, Gesenius, and Hengstenberg. The word rendered 'he made' (וַיִּתֵּן, from נָתַן *nâthăn*) is a word of very frequent occurrence in the Scriptures. According to Gesenius, it means—1. *To give*, as (*a*) to give the hand to a victor; (*b*) to give into the hand of any one, *i.e.*, the power; (*c*) to give, *i.e.*, to turn the back; (*d*) to give, *i.e.*, to yield fruit as a tree; (*e*) to give, *i.e.*, to show compassion; (*f*) to give honour, praise, &c.; (*g*) to give into prison, or into custody. 2. *To sit*, place, put, lay; (*a*) to set before any one; (*b*) to set one over any person or thing; (*c*) to give one's heart to anything; *i.e.*, to apply the mind, &c. 3. *To make;* (*a*) to make or constitute one as anything; (*b*) to make a thing *as* something else. The notion of *giving*, or *giving over*, is the essential idea of the word, and not that of *making*, as our translation would seem to imply; and the sense is, that he was *given by design* to the grave of the wicked, or it was *intended* that he should occupy such a grave. The meaning then would be,

And his grave was appointed with the wicked;
But he was with a rich man in his death—
Although he had done no wrong,
Neither was there any guile in his mouth.

But who gave, or appointed him? I answer—1. The word may either here be used impersonally, as in Ps. lxxii. 15. 'to him shall be given,' marg. 'one shall give,' Eccl. ii. 21, meaning, that *some one* gave, or appointed his grave with the wicked; *i.e.*, his grave *was* appointed with the wicked; or, 2. The phrase 'my people' (עַמִּי) must be supplied; my people appointed his grave to be with the wicked; or, 3. God gave, or appointed his grave with the wicked. It seems to me that it is to be regarded as used *impersonally*, meaning that his grave was appointed with the wicked; and then the sense will be, that it was designed that he should be buried with the wicked, without designating the person or persons who intended it. So it is correctly rendered by Lowth and Noyes, 'His grave was appointed with the wicked.' ¶ *With the wicked.* It was designed that he should be buried with the wicked. The sense is, that it was not only intended to put him to death, but also to heap the highest indignity on him. Hence, it was intended to deny him an honourable burial, and to consign him to the same ignominious grave with the violators of the laws of God and man. One part of an ignominious punishment has often been to deny to him who has been eminent in guilt an honourable burial. Hence, it was said of Ahab (1 Kings xxi. 19), that the dogs should lick his blood; and of Jezebel that the dogs should eat her (1 Kings xxi. 23). Thus of the king of Babylon (Isa. xiv. 19), that he should 'be cast out of his grave as an abominable branch' (see Note on that place). Hence those who have been peculiarly guilty are sometimes quartered, and their heads and other parts of the body suspended on posts, or they are hung in chains, and their flesh left to be devoured by the fowls of heaven. So Josephus (*Ant.* iv. 8. 6), says, 'He that blasphemeth God, let him be stoned; and let him hang on a tree all that day, and then let him be buried in an ignominious and obscure manner.' The idea here is, that it was intended to cast the highest possible indignity on the Messiah; not only to put him to death, but even to deny him the privilege of an honourable burial, and to commit him to the same grave with the wicked. How remarkably was this fulfilled! As a matter of course, since he was put to death with wicked men, he would naturally have been buried with them, unless there had been some special interposition in his case. He was given up to be treated as a criminal; he was made to take the vacated place of a murderer—Barabbas—on the cross; he was subjected to the same indignity and cruelty to which the two malefactors were; and it was evidently designed also that he should be buried in the same manner, and probably in the same grave. Thus in John xix. 31, it is said that the Jews, because it was the preparation, in order that their bodies should not remain on the cross on the Sabbath day, 'besought Pilate that their legs might be broken, and that they might be taken away;' intending evidently that their death should be hurried in the same cruel manner, and that they should be buried in the same way. Who can but wonder at the striking accuracy of the prediction! ¶ *And with the rich* (עָשִׁיר). The words 'he was,' are here to be supplied. 'But he was with a rich man in his death.' The particle וְ, rendered *and*, is properly here adversative, and means *but, yet.* The meaning is, that although he had been executed with criminals, and it had been expected that he would be interred with them, yet he was associated with a rich man in his death; *i.e.*, in his burial. The purpose which had been cherished in regard to his burial was not accomplished. The word עָשִׁיר (from עָשַׁר, *to be straight*, to prosper, to be happy, and then to be rich), means properly *the rich*, and then the honourable and noble. It occurs very often in the Bible (*see* Taylor's *Concord.*), and is in all cases in our English version rendered 'rich.' Gesenius contends, however, that it sometimes is to be taken in a bad sense, and that it means proud, arrogant, impious, because riches are a source of pride, and pride to a Hebrew is synonymous with impiety. He appeals to Job xxvii. 19, in proof of this. But it is evident that the place in Job, 'The rich man shall lie down, but he shall not be gathered,' may be understood as speaking of a rich man as he is commonly found; and the *word* there does not mean proud, or wicked, but it means *a rich man* who is without religion. In all places where the word occurs in the Bible, the primary idea is that of *a rich man*—though he may be righteous or wicked, pious or impious, a friend of God or an enemy. That is to be determined by the connection. And the natural and proper idea here is that of a man who is wealthy, though without any intimation with regard to his moral character. It is rather implied that the man referred to would have a character different from 'the wicked,' with whom his grave was appointed. Several interpreters, however, of the highest character, have supposed that the word here refers to *the ungodly*, and means, that in his death he was associated with the ungodly. Thus Calvin supposes that it refers to the Scribes and Pharisees, and the impious and violent Romans who rushed upon him to take his life. Luther remarks that it means, 'a rich man; one who gives himself to the pursuit of wealth; *i.e.*, an ungodly man.' But the objection is insuperable that the word in the Bible *never* is used in this sense, to denote simply a wicked or an ungodly man. It may denote a rich man who *is* ungodly—but that must be determined by the connection. The simple idea in the word is that of *wealth*, but whether the person referred to be a man of fair or unfair, pure or impure character, is to be determined by other circumstances than the mere use of the word. So the word 'rich' is used in our language, and in all languages. The principal reason why it has here been supposed to mean *ungodly* is, that the parallelism is supposed to require it. But this is not necessary. It may be designed to intimate that there was a distinction between the *design* which was cherished in regard to his burial, and the *fact*. It was intended that he should have been interred with the wicked; but in fact, he was with the rich in his death. ¶ *In his death.* Marg. 'Deaths' (בְּמֹתָיו). Lowth renders this, 'His tomb.' He understands the letter ב as *radical* and not *servile;* and supposes that the word is בָּמוֹת *bâmōth* (*hills*); *i.e.*, sepulchral hills. Tombs, he observes, correctly, were often hills or *tumuli* erected over the bodies of the dead; and he supposes that the word *hill*, or *high place*, became synonymous with a *tomb*, or sepulchre. This interpretation was first suggested by Aben Ezra, and has been approved by Œcolampadius, Zuingle, Drusius, Ikin, Kuinoel, and others. But the interpretation is liable to great objections. 1. It is opposed to all the ancient versions. 2. There is no evidence that the word בָּמוֹת *bâmōth* is ever used except in one place (Ezek. xliii. 7, where it means also primarily *high places*, though there perhaps denoting a burial-place), in the sense of *βωμός*, a tomb, or place of burial. It denotes a high place or height; a stronghold, a fastness, a fortress; and then an elevated place, where the rites of idolatry were celebrated; and though it is not improbable that those places became burial-places—as we bury in the vicinity of a place of worship—yet the word simply and by itself does not denote a *tumulus*, or an elevated place of burial. The word here, therefore, is to be regarded as a noun from מָוֶת *mâvĕth*, or מוֹת *mōth*, plural מוֹתִים *mōthīm*, meaning the same as 'after his death'—'the grave.' The plural is used instead of the singular in Ezek. xxviii. 8–10; and also Job xxi. 32: 'Yet he shall be brought to the grave;' Marg. as Heb. 'graves.' The sense, therefore, is, that after his death he would be with a man of wealth, but without determining anything in regard to his moral character. The exact fulfilment of this may be seen in the account which is given of the manner of the burial of the Saviour by Joseph of Arimathea (Matt. xxvii. 57–60. Joseph was a rich man. He took the body, and wound it in a clean linen cloth, and laid it in his own new tomb, a tomb hewn out of a rock—that is, a grave designed for himself; such as a rich man would use, and where it was designed that a rich man should be laid. He was buried with spices (John xix. 39, 40); embalmed with a large quantity of myrrh and aloes, 'about a hundred pound weight,' in the mode in which *the rich* were usually interred. How different this from the interment of malefactors! How different from the way in which he would have been buried if he had been interred with them as it had been designed! And how very striking and minutely accurate this prophecy in circumstances which could not *possibly* have been the result of conjecture! How *could* a pretended prophet, seven hundred years before the event occurred, conjecture of one who was to be executed as a malefactor, and with malefactors, and who would in the ordinary course of events be buried *with* malefactors, conjecture that he would be rescued from such an ignominious burial by the interposition of a rich man, and buried in a grave designed for a man of affluence, and in the manner in which the wealthy are buried? ¶ *Because* (עַל *ăl*). This word here has probably the signification of *although*. It is used for עַל אֲשֶׁר *ăl ăshĕr*. Thus it is used in Job xvi. 17: 'Not for *any* injustice in my hands;' Heb. 'Although there is no injustice in my hands.' The *sense* here demands this interpretation. According to our common version, the meaning is, that he was buried with the rich man *because* he had done no violence, and was guilty of no deceit; whereas it is rather to be taken in connection with the entire strain of the passage, and to be regarded as meaning, that he was wounded, rejected, put to death, and buried by the hands of men, *although* he had done no violence. ¶ *He had done no violence.* The precise sense of the expression is, that he had not by harsh and injurious conduct provoked them to treat him in this manner, or deserved this treatment at their hands. In accordance with this, and evidently with this passage in his eye, the apostle Peter says of the Lord Jesus, 'who did no sin, neither was guile found in his mouth' (1 Pet. ii. 20–22). ¶ *Neither* was any *deceit in his mouth.* He was no deceiver, though he was regarded and treated as one. He was perfectly candid and sincere, perfectly true and holy. No one can doubt but this was exactly fulfilled in the Lord Jesus; and however it may be accounted for, it was true to the life, and it is applicable to him alone. Of what other dweller on the earth can it be said that there was *no* guile found in his mouth? Who else has lived who has *always* been perfectly free from deceit?

10 Yet it pleased the LORD to
bruise him; he hath put *him* to
grief: [1]when thou shalt make his
soul an [a]offering for sin, he shall
see *his* seed, he shall prolong *his*
days, and the pleasure [b]of the LORD
shall prosper in his hand.

1 or, *his soul shall make.*
a 2Co.5.21; He.9.24-26. b 2Th.1.11.

10. *Yet it pleased the* LORD *to bruise him.* In this verse, the prediction respecting the final glory and triumph of the Messiah commences. The design of the whole prophecy is to state, that in consequence of his great sufferings, he would be exalted to the highest honour (see Notes on ch. lii. 13). The sense of this verse is, 'he was subjected to these sufferings, not on account of any sins of his, but because, under the circumstances of the case, his sufferings would be pleasing to JEHOVAH. He saw they were necessary, and he was willing that he should be subjected to them. He has laid upon him heavy sufferings. And when he has brought a sin-offering, he shall see a numerous posterity, and the pleasure of the Lord shall prosper through him.' The LORD was 'pleased' with his sufferings, not because he has delight in the sufferings of innocence; not because the sufferer was in any sense guilty or ill-deserving; and not because he was at any time displeased or dissatisfied with what the Mediator did, or taught. But it was—1. Because the Messiah had *voluntarily* submitted himself to those sorrows which were necessary to show the evil of sin; and in view of the great object to be gained, the eternal redemption of his people, he was *pleased* that he would subject himself to so great sorrows to save them. He was pleased with the end in view, and with all that was necessary in order that the end might be secured. 2. Because these sufferings would tend to illustrate the Divine perfections, and show the justice and mercy of God. The gift of a Saviour, such as *he* was, evinced boundless benevolence; his sufferings in behalf of the guilty showed the holiness of his nature and law; and all demonstrated that he was at the same time disposed to save, and yet resolved that no one should be saved by dishonouring his law, or without expiation for the evil which had been done by sin. 3. Because these sorrows would result in the pardon and recovery of an innumerable multitude of lost sinners, and in their eternal happiness and salvation. The whole work was one of benevolence, and JEHOVAH was pleased with it *as* a work of pure and disinterested love. ¶ *To bruise him* (see Notes on ver. 5). The word here is the infinitive of Piel. 'To bruise him, or his being bruised, was pleasing to JEHOVAH;' that is, it was acceptable to him that he should be *crushed* by his many sorrows. It does not of necessity imply that there was any *positive* and *direct* agency on the part of JEHOVAH in bruising him, but only that the fact of his being thus crushed and bruised was acceptable to him. ¶ *He hath put* him *to grief.* This word, 'hath grieved him,' is the same which in another form occurs in ver. 4. It means that it was by the agency, and in accordance with the design of JEHOVAH, that he was subjected to these great sorrows. ¶ *When thou shalt make his soul.* Marg. 'His soul shall make.' According to the translation in the text, the speaker is the prophet, and it contains an address to JEHOVAH, and JEHOVAH is himself introduced as speaking in ver. 11. According to the margin, JEHOVAH himself speaks, and the idea is, that his soul should make an offering for sin. The Hebrew will bear either. Jerome renders it, 'If he shall lay down his life for sin.' The LXX. render it in the plural, 'If you shall give [an offering] for sin, your soul shall see a long-lived posterity.' Lowth renders it, 'If his soul shall make a propitiatory sacrifice.' Rosenmüller renders it, 'If his soul, *i.e.*, he himself, shall place his soul as an expiation for sin.' Noyes renders it, 'But since he gave himself a sacrifice for sin.' It seems to me that the margin is the correct rendering, and that it is to be regarded as in the third person. Thus the whole passage will be connected, and it will be regarded as the assurance of JEHOVAH himself, that when his life should be made a sacrifice for sin, he would see a great

multitude who should be saved as the result of his sufferings and death. ¶ *His soul.* The word here rendered 'soul' (נֶפֶשׁ) means properly *breath,* spirit, the life, the vital principle (Gen. i. 20–30; ix. 4; Lev. xvii. 11; Deut. xii. 23). It sometimes denotes the rational soul, regarded as the seat of affections and emotions of various kinds (Gen. xxxiv. 3; Ps. lxxxvi. 4; Isa. xv. 4; xlii. 1; Cant. i. 7; iii. 1–4). It is here equivalent to *himself*—when he himself is made a sin-offering, or sacrifice for sin. ¶ *An offering for sin* (אָשָׁם). This word properly means, *blame,* guilt which one contracts by transgression (Gen. xxvi. 10; Jer. li. 5); also a sacrifice for guilt; a sin-offering; an expiatory sacrifice. It is often rendered 'trespass-offering' Lev. v. 19; vii. 5; xiv. 21; xix. 21; 1 Sam. vi. 3, 8, 17). It is rendered 'guiltiness' (Gen. xxvi. 10); 'sin' (Prov. xiv. 9); 'trespass' (Num. v. 8). The idea here is, clearly, that he would be made an offering, or a sacrifice for sin; that by which guilt would be expiated and an atonement made. In accordance with this, Paul says (2 Cor. v. 21), that God 'made him to be sin for us' (ἁμαρτίαν), *i.e.*, a sin-offering; and he is called ἱλασμὸς and ἱλαστήριον, a propitiatory sacrifice for sins (Rom. iii. 25; 1 John ii. 2; iv. 10). The idea is, that he was himself innocent, and that he gave up his soul or life in order to make an expiation for sin—as the innocent animal in sacrifice was offered to God as an acknowledgment of guilt. There could be no more explicit declaration that he who is referred to here, did not die as a martyr merely, but that his death had the high purpose of making expiation for the sins of men. Assuredly this is not language which can be used of any martyr. In what sense could it be said of Ignatius or Cranmer that their souls or lives were made *an offering* (אָשָׁם or ἱλασμὸς) for sin? Such language is never applied to martyrs in the Bible; such language is never applied to them in the common discourses of men. ¶ *He shall see* his *seed.* His posterity; his descendants. The language here is taken from that which was regarded as the highest blessing among the Hebrews. With them length of days and a numerous posterity were regarded as the highest favours, and usually as the clearest proofs of the Divine love. 'Children's children are the crown of old men' (Prov. xvii. 6). See Ps. cxxvii. 5; cxxviii. 6: 'Yea, thou shalt see thy children's children, and peace upon Israel.' So one of the highest blessings which could be promised to Abraham was that he would be made the father of many nations (Gen. xii. 2; xvii. 5, 6). In accordance with this, the Messiah is promised that he shall see a numerous spiritual posterity. A similar declaration occurs in Ps. xxii. 30, which is usually applied to the Messiah. 'A seed shall serve him; it shall be accounted to the Lord for a generation.' The natural relation between father and son is often transferred to spiritual subjects. Thus the name *father* is often given to the prophets, or to teachers, and the name *sons* to disciples or learners. In accordance with this, the idea is here, that the Messiah would sustain this relation, and that there would be multitudes who would sustain to him the relation of spiritual children. There may be emphasis on the word 'see'—he shall *see* his posterity; for it was regarded as a blessing not only to *have* posterity, but to be permitted to live and *see* them. Hence the joy of the aged Jacob in being permitted to *see* the children of Joseph (Gen. xlviii. 11): 'And Israel said unto Joseph, I had not thought to see thy face; and lo, God hath showed me also thy seed.' ¶ *He shall prolong* his *days.* His life shall be long. This also is language which is taken from the view entertained among the Hebrews that long life was a blessing, and was a proof of the Divine favour. Thus, in 1 Kings iii. 14, God says to Solomon, 'if thou wilt walk in my ways, and keep my statutes and my commandments, as thy father David did walk, then I will lengthen thy days' (see Deut. xxv. 15; Ps. xxi. 4; xci. 16; Prov. iii. 2). The meaning here is, that the Messiah, though he should be put to death, would yet see great multitudes who should be his spiritual children. Though he should die, yet he would live again, and his days should be lengthened out. It is fulfilled in

11 He shall see of the travail of his soul, *and* shall be satisfied: by his [a] knowledge shall my righteous servant [b] justify [c] many; for he shall bear their iniquities.

[a] Jn.17.3; 2Pe.1.2,3. [b] 2 Jn.1.3. [c] Ro.3.24.

the reign of the Redeemer on earth, and in his eternal existence and glory in heaven. ¶ *And the pleasure of the* LORD. That is, that which shall please JEHOVAH; the work which he desires and appoints. ¶ *Shall prosper* (see Notes on ch. lii. 13, where the same word occurs). ¶ *In his hand.* Under his government and direction. Religion will be promoted and extended through him. The reward of all his sufferings in making an offering for sin would be, that multitudes would be converted and saved; that his reign would be permanent, and that the work which JEHOVAH designed and desired would prosper under his administration.

11. *He shall see of the travail of his soul.* This is the language of JEHOVAH, who is again introduced as speaking. The sense is, he shall see the fruit, or the result of his sufferings, and shall be satisfied. He shall see *so much good* resulting from his great sorrows; so much happiness, and so many saved, that the benefit shall be an ample compensation for all that he endured. The word here rendered 'travail' (עָמָל), denotes properly *labour, toil;* wearisome labour; labour and toil which produce exhaustion; and hence sometimes vexation, sorrow, grief, trouble. It is rendered 'labour' (Ps. xc. 10; cv. 44; Jer. xx. 18; Eccl. ii. 11–20); 'perverseness' (Num. xxi. 21); 'sorrow' (Job iii. 10); 'wickedness' (Job iv. 8); 'trouble' (Job v. 6, 7; Ps. lxxiii. 5); 'mischief' (Job xv. 35; Ps. vii. 13; x. 7–14; xciv. 20); 'travail,' meaning labour, or toil (Eccl. iv. 4–6); 'grievousness' (Isa. x. 1); 'iniquity' (Hab. i. 13); 'toil' (Gen. xli. 51); 'pain' (Ps. xxv. 18); and 'misery' (Prov. xxxi. 7). The word 'travail' with us has two senses, first, labour with pain, severe toil; and secondly, the pains of childbirth. The word is used here to denote excessive toil, labour, weariness; and refers to the arduous and wearisome labour and trial involved in the work of redemption, as that which exhausted the powers of the Messiah as a man, and sunk him down to the grave. ¶ And *shall be satisfied.* That is, evidently, he shall be permitted to see so much fruit of his labours and sorrows as to be an ample recompence for all that he has done. It is not improbable that the image here is taken from a husbandman who labours in preparing his soil for the seed, and who waits for the harvest; and who, when he sees the rich and yellow field of grain in autumn, or the wain heavily laden with sheaves, is abundantly satisfied for what he has done. He has pleasure in the contemplation of his labour, and of the result; and he does not regret the wearisome days and the deep anxiety with which he made preparation for the harvest. So with the Redeemer. There will be rich and most ample results for all that he has done. And when he shall look on the multitude that shall be saved; when he shall see the true religion spreading over the world; when he shall behold an immense host which no man can number gathered into heaven; and when he shall witness the glory that shall result to God from all that he has done, he shall see enough to be an ample compensation for all that he has endured, and he shall look on his work and its glorious results with pleasure. We may remark here that this implies that *great* and *most glorious* results will come out of this work. The salvation of a large portion of the race, of multitudes which no man can number, will be necessary to be any *suitable* remuneration for the sufferings of the Son of God. We may be assured that he will be 'satisfied,' only when multitudes are saved; and it is, therefore, morally certain that a large portion of the race, taken as a whole, will enter into heaven. Hitherto the number has been small. The great mass have rejected him, and have been lost. But there are brighter times before the church and the world. The pure gospel of the Redeemer is yet to spread around the globe, and it is yet to become, and to be for ages, the religion of the world.

Age after age is to roll on when all shall know him and obey him; and in those future times, what immense multitudes shall enter into heaven! So that it may yet be seen, that the number of those who will be lost from the whole human family, compared with those who will be saved, will be no greater in proportion than the criminals in a well-organized community who are imprisoned are, compared with the number of obedient, virtuous, and peaceful citizens. ¶ *By his knowledge.* That is, by the knowledge of him. The idea is, by becoming fully acquainted with him and his plan of salvation. The word *knowledge* here is evidently used in a large sense to denote *all* that constitutes acquaintance with him. Thus Paul says (Phil. iii. 10), 'That I may know him, and the power of his resurrection.' It is only by the knowledge of the Messiah; by an acquaintance with his character, doctrines, sufferings, death, and resurrection, that any one can be justified. Thus the Saviour says (John xvii. 3), 'And this is life eternal, that they might know thee the only true God, and Jesus Christ whom thou hast sent.' Men are to become acquainted with him; with his doctrines, and with his religion, or they can never be regarded and treated as righteous in the sight of a holy God. ¶ *Shall my righteous servant.* On the meaning of the word 'servant,' as applied to the Messiah, see Notes on ch. lii. 13. The word 'righteous' (צַדִּיק), Lowth supposes should be omitted. His reasons are—1. That three MSS., two of them ancient, omit it. 2. That it makes a solecism in this place; for, according to the constant usage of the Hebrew language, the adjective, in a phrase of this kind, ought to follow the substantive; and, 3. That it makes the hemistich too long. But none of these reasons are sufficient to justify a change in the text. The phrase literally is, 'the righteous, my servant;' and the sense is, evidently, 'my righteous servant.' The word *righteous*, applied to the Messiah, is designed to denote not only his personal holiness, but to have reference to the fact that he would make many *righteous* (יַצְדִּיק). It is applicable to him, because he was eminently holy and pure, and because also he was the source of righteousness to others; and in the work of justification it is important in the highest degree to fix the attention on the fact, that he by whom the sinner was to be justified was himself perfectly holy, and able to secure the justification and salvation of all who intrusted their souls to him. No man could feel secure of salvation unless he could commit his soul to one who was perfectly holy, and able to 'bring in everlasting righteousness.' ¶ *Justify* (יַצְדִּיק). The word צָדַק is of very frequent occurrence in the Bible; and no word is more important to a correct understanding of the plan of salvation than this, and the corresponding Greek word δικαιῶ. On the meaning of the Greek word, see Notes on Rom. i. 17. The Hebrew word means to be right, straight, as if spoken of a way (Ps. xxiii. 3). Hence, 1. To be just, righteous, spoken of God in dispensing justice (Ps. lv. 6); and of laws (Ps. xix. 10). 2. To have a just cause, to be in the right; (*a*) in a forensic sense (Gen. xxviii. 26; Job ix. 16–20; x. 15; xiii. 18); (*b*) of disputants, to be in the right (Job xxiii. 12); (*c*) to gain one's cause, to be justified (Isa. xliii. 9–26). In this sense it is now often used in courts of justice, where a man who is charged with crime shows that he did not do the deed, or that having done it he had a right to do it, and the law holds him innocent. 3. To be righteous, upright, good, innocent. In this sense the word is often used in the Bible (Job xv. 14; xxiii. 9; Ps. cxliii. 2). But in this sense the Messiah will *justify* no one. He did not come to declare that men *were* upright, just, innocent. Nor will he justify them because they can show that they have not committed the offences charged on them, or that they had a right to do what they have done. The whole work of justification through the Redeemer proceeds on the supposition that men are *not* in fact innocent, and that they cannot vindicate their own conduct. 4. In Hiphil, the word means, to pronounce just, or righteous. In a forensic sense, and as applied to the act of justification before

12 Therefore will I divide him *a portion* with the great, and he shall divide the spoil with the strong; because [a]he hath poured out his soul unto death: and he was numbered with the transgressors: and he bare the sin of many, and made intercession [b]for the transgressors.

a He.12.2.

b He.7.28; 1 Jn.2.1.

God, it means to declare righteous, or to admit to favour as a righteous person; and in connection with the pardon of sin, to resolve to treat as righteous, or as if the offence had not been committed. It is more than mere pardon; it involves the idea of a purpose to *treat as* righteous, and to acknowledge as such. It is not to declare that the person is innocent, or that he is not ill deserving, or that he had a right to do as he had done, or that he has a claim to mercy—for this is not true of any mortal; but it is to pardon, and to accept him *as if* the offence had not been committed—to regard him in his dealings with him, and treat him ever onward as if he were holy. This sense of the word here is necessary, because the whole passage speaks of his bearing sin, and suffering for others, and thus securing their justification. It does not speak of him as instructing men and thus promoting religion; but it speaks of his dying for them, and thus laying the foundation for their justification. They are justified only in connection with his bearing their iniquities; and this shows that the word is here used in the *forensic* sense, and denotes that they will be regarded and treated as righteous on account of what he has suffered in their behalf. ¶ *For he shall bear.* On the meaning of the word *bear*, see Notes on ver. 4. ¶ *Their iniquities.* Not that he became a sinner, or that sin can be transferred, which is impossible. Guilt and ill desert are personal qualities, and cannot be transferred from one to another. But the *consequences* of guilt may pass over to another; the *sufferings*, which would be a proper expression of the evil of sin, may be assumed by another. And this was done by the Redeemer. *He stood between the stroke of justice and the sinner, and received the blow himself.* He *intercepted*, so to speak, the descending sword of justice that would have cut the sinner down, and thus saved him. He thus bore their iniquities; *i.e.*, he bore in his own person what would have been a proper expression of the evil of sin if he had been himself the sinner, and had been guilty (see Notes on ver. 6). It is in connection with this that men become justified; and it is only by the fact that he has thus borne their iniquities that they can be regarded as righteous in the sight of a holy God. *They become interested in his merits just as he became interested in their iniquities.* There is in neither case any transfer of personal properties; but there is in both cases a participation in the *consequences* or the *results* of conduct. *He* endured the consequences or results of sin; *we* partake of the consequences or the results of his sufferings and death in our behalf. This is the great cardinal doctrine of justification; the peculiarity of the Christian scheme; the glorious plan by which lost men may be saved, and by which the guilty may become pardoned, and be raised up to endless life and glory; the *articulus stantis vel cadentis ecclesiæ*. Luther.*

12. *Therefore will I divide him.* I will divide *for* him (לוֹ *lo*). This verse is designed to predict the triumphs of the Messiah. It is language appropriate to him as a prince, and designed to celebrate his glorious victories on earth. The words here used are taken from the custom of distributing the spoils of victory after a battle, and the idea is, that as a conqueror takes valuable spoils, so the Messiah would go forth to the spiritual conquest of the world, and subdue it to himself. Rosenmüller renders this, *Dispertsam ei multos*—'I will divide to him the many;' *i.e.*, he shall have many as his portion. Hengsten-

* See Supplementary Notes, Gal. iii. 13; 2 Cor. v. 19, 21; and Rom. iv., v., in which the reader will see that the doctrine of imputation involves no such transference of moral character, no such infusion of sin or righteousness, as the author here and elsewhere alleges.

berg, 'I will give him the mighty for a portion.' So the LXX. 'Therefore he shall inherit (κληρονομήσει) many.' So Lowth, 'Therefore will I distribute to him the many for his portion.' But it seems to me that the sense is, that his portion would be *with* the mighty or the many (בָּרַבִּים) and that this interpretation is demanded by the use of the preposition ב in this case, and by the corresponding word אֶת prefixed to the word 'mighty.' The sense, according to this, is, that the spoils of his conquests would be *among* the mighty or the many; that is, that his victories would not be confined to a few in number, or to the feeble, but the triumphs of his conquests would extend afar, and be found among the potentates and mighty men of the earth. The word rendered here 'the great' (רַבִּים *răbbīm*), may mean either *many* or *powerful* and *great*. The parallelism here with the word עֲצוּמִים (*the mighty*), seems to demand that it be understood as denoting the great, or the powerful, though it is differently rendered by the Vulgate, the LXX., the Chaldee, by Castellio, and by Junius and Tremellius. The sense is, I think, that his conquests would be among the great and the mighty. He would overcome his most formidable enemies, and subdue them to himself. Their most valued objects; all that constituted their wealth, their grandeur, and their power, would be among the spoils of his victories. It would not be merely his feeble foes that would be subdued, but it would be the mighty, and there would be no power, however formidable, that would be able to resist the triumphs of his truth. The history of the gospel since the coming of the Redeemer shows how accurately this has been fulfilled. Already he has overcome the mighty, and the spoils of the conquerors of the world have been among the trophies of his victories. The Roman empire was subdued; and his conquests were among these conquerors, and his were victories over the subduers of nations. It will be still more signally fulfilled in coming times, when the kingdoms of this world shall become the kingdom of our Lord and of his Christ, and he shall reign for ever and ever (Rev. xi. 15). ¶ *And he shall divide the spoil with the strong.* And with the mighty, or with heroes, shall he divide the plunder. The idea here is not materially different from that which was expressed in the former member of the sentence. It is language derived from the conquests of the warrior, and means that his victories would be among the great ones of the earth; his conquests over conquerors. It was from language such as this that the Jews obtained the notion, that the Messiah would be a distinguished conqueror, and hence they looked forward to one who as a warrior would carry the standard of victory around the world. But it is evident that it may be applied with much higher beauty to the spiritual victories of the Redeemer, and that it expresses the great and glorious truth that the conquests of the true religion will yet extend over the most formidable obstacles on the earth. ¶ *Because he hath poured out his soul unto death.* His triumphs would be an appropriate reward for his sufferings, his death, and his intercession. The expression 'he poured out his soul,' or *his life* (נַפְשׁוֹ; see Notes on ver. 10), is derived from the fact that the life was supposed to reside in the blood (see Notes on Rom. iii. 25); and that when the blood was poured out, the life was supposed to flow forth with it. As a reward for his having thus laid down his life, he would extend his triumphs over the whole world, and subdue the most mighty to himself. ¶ *And he was numbered with the transgressors.* That is, he shall triumph *because* he suffered himself to be numbered with the transgressors, or to be put to death with malefactors. It does not mean that he was a transgressor, or in any way guilty; but that in his death he was in fact numbered with the guilty, and put to death with them. In the public estimation, and in the sentence which doomed him to death, he was regarded and treated as if he had been a transgressor. This passage is expressly applied by Mark to the Lord Jesus (Mark **xv**. 28). ¶ *And he bare the sin of many* (נָשָׂא *nâsâ*). On the meaning of this word 'bare,' see Notes on ver. 4;

and on the doctrine involved by his bearing sin, see the Note on ver. 4–6, 10. The idea here is, that he would triumph *because* he had thus borne their sins. As a reward for this God would bless him with abundant spiritual triumphs among men, and extend the true religion afar. ¶ *And made intercession for the transgressors.* On the meaning of the word here rendered 'made intercession' (יַפְגִּיעַ), see Notes on ver. 6, where it is rendered 'hath laid on him.' The idea is that of causing to meet, or to rush; and then to *assail*, as it were, with prayers, to supplicate for any one, to entreat (see Isa. lix. 16; Jer. xxxvi. 25). It may not refer here to the mere act of making prayer or supplication, but rather perhaps to the whole work of the intercession, in which the Redeemer, as High Priest, presents the merit of his atoning blood before the throne of mercy and pleads for men (see Rom. viii. 34; Heb. vii. 25; 1 John ii. 1). This is the closing part of his work in behalf of his people and of the world; and the sense here is, that he would be thus blessed with abundant and wide extended triumph, *because* he made intercession. All his work of humiliation, and all his toils and sufferings, and all the merit of his intercession, became necessary in order to his triumph, and to the spread of the true religion. In consequence of all these toils, and pains, and prayers, God would give him the victory over the world, and extend his triumphs around the globe. Here the work of the Mediator *in behalf* of men will cease. There is to be no more suffering, and beyond his intercessions he will do nothing for them. He will come again indeed, but he will come to judge the world, not to suffer, to bleed, to die, and to intercede. All his future conquests and triumphs will be in consequence of what he has already done; and they who are not saved *because* he poured out his soul unto death, *and* bare the sin of many, *and* made intercession, will not be saved at all. There will be no more sacrifice for sin, and there will be no other advocate and intercessor.

WE have now gone through, perhaps at tedious length, this deeply interesting and most important portion of the Bible. Assuming now (see the remarks prefixed to ch. lii. 13, *sq.*) that this was written seven hundred years before the Lord Jesus was born, there are some remarks of great importance to which we may just refer in the conclusion of this exposition.

1. The first is, the *minute* accuracy of the statements here as applicable to the Lord Jesus. While it is apparent that there has been no other being on earth, and no "collective body of men," to whom this can be applied, it is evident that the whole statement is applicable to the Redeemer. It is not the general accuracy to which I refer; it is not that there is some resemblance in the *outline* of the prediction; it is, that the statement is *minutely* accurate. It relates to his appearance, his rejection, the manner of his death, his being pierced, his burial. It describes, as minutely as could have been done after the events occurred, the manner of his trial, of his rejection, the fact of his being taken from detention and by a judicial sentence, and the manner in which it was designed that he should be buried, and yet the remarkable fact that this was prevented, and that he was interred in the manner in which the rich were buried (see Notes on vers. 2, 3, 7–10).

2. This coincidence could never have occurred if the Lord Jesus had been an impostor. To say nothing of the difficulty of attempting to fulfil a prediction by imposture and the general failure in the attempt, there are many things here which would have rendered *any* attempt of this kind utterly hopeless. A very large portion of the things referred to in this chapter were circumstances over which an impostor could have no control, and which he could bring about by no contrivance, no collusion, and no concert. They depended on the arrangements of Providence, and on the voluntary actions of men, in such a way that he could not affect them. How could he so order it as to grow up as a root out of a dry ground; to be despised and rejected of men; to be taken from detention and from a judicial sentence though innocent; to have it designed that he should be buried with malefactors, and to be numbered with transgressors, and yet to be rescued by a rich man, and placed in his tomb? This consideration becomes more striking when it is remembered that not a few men claimed to be the Messiah, and succeeded in imposing on many, and though they were at last abandoned or punished, yet between *their* lives and death, and the circumstances here detailed, there is not the shadow of a coincidence. It is to be remembered also that an impostor *would* not have aimed at what would have constituted a fulfilment of this prophecy. Notwithstanding

the evidence that it refers to the Messiah, yet it is certain also that the Jews expected no such personage as that here referred to. They looked for a magnificent temporal prince and conqueror; and an impostor *would* not have attempted to evince the character, and to go through the circumstances of poverty, humiliation, shame, and sufferings, here described. What impostor ever *would* have attempted to fulfil a prophecy by subjecting himself to a shameful death? What impostor *could* have brought it about in this manner if he had attempted it? No; it was only the true Messiah that either would or could have fulfilled this remarkable prophecy. Had an impostor made the effort, he must have failed; and it was not in human nature to attempt it under the circumstances of the case. All the claims to the Messiahship by impostors have been of an entirely different character from that referred to here.

3. We are then prepared to ask an infidel how he will dispose of this prophecy. That it existed seven hundred years before Christ is as certain as that the poems of Homer or Hesiod had an existence before the Christian era; as certain as the existence of any ancient document whatever. It will not do to say that it was forged—for this is not only without proof, but would destroy the credibility of all ancient writings. It will not do to say that it was the result of natural sagacity in the prophet—for whatever may be said of conjectures about empires and kingdoms, no natural sagacity can tell what will be the character of an individual man, or whether such a man as here referred to would exist at all. It will not do to say that the Lord Jesus was a cunning impostor and resolved to fulfil this ancient writing, and thus establish his claims; for, as we have seen, such an attempt would have belied human nature, and if attempted, could not have been accomplished. It remains then to ask what solution the infidel will give of these remarkable facts. We present him the prophecy—not a rhapsody, not conjecture, not a general statement; but minute, full, clear, unequivocal, relating to points which could not have been the result of conjecture, and over which the individual had no control. And then we present him with the record of the life of Jesus—minutely accurate in all the details of the fulfilment—a coincidence *as* clear as that between a biography and the original—and ask him to explain it. And we demand a definite and consistent answer to this. To turn away from it does not answer it. To laugh, does not answer it; for there is no argument in a sneer or a jibe. To say that it is not worth inquiry is not true, for it pertains to the great question of human redemption. But if he *cannot* explain it, then he should admit that it is such a prediction as only God could give, and that Christianity is true.

4. This chapter proves that the Redeemer died as an atoning sacrifice for men. He was not a mere martyr, and he did not come and live merely to set us an example. Of what martyr was the language here ever used, and how could it be used? How could it be said of any martyr that he bore our griefs, that he was bruised for our iniquities, that our sins were made to rush and meet upon him, and that he bare the sin of many? And if the purpose of his coming was merely to *teach* us the will of God, or to set us an example, why is such a prominence here given to his sufferings in behalf of others? Scarcely an allusion is made to his example, while the chapter is replete with statements of his sufferings and sorrows in behalf of others. It would be impossible to state in more explicit language the truth that he died as a sacrifice for the sins of men; that he suffered to make proper expiation for the guilty. No confession of faith on earth, no creed, no symbol, no standard of doctrine, contains more explicit statements on the subject. And if the language here used does not demonstrate that the Redeemer was an atoning sacrifice, it is impossible to conceive how such a doctrine could be taught or conveyed to men.

5. This whole chapter is exceedingly important to Christians. It contains the most full, continuous statement in the Bible of the design of the Redeemer's sufferings and death. And after all the light which is shed on the subject in the New Testament; after all the full and clear statements made by the Redeemer and the apostles; still, if we wish to see a full and continuous statement on the great doctrine of the atonement, we naturally recur to this portion of Isaiah. If we wish our faith to be strengthened, and our hearts warmed by the contemplation of his sufferings, we shall find no part of the Bible better adapted to it than this. It should not only be the subject of congratulation, but of much fervent prayer. No man can study it too profoundly. No one can feel too much anxiety to understand it. Every verse, every phrase, every word should be pondered until it fixes itself deep in the memory, and makes an eternal impression on the heart. If a man understands this portion of the Bible, he will have a correct view of the plan of salvation. And it should be the subject of profound and prayerful contemplation till the heart glows with love to that merciful God who was willing

to give the Redeemer to such sorrow, and to the gracious Saviour who, for our sins, was willing to pour out his soul unto death. I bless God that I have been permitted to study it; and I pray that this exposition—cold and imperfect as it is—may be made the means yet of extending correct views of the design of the Redeemer's death among his friends, and of convincing those who have doubted the truth of the Bible, that a prophecy like this demonstrates that the Book in which it occurs must be from God.

CHAPTER LIV.

ANALYSIS.

This chapter, probably closely connected in sense with the preceding, and growing out of the great truths there revealed respecting the work of the Messiah, contains a promise of the enlargement, the moral renovation, and the future glory of the kingdom of God, especially under the Messiah. Like the preceding and succeeding chapters, it may have been primarily designed to give consolation to the exiles in Babylon, but it was consolation to be derived from what would occur in distant times under the Messiah, and in the spread of the true religion. Few and feeble as they were then; oppressed and captive; despised and apparently forsaken, they were permitted to look forward to future days, and had the assurance of a vast increase from the Gentile world, and of permanent glory. The design of the whole chapter is *consolatory*, and is a promise of what would certainly result from the purpose of sending the Messiah to die for the world.

The chapter may be regarded as divided into the following portions:—

I. An address to the people of God, or to Jerusalem, regarded as then feeble, and promising great enlargement (1–6). 1. Promise of a great increase, under a two-fold image; first, Of a woman who had been barren, and who subsequently had many children (1); and, secondly, Of a *tent* that was to be enlarged, in order to accommodate those who were to dwell in it (2, 3). 2. The foundation of this promise or assurance, that Jehovah was the husband and protector of his people (4–6).

II. The covenant which Jehovah had made with his people was firm and immovable (7, 10). 1. He had indeed forsaken them for a little while, but it was only to gather them again with eternal and unchanging favour (7, 8). 2. His covenant with them would be as firm as that which he had made with Noah, and which he had so steadily observed (9). 3. It would be even more firm than the hills (10). They would depart, and the mountains would be removed; but his covenant with his people would be unshaken and eternal.

III. A direct address to his people, as if agitated and tossed on a heaving sea, promising future stability and glory (11–14). 1. They were then like a ship on the stormy ocean, and without comfort. 2. Yet there would be a firm foundation laid. These agitations would cease, and she would have stability. 3. The future condition of his people would be glorious. His church would rise on the foundation—the foundation of sapphires—like a splendid palace made of precious stones (11, 12). 4. All her children would be taught of Jehovah, and their peace and prosperity be great (13). 5. She would be far from oppression and from fear (14).

IV. She would be safe from all her foes. No weapon that should be formed against her would prosper. All they who made any attack on her were under his control, and God would defend her from all their assaults (15–17).

SING, [a] O barren, thou *that* didst not bear; break forth into singing, and cry aloud, thou *that* didst not travail with child: for more *are* the children of the desolate, than the children of the married wife, saith the Lord.

a Zep.3.14; Ga.4.27.

CHAPTER LIV.

1. *Sing, O barren.* That is, shout for joy, lift up the voice of exultation and praise. The 'barren' here denotes the church of God under the Old Testament, confined within the narrow limits of the Jewish nation, and still more so in respect to the very small number of true believers, and which seemed sometimes to be deserted of God, her husband (Lowth). It is here represented under the image of a female who had been destitute of children, and who now has occasion to rejoice on the reconciliation of her husband (ver. 6; Lowth), and on the accession of the Gentiles to her family. The Chaldee renders it, 'Rejoice, O Jerusalem, who hast been as a sterile woman that did not bear.' The church is often in the Bible compared to a female, and the connection between God and his people is often compared with that between husband and wife (comp. Isa. lxii. 5;

2 Enlarge the place of thy tent,
and let them stretch forth the curtains of thine habitations: spare not,
lengthen thy cords, and strengthen
thy stakes:
3 For thou shalt break forth on
the right hand and on the left; and
thy seed shall inherit the Gentiles,
and make the desolate cities to be
inhabited.
4 Fear not; for thou shalt not
be ashamed: neither be thou confounded; for thou shalt not be put
to shame; for thou shalt forget the
shame of thy youth, and shalt not remember the reproach of thy widowhood any more.

Ezek. xvi.; Rev. xxi. 2–9; xxii. 17). ¶ *Thou* that *didst not bear.* Either referring to the fact that the church was confined within the narrow limits of Judea; or that there had been in it a small number of true believers; or addressed to it in Babylon when it was oppressed, and perhaps constantly diminishing in number. I think it probable that it refers to the latter; and that the idea is, that she saw her sons destroyed in the siege and destruction of Jerusalem, and that she was not augmented by any accessions while in Babylon, but would have great occasion for rejoicing on her return, and in her future increase under the Messiah by the accession of the Gentiles. ¶ *Break forth into singing* (comp. ch. xiv. 7; xliv. 23; xlix. 13). ¶ *For more* are *the children of the desolate.* The 'desolate' here refers to Jerusalem, or the church. By the 'married woman,' Rosenmüller supposes the prophet means other nations which flourished and increased like a married woman. Grotius supposes that he means other cities which were inhabited, and that Jerusalem would surpass them all in her prosperity and in numbers. But the phrase seems to have somewhat of a proverbial cast, and probably the idea is that there would be a great increase, a much greater increase than she had any reason to apprehend. As if a promise was made to a barren female that she should have more children than those who were married usually had, so Jerusalem and the church would be greatly enlarged, far beyond what usually occurred among nations. The fulfilment of this is to be looked for in the accession of the Gentiles (ver. 3). 'The conversion of the Gentiles is all along considered by the prophet as a new accession of adopted children, admitted into the original church of God, and united with it' (Lowth). See the same idea presented at greater length in ch. xlix. 20–22.

2. *Enlarge the place of thy tent.* The same idea occurs in ch. xlix. 19, 20 (see the Notes on that chapter). *The curtains of thy habitations.* The word 'curtain' does not quite express the sense here. It is commonly with us used to denote the cloth hanging round a bed or at a window, which may be spread or drawn aside at pleasure, or the hanging in theatres to conceal the stage from the spectators. The word here, however, denotes the canopy or cloth used in a tent; and the idea is, that the boundaries of the church were to be greatly enlarged, in order to accommodate the vast accession from the pagan world. ¶ *Spare not.* Do not be parsimonious in the provision of the materials for greatly enlarging the tent to dwell in. ¶ *Lengthen thy cords* (see Note on ch. xxxiii. 20).

3. *For thou shalt break forth* (see Notes on ch. xlix. 19, 20). ¶ *And make the desolate cities* (see Notes on ch. xliv. 26).

4. *Fear not,* &c. (see Notes on ch. xli. 10, 14). ¶ *Neither shalt thou be confounded.* All these words mean substantially the same thing; and the design of the prophet is to affirm, in the strongest possible manner, that the church of God should be abundantly prospered and enlarged. The image of the female that was barren is kept up, and the idea is, that there should be no occasion of the shame which she felt who had no children. ¶ *For thou shalt forget the shame of thy youth.* In the abundant increase and glory of future times, the circumstances of shame which attended their early history shall be forgotten. The 'youth' of the Jewish people refers doubtless to the bondage

5 For thy Maker *is* thine husband;
the [a] LORD of hosts *is* his name; and
thy Redeemer, the Holy One of Israel; the God of the whole earth
shall he be called.

6 For the LORD hath called thee
as a woman forsaken and grieved
in spirit, and a wife of youth, when
thou wast refused, saith thy God.

[a] Je.3.14.

of Egypt, and the trials and calamities which came upon them there. So great should be their future prosperity and glory, that all this should be forgotten. ¶ *The reproach of thy widowhood.* The captivity at Babylon, when they were like a woman bereft of her husband and children (see Notes on ch. xlix. 21).

5. *For thy Maker* is *thine husband.* Both these words, 'maker' and 'husband,' in the Hebrew are in the plural number. But the form is evidently the *pluralis excellentiæ*—a form denoting majesty and honour (see 1 Sam. xix. 13, 16; Ps. cxlix. 2; Prov. ix. 10; xxx. 3; Eccl. xii. 1; Hos. xii. 1). Here it refers to 'JEHOVAH of hosts,' necessarily in the singular, as JEHOVAH is ONE (Deut. vi. 4). No argument can be drawn from this phrase to prove that there is a distinction of persons in the Godhead, as the form is so often used evidently with a singular signification.* That the words here properly have a singular signification was the evident understanding of the ancient interpreters. Thus Jerome, *Quia dominabitur tui qui fecit te*—'Because he shall rule over thee who made thee.' So the LXX, Ὅτι κύριος ὁ ποιῶν σε, κ.τ.λ.—'For the Lord who made thee, the Lord of Sabaoth,' &c. So the Chaldee and the Syriac. Lowth renders it, 'For thy husband is thy Maker.' The word rendered 'husband,' from בַּעַל, denotes properly the lord, maker, or ruler of any one; or the owner of anything. It often, however, means, to be a husband (Deut. xxi. 13; xxiv. 1; Isa. lxii. 5; Mal. ii. 11), and is evidently used in that sense here. The idea is, that JEHOVAH would sustain to his people the relation of a husband; that he who had made them, who had originated all their laws and institutions, and moulded them as a people (see Note on ch. xliii. 1), would now take his church under his protection and care (see Notes on ch. lxii. 5). ¶ *And thy Redeemer,* &c. (see Notes on ch. xliii. 1–3.) ¶ *The God of the whole earth.* He shall no more be regarded as peculiarly the God of the Jewish people, but shall be acknowledged as the only true God, the God that rules over all the world. This refers undoubtedly to the times of the gospel, when he should be acknowledged as the God of the Gentiles as well as the Jews (see Rom. iii. 29).

6. *For the* LORD *hath called thee.* This is designed to confirm and illustrate the sentiment in the previous verse. God there says that he would be a husband to his people. Here he says, that although he had for a time apparently forsaken them, as a husband who had forsaken his wife, and although they were cast down and dejected like a woman who had thus been forsaken, yet he would now restore them to favour. ¶ *Hath called thee.* That is, will have called thee to himself—referring to the future times when prosperity should be restored to them. ¶ *As a woman forsaken.* Forsaken by her husband on account of her offence. ¶ *And grieved in spirit.* Because she was thus forsaken. ¶ *And a wife of youth.* The LXX. render this very strangely, 'The Lord hath not called thee as a wife forsaken and disconsolate; *nor* as a wife that hath been hated from her youth;' showing conclusively that the translator here did not understand the meaning of the passage, and vainly endeavoured to *supply* a signification by the insertion of the negatives, and by endeavouring to *make* a meaning. The idea is that of a wife wedded in youth; a wife towards whom there was early and tender love, though she was afterwards rejected. God had loved the Hebrew people as his people in the early days of their history. Yet for their idolatry he had seen occasion afterwards to cast them off, and to doom them to a long and painful exile. But he would yet love them with all the former ardour of affection, and would greatly increase and prosper them. ¶ *When thou wast refused.* Or, that

* See the Supplementary Note on ch. vi 8.

7 For a small moment [a]have I forsaken thee; but with great mercies will I gather thee.
8 In a little wrath I hid my face from thee for a moment; but with everlasting kindness will I have mercy on thee, saith the LORD thy Redeemer.
9 For this *is as* the waters of Noah

a 2 Co.4.17.

hath been rejected. Lowth, 'But afterwards rejected.' It may be rendered, 'Although (כִּי *kī* has often the sense of *although*) thou wert rejected,' or 'although she was rejected.' The idea is, that she had been married in youth, but had been afterwards put away.

7. *For a small moment.* The Chaldee and Syriac render this, 'In a little anger.' Lowth has adopted this, but without sufficient authority. The Hebrew means, 'For a little moment;' a very short time. The reference here is probably to the captivity at Babylon, when they were apparently forsaken by JEHOVAH. Though to them this appeared long, yet compared with their subsequent prosperity, it was but an instant of time. Though this had probably a primary reference to the captivity then, yet there can be no impropriety in applying it to other similar cases. It contains an important principle; that is, that though God appears to forsake his people, yet it will be comparatively but for a moment. He will remember his covenant, and however long their trials may seem to be, yet compared with the subsequent mercies and the favours which shall result from them, they will seem to be but as the sorrows of the briefest point of duration (comp. 2 Cor. iv. 17). ¶ *But with great mercies.* The contrast here is not that of *duration* but of *magnitude.* The forsaking was 'little,' the mercies would be 'great.' It would be mercy that they would be recalled at all after all their faults and crimes; and the mercy which would be bestowed in the enlargement of their numbers would be inexpressibly great. ¶ *Will I gather thee.* Will I collect thee from thy dispersions, and gather thee to myself as my own people.

8. *In a little wrath.* The Syriac renders this, 'In great wrath.' The Vulgate, 'In a moment of indignation.' The LXX. 'In a little wrath.' Noyes renders it in accordance with the view of Rosenmüller, 'In overflowing wrath.' This variety of interpretation has arisen from the various meanings affixed to the unusual word שֶׁצֶף. This word occurs nowhere else in the Bible. Gesenius supposes that it is used for the sake of paronomasia with קֶצֶף *qĕtzĕph,* 'wrath,' instead of שֶׁטֶף *shĕtĕph.* This word frequently occurs, and means a gushing out, an overflowing, an inundation, a flood (Neh. i. 8; Job xxxviii. 25; Ps. xxxii. 6; Prov. xxvii. 4). According to this it would mean, 'in my overflowing anger,' in accordance with the expression in Prov. xxvii. 4, 'anger is outrageous,' more correctly in the margin, 'An overflowing.' The parallelism, however, seems to demand the sense of *short* or *momentary,* as it stands opposed to 'everlasting.' But it is not possible to demonstrate that the Hebrew word has this signification. Rosenmüller agrees with Gesenius in the opinion that it should be rendered 'In overflowing wrath;' and perhaps as the parallelism of the word 'everlasting' will be sufficiently secured by the phrase 'for a moment,' the probability is in favour of this interpretation. Then it will mean that the wrath, though it was but for a moment, was overflowing. It was like a deluge; and all their institutions, their city, their temple, their valued possessions, were swept away. ¶ *I hid my face from thee.* This is expressive of displeasure (see Note on ch. liii. 3; comp. Job xiii. 24; xxxiv. 29; Ps. xxx. 7; xliv. 24; Isa. viii. 17). Here it refers to the displeasure which he had manifested in the punishment which he brought on them in Babylon. ¶ *For a moment* (see Note on ver. 7). This stands opposed to the 'everlasting kindness' which he would show to them. ¶ *But with everlasting kindness.* This is true—1. Of the church at large under the Messiah. It is the object of the unchanging affection and favour of God. 2. Of each individual Christian. He will make him blessed in an eternal heaven.

9. *For this* is as *the waters of Noah*

unto me: for *as* I have sworn that
the waters of Noah should no more
go over the earth; so have I sworn
that I would not be wroth with thee,
nor rebuke thee.
10 For [a] the mountains shall depart, and the hills be removed; but
my kindness shall not depart from
thee, neither shall the covenant [b] of
my peace be removed, saith the LORD
that hath mercy on thee.
11 O thou afflicted, tossed with
tempest, *and* not comforted, behold, I will lay thy stones [c] with
fair colours, and lay thy foundation with sapphires.

[a] Ro.11.29. [b] 2Sa.23.5. [c] Re.21.18.

unto me. As it was in the time of the flood of waters, so shall it be now. 'I then solemnly promised that the waters should not again drown the earth, and I have kept that promise. I now promise with equal solemnity that I will bestow perpetual favour on my true people, and will shed upon them eternal and unchanging blessings.' 'The waters of Noah,' here mean evidently the flood that came upon the world in his time, and from which he and his family were saved. Lowth, on the authority of one MS. and of the Vulg., Syr., Sym., and Theod., reads this, 'In the days of Noah.' But the authority is not sufficient to change the Hebrew text, and the sense is as clear as if it were changed. ¶ As *I have sworn* (Gen. viii. 21, 22). God appeals to this not only because the oath and promise had been *made*, but because it had been *kept*. ¶ *That I would not be wroth.* The idea seems here to be that no calamities should spread over the *whole* church, and sweep it away, as the waters swept over the world in the time of Noah, or as desolation swept over Jerusalem and the whole land of Canaan in the time of the exile at Babylon. There would be indeed persecutions and calamities, but the church would be safe amidst all these trials. The period would never arrive when God would forsake the church, and when he would leave it to perish. One has only to recollect how God has guarded the church, even during the most dangerous periods, to see how remarkably this has been fulfilled. His covenant has been as sure as that which was made with Noah, and it will be as secure and firm to the end of time.

10. *For the mountains shall depart* (see Notes on ch. li. 6). ¶ *The covenant of my peace.* That is, the covenant by which I promise peace and prosperity to thee.

11. *O thou afflicted.* In the previous verses, JEHOVAH had merely promised protection, and had in general terms assured them of his favour. Here he shows that they should not only be defended, but that his church would rise with great beauty, and be ornamented like a most splendid palace or temple. This is to be regarded as addressed primarily to the exiles in Babylon near to the close of their seventy years' captivity. But nothing forbids us to apply it to the church in all *similar* circumstances when persecuted, and when she is like a ship rolling on the heaving billows of the ocean. ¶ *Tossed with tempest.* Lowth, 'Beaten with the storm.' The idea is that of a ship that is driven by the tempest; or any object that is tossed about with a whirlwind (סֹעֲרָה). See Jonah i. 11–13; Hos. xiii. 3; Heb. iii. 14. The figure is peculiarly striking in an Oriental country. Tempests and whirlwinds there, are much more violent than they are with us, and nothing there can stand before them (see Harmer's *Obs.* vol. i. p. 92, *sq.* Ed. Lond. 1808). ¶ And *not comforted.* They were far away from all the comforts which they had enjoyed in their own land, and they were apparently forsaken by God. ¶ *Behold, I will lay thy stones.* It is not uncommon in the Scriptures to compare the prosperity of the church to a splendid temple or palace. In the book of Tobit (ch. xiii. 16, 17) a description of Jerusalem occurs, which has all the appearance of having been copied from this, or at least shows that the writer had this passage in his eye. 'For Jerusalem shall be built up with sapphires, and emeralds, and precious stones; thy walls, and battlements, and towers, of pure gold. And the streets of Jerusalem shall be paved with beryl, and carbuncle, and stones of Ophir.'

12 And I will make thy windows of agates, and thy gates of carbuncles, and all thy borders of pleasant stones.

And in the book of Revelation (ch. xxi. 18–21), a similar description occurs of the New Jerusalem. Possibly John had his eye upon this passage in Isaiah, though he has greatly amplified the description. The passage here undoubtedly contains a figurative description of the future prosperity and glory of the church of God. Lowth remarks on it, justly, 'These seem to be general images to express beauty, magnificence, purity, strength, and solidity, agreeably to the ideas of eastern nations; and to have never been intended to be strictly scrutinized or minutely and particularly explained, as if they had each of them some precise moral and spiritual meaning.' The phrase 'I will lay thy stones,' refers to the work of masonry in laying down the foundation of a building, or the stones of which a building is composed, in mortar or cement. Literally, 'I cause to lie down.' The word here used (רָבַץ) is usually appropriated to an animal that crouches or lies down. ¶ *With fair colours.* This translation by no means conveys the idea of the original. The sense is not that the stones would *have* fair colours, but that the *cement* which would be used would be that which was commonly employed to make the most valued colours. The edifice which would be reared would be as costly and magnificent as if the very cement of the stones consisted of the most precious colouring matter; the purest vermilion. The word here rendered 'fair colours' (פּוּךְ *pŭkh*) denotes properly, sea-weed, from which an alkaline paint was prepared; then paint itself, dye, *fucus*, and also that with which the Hebrew women tinged their eyelashes (*stibium*). This is composed of the powder of lead ore, and was drawn with a small wooden bodkin through the eyelids, and tinged the hair and the edges of the eyelids with a dark sooty colour, and was esteemed to be a graceful ornament. This practice is of great antiquity. It was practised by Jezebel (see 2 Kings ix. 30, where the same word is used as here); it was practised among the Greeks and Romans (Xen. *Cyr.* i. 11); and it is still practised in Africa (see Shaw's *Travels*, pp. 294, 295). The word here used is rendered 'paint,' or 'painted' (2 Kings ix. 30; Jer. xl. 30); and 'glistening stones' (1 Chron. xxix. 2). It does not occur elsewhere. In the passage in Chronicles it may mean the carbuncle, as it is rendered here by the LXX. (ἄνθρακα); but it here denotes, doubtless, the valued paint or dye which was used as an ornament. The description here is that the very stones should be laid in cement of this description, and is of course equivalent to saying that it would be in the most costly and magnificent manner. It may be added, however, that it would not be the mere fact that the stibium would constitute the cement that the prophet seems to refer to, but probably he also means to intimate that this would contribute greatly to the *beauty* of the city. The cement in which bricks or stones is laid in a building is partly visible, and the beauty of the structure would be augmented by having that which was regarded as constituting the highest ornament used for cement. ¶ *And thy foundations with sapphires.* The sapphire is a well-known gem distinguished for its beauty and splendour. In hardness it is inferior to the diamond only. Its colours are blue, red, violet, green, white, or limpid.

12. *And I will make thy windows.* The word here rendered 'windows' is rendered by Jerome *propugnacula*—'fortresses,' bulwarks, ramparts; and by the LXX. Επαλξεις—'Bulwarks,' or rather, *pinnacles* on the walls. The Hebrew word שִׁמְשׁוֹת is evidently derived from שֶׁמֶשׁ *shêmêsh* (the sun); and has some relation in signification to the sun, either as letting in light, or as having a radiated appearance like the sun. Gesenius renders it, 'notched battlements, the same as sun, or rays of the sun.' Faber (*Hebrew Archæol.*, p. 294) supposes that the name was given to the turrets or battlements here referred to, because they had some resemblance to the rays of the sun. I think it prob-

13 And all thy children *shall be* taught of the LORD; and great *shall be* the peace of thy children.

---

able that the prophet refers to some radiated ornament about a building, that had a resemblance to the sun, or to some gilded turrets on the walls of a city. I see no evidence in the ancient versions that the word refers to *windows*. ¶ *Of agates.* Agates are a class of silicious, semi-pellucid gems, of many varieties, consisting of quartz-crystal, flint, horn-stone, chalcedony, amethyst, jasper, cornelian, &c., variegated with dots, zones, filaments, ramifications, and various figures. They are esteemed the least valuable of all the precious stones. They are found in rocks, and are used for seals, rings, &c. (Webster.) The Hebrew word כַּדְכֹּד *kădhkōd*, from כָּדַד *kâdhădh, to beat,* to pound, and then to strike fire, seems to denote a sparkling gem or ruby. It is not often used. It is rendered by Jerome, *Jaspidem*. The LXX. Ιασπιν—'Jasper,' a gem of a green colour. It may be observed that it is not probable that such a stone would be used for a *window*, for the purpose of letting in light. ¶ *And thy gates.* See Rev. xxi. 21—'And the twelve gates were twelve pearls; every several gate was of one pearl.' The gates of the city would be made of most precious stones. ¶ *Of carbuncles.* The carbuncle is a beautiful gem of a deep red colour, with a mixture of scarlet, called by the Greeks *anthrax*, found in the East Indies. It is usually about a quarter of an inch in length. When held up to the sun it loses its deep tinge, and becomes exactly the colour of a burning coal (Webster). Hence its name in Greek. The Hebrew name אֶקְדָּח is derived from קָדַח, *to burn*, and denotes a flaming or sparkling gem. The word occurs nowhere else in the Hebrew Bible. ¶ *And all thy borders.* All thy boundaries; or the whole circuit of thy walls. See Rev. xxi. 18—'And the building of the wall of it was of jasper.' The idea is, that the whole city would be built in the most splendid manner. Its foundations and all its stones would be laid in the most precious cement; its turrets, towers, battlements, gates, and the circuit of its walls, would be made of the most precious gems. In general, there can be no doubt that this is designed to represent the future glory of the church under the Redeemer, and perhaps also to furnish an emblematic representation of heaven (comp. Rev. xxi. 2). Kimchi supposes that this may possibly be taken literally, and that Jerusalem may be yet such as is here described. Abarbanel supposes that it may refer to the time when the Oriental world, where these gems are principally found, shall be converted, and come and join in rebuilding the city and the temple. But the whole description is one of great beauty as applicable to the church of God; to its glories on earth; and to its glory in heaven. Its future magnificence shall be as much greater than anything which has yet occurred in the history of the church, as a city built of gems would be more magnificent than Jerusalem was in the proudest days of its glory. The language used in this verse is in accordance with the Oriental manner. The style of speaking in the East to denote unexampled splendour is well illustrated in the well-known Oriental tale of Aladdin, who thus gives his instructions: 'I leave the choice of materials to you, that is to say, porphyry, jasper, agate, lapis lazuli, and the finest marble of the most varied colours. But I expect that in the highest story of the palace, you shall build me a large hall with a dome, and four equal fronts; and that instead of layers of bricks, the walls be made of massy gold and silver, laid alternately: and that each front shall contain six windows, the lattices of all which, except one, which must be left unfinished and imperfect, shall be so enriched with art and symmetry, with diamonds, rubies, and emeralds, that they shall exceed everything of the kind ever seen in the world.'—(*Pictorial Bible.*)

13. *And all thy children.* All that dwell in this splendid city; all that are the true friends of the Redeemer. It shall be a part of their future glory that

14 In righteousness shalt thou be established, thou shalt be far from oppression; for thou shalt not fear: and from terror; for [a]it shall not come near thee.

15 Behold, they shall surely gather together, *but* not by me; whosoever shall gather together against thee shall fall for thy sake.

a Pro.3.25,26.

they shall be all under Divine instruction and guidance. See Jer. xxxi. 34—'And they shall teach no more every man his neighbour, and every man his brother, saying, Know the LORD; for they shall all know me, from the least of them unto the greatest of them.' ¶ *And great* shall be *the peace of thy children.* (see Notes on ch. ii. 4; ix. 6).

14. *In righteousness shalt thou be established.* This is language which is appropriately addressed to a city or commonwealth. The idea is, that it would not be built up by fraud, and rapine, and conquest, as many cities had been, but by the prevalence of justice. ¶ *Thou shalt be far from oppression.* That is, thou shalt be far from being oppressed by others. So the connection demands. The Hebrew would bear an *active* signification, so that it might be read, 'be thou far from oppression,' *i.e.*, be far from oppressing others. But the design of the prophet is rather to promise than to command; and the idea is, that they should have no occasion to fear the violence of others any more. ¶ *For it shall not come near thee.* This doubtless refers to the security, perpetuity, and prosperity of the church under the Messiah.

15. *Behold, they shall surely gather together.* The idea in this verse is, that the enemies of the people of God would indeed form alliances and compacts against them, but it would not be under the Divine direction, and they would not be able to prevail against the church. The word here rendered 'gather together' (גּוּר) means properly *to turn aside from the way;* then to sojourn for a time; then to assemble against any one. It seems here to refer to the gathering together of hostile forces to form an alliance, or to wage war. Great variety, however, has prevailed in the interpretation of the passage, but this seems to be the sense of it. Jerome renders it, 'Lo, a foreigner shall come who was not with me, the stranger shall hereafter be joined to thee,' and seems to understand it of the proselytes that should be made. This sense is found expressly in the LXX., 'Lo, proselytes shall come to thee through me, and they shall sojourn with thee, and fly to thee.' The Chaldee renders it, 'Lo, the captivity of thy people shall be surely gathered unto thee, and in the end the kings of the people which were assembled to afflict thee, O Jerusalem, shall fall in the midst of thee.' But the above seems to be the correct sense. Alliances would be formed; compacts would be entered into; leagues would be made by the enemies of the people of God, and they would be assembled to destroy the church. This has often been done. Formidable confederations have been entered into for the purpose, and deep-laid plans have been devised to destroy the friends of the Most High. See Ps. ii. 2: 'The kings of the earth set themselves, and the rulers take counsel together against the LORD, and against his Anointed.' No small part of history is a record of the combinations and alliances which have been entered into for the purpose of driving the true religion from the world. ¶ But *not by me.* Not under my direction, or by my command. ¶ *Shall fall for thy sake.* Heb. עָלַיִךְ—'Shall fall unto thee.' Lowth, 'Shall come over to thy side.' The phrase seems to mean that they should 'fall to them,' *i.e.*, that they should lay aside their opposition, break up their alliances *against* the church, and come over *to* it. In proof of this interpretation, Rosenmüller appeals to the following places:—1 Chron. xii. 19, 20; 2 Chron. xv. 9; Jer. xxi. 9; xxxix. 9. The passage, therefore, looks to the future conversion of the enemies of the church to the true faith. It has, doubtless, been partially fulfilled in the conversion of nations that have been leagued against the gospel of the Redeemer. There was a striking fulfilment in the times that succeeded the persecutions

16 Behold, I have created the smith that bloweth the coals in the fire, and that bringeth forth an instrument for his work; and I [a] have created the waster to destroy.

17 No weapon that is formed against thee shall prosper: and every [b] tongue *that* shall rise against thee in judgment thou shalt condemn. This *is* the heritage of the servants of the LORD; and their righteousness [c] *is* of me, saith the LORD.

[a] ch.37.26,27. [b] Ro.8.1,33. [c] Ps.71.16,19; Phi.3.9.

of Christians in the Roman empire. After all the power of the empire had been enlisted in ten successive persecutions to destroy the church, the very empire that had thus opposed the church was converted to the Christian faith. In a still more signal manner will this be fulfilled when all the powers of the earth now leagued against the gospel shall be converted, and when all nations shall be brought under the influences of the true religion.

16. *Behold, I have created the smith.* The sense of this verse is, 'Everything that can effect your welfare is under my control. The smith who manufactures the instruments of war or of torture is under me. His life, his strength, his skill, are all in my hands, and he can do nothing which I shall not deem it best to permit him to do. So with the enemy of the church himself—the waster who destroys. I have made him, and he is wholly under my control and at my disposal.' The smith who bloweth the coals, denotes the man who is engaged in forging instruments for war, or for any other purpose. Here it refers to him who should be engaged in forging instruments of battle to attack the church; and why should it not refer also to him who should be engaged in making instruments *of torture*—such as are used in times of persecution? ¶ *That bringeth forth an instrument for his work.* Lowth, 'According to his work.' Noyes, 'By his labour.' The idea is, that he produces an instrument as the result of his work. ¶ *I have created the waster to destroy.* I have formed every man who is engaged in spreading desolation by wars, and I have every such man under my control (see Notes on ch. x. 5–7; xxxvii. 26, 27; xlvi. 1–6). The sense here is, that as God had all such conquerors under his control, they could accomplish no more than he permitted them to do.

17. *No weapon that is formed.* No instrument of war, no sword, or spear; no instrument of persecution or torture that is made by the smith, ver. 16. ¶ *Shall prosper.* On the meaning of this word, see Notes on ch. lii. 13. The sense here is, that it shall not have final and ultimate prosperity. It might be permitted for a time to appear to prosper—as persecutors and oppressors have done; but there would not be final and complete success. ¶ *And every tongue.* No one shall be able to injure you by words and accusations. If a controversy shall arise; if others reproach you and accuse you of imposture and deceit, you will be able ultimately to convince them of error, and, by manifestation of the truth, to condemn them. The *language* here is derived probably from courts of justice (see Notes on ch. xli. 1); and the idea is, that truth and victory, in every strife of words, would be on the side of the church. To those who have watched the progress of discussions thus far on the subject of the true religion, it is needless to say that this has been triumphantly fulfilled. Argument, sophism, ridicule, have all been tried to overthrow the truth of the Christian religion. Appeals have been made to astronomy, geology, antiquities, history, and indeed to almost every department of science, and with the same want of success. Poetry has lent the charm of its numbers; the grave historian has interwoven with the thread of his narrative covert attacks and sly insinuations against the Bible; the earth has been explored to prove that 'He who made the world and revealed its age to Moses was mistaken in its age;' and the records of Oriental nations, tracing their history up cycles of ages beyond the Scripture account of the creation of the world, have been appealed to, but thus far in all these contests ultimate victory has declared in favour of the

CHAPTER LV.

ANALYSIS.

This chapter is closely connected in sense with the preceding chapter. It flows from the doctrines stated in ch. liii., and is designed to state what would follow from the coming of the Messiah. It would result from that work that the most free and full invitations would be extended to all men to return to God, and to obtain his favour. There would be such ample provision made for the salvation of men, that the most liberal invitations could be extended to sinners. The main idea in the chapter, I conceive to be, *that the effect of the work of the Redeemer would be to lay the foundation for a universal invitation to men to come and be saved.* So ample would be the merits of his death (ch. liii.), that *all might come* and partake of eternal life. To state this, I suppose to be the main design of this chapter. It may be regarded as comprising the following parts:—

I. A universal invitation to come and embrace the provisions of mercy. 1. All were invited to come, even they who were the most poor and needy, who had no money, as freely as to running waters and streams (1). 2. They were now regarded as spending their money and their labour for that which produced no permanent satisfaction—descriptive of the world in its vain efforts to find enjoyment (2). 3. If they would come to God they should live, and he would make with them an eternal covenant (3).

II. To encourage them to this, the assurance is presented that God had given the Messiah to be a leader of the people, and that under him distant nations should embrace the truth and be saved (4, 5).

III. In view of the fulness of the provisions of mercy, and of the fact that a great leader had been provided, all are encouraged to come and seek God. This invitation is pressed on their attention by several considerations:—1. Jehovah might now be found, and he was ready to pardon abundantly all sinners who were disposed to forsake the error of their way and to return to him (6, 7). 2. God shows that his plans were high above those of men, and his thoughts more elevated than theirs, and his counsels should stand. The rain descended on the earth and accomplished his great plans, and so it would be with his word. His promises would be fulfilled, and his designs would take effect, and there was, therefore, every encouragement to come, and partake of his favour and his grace (8–11). 3. There should be rich and abundant blessings attending their return to God, and universal rejoicing from their embracing the religion of the Redeemer, and becoming interested in his mercy and salvation (12, 13).

There is not to be found in the Bible a chapter more replete with rich invitations than this, nor perhaps is there anywhere to be found one of more exquisite beauty. To the end of the world it will stand as the fullest conceivable demonstration that God *intended* that the offers of salvation should be made to all men, and that he designs that his gospel shall accomplish the great plans which he had in view when he devised the scheme of redemption. While this precious chapter remains in the book of God, no sinner need despair of salvation who is disposed to return to him; no one can plead that he is too great a sinner to be saved; no one can maintain successfully that the provisions of mercy are limited in their nature or their appli-

---

Bible. And no matter from what quarter the attack has come, and no matter how much learning and talent have been evinced by the adversaries of the Bible, God has raised up some Watson, or Lardner, or Chalmers, or Buckland, or Cuvier, or Wiseman, to meet these charges, and to turn the scales in favour of the cause of truth. They who are desirous of examining the effects of the controversy of Christianity with science, and the results, can find them detailed with great learning and talent in Dr. Wiseman's *Lectures on the connection between Science and Revealed Religion*, Andover, 1837. ¶ *This* is *the heritage.* The inheritance which awaits those who serve God is truth and victory. It is not gold and the triumph of battle. It is not the laurel won in fields of blood. But it is, the protection of God in all times of trouble; his friendship in all periods of adversity; complete victory in all contests with error and false systems of religion; and preservation when foes rise up in any form and endeavour to destroy the church, and to blot out its existence and its name. ¶ *And their righteousness* is *of me.* Or rather, 'this is the righteousness, or the justification which they obtain of me; this is that which I impart to them as their justification.' The idea is not that their righteousness is of him, but that this justification or vindication from him is a part of their inheritance and their portion.

cability to any portion of the race; and no minister of the gospel need be desponding about the success of the work in which he is engaged. The gospel shall just as certainly produce the effect which God intended, as the rain which comes down in fertilizing showers upon the dry and thirsty earth.

HO, every one that thirsteth, come [a] ye to the waters, and he that hath no money; come ye, buy [b] and eat; yea, come, buy wine [c] and milk, without money, and without price.

a Jn.4.10,14; 7.37; Re.21.6; 22.17. b Mat.13.44-46; Re.3.18. c Ca.5.1.

CHAPTER LV.

1. *Ho* (הוֹי). This word here is designed to call attention to the subject as one of importance. ¶ *Every one that thirsteth.* The word 'thirst' often indicates intense *desire,* and is thus applied to the sense of want which sinners often have, and to their anxious wishes for salvation. It is not improbable that the Saviour had this passage in his eye when he pronounced the blessing on those who hunger and thirst after righteousness (Matt. v. 6). No wants are so keen, none so imperiously demand supply, as those of hunger and thirst. They occur daily; and when long continued, as in the case of those who are shipwrecked, and doomed to wander months or years over burning sands with scarcely any drink or food, nothing is more distressing. Hence the figure is often used to denote any intense desire for anything, and especially an ardent desire for salvation (see Ps. xlii. 2; lxiii. 1; cxliii. 6; John vii. 37). The invitation here is made to all. 'Every one' (כָּל) is entreated to come. It is not offered to the elect only, or to the rich, the great, the noble; but it is made to all. It is impossible to conceive of language more universal in its nature than this; and while this stands in the Word of God, the invitation *may* be made to all, and *should* be made to all, and *must* be made to all. It *proves* that provision is made for all. Can God invite to a salvation which has not been provided? Can he ask a man to partake of a banquet which has no existence? Can he ask a man to drink of waters when there are none? Can he tantalize the hopes and mock the miseries of men by inviting them to enter a heaven where they would be unwelcome, or to dwell in mansions which have never been provided? (comp. Matt. xi. 28; Mark xvi. 15; John vii. 37; Rev. xxii. 17). ¶ *Come ye to the waters.* Water, floods, overflowing streams, or copious showers, are often used in the Scriptures to denote abundant blessings from God, and especially the blessings which would exist under the Messiah (see Isa. xxxv. 6; xliii. 20; xliv. 3). ¶ *And he that hath no money.* The poor; they who would be unable to purchase salvation if it were to be sold. The idea here is the absolute freeness of the offer of salvation. No man can excuse himself for not being a Christian because he is poor; no man who is rich can ever boast that he has *bought* salvation, or that he has obtained it on more easy terms because he had property. ¶ *Come ye, buy and eat* (comp. Matt. xiii. 44–46). That is, procure it without paying a price. The word rendered here 'buy' (שָׁבַר *shâbhăr*), properly means *to break,* then to purchase, &c. (*grain*), as that which is *broken* in a mill (Gesenius), or that which *breaks* hunger; comp. Eng. *breakfast* (Castell.) ¶ *Buy wine* (יַיִן). Wine was commonly used in their feasts, and indeed was an article of common drink (see Notes on ch. xxv. 6). Here it is emblematic of the blessings of salvation spoken of as a feast made for men. Wine is usually spoken of as that which exhilarates, or makes glad the heart (Judg. ix. 13; 2 Sam. xiii. 28; Ps. civ. 15), and it is possible that the image here may be designed specifically to denote that the blessings of salvation make men happy, or dissipate the sorrows of life, and cheer them in their troubles and woes. ¶ *And milk* Milk, in the Scriptures, is used to denote that which nourishes, or is nutritious (Deut. xxxii. 14; Judg. iv. 1; v. 25; Isa. vii. 22; 1 Cor. ix. 7). It is mentioned as used with wine in Cant. v. 1, 'I have drunk my wine with my milk;' and with honey (iv. 11), 'Honey and milk are under my tongue.' The sense here is, that the blessings of the gospel are fitted to nourish and support the soul as well as to make it glad and

2 Wherefore do ye [1] spend money for *that which is* not bread, and your labour for *that which* satisfieth not? Hearken diligently [a] unto me, and eat ye *that which is* good, and let your soul delight itself in [b] fatness.

3 Incline your ear and come unto me: hear, and your soul shall live; and I will make an everlasting covenant [c] with you, *even* the sure mercies [d] of David.

1 *weigh.* a Mat.22.4. b Ps.63.5. c 2 Sa.23.5; Je.32.40. d Ac.13.34.

cheerful. ¶ *Without money,* &c. None are so poor that they cannot procure it; none are so rich that they can purchase it with gold. If obtained at all by the poor or the rich, it must be without money and without price. If the poor are willing to accept of it as a gift, they are welcome; and if the rich will not accept of it as a gift, they cannot obtain it. What a debt of gratitude we owe to God, who has thus placed it within the reach of all! How cheerfully and thankfully should we accept that as a gift which no wealth, however princely, *could* purchase, and which, being purchased by the merits of the Redeemer, is put within the reach of the humblest child of Adam!

2. *Wherefore do ye spend money.* Marg. 'Weigh.' That is, in Hebrew, 'weigh silver.' Before money was coined, the precious metals were *weighed,* and hence to make a payment is represented as *weighing out silver* (Gen. xxiii. 16). ¶ *For* that which is *not bread.* The idea here is, that men are endeavouring to purchase happiness, and are disappointed. Bread is the support of life; it is therefore emblematic of whatever contributes to support and comfort. And in regard to the pursuit of happiness in the pleasures of life, and in ambition, vanity, and vice, men are as much disappointed, as he would be who should spend his money, and procure nothing that would sustain life. ¶ *And your labour for* that which *satisfieth not.* You toil, and expend the avails of your labour for that which does not produce satisfaction. What a striking description of the condition of the world! The immortal mind will not be *satisfied* with wealth, pleasure, or honour. It never has been. Where is the man who is *satisfied* with his wealth, and who says it is enough? Where is there one who is satisfied with pleasure, and vanity, and gaiety? There is a void in the heart which these things do not, cannot fill. There is a consciousness that the soul was made for higher and nobler purposes, and that nothing but God can meet its boundless desires. Where is the man who has ever been satisfied with ambition? Alexander wept on the throne of the world; and though Diocletian and Charles V. descended voluntarily from the throne to private life, it was because there was nothing *in* royalty to satisfy the soul, and not because they found happiness *enough* there. There never was a more simple and true description of this whole world than in this expression of Isaiah, that men are spending their money and their labour for that which satisfieth not. ¶ *Hearken diligently unto me.* The idea is, that by attending to his words and embracing his offers, they would find that without money or price which they were vainly seeking at so much expense and with so much toil. ¶ *And eat,* &c. The prophet here returns to the image in the former verse. They were invited to partake of that which would nourish the soul, and which would fill it with joy. ¶ *And let your soul delight itself in fatness.* 'Fatness' in the Scriptures is used to denote the richest food (Gen. xxvii. 28–39; Job xxxvi. 16; Ps. lxv. 11), and hence is an emblem of the rich and abundant blessings resulting from the favour of God (Ps. xxxvi. 9; lxiii. 5).

3. *Hear, and your soul shall live.* That is, if you attend to my command and embrace my promises, you shall live. Religion in the Scriptures is often represented as *life* (John v. 40; vi. 33; viii. 13; xx. 31; Rom. v. 17, 18; vi. 4; viii. 6; 1 John v. 12; Rev. ii. 7–10). It stands opposed to the death of sin—to spiritual and eternal death. ¶ *And I will make an everlasting covenant with you.* On the word 'covenant,' see Notes on ch. xxviii. 18; xlii. 6; xlix. 8. Here it means that God would bind himself to be their God, their protector, and their friend. This covenant would

4 Behold, I have given him [a] *for* a witness [b] to the people, a leader and commander [c] to the people.

5 Behold, thou shalt call a nation *that* thou knowest not; and nations *that* [d] knew not thee shall run unto

a Eze.34.23. b Jn.18.37; Re.1.5. c Ep.5.24. d ch.60.5; Zec.8.23.

be made with *all* who would come to him. It would not be with the nation of the Jews, as such, or with any community, as such, but it would be with all who should embrace the offers of life and salvation. ¶ Even *the sure mercies of David.* I will confirm to you, and fulfil in you, the solemn promises made to David. The transaction here referred to is that which is celebrated in Ps. lxxxix. 2–4:—

For I have said, mercy shall be built up for ever;
Thy faithfulness hast thou established in the very heavens.
I have made a covenant with my chosen,
I have sworn unto David my servant,
Thy seed will I establish for ever,
And build up thy throne to all generations.

A kingdom had thus been promised to David, and he had been assured that the true religion should flourish among those who were to succeed him in Israel. The prophet here says that this solemn promise would be fulfilled in those who should embrace the Messiah, and that God would ratify with them this covenant. The word here rendered 'mercies' (חֶסֶד), properly means *kindness,* goodwill, pity, compassion; then goodness, mercy, grace. The word rendered 'sure,' denotes that which is established, or confirmed; that in which *confidence* may be placed. The whole expression denotes that the covenant made with David was one which *promised* great favours, and was one which was not to be abrogated, but which was to be perpetual. With all who embraced the Messiah, God would enter into such an unchanging and unwavering covenant—a covenant which was not to be revoked.

4. *Behold, I have given him.* This is evidently the language of God respecting the Messiah, or of David as representing the Messiah. Rosenmüller supposes that the name David here is used to designate the Messiah, and in support of this appeals to Ezek. xxxiv. 23, 24; xxxvii. 24, 25; Jer. xxx. 9; Hos. iii. 5. An examination of these passages will show that they *all* refer to the Messiah by the name of David; and it is morally certain that in the passage before us, the name David (ver. 3) suggested the Messiah. It seems to me that this is to be regarded as a *direct address* respecting the Messiah, and that the object of the speaker here is to state a reason why he should be embraced. That reason was that God had constituted him as a leader. The Chaldee renders this, 'Lo, I have constituted him as a prince to the people, a king and ruler over all kingdoms.' Kimchi says that it means that the Messiah would be a monitor or a mediator between men and him who would accuse them. Grotius supposes that *Jeremiah* is intended here; but in that opinion he is destined undoubtedly to stand for ever alone. The almost unbroken interpretation, from the earliest times, is that which refers it directly to the Messiah. ¶ For *a witness to the people.* Noyes renders this, 'A ruler.' Rosenmüller, 'A monitor,'—one whose office it was publicly to admonish, or reprove others in the presence of witnesses. Jerome renders it, 'A witness.' The LXX. Μαρτύριον—'A testimony.' The Chaldee (רַב *rābh*), 'A prince.' The Hebrew word (עֵד) means properly a witness (Prov. xix. 5–9); then testimony, witness borne (Ex. xx. 13; Deut. v. 17); then a prince, chief, lawgiver, commander. Comp. the use of the verb in 2 Kings xvii. 13; Ps. l. 7; lxxxi. 9; Lam. ii. 13. The parallelism requires us to understand it in this sense here—as one who stood forth to bear solemn testimony in regard to God—to his law, and claims, and plans; and one who, therefore, was designated to be the instructor, guide, and teacher of men. ¶ *A leader.* Chaldee, 'A king.' The idea is, that he would sustain the relation of a sovereign. One of the important offices of the Messiah is that of *king.* ¶ *A commander.* Or, rather, a lawgiver. He would originate the laws and institutions of his people.

5. *Behold, thou shalt call,* &c. This is evidently an address to the Messiah, and is a promise that the Gentiles should be called by him to the fellowship of the gospel. ¶ That *thou knowest not.*

thee, because of the LORD thy God, and for the Holy One of Israel; for he hath glorified thee.

6 Seek ye the LORD while [a] he may be found, call ye upon him while he is near.

a Jn.7.34; He.2.3.

The phrase 'thou knowest not,' means a nation that had not been regarded as his own people. ¶ *And nations* that *knew not thee.* The heathen nations that were strangers to thee. ¶ *Shall run unto thee.* Indicating the haste and anxiety which they would have to partake of the benefits of the true religion. ¶ *Because of the* LORD *thy God.* From respect to the God who had appointed the Messiah, and who had organized the Church. ¶ *For he hath glorified thee* (John xvi. 5). God had glorified him by appointing him to be the Messiah; and he would glorify him in the future triumphs of the gospel, in the day of judgment, and in the eternal splendours of heaven.

6. *Seek ye the* LORD. The commencement of religion in the heart is often represented as seeking for God, or inquiring for his ways (Deut. iv. 29; Job v. 8; viii. 5; Ps. ix. 10; xiv. 2; xxvii. 8). This is to be regarded as addressed not to the Jewish exiles only or peculiarly, but to all in view of the coming and work of the Messiah. That work would be so full and ample that an invitation could be extended to all to seek after God, and to return to him. It is implied here—1. That men are by nature ignorant of God—since they are directed to 'seek' for him. 2. That if men will obtain his favour it must be sought. No man becomes his friend without desiring it; no one who does not earnestly seek for it. 3. That the invitation to seek God should be made to all. In this passage it is unlimited (comp. ver. 7). Where there are sinners, there the invitation is to be offered. 4. That the knowledge of God is of inestimable value. He would not command men to seek that which was worthless; he would not urge it with so much earnestness as is here manifested if it were not of inexpressible importance. ¶ *While he may be found.* It is implied here—1. That God may now be found. 2. That the time will come when it will be impossible to obtain his favour. The leading thought is, that under the Messiah the offer of salvation will be made to men fully and freely. But the period will come when it will be withdrawn. If God forsakes men; if he wholly withdraws his Spirit; if they have committed the sin which hath never forgiveness; or if they neglect or despise the provisions of mercy and die in their sins, it will be too late, and mercy cannot then be found. How unspeakably important, then, is it to seek for mercy at once—lest, slighted now, the offer should be withdrawn, or lest death should overtake us, and we be removed to a world where mercy is unknown! How important is the present moment—for another moment may place us beyond the reach of pardon and of grace! How amazing the stupidity of men who suffer their present moments to pass away unimproved, and who, amidst the gaieties and the business of life, permit the day of salvation to pass by, and lose their souls! And how just is the condemnation of the sinner! If a man will not do so simple a thing as to ASK for pardon, he OUGHT to perish. The universe will approve the condemnation of such a man; and the voice of complaint can never be raised against that Holy Being who consigns such a sinner to hell. ¶ *Call ye upon him.* That is, implore his mercy (see Rom. x. 13; comp. Joel ii. 32). How easy are the terms of salvation! How just will be the condemnation of a sinner if he will not call upon God! Assuredly if men will not breathe out one broken-hearted petition to the God of heaven that they may be saved, they have only to blame themselves if they are lost. The terms of salvation *could* be made no easier; and man *can* ask nothing more simple. ¶ *While he is near.* In an important sense God is equally near to us at all times. But this figurative language is taken from the mode of speaking among men, and it denotes that there are influences more favourable for seeking him at some periods than others. Thus God comes near to us in the preaching of his

7 Let the wicked forsake his
way, and the [1] unrighteous man
his thoughts; [a] and let him return
unto the LORD, and he will have
mercy upon him: and to our God,
for he will [2] abundantly [b] pardon.
8 For my thoughts *are* not your
thoughts, neither *are* your ways my
ways, saith the LORD.

1 *man of iniquity.* [a] Mar.7.21,23.
2 *multiply to pardon.* [b] Ps.130.7.

word, when it is borne with power to the conscience; in his providences, when he strikes down a friend and comes into the very circle where we move, or the very dwelling where we abide; when he lays his hand upon us in sickness, he is *near* us by day and by night; in a revival of religion, or when a pious friend pleads with us, God is near to us then, and is calling us to his favour. These are favourable times for salvation; times which, if they are suffered to pass by unimproved, return no more; periods which will all soon be gone, and when they are gone, the sinner irrecoverably dies.

7. *Let the wicked*, &c. In this verse we are told what is necessary in order to seek God and to return to him, and the encouragement which we have to do it. The first step is for the sinner to forsake his way. He must come to a solemn pause, and resolve to abandon all his transgressions. His evil course; his vices; his corrupt practices; and his dissipated companions, must be forsaken. ¶ *And the unrighteous man.* Marg. 'Man of iniquity.' This is a literal translation. The address is made to all men; for all are such. ¶ *His thoughts.* The Hebrew word denotes all that is the object of *thought;* and the idea is, that the man must abandon his plans and purposes of life. The thoughts, in the sight of a holy God, are not less important than the external deportment; and no man can obtain his favour who is not ready to abandon his erroneous opinions, his pride and vanity, his plans of evil, and his purposes of life that are opposed to God. ¶ *And let him return unto the* LORD. Man, in the Scriptures, is everywhere described as having wandered away from the true God. Religion consists in *returning* to him for pardon, for consolation, for protection, for support. The true penitent is desirous of returning to him, as the prodigal son returned to his father's house; the man who loves sin chooses to remain at a distance from God. ¶ *And to our God.* The God of his people; the God of the speaker here. It is the language of those who have found mercy. The idea is, that he who has bestowed mercy on *us*, will be ready to bestow it on others. '*We* have returned to God. We have had experience of his compassion, and we have such a conviction of his overflowing mercy, that we can assure all others that if they will return to *our* God, he will abundantly pardon them.' The doctrine is, that they who have found favour have a deep conviction of the abounding compassion of God, and such a sense of the fulness of his mercy, that they are disposed to offer the assurance to all others, that they may also obtain full forgiveness. Compare Rev. xxii. 17—'And let him that heareth say, Come.' ¶ *For he will abundantly pardon.* Marg. as Heb. 'Multiply to pardon.' He abounds in forgiveness. This is the conviction of those who are pardoned; this is the promise of inestimable worth which is made to all who are willing to return to God. On the ground of this promise all may come to him, and none who come shall be sent empty away.

8. *For my thoughts* are *not your thoughts.* Interpreters have differed in regard to the *connection* of this verse with the preceding. It is evident, I think, that it is properly connected with the subject of *pardon;* and the sense must be, that the plans and purposes of God in regard to forgiveness are as far *above* those of men as the heavens are higher than the earth, ver. 9. But in what respects his plan of pardon differs from those of men, the prophet does not intimate, and can be understood only by the views which are presented in other parts of the Bible. The connection here would seem to demand some such view as the following—1. Men find it difficult to pardon at all. They harbour malice; they seek revenge; they are

9 For [a] *as* the heavens are higher than the earth, so are my ways higher than your ways, and my thoughts than your thoughts.

10 For as the rain [b] cometh down, and the snow, from heaven, and returneth not thither, but watereth the earth, and maketh it bring forth and bud, that it may give seed to the sower, and bread to the eater;

a Ps.103.11. *b* De.32.2.

slow to forgive an injury. Not so with God. He harbours no malice; he has no desire of revenge; he has no reluctance to forgive. 2. It may refer to *the number of offences.* Men, if they forgive once, are slow to forgive a second time, and still more reluctant to forgive a third time, and if the offence is often repeated they refuse to forgive altogether. Not so with God. No matter how often we have violated his law, yet he can multiply forgiveness in proportion to our faults. 3. *The number of the offenders.* Men *may* pardon one, or a few who injure them, but if the number is greatly increased, their compassions are closed, and they feel that the world is arrayed against them. Not so with God. No matter how numerous the offenders—though they embrace the inhabitants of the whole world—yet he can extend forgiveness to them all. 4. In regard to the *aggravation* of offences. A slight injury men forgive. But if it is aggravated, they are slow to pardon. But not so with God. No matter how aggravated the offence, he is ready to forgive. It may be added—5. That his thoughts in regard to the *mode* of pardon are far above ours. The plan of forgiveness through a Redeemer—the scheme of pardon so fully illustrated in ch. liii., and on which the reasoning of the prophet here is based—is as far above any of the modes of pardon among men, as the heavens are above the earth. The scheme which contemplated the incarnation of the Son of God; which proffered forgiveness only through his substituted sufferings, and in virtue of his bitter death, was one which man could not have *thought* of, and which surpasses all the schemes and plans of men. In this respect, God's ways are not our ways, and his thoughts are not our thoughts.—But at the same time that this passage refers primarily to the subject of pardon, and should be interpreted as having a main reference to that, it is also true of the ways of God in general. His ways are not our ways, and his thoughts are not ours in regard to his plans in the creation and government of the world. He has plans for accomplishing his purposes which are different from ours, and he secures our own welfare by schemes that cross our own. He disappoints our hopes; foils our expectations; crosses our designs; removes our property, or our friends; and thwarts our purposes in life. He leads us in a path which we had not intended; and secures our ultimate happiness in modes which are contrary to all our designs and desires. It follows from this—1. That we should form our plans with submission to the higher purposes of God. 2. We should resign ourselves to him when he chooses to thwart our plans, and to take away our comforts.

9. *For* as *the heavens,* &c. This verse is designed merely to illustrate the idea in the former. There is as great a difference between the plans of God and those of men, as between the heavens and the earth. A similar comparison occurs in Ps. ciii. 11—

For as the heaven is high above the earth,
So great is his mercy toward them that fear him.

Comp. Ps. lvii. 10—

For thy mercy is great unto the heavens,
And thy truth unto the clouds.

Also Ps. lxxxix. 2—

Mercy shall be built up for ever,
Thy faithfulness shalt thou establish in the very heavens.

The idea in all these passages is substantially the same—that the mercy and compassion of God are illimitable.

10. *For as the rain cometh down.* The meaning of this verse and the following is plain. This refers evidently, as the whole passage does, to the times which should succeed the coming of the Messiah. The hearts of men by nature are what the earth would be without the rains of heaven—barren and sterile. But God says that his truth shall certainly accomplish an

11 So shall my word be that goeth forth out of my mouth: it shall not return unto me void; [a] but it shall accomplish that which I please, and it shall prosper *in the thing* whereto I sent it.

[a] Mat.24.35.

effect similar to that produced by descending showers. The rain never descends in vain. It makes the earth fertile, beautiful, and lovely. So would it be with his truth in the moral world. The comparison of truth with descending rain or dews is exceedingly beautiful, and occurs not unfrequently in the Bible. See Deut. xxxii. 2—

> My doctrine shall drop as the rain,
> My speech shall distil as the dew,
> As the small rain upon the tender herb,
> And as the showers upon the grass.

Comp. 2 Sam. xxiii. 4; Ps. lxxii. 6; Isa. v. 6; Note on xliv. 3. ¶ *And the snow.* This is a part of the emblem or symbol designed to denote the fertilizing effect of the truth of God. The snow, as well as the rain, accomplishes important purposes in rendering the earth fertile. It constitutes a covering that contributes to the warmth and preservation of plants and vegetation in the colder latitudes, and on the hills and mountains is accumulated in the winter months to fill the streams, or produce the overflowing of the rivers in the spring and the summer. This expression should not, however, be pressed *ad unguem* in the interpretation, as if it contained any special spiritual signification. It is a part of the general description of that which descends from heaven to render the earth fertile. ¶ *From heaven.* From the clouds. ¶ *And returneth not thither.* That is, not in the form in which they descend on the earth. They return not thither *as* rain and snow. The main idea is, they do not return without accomplishing the effect which God intends. ¶ *And bud.* Put forth its increase; causes it to sprout up, or germinate. The word 'bud' is applied rather to the small protuberance on the ends of limbs and branches, which contains the germ of the future leaf or flower. This word צָמַח means rather *to germinate,* or to cause to vegetate in general. It is applied to the putting forth of vegetation on the earth when the showers descend.

11. *So shall my word be.* All the truth which God reveals is as much adapted to produce an effect on the hard and sterile hearts of men as the rain is on the earth. ¶ *It shall not return unto me void.* It shall not return to me without accomplishing that which I intend. ¶ *And it shall prosper* (see Note on ch. lii. 13). This proves—1. That God has a design in giving his Word to men. He has as distinct an intention in his Word as he has in sending down rain upon the earth. 2. That whatever is his design in giving the gospel, it shall be accomplished. It is never spoken in vain, and never fails to produce the effect which he intends. The gospel is no more preached in vain than the rain falls in vain. And though that often falls on barren rocks, or on arid sands; on extended plains where no vegetation is produced, or in the wilderness 'where no man is,' and seems to our eyes in vain, yet it is not so. God has a design in each drop that falls on sands or rocks, as really as in the copious shower that falls on fertile fields. And so the gospel often falls on the hard and barren hearts of men. It is addressed to the proud, the sensual, the avaricious, and the unbelieving, and seems to be spoken in vain, and to return void unto God. But it is not so. He has some design in it, and that will be accomplished. It is proof of the fulness of his mercy. It leaves men without excuse, and justifies himself. Or when long presented—apparently long in vain—it ultimately becomes successful, and sinners are at last brought to abandon their sins, and to turn unto God. It is indeed often rejected and despised. It falls on the ears of men apparently as the rain falls on the hard rock, and there are, so to speak, large fields where the gospel is preached as barren and unfruitful of any spiritual good as the extended desert is of vegetation, and the gospel seems to be preached to almost entire communities with as little effect as is produced when the rains fall on the deserts of Arabia, or of Africa. But there will

12 For ye shall go out with joy, and be led forth with peace: the mountains and the hills shall break forth before you into singing, and all the trees of the field shall clap *their* hands.

[a] Ro.6.19.

13 Instead [a] of the thorn shall come up the fir-tree, and instead of the brier shall come up the myrtle-tree: and [b] it shall be to the LORD for a name, for an everlasting sign, *that* shall not be cut off.

[b] Je.13.11.

be better and happier times. Though the gospel may not now produce all the good effects which we may desire, yet it will be ultimately successful to the full wish of the widest benevolence, and the whole world shall be filled with the knowledge and the love of God.

12. *For ye shall go out with joy.* This *language* is that which is properly applicable to the exiles in Babylon, but there can be no doubt that the prophet looks also to the future happier times of the Messiah (comp. Notes on ch. lii. 7). ¶ *The mountains and the hills.* Language like this is common in Isaiah, where all nature is called on to rejoice, or where inanimate objects are represented as expressing their sympathy with the joy of the people of God (see Note on ch. xiv. 8; xxxv. 1, 2, 10; xlii. 10, 11; xliv. 23). Indeed, this imagery is common in all poetry. Thus Virgil—

> Ipsi lætitia voces ad sidera jactant,
> Intonsi montes: ipsæ jam carmina rupes,
> Ipsa sonant arbusta.
>
> *Ec.* v. 62, *sq.*

> The untill'd mountains strike the echoing sky;
> And rocks and towers the triumph speed abroad.
>
> WRANGHAM.

Such language occurs especially in the poetry of the Orientals. Thus, when the god Ramar was going to the desert, says Roberts, it was said to him, 'The trees will watch for you; they will say, He is come, he is come; and the white flowers will clap their hands. The leaves as they shake will say, Come, come, and the thorny places will be changed into gardens of flowers.' ¶ *And all the trees of the field shall clap* their *hands.* To clap the hands is expressive of joy and rejoicing (comp. 2 Kings xi. 12; Ps. xlvii. 1). Thus, in Ps. xcviii. 8, it is said:

> Let the floods clap their hands;
> Let the hills be joyful together.

Among the Jews the language was sometimes used to express *malignant* joy at the calamity of others (comp. Job xxvii. 3; xxxiv. 37; Lam. ii. 15; Ezek. xxv. 6). Here it is an expression of the universal rejoicing which would attend the extension of the kingdom of God on the earth.

13. *Instead of the thorn* (comp. Notes on ch. xi. 6–8; xxxv. 1, 2; xli. 19; xlii. 20). The word rendered 'thorn' (נַעֲצוּץ) occurs only here and in Isa. vii. 19. It evidently means a thorn, hedge, or thorny-bush. ¶ *Shall come up the fir-tree* (בְּרוֹשׁ *bĕrōsh;* see Notes on ch. xiv. 8; xxxvii. 24; lx. 13; Zech. xi. 2). A change would be produced in the moral condition of man as great as if in the natural world the rough and useless thorn should be succeeded by the beautiful and useful cypress (comp. ch. lx. 13). ¶ *And instead of the brier.* The brier is everywhere an emblem of desolation, and of an uncultivated country (see ch. v. 6; vii. 23, 24). ¶ *The myrtle-tree* (see Notes on ch. xli. 19). The idea here is, that under the gospel the change would be as great in the moral world as if a field all overrun with briers should at once become thick set with myrtles. ¶ *And it shall be to the* LORD. The reference here is to all that had been said in the chapter. The gift of the Messiah; the universal offer of the gospel; the bestowing of pardon; the turning of the wicked unto God; and the great and salutary changes produced by the gospel, would all be a memorial of the benevolence and glory of JEHOVAH. ¶ *For a name.* It should tend to diffuse his name; to spread abroad a knowledge of himself. ¶ *An everlasting sign.* On the meaning of the word rendered 'sign,' see Notes on ch. vii. 14. Here it means that it would be an eternal memorial of the mercy and goodness of JEHOVAH. ¶ That *shall not be cut off.* The gospel with its rich and varied blessings shall erect enduring monuments in the earth, to the praise

CHAPTER LVI.

ANALYSIS.

THIS chapter, to ver. 9, is evidently a continuation of the same general subject which is discussed in the previous chapters, and is closely connected with the great truths communicated in ch. lii. 13–15, and ch. liii., respecting the work of the Messiah. The general design of the prophet seems to be to state the happy results which would follow his coming. In ch. liv., he states that that work would render the establishment and perpetuity of the church certain. In ch. lv., he states that it would lay the foundation for the offer of the gospel to all men, and that it should certainly be successful on the earth and finally triumph, and produce great and important changes. In this chapter (1–9) the same idea is presented in another form, that no one would be excluded from the offer of salvation, and that strangers and foreigners would become connected, with equal privileges, with the people of God. At ver. 9, a new subject is introduced—the invasion of the land of Judea by foreign armies, and the consequent punishment of the wicked and idolatrous part of the nation. This subject is continued in the following chapter. The following analysis will present a view of the design and scope of this.

I. The kingdom of God was near. The great work of man's redemption, to which the prophet referred, would not be long delayed, and those who were expecting the coming of the Messiah should be holy (1).

II. The blessedness of those who should be admitted to the privileges connected with the kingdom of God, and the coming of the Messiah. 1. Who they would be. (1.) The man who kept the Sabbath (2–4). (2.) The stranger and foreigner (3–6). (3.) The eunuch (3, 4). 2. The privileges of thus being admitted to the favour and friendship of God. (1.) They should be brought to his holy mountain. (2.) They should be made joyful in the house of prayer. (3.) Their offerings should be accepted. (4.) These favours should be extended to all people (7, 8).

III. A prophecy respecting the invasion of the land on account of the crimes of the nation. 1. The invasion is represented under the image of wild beasts coming to devour (9). 2. The cause of this. (1.) The indolence and unfaithfulness of the watchmen. (2.) Their selfishness, avarice, and covetousness. (3.) Their revelry and intemperance (10–12).

THUS saith the LORD, Keep ye [a]judgment, and do justice: for my salvation *is* near to come, and my righteousness to be revealed.

[a] or, *equity*.

and honour of God. It will be more enduring as a memorial of him than all altars and statues, and temples erected to celebrate and perpetuate idolatry; as wide-diffused as are his works of creation, and more fruitful of blessings than anything elsewhere conferred on man.

CHAPTER LVI.

1. *Thus saith the* LORD. That is, in view of the fact that the kingdom of God was to come at no distant period. JEHOVAH states what was necessary to prepare themselves for it, and what was the character which he demanded of those who were disposed to embrace its offers, and who would be admitted to its privileges. ¶ *Keep ye judgment.* Marg. 'Equity.' Break off your sins, and be holy. A somewhat similar declaration was made by John the Baptist when he announced the coming of the Messiah: 'Repent ye, for the kingdom of heaven is at hand' (Matt. iii. 2). The general idea is, that it was not only *appropriate* that the prospect of his coming and his near approach should lead them to a holy life, but it was *necessary* in order that they might escape his indignation. ¶ *My salvation* is *near to come.* It is to be borne in mind that this was regarded as addressed to the Jews in exile in Babylon, and there is probably a primary reference in the words to the deliverance which they were about to experience from their long and painful captivity. But at the same time the language is appropriate to the coming of the kingdom of God under the Messiah, and the whole scope of the passage requires us to understand it of that event. Language similar to this occurs frequently in the New Testament, where the sacred writers seem to have had this passage in their eye (see Matt. iii. 2; Luke xxi. 31; Rom. xiii. 11; comp. Isa. lxii. 1–11). It is to be regarded, therefore, as having a reference to the future coming of the Messiah—perhaps as designed to describe the *series* of deliverances which were to close the painful bondage in Babylon, and to bring the people of

2 Blessed [a] *is* the man *that* doeth
this, and the son of man *that* layeth
hold on it; that keepeth the Sabbath [b] from polluting it, and keepeth his hand from doing any evil.
3 Neither let the son of the
stranger, [c] that hath joined himself
to the LORD, speak, saying, The
LORD hath utterly separated me
from his people: neither let the
eunuch [d] say, Behold, I *am* a dry
tree.

a Lu.12.43. b ch.58.13. c Nu.18.4,7; Ac.10.34,35. d Ac.8.27,&c.

God to perfect freedom, and to the full fruition of his favour. Though the actual coming of the Messiah at the time of the exile was at a period comparatively remote, yet the commencement of the great work of their deliverance was near at hand. They were soon to be rescued, and this rescue was to be but the first in the train of deliverances that would result in the entire redemption of the people of God, and was to be the public pledge that all that he had promised of the redemption of the world should be certainly effected. ¶ *To be revealed.* To be made known; to be publicly manifested.

2. *Blessed* is *the man.* Heb. 'The blessings of the man' (see Ps. i. 1). The sense is, 'happy is the man.' The word here rendered 'man' (אֱנוֹשׁ) usually denotes a man in humble life or in a subordinate rank, in contradistinction from אִישׁ, a man in elevated rank. As the object of the prophet here is particularly to say, that the 'stranger' and the 'eunuch' would be admitted to these privileges, it is possible that he designedly used a word denoting one in humble life. The particular blessing to which he refers is specified in ver. 7, 8. ¶ That *doeth this.* That is, this which the prophet soon specifies—keeping the Sabbath, and abstaining from evil. ¶ *And the son of man.* Another form of expression denoting man. ¶ That *layeth hold on it.* Heb. 'Binds himself fast to it;' or seizes upon it with strength. That is, he adheres firmly to the purpose, as a man seizes upon a thing with an intention not to let it go. ¶ *That keepeth the Sabbath from polluting it.* Who sacredly observes the day of holy rest which God has appointed. The Sabbath was one of the peculiar rites of the Jewish religion, and one of the most important of their institutions. Its observance entered essentially into the idea of their worship, and was designed to be the standing memorial or sign between God and the Jewish nation (Ex. xxxi. 13–17). At home, in their own nation, it kept up the constant sense of religion; abroad, when they travelled among strangers, it would serve to remind all of the peculiar nature of their institutions, and be the public evidence that they were the worshippers of JEHOVAH. Hence, as this served to distinguish them from other people, it comes to be used here to signify the observance of the rites which pertained to the public worship of God; and evidently includes whatever was to be perpetual and unchanging in the public worship of the Creator. It is remarkable that the prophet does not pronounce a blessing on him who came to bloody altars with sacrifices, or him who burned incense, or him who conformed to the peculiar rites of the Jewish religion. These rites were to pass away, and the obligation to observe them was to cease; and in this indirect manner the sacred writer has given an intimation that there would be blessings on those who did *not* observe those rites, and that the period would arrive when the Divine favour and mercy would descend on men in a different channel. In regard to the importance of the Sabbath, see Notes on the close of chapter lviii. ¶ *And keepeth his hand,* &c. That is, is an upright, holy, honest man. He not only worships God and keeps the Sabbath, but he is upright in the discharge of all the duties which he owes to his fellow-men. These two specifications are evidently designed to include all the influences of religion—the proper service and worship of God, and an upright and holy life. Never in fact are they separated, and the religion of the Bible was designed to secure the one as much as the other.

3. *Neither let the son of the stranger.*

4 For thus saith the LORD unto
the eunuchs that keep my sabbaths,
and choose *the things* that please
me, and take hold of my covenant;
5 Even unto them will I give in
mine house, [a]and within my walls,
a place and a name better [b]than of
sons and of daughters: I will give
them an everlasting name, that shall
not be cut off.

a 1Ti.3.15. b Jn.1.12.

The foreigner who shall become a proselyte to the true religion. ¶ *That hath joined himself.* That has embraced the true faith, and become a worshipper of the true God. It is evidently implied here that there would be such proselytes, and that the true religion would be extended so as to include and embrace them. The idea is, that they should be admitted to the same privileges with those who had been long recognized as the people of God. ¶ *The* LORD *hath utterly separated.* Let him not esteem himself to be an outcast, or cut off from the privileges of the people of God. This language is used with reference to the opinion which prevailed among the Jews, that the Gentiles were excluded from the privileges of the people of God, and it is designed to intimate that hereafter all such barriers would be broken down. They who entered the church as proselytes from the heathen world, were not to come in with any sense of inferiority in regard to their rights among his people; but they were to feel that all the barriers which had heretofore existed were now broken down, and that all men were on a level. There is to be no assumption of superiority of one nation or rank over another; there is to be no sense of inferiority of one class in reference to another. ¶ *Neither let the eunuch say.* This class of men was usually set over the harems of the East (Est. ii. 3, 14, 15; iv. 5); and they were employed also as high officers at court (Est. i. 10, 12, 15; Dan. i. 3; Acts viii. 27). The word is sometimes used to denote a minister of court; a court officer in general (Gen. xxxvii. 6; xxxix. 1). The Targum often renders the word by רַבָּא, *a prince.* ¶ *Behold, I* am *a dry tree.* A dry tree is an emblem of that which is barren, useless, unfruitful. By the law of Moses such persons could not be enrolled or numbered in the congregation of the Lord (Deut. xxiii. 2). The sense here is, that they should not hereafter be subjected to the religious and civil disabilities to which they had been. These external barriers to the full privileges among the people of God, would be removed. All classes and ranks would be admitted to the same privileges; all would be on the same level (see ver. 5).

4. *For thus saith the* LORD *unto the eunuchs.* Even the eunuchs, who have hitherto been excluded from the privileges of the people of God, and who have been regarded as a separated and degraded people, shall be admitted to the same privileges as others. ¶ *That keep my sabbaths.* The word is here used in the plural, though the weekly Sabbath is probably particularly intended. It may be, however, that the word is used to represent religious observances in general (see Notes on ver. 2). ¶ *And choose* the things *that please me.* Who will be willing to sacrifice their own pleasure and preferences to those things which I choose, and in which I delight. ¶ *And take hold of my covenant.* Hold fast, or steadily maintain my covenant. On the meaning of the word 'covenant,' see Notes on ch. xxviii. 18; xlii. 6; xlix. 8; liv. 10.

5. *Will I give in mine house.* That is, they shall be admitted to all the privileges of entering my house of prayer, and of being regarded as my true worshippers, and this shall be to them a more invaluable privilege than would be any earthly advantages. The word 'house' here refers undoubtedly to the temple, regarded as emblematic of the place of public worship in all ages. ¶ *And within my walls.* The walls of the city where God dwelt, referring primarily to the walls of Jerusalem. They should be permitted to dwell with God, and be admitted to all the privileges of others. All, of all classes and conditions, under the reign of the Messiah, should be regarded as on a level, and entitled

6 Also the sons of the stranger that join [a] themselves to the LORD, to serve him, and to love the name of the LORD, to be his servants, every one that keepeth the sabbath from polluting it, and taketh hold of my covenant;

7 Even [b] them will I bring to my holy mountain; and make them joyful in my house of prayer; their burnt-offerings and their sacrifices *shall be* [c] accepted upon mine altar: for [d] mine house shall be called an house of prayer for all people.

a Je.50.5. b Ep.2.11-13. c 1 Pe.2.5. d Mat.21.13.

to equal advantages. There should be no religious disabilities arising from *caste*, age, country, colour, or rank of life. Those who had any physical defect should not on that account be excluded from his favour, or be regarded as not entitled to his offers of mercy. The lame, therefore, the halt, the blind; the man of colour, the AFRICAN, the red man of the woods; the Hindoo and the Islander; all are to be regarded as alike invited to participate in the favour of God, and none are to be excluded from the 'house' erected to his praise, and from within the 'walls' of the holy city where he dwells. ¶ *A place.* Heb. יָד—'A hand.' The word is, however, used to denote 'a place' (Deut. xxiii. 13; Num. ii. 17; Josh. viii. 10). It is sometimes used in the sense of 'monument,' or 'trophy' (1 Sam. xv. 12; 2 Sam. xviii. 18), as if a monument were *a hand* pointing out or showing anything. The word here denotes, however, *a place*, and means that the excluded foreigner and the eunuch should be admitted to a place in the temple of God; that is, should be admitted to the favour of God, and be permitted to dwell with him. ¶ *And a name.* As it was regarded among the Hebrews as one of the highest honours to have a numerous posterity, the idea here is, that they should be admitted to the highest possible honour—the honour of being regarded as the children of God, and treated as his friends. ¶ *And I will give them an everlasting name.* Their memory shall not perish. They shall be admitted to eternal and unchangeable honours—the everlasting honour of being treated as the friends of God.

6. *Also the sons of the stranger* (see Note on ver. 3). The conditions on which they should be admitted to the same privileges are specified, and are the following:—1. They were to 'join themselves to the LORD' (see Note on ver. 3). 2. This should be with a purpose to 'serve him.' Their aim and design should be to keep his commandments and to do his will. 3. They were to 'love the name of the LORD;' that is, to love JEHOVAH himself, for the 'name' of the Lord is often used as denoting the Lord himself. 4. They were to keep his Sabbaths (see Notes on ver. 4). 5. They were to take hold of his covenant (see Notes on ver. 4). On these conditions the sons of the foreigner were to be admitted to all the privileges of the children of God, and to be united with all who love and serve him.

7. *Even them will I bring to my holy mountain* (see Notes on ch. ii. 3). That is, they should be admitted to the fellowship and privileges of his people. ¶ *And make them joyful.* In the participation of the privileges of the true religion, and in the service of God, they shall be made happy. ¶ *In my house of prayer.* In the temple—here called the house of prayer. The *language* here is all derived from the worship of the Jews, though the meaning evidently is, that under the new dispensation, all nations would be admitted to the privileges of his people, and that the appropriate services of religion which they would offer would be acceptable to God. ¶ *Their burnt-offerings.* That is, their worship shall be as acceptable as that of the ancient people of God. This evidently contemplates the future times of the Messiah, and the sense is, that in those times, the Gentiles would be admitted to the same privileges of the people of God, as the Jewish nation had been. It is true that proselytes were admitted to the privileges of religion among the Jews, and were permitted to offer burnt-offerings and sacrifices, nor can there be a doubt that they were then acceptable to God. But it is also true that there

8 The LORD God, which gathereth the outcasts [a] of Israel, saith, Yet will I gather *others* [b] to him, besides [1] those that are gathered unto him.

[a] Ps.147.2. [b] Jn.10.16. [1] to his gathered.

was a conviction that they were admitted *as* proselytes, and that there would be a superiority felt by the native-born Jews over the foreigners who were admitted to their society. Under the Jewish religion this distinction was inevitable, and it would involve, in spite of every effort to the contrary, much of the feeling of *caste*—a sense of superiority on the one hand, and of inferiority on the other; a conviction on the one part that they were the descendants of Abraham, and the inheritors of the ancient and venerable promises, and on the other that they had come in *as* foreigners, and had been admitted by special favour to these privileges. But all this was to be abolished under the Messiah. No one was to claim superiority on account of any supposed advantage from birth, or nation, or country; no one, however humble he might feel in respect to God and to his own deserts, was to admit into his bosom any sense of inferiority in regard to his origin, his country, his complexion, his former character. All were to have the same near access to God, and the offering of one was to be as acceptable as that of another. ¶ *For mine house.* This passage is quoted by the Saviour (Matt. xxi. 13), to show the impropriety of employing the temple as a place of traffic and exchange. In that passage he simply quotes the declaration that it should be 'a house of prayer.' There are two ideas in the passage as used by Isaiah; first, that the temple should be regarded as a house of prayer; and, secondly, that the privileges of that house should be extended to all people. The main design of the temple was that God might be there invoked, and the inestimable privilege of calling on him was to be extended to all the nations of the earth.

8. *The* LORD *God.* This verse is a continuation of the promise made in the previous verses, that those of other nations would be united to the ancient people of God. The sense is, that JEHOVAH would not only gather back to their country those who were scattered abroad in other lands, but would also call to the same privileges multitudes of those who were now aliens and strangers. ¶ *Which gathereth the outcasts of Israel.* Who will collect again and restore to their own country those of the Jews who were scattered abroad—the exiles who were in distant lands. ¶ *Yet will I gather* others *to him.* To Israel; that is, to the Jews (see John x. 16). ¶ *Besides those.* Marg. 'To his gathered.' To those who are collected from their exile and restored to their own country, I will add many others of other nations. This completes the promise referred to in this and the previous chapters. The next verse introduces a new subject, and here a division should have been made in the chapters. The great truth is here fully expressed, that under the Messiah the heathen world would be admitted to the privileges of the people of God. The formidable and long-existing barriers between the nations would be broken down. No one nation would be permitted to come before God claiming any peculiar privileges; none should regard themselves as in any sense inferior to any other portion of the world on account of their birth, their rank, their privileges by nature. Under this economy we are permitted to live—happy now in the assurance that though we were once regarded as strangers and foreigners, yet we are 'now fellow-citizens with the saints and of the household of God' (Eph. ii. 19). The whole world lies on a level before God in regard to its origin —for God 'has made of one blood all the nations of men to dwell on the face of all the earth' (Acts xviii. 26). The whole race is on a level in regard to moral character—for all have sinned, and come short of the glory of God. And the whole race is on a level in regard to redemption—for the same Saviour died for all; the same heaven is offered to all; and the same eternal and most blessed God is ready to admit all to his favour, and to confer on all everlasting life. What thanks do we owe to the God of grace for the blessings of the eternal gospel; and how anxious should we be that the offers of salvation should

9 All ye beasts of the field, come to devour; *yea*, all ye beasts in the forest.

10 His watchmen *are* blind; they are all ignorant, they *are* all dumb dogs, they cannot bark; [1] sleeping, lying down, loving to slumber.

1 or, *dreaming; or, talking in their sleep.*

in fact be made known to all men! The wide world may be saved, and there is not one of the human race so degraded in rank, or colour, or ignorance, that he may not be admitted to the same heaven with Abraham and the prophets, and whose prayers and praises would not be as acceptable to God as those of the most magnificent monarch who ever wore a crown.

9. *All ye beasts of the field.* This evidently commences a new subject, and refers to some invasion of the land of Judea. In the previous chapter, the prophet had comforted the people by the assurance of the coming of the Messiah, and by the fact that they should be enlarged by the accession of the Gentiles. He proceeds here to a more disagreeable part of the subject. The design is, to reprove particularly the sins of the rulers of the people, and to assure them that such conduct would incur the vengeance of Heaven. The sins reproved are indolence and inattention to duty (ver. 10–12); a spirit of self-indulgence and of slumber, avarice and selfishness, and luxury and intemperance. The vengeance here referred to, Lowth supposes to be the invasion of the land by the Chaldeans, and perhaps by the Romans. Grotius supposes that it refers to the Egyptians, and to bands of robbers from the Chaldeans, Syrians, Moabites, and Ammonites. Vitringa strangely enough refers it to the barbarous nations which broke in upon the Christian church to lay it waste and destroy it during the decline of the Roman empire, particularly the Huns, Saracens, Turks, Turcomans, Tartars, &c. But the connection seems to demand that it should be understood of some events, not far distant from the time of the prophet, which would be a proper punishment of the crimes then existing. According to this interpretation, the reference here, I suppose, is to the invasion of the land by the Chaldeans. They would come as wild beasts, to spread terror and devastation before them. And so great were the national crimes, that the prophet *calls* on them to come and devour all before them. The comparison of invaders to wild beasts is not uncommon in the Scriptures. Thus Jer. xii. 9—

Mine heritage is unto me as a speckled bird,
The birds round about are against her;
Come ye, assemble all the beasts of the field,
Come to devour.

So Jer. l. 17—

Israel is a scattered sheep;
The lions have driven him away;
First the king of Assyria hath devoured him,
And last this Nebuchadrezzar, king of Babylon,
hath broken his bones.

See also Isa. ix. 11.

10. *His watchmen.* The prophet proceeds to specify the sins which had thus induced God to send the desolating armies of foreign nations. The first is specified in this verse, the apathy, indifference, and unfaithfulness, which prevailed among those who were appointed to guard their interests and defend the cause of truth. The word rendered 'his watchmen' (צֹפָו) is derived from צָפָה, *to look about;* to view from a distance; to see afar. It is applied appropriately to those who were stationed on the walls of a city, or on a tower, in order that they might see the approach of an enemy (1 Sam. xiv. 16; 2 Sam. xiii. 34; xviii. 24). It is then applied to *prophets*, who are as it were placed on an elevated post of observation, and who are able to cast the eye far into future scenes, and to predict future events (Jer. vi. 17; Ezek. iii. 17; Note on Isa. xxi. 6–11; lii. 8; comp. lxii. 6). Here it refers undoubtedly to the public teachers of the Jews who had failed to perceive the crimes and dangers of the people; or who, if they had seen them, had neglected to warn them of the prevalence of sin, and of the dangers to which they were exposed. ¶ Are *blind.* They have become wilfully blind to the existence of idolatry and vice, or they are so corrupt in sentiment and practice, that they fail to notice the existence of the prevailing

11 Yea, *they are* [1]greedy dogs *which* can [2]never have enough, and they *are* shepherds *that* cannot understand; they all look to their own

1 *strong of appetite.*

2 *know not to be satisfied.*

---

sins. ¶ *They are all ignorant.* Heb. 'They do not know.' This may either mean that they were not possessed of the proper qualifications for the office of prophets, or that they were so immersed in sin themselves, and so indolent, that they did not observe the existence of the national sins. In either case, they were unfit for the station. ¶ *They* are *all dumb dogs.* Dogs are appointed to guard a house or flock, and to give notice of the approach of a robber by night (Job xxx. 1). They are thus an emblem of a prophet — appointed to announce danger. Generally in the Scriptures the *dog* is mentioned as the symbol of uncleanness, of vileness, of apostasy, of that which deserved the utmost contempt (Deut. xxiii. 18; 1 Sam. xxiv. 14; 2 Sam. ix. 8; Prov. xxvi. 11; Phil. iii. 2; 2 Pet. ii. 22; Rev. xxi. 8; xxii. 15; comp. Virg. *Georg.* i. 470). But here the dog is an emblem of vigilance. The phrase 'dumb dogs,' is applicable to prophets who from any cause failed to warn the nation of their guilt and danger. ¶ *They cannot bark.* They cannot give warning of the danger which threatens. The reason why they *could* not do this the prophet immediately states. They loved to slumber—they delighted in indolence and repose. ¶ *Sleeping.* Marg. 'Dreaming,' or 'Talking in their sleep.' The word הֹזִים (*hōzīm*), is from הָזָה (*hâzâ*), *to dream, to talk in one's dreams.* It is kindred to חָזָה (*hhâzâ*), to see, and the primary idea seems to be that of nocturnal *visions.* The LXX. render it, Ενυπνιαζόμενοι κοίτην—'Sleeping in bed.' Aquila, Φανταζόμενοι—'Having visions,' or phantasms. The idea is that probably of dreaming, or drowsing; a state of indolence and unfaithfulness to their high trust. Perhaps also there is included the idea of their being deluded by vain imaginations, and by false opinions, instead of being under the influence of truth. For it is commonly the case that false and unfaithful teachers of religion are not *merely inactive;* they act under the influence of deluding and delusive views—like men who are dreaming and who see nothing real. Such was probably the case with the false prophets in the time of Isaiah. ¶ *Lying down.* As dogs do who are indolent. They are inactive, unfaithful, and delighting in ease. ¶ *Loving to slumber.* Perhaps there was never a more graphic and striking description of an indolent and unfaithful ministry than this. Alas, that it should be too true of multitudes who bear the sacred office, and who are appointed to warn their fellow-men of danger! How many come still under the description of 'dumb dogs who cannot bark, and who love to slumber!' Some are afraid of giving offence; some have no deep sense of the importance of religious truth, and the actual danger of the ungodly; some embrace false opinions—led on by day-dreams and fictions of the imagination, as unreal, as vain, and as inconsistent, as are the incoherent expressions which are uttered in sleep; some engage in worldly projects, and fill up their time with the cares and plans of this life; and some are invincibly indolent. Nothing will rouse them; nothing induce them to forego the pleasures of sleep, and ease, and of an inactive life. The friends of God are unrebuked when they err; and an inactive and unfaithful ministry suffers the great enemy to come and bear away the soul to death, as an unfaithful mastiff would suffer the thief to approach the dwelling without warning the inmates. But the mastiff is usually *more* faithful than an indolent ministry. To the deep shame of man be it spoken, there are more ministers of religion who are indolent, inactive, and unfaithful, than there are of the canine race. Instinct prompts *them* to act the part which God intends; but alas, there *are* MEN —men in the ministry—whom neither instinct, nor conscience, nor reason, nor hope, nor fear, nor love, nor the command of God, nor the apprehension of eternal judgment, will rouse to put forth unwearied efforts to save souls from an eternal hell!

11. *Yea,* they are *greedy dogs.* Marg.

way, every one for his gain from his
quarter.
12 Come ye, *say they*, I will fetch
wine, and we will fill ourselves with
strong drink; and to-morrow shall
be as this day, *and* much more
abundant.

'Strong of appetite.' Literally, 'Strong of soul' (עַזֵּי־נֶפֶשׁ). Jerome renders it, *Canes impudentissimi*. So the LXX. Κύνες ἀναιδεῖς τῇ ψυχῇ—'Dogs impudent in soul.' They were greedy and insatiable in that which the soul or the appetite demands. The idea here is, that the prophets to whom reference is here made were sensual, and disposed to gorge themselves; living only for carnal indulgence, insensible to the rights of others, and never satisfied. ¶ *And they* are *shepherds* that *cannot understand*. Who are ignorant of the wants of the people, and who cannot be made to comprehend what is needed by them (see ver. 10). ¶ *They all look to their own way*. That is, they are all selfish. The ministers of religion are set apart not to promote their own interests but the welfare and salvation of others. ¶ *Every one for his gain*. For his own private ends and emoluments. ¶ *From his quarter*. Lowth, 'From the highest to the lowest.' So Rosenmüller. LXX. Κατὰ τὸ ἑαυτοῦ—'Each one according to his own purpose.' The Heb. is literally, 'From his end,' or extremity. Gen. xix. 4: 'From every quarter' (מִקָּצֶה) that is, from one end to the other; one and all, the whole. This seems to be the idea here, that one and all were given to selfishness, to covetousness, and to indulgence in luxury and sensuality.

12. *Come ye*, say they (comp. Notes on ch. xxii. 13). That is, one says to another, 'I will fetch wine;' or as *we* would say, 'I will take another glass.' The object is to describe a *drinking-bout*, or *carousal*, when the glass is shoved around, and there is drinking to excess. The language denotes the state of exhilaration and excitement when sitting at the table, and already under the influence of wine. This is not designed to be descriptive of the people at large, but of the 'watchmen,' or public teachers of the nation, and it certainly shows a state of most lamentable degeneracy and corruption. Unhappily, however, it has not been confined to the times of Manasseh. There have been periods in the history of the Christian church, and there are still portions of that church, where the language here used with so much severity would be an appropriate description even of the Christian ministry; scenes where the professed heralds of salvation sit long at the wine, and join with the gay, the worldly, and the profane, in 'shoving round' the sparkling cup. No severer language is used in the prophets to describe and denounce any class of sinners than is appropriated to such men; at no time has the church more occasion to sit in the dust and to weep, than when her ministers 'rise up early in the morning, that they may follow strong drink; and continue until night, till wine inflame them (Isa. v. 11). ¶ *We will fill ourselves with strong drink* (see Notes on ch. v. 11). ¶ *And to-morrow*, &c. That is, indulgence of this kind was habitual. There was an *intention* to continue it. It was not that they had been once overtaken and had erred; but it was that they loved it, and meant to drink deeper and deeper. So now the guilt of ministers is greatly aggravated in the same way. It is not *merely* that they drink wine; it is not even that they on a single occasion drink too much, and say and do foolish and wicked things—liable as all are to this who indulge in drinking wine at all, and certainly as ministers will do it who indulge in the habit;—it is that they *mean* to do it; they resolve *not* to abandon it, but purpose to persevere in the habit 'to-morrow.' Hence, such men refuse to join a Society of Temperance; hence they oppose such societies as ultra and fanatical; and hence, by *not* joining them, they proclaim to the world, 'Come ye, and I will take another glass, and to-morrow shall be as this day, and much more abundant.' It is this *settled* purpose—this fixed resolution, stretching into future time, and embracing coming years, that

CHAPTER LVII.

ANALYSIS.

THIS chapter is evidently closely connected in sense with ch. lvi. 9-12. In the closing part of the last chapter the prophet had said that the land of Israel would be invaded by foreign armies, represented under the image of ravening beasts come to devour. One of the causes of this he had also stated, viz., the general licentiousness, avarice, and intemperance of the rulers of the nation. The same general subject is pursued in this chapter, which has been very improperly separated from the preceding. In this the prophet states specifically the sins of the nation at large, evidently as a reason why the calamities of the foreign invasion were coming upon them. It is probable that the chapter has primary reference to the times of Manasseh. Of the characteristics of his cruel reign, see the Introduction, § 3. It was a time of persecution and blood. The righteous were put to death; the public service of God was profaned and desecrated; and the evils of idolatry were seen and felt, under the royal patronage, throughout the land. Yet notwithstanding this, the nation was stupid and insensible. They were not affected as they should have been by the fact that the righteous were cut off by persecution, and that idolatry was patronized throughout the land. A few, like the prophets, felt, and deeply felt. Their hearts were desponding, and their spirits drooped. To encourage them, and to rebuke the mass of the stupid and guilty nation, was the design of this chapter.

It may be regarded as divided into three parts:—

I. The fact that the righteous were put to death, and yet that the nation was sunk in deep and deplorable stupidity. 1. The proof of the insensibility of the nation, visible in the fact that the just were taken away, and that they were unmoved (1.) 2. A statement of the comparative happy condition of the righteous, though they suffered under persecution, and were put to a violent death (ver. 1, last part, ver. 2). So far as *they* were concerned it was well, for (1.) They were taken away from more fearful approaching evils. (2.) They entered into rest.

II. A solemn address of JEHOVAH, himself sitting as judge on the tribunal, and stating the crimes and demonstrating the guilt of the nation (3-14). 1. The nation summoned before him as having been apostatized—under the image so common in the prophets of their being guilty of adultery (3). 2. They were guilty of falsehood and unfaithfulness to him, and of deriding his government and laws (4). 3. The statement of the prevalence of idolatry in all parts of the nation, under every green tree, in every valley, in the clefts of the rocks, upon every mountain, and in every secret place (5-8). 4. They had gone and sought alliance with foreign powers; under the image of a woman unfaithful to her marriage vow (9). 5. They had not feared God in the prevalence of the evil and in the corruption of the nation (10, 11). 6. For all this God denounces heavy judgment (12-14). Their works should not profit them (12); nothing on which they relied could deliver them (13, first part); but the pious who confided in God should be protected (13, last part); and the stumbling-block should be taken up out of the way of his people (14).

III. Consolation and assurances of pardon, protection, and peace to those who would repent and put their trust in God. Their state contrasted with that of the wicked (15-21). 1. The righteous (15-19). (1.) Though God was high and great and holy, yet he dwelt with the lowly and the penitent. They were, therefore, encouraged to return (15). (2.) Though he had entered into controversy with his people for their sins, yet he would not continue it for ever. The feeble powers of man could not long endure the expressions of his displeasure, and he therefore would withdraw the tokens of his wrath (16). (3.) He had indeed punished his people for their covetousness, but he would restore comfort to those who mourned over their sins (17, 18). (4.) He was the author of peace, and all who were afar off, and all who were near, who would return to him, should enjoy it (19). 2. The wicked. Their condition was one strongly contrasted with that of the righteous (20, 21). (1.) They were like the troubled sea (20). (2.) They had no peace (21).

---

is so offensive to God. And there is not on earth a condition of more public iniquity than when the ministers of religion take this bold and open stand, and resolve that they *will not* abandon intoxicating drinks, but will continue to drink 'to-morrow,' and ever onward. Hopeless is the work of reformation when the ministers of religion take this stand; and dark is the prospect for the church on earth, when the messengers of salvation cannot be induced to stand before the church of God as examples and advocates for temperance on the most strict and uncompromising principles.

THE righteous perisheth, and no man layeth *it* to heart: and merciful [1]men *are* taken away, none considering that the righteous *is* taken away from [2]the evil *to come.*

1 *men of kindness,* or, *godliness.*

2 or, *that which is evil.*

CHAPTER LVII.

1. *The righteous perisheth.* This refers, as I suppose, to the time of Manasseh (see Introd. § 3). Grotius supposes, that it refers to king Josiah; Vitringa, that it refers to martyrs in general. But it seems probable to me that the prophet designs to describe the state of stupidity which prevailed in his own time, and to urge as one proof of it, that the pious part of the nation was taken away by violent death, and that the nation was not affected by it. Such was the guilt of Manasseh; so violent was the persecution which he excited against the just, that it is said of him that he 'shed innocent blood very much, till he had filled Jerusalem from one end to another' (2 Kings xxii. 16). There is evidence (see Introd. § 2), that Isaiah lived to his time, and it is probable that he himself ultimately fell a victim to the rage of Manasseh. Though he had, on account of his great age, retired from the public functions of the prophetic office, yet he could not be insensible to the existence of these evils, and his spirit would not suffer him to be silent, even though bowed down by age, when the land was filled with abominations, and when the best blood of the nation was poured out like water. The word rendered 'perisheth' (אָבַד) as well as the word rendered 'taken away' (אָסַף) denotes violence, and is indicative of the fact that they were removed by a premature death. ¶ *And no man layeth* it *to heart.* No one is aroused by it, or is concerned about it. The sentiment of the passage is, that it is proof of great stupidity and guilt when men see the righteous die without concern. If the pious die by persecution and others are not aroused, it shows that they acquiesce in it, or have no confidence in God, and no desire that his people should be preserved; if they die in the ordinary mode and the people are unaffected, it shows their stupidity. The withdrawment of a pious man from the earth is a public calamity. His prayers, his example, his life, were among the richest blessings of the world, and men should be deeply affected when they are withdrawn; and it shows their guilt and stupidity when they see this with indifference. It increases the evidence of this guilt when, as is sometimes the case, the removal of the righteous by death is an occasion of joy. The wicked hate the secret rebuke which is furnished by a holy life, and they often feel a secret exultation when such men die. ¶ *And merciful men.* Marg. 'Men of kindness,' or 'godliness.' Lowth and Noyes render it, 'Pious men.' The LXX. Ἄνδρες δίκαιοι—'Just men.' The Hebrew word denotes *mercy* or kindness (חֶסֶד). Here it probably means, 'Men of mercy;' that is, men who are the subjects of mercy; men who are pious, or devoted to God. ¶ Are *taken away.* Heb. 'Are gathered.' That is, they are gathered to their fathers by death. ¶ *None considering.* They were not anxious to know what was the design of Divine Providence in permitting it. ¶ *From the evil* to come. Marg. 'That which is evil.' The idea here evidently is, that severe calamities were coming upon the nation. God was about to give them up to foreign invasion (ch. lvi. 9, *sq.*); and the true reason why the just were removed was, that they may not be subject to the Divine wrath which should come upon the nation; they were not to be required to contemplate the painful state of things when an enemy should fire the cities, the palaces, and the temple, and cause the sacred services of religion to cease. It was a less evil for them to be removed by death—even by the painful death of persecution—than to be compelled to participate in these coming sorrows. At the same time this passage may be regarded as inculcating a more general truth still. It is, that the pious are often removed in order that they may not be exposed to evils which they would experience should they live. There might be the pains and sorrows of persecution; there

2 He shall [1]enter into peace: they shall rest in their beds, *each one* walking [2]*in* his [a]uprightness.

3 But draw near hither, ye sons of the sorceress, the seed of the adulterer and the whore.

1 *go in peace.* 2 or, *before him.*

a Re.14.13.

might be long and lingering disease; there might be poverty and want; there might be the prevalence of iniquity and infidelity over which their hearts would bleed; there might be long and painful conflicts with their own evil hearts, or there might be danger that *they* would fall into sin, and dishonour their high calling. For some or all these reasons the righteous may be withdrawn from the world; and could we see those reasons as God does, nothing more would be necessary to induce us to acquiesce entirely in the justice of his dealings.

2. *He shall enter into peace.* Lowth, 'He shall go in peace.' So the margin. Vulg. 'Peace shall come.' LXX. 'His sepulture (ἡ ταφὴ αὐτοῦ) shall be in peace.' The idea is, that by his death the righteous man shall enter into rest. He shall get away from conflict, strife, agitation, and distress. This may either refer to the peaceful rest of the grave, or to that which awaits the just in a better world. The direct meaning here intended is probably the former, since the grave is often spoken of as a place of rest. Thus Job (iii. 17), speaking of the grave, says:

> There the wicked cease from troubling;
> And there the weary be at rest.

The connection here seems also to demand the same sense, as it is immediately added, 'they shall rest in their beds.' The grave is a place of peace:

> Nor pain, nor grief, nor anxious fear,
> Invade thy bounds; no mortal woes
> Can reach the peaceful sleeper here,
> While angels watch the soft repose.—WATTS.

At the same time it is true that the dying saint '*goes* in peace!' He has calmness *in his dying*, as well as peace *in his grave*. He forgives all who have injured him; prays for all who have persecuted him; and peacefully and calmly dies. He lies in a peaceful grave—often represented in the Scriptures as a place of repose, where the righteous 'sleep' in the hope of being awakened in the morning of the resurrection. He enters into the rest of heaven—the world of perfect and eternal repose. No persecution comes there; no trial awaits him there; no calamity shall meet him there. Thus, in all respects, the righteous leave the world in peace; and thus death ceases to be a calamity, and this most dreaded of all evils is turned into the highest blessing. ¶ *They shall rest in their beds.* That is, in their graves. ¶ Each one *walking* in *his uprightness.* Marg. 'Before him.' The word נְכֹחַ means *straight, right,* and is used of one who walks straight forward. It here means an upright man, who is often represented as walking in a straight path in opposition to sinners, who are represented as walking in crooked ways (Ps. cxxv. 5; Prov. ii. 15; Isa. lix. 8; Phil. ii. 15). The sense here is, that all who are upright shall leave the world in peace, and rest quietly in their graves.

3. *But draw near hither.* That is, come near to hear the solemn sentence which God pronounces in regard to your character and doom. This is addressed to the impenitent and unbelieving part of the nation, and is designed to set before them the greatness of their sin, and the certainty that they would be punished. ¶ *Ye sons of the sorceress.* You who are addicted to sorcery and enchantments; who consult the oracles of the heathen rather than the only true God. On the meaning of the word used here, see Notes on ch. ii. 6. The Hebrews, like other inhabitants of the East, were much addicted to this, and particularly in the time of Manasseh (2 Kings xxi. 6): 'And he made his sons pass through the fire, and observed times, and used enchantments, and dealt with familiar spirits, and wizards.' So much were they devoted to this in his time, that they might be called, by way of eminence, '*the sons* of the sorceress;' as if a sorceress had been their mother, and they had grown up to walk in her steps, and to imitate her example. ¶ *The seed of the adulterer.* Implying

4 Against whom do ye sport yourselves? against whom make ye a wide mouth, *and* draw out the tongue? *are* ye not children of transgression, a seed of falsehood.

5 Inflaming yourselves [1] with idols under [a] every green tree, slaying the children [b] in the valleys under the clefts of the rocks?

1 or, *among the oaks.* a 2 Ki.17.10,&c. b 2 Ki.16.3.4.

that the obligations of the marriage contract were disregarded, and that licentiousness prevailed in the nation. Amidst the other abominations which existed under the wicked and corrupt reign of Manasseh (2 Kings xxi.), there is every probability that these sins also abounded. Licentiousness had been the invariable attendant on idol-worship; and dissoluteness of manners is the usual accompaniment of all other crimes. It is observable also that the Saviour often charges the same sin on the nation in his own time (Matt. xii. 39; xvi. 4; John viii. 1, *sq.*) In the language here, however, there is a reference to the fact that the nation had apostatized from God, and they were guilty of *spiritual* adultery—that is, of unfaithfulness to God. They fixed their affections on other objects than God, and loved the images of idol-worship more than they did their Creator.

4. *Against whom do ye sport yourselves?* The word here rendered 'sport' (עָנַג) means properly *to live delicately* and tenderly; then to rejoice, to take pleasure or delight. Here, however, it is evidently used in the sense of to sport one's self over any one, *i.e.*, to deride; and the idea is, probably, that they made a sport or mockery of God, and of the institutions of religion. The prophet asks, with deep indignation and emotion, against whom they did this. Were they aware of the majesty and glory of that Being whom they thus derided? ¶ *Against whom make ye a wide mouth?* That is, in derision or contempt (Ps. xxxv. 21): 'Yea, they opened their mouth wide against me.' ¶ And *draw out the tongue?* Lowth, 'Loll the tongue;' or, as we would say, 'run out the tongue.' Perhaps it was done with a rapid motion, as in mockery of the true prophets when they delivered the message of God (comp. 2 Chron. xxxvi. 16). Contempt was sometimes shown also by protruding the lips (Ps. xxii. 7): 'They shoot out the lip;' and also by *gaping* upon a person (Ps. xxii. 13); 'They gaped upon me with their mouths.' ¶ Are *ye not children of transgression?* That is, in view of the fact that you make a sport of sacred things, and deride the laws and the prophets of God. ¶ *A seed of falsehood.* A generation that is unfaithful to God and to his cause.

5. *Inflaming yourselves.* Burning, *i.e.*, with lust. The whole language here is derived from adulterous intercourse. The sense is, that they were greatly addicted to idolatry, and that they used every means to increase and extend the practice of it. The Vulgate, however, renders this, 'Who console yourselves.' The LXX. render it, 'Invoking (παρακαλοῦντες) idols.' But the proper meaning of the Hebrew word חָמַם is, *to become warm;* to be inflamed, or to burn as with lust. ¶ *With idols.* Marg. 'Among the oaks.' Heb. בָּאֵלִים. Vulg. *In diis*—'With the gods.' LXX. Εἴδωλα—'Idols.' So the Chaldee and Syriac. The Hebrew may denote 'with gods,' *i.e.*, with idol-gods; or it may denote, as in the margin, 'among the oaks,' or the terebinth groves, from אֵיל. plural אֵילִים, or אֵלִים (*the terebinth*). See the word explained in the Note on ch. i. 29. Kimchi and Jarchi here render it by 'the terebinth tree.' Lowth renders it, 'Burning with the lust of idols;' and probably this is the correct interpretation; for, if it had meant oaks or the terebinth tree, the phrase would have been *under* (תַּחַת) instead of *in* or *with* (ב). ¶ *Under every green tree* (see Notes on ch. i. 29; comp. Deut. xxii. 2; 2 Kings xvii. 10; 2 Chron. xxviii. 4). ¶ *Slaying the children.* That is, sacrificing them to the idol-gods. This was commonly done by burning them, as when they were offered to Moloch, though it is not improbable that they were sometimes sacrificed in other ways. It was a common custom among the worshippers of Moloch. Thus

6 Among the smooth *stones* of the stream *is* thy portion; they, they *are* thy lot; even to them hast thou poured a drink-offering, thou hast offered a meat-offering. Should I receive comfort in these?

---

it is said of Ahaz (2 Chron. xxviii. 3), that he 'burnt incense in the valley of the son of Hinnom, and burnt his children in the fire.' The same thing is said of Manasseh, to whose time the prophet most probably refers. 'And he caused his children to pass through the fire in the valley of the son of Hinnom' (2 Chron. xxxiii. 6; comp. Jer. vii. 31). The same thing was practised in the countries of the Babylonian empire (2 Kings xvii. 31), and from Deut. xii. 31, it is evident that it was commonly practised by heathen nations. The Phenicians, according to Eusebius (Præp. Evan. iv. 16), and the Carthagenians, according to Diodorus Siculus (xx. 14), practised it. ¶ *In the valleys.* The place where these abominations were practised by the Jews was the valley of the son of Hinnom (see the references above); that is, the valley of Jehoshaphat, lying to the south and the south-east of Jerusalem. A large hollow, brazen statue was erected, and the fire was enkindled within it, and the child was placed in his heated arms, and thus put to death. The cries of the child were drowned by the music of the תֹּף *toph*, or kettle-drums (see Notes on ch. v. 12, where this instrument is fully described), and hence the name of the valley was *Tophet.* ¶ *Under the clefts of the rocks.* Dark and shady groves, and deep and sombre caverns were the places where the abominable rites of the heathen superstitions were practised (comp. Notes on ch. xi. 21).

6. *Among the smooth* stones *of the streams.* In the original here, there is a paronomasia, which cannot be fully retained in our English version. There has been also considerable diversity of opinion in regard to the sense of the passage, from the ambiguity of the words in the original. Jerome (Vulg.) renders it, *In partibus torrentis pars tua*—'Thy portion is in the parts of the torrent.' The LXX. translate it, 'This is thy portion; this is thy lot.' The word rendered in our version 'smooth stones' (חֵלֶק *hhêlĕq*), means properly *smoothness,* hence, barrenness or bare place; and supposes that the idea is, their lot was in the bare places of the valley, *i.e.*, in the open (not wooded) places where they worshipped idols—an interpretation not very consistent with the fact that groves were commonly selected as the place where they worshipped idols. It seems to me, therefore, that the idea of *smoothness* here, whether of the valley or of the stones, is not the idea intended. Indeed, in no place, it is believed, does the word mean 'smooth stones;' and it is difficult to conceive what was the exact idea which our translators intended to convey, or why they supposed that such worship was celebrated among the smooth or much-worn stones of the running stream. The true idea can probably be obtained by reverting to the primitive sense of the word as derived from the verb. The verb חָלַק *hhâhlăq* means—1. *To smooth.* 2. *To divide,* to distribute, to appropriate—as the dividing of spoil, &c. Hence the noun also means *dividing,* or portion, as that which is *divided*—whether an inheritance, or whether the dividings of spoil after battle. Retaining this idea, the literal sense, as I conceive, would be this—in which also something of the paronomasia will be retained: 'Among the dividings of the valley is thy dividing,' *i.e.*, thy portion. In the places where the valley divides, is thy lot. Thy lot is there instead of the place which God appointed. There you worship; there you pour out your libations to the false gods; and there you must partake of the protection and favour which the gods whom you worship can give. You have chosen that as your inheritance, and by the results of that you must abide. ¶ *Of the stream.* The word here rendered 'stream' (נַחַל *năhhăl*), means either a stream, or a rivulet of water (Num. xxxiv. 5; Josh. xv. 4–47); or it means a *valley* with a brook or torrent; a low place with water. Here it means evidently the latter—as it cannot be supposed they would worship *in* a stream, though they

7 Upon a lofty and high mountain hast thou set thy bed: even thither wentest thou up to offer sacrifice.
8 Behind the doors also and the posts hast thou set up thy remembrance; for *a* thou hast discovered *thyself to another* than me, and art gone up: thou hast enlarged thy bed, and [1] made thee *a covenant* with them; thou lovedst their bed where [2] thou sawest *it*.

a Eze.16.25,&c.; 23.2,&c.

1 or, *hewed it for thyself* larger *than theirs*.
2 or, *thou providest room*.

undoubtedly worshipped in a vale or low place where there was occasionally a rivulet of water. This entire description is strikingly applicable to the valley of Jehoshaphat—a low vale, broken by chasms and by projecting and overhanging rocks, and along the centre of which flowed a small brook, much swelled occasionally by the waters that fell from the adjacent hills. At some seasons of the year, however, the valley was entirely dry. The idea here is, that they had chosen their portion in the dividings of that valley instead of the adjacent hills on which the worship of God was celebrated. That valley became afterwards the emblem of punishment: and may it not be implied in this passage that they were to inherit whatever would descend on that valley; that is, that they were to participate in the punishment which would be the just expression of the Divine displeasure? ¶ *Even to them hast thou poured out.* That is, to these idols erected in the valleys. ¶ *A drink-offering.* A libation, or drink-offering was usually poured out in the worship of heathen gods (Jer. vii. 18). It was common also in the worship of the true God (see Gen. xxxv. 14). Among the Hebrews it consisted of wine and oil (Ex. xxix. 40; Num. xv. 5–7; Lev. xxiii. 13). ¶ *Thou hast offered a meat-offering.* On the word used here (מִנְחָה *minhhâ*) see Notes on ch. i. 13; xliii. 23. The word 'meat' formerly denoted in the English language *food* in general, and was not confined as it is now to animal food. Hence the word 'meat-offering' is so often used in the Scriptures when a sacrifice is intended which was not a bloody sacrifice. The *minhha* was in fact an offering of *meal*, fine flour, &c., mingled with oil (Lev. xiv. 10; Num. vii. 13), and was distinguished expressly from the bloody sacrifice. The word '*meal*-offering' would much more appropriately express the sense of the original than '*meat*-offering.' This was a common offering made to idols as well as to the true God, and was designed as an expression of thankfulness. ¶ *Should I receive comfort in these?* It is implied that God could not behold them but with displeasure, and that for them he would punish them. The Vulg. and the LXX. well express it, 'On account of these things shall I not be enraged?'

7. *Upon a lofty and high mountain.* The design of this verse and the following, is, to show the extent, the prevalence, the publicity, and the grossness of their idolatry. The language is that which would appropriately express adulterous intercourse, and is designed to show the abhorrence in which God held their conduct. The language is easy to be understood, and it would not be proper to go into an extended explanation of the phrases used. It is common in the Scriptures to compare idolatry among the people of God, with unfaithfulness to the marriage vow. The declaration that they had placed their bed on a high mountain, means, that in the rites of idolatrous worship, there was no concealment. It was public and shameless.

8. *Behind the doors.* In every part of their habitations—behind the doors and posts and beams of their houses, they had erected the memorials of idolatrous worship. ¶ *Hast thou set up thy remembrance.* That is, they had filled their houses with the images of tutelary gods, or with something dedicated to them. The Greeks and Romans had their *Lares* and *Penates*—their household or domestic gods—the images of which were in every family. The same was true of the apostate Hebrews. They had filled their houses with the memorials of idol-worship, and there was no part of their dwellings in which such memorials were not to be found.

9 And thou [1] wentest to the king
with ointment, [a] and didst increase
thy perfumes, and didst send thy
messengers far off, and didst debase
thyself even unto hell.

1 or, *respectedst.* a Ho.12.1.

When a people forget God, the memorials of their apostasy will be found in every part of their habitations. The shrines of idol-gods may not be there; the beautiful images of the Greek and Roman mythology, or the clumsy devices of less refined heathens, may not be there; but the furniture, the style of living, will reveal from 'behind every door and the posts' of the house that God is forgotten, and that they are influenced by other principles than a regard to his name. The sofa, the carpet, the chandelier, the centre-table, the instruments of music, the splendid mirror, *may be* of such workmanship as to show, as clearly as the image of a heathen god, that Jehovah is not honoured in the dwelling, and that his law does not control the domestic arrangements. It may be added here that this custom of the Hebrews of placing the images of idols in their dwellings, was in direct violation of the law of Moses. They were expressly directed to write the laws of God on the posts of the house and on the gates (Deut. vi. 9; xi. 20); and a curse was denounced against the man who made a graven or molten image and put it in a secret place (Deut. xxvii. 15). ¶ *For thou hast discovered* thyself. This language is taken from adulterous intercourse, and is designed to show the love which they had for idolatrous worship, and the extent of their unfaithfulness to God. ¶ *And made thee* a covenant *with them.* Marg. 'Hewed it for thyself larger than theirs.' The true sense is, that they had made an agreement with idolaters, or had entered into a covenant with them. ¶ *Thou lovedst their bed.* Marg. 'Thou providest room.' Literally, 'Thou lovest their bed; thou hast provided a place for it.' The word יָד, here rendered 'where,' means literally *a hand;* then a side, a place (see Notes on ch. lvi. 5). The passage means, that they had delighted in the temples, altars, groves, and sacrifices of idolatry, and had provided a place for them in their own land.

9. *And thou wentest to the king.* Marg. 'Respectedst.' Jerome renders this, 'Thou hast adorned thyself with royal ointment, and hast multiplied thy painting;' and evidently understands it as a continuance of the sentiment in the previous verses as referring to the kind of decoration which harlots used. The LXX. render it, 'Thou hast multiplied thy fornication with them, and hast done it with many who are far from thee.' The Chaldee renders it, 'When thou didst keep the law thou wert prosperous in the kingdom; and when thou didst abound in good works, then thine armies were multiplied.' Lowth supposes that the king of Egypt or Assyria is intended, and that the prophet refers to the fact, that the Hebrews had sought an alliance with them, and in order to secure it, had carried a present of valuable unguents, after the manner of the East. Rosenmüller supposes, that by the king an idol was intended, and that the sense is, that they had anointed themselves with oil, and prepared perfumes, in order to be acceptable to the idol; that is, had decorated themselves as harlots did. Grotius supposes that it means that they had imitated foreign kings, and copied the customs of other nations, and refers to the example of Ahaz (2 Kings xvi. 10). Others suppose that the word 'king' is to be taken collectively, and that it means that they had sought the alliance, and imitated the customs of foreign nations in general. It is probable that the prophet refers to some such fact. On former occasions, they had sought the alliance of the king of Assyria (see ch. vii. *sq.*); and on one occasion, at least, they had meditated an alliance with the king of Egypt (ch. xxx. 2, *sq.*) The essential idea is, that they had proved unfaithful to Jehovah. This idea is presented here under the image of a female unfaithful to her husband, who had decorated and perfumed herself that she might allure others. Thus the Jews had forsaken God, and had endeavoured to make themselves agreeable in the sight of other nations, and had courted

10 Thou art wearied in the greatness [a] of thy way; *yet* saidst thou not, There is no hope: thou hast found the life [1] of thine hand; therefore thou wast not grieved.

[a] Je.2.36. [1] or, *living.*

their friendship and alliance. The word 'king,' according to this, refers not to idols, but to foreign princes, whose assistance had been sought. ¶ *And didst increase thy perfumes.* That is, for the purpose of rendering thyself agreeable, after the manner of a licentious female (see Prov. vii. 17). The custom of perfuming the person was common in the East, and is still practised there. ¶ *And didst send thy messengers.* That is, to distant nations, for the purpose of securing their alliance. ¶ *And didst debase* thyself even *unto hell.* On the meaning of the word 'hell,' see Notes on ch. v. 14. The idea is, that they had sunk to the deepest possible debasement. In forsaking Jehovah; in seeking foreign alliances; in their anxiety to secure their aid when Jehovah was abundantly able and willing to protect them, they had sunk to the lowest degradation of character and condition. The sentiment is, that men degrade themselves when they do not put confidence in God, and when, distrusting his ability, they put reliance on any other aid than his. If men have God for their protector, why should they court the friendship of earthly princes and kings?

10. *Thou art wearied in the greatness of thy way.* That is, in the length of thy journeys in order to procure foreign aid. Thou hast travelled to distant nations for this purpose, and in doing it, hast become weary without securing the object in view. ¶ Yet *saidst thou not, There is no hope.* 'Thou didst not say it is to be despaired of (נוֹאָשׁ), or it is vain. Though repulsed in one place, you applied to another; though weary, you did not give it up. Instead of returning to God and seeking his aid, you still sought human alliances, and supposed you would find assistance from the help of men.' This is a striking illustration of the conduct of men in seeking happiness away from God. They wander from object to object; they become weary in the pursuit, yet they do not abandon it; they still cling to hope though often repulsed—and though the world gives them no permanent comfort—though wealth, ambition, gaiety, and vice all fail in imparting the happiness which they sought, yet they do not give it up in despair. They still feel that it is to be found in some other way than by the disagreeable necessity of returning to God, and they wander from object to object, and from land to land, and become exhausted in the pursuit, and still are not ready to say, 'there is no hope, we give it up in despair, and we will now seek happiness in God.' ¶ *Thou hast found the life of thine hand.* Marg. 'Living.' Lowth, 'Thou hast found the support of thy life by thy labour.' Noyes, 'Thou yet findest life in thy hand.' Much diversity of opinion has prevailed in regard to the interpretation of this passage. Vitringa interprets the whole passage of their devotion to idols, and supposes that this means that they had borne all the expense and difficulty and toil attending it because it gratified their hearts, and because they found a pleasure in it which sustained them. Calvin supposes that it is to be understood *ironically.* 'Why didst thou not repent and turn to me? Why didst thou not see and acknowledge thy madness? It was because thou didst find thy life in thy hand. All things prospered and succeeded according to thy desire, and conferred happiness.' The LXX. render it, 'Because in full strength (ἐνισχύουσα) thou hast done this; therefore thou shouldst not supplicate me.' Jerome explains it to mean, 'because they have done the things referred to in the previous verses, therefore they had not supplicated the Lord, trusting more in their own virtues than in God.' The Syriac renders it, 'The guilt of thy hand has contracted rust for thee, therefore thou hast not offered supplication.' The Chaldee renders it, 'Thou hast amassed wealth, therefore thou didst not repent.' Kimchi explains it to mean, 'Thou hast found something which is as pleasant to thee as the food is which is the life of man.' The phrase 'life of thy hand'

11 And of whom hast thou been afraid or feared, that thou hast lied, and hast not remembered me, nor laid *it* to thy heart? have [a]not I held my peace even of old, and thou fearest me not?

[a] Ps.50.21.

---

occurs nowhere else. The hand is the instrument by which we execute our purposes; and by the life of the hand here, there seems to be meant that which will give full and continued employment. They had found in these things that which effectually prevented them from repenting and returning to God. They had relied on their own plans rather than on God; they had sought the aid of foreign powers; they had obtained that which kept them from absolute despair, and from feeling their need of the assistance of God. Or, if it refers to their idol-worship, as Vitringa supposes, then it means that, notwithstanding all the trouble, toil, and expense which they had experienced, they had found so much to gratify them that they continued to serve them, and were unwilling to return to God. ¶ *Therefore thou wast not grieved.* Lowth, 'Thou hast not utterly fainted.' The word used here (חָלָה) means *to be polished;* then to be worn down in strength; to be weak or exhausted (Judg. xvi. 7); then to be sick, diseased, made weak. Here it means, that either by the aid which they had obtained by foreign alliances, or by the gratification experienced in the service of idols, they had found so much to uphold them that they had not been in utter despair. And the passage may teach the general truth, that notwithstanding all the trials and disappointments of life, still sinners find *so much* comfort in the ways of sin, that they are not utterly overwhelmed in despair. They still find the 'life of their hand in them.' If a plan fails, they repeat it, or they try another. In the pursuits of ambition, of wealth, and of fashion, notwithstanding all the expense, and irksomeness, and disappointment, they find *a kind* of pleasure which sustains them, and *enough* success to keep them from returning to God. It is this imperfect pleasure and success which the world gives amidst all its disappointments, and this hope of less diminished joys and more ample success in schemes of gain, and pleasure, and ambition, that sustains the votaries of this world in their career, and keeps them from seeking the pure and unmingled pleasures of religion. When the world becomes *all* gloom, and disappointment, and care, then there is felt the necessity of a better portion, and the mind is turned to God. Or when, as is more common, the mind becomes convinced that all the joys which the world can give—allowing the utmost limit to what is said by its friends of its powers—are poor and trifling compared with the joys which flow from the eternal friendship of God, then the blessings of salvation are sought with a full heart; and then man comes and consecrates the fulness of his energies and his immortal vigour to the service of the God that made him.

11. *And of whom hast thou been afraid.* The sense of this verse is exceedingly obscure. The design is evidently to reprove the Jews for the course which they had been pursuing in practising idolatry, and in seeking the alliance of foreign powers. The main scope of the passage seems to be, to state that all this was proof that they did not fear God. Their conduct did not originate from any reverence for him, or any respect to his commands. And the question, 'of whom hast thou been afraid?' seems to mean that they had not been afraid of God. If they had had any reverence for any being or object that had led to the course which they had pursued, it was not for God. ¶ *That thou hast lied.* That thou hast been false and unfaithful to God. The image is here kept up of unfaithfulness to the marriage vow (ver. 6–8). ¶ *And hast not remembered me.* The proof of this was, that they had fallen into idolatry, and had sought the alliance and friendship of foreign powers. ¶ *Have not I held my peace.* The idea here seems to be, that God had been silent a long time, and they had, therefore, been emboldened to sin. He had, as it were, connived at their apostasy

12 I will declare thy righteousness, and thy works; for they shall
not profit thee.
13 When thou criest, let thy
companies deliver thee: but the
wind shall carry them all away;
vanity shall take *them:* but he that
putteth [a] his trust in me shall possess the land, and shall inherit my
holy mountain.
14 And shall say, Cast ye up,
cast ye up, prepare the way, take
up the stumbling-block [b] out of the
way of my people.
15 For thus saith the high and
lofty One that inhabiteth eternity,

a Ps.37.3,9.

b 1 Co.1.23.

and infidelity; and they had thus cast off the fear of him, and given themselves wholly to idolatry. Comp. Eccl. viii. 11.

12. *I will declare thy righteousness.* This is evidently spoken ironically. The sense is, 'you have devoted yourselves to idols, and you have sought the aid of foreigners. I will now announce to you the true nature of the deliverance which they can bring to you.' This is done in the following verse.

13. *When thou criest.* That is, when you are in trouble, and feel your need of help. ¶ *Let thy companies deliver thee.* The word here used (קִבּוּץ) means, properly, a gathering; a throng; a collection. Here it refers either to the *throngs* of the idols which they had collected, and on which they relied; or to the collection of foreigners which they had summoned to their assistance. The idea is, that if men trust to other objects for aid than the arm of God, they will be left in the day of trial to such assistance as they can render them. ¶ *But the wind shall carry.* They shall be like the protection which the wind sweeps away. The Saviour expresses a similar sentiment in Matt. vii. 26, 27. ¶ *Vanity shall take* them. Lowth and Noyes, 'A breath shall take them off.' The word הֶבֶל *hêbhêl*, properly means *a breath;* and probably denotes here a gentle breeze, the slightest breath of air, denoting the entire instability of the objects on which they trusted, when they could be so easily swept off. ¶ *Shall possess the land.* The assurances of the favour and friendship of God are usually expressed in this way (comp. Notes on ch. xlix. 8). See Ps. xxxvii. 11; 'The meek shall inherit the earth.' Comp. Ps. lxix. 35, 36; Matt. v. 5. ¶ *And shall inherit my holy mountain.* In Jerusalem. That is, they shall be admitted to elevated spiritual privileges and joys—as great as if they had possession of a portion of the mount on which the temple was built, and were permitted to dwell there.

14. *And shall say.* Lowth, 'Then will I say.' Noyes, 'Men will say.' The word אָמַר seems to be used here *impersonally*, and to mean, 'One shall say;' *i.e.* it shall be said. The LXX. and the Syriac render it, 'They shall say.' The idea is, that the obstacles would be removed from the path of those who put their trust in God. The *language* is derived from the return from the exile, as if persons should go before them, and should cry, 'Cast ye up;' or as if the cry of the people all along their journey should be, 'Remove the obstacles to their return.' ¶ *Cast ye up, cast ye up.* That is, remove the obstacles; level the hills; take up any obstruction out of the way (comp. Notes ch. xxxv. 8; xl. 3, 4). This cry is often heard before the coming of a distinguished prince or conqueror in the East. The Rev. Joseph Wolff stated, in a lecture in Philadelphia (Sept. 18, 1837), that, on entering Jerusalem from the west, in the direction of Gaza, the road, for a considerable distance from Jerusalem, was so full of stones, that it was impracticable to ride, and those who were entering the city were obliged to dismount. When the Pasha (Ibrahim, son of Mehemet Ali) approached Jerusalem, it was customary for a considerable number of labourers to go before him, and remove the stones from the way. This was done amidst a constant cry, 'Cast up, cast up the way; remove the stones, remove the stones.' And on a placard, or standard, it was written, 'the Pasha is coming;' and everywhere the cry was heard, 'the Pasha is coming, the Pasha is coming; cast up the way, remove the stones.'

15. *For thus saith.* The design of

whose name *is* Holy ; I dwell in
the high and [a]holy *place*, with him
also [b] *that is* of a contrite and humble
spirit, to revive [c]the spirit of the
humble, and to revive the heart of
the contrite ones.

16 For [d]I will not contend for
ever, neither will I be always wroth:
for the spirit should fail before me,
and the souls *which* I have made.

a Zec.2.13. b ch.66.1,2; Ps.34.18; 138.6. c Mat.5.4. d Ps.103.9; Mi.7.18.

this verse is, to furnish the assurance that the promise made to the people of God would certainly be accomplished. It was not to be presumed that he was so high and lofty, that he did not condescend to notice the affairs of men; but though he, in fact, dwelt in eternity, yet he also had his abode in the human heart. Many of the ancient heathens supposed that God was so lofty that he did not condescend to notice human affairs. This was the view of the Epicureans (see Notes on Acts xvii. 18); and the belief extensively prevailed in the Oriental world, that God had committed the management of the affairs of men to inferior beings which he had created. This was the basis of the Gnostic philosophy. According to this, God reposed far in the distant heavens, and was regardless of the affairs and plans of mortals, and personally unconcerned in the government of this lower world. But the Bible reveals him as a very different being. True, he is vast and illimitable in his existence and perfections; but, at the same time, he is the most condescending of all beings. He dwells with men, and he delights in making his abode with the penitent and the contrite. ¶ *The high and lofty One.* One MS. reads 'Jehovah,' before 'saith;' and Lowth has adopted the reading; but the authority is not sufficient. The sense is, that he who is here spoken of is, by way of eminence, THE high and holy One; the most high and the most exalted being in the universe. He is so far above all creatures of all ranks that it is not needful to specify his name in order to designate him. No one can be compared with him; no one so nearly approaches him that there can be any danger of confounding him with other beings. ¶ *That inhabiteth eternity* (comp. Notes on ch. ix. 6). The word 'eternity' here evidently stands in contrast with the 'contrite and humble spirit;' and it seems to be used to denote the elevated *place* of an eternal dwelling or heaven. He dwells not only among men, but he dwells in eternity —where time is unknown—in a world where succession is not marked—and long before the interminable duration was broken in upon by the revolutions of years and days. ¶ *Whose name* is *Holy* (see Notes on ch. i. 4; xxx. 11; xli. 14; xliii. 3, 8, 14; xlvii. 4). ¶ *I dwell in the high and holy* place. In heaven—uniformly represented as far exalted above the earth, and as the peculiar home or dwelling-place of God. Thus, in ch. lxiii. 15, heaven is called the habitation of the holiness and glory of Jehovah. ¶ *With him also* that is *of a contrite and humble spirit.* The word 'contrite' (דַּכָּא) means properly that which is broken, crushed, beaten small, trodden down. Here it denotes a soul that is borne down with a sense of sin and unworthiness; a heart that is, as it were, *crushed* under a superincumbent weight of guilt (see Ps. xxxiv. 18; cxxxviii. 6). ¶ *To revive the spirit.* Literally, 'to make alive.' The sense is, he imparts spiritual life and comfort. He is to them what refreshing rains and genial suns and dews are to a drooping plant.

16. *For I will not contend for ever.* I will not be angry with my people for ever, nor always refuse to pardon and comfort them (see Ps. ciii. 9). This is to be regarded as having been primarily addressed to the Jews in their long and painful exile in Babylon. It is, however, couched in general language; and the idea is, that although God would punish his people for their sins, yet his wrath would not be perpetual. If they were his children, he would visit them again in mercy, and would restore to them his favour. ¶ *For the spirit should fail before me.* Critics have taken a great deal of pains on this part of the verse, which they suppose to be very obscure. The simple meaning seems to be, that if God should con-

17 For the iniquity of his [a] covetousness was I wroth, and smote him: I hid me, and was wroth, and he went on [1] frowardly in the way of his heart.

18 I have seen his ways, and will heal [b] him: I will lead him also, and restore comforts unto him and to his mourners.

a Je.6.13. 1 *turning away.* b Je.30.3; 33 6; Ho.14.4.

tinue in anger against men they would be consumed. The human soul could not endure a long-continued controversy with God. Its powers would fail; its strength decay; it must sink to destruction. As God did not intend this in regard to his own people; as he meant that his chastisements should not be for their destruction, but for their salvation; and as he knew how much they could bear, and how much they needed, he would lighten the burden, and restore them to his favour. And the truth taught here is, that if we are his children, we are safe. We may suffer much and long. We may suffer so much that it seems scarcely possible that we should endure more. But he knows how much we can bear; and he will remove the load, so that we shall not be utterly crushed. A similar sentiment is found in the two following elegant passages of the Psalms, which are evidently parallel to this, and express the same idea:—

But he being full of compassion,
Forgave their iniquity, and destroyed them not;
Yea many a time turned he his anger away,
And did not stir up all his wrath.
For he remembered that they were but flesh;
A wind that passeth away and returneth not again. Ps. lxxviii. 38, 39.

He will not always chide;
Neither will he keep his anger for ever.
Like as a father pitieth his children,
So the Lord pitieth them that fear him.
For he knoweth our frame;
He remembereth that we are dust.
Ps. ciii. 9, 13, 14.

The Hebrew word which is here rendered 'should fail' (עָטַף), means properly *to cover*, as with a garment; or to envelope with anything, as darkness. Then it is used in the sense of having the mind covered or muffled up with sorrow; and means to languish, to be faint or feeble, to fail. Thus it is used in Ps. lxi. 2; cvii. 5; cxlii. 3; Lam. ii. 11, 12, 19; Jonah ii. 7. Other interpretations of this verse may be seen in Rosenmüller; but the above seems to be the true sense. According to this, it furnishes ground of encouragement and comfort to all the children of God who are afflicted. No sorrow will be sent which they will not be able to endure, no calamity which will not be finally for their own good. At the same time, it is a passage full of alarm to the sinner. How *can* he contend for ever with God? How *can* he struggle always with the Almighty? And what *must* be the state in that dreadful world, where God *shall* contend for ever with the soul, and where all its powers shall be crushed beneath the vengeance of his eternal arm!

17. *For the iniquity of his covetousness.* The guilt of his avarice; that is, of the Jewish people. The word here rendered 'covetousness' (בֶּצַע) means plunder, rapine, prey; then unjust gains, or lucre from bribes (1 Sam. vii. 3; Isa. xxxiii. 15); or by any other means. Here the sense is, that one of the prevailing sins of the Jewish people which drew upon them the Divine vengeance, was avarice, or the love of gain. Probably this was especially manifest in the readiness with which those who dispensed justice received bribes (comp. ch. ii. 7). See also Jer. vi. 13: 'For from the least of them even unto the greatest of them every one is given to covetousness.' ¶ *And smote him.* That is, I brought heavy judgments on the Jewish people. ¶ *I hid me.* I withdrew the evidences of my presence and the tokens of my favour, and left them to themselves. ¶ *And he went on frowardly.* Marg. 'Turning away.' That is, abandoned by me, the Jewish people declined from my service and sunk deeper into sin. The idea here is, that if God withdraws from his people, such is their tendency to depravity, that they will wander away from him, and sink deeper in guilt—a truth which is manifest in the experience of individuals, as well as of communities and churches.

18. *I have seen his ways.* That is, either his ways of sin, or of repentance

19 I create the fruit [a] of the lips;
Peace, peace to *him that is* far [b] off,
and to *him that is* near, saith the
LORD; and I will heal him.
20 But the wicked *are* like the

a Ho.14.2; He.13.15. b Ep.2.13,17.

Most probably it means the former; and the idea is, that God had seen how prone his people were to sin, and that he would now interpose and correct their proneness to sin against him, and remove from them the judgments which had been brought upon them in consequence of their crimes. ¶ *And will heal him.* That is, I will pardon and restore him. Sin, in the Scriptures, is often represented as a disease, and pardon and salvation as a healing of the disease (2 Chron. vii. 14; Ps. xli. 4; Jer. iii. 22; xvii. 4; xxxii. 6; Hos. xiv. 4; see Notes on Isa. vi. 10). ¶ *And to his mourners.* To the pious portion that mourned over their sin; or to the nation which would sigh in their long and painful captivity in Babylon.

19. *I create the fruit of the lips.* The Chaldee and Syriac render this, 'The words of the lips.' The 'fruit' of the lips is that which the lips produce, that is, *words;* and the reference here is doubtless to offerings of praise and thanksgiving. See Heb. xiii. 15; where the phrase, 'fruit of the lips' (καρπὸς χειλέων), is explained to mean *praise.* Compare Hos. xiv. 2, where the expression, 'we will render the calves of the lips,' means that they would offer praise. The sense here is, that God bestowed such blessings as made thanksgiving proper, and thus, he '*created* the fruit of the lips.' ¶ *Peace, peace.* The great subject of the thanksgiving would be peace. The peace here referred to probably had a primary reference to the cessation of the calamities which would soon overwhelm the Jewish nation, and their restoration again to their own land. But the whole strain of the passage also shows that the prophet had a more general truth in his view, and that he refers to that peace which would diffuse joy among all who were far off, and those who were nigh. Paul evidently alludes to this passage in Eph. ii. 14-17. Thus understood, the more general reference is to the peace which the Messiah would introduce, and which would lay the foundation for universal rejoicing and praise (comp. Notes on ch. ii. 4; ix. 5). ¶ *To* him that is *far off.* Applied by the apostle Paul to the Gentiles, who are represented as having been far off from God, or as aliens or strangers to him (Eph. ii. 17). ¶ *And to* him that is *near.* That is, to the Jewish people (Eph. ii. 17), represented as having been comparatively near to God in the enjoyment of religious privileges.

20. *But the wicked.* All who are transgressors of the law and who remain unpardoned. The design of this is to contrast their condition with that of those who should enjoy peace. The proposition is, therefore, of the most general character. *All* the wicked are like the troubled sea. Whether prosperous or otherwise; rich or poor; bond or free; old or young; whether in Christian, in civilized, or in barbarous lands; whether living in palaces, in caves, or in tents; whether in the splendour of cities, or in the solitude of deserts; ALL are like the troubled sea. ¶ Are *like the troubled sea.* The agitated (נִגְרָשׁ), ever-moving and restless sea. The sea is always in motion, and never entirely calm. Often also it lashes into foam, and heaves with wild commotion. ¶ *When it cannot rest.* Lowth renders this, 'For it never can be at rest.' The Hebrew is stronger than our translation. It means that there is no possibility of its being at rest; it is *unable to be still* (כִּי הַשְׁקֵט לֹא יוּכָל). The LXX. render it, 'But the wicked are tossed like waves (κλυδωνισθήσονται), and are not able to be at rest.' The idea, as it seems to me, is not exactly that which seems to be conveyed by our translation, that the wicked are like the sea, *occasionally* agitated by a storm and driven by wild commotion, but that, like the ocean, there is *never* any peace, as there is no peace to the restless waters of the mighty deep. ¶ *Whose waters.* They who have stood on the shores of the ocean and seen the waves—especially in a storm—foam, and roll, and dash on the beach, will be able to appreciate the force of this beautiful figure,

troubled sea, when it cannot [a] rest, whose waters cast up mire and dirt.

21 *There is* no [b] peace, saith my God, to the wicked.

a Pr.4.16,17.

b 2Ki.9.22.

and cannot but have a vivid image before them of the unsettled and agitated bosoms of the guilty. The figure which is here used to denote the want of peace in the bosom of a wicked man, is likewise beautifully employed by Ovid :

Cumque sit hibernis agitatum fluctibus æquor,
Pectora sunt ipso turbidiora mari.
Trist. i. x. 33.

The agitation and commotion of the sinner here referred to, relates to such things as the following :—1. There is no permanent happiness or enjoyment. There is no calmness of soul in the contemplation of the Divine perfections, and of the glories of the future world. There is no substantial and permanent peace furnished by wealth, business, pleasure; by the pride, pomp, and flattery of the world. All leave the soul *un*satisfied, or *dis*satisfied ; all leave is unprotected against the rebukes of conscience, and the fear of hell. 2. Raging passions. The sinner is under their influence, and they may be compared to the wild and tumultuous waves of the ocean. Thus the bosoms of the wicked are agitated with the conflicting passions of pride, envy, malice, lust, ambition, and revenge. These leave no peace in the soul ; they make peace impossible. Men may learn in some degree to control them by the influence of philosophy ; or a pride of character and respect to their reputation may enable them in some degree to restrain them ; but they are like the smothered fires of the volcano, or like the momentary calm of the ocean that a gust of wind may soon lash into foam. To restrain them is not to subdue them ; for no man can tell how soon he may be excited by anger, or how soon the smothered fires of lust may burn. 3. Conscience. Nothing more resembles an agitated ocean casting up mire and dirt, than a soul agitated by the recollections of past guilt. A deep dark cloud in a tempest overhangs the deep ; the lightnings play and the thunder rolls along the sky, and the waves heave with wild commotion. So it is with the bosom of the sinner. Though there may be a temporary suspension of the rebukes of conscience, yet there is no permanent peace. The soul *cannot* rest ; and in some way or other the recollections of guilt will be excited, and the bosom thrown into turbid and wild agitation. 4. The fear of judgment and of hell. Many a sinner has no rest, day or night, from the fear of future wrath. His troubled mind looks onward, and he sees nothing to anticipate but the wrath of God, and the horrors of an eternal hell.—How invaluable then is religion ! All these commotions are stilled by the voice of pardoning mercy, as the billows of the deep were hushed by the voice of Jesus. How much do we owe to religion ! Had it not been for this, there had been no peace in this world. Every bosom would have been agitated with tumultuous passion ; every heart would have quailed with the fear of hell. How diligently should we seek the influence of religion ! We all have raging passions to be subdued. We all have consciences that may be troubled with the recollections of past guilt. We are all travelling to the bar of God, and have reason to apprehend the storms of vengeance. We all must soon lie down on beds of death, and in all these scenes there is nothing that can give permanent and solid peace but the religion of the Redeemer. Oh ! *that* stills all the agitation of a troubled soul ; lays every billow of tumultuous passion to rest ; calms the conflicts of a guilty bosom ; reveals God reconciled through a Redeemer to our souls, and removes all the anticipated terrors of a bed of death and of the approach to the judgment bar. Peacefully the Christian can die —not as the troubled sinner, who leaves the world with a bosom agitated like the stormy ocean—but as peacefully as the gentle ripple dies away on the beach.

How blest the righteous when they die,
When holy souls retire to rest!
How mildly beams the closing eye,
How gently heaves the expiring breast!

So fades a summer cloud away;
So sinks the gale when storms are o'er;
So gently shuts the eye of day;
So dies a wave along the shore.—BARBAULD.

CHAPTER LVIII.

ANALYSIS.

THE design of this chapter is to reprove the Jews for a vain dependence on the performance of the outward forms of worship. The nation is represented as diligent in the performance of the external rites of their religion, and as expecting to avert the Divine judgments by the performance of those rites. They are represented as filled with amazement, that though they were thus diligent and faithful, they had no tokens of the Divine approbation, but were left as if forsaken by God. The main scope of the chapter is to state the reasons why their religious services met with no tokens of the Divine acceptance, and the blessings which would follow the proper performance of their duties.

It is not certainly known to what period the prophet refers, whether to the Jews in his own time, or to the Jews regarded as in Babylon. Rosenmüller supposes the reference is wholly to the Jews suffering in their captivity, and practising their religious rites with a view of obtaining the Divine favour and a release. He argues this because there is no reference here to sacrifices, but merely to fasting, and the observance of the Sabbath; duties which they could perform even when far away from the temple, and from their own land. But it seems more probable that the reference here to fasting is designed as an instance or specimen of the character of the people, and that this is made so prominent because they abounded so much in it, and were so hypocritical in its observance. It is possible that it was composed at or near the time of some of the public fasts during the reign of Manasseh, and that the fact that the external rites of religion were observed amidst the abominations of that wicked reign roused the indignation of the prophet, and led him to pour forth this severe reproof of the manner in which they approached God.

The chapter comprises the following subjects:—

I. A direction to the prophet openly and boldly to reprove the sins of the nation (1).

II. The fact that the Jewish people were regular and diligent in the observance of the external duties of religion, and that they expected the Divine favour on the ground of those observances (2, 3).

III. The prophet states the reason why their excessive and punctual religious duties had not been accepted or followed with the Divine favour and blessing. 1. They still continued their heavy exactions on others, and made everything tributary to their own pleasure (3). 2. They did it for strife and debate; with hoarse contentions and angry passions (4). 3. It was with an affected and hypocritical seriousness and solemnity, not as a proper expression of a deep sense of sin (5).

IV. The prophet states the true ways in which the favour of God might be obtained, and the happy results which would follow the proper observance of his commands, and the proper discharge of the duties of religion. 1. The proper mode of fasting, and the happy results (6-9). (1.) The kind of fasting which God had chosen (6, 7). It was to loose the bands of wickedness, and undo the heavy burdens, and let the oppressed go free, and to aid the poor and needy. (2.) The consequence of this (8, 9). Their light would break forth as the morning, and the nation would prosper, and their prayers would be heard. 2. The special duty of removing the yoke of oppression, and of regarding the poor and the oppressed, and the consequences (9-12). (1.) The duty. God requires the yoke of oppression to be put away, and the oppressed and the poor to be regarded by his people (9, last clause, 10). (2.) The consequences which would follow from this (10-12). Their light would rise in obscurity, and their darkness would be as noonday; JEHOVAH would be their guide, and the waste places would be repaired, and the desolations cease. 3. The duty of keeping the Sabbath, and the consequences (13, 14). (1.) The duty (13). They were to cease to do their own pleasure, and to call it holy, and to regard it with delight. (2.) The consequences (14). They would then find delight in the service of JEHOVAH; and they would ride upon the high places of the earth, and be abundantly blessed and prospered.

CRY [1] aloud, spare not; lift up thy voice like a trumpet, and show my people their transgressions, and the house of Jacob their sins.

1 *with the throat.*

---

21. There is *no peace* (see Note on ch. xlviii. 22).

CHAPTER LVIII.

1. *Cry aloud.* Marg. 'With the throat;' that is, says Gesenius, with open throat, with full voice coming from the throat and breast; while one who speaks low uses only the lips and tongue (1 Sam. i. 13). The Chaldee here introduces the word *prophet*, 'O

2 Yet [a] they seek me daily, and delight to know my ways, as a nation that did righteousness, and forsook not the ordinance of their God: they ask of me the ordinances of justice; they take delight in approaching to God.

a De.5.28.29.

prophet, cry aloud.' The LXX. render it, 'Cry with strength' (ἐν ἰσχύϊ). ¶ *Spare not.* That is, do not spare, or restrain the voice. Let it be full, loud, and strong. ¶ *Lift up thy voice like a trumpet.* Speak loud and distinct, so that the language of reproof may be heard. The sense is, the people are insensible and stupid. They need something to rouse them to a sense of their guilt. Go and proclaim it so that all may hear. Speak not in whispers; speak not to a part, but speak so earnestly that their attention will be arrested, and so that all shall hear (comp. Notes on ch. xl. 9). ¶ *And show my people.* This either refers to the Jewish people in the time of the prophet; or to the same people in their exile in Babylon; or to the people of God after the coming of the Messiah. Vitringa supposes that it refers to the nominally Christian Church when it should have sunk into the sins and formalities of the Papacy, and that the direction here is to the true ministers of God to proclaim the sins of a corrupt and degenerate church. The main reason assigned by him for this is, that there is no reference here to the temple, to the sacrifices, or to the idolatry which was the prevailing sin in the time of Manasseh. Rosenmüller, for a similar reason, supposes that it refers to the Jews in Babylon. But it has already been remarked (see the analysis to the chapter), that this reason does not appear to be satisfactory. It is true that there is no reference here to the temple or to sacrifices, and it may be true that the main sin of the nation in the time of Manasseh was idolatry; but it is also true that formality and hypocrisy were prominent sins, and that these deserved reproof. It is true that while they adhered to the public forms of religion, the heart was not in them; and that while they relied on those forms, and were surprised that the Divine favour was not manifested to them on account of their observance, there was a good reason why that favour was withheld, and it was important that that reason should be stated clearly and fully. It is probable, therefore, that the reference here is to the times of the prophet himself, and that the subject of rebuke is the formality, hypocrisy, and prevalent sins of the reign of Manasseh.

2. *Yet they seek me daily.* The whole description here is appropriate to the character of formalists and hypocrites; and the idea is, that public worship by sacrifice was celebrated daily in the temple, and was not intermitted. It is not improbable also that they kept up the regular daily service in their dwellings. ¶ *And delight to know my ways.* Probably this means, they *profess* to delight to know the ways of God; *i.e.*, his commands, truths, and requirements. A hypocrite has no real delight in the service of God, or in his truth, but it is true at the same time that there may be a great deal of *professed* interest in religion. There may be a great deal of busy and bustling solicitude about the *order* of religious services; the external organization of the church; the ranks of the clergy; and the claims of a liturgy. There may be much pleasure in theological discussion; in the metaphysics of theology; in the defence of what is deemed orthodoxy. There may be much pleasure in the mere *music* of devotion. There may be pleasure in the voice of a preacher, and in the power of his arguments. And there may be much pleasure in the advancement of the denomination to which we are attached; the conversion of men not *from sin*, but from a side opposite to us; and not *to holiness* and *to God*, but to our party and denomination.—True delight in religion is *in religion itself;* in the service of God as such, and because it is holy. It is not mere pleasure in creeds, and liturgies, and theological discussions, and in the triumph of our cause,

3 Wherefore [a] have we fasted, *say they*, and thou seest not? *wherefore* have we afflicted [b] our soul, and thou takest no knowledge? Behold, in the day of your fast you find pleasure, and exact all your labours.[1]

a Mal.3.14. b Le.16.29.
1 *griefs*, or, *things wherewith ye grieve others*.

nor even in the triumph of Christianity as a mere party measure; but it is delight in God as he is, in his holy service, and in his truth. ¶ *As a nation that did righteousness.* As a people would do who really loved the ways of righteousness. ¶ *They ask of me the ordinances of justice.* Their priests and prophets consult about the laws and institutions of religion, as if they were really afraid of violating the Divine commands. At the same time that they are full of oppression, strife, and wickedness, they are scrupulously careful about violating any of the commands pertaining to the rites of religion. The same people were subsequently so conscientious that they did not dare to enter the judgment-hall of Pilate lest they should disqualify themselves from partaking of the Passover, at the same time that they were meditating the death of their own Messiah, and were actually engaged in a plot to secure his crucifixion! (John xix. 28.) It is often the case that hypocrites are most scrupulous and conscientious about forms just as they are meditating some plan of enormous guilt, and accomplishing some scheme of deep depravity. ¶ *They take delight in approaching to God.* There *is* a pleasure which even a hypocrite has in the services of religion, and we should not conclude that *because* we find pleasure in prayer and praise, that *therefore* we are truly pious. Our pleasure may arise from a great many other sources than any just views of God or of his truth, or an evidence that we have that we are his friends.

3. *Wherefore have we fasted.* They had fasted much, evidently with the expectation of delivering themselves from impending calamities, and securing the Divine favour. They are here introduced as saying that they had been disappointed. God had not interposed as they had expected. Chagrined and mortified, they now complain that he had not noticed their very conscientious and faithful regard for the duties of religion. ¶ *And thou seest not?* All had been in vain. Calamities still impended; judgments threatened; and there were no tokens of the Divine approbation. Hypocrites depend on their fastings and prayers as laying God under *obligation* to save them. If he does not interpose, they complain and murmur. When fasting is the result of a humble and broken heart, it is acceptable; when it is instituted as a means of *purchasing* the Divine favour, and as laying God under *obligation*, it can be followed by no happy result to the soul. ¶ *Have we afflicted our soul.* By fasting. Twenty-one MSS. (six ancient), says Lowth, have this in the plural number —'our souls' and so the LXX., Chaldee, and Vulgate. The sense is not materially affected, however. It is evident here that they regarded their numerous fastings as laying the foundation of a claim on the favour of God, and that they were disposed to complain when that claim was not acknowledged. Fasting, like other religious duties, is proper; but in that, as in all other services of religion, there is danger of supposing that we bring God under *obligation*, and that we are laying the foundation of a *claim* to his favour. ¶ *Thou takest no knowledge.* Thou dost not regard our numerous acts of self-denial. ¶ *Behold, in the day of your fast you find pleasure.* The prophet here proceeds to state the reasons why their fastings were not succeeded as they supposed they would be, by the Divine favour. The first reason which he states is, that even when they were fasting, they were giving full indulgence to their depraved appetites and lusts. The Syriac has well rendered this, 'In the day of your fasting you indulge your lusts, and draw near to all your idols.' This also was evidently the case with the Jews in the time of the Saviour. They were characterized repeatedly by him as 'an evil and *adulterous* generation,' and yet no generation perhaps was ever more punctual and strict in the external duties

4 Behold, ye fast for strife and
debate, and to smite [a] with the fist
of wickedness: ye [1] shall not fast
as *ye do this* day, to make your
voice to be heard on high.

a 1 Ki.21.12. 1 or, *fast not as this day*.

of fasting and other religious ceremonies. ¶ *And exact all your labours.* This is the second reason why their fasting was attended with no more happy results.—The margin renders this 'griefs,' or 'things wherewith ye grieve others.' Lowth renders it, 'All your demands of labour ye rigorously exact.' Castellio renders it, 'And all things which are due to you, you exact.' The word here rendered 'labours' denotes usually hard and painful labour; toil, travail, &c. The LXX. render it here, 'And goad (ὑπονύσσετε) all those who are under your control' (τοὺς ὑποχειρίους ὑμῶν). The idea seems to be that they were at that time oppressive in exacting all that was due to them; they remitted nothing, they forgave nothing. Alas, how often is this still true! Men may be most diligent in the external duties of religion; most abundant in fasting and in prayer, and at the same time most unyielding in demanding all that is due to them. Like Shylock—another Jew like those in the time of Isaiah—they may demand 'the pound of flesh,' at the same time that they may be most formal, punctual, precise, and bigoted in the performance of the external duties of religion. The sentiment taught here is, that if we desire to keep a fast that shall be acceptable to God, it must be such as shall cause us to unbind heavy burdens from the poor, and to lead us to relax the rigour of the claims which would be oppressive on those who are subject to us (see ver. 6).

4. *Behold, ye fast for strife and debate.* This is a third characteristic of their manner of fasting, and a third reason why God did not regard and accept it. They were divided into parties and factions, and probably made their fastings an occasion of augmented contention and strife. How often has this been seen! Contending denominations of Christians fast, not laying aside their strifes; contending factions in the church fast in order to strengthen their party with the solemn sanctions of religion. One of the most certain ways for bigots to excite persecution against those who are opposed to them is to 'proclaim a fast;' and when together, their passions are easily inflamed, their flagging zeal excited by inflammatory harangues, and their purpose formed to regard and treat their dissentient brethren as incorrigible heretics and irreconcilable foes. It may be added, also, that it is possible thus to prostitute all the sacred institutions of religion for party and inflammatory purposes. Even the ordinance of the Lord's Supper may be thus abused, and violent partisans may come around the sacred memorials of a Saviour's body and blood, to bind themselves more closely together in some deed of persecution or violence, and to animate their drooping courage with the belief that what has been in fact commenced with a view to power, is carried on from a regard to the honour of God. ¶ *And to smite with the fist of wickedness.* Lowth renders this, in accordance with the LXX. 'To smite with the fist the poor;' but this translation can be obtained only by a most violent and wholly unauthorized change in the Hebrew text. The idea is plain, that 'even when fasting' they were guilty of strife and personal combats. Their passions were unsubdued, and they gave vent to them in disgraceful personal encounters. This manifests a most extraordinary state of society, and is a most melancholy instance to show how much men may keep up the forms of religion, and even be punctual and exact in them, when the most violent and ungovernable passions are raging in their bosoms, and when they seem to be unconscious of any *discrepancy* between the religious service and the unsubdued passions of the soul. ¶ *Ye shall not fast, &c.* It is not acceptable to God. It must be offensive in his sight. ¶ *To make your voice to be heard on high.* That is, in strife and contention. So to contend and strive, says Grotius, that your voice can be heard on the mountain top. Rosenmüller, however, supposes that it means, that their fast was so conducted that they could not expect that their prayers would ascend

5 Is it such [a]a fast that I have chosen? a [1]day for a man to afflict his soul? *is it* to bow down his head as a bulrush, and to spread sackcloth [b]and ashes *under him?* wilt thou call this a fast, and an acceptable day to the LORD?

a Zec.7.5. 1 or, *to afflict his soul for a day.* *b* De.9.3.

to heaven and be heard by God. But it seems to me that the former is the correct interpretation. Their fastings were accompanied with the loud and hoarse voice of contention and strife, and on that account could not be acceptable to God.

5. *Is it such a fast that I have chosen?* Is this such a mode of fasting as I have appointed and as I approve? ¶ *A day for a man to afflict his soul?* Marg. 'To afflict his soul for a day.' The reading in the text is the more correct; and the idea is, that the pain and inconvenience experienced by the abstinence from food was not the *end* in view in fasting. This seems to have been the mistake which they made, that they supposed there was something meritorious in the very *pain* incurred by such abstinence. Is there not danger of this now? Do we not often feel that there is something meritorious in the very inconveniences which we suffer in our acts of self-denial? The important idea in the passage before us is, that the pain and inconvenience which we may endure by the most rigid fasting are not meritorious in the sight of God. They are not that at which he aims by the appointment of fasting. He aims at justice, truth, benevolence, holiness (ver. 6, 7); and he esteems the act of fasting to be of value only as it will be the means of leading us to reflect on our faults, and to amend our lives. ¶ Is it *to bow down his head.* A bulrush is the large reed that grows in marshy places. It is, says Johnson, without knots or joints. In the midst of water it grows luxuriantly, yet the stalk is not solid or compact like wood, and, being unsupported by joints, it easily bends over under its own weight. It thus becomes the emblem of a man bowed down with grief. Here it refers to the sanctimoniousness of a hypocrite when fasting—a man without real feeling who puts on an air of affected solemnity, and 'appears to others to fast.' Against that the Saviour warned *his* disciples, and directed them, when they fasted, to do it in their ordinary dress, and to maintain an aspect of cheerfulness (Matt. vi. 17, 18). The hypocrites in the time of Isaiah seemed to have supposed that the object was gained if they assumed this affected seriousness. How much danger is there of this now! How often do even Christians assume, on all the more solemn occasions of religious observance, a forced sanctimoniousness of manner; a demure and dejected air; nay, an appearance of melancholy—which is often understood by the world to be misanthropy, and which easily slides into misanthropy! Against this we should guard. Nothing more injures the cause of religion than sanctimoniousness, gloom, reserve, coldness, and the conduct and deportment which, whether right or wrong, will be construed by those around us as misanthropy. Be it not forgotten that the seriousness which religion produces is always consistent with cheerfulness, and is always accompanied by benevolence; and the moment we feel that our religious acts consist in merely bowing down the head like a bulrush, that moment we may be sure we shall do injury to all with whom we come in contact. ¶ *And to spread sackcloth and ashes* under him. On the meaning of the word 'sackcloth,' see Notes on ch. iii. 24. It was commonly worn around the loins in times of fasting and of any public or private calamity. It was also customary to sit on sackcloth, or to spread it under one either to lie on, or to kneel on in times of prayer, as an expression of humiliation. Thus in Est. iv. 3, it is said, 'and many lay on sackcloth and ashes;' or, as it is in the margin, 'sackcloth and ashes were laid under many;' (comp. 1 Kings xxi. 27). A passage in Josephus strongly confirms this, in which he describes the deep concern of the Jews for the danger of Herod Agrippa, after having been stricken suddenly with a violent disorder in the theatre of Cæsarea. 'Upon the news

6 *Is* not this the fast that I have chosen? to loose [a] the bands of wickedness, to undo the [1] heavy burdens, [b] and to let the [2] oppressed go free, [c] and that ye break every yoke?

a Jonah 3.5-10. 1 *bundles of the yoke.* b Ne.5.10,12. 2 *broken.* c Je.34.8.

of his danger, immediately the multitude, with their wives and children, *sitting upon sackcloth according to their country rites*, prayed for the king; all places were filled with wailing and lamentation; while the king, who lay in an upper room, beholding the people below thus falling prostrate on the ground, could not himself refrain from tears.'—(*Antiq.* xix. 8. 2.) We wear crape—but for a somewhat different object. With us it is a mere *sign* of grief; but the wearing of sackcloth or sitting on it was not a mere *sign* of grief, but was regarded as tending to *produce* humiliation and mortification. Ashes also were a symbol of grief and sorrow. The wearing of sackcloth was usually accompanied with ashes (Dan. ix. 3; Est. iv. 1, 3). Penitents, or those in affliction, either sat down on the ground in dust and ashes (Job ii. 8; xlii. 6; Jonah iii. 6); or they put ashes on their head (2 Sam. xiii. 19; Lam. iii. 16); or they mingled ashes with their food (Ps. cii. 9). The Greeks and the Romans had also the same custom of strewing themselves with ashes in mourning. Thus Homer (*Iliad*, xviii. 22), speaking of Achilles bewailing the death of Patroclus, says:

> Cast on the ground, with furious hands he spread
> The scorching ashes o'er his graceful head,
> His purple garments, and his golden hairs;
> Those he deforms, and these he tears.

Laertes (*Odys.* xxiv. 315), shows his grief in the same manner:

> Deep from his soul he sighed, and sorrowing spread
> A cloud of ashes on his hoary head.

So Virgil (*Æn.* x. 844), speaking of the father of Lausus, who was brought to him wounded, says:

> Canitiem immundo deformat pulvere.

¶ *Wilt thou call this a fast?* Wilt thou suppose that these observances can be such as God will approve and bless? The truth here taught is, that no mere outward expressions of penitence can be acceptable to God.

6. Is *not this the fast that I have chosen?* Fasting is right and proper; but that which God approves will prompt to, and will be followed by, deeds of justice, kindness, charity. The prophet proceeds to specify very particularly what God required, and when the observance of seasons of fasting would be acceptable to him. ¶ *To loose the bands of wickedness.* This is the first thing to be done in order that their fasting might be acceptable to the Lord. The idea is, that they were to dissolve every tie which unjustly bound their fellow-men. The Chaldee renders it, 'Separate the congregation of impiety;' but the more probable sense is, that if they were exercising any unjust and cruel authority over others; if they had bound them in any way contrary to the laws of God and the interests of justice, they were to release them. This might refer to their compelling others to servitude more rigidly than the law of Moses allowed; or to holding them to contracts which had been fraudulently made; or to their exacting strict payment from persons wholly incapacitated to meet their obligations; or it might refer to their subjecting others to more rigid service than was allowed by the laws of Moses, but it would not require a very ardent imagination for any one to see, that if he held slaves *at all*, that this came fairly under the description of the prophet. A man with a tender conscience who held slaves would have been likely to suppose that this part of the injunction applied to himself. ¶ *To undo the heavy burdens.* Marg. 'Bundles of the yoke.' The LXX. render it, 'Dissolve the obligations of onerous contracts.' The Chaldee, 'Loose the obligations of the writings of unjust judgment.' The Hebrew means, 'Loose the bands of the yoke,' a figure taken from the yoke which was borne by oxen, and which seems to have been attached to the neck by cords or bands (*see* Fragments to Taylor's *Calmet*, No. xxviii.) The yoke, in the Scripture, is usually regarded as an emblem of oppression, or compulsory toil, and is undoubtedly

so used here. The same word is used to denote 'burden' (מוֹטָה), which in the subsequent member is rendered 'yoke,' and the word which is rendered 'undo' (הַתֵּר from נָתַר), is elsewhere employed to denote emancipation from servitude. The phrase here employed would properly denote the release of captives or slaves, and would doubtless be so understood by those whom the prophet addressed. Thus in Ps. cv. 17–20:

He sent a man before them, even Joseph,
Who was sold for a servant;
Whose feet they hurt with fetters;
He was laid in iron:
Until the time when his word came,
The word of the Lord tried him.
The king sent and loosed him (וַיַּתִּירֵהוּ),
Even the ruler of the people, and let him go free.

¶ *And let the oppressed go free.* Marg. 'Broken.' The Hebrew word רְצוּצִים is from the word רָצַץ, meaning *to break*, to break down (see Notes on ch. xlii. 3); to treat with violence, to oppress. It may be applied to those who are treated with violence in any way, or who are broken down by hard usage. It may refer, therefore, to slaves who are oppressed by bondage and toil; or to inferiors of any kind who are subjected to hard usage by those who are above them; or to the subjects of a tyrant groaning under his yoke. The use of the phrase here, 'go free,' however, seems to limit its application in this place to those who were held in bondage. Jerome renders it, 'Free those who are broken' (*confracti*). The LXX. Τεθραυσμένους—'Set at liberty those who are broken down.' If *slavery* existed at the time here referred to, this word would be appropriately understood as including that—at least would be so understood by the slaves themselves—for if any institution deserves to be called *oppression*, it is that of slavery. This interpretation would be confirmed by the use of the word rendered *free*. That word (חָפְשִׁים *hhŏphshīm*) evidently refers to the act of freeing a slave. The person who had once been a slave, and who had afterwards obtained his freedom, was denominated חָפְשִׁי *hhŏphshī* (see Jahn, *Bib. Ant.* § 171). This word occurs, and is so used, in the following places; Ex. xxi. 12, 'And the seventh [year] he shall go out *free;*' ver. 5, 'I will not go out *free;*' xxvi. 27, 'He shall let him go *free;*' Deut. xv. 12, 'Thou shalt let him go *free;*' ver. 13, 'When thou sendest him out *free;*' ver. 18, 'When thou sendest him away *free;*' Job iii. 19, 'The servant is *free* from his master;' that is, in the grave, where there is universal emancipation. Comp. Jer. xxxiv. 9–11, 14, 16, where the same Hebrew word is used, and is applied expressly to the emancipation of slaves. The word is used in no other places in the Bible except the following: 1 Sam. xvii. 25, 'And make his father's house *free* in Israel,' referring to the favour which was promised to the one who would slay Goliath of Gath. Job xxxix. 5: 'Who hath sent out the wild ass *free?*' Ps. lxxxviii. 5: '*Free* among the dead.' The usage, therefore, is settled that the word properly refers to deliverance from servitude. It would be naturally understood by a Hebrew as referring to that, and unless there was something in the connection which made it necessary to adopt a different interpretation, a Hebrew would so understand it of course. In the case before us, such an interpretation would be obvious, and it is difficult to see how a Jew *could* understand this direction in any other way, if he was an owner of slaves, than that he should set them at once at liberty. ¶ *And that ye break every yoke.* A yoke, in the Scriptures, is a symbol of oppression, and the idea here is, that they were to cease all oppressions, and to restore all to their just and equal rights. The prophet demanded, in order that there might be an acceptable 'fast,' that *everything* which could properly be described as a 'yoke' should be broken. How could this command be complied with by a Hebrew if he continued to retain his fellow-men in bondage? Would not its fair application be to lead him to emancipate those who were held as slaves? Could it be true, whatever else he might do, that he would fully comply with this injunction, unless this were done? If now this whole injunction were fairly complied with in *this* land, who can doubt that it would lead to the emancipation of the slaves? The language is such that it cannot well

7 *Is it* not to deal thy bread to the hungry, and that thou bring the poor that are [1] cast out to thy house? when thou seest the naked, that thou cover him; and that thou hide not thyself from thine own flesh?

8 Then [a] shall thy light break forth as the morning, and thine health shall spring forth speedily; and thy righteousness shall go before thee: the glory of the LORD shall [2] be thy rere-ward.

1 or, *afflicted.* a Job 11.17. 2 or, *gather thee up.*

be misunderstood. The prophet undoubtedly specifies those things which properly denote slavery, and demands that they should all be abandoned in order to an acceptable 'fast to the Lord,' and the fair application of this injunction would soon extinguish slavery throughout the world.

7. Is it *not to deal thy bread to the hungry?* The word renderd 'deal' (פָּרַס), means *to divide, to distribute.* The idea is, that we are to apportion among the poor that which will be needful for their support, as a father does to his children. This is everywhere enjoined in the Bible, and was especially regarded among the Orientals as an indispensable duty of religion. Thus Job (xxxi. 16–22) beautifully speaks of his own practice:

If I have withheld the poor from his desire,
Or have caused the eyes of the widow to fail;
Or have eaten my morsel myself alone,
And the fatherless hath not eaten thereof;
If I have seen any perish for want of clothing,
Or any poor without covering;— . . . .
Then let mine arm fall from my shoulder blade,
And mine arm be broken from the bone.

¶ *And that thou bring the poor that are cast out to thy house.* Marg. 'Afflicted.' Hospitality to all, and especially to the friendless and the stranger, was one of the cardinal virtues in the Oriental code of morals. Lowth renders this, 'The wandering poor.' ¶ *When thou seest the naked,* &c. This duty is also plain, and is everywhere enjoined in the Bible (comp. Matt. xxv. 38). ¶ *And that thou hide not thyself from thine own flesh.* That is, from thine own kindred or relations who are dependent on thee. Compare Gen. xxix. 14; xxxvii. 27; where the word 'flesh' is used to denote near relations—relations as intimate and dear as if they were a part of our flesh and blood (Gen. ii. 23). To hide one's self from them may denote either, first, to be ashamed of them on account of their poverty or humble rank in life; or, secondly, to withhold from them the just supply of their wants. Religion requires us to treat all our kindred, whatever may be their rank, with kindness and affection, and enjoins on us the duty of providing for the wants of those poor relatives who in the providence of God are made dependent on us.

8. *Then shall thy light* (see Notes on ch. xliv. 7). The idea here is, that if they were faithful in the discharge of their duty to God, he would bless them with abundant prosperity (comp. Job xi. 17). The image is, that such prosperity would come on the people like the spreading light of the morning. ¶ *And thine health.* Lowth and Noyes render this, 'And thy wounds shall be speedily healed over.' The authority on which Lowth relies, is the version of Aquila as reported by Jerome, and the Chaldee. The Hebrew word here used, (אֲרוּכָה), means properly *a long bandage* (from אָרַךְ, *to make long*), such as is applied by surgeons to heal a wound (comp. Notes on ch. i. 6). It is then used to denote the healing which is secured by the application of the bandage; and figuratively here means their restoration from all the calamities which had been inflicted on the nation. The word rendered 'spring forth' (from צָמַח) properly relates to the manner in which plants germinate (comp. Notes on ch. xlii. 9). Here the sense is, that if they would return to God, they would be delivered from the calamities which their crimes had brought on them, and that peace and prosperity would again visit the nation. ¶ *And thy righteousness shall go before thee.* Shall be thy leader—as an army is conducted. The idea is that their conformity to the Divine laws would serve the purpose of a leader to conduct them in the ways of peace, happiness, and prosperity. ¶ *The glory of the* LORD. The allusion here is doubtless to the mode in which the children of Israel came out of Egypt (see Notes

9 Then shalt thou call, and the
Lord shall answer; thou shalt cry,
and he shall say, Here I *am*. If
thou take away from the midst of
thee the yoke, the putting forth of
the finger, and speaking vanity:
10 And *if* thou draw out thy
soul to the hungry, and satisfy the
afflicted soul; then shall thy light
rise in obscurity, and thy darkness
be as the noon-day.
11 And the Lord shall guide
thee continually, and satisfy thy
soul in [1] drought, [a] and make fat
thy bones: and thou shalt be like
a watered garden, and like a spring
of water, whose waters [2] fail not.

1 *droughts.* a Ps.37.19. 2 *lie,* or, *deceive.*

on ch. vi. 5). ¶ *Shall be thy rere-ward.* Marg. 'Shall gather thee up.' That is, shall bring up the rear (see Notes on ch. lii. 12).

9. *Then shalt thou call.* The sense is, that if we go before God renouncing all our sins, and desirous of doing our duty, then we have a right to expect that he will hear us. But if we go indulging still in sin; if we are false and hollow and hypocritical in our worship; or if, while we keep up the regular forms of devotion, we are nevertheless guilty of oppression, cruelty, and dishonesty, we have no right to expect that he will hear us (see Notes on ch. i. 15). ¶ *If thou take away—the yoke* (see Notes on ver. 6). ¶ *The putting forth of the finger.* That is, if you cease to contemn and despise others; if you cease to point at them the finger of scorn. It was usual to make use of the middle finger on such occasions. Thus Martial, ii. 28, 2:

> Rideto multum ——
> —— et digitum porrigito medium.

So Juvenal, *Sat.* x. 52:

> —— mediumque ostenderet unguem.

¶ *And speaking vanity.* Lowth and Noyes render it thus, 'The injurious speech.' Kimchi understands it of words of contention and strife. The word here used (אָוֶן) denotes either nothingness, vanity, a vain and empty thing (Isa. xli. 29; Zech. x. 2); or falsehood, deceit (Ps. xxxvi. 4; Prov. xvii. 4); or unworthiness, wickedness, iniquity (Job xxxvi. 21; Isa. i. 13); here it means, probably, every kind of false, harsh, and unjust speaking—all of which probably abounded among the Jews. The LXX. render it, 'Ῥῆμα γογγυσμοῦ—' The word of murmuring.'

10. *And if thou draw out thy soul to the hungry.* Lowth, on the authority of eight MSS., renders this, 'If thou bring forth *thy bread* to the hungry.' So the Syriac and Noyes. But the authority is not sufficient to justify the change in the text, nor is it necessary. The word 'soul' here is synonymous with heart, or benevolent affection; and the idea is, if they expressed benevolent affection or kindness towards those in want. ¶ *Then shall thy light rise in obscurity.* That is, it will be as if the cheerful light of the sun should rise amidst the shades of midnight. The sense is, that their calamities and trials would be suddenly succeeded by the bright and cheerful light of prosperity.

11. *And the* Lord *shall guide thee continually.* Jehovah will go before you and will lead you always. ¶ *And satisfy thy soul in drought* (see Notes on ch. xli. 17, 18). The word rendered 'drought' (Marg. 'droughts;' Heb. צַחְצָחוֹת) means *dry places*—places exposed to the intense heat of a burning sun and parched up for the want of moisture. The idea is, that God would provide for them as if in such places copious rains were to fall, or refreshing fountains to burst forth. ¶ *And make fat thy bones.* Lowth, 'Shall renew thy strength.' Noyes, 'Strengthen thy bones.' Jerome renders it, 'Shall liberate thy bones.' The LXX. 'Thy bones shall be made fat.' The idea is undoubtedly that of vigorous prosperity, and of strength. Job (xxi. 24) expresses a similar idea of a strong man dying:

> 'His watering places for flocks abound with milk,
> And his bones are moist with marrow.'

For the propriety of this translation, which differs from the common version, see my Notes on Job, *in loco.* The word here used (חָלַץ), however, does not often, if ever, denote *to make fat.* It

12 And *they that shall be* of thee shall build the old waste places: thou shalt raise up the foundations of many generations; and thou shalt be called, The repairer of the breach, The restorer of paths to dwell in.

---

rather means to be manful, active, brave, ready for war; and the idea here is, probably, derived from the preparation which is made for the active services of war, rather than that of being made fat. ¶ *And thou shalt be like a watered garden.* Syriac, 'Like paradise.' This is a most beautiful image to denote continued prosperity and blessedness—an image that would be particularly striking in the East. The ideas of happiness in the Oriental world consisted much in pleasant gardens, running streams, and ever-flowing fountains, and nothing can more beautifully express the blessedness of the continued favour of the Almighty. The following extract from Campbell (*African Light*), may illustrate this passage: 'In a hot climate, where showers seldom fall, except in what is called the rainy season, the difference between a well and ill watered garden is most striking. I remember some gardens in Africa, where they could lead no water upon them, the plants were all stinted, sickly, or others completely gone, only the hole left where the faded plant had been. The sight was unpleasant, and caused gloom to appear in every countenance; they were pictures of desolation. But in other gardens, to which the owners could bring daily supplies of water from an overflowing fountain, causing it to traverse the garden, every plant had a green, healthy appearance, loaded with fruit, in different stages towards maturity, with fragrant scent proceeding from beds of lovely flowers; and all this produced by the virtue God hath put into the single article of water.' ¶ *Whose waters fail not.* Marg. 'Lie,' or 'Deceive.' Heb. כָּזַב—'Lie.' Waters or springs lie or deceive when they become dried up, or fail in the dry seasons of the year. They deceive the shepherd who expected to obtain water there for himself or his flock; they deceive the caravan which had travelled to the well-known fountain where it had been often refreshed, and where, it is now found, its waters are dried up, or lost in the sand. Hence such a brook or fountain becomes an emblem of a false and deceitful friend (Job vi. 15):

> My brethren have dealt deceitfully as a brook,
> As the stream of brooks they pass away.

But in the supplies which God makes for his people there is no such deception. The fountains of pardon, peace, and joy are ever open and ever full. The streams of salvation are always flowing. The weary pilgrim may go there at any season of the year, and from any part of a desolate world, and find them always full, refreshing, and free. However far may be the pilgrimage to them from amidst the waste and burning climes of sin, however many come to slake their thirst, and however frequently they come, they find them always the same. They never fail; and they will continue to flow on to the end of time.

12. *And* they that shall be *of thee*. They that spring from thee; or thy people. ¶ *Shall build the old waste places.* Shall repair the old ruins, and restore the desolate cities and fields to their former beauty. This language is taken from the condition of Judea during the long captivity at Babylon. The land would have been desolated by the Chaldeans, and lain waste for a period of seventy years. Of course all the remains of their former prosperity would have gone to decay, and the whole country would be filled with ruins. But all this, says the prophet, would be restored if they were obedient to God, and would keep his law. Their descendants would be so numerous that the land would be entirely occupied and cultivated again, and cities and towns would rise with their former beauty and magnificence. ¶ *Thou shalt raise up the foundations of many generations.* That is, the foundations which had endured for generations. The word 'foundations' here (מוֹסָד), means properly the foundation of a building, *i.e.*, on which a building rests. Here it means the foundation when that alone remains; and is equivalent to ruins. The Hebrew phrase translated 'of many generations' (דוֹר־וָדוֹר, *generation and generation*),

13 If thou turn away thy foot from the sabbath, *from* doing thy pleasure on my holy day; and call the sabbath a delight, the holy of the LORD, honourable; and shalt honour him, not doing thine own ways, nor finding thine own pleasure, nor speaking *thine own* words:

is equivalent to one generation after another, and is the usual form of the superlative degree. The exact amount of time is not designated; but the phrase is equivalent to a long time—while one generation passes away after another. Vitringa applies this to the gospel, and supposes that it means that the church, after long decay and desolation, would rise to its former beauty and glory. The promise is indeed *general;* and though the *language* is taken from the recovery of Palestine from its ruins after the captivity, yet there can be no objection to applying it in a more general sense, as teaching that the people of God, if they are faithful in keeping his commandments, and in manifesting the spirit which becomes the church, will repair the ruins which sin has made in the world, and rebuild the wastes and the desolations of many ages. Sin has spread its desolations far and wide. Scarce the foundations of righteousness remain in the earth. Where they do remain, they are often covered over with ruined fragments, and are surrounded by frightful wastes. The world is full of the ruins which sin has caused; and there could be no more striking illustration of the effects of sin on all that is good, than the ruins of Judea during the seventy years of exile, or than those of Palmyra, of Baalbec, of Tyre, of Ephesus, and of Persepolis, at present. It is for the church of God to rebuild these wastes, and to cause the beauties of cultivated fields, and the glories of cities rebuilt, to revisit the desolate earth; in other words, to extend the blessings of that religion which will yet clothe the earth with moral loveliness, as though sin had not spread its gloomy and revolting monuments over the world. ¶ *And thou shalt be called.* The name which shall appropriately designate what you will do. ¶ *The repairer of the breach.* Lowth, 'The repairer of the broken mound.' The phrase properly means, 'the fortifier of the breach;' *i.e.*, the one who shall build up the breach that is made in a wall of a city, either by the lapse of time, or by a siege. ¶ *The restorer of paths to dwell in.* Lowth and Noyes render this, 'The restorer of paths to be frequented by inhabitants.' The LXX. render it, 'And thou shalt cause thy paths to rest in the midst of thee;' and Jerome, *Avertens semitas in quietem*—'Turning the paths into rest,' which the Jewish exposition explains to mean, 'Thou shalt build walls so high that no enemy can enter them.' So Grotius renders it, 'Turning thy paths to rest;' that is, thou shalt leave no way of access to robbers. The Chaldee renders it, 'Converting the wicked to the law.' The common English version has probably expressed correctly the sense. The idea is, that they would repair the public highways which had long lain desolate, by which access was had to their dwelling-places. It does not mean, however, that the paths or ways were to be places in which to dwell, but that the ways which led to their dwelling-places were to be restored, or repaired. These roads, of course, in the long desolations would be ruined. Thorns, and brambles, and trees would have grown upon them; and having been long neglected, they would be impassable. But the advantages of a free intercourse from one dwelling and one city to another, and throughout the land, would be again enjoyed. Spiritually applied, it means the same as the previous expression, that the church of God would remove the ruins which sin has caused, and diffuse comfort and happiness around the world. The obstructed and overrun paths to a quiet and peaceable dwelling on earth would be cleared away, and the blessings of the true religion would be like giving free and easy access from one tranquil and prosperous dwelling-place to another.

13. *If thou turn away thy foot from the Sabbath.* The evident meaning of this is, that they were sacredly to observe the Sabbath, and not to violate or pollute it (see Notes on ch. lvi. 2). The

idea, says Grotius, is, that they were not to travel on the Sabbath-day on ordinary journeys. The 'foot' is spoken of as the instrument of motion and travel. 'Ponder the paths of thy feet' (Prov. ii. 26); *i.e.*, observe attentively thy goings. 'Remove thy foot from evil' (Prov. iv. 27); *i.e.*, abstain from evil, do not go to execute evil. So here, to restrain the foot *from* the Sabbath, is not to have the foot employed on the Sabbath; not to be engaged in travelling, or in the ordinary active employments of life, either for business or pleasure. ¶ From *doing thy pleasure on my holy day.* Two things may here be observed—1. God claims the day as *his*, and as holy on that account. While all time is his, and while he requires all time to be profitably and usefully employed, he calls the Sabbath peculiarly his own—a day which is to be observed with reference to himself, and which is to be regarded as belonging to him. To take the hours of that day, therefore, for *our* pleasure, or for work which is not necessary or merciful, is to ROB God of that which he claims as his own. 2. We are not to do our own pleasure on that day. That is, we are not to pursue our ordinary plans of amusement; we are not to devote it to feasting, to riot, or to revelry. It is true that they who love the Sabbath as they should will find 'pleasure' in observing it; for they have happiness in the service of God. But the idea is, here, that we are to do the things which God requires, and to consult *his* will in the observance. It is remarkable that the thing here adverted to, is the very way in which the Sabbath is commonly violated. It is not extensively a day of business, for the propriety of a periodical cessation from toil is so obvious, that men *will* have such days recurring at moderate intervals. But it is a day of pastime and amusement; a day not merely of relaxation from toil, but also of relaxation from the restraints of temperance and virtue. And while the Sabbath is God's great ordinance for perpetuating religion and virtue, it is also, by perversion, made Satan's great ordinance for perpetuating intemperance, dissipation, and sensuality. ¶ *And call the Sabbath a delight.* This appropriately expresses the feelings of all who have any just views of the Sabbath. To them it is not wearisome, nor are its hours heavy. They love the day of sweet and holy rest. They esteem it a privilege, not a task, to be permitted once a week to disburden their minds of the cares, and toils, and anxieties of life. It is a 'delight' to them to recall the memory of the institution of the Sabbath, when God rested from his labours; to recall the resurrection of the Lord Jesus, to the memory of which the Christian Sabbath is consecrated; to be permitted to devote *a whole day* to prayer and praise, to the public and private worship of God, to services that expand the intellect and purify the heart. To the father of a family it is the source of unspeakable delight that he may conduct his children to the house of God, and that he may instruct them in the ways of religion. To the Christian man of business, the farmer, and the professional man, it is a pleasure that he may suspend his cares, and may uninterruptedly think of God and of heaven. To all who have any just feeling, the Sabbath is a 'delight;' and for them to be compelled to forego its sacred rest would be an unspeakable calamity. ¶ *The holy of the* LORD, *honourable.* This more properly means, 'and call the holy of JEHOVAH honourable.' That is, it does not mean that they who observed the Sabbath would call it 'holy to JEHOVAH *and* honourable;' but it means that the Sabbath was, in fact, 'the holy of JEHOVAH,' and that *they* would regard it as 'honourable.' A slight inspection of the Hebrew will show that this is the sense. They who keep the Sabbath aright will esteem it a day *to be honoured* (מְכֻבָּד). ¶ *And shalt honour him.* Or rather, shalt honour *it;* to wit, the Sabbath. The Hebrew will bear either construction, but the connection seems to require us to understand it of the Sabbath rather than of the LORD. ¶ *Not doing thine own ways.* This is evidently explanatory of the phrase in the beginning of the verse, 'if thou turn away thy foot.' So the LXX. understand it: Οὐκ ἀρεῖς τὸν πόδα σου ἐπ' ἔργῳ—'And will not lift up thy foot to any work.' They were not

14 Then shalt thou delight thyself in the LORD; and I will cause thee to ride upon the high places of the earth, and feed thee with the heritage of Jacob thy father: for the mouth of the LORD hath spoken *it*.

to engage in secular labour, or in the execution of their own plans, but were to regard the day as belonging to God, and to be employed in his service alone. ¶ *Nor finding thine own pleasure.* The Chaldee renders this, 'And shalt not provide on that day those things which are necessary for thee.' ¶ *Nor speaking* thine own *words.* Lowth and Noyes render this, 'From speaking vain words.' The LXX. 'Nor utter a word in anger from thy mouth.' The Chaldee renders it, 'Words of violence.' It is necessary to add some epithet to make out the sense, as the Hebrew is literally, 'and to speak a word.' Probably our common translation has expressed the true sense, as in the previous members of the verse the phrase 'thine own' thrice occurs. And according to this, the sense is, that on the Sabbath our conversation is to be such as becomes a day which belongs to God. It is not less important that our conversation should be right on the Sabbath than it is that our conduct should be.

14. *Then shalt thou delight thyself in the* LORD. That is, as a consequence of properly observing the Sabbath, thou shalt find pleasure in JEHOVAH. It will be a pleasure to draw near to him, and you shall no longer be left to barren ordinances and to unanswered prayers. The delight or pleasure which God's people have in him is a direct and necessary consequence of the proper observance of the Sabbath. It is on that day set apart by his own authority, for his own service, that he chooses to meet with his people, and to commune with them and bless them; and no one ever properly observed the Sabbath who did not find, as a consequence, that he had augmented pleasure in the existence, the character, and the service of JEHOVAH. Compare Job xxii. 21–26, where the *principle* stated here—that the observance of the law of God will lead to happiness in the Almighty—is beautifully illustrated (see also Ps. xxxvii. 4). ¶ *And I will cause thee to ride upon the high places of the earth.* A phrase like this occurs in Deut. xxxii. 13: 'He made him ride on the high places of the earth, that he might eat the increase of fields.' In Hab. iii. 19, the phrase also occurs: 'He will make my feet like hinds' feet, and he will make me to walk upon mine high places.' So also Ps. xviii. 33: 'He maketh my feet like hinds' feet, and setteth me upon my high places.' In Amos iv. 13, it is applied to God: 'He maketh the morning darkness, and treadeth upon the high places of the earth.' Kimchi, Calvin, and Grotius suppose that the idea here is, that God would restore the exiled Jews to their own land—a land of mountains and elevated places, more lofty than the surrounding regions. Vitringa says that the phrase is taken from a conqueror, who on his horse or in his chariot, occupies mountains, hills, towers, and monuments, and subjects them to himself. Rosenmüller supposes it means, 'I will place you in lofty and inaccessible places, where you will be safe from all your enemies.' Gesenius also supposes that the word 'high places' here means fastnesses or strongholds, and that to walk over those strongholds, or to ride over them, is equivalent to possessing them, and that he who has possession of the fastnesses has possession of the whole country (see his *Lexicon* on the word בָּמָה, No. 2). I give these views of the most distinguished commentators on the passage, not being able to determine satisfactorily to myself what is the true signification. Neither of the above expositions seems to me to be entirely free from difficulty. The general idea of prosperity and security is undoubtedly the main thing intended; but what is the specific sense couched under the phrase 'to *ride* on the high places of the earth,' does not seem to me to be sufficiently explained. ¶ *And feed thee with the heritage of Jacob thy father.* That is, thou shalt possess the land promised to Jacob as an inheritance. ¶ *For the mouth of the* LORD *hath spoken*

REMARKS ON THE CHAPTER.

I. From ver. 1–6, and the exposition given of these verses, particularly ver. 6, we may make the following remarks respecting slavery.

1. That the prophets felt themselves at entire liberty to animadvert on slavery as an evil. They did not feel themselves restrained from doing it by the fact that slavery was sustained by law, or by the plea that it was a civil institution, and that the ministers of religion had nothing to do with it. The holy men who were sent by God as his ambassadors, did not suppose that, in lifting up the voice against this institution, they were doing anything contrary to what fairly came within their notice as religious teachers, nor did they regard it as, in such a sense, a civil institution that they were not to advert to it.

It is often said in our country that slavery is a civil institution; that it pertains solely to political affairs; that the constitution and the laws suppose its existence, and make provision for its perpetuity; that it is not appropriate for the ministers of religion, and for ecclesiastical bodies to intermeddle with it. This plea, however, might have been urged with much more force among the Hebrews. *Their* constitution was, what ours is not, of Divine appointment, and it would have been easy for a friend of slavery to say that the prophets were interfering with what was sanctioned by the laws, and with the arrangements which were made for its perpetuity in the commonwealth. Why would not such an argument have as much weight then as it should be allowed to have now?

2. The prophet Isaiah felt himself at entire liberty to exhort the people to restore their slaves to freedom. He considered that slavery was as proper a subject for him to discuss as any other. He treated it as entirely within his province, and did not hesitate at all to express his views on it as an evil, and to demand that the evil should cease, in order to an acceptable worship of God.

3. He does not speak of it as a good and desirable institution, or as contributing to the welfare of the community. It is, in his view, a hard and oppressive system; a system which should be abandoned if men would render acceptable service to God. There is no apology made for it; no pleading for it as a desirable system; no attempt made to show that it is in accordance with the laws of the land and with the laws of God. It would not be difficult to imagine what would be the emotions of Isaiah, if, after he had written this 58th chapter of his prophecies, it should be represented that he was the friend of slavery, or if he were to read some of the vindications of the systems published in this Christian land by ministers of the gospel, and by ecclesiastical bodies, or should hear the sentiments uttered in debate in Synods, Assemblies, Conferences, and Conventions.

4. It may be inferred from the exposition given, that Isaiah did not suppose that slavery was in accordance with the spirit of the Mosaic institutions, or that those institutions were designed to perpetuate it. His treatment of it is just such as would be natural on the supposition that the Mosaic institutions were so made that, while it was for a while *tolerated*—just as polygamy and divorce were—yet that it was the tendency and design of the Mosaic system ultimately to remove the evil entirely, and to make the Hebrews throughout a free people, and that it was therefore proper for him, as a prophet, to enjoin on them the duty of letting all the oppressed go free. It may be added, that if this was proper in the time of Isaiah, it cannot be *less* proper under the light of the gospel and in the nineteenth century.

II. From the closing portion of this chapter (ver. 13, 14), we may derive the following important inferences respecting the Sabbath:—

1. It is to be of perpetual obligation. The whole chapter occurs in the midst of statements that relate to the times of the Messiah. There is no intimation that the Sabbath was to be abolished, but it is fairly implied that its observance was to be attended with most happy results in those future times. At all events, Isaiah regarded it as of binding obligation, and felt that its proper observance was identified with the national welfare.

2. We may see the manner in which the Sabbath is to be observed. In no place in the Bible is there a more full account of the proper mode of keeping that holy day. We are to refrain from ordinary travelling and employments; we are not to engage in doing our own pleasure; we are to regard it with delight, and to esteem it a day worthy to be honoured; and we are to show respect to it by not performing our own ordinary works, or pursuing pleasures, or engaging in the common topics of conversation. In this descrip-

---

it. This formula often occurs when an important promise is made, and it is regarded as ample security for the fulfilment that Jehovah has promised it. What more ample security can be required, or conceived, than the promise of the eternal God?

tion there occurs nothing of peculiar Jewish ceremony, and nothing which indicates that it is not to be observed in this manner at all times. Under the gospel, assuredly, it is as proper to celebrate the Sabbath in this way, as it was in the times of Isaiah, and God doubtless intended that it should be perpetually observed in this manner.

3. Important benefits result from the right observance of the Sabbath. In the passage before us, these are said to be, that they who thus observed it would find pleasure in JEHOVAH, and would be signally prospered and be safe. But those benefits are by no means confined to the Jewish people. It is as true now as it was then, that they who observe the Sabbath in a proper manner find happiness in the Lord—in his existence, perfections, promises, law, and in communion with him—which is to be found nowhere else. Of this fact there are abundant witnesses now in every Christian church, and they will continue to be multiplied in every coming age. And it is *as* true that the proper observance of the Sabbath contributes to the prosperity and safety of a nation now, as it ever did among the Jewish people. It is not merely from the fact that God promises to bless the people who keep his holy day; though this is of more value to a nation than all its armies and fleets; but it is, that there is in the institution itself much that tends to the welfare and prosperity of a country. It is a time when worldliness is broken in upon by a periodical season of rest, and when the thoughts are left free to contemplate higher and purer objects. It is a time when more instruction is imparted on moral and religious subjects, than on all the other days of the week put together. The public worship of God tends to enlarge the intellect, and purify the heart. No institution has ever been originated that has contributed so much to elevate the common mind; to diffuse order, peace, neatness, decency among men, and thus to perpetuate and extend all that is valuable in society, as the Sabbath. Any one may be convinced of this, who will be at the pains to compare a neighbourhood, a village, or a city where the Sabbath is *not* observed with one where it is; and the difference will convince him at once, that society owes more to the Sabbath than to any single institution besides, and that in no way possible can one-seventh portion of the time be so well employed as in the manner contemplated by the Christian day of rest.

4. Society *will* have seasons of cessation from labour, and when they are not made occasions for the promotion of virtue, they will be for the promotion of vice. Thus among the Romans an annual *Saturnalia* was granted to all, as a season of relaxation from toil, and even from the restraints of morality, besides many other days of periodical rest from labour. Extensively among heathen nations also, the seventh day of the week, or a seventh portion of the time, has been devoted to such relaxation. Thus Hesiod says, Ἑβδομον ἱερον ἠμαρ—'The seventh day is holy.' Homer and Callimachus give it the same title. Philo says of the seventh day, Ἑόρτη γὰρ οὐ μιας πολέως ἢ χώρας ἐστὶν ἀλλὰ τοῦ παντὸς—'It is a feast, not of one city or one country only, but of all.' Josephus (*Contra Apion.* ii.), says, 'There is no city, however barbarous, where the custom of observing the seventh day which prevails among the Jews is not also observed.' Theophilus of Antioch (ii.), says, 'Concerning the seventh day, which all men celebrate.' Eusebius says, 'Almost all the philosophers and poets acknowledge the seventh day as holy.' *See* Grotius, *De Veritate*, i. It is evident that this custom did not originate by chance, nor was it kept up by chance. It must have been originated by far-spreading tradition, and must have been observed either because the day was esteemed to be holy, or because it was found to be convenient or advantageous to observe such a periodical season of rest. In accordance with this feeling, even the French nation during the Revolution, while they abolished the Christain Sabbath, felt so deeply the necessity of a periodical rest from labour, that they appointed the *decade*—or one day in ten, to be observed as a day of relaxation and amusement. Whatever, therefore, may have been the origin of the Sabbath, and whatever may be the views which may be entertained of its sacredness, it is now reduced to a moral certainty that men *will* have a periodical season of cessation from labour. The only question is, In what way shall it be observed? Shall it be devoted to amusement, pleasure, and vice; or shall it be employed in the ways of intelligence, virtue, and religion? It is evident that such a periodical relaxation *may be* made the occasion of immense good to any community; and it is not less evident that it *may be* the occasion of extending far the evils of intemperance, profaneness, licentiousness, and crime. It is vain to attempt to blot out wholly the observance of the Christian Sabbath; and since it *will* and *must* be observed as a day of cessation from toil, all that remains is for society to avail itself of the advantages which may be derived from its proper observance, and to make it the handmaid of temperance, intelligence, social order, and pure religion

5. It is deeply, therefore, to be regretted that this sacred institution has been, and is so widely abused in Christian lands. As it is, it is exte..-

sively a day of feasting, amusement, dissipation, and revelry. And while its observance is, more decidedly than anything else, the means of perpetuating virtue and religion on earth, it is perhaps not too much to say that it is the occasion of more intemperance, vice, and crime than all the other days of the week put together. This is particularly the case in our large cities and towns. A community cannot be disbanded from the restraints of labour one-seventh part of the time without manifest evil, unless there are salutary checks and restraints. The merchant cannot safely close his counting-room; the clerk and apprentice cannot safely be discharged; the common labourer cannot safely be dismissed from toil, unless there is something that shall be adapted on that day to enlarge the understanding, elevate the morals, and purify the heart. The welfare of the community demands that; and nowhere more than in this country. Who can doubt that a proper observance of the holy Sabbath would contribute to the prosperity of this nation? Who can doubt that the worship of God; the cultivation of the heart; the contemplation of moral and religious truth; and the active duties of benevolence, would contribute more to the welfare of the nation, than to devote the day to idleness, amusement, dissipation, and sin?

6. While the friends of religion, therefore, mourn over the desecration of the Christian Sabbath, let them remember that *their* example may contribute much to secure a proper observance of that day. On the friends of the Redeemer it devolves to rescue the day from desecration; and by the Divine blessing it may be done. The happiness of every Christian is indissolubly connected with the proper observance of the Sabbath. The perpetuity of the true religion, and its extension throughout the earth, is identified with the observance of the Sabbath. And every true friend of God the Saviour, as he values his own peace, and as he prizes the religion which he professes to love, is bound to restrain his foot on the Sabbath; to cease to find his own pleasure, and to speak his own words on that holy day; and to show that the Sabbath is to him a delight, and that he esteems it as a day to be honoured and to be loved.

CHAPTER LIX.

ANALYSIS.

This chapter is closely connected in sense with the preceding, and is designed to illustrate the same general sentiment; that the reason why the religious services of the nation were not accepted, and the nation delivered from calamity, was their hypocrisy and their other sins. The previous chapter contained a bold and energetic reproof of their expectation of the Divine favour, when they were observing only external rites without repentance, and even when they continued to practise oppression and cruelty. This beautiful chapter states more in detail their sins, and the consequences of their transgressions. The following arrangement of the parts of the chapter, will show its design and scope at a single view.

I. It was not because Jehovah was unable to save them that they were exposed to such judgments, and visited with such calamities (1). They were, therefore, not to blame him. This general principle is stated, in order to prevent what commonly occurs when men suffer much—a disposition to throw the blame on God.

II. It was for their sins that they were exposed to these judgments (2–8). The prophet proceeds to specify those sins in detail, with a view to bring them to conviction and to repentance. 1. The general principle is stated, that it was their sins alone which had separated between them and God (2). 2. Their hands were defiled with blood (3, part first). 3. Their lips had spoken falsehood (3, last part). 4. There was no justice among them (4, part first). 5. Their plans were mischievous (4, second part). 6. Their actions were like the egg of the cockatrice, hateful and destructive as that egg when hatched (5). 7. Their works were like the web of a spider, which could never be a covering of righteousness (6). 8. Their feet run to evil (7, part first). 9. Their thoughts were evil (7, second part). 10. They were strangers to the way of peace (8).

III. After this statement of the prevalent sins of the nation, the prophet introduces the people as making *confession*, that it was for these and similar sins that they were exposed to the Divine displeasure. Identifying himself with the people, he enumerates the calamities to which they were exposed, as a consequence of the sins which prevailed (9–14). They were in darkness; they waited in vain for light; they stumbled at noonday; they vented their sorrows like the roaring of bears, or the plaintive cry of the dove, but all in vain.

IV. Jehovah is represented as seeing this state of deep guilt; a state where there was deep conviction of that guilt, and a readiness to make confession; and as wondering that there was no intercessor, and as *himself* interposing to bring deliverance and salvation (15–18). The *characteristics* of him who should come to accomplish these purposes, were righteousness, salvation, vengeance, and zeal (17). He would come to take recompence on his foes, and to reward the wicked according to their deeds (18).

V. The *effect* of this would be that the name of JEHOVAH would be feared from the rising to the setting sun. JEHOVAH would erect a barrier against the enemy when he should come in like a flood; and the Redeemer would come to Zion to effect deliverance for those who should truly repent (19–20).

VI. A covenant would be established between God and those who would turn away from transgressions (21). The *nature* of that covenant was, that its blessings would be perpetual. The spirit which God would give, and the words which he would put into their mouths, would abide with them and their posterity for ever.

'As this chapter,' says Lowth, 'is remarkable for the beauty, strength, and variety of the images with which it abounds; so it is peculiarly distinguished by the eloquence of the composition, and the exact construction of the sentences. From the first verse to the two last, it falls regularly into stanzas of four lines.' This poetical form of the chapter must be apparent to the slightest observation of the reader; and there is perhaps no instance of more regular construction of the various members and parts of a composition in the writings of the Hebrews.

The chapter has evidently a primary reference to the character of the nation in the times of Isaiah. The deep depravity which is described, is such as existed in the times of Manasseh; and one object of the prophet was manifestly to bring them to conviction for their sins; and to show them why they were suffering, or about to suffer, from the expressions of the Divine displeasure. But the chapter evidently also looks forward to future times, and the close of it refers so manifestly to the times of the Messiah, that it is impossible not to apply it to him.

BEHOLD, the LORD's hand is not shortened, that it cannot save; neither his ear heavy, that it cannot hear;
2 But your iniquities have separated between you and your God, and your sins have [1] hid *his* face from you, that he will not hear.

1 or, *made him hide.*

CHAPTER LIX.

1. *Behold, the* LORD's *hand is not shortened.* On the meaning of this phrase, see Notes on ch. l. 2. ¶ *Neither his ear heavy, that it cannot hear.* On the meaning of this phrase, see Notes on ch. vi. 10.

2. *But your iniquities.* That is, the sins which the prophet had specified in the previous chapter, and which he proceeds further to specify in this. ¶ *Have separated.* The word here used (בָּדַל) conveys the idea of division, usually by a curtain or a wall (Ex. xxvi. 33; xlii. 26). Thus the 'firmament' (רָקִיעַ, *expanse*) is said to have *divided* or separated (מַבְדִּיל) the waters from the waters (Gen. i. 6). The idea here is, that their sins were like a partition between them and God, so that there was no intercourse between them and him. ¶ *And your sins have hid* his *face from you.* Marg. 'Made him hide.' The Hebrew word here is in Hiphil, meaning 'to *cause* to hide.' Kimchi and Aben Ezra understand it as *causing* him to hide his face; Vitringa as hiding his face. The metaphor, says Vitringa, is not taken from a man who turns away his face from one because he does not choose to attend to what is said, but from something which comes between two persons, like a dense cloud, which hides one from the other. And, according to this, the idea is, that their sins had risen up like a thick, dark cloud between them and God, so that they had no clear view of him, and no intercourse with him—as a cloud hides the face of the sun from us. A similar idea occurs in Lam. iii. 44:

> Thou hast covered thyself with a cloud,
> That our prayers should not pass through.

But it seems to me more probable that the Hiphil signification of the verb is here to be retained, and that the idea is, that their sins had *caused* JEHOVAH to hide or turn away his face from their prayers from an unwillingness to hear them when they were so deeply immersed in sin. Thus the LXX. 'On account of your sins he has turned away his face (ἀπέστρεψε τὸ πρόσωπον) from you, so that he will not have mercy' (τοῦ μὴ ἐλεῆσαι). It is universally true that indulgence in sin causes God to turn away his face, and to withhold mercy and compassion. He cannot pardon those who indulge in transgression, and

3 For [a]your hands are defiled
with blood, and your fingers with
iniquity; your lips have spoken
lies, your tongue hath muttered
perverseness.
4 None calleth for justice, nor
any pleadeth for truth: they trust
in vanity, and speak lies; they
conceive mischief, and bring forth
iniquity.
5 They hatch [1] cockatrices' eggs,
and weave the spider's web: he
that eateth of their eggs dieth,

[a] ch.1.15. [1] or, *adders'*.

who are unwilling to abandon the ways of sin (comp. Notes on ch. i. 15).

3. *For your hands are defiled with blood.* The prophet proceeds here more particularly to specify the sins of which they were guilty; and in order to show the extent and depth of their depravity, he specifies the various members of the body—the hands, the fingers, the lips, the tongue, the feet, as the agents by which men commit iniquity. See a similar argument on the subject of depravity in Rom. iii. 13–15, where a part of the description which the prophet here gives is quoted by Paul, and applied to the Jews in his own time. The phrase 'your hands are defiled with blood,' means with the blood of the innocent; that is, they were guilty of murder, oppression, and cruelty. See a similar statement in ch. i. 15, where the phrase 'your hands *are full* of blood' occurs. The word here rendered 'defiled' (גָּאַל) means commonly *to redeem, to ransom;* then to avenge, or to demand and inflict punishment for bloodshed. In the sense of *defiling* it occurs only in the later Hebrew writers—*perhaps* used in this sense because those who were avengers became covered, *i.e.*, defiled with blood. ¶ *And your fingers with iniquity.* The *fingers* in the Scriptures are represented as the agents by which any purpose is executed (Isa. ii. 8), 'Which their own fingers have made' (comp. ch. xvii. 8). Some have supposed that the phrase here used means the same as the preceding, that they were guilty of murder and cruelty. But it seems more probable that the idea suggested by Grotius is the true sense, that it means that they were guilty of rapine and theft. The fingers are the instruments by which theft—especially the lighter and more delicate kinds of theft—is executed. Thus we use the word 'light-fingered' to denote any one who is dexterous in taking and conveying away anything, or any one who is addicted to petty thefts. ¶ *Your lips have spoken lies.* The nation is false, and no confidence can be reposed in the declarations which are made. ¶ *Your tongue hath muttered.* On the word rendered 'muttered' (הָגָה), see Notes on ch. viii. 19. Probably there is included in the word here, the idea that they not only *spoke* evil, but that they did it with a murmuring, discontented, or malicious spirit. It may also mean that they calumniated the government of God, and complained of his laws; or it may mean, as Grotius supposes, that they calumniated others—that is, that slander abounded among them. ¶ *Perverseness.* Heb. עַוְלָה—'Evil'—the word from which our word *evil* is derived.

4. *None calleth for justice.* Or rather, there is no one who brings a suit with justice; no one who goes into court for the purpose of obtaining justice. There is a love of litigation; a desire to take all the advantage which the law can give; a desire to appeal to the law, not for the sake of having strict justice done, but for the sake of doing injury to others, and to take some undue advantage. ¶ *Nor* any *pleadeth for truth.* Or, no one pleadeth *with* truth. He does not state the cause as it is. He makes use of cunning and falsehood to gain his cause. ¶ *They trust in vanity.* They confide in quirks and evasions rather than in the justice of their cause. ¶ *They conceive mischief.* They form plans of evil, and they execute them when they are fully ripe. Compare Job xv. 35, where the same phrase occurs. The sense is, that they form plans to injure others, and that they expect to execute them by fraud and deceit.

5. *They hatch cockatrices' eggs.* Marg. 'Adders'.' On the meaning of the word here rendered 'cockatrice,' see Notes on ch. xi. 8. Some poisonous serpent is intended, probably the adder,

and that which is crushed [1] breaketh out into a [a] viper.

6 Their webs shall not become garments, neither shall they cover

1 or, *sprinkled*, as if *there brake out a viper*.

a Mat.3.7; 12.34.

or the serpent known among the Greeks as the basilisk, or cerastes. This figurative expression is designed to show the evil nature and tendency of their works. They were as if they should carefully nourish the eggs of a venomous serpent. Instead of crushing them with the foot and destroying them, they took pains to hatch them, and produce a venomous race of reptiles. Nothing can more forcibly describe the wicked character and plans of sinners than the language here used—plans that are as pernicious, loathsome, and hateful as the poisonous serpents that spread death and ruin and alarm everywhere. ¶ *And weave the spider's web.* This phrase, in itself, may denote, as some have understood it, that they formed plans designed to seize upon and destroy others, as spiders weave their web for the purpose of catching and destroying insects. But the following verse shows that the language is used rather with reference to the tenuity and gossamer character of the web, than with any such design. Their *works* were like the web of the spider. They bore the same relation to true piety which the web of the spider did to substantial and comfortable raiment. They were vain and useless. The word here rendered 'web' properly denotes the cross-threads in weaving, the woof or filling; and is probably derived from a word signifying a *cross-beam* (see Rosenmüller *in loco;* also Bochart, *Hieroz.* ii. 4. 23). ¶ *He that eateth of their eggs dieth.* That is, he who partakes of their counsels, or of the plans which they form, shall perish. Calvin says that the meaning is, that 'whosoever had anything to do with them would find them destructive and pestiferous.' Similar phrases, comparing the plans of the wicked with the eggs and the brood of the serpent, are common in the East. 'It is said,' says Roberts, speaking of India, 'of the plans of a decidedly wicked and talented man, "That wretch! he hatches serpents' eggs." "Beware of the fellow, his eggs are nearly hatched." "Ah, my friend, touch not that affair, meddle not with that matter; there is a serpent in the shell."' ¶ *And that which is crushed breaketh out into a viper.* On the meaning of the word here rendered 'viper,' see Notes on ch. xxx. 6. Marg. 'Sprinkled, *is as if* there brake out a viper.' Jerome renders it, 'Which, if pierced, breaks out into a basilisk.' The LXX. render it, 'And he who was about to eat of their eggs, having broken one that was putrid (συντρίψας οὔριον), found in it a basilisk (βασίλισκον).' The difference of translation in the text and the margin of the common version has arisen from the fact that the translators supposed that the word here used (זוּרֶה) might be derived from זָרָה *zârâh, to sprinkle,* or *to scatter.* But it is formed from the word זוּר *zûr, to squeeze, to press, to crush;* and in Job xxxix. 15, is applied to the fact that the ostrich might *crush* her eggs with her foot. The sense here is, that when their plans were developed, they would be found to be evil and pernicious—as when an egg should be broken open, a venomous serpent would come forth. The viper, it is true, brings forth its young alive, or is a viviparous animal. But Bochart has remarked, that though it produces its young in this manner, yet that during the period of gestation the young are included in eggs which are broken at the birth.—This is a very impressive illustration of the character and plans of the wicked. The serpents here referred to are among the most venomous and destructive that are known. And the comparison here includes two points—1. That their plans resembled the *egg* of the serpent. The nature of the egg cannot be easily known by an inspection. It may have a strong resemblance to those which would produce some inoffensive and even useful animals. It is only when it is hatched that its true nature is fully developed. So it is with the plans of the wicked. When forming, their true nature may not be certainly known, and it may not be easy to determine their real character. 2. Their

themselves with their works: their works *are* works of iniquity, and the act of violence *is* in their hands.

7 Their [a] feet run to evil, and they make haste to shed innocent blood: their thoughts *are* thoughts of iniquity; wasting and [1] destruction *are* in their paths.

8 The way of peace they know

a Ro.3.15,&c. 1 *breaking.*

plans, when developed, are like the poisonous and destructive production of the serpent's egg. The true nature is then seen; and it is ruinous, pernicious, and evil.

6. *Their webs shall not become garments.* The spider's web is unfit for clothing; and the idea here is, that their works are as unfit to secure salvation as the attenuated web of a spider is for raiment. The sense is, says Vitringa, that their artificial sophisms avail nothing in producing true wisdom, piety, virtue, and religion, or the true righteousness and salvation of men, but are airy speculations. The works of the self-righteous and the wicked; their vain formality, their false opinions, their subtle reasonings, and their traditions, are like the web of the spider. They hide nothing, they answer none of the purposes of a garment of salvation. The doctrine is, that men must have some better righteousness than the thin and gossamer covering which their own empty forms and ceremonies produce (comp. ch. lxiv. 6).

7. *Their feet run to evil.* In accordance with the design of the prophet to show the *entireness* of their depravity, he states that all their members were employed in doing evil. In ver. 3–6, he had remarked that depravity had extended to their hands, their fingers, their lips, and their tongue; he here states that their *feet* also were employed in doing evil. Instead of treading the paths of righteousness, and hastening to execute purposes of mercy and justice, they were employed in journeyings to execute plans of iniquity. The words 'run,' and 'make haste,' are designed to intimate the intensity of their purpose to do wrong. They did not walk slowly; they did not even take time to deliberate; but such was their desire of wrong-doing, that they *hastened* to execute their plans of evil. Men usually walk slowly and with a great deal of deliberation when any *good* is to be done; they walk rapidly, or they run with haste and alacrity when *evil* is to be accomplished. This passage is quoted by the apostle Paul (Rom. iii. 15), and is applied to the Jews of his own time as proof of the depraved character of the entire nation. ¶ *They make haste to shed innocent blood.* No one can doubt that this was the character of the nation in the time of Manasseh (see Introd. § 3). It is not improbable that the prophet refers to the bloody and cruel reign of this prince. That it was also the character of the nation when Isaiah *began* to prophesy is apparent from ch. i. 15–21. ¶ *Their thoughts.* That is, their plans and purposes are evil. It is not merely that evil is *done*, but they *intended* that it should be done. They had no plan for doing good; and they were constantly laying plans for evil. ¶ *Wasting.* That is, violence, oppression, destruction. It means that the government was oppressive and tyrannical; and that it was the general character of the nation that they were regardless of the interests of truth and righteousness. ¶ *And destruction.* Marg. 'Breaking.' The word commonly means *breaking* or *breach;* then a breaking down, or destruction, as of a kingdom (Lam. ii. 11; iii. 47); or of individuals (Isa. i. 28). Here it means that they broke down or trampled on the rights of others. ¶ Are *in their paths.* Instead of marking their ways by deeds of benevolence and justice, they could be tracked by cruelty and blood. The path of the wicked through the earth can be seen usually by the desolations which they make. The path of conquerors can be traced by desolated fields, and smouldering ruins, and forsaken dwelling-places, and flowing blood; and the course of all the wicked can be traced by the desolations which they make in their way.

8. *The way of peace they know not.* The phrase 'way of peace' may denote either peace of conscience, peace with

not; and *there is* no [1]judgment in their goings: they have made them crooked [a]paths: whosoever goeth therein shall not know peace.

9 Therefore [b]is judgment far from us, neither doth justice overtake us; we wait for light, but behold obscurity; for brightness, *but* we walk in darkness.

10 We [c]grope for the wall like the blind, and we grope as if *we had* no eyes: [d]we stumble at noonday as in the night; we *are* in desolate places as dead *men*.

1 or, *right*. a Ps.125.5; Pr.28.18. b La.5.16,17. c De.28.29. d Am.8.9.

God, peace among themselves, or peace with their fellow-men. Possibly it may refer to all these; and the sense will be, that in their whole lives they were strangers to true contentment and happiness. From no quarter had they peace, but whether in relation to God, to their own consciences, to each other, or to their fellow-men, they were involved in continual strife and agitation (see Notes on ch. lvii. 20, 21). ¶ *And there is no judgment in their goings.* Marg. '*Right.*' The sense is, that there was no justice in their dealings; there was no disposition to do right. They were full of selfishness, falsehood, oppression, and cruelty. ¶ *They have made them crooked paths.* A crooked path is an emblem of dishonesty, fraud, deceit. A straight path is an emblem of sincerity, truth, honesty, and uprightness (see Ps. cxxv. 5; Prov. ii. 15; and Notes on ch. xl. 4). The idea is, that their counsels and plans were perverse and evil. We have a similar expression now when we say of a man that he is '*straightforward*,' meaning that he is an honest man.

9. *Therefore is judgment far from us.* This is the confession of the people that they were suffering not unjustly on account of their crimes. The word 'judgment' here is evidently to be taken in the sense of vengeance or vindication. The idea is this, 'we are subjected to calamities and to oppressions by our enemies. In our distresses we cry unto God, but on account of our sins he does not hear us, nor does he come to vindicate our cause.' ¶ *Neither doth justice overtake us.* That is, God does not interpose to save us from our calamities, and to deliver us from the hand of our enemies. The word *justice* here is not to be regarded as used in the sense that they had a claim on God, or that they were now suffering unjustly, but it is used to denote the attribute of justice in God; and the idea is, that the just God, the avenger of wrongs, did not come forth to vindicate their cause, and to save them from the power of their foes. ¶ *We wait for light.* The idea here is, that they anxiously waited for returning prosperity. ¶ *But behold obscurity.* Darkness. Our calamities continue, and relief is not afforded us. ¶ *For brightness.* That is, for brightness or splendour like the shining of the sun—an emblem of happiness and prosperity.

10. *We grope for the wall like the blind.* A blind man, not being able to see his way, feels along by a wall, a fence, or any other object that will guide him. They were like the blind. They had no distinct views of truth, and they were endeavouring to *feel* their way along as well as they could. Probably the prophet here alludes to the threatening made by Moses in Deut. xxviii. 28, 29, 'And the LORD shall smite thee with madness, and blindness, and astonishment of heart; and thou shalt grope at noon-day as the blind gropeth in darkness, and thou shalt not prosper in thy ways.' ¶ *We stumble at noon-day as in the night.* The idea here is, that they were in a state of utter disorder and confusion. Obstacles were in their way on all hands, and they could no more walk than men could who at noon-day found their path filled with obstructions. There was no remission, no relaxation of their evils. They were continued at all times, and they had no intervals of day. Travellers, though at night they wander and fall, may look for approaching day, and be relieved by the returning light. But not so with them. It was all night. There were no returning intervals of light, repose and peace. It was as if the sun was blotted out, and all was one long,

11 We roar all like bears, and mourn[a] sore like doves: we look for[b] judgment, but *there is* none; for salvation, *but* it is far from us.

a Eze.7.16. b Je.7.15.

uninterrupted, and gloomy night. ¶ *We are in desolate places.* There has been great variety in the interpretation of this phrase. Noyes, after Gesenius, translates it, 'In the midst of fertile fields we are like the dead.' One principal reason which Gesenius gives for this translation (*Comm. in loc.*) is, that this best agrees with the sense of the passage, and answers better to the previous member of the sentence, thus more perfectly preserving the parallelism :

> *At noon-day* we stumble as in the night;
> *In fertile fields* we are like the dead.

Thus the idea would be, that even when all seemed like noon-day they were as in the night; and that though they were in places that seemed luxuriant, they were like the wandering spirits of the dead. Jerome renders it, *Caliginosis quasi mortui.* The LXX. 'They fall at mid-day as at midnight; they groan as the dying' (ὡς ἀποθνήσκοντες στενάζουσιν). The Syriac follows this, 'We groan as those who are near to death.' The Chaldee renders it, 'It (the way) is closed before us as the sepulchre is closed upon the dead;' that is, we are enclosed on every side by calamity and trial, as the dead are in their graves. The derivation of the Hebrew word אַשְׁמַנִּים is uncertain, and this uncertainty has given rise to the variety of interpretation. Some regard it as derived from שָׁמַם *shâmăm, to be laid waste, to be desolate;* and others from שָׁמַן *shâmăn, to be,* or *become fat.* The word שְׁמַנִּים *shemannim,* in the sense of fatness, *i. e.,* fat and fertile fields, occurs in Gen. xxvii. 28, 39; and this is probably the sense here. According to this, the idea is, we are in fertile fields like the dead. Though surrounded by lands that are adapted to produce abundance, yet we are cut off from the enjoyment of them like the dead. Such is the disturbed state of public affairs; and such the weight of the Divine judgments, that we have no participation in these blessings and comforts. The idea which, I suppose, the prophet means to present is, that the land was fitted to produce abundance, but that such was the pressure of the public calamity, that all this now availed them nothing, and they were like the dead who are separated from all enjoyments. The original reference here was to the Jew suffering for their sins, whether regarded as in Palestine under their heavy judgments, or as in Babylon, where all was night and gloom. But the *language* here is strikingly descriptive of the condition of the world at large. Sinners at noon-day grope and stumble as in the night. In a world that is full of the light of Divine truth as it beams from the works and the word of God, they are in deep darkness. They feel their way as blind men do along a wall, and not a ray of light penetrates the darkness of their minds. And in a world full of fertility, rich and abundant and overflowing in its bounties, they are still like 'the dead.' True comfort and peace they have not; and they seem to wander as in the darkness of night, far from peace, from comfort, and from God.

11. *We roar all like bears.* This is designed still further to describe the heavy judgments which had come upon them for their sins. The word here rendered 'roar' (from הָמָה *hâmâ,* like Eng. *to hum,* Germ. *hummen,* spoken of bees), is applied to any murmuring, or confused noise or sound. It sometimes means to *snarl,* as a dog (Ps. lix. 7, 15); to *coo,* as a dove (Ezek. vii. 16); it is also applied to waves that roar (Ps. xlvi. 4; Isa. li. 15); to a crowd or tumultuous assemblage (Ps. xlvi. 7); and to music (Isa. xvi. 11; Jer. xlviii. 36). Here it is applied to the low growl or groan of a bear. Bochart (*Hieroz.* i. 3. 9), says, that a bear produces a melancholy sound; and Horace (*Epod.* xvi. 51), speaks of its low groan :—

> Nec vespertinus circumgemit ursus ovile.

Here it is emblematic of mourning, and is designed to denote that they were suffering under heavy and long-continued calamity. Or, according to Gesenius (*Comm. in loc.*), it refers to a bear which

12 For [a]our transgressions are multiplied before thee, and our sins testify against us: for our transgressions *are* with us; and *as for* our iniquities, we know them:

13 In transgressing and lying against[b] the LORD, and departing away from our God, speaking oppression and revolt, conceiving and uttering from the [c]heart words of falsehood.

14 And judgment is turned away backward, and justice standeth afar off: for truth is fallen in the street, and equity cannot enter.

15 Yea, truth faileth; and he *that* departeth from evil [1]maketh himself a prey: and the LORD saw *it*, and it [2]displeased him that *there was* no judgment.

[a] Da.9.5,&c. [b] ch.48.8; Je.2.19-21. [c] Mat.12.34.
1 or, *is accounted mad.* 2 or, *was evil in his eyes.*

is hungry, and which growls, impatient for food, and refers here to the *complaining*, dissatisfaction, and murmuring of the people, because God did not come to vindicate and relieve them. ¶ *And mourn sore like doves.* The cooing of the dove, a plaintive sound, is often used to denote grief (see Ezek. vii. 16; comp. Notes on ch. xxxviii. 14). ¶ *We look for judgment,* &c. (see Notes on ver. 9.)

12. *Our sins testify against us.* Heb. 'Answer against us.' The idea is, that their past lives had been so depraved that they became witnesses against them (comp. Notes on ch. iii. 9). ¶ *We know them.* We recognize them as *our* sins, and we cannot conceal from ourselves the fact that we are transgressors.

13. *In transgressing.* That is, we have been guilty of this as a *continuous* act. ¶ *And lying against the* LORD. We have proved false to JEHOVAH. Though we have been professedly his people, yet we have been secretly attached to idols, and have in our hearts been devoted to the service of false gods. ¶ *And departing away from our God.* By the worship of idols, and by the violation of his law. ¶ *Speaking oppression and revolt.* Forming plans to see how we might best take advantage of the poor and the defenceless, and to mature our plans of revolt against God. ¶ *Conceiving and uttering from the heart* (see Notes on ver. 4). The idea is, that they had formed in their hearts schemes of deception, and that in their conversation and their lives they had given utterance to them. All this is the language of genuine contrition, where there is a consciousness of deep guilt in the sight of God. There is an overpowering sense of the evil of sin, and a willingness to make the most full and ample acknowledgment, *however mortifying it may be,* of the errors and follies of the life.

14. *And judgment is turned away backward.* The word 'judgment' is not used, as in ver. 9, to denote the Divine interposition to avenge and deliver them, but it is used in the sense of justice, or just decisions between man and man. The verse contains a further confession of the evil of their course of life; and, among other things, they acknowledged that they had been *unjust* in their legal decisions. They had been influenced by partiality and by bribes; they had condemned the innocent, they had acquitted the guilty. Judgment had thus been *turned back* by their sins when it seemed to be approaching and entering the city. ¶ *And justice standeth afar off.* This is a beautiful figure. Justice is represented as standing at a distance from the city. Deterred by their sins, it would not enter. They prevented its approach, and it was unknown among them. ¶ *For truth is fallen in the street.* Or rather, perhaps, *in the gate*—the place where justice was administered. The language here is all taken from courts of justice, and the idea is, that there was no justice in their decisions, but that their courts were unprincipled and corrupt. ¶ *And equity cannot enter.* It stood at a distance, and the impenetrable mass of guilt effectually prevented its approach to the capital.

15. *Yea, truth faileth.* That is, it is not to be found, it is wanting. The word here used (from עָדַר) means to be left, to remain (2 Sam. xvii. 22); then to be wanting or lacking (1 Sam. xxx. 19; Isa. xl. 26). Here it means that truth had no existence there. ¶ *And he* that *departeth from evil maketh*

16 And [a] he saw that *there was* no man, and wondered that *there was* no intercessor; therefore his arm [b] brought salvation unto him; and his righteousness it sustained him.

a Eze.22.30. b Ps.98.1.

himself a prey. Marg. 'Is accounted mad.' Noyes renders this, 'And he that departeth from evil is plundered.' Grotius renders it, 'The innocent man lies open to injury from all.' The LXX. 'They took away the mind from understanding;' or, 'They substituted opinion in the place of knowledge.'—(Thompson's *Translation.*) The phrase, 'He that departeth from evil,' means evidently a man who did not, and would not, fall in with the prevailing iniquitous practices, but who maintained a life of honesty and piety. It was one of the evils of the times that such a man would be harassed, plundered, ill-treated. The word rendered 'maketh himself a prey' (מִשְׁתּוֹלֵל from שָׁלַל), is a word usually signifying to strip off, to plunder, to spoil. Some have supposed that the word means to make foolish, or to account mad, in Job xii. 17, 19. Thus, in the passage before us, the LXX. understood the word, and this sense of the word our translators have placed in the margin. But there is no reason for departing here from the usual signification of the word as denoting to plunder, to spoil; and the idea is, that the men of honesty and piety were subject to the rapacity of the avaricious, and the oppression of the mighty. They regarded them as lawful prey, and took every advantage in stripping them of their property, and reducing them to want. This completes the statement of the crimes of the nation, and the existence of such deeds of violence and iniquity constituted the basis on which God was led to interpose and effect deliverance. Such a state of crime and consequent suffering demanded the Divine interposition; and when JEHOVAH saw it, he was led to provide a way for deliverance and reform.

The passage before us had a primary reference to the prevalence of iniquity in the Jewish nation. But it is language also that will quite as appropriately describe the moral condition of the world as laying the foundation for the necessity of the Divine interposition by the Messiah. Indeed, the following verses undoubtedly refer to him. No one, it is believed, can attentively read the passage, and doubt this. The mind of the prophet is fixed upon the depravity of the Jewish nation. The hands, the tongue, the eyes, the feet, the fingers, were all polluted. The whole nation was sunk in moral corruption; and this was but a partial description of what was occurring everywhere on the earth. In such a state of things in the Jewish nation, and in the whole world, the question could not but arise, whether no deliverer could be found. Was there no way of pardon; no way by which deserved and impending wrath could be diverted? From this melancholy view, therefore, the prophet turns to him who was to be the Great Deliverer, and the remainder of the chapter is occupied with a most beautiful description of the Redeemer, and of the effect of his coming. The sentiment of the whole passage is, *that the deep and extended depravity of man was the foundation of the necessity of the Divine interposition in securing salvation, and that in view of the guilt of men, God provided one who was a Glorious Deliverer, and who was to come to Zion as the Redeemer.* ¶ *And the* LORD *saw* it. He saw there was no righteousness; no light; no love; no truth. All was violence and oppression; all was darkness and gloom. ¶ *And it displeased him.* Marg. 'Was evil in his eyes.' So Jerome, 'It appeared evil in his eyes.' LXX. Καὶ οὐκ ἤρεσεν αὐτῷ—'And it did not please him.' The Heb. וַיֵּרַע means, literally, 'It was evil in his eyes.' That is, it was painful or displeasing to him. The existence of so much sin and darkness was contrary to the benevolent feelings of his heart. ¶ *That* there was *no judgment.* No righteousness; no equity; and that iniquity and oppression abounded.

16. *And he saw that* there was *no man.* That is, no wise and prudent man qualified to govern the affairs of the people. Or, that there was no man qualified to interpose and put an end to

17 For he put on righteousness as [a] a breastplate, and an helmet of salvation upon his head; and he put on the garments of vengeance *for* clothing, and was clad with zeal [b] as a cloak.

a Ep.6.14,17.
b Jn.2.17.

these evils; no one qualified to effect a reformation, and to save the nation from the calamities which their sins deserved. The reason why God provided a Redeemer was, that such was the extent and nature of human depravity, that no one on earth could arrest it, and save the world. A similar expression occurs in ch. xli. 28. ¶ *And wondered.* This is language adapted to the mode of speaking among men. It cannot be taken literally, as if God was amazed by suddenly coming to the knowledge of this fact. It is designed to express, with great emphasis, the truth, that there was no one to intercede, and that the wicked world was lying in a helpless condition. ¶ *That* there was *no intercessor.* On the meaning of the word here rendered 'intercessor,' see Notes on ch. liii. 6. The Chaldee renders it, 'There was no man who could stand and pray for them.' In ch. lxiii. 5, Isaiah expresses the idea in the following language: 'I looked, and there was none to help; and I wondered that there was none to uphold.' ¶ *Therefore his arm.* On the meaning of this phrase, see Notes on ch. xl. 10 (comp. ch. li. 5; lxiii. 5). The idea is, that salvation was to be traced to God alone. It did not originate with man, and it was not accomplished by his agency or help. ¶ *And his righteousness, it sustained him.* Sustained by the consciousness that he was doing right, he went forward against all opposition, and executed his plan. This is language derived from the mode of speaking among men, and it means that as a man who is engaged in a righteous cause is sustained amidst much opposition by the consciousness of integrity, so it is with God. The cause of redemption is *the* great cause of righteousness on earth. In this cause the Redeemer was sustained by the consciousness that he was engaged in that which was designed to vindicate the interests of truth and justice, and to promote righteousness throughout the universe.

17. *For he put on righteousness.* That is, God the Redeemer. The prophet here introduces him as going forth to vindicate his people clad like an ancient warrior. In the declaration that he 'put on righteousness,' the essential idea is, that he was pure and holy. The same image is used by the prophet in another figure in ch. xi. 5 (see Notes on that place). ¶ *As a breastplate.* The breastplate was a well-known piece of ancient armour, designed to defend the breast from the darts and the sword of an enemy. The design here is, to represent the Redeemer as a hero; and accordingly allusion is made to the various parts of the armour of a warrior. Yet he was not to be *literally* armed for battle. Instead of being an earthly conqueror, clad in steel, and defended with brass, his weapons were moral weapons, and his conquests were spiritual. The various parts of his weapons were 'righteousness,' 'salvation,' and 'zeal.' This statement should have been, in itself, sufficient to keep the Jews from anticipating a Messiah who would be a bloody warrior, and distinguished for deeds of conquest and blood. This figure of speech is not uncommon. Paul (in Eph. vi. 14–17; comp. 2 Cor. vi. 7) has carried it out to greater length, and introduced more particulars in the description of the spiritual armour of the Christian. ¶ *And an helmet of salvation.* The helmet was a piece of defensive armour for the head. It was made of iron or brass, and usually surmounted by a crest of hair. It was designed to guard the head from the stroke of a sword. No particular stress should be laid on the fact, that it is said that 'salvation' would be the helmet. The design is to represent the Redeemer by the figure of a hero clad in armour, yet there seems to be no particular reason why salvation should be referred to as the helmet, or righteousness as the cuirass or breastplate. Nothing is gained by a fanciful attempt to spiritualize or explain them. ¶ *And he put on the garments of vengeance* for *clothing.* By 'garments,'

18 According to *their* [1]deeds accordingly he will repay, fury to his adversaries, recompence to his enemies; [a]to the islands he will repay recompence.

19 So [b]shall they fear the name

1 *recompences.* a Lu.19.27. b Mal.1.11.

here, Vitringa supposes that there is reference to the *interior* garments which were worn by the Orientals corresponding to the tunic of the Romans. But it is more probable that the allusion is to the other parts of the dress or armour in general of the ancient warrior. The statement that he was clad in the garments of vengeance means, that he would go forth to vindicate his people, and to take vengeance on his foes. It would not be for mere defence that he would be thus armed for battle; but he would go forth for aggressive movements, in subduing his enemies and delivering his people (comp. ch. lxiii. 1–6). ¶ *And was clad with zeal as a cloak.* The cloak worn by men in military as well as in civil life, was a loose flowing robe or mantle that was thrown over the body, usually fastened on the right shoulder by a hook or clasp, and suffered to flow in graceful folds down to the feet. In battle, it would be laid aside, or secured by a girdle about the loins. Vitringa remarks, that, as it was usually of purple colour, it was adapted to represent the zeal which would burn for vengeance on an enemy. But the whole figure here is that drawn from a warrior or a conqueror; a hero prepared alike for defence and offence. The idea is, that he would be able to defend and vindicate his people, and to carry on aggressive warfare against his enemies. But it was not to be a warfare literally of blood and carnage. It was to be such as would be accomplished by righteousness, and zeal, and a desire to secure salvation. The triumph of righteousness was the great object still; the conquests of the Redeemer were to be those of truth.

18. *According to* their *deeds.* The general sentiment of this verse is plain, though there is not a little difficulty in the construction of the Hebrew. Lowth pronounces the former part of the verse, as it stands in the Hebrew text, to be 'absolutely unintelligible. By a slight change in the Hebrew as it now stands (reading בַּעַל, *lord,* instead of כְּעַל *as according to*), Lowth supposes that he has obtained the true sense, and accordingly translates it:

He is mighty to recompense;
He that is mighty to recompense shall requite.

This translation is substantially according to the Chaldee, but there is no authority from MSS. to change the text in this place. Nor is it necessary. The particle כְּעַל *kĕăl* occurs as a preposition in ch. lxiii. 7, in the sense of 'as according to,' or 'according to,' and is similar in its form to the word מֵעַל *mēăl*, which often occurs in the sense of *from above,* or *from upon* (Gen. xxiv. 64; xl. 19; Isa. xxxiv. 16; Jer. xxxvi. 11; Amos vii. 11). The sense of the verse before us is, that God would inflict just punishment on his enemies. It is a *general* sentiment, applicable alike to the deliverance from Babylon and the redemption of his church and people at all times. In order to effect the deliverance of his people it was necessary to take vengeance on those who had oppressed and enslaved them. So in order to redeem his church, it is often necessary to inflict punishment on the nations that oppose it, or to remove by death the adversaries that stand in his way. This punishment is inflicted strictly according to their deeds. The principal thought here is, undoubtedly, that as they had opposed and oppressed the people of God, so he would take vengeance on them. He would remove his enemies, and prepare the way in this manner for the coming of his kingdom. ¶ *To the islands.* On the use of the word 'islands' in Isaiah, see Notes on ch. xli. 1. The idea here is, that he would 'repay recompence' or take vengeance on the foreign nations which had oppressed them.

19. *So shall they fear.* That is, the result of the Divine interposition to punish his enemies, shall be to secure the acknowledgment of the existence and perfections of JEHOVAH in every part of the world. See especially the Notes on ch. xlv. 6. ¶ *When the enemy shall come in.* There has been great variety

of the Lord from the west, and his glory from the rising of the sun. When the enemy shall come in like [a] a flood, the Spirit of the Lord shall [1] lift up a standard against him.

[a] Re.12.15,16.

[1] *put him to flight.*

in the interpretation of this passage, and it is remarkable that our translators have departed from all the ancient versions, and that the present translation differs from nearly all the modern expositions of the place. Lowth renders it:

When he shall come like a river straitened in
his course,
Which a strong wind driveth along.

Jerome (Vulg.) renders it, 'When he shall come as a violent river which the Spirit of the Lord (*spiritus Domini*, or the wind of the Lord, *i.e.*, a strong wind) drives along.' The LXX. 'For the wrath of the Lord will come like an impetuous stream; it will come with fury.' The Chaldee, 'When they shall come who oppress, like an overflowing of the river Euphrates.' The Syriac, 'Because when the oppressor shall come as a river, the Spirit of the Lord shall humble him.' The reason of this variety of interpretation is the ambiguity of the Hebrew words which occur in the verse. The word which in our common version is rendered 'the enemy' (צַר *tzâr*, from צָרַר *tzârăr*, to press, compress, bind up together; *intrans.* to be straitened, or compressed), may mean either—1. *An adversary, enemy, persecutor*, synonymous with אוֹיֵב, as in Num. x. 9; Deut. xxxii. 27; Job xvi. 9; or, 2. *Straits, affliction* (Ps. iv. 2; xviii. 7; xliv. 11); or, 3. *Strait, narrow* (Num. xxii. 26; Job xli. 7). It may be, therefore, here either a noun meaning an enemy; or it may be an adjective qualifying the word river, and then will denote a river that is closely confined within its banks, and that is urged forward by a mass of accumulating waters, or by a mighty wind. According to this, it will mean that Jehovah will come to take vengeance with the impetuosity of a river that swells and foams and is borne forward with violence in its course. The comparison of a warrior or hero with such a mighty and impetuous torrent, is exceedingly forcible and beautiful, and is not uncommon (see Notes on ch. viii. 7). The phrase rendered 'the Spirit of the Lord' (רוּחַ יְהוָֹה), may denote 'the wind of Jehovah,' or a strong, violent, mighty wind. The appropriate signification of the word רוּחַ *rūăh*, is *wind*, or *breath;* and it is well known that the name of God is often in the Scriptures used to denote that which is mighty or vast, as in the phrase, mountains of God, cedars of God, &c. There is no reason why it should be here regarded as denoting 'the Spirit of God,'—the great agent of enlightening and reforming the world. It may be understood, as Lowth and others have applied it, to denote a strong and violent wind—a wind urging on a mass of waters through a compressed and straitened place, and thus increasing their impetuosity and violence. The phrase 'Spirit of God' (רוּחַ אֱלֹהִים), is used to denote a strong wind, in 1 Kings xviii. 12; 2 Kings ii. 16; Isa. xl. 7; Ezek. ii. 24; iii. 14. The word rendered in our version, 'shall lift up a standard' (נֹסְסָה), rendered in the margin, 'put him to flight,' if derived from נָסַס *nâsăs*, and if written with the points נָסְסָה *nâsĕsâh*, would denote to lift up, to elevate, as a standard or banner, or anything to oppose and retard a foe. But the word is probably derived from נוּס *nūs, to flee*, in Piel נוֹסֵס, to impel, to cause to flee. Here it means, then, that the mighty wind impels or drives on the compressed waters of the stream, and the whole passage means that Jehovah would come to deliver his people, and to prostrate his foes with the impetuosity of a violent river compressed between narrow banks, and driven on by a mighty wind. True, therefore, as it is, that when a violent enemy assails the church; when he comes in with error, with violence, and with allies, like a flood, Jehovah will rear a standard against him, and the influences of the Spirit of God may be expected to interpose to arrest the evil; yet *this* passage does not teach that doctrine, nor

20 And [a]the Redeemer shall come to Zion, and unto them that turn [b]from transgression in Jacob, saith the LORD.

21 As for me, this *is* my [c]covenant with them, saith the LORD; My Spirit that *is* upon thee, and my words which I have put in thy mouth, shall not depart out of thy mouth, nor out of the mouth of thy seed, nor out of the mouth of thy seed's seed, saith the LORD, from henceforth and for ever.

[a] Ro.11.16. [b] He.12.14. [c] He.8.8,&c.

should it be so applied. It *does* teach that JEHOVAH will go forth with energy and power to defend his people and to prostrate his foes.

20. *And the Redeemer shall come.* On the meaning of the word here rendered 'Redeemer,' see Notes on ch. xliii. 1. This passage is applied by the apostle Paul to the Messiah (Rom. xi. 26); and Aben Ezra and Kimchi, among the Jews, and Christians generally, suppose that it refers to him. ¶ *To Zion.* On the word 'Zion,' see Notes on ch. i. 8. The LXX. render this, Ἕνεκεν Σιὼν—'On account of Zion.' The apostle Paul (Rom. xi. 26), renders this, 'There shall come out of Zion (ἐκ Σιὼν) the Deliverer,' meaning that he would arise among that people, or would not be a foreigner. The idea in Isaiah, though substantially the same, is rather that he would come as a deliverer from abroad; that is, he would come from heaven, or be commissioned by God. When it is said that he would come *to* Zion, it is not meant that he would come exclusively to the Jews, but that his mission would be primarily to them. ¶ *And unto them that turn from transgression in Jacob.* There is much variety in the interpretation of this passage. Paul (Rom. xi. 26) quotes it thus, 'and shall turn away ungodliness from Jacob;' and in this he has literally followed the Septuagint. The Vulgate renders it as in our translation. The Chaldee, 'And shall turn transgressors of the house of Jacob to the law.' The Syriac, 'To those who turn iniquity from Jacob.' Lowth has adopted the rendering of the LXX., and supposes that an error has crept into the Hebrew text. But there is no good authority for this supposition. The LXX. and the apostle Paul have retained substantially, as Vitringa has remarked, the sense of the text. The main idea of the prophet is, that the effect of the coming of the Messiah would be to turn men from their sins. He would enter into covenant only with those who forsook their transgressions, and the only benefit to be derived from his coming would be that many would be thus turned from their iniquities.

21. *As for me.* In the previous part of the chapter, the prophet has spoken. Here JEHOVAH is introduced as speaking himself, and as declaring the nature of the covenant which he would establish. In the verse previous, it had been stated that the qualifications on the part of men for their partaking of the benefits of the Redeemer's work, were, that they should turn from transgression. In this verse, JEHOVAH states what he would do in regard to the covenant which was to be established with his people. 'So far as I am concerned, I will enter into a covenant with them and with their children.' ¶ *This* is *my covenant with them* (comp. Notes on ch. xlii. 6; xlix. 8; liv. 10). The covenant here referred to, is that made with men under the Messiah. In important respects it differed from that made with the Jewish people under Moses. The word 'covenant' here is evidently equivalent, as it is commonly, when applied to a transaction between God and men, to a most solemn promise on his part; and the expression is a most solemn declaration that, under the Messiah, God would impart his Spirit to those who should turn from transgression, and would abundantly bless them and their offspring with the knowledge of his truth. When it is said, 'this is my covenant,' the import evidently is, 'this is the nature or the tenure of my covenant, or of my solemn promises to my people under the Messiah. It shall certainly occur that my Spirit will be continually imparted to thy seed, and that my words will abide with thee and them for ever.' ¶ *My Spirit that* is *upon thee.* The

word 'thee' here does not refer, as Jerome and others suppose, to the prophet, but to the pious Hebrew people. The covenant under the Messiah, was not made peculiarly with the prophet or his posterity, but is a promise made to the church, and here evidently refers to the true people of God: and the idea is, that the Spirit of God would be continually imparted to his people, and to their descendants for ever. It is a covenant made with true believers and with their children. ¶ *And my words.* The Chaldee understands this of prophecy. But it seems rather to refer to the truth of God in general which he had revealed for the guidance and instruction of his church. ¶ *Shall not depart out of thy mouth.* This phrase probably means, that the truth of God would be the subject of perpetual meditation and conversation. The covenant would be deemed so precious that it would constantly dwell on the tongues of those who were interested in it. ¶ *Thy seed's seed.* Thy descendants; thy posterity. ¶ *From henceforth and for ever.* This is in accordance with the promises which everywhere occur in the Scriptures, that God would bless the posterity of his people, and that the children of the pious should partake of his favour. See Ex. xx. 6: 'Showing mercy unto thousands (*i.e.*, thousands of generations) of them that love me and keep my commandments.' Compare Deut. iv. 37; v. 29; vii. 9; Ps. lxxxix. 24, 36; Jer. xxxii. 39, 40. There is no promise of the Bible that is more full of consolation to the pious, or that has been more strikingly fulfilled than this. And though it is true that not *all* the children of holy parents become truly pious; though there are instances where they are signally wicked and abandoned, yet it is also true that rich spiritual blessings *are* imparted to the posterity of those who serve God and who keep his commandments. The following facts are well known to all who have ever made any observation on this subject:—1. The great majority of those who become religious are the descendants of those who were themselves the friends of God. Those who now compose the Christian churches, are not those generally who have been taken from the ways of open vice and profligacy; from the ranks of infidelity; or from the immediate descendants of scoffers, drunkards, and blasphemers. Such men usually tread, for a few generations at least, in the footsteps of their fathers. The church is composed mainly of the descendants of those who have been true Christians, and who trained their children to walk in the ways of pure religion. 2. It is a fact that comparatively a large proportion of the descendants of the pious themselves for many generations become true Christians. I know that it is often thought to be otherwise, and especially that it is often said that the children of clergymen are less virtuous and religious than others. But it should be remembered that such cases are more prominent than others, and especially that the profane and the wicked have a malicious pleasure in making them the subject of remark. The son of a drunkard will be intemperate without attracting notice—for such a result is expected; the son of an infidel will be an infidel; the son of a scoffer will be a scoffer; of a thief a thief; of a licentious man licentious, without being the subject of special observation. But when the son of an eminent Christian treads the path of open profligacy, it at once excites remark, because *such is not the usual course, and is not usually expected;* and because a wicked world has pleasure in marking the case, and calumniating religion through such a prominent instance of imperfection and sin. But such is not the common result of religious training. Some of the most devotedly pious people of this land are the descendants of the Huguenots who were expelled from France. A very large proportion of all the piety in this country has been derived from the 'Pilgrims,' who landed on the rock of Plymouth, and God has blessed their descendants in New England and elsewhere with numerous revivals of religion. I am acquainted with the descendants of John Rogers, the first martyr in Queen Mary's reign, of the tenth and eleventh generations. With a single exception, the oldest son in the family has been a clergymen—some of them eminently distinguished for learning and piety;

CHAPTER LX.

ANALYSIS.

IN this chapter there is commenced a most glowing and beautiful description of the 'golden age' under the Messiah. The description is continued to the close of ch. lxii. It is adorned with the highest ornaments of poetry; the future glory of the church is displayed under the most splendid colours, and with every variety of imagery. It is designed to set forth the glory of that time when the Gentiles shall be gathered into the church, and when the whole world shall become tributary to the Messiah, and be illuminated with the light of Christian truth. The main design of the chapter is to foretell the conversion of the heathen world, and the happy and peaceful times which shall exist when that has occurred. In doing this, the highest beauties of prophetic imagery are introduced, and the powers of the inspired prophet seem to have been taxed to the utmost to convey a just view of the glory of the scene.—That it refers to the time of the Messiah no one can doubt who reads it. And that it refers to events which have not yet fully occurred is, I think, equally clear, and will be made apparent in the Notes. In accordance with the usual mode in Isaiah (see Introd. § 7, 4), the prophet throws himself into the midst of the future scene (ver. 1), and the events are described as passing in vision before his eyes. He sees the light as already shining, and the glory of JEHOVAH as actually arisen upon the church;—he sees the Gentiles flocking to the Redeemer, and bringing their most valued and precious objects, and laying them at his feet.

The chapter may, for convenience, be regarded as consisting of three parts:

I. An invocation to the church to arise, and to enjoy and diffuse the light which had risen upon her (1, 2), the earth elsewhere was enveloped in deep darkness, but the light of Messiah's reign and of truth was with her.

II. The declaration that the Gentile world would be converted to the true religion, and would participate in the blessings of the reign of the Messiah. 1. The assurance that this event would occur (3). 2. The church directed to look around, and behold the multitudes that were flocking to her (4). 3. Specifications of those who would come and participate in the benefits of the reign of the Messiah. (1.) The abundance of the sea would come. (2.) The wealth of the Gentiles (5). (3.) The camels and dromedaries

---

and there are few families now in this land a greater proportion of whom are pious than of that. The following statistical account made of a limited section of the country, not more favoured or more distinguished for piety than many others, accords undoubtedly with similar facts which are constantly occurring in the families of those who are the friends of religion. The Secretary of the Massachusetts Sabbath School Society made a limited investigation, in the year 1838, for the purpose of ascertaining the facts about the religious character of the families of ministers and deacons with reference to the charge so often urged that the 'sons and daughters of ministers and deacons were worse than common children.' The following is the result. In 268 families which he canvassed, he found 1290 children over fifteen years of age. Of these children 884, *almost three-fourths, are hopefully pious;* 794 have united with the churches; sixty-one entered the ministry; only seventeen are dissipated, and about half only of these became so while with their parents. In eleven of these families there are 123 children, and *all* but seven pious. In fifty-six of these families there are 249 children over fifteen, and *all* hopefully pious. When and where can any such result be found in the families of infidels, of the vicious, or of irreligious men? Indeed, it is the great law by which religion and virtue are perpetuated in the world, that God is faithful to this covenant, and that he blesses the efforts of his friends to train up generations for his service. 3. All pious parents should repose on this promise of a faithful God. They may and should believe that it is his design to perpetuate religion in the families of those who truly serve and obey him. They should be faithful in imparting religious truth; faithful in prayer, and in a meek, holy, pure, and benevolent example; they should so live *that their children may safely tread in their footsteps;* they should look to God for his blessing on their efforts, and their efforts will not be in vain. They shall see their children walk in the ways of virtue; and when they die, they may leave the world with unwavering confidence that God will not suffer his faithfulness to fail; that he will not break his covenant, nor alter the thing that is gone out of his lips (Ps. lxxxix. 33, 34).

from Midian, Ephah, and all they who resided in Sheba would come with their gold and incense (6). (4.) The flocks of Kedar, and the rams of Nebaioth would be offered (7). (5.) The multitude would be so great as to excite astonishment, and lead to the inquiry who they were. They would come like clouds; they would fly for safety as doves do to their windows in an approaching tempest (8). (6.) The distant islands—the heathen coasts, would wait for the gospel; and the commerce of the world be made tributary to the spread of truth (9). (7.) The sons of strangers would be employed in defending Zion, and kings would become the servants of the church (10.) 4. So great would be the anxiety to embrace the provisions of mercy, and so numerous the converts from the Pagan world, that the gates of Zion would never be closed day or night (11). 5. The nation that refused this homage would be certainly destroyed (12). 6. Then follows a beautiful poetical description of the conversion of the Pagan world, and of the fact that the most valued and valuable objects of the Gentiles would be consecrated to the church, under the image of bringing the beautiful trees of Lebanon to adorn the grounds around the temple (13, 14). 7. Zion would be made an eternal excellency (15). 8. There would thus be furnished the fullest proof of the faithfulness of God, and of the fact that JEHOVAH was the Redeemer and Saviour of his people.

III. The happy state of the church in those times. 1. It would be an age when peace and justice would characterize the rulers (17). 2. Violence, contention, wasting, would be known no more (18). 3. There would be uninterrupted prosperity, and the constant reign of truth (19, 20). 4. The people would be all holy (21). 5. Their numbers would be greatly augmented, as if a small one should become a strong nation (22).

ARISE, [1] shine; for thy light *is* [a] come, and the glory of the LORD is risen upon thee.

1 or, *be enlightened, for thy light cometh.* a Ep.5.8.

CHAPTER LX.

1. *Arise.* This is evidently addressed to the church, or to Zion regarded as the seat of the church. It is represented as having been in a state of affliction and calamity (comp. Notes on ch. iii. 26; lii. 1, 2). She is now called on to arise from the dust, and to impart to others the rich privileges which were conferred on her. ¶ *Shine* (אוֹרִי). Lowth renders this, 'Be thou enlightened.' Marg. 'Be enlightened, for thy light cometh.' Noyes, 'Enjoy light.' LXX. Φωτίζου φωτίζου—'Be enlightened; be enlightened, O Jerusalem.' Herder renders it, 'Be light.' Vitringa regards the expression as equivalent to this, 'pass into a state of light. That is, enjoy light thyself, and impart it freely to others.' Gesenius renders it, 'Shine, be bright; that is, be surrounded and resplendent with light.' The idea probably is this, 'rise now from a state of obscurity and darkness. Enter into light; enter into times of prosperity.' It is not so much a command to impart light to others as it is to be encompassed with light and glory. It is the language of prophecy rather than of command; a call rather to participate in the light that was shining than to impart it to others. The LXX. and the Chaldee here add the name 'Jerusalem,' and regard it as addressed directly to her. ¶ *Thy light* is *come.* On the word 'light,' see Notes on ch. lviii. 8, 10. The light here referred to is evidently that of the gospel; and when the prophet says that that light 'is come,' he throws himself into future times, and sees in vision the Messiah as having already come, and as pouring the light of salvation on a darkened church and world (comp. Notes on ch. ix. 2). ¶ *And the glory of the* LORD. There is reference here, doubtless, to the Shechinah or visible splendour which usually accompanied the manifestations of God to his people (see Notes on ch. iv. 5). As JEHOVAH manifested himself in visible glory to the Israelites during their journey to the promised land, so he would manifest himself in the times of the Messiah as the glorious protector and guide of his people. The Divine character and perfections would be manifested like the sun rising over a darkened world. ¶ *Is risen upon thee.* As the sun rises. The word here used (זָרַח) is commonly applied to the rising of the sun (Gen. xxxii. 31; Ex. xxii. 2; 2 Sam. xxiii. 4; Ps. civ. 22). The comparison of the gospel to the sun rising upon a dark world is exceedingly

2 For behold, the darkness shall cover the earth, and gross darkness the people; but the LORD [a] shall arise upon thee, and his glory shall be seen upon thee.

3 And the Gentiles shall come to thy light, and kings [b] to the brightness of thy rising.

4 Lift up thine eyes round about, and see: all they gather themselves together, they come to thee: thy sons shall come from far, and thy daughters shall be nursed at *thy* side.

[a] Mal.4.2; 2 Co.4.6. [b] ch.49.6,23; Re.21.24.

beautiful, and often occurs in the Bible (comp. Mal. iv. 2; Luke i. 78, marg.) ¶ *Upon thee.* Upon thee, in contradistinction from other nations and people. The gospel shed its first beams of glory on Jerusalem.

2. *For behold.* Lo, darkness covers the earth. This is designed to turn the attention to the fact that all the rest of the world would be enveloped in deep spiritual night. ¶ *Darkness* (see Notes on ch. xlv. 7). ¶ *Shall cover the earth.* Shall envelope the whole world except where it is illuminated by the gospel. It is needless to say that this was the fact when the Messiah came, and that it is still extensively true also. ¶ *And gross darkness.* Lowth renders this, 'A thick vapour.' Herder, 'Deep obscurity.' LXX. Γνόφος—Cloud, shade, tempest. The Hebrew word (עֲרָפֶל) usually denotes thick cloud, cloudy darkness, gloom; and is often applied to the thick clouds of a tempest (Ex. xx. 18; Deut. iv. 11; Ps. xviii. 10). It is a word of intenser meaning than that which is rendered 'darkness' (חֹשֶׁךְ) and the idea here is, that the nations would be enveloped in a cloud of ignorance and sin so dense and obscure that no light could penetrate it—a description strikingly applicable to the whole heathen world. ¶ *But the* LORD *shall arise upon thee.* Like the sun. That is, JEHOVAH would manifest his perfections to them in a glorious manner. ¶ *Shall be seen upon thee.* There is more emphatic meaning in the original here than is conveyed in our translation. The Hebrew word (נִרְאָה) does not mean merely that that glory would be *visible,* but that it would be *conspicuous.* It would be so bright and luminous that it would be *seen* afar—like a cloud or column of glory standing over Jerusalem that would be conspicuous to far distant people.

3. *And the Gentiles shall come.* So splendid shall be that glory, that it will attract the distant nations, and they shall come and participate in the blessings of the gospel. This contains the main statement which it is the design of this chapter to illustrate. The prophet had frequently made this statement before in general terms (comp. ch. ii. 3; xi. 10; xlix. 22; liv. 3); but he here goes into a more particular account, and more fully describes the blessings which would result from this accession to the true church. ¶ *And kings* (comp. Notes on ch. xlix. 7, 23; lii. 15). ¶ *To the brightness of thy rising.* This does not mean that the church was to arise with the splendour of the sun; but 'thy rising' means the rising *upon her*—called *her* rising, because it would shed its beams on her. It is correctly rendered by Lowth—'The brightness of thy sunrising;' by Noyes and Herder, 'The brightness that riseth upon thee.'

4. *Lift up thine eyes.* Jerusalem is here addressed as a female with eyes cast down from grief. She is directed to lift them up, and to see the great multitudes that were flocking to her. Wherever she could turn her eyes, she would behold them hastening to come to her. In this verse and the following verses, the prophet goes into a particular statement of what he referred to in general terms in ver. 3. The first thing which he specifies is, that the dispersed sons and daughters of the Jewish people would be gathered back. ¶ *Thy sons shall come from far.* They who have been driven into exile into distant lands shall again return. This is in accordance with the predictions so often made in Isaiah, that the scattered sons of the Jewish people would be again collected (see Notes on ch. xlix. 17, 18. ¶ *And thy daughters shall be nursed at* thy

5 Then thou shalt see, and flow
together, and thine heart shall fear,
and be enlarged; because [a]the
abundance[1] of the sea shall be
converted unto thee, the [2]forces of
the Gentiles shall come unto thee.

a Ro.11.25.

1 or, *noise of the sea shall be turned toward thee.*
2 or, *wealth,* ver. 11; ch.61.6.

side. The LXX. render this, 'And thy daughters shall be borne upon the shoulders' (ἐπ' ὤμων ἀρθήσονται). Lowth also says, that one MS. reads it 'upon the shoulders,' and another has both 'shoulders' and 'side.' The translation of the LXX., and these different readings of the MSS. have probably been caused by the supposed improbability of the fact, that children were nursed or carried on the side (comp. ch. xlix. 22). But Sir John Chardin says that it is the general custom in the East to carry the children astride upon the hip, with the arms around the body. The word, however, which is rendered 'nursed' in our translation (תֵּאָמַנָה from אָמַן), means, properly, to stay, to sustain, support; to bear or carry a child (Num. xi. 12); hence to be faithful, firm. It is not certain that it is in any instance used in the sense of nursing; but it more probably means here, they shall be borne. It implies that the church would evince deep solicitude for the education and welfare of the young—as a mother does for her children; and that it would be one of the blessings of those times that that solicitude should be felt and manifested.

5. *Then shalt thou see.* Lowth renders this, 'Then shalt thou fear and overflow with joy;' and supposes that it refers to the agitation and anxiety of mind attending the scene, and to the joy consequent on the numerous conversions. His authority for this change is, that forty MSS. (two of them ancient) have תיראי, 'thou shalt fear,' instead of תִּרְאִי, 'thou shalt see.' But though the change is of a single letter, there is not sufficient authority to make it, nor does the sense require it. The Vulgate, LXX., Chaldee, Syriac, Arabic, and Castellio, all render it in accordance with the present reading of the Hebrew text. The idea is, that Jerusalem would look with deep interest on the great multitude that would be converted to her, and that the effect would be to cause the heart to overflow with joy. ¶ *And flow together.* This translation, it is believed, by no means conveys the true sense of the passage. Indeed, it is difficult to make sense of the translation. It is true that the Hebrew word נָהַר, *nâhăr,* means to flow, to flow together; whence the word נָהָר, *nâhâr,* 'river.' But it may be used in the sense of flowing, or overflowing *with joy;* or it may seem to shine, to be bright, the same as נוּר, *nûr* (Gesenius); and thence to be cheered, to rejoice, as when the countenance is bright and cheerful (comp. Job iii. 4). Taylor (*Heb. Con.*) renders it, 'And be enlightened, or have the light flow upon thee.' The true idea is, doubtless, that of rejoicing; denoting the happiness which will always exist in the church when many are *seen* to come and give themselves to God. ¶ *And thine heart shall fear.* The heart shall be *ruffled,* agitated, deeply excited by the view of the numbers that are converted, and by the evidence thus furnished of the Divine favour and presence. The effect of numerous simultaneous conversions in a revival of religion, is always to produce awe and reverence. There is a conviction that God is near, and that this is his work; and a deep veneration produced by the demonstrations of his power which does not exist in other circumstances. This effect is described also by Jeremiah, ch. xxxiii. 9: 'And they shall fear and tremble for all the goodness and for all the prosperity that I shall procure unto her' [Jerusalem]. ¶ *And be enlarged.* Shall be swelled or filled with joy. ¶ *Because the abundance of the sea.* Marg. 'Noise of the sea shall be turned unto thee.' Lowth and Noyes render it, 'The riches of the sea.' So the LXX. Πλοῦτος θαλάσσης. The Chaldee renders it, 'There shall be transferred to thee the wealth of the west' (עוֹתַר מַעְרְבָא). The Hebrew word הֲמוֹן properly denotes a noise or sound; as of rain, of the raging of the ocean, or of

6 The multitude of camels shall
cover thee, the dromedaries of
Midian [a] and Ephah ; all they from
Sheba [b] shall come: they shall bring
gold [c] and incense: and they shall
show forth the praises of the LORD.

[a] Ge.25.4,13. [b] Ps.72.10. [c] Mat.2.11.

a multitude of men. Then it denotes a multitude or crowd of men itself (Isa. xiii. 4; xxxiii. 3; Dan. x. 6); a host or army (Judg. iv. 7; Dan. xi. 11–13); a multitude of waters (Jer. x. 13; li. 16). It then denotes a multitude of possessions; a vast amount of wealth (Ps. xxxvii. 16; Eccl. v. 9). Here it may refer either to the multitude of the *people* that dwelt on the islands of the sea, or to their *wealth* that would be brought and devoted to Zion. As various kinds of *property* are immediately specified, it seems most natural to refer it to that; and then the idea is, that the wealth possessed by lands beyond the sea, or surrounded by the sea, would be devoted to the church of God. It will be remembered, that nearly all the wealth that was imported by Solomon and others to Judea came from beyond sea, and that it was natural to speak of such places as abounding in riches. The idea is, that the wealth of all those distant lands would be consecrated to the church—an idea denoting its great prosperity and glory when all lands should come under the influence of the truth. ¶ *Shall be converted.* Heb. 'Shall be turned.' Instead of being employed in idolatry and sin; in purposes of pleasure and mere magnificence, it *shall be turned* to a different purpose. ¶ *The forces of the Gentiles.* Marg. 'wealth.' The margin has undoubtedly the correct interpretation. The word here used (חַיִל, constr. חֵיל), usually, indeed, denotes strength, might, valour; an army, forces, host; but it also means riches, wealth (Ge. xxiv. 29; Deut. viii. 17, 18; Ruth iv. 11; Job xx. 15). The LXX. renders the passage, 'The riches of the sea, and of the nations, and of the people will come over to thee.' The sense is, that the wealth of the heathen world would be consecrated to the service of the church. To some extent, this has been the case. No small part of the great wealth of the Roman empire was devoted to the service of the Christian church; and the wealth of what was then Pagan Europe, and of what was then Pagan and unknown America, has been, to a considerable extent, devoted to the Redeemer. The time will come when the wealth of India, of China, of Africa, and of the entire world, shall be devoted to the service of God, in a manner far more decided than has yet occurred in the most favoured Christian lands.

6. *The multitude of camels.* Lowth renders this, 'An inundation of camels.' The Hebrew word properly denotes an inundation or overflowing of waters, but it is not improperly applied to a numerous caravan or company of animals. The camel is a well-known useful animal that constitutes the principal beast of burden in Arabia, and that may, indeed, be said to constitute its wealth. It is frequently spoken of as 'the ship of the desert.' The description here is strictly applicable to Arabia; and, undoubtedly, the prophet meant to say, that that country would be blessed with the true religion, and that her merchandise and wealth would become tributary to the church of God. ¶ *Shall cover thee.* Shall come in such multitudes as to fill thee, and to be spread out all over thee. Thus we speak of a land being covered with flocks and herds. ¶ *The dromedaries.* The dromedary

DROMEDARY (*Camelus Dromedarius*).

is a species of camel that is found principally in Arabia, with one bunch or protuberance on its back, in distinction from the Bactrian camel, which has two bunches (Webster). 'It is found,' says

Dr. Shaw, 'in Barbary, though much more rarely there than in the Levant. It is chiefly remarkable for its prodigious swiftness; the Arabs affirming that it will run over as much ground in one day as one of their best horses will perform in eight or ten. The Shiekh who conducted us to Mount Sinai rode upon a camel of this kind, and would frequently divert us with an instance of its great abilities. For he would depart from our caravan, reconnoitre another just in view, and return to us again in less than a quarter of an hour. It differeth from the common camel in being of a finer and rounder shape, and in

BACTRIAN CAMEL (*Camelus Bactrianus*).

having on its back a lesser bunch or protuberance.'—(Shaw's *Travels*, p. 240.) Hence, in Jer. ii. 23, the prophet speaks of the 'swift dromedary.' The idea here is, that these fleet animals, so valuable to the inhabitants of Arabia, would come bringing their merchandise for the service of the church of God; that is, the wealth of Midian and Ephah would be devoted to him. ¶ *Midian.* Midian was the fourth son of Abraham and Keturah (Gen. xxv. 2), and was the father of the Midianites. The Midianites are frequently mentioned in the Scriptures (Gen. xxxvii. 28–36; Num. xxv. 17; xxxi. 2; Judg. vi. 7–16; vii. 23, 25, *et al.*) As early as the time of Jacob they were employed in traffic, and were associated with the Ishmaelites in this business, for it was to a company of these men that Joseph was sold by his brethren (Gen. xxxvii. 28). 'The original and appropriate district of the Midianites seems to have been on the east side of the Elanitic branch of the Red Sea, where the Arabian geographers place the city of *Madian*. But they appear to have spread themselves northward, probably along the desert coast of Mount Seir, to the vicinity of the Moabites; and on the other side, also, they covered a territory extending to the neighbourhood of Mount Sinai.'—(Robinson's *Calmet*.) Generally, the names Midianites and Ishmaelites seem to have been nearly synonymous. ¶ *Ephah.* Ephah was the eldest son of Midian (Gen. xxv. 4), and dwelt in Arabia Petræa, and gave name to the city of Ephah, called here by the LXX. Γαιφά (*Gæpha*). This city, and the small extent of country around it, constituted a part of Midian on the eastern shore of the Dead Sea, to which the territories of Midian extended. It abounded in dromedaries and camels (Judg. vi. 6). ¶ *All they from Sheba shall come.* Sheba is celebrated in the Scriptures chiefly as the place whence the Queen of that country came to visit Solomon (1 Kings x. 1; 2 Chron. ix. 1). That it abounded in wealth, may be inferred from the train which accompanied her, and from the presents with which she came to Solomon. 'And she came to Jerusalem with a very great train, with camels that bare spices, and much fine gold, and precious stones' (1 Kings x. 2). Whether it was the same country as *Seba* has been a matter of uncertainty (comp. Notes on ch. xliii. 3). It is elsewhere (Ps. lxxii. 10) mentioned as a place from whence presents should be brought to Solomon—

The kings of Tarshish and of the isles shall bring presents;
The kings of Sheba and Seba shall offer gifts.

It is usually mentioned as a place in which gold and incense abounded. 'To him shall be given the gold of Sheba (Ps. lxx. 15); 'To what purpose cometh there to me incense from Sheba' (Jer. vi. 20); 'The merchants of Sheba were thy merchants' (Ezek. xxvii. 22). According to Bruce, it was situated in Abyssinia in Ethiopa, and this has been the common opinion. It was south of Egypt, and the intercourse between Sheba and Jerusalem was not difficult; and probably a constant traffic was maintained between the two countries. In

7 All the flocks of Kedar shall be gathered together unto thee, the rams of Nebaioth shall minister unto thee: they shall come up with acceptance on mine altar, and I will [a]glorify the house of my glory.

[a] Hag.2.7,9.

the time of the Mamelukes, before the conquest of Egypt and Arabia by Selim, a caravan constantly set out from Abyssinia for Jerusalem (comp. Notes on ch. xlv. 14). ¶ *They shall bring gold and incense.* That this country abounded in incense, see the passages of Scripture referred to above. On the meaning of the wood 'incense,' see Notes on ch. i. 13. The idea is, that they would bring the most valuable productions of their country and devote them to God—perhaps designed to show that the wealth of Africa should yet be consecrated to the cause of the true religion. ¶ *And they shall show forth.* These distant lands shall join in the worship of JEHOVAH.

7. *All the flocks of Kedar.* On the word 'Kedar,' see Notes on ch. xxi. 16. The Kedarenians were a wandering tribe that frequently changed their residence, though it is probable they usually dwelt in the south part of Arabia Deserta, or the north of Arabia Petræa. They are mentioned as dwelling in beautiful tents (Cant. i. 5): 'I am black, but comely as the tents of Kedar,' see Ps. cxx. 5; comp. Isa. xxi. 16, 17; xlii. 11. The language here also means that that which constituted their principal wealth would come and enrich Jerusalem, or the church of God. ¶ *The rams of Nebaioth.* Nebaioth was also a son of Ishmael (Gen. xxv. 13; 1 Chron. i. 29), and was the father of the Nabatheans. They were a people of Arabia Petræa, and lived principally by plunder, trade, and the keeping of flocks. The country of Nabathea extended, it is supposed, from the Euphrates to the Red Sea, and embraced Petra, the capital of Arabia Deserta, and also Medaba. It is not possible, however, to fix the exact boundaries of the various tribes of Arabians. The general idea is, that their most valuable possessions would be devoted to God. ¶ *Shall minister unto thee.* That is, by coming up as an acceptable sacrifice on the altar. ¶ *They shall come up with acceptance on mine altar.* It is by no means necessary to understand this literally. The Jews were accustomed to express their ideas of worship by sacrifices, and the prophet naturally employed that language. The sense is, that the conversion of the wandering tribes of Arabia would be as certain and as signal as if the numerous flocks of Kedar and Nebaioth should be devoted to JEHOVAH in sacrifice. All that was valuable there would be employed in his service; the people would come with their most precious offerings and consecrate them to God. It is evident that this remains to be fulfilled. Paul, indeed, preached in Arabia (Gal. i. 17); and, doubtless, there were some conversions to Christianity there. But, as a people, they never have been converted to the true God; and in all ages they have been the victims of either idolatry or superstition. The time will come, however, when Arabia, so interesting as settled by the descendants of Abraham; so interesting in the bold, active, and energetic character of its tribes; so interesting as using a language that is one of the most refined and far-spoken of the earth; and so interesting as being, in some parts at least, among the most fertile and beautiful of the earth, shall be converted to God. Probably the most balmy, pure, and pleasant climate of the world is the southern part of Arabia Felix — the country of Yemen; and when the Arabs shall bring their energy of character to the service of the true God, and the gospel shall be preached in their language to all their tribes, no one can predict the effect which this shall have on the entire conversion of the world. ¶ *And I will glorify.* I will honour my glorious house, *i.e.*, the temple. Lowth, 'And my beauteous house I will yet beautify.' The idea is, that he would adorn the temple by bringing the distant nations, with their most valuable possessions, to worship there. That is, the true religion would yet appear glorious when the nation should acknowledge it and submit to its requirements.

8 Who *are* these *that* fly as a
cloud, and as the doves to their
windows?
9 Surely the isles [a] shall wait for
me, and the ships of Tarshish first,
to bring thy sons from far, their
silver [b] and their gold with them,
unto the name of the LORD thy
God, and to the Holy One of Israel,
because he hath glorified thee.

[a] ch.42.4.

[b] Ps.68.30,31; Zec.14.14.

8. *Who* are *these* that *fly as a cloud?* In multitudes so numerous, that they appear as a dense cloud. The prophet, in vision, sees a vast multitude coming to Jerusalem, or hastening to embrace the true religion—so numerous as to excite surprise, and to lead to the question, Who can they be? (comp. ch. xlix. 21.) It is not uncommon to compare a multitude of persons to a cloud. Thus Livy (xxxv. 49), *Rex contra peditum equitumque nubes jactat.* Thus in Heb. xii. 1, the number of witnesses who are said to encompass Christians is compared to a cloud (νέφος μαρτύρων). So Virgil (*Geor.* iv. 60) compares a swarm of bees to a cloud—*obscuramque trahi vento mirabere nubem.* The Chaldee understands this of *swift* clouds, and takes the point of the comparison to be the *velocity* with which they would come. 'Who are these that come publicly (בְּגָלֵי) *as swift clouds?*' But the comparison relates probably to the *number*, rather than to the *swiftness* with which they would come. Converts would be multiplied in such numbers, that they would seem to be like dense clouds making their way to Zion. This strikingly expresses the fact of the numerous conversions among the Gentiles, and is a most beautiful description of a revival of religion. ¶ *And as the doves to their windows.* Lowth renders this, 'Like doves upon the wing'—supposing with Houbigant, that there is a slight error in the Hebrew text. The LXX. render it, Σὺν νοσσοῖς—'With their young.' But the true idea is contained in the common version. Doves fly to their houses, or to their windows, in an approaching storm. In like manner converts would hasten to Zion from the heathen world. They would come in great numbers, and would feel that if there they would be safe. Morier, in his *Second Journey*, p. 140, has well illustrated this passage—'In the environs of the city' [Ispahan], says he, 'to the westward, near Zainderood, are many pigeon-houses, erected at a distance from habitations, for the purpose of collecting pigeon's dung for manure. They are large, round towers, rather broader at the bottom than at the top, crowned by conical spiracles, through which the pigeons descend. Their interior resembles a honey-comb, pierced with a thousand holes, each of which forms a snug retreat for a nest. The extraordinary flights of pigeons which I have seen upon one of these buildings affords, perhaps, a good illustration of Isa. lx. 8. Their great numbers, and the compactness of their mass, literally looked like a cloud at a distance, and obscured the sun in their passage.' The prediction here has already, in part at least, been fulfilled. The rapid conversions in the time of the apostles accorded with this prediction. In numerous revivals of religion, also, has there been a fulfilment of it; and we are yet to anticipate a far more striking and glorious completion of it in the conversion of the heathen world to the Christian faith.

9. *Surely the isles.* On the meaning of the word 'isles' in Isaiah, see Notes on ch. xli. 1. ¶ *Shall wait for me* (see Notes on ch. xli. 4). ¶ *And the ships of Tarshish* (see Notes on ch. ii. 16). The main idea here is clear. These ships were the principal vessels known to the Hebrews as employed in foreign commerce, and the prophet employs the name to denote ships in general that sailed to distant ports. They will be employed in importing the most valuable productions of distant climes to Zion, and in collecting those who should be converted to God; that is, the commerce of the world would be made tributary to religion, and the ships that sail to distant lands would be employed in advancing the cause of salvation. ¶ *First.* Among the first, in the first rank; they shall be among the most

10 And the sons of strangers shall [a] build up thy walls, and their kings shall minister unto thee: for in [b] my wrath I smote thee, but in my favour have I had mercy on thee.

11 Therefore thy gates shall be open [c] continually: they shall not be shut day nor night; that *men* may bring unto thee the forces of the Gentiles, and *that* their kings *may be* brought.

[a] Zec.6.15. [b] ch.57.17. [c] Re.21.25.

active and useful agents in diffusing the knowledge of the truth. Twenty-five MSS. and the Syriac read it, 'As at the first.' Jarchi and Kimchi suppose it means, as at the first; that is, as in the time of Solomon. But the idea is, that the ships which trade to the most distant regions will be among the principal instrumentalities employed in the conversion of the heathen world to Christianity. To some extent this has already been done. The servants of God have been borne already to almost every heathen land; and the time *may* come when it shall be deemed an essential object of those engaged in foreign commerce to diffuse a knowledge of civilization, and of the arts of life; of science, and of pure religion. ¶ *To bring thy sons from far.* Those who shall be converted from distant lands—as if they were to come personally and worship at Jerusalem (see Notes on ch. xlix. 22). ¶ *Unto the name of the* LORD *thy God.* Lowth renders this, 'Because of the name.' So the LXX. Διὰ τὸ ὄνομα, κ.τ.λ. The idea is, that all this wealth would be devoted to JEHOVAH, and employed in his service. ¶ *Because he hath glorified thee.* He has honoured thee by imparting to thee the true religion, and making me the means of diffusing it around the world.

10. *And the sons of strangers.* They who have been devoted to a foreign and a false religion shall become devoted to the true religion, and engage in the service of the true God. ¶ *Shall build up thy walls.* Jerusalem is represented as a ruined city. Her walls had been thrown down, and were lying prostrate. In restoring her to her former magnificence, strangers and foreigners would lend their cheerful aid. The idea is, that they would become tributary to the church, and esteem it a privilege to be engaged in any service, however laborious, that would promote its best interests. ¶ *And their kings* (see Notes on ch. xlix. 23). ¶ *For in my wrath I smote thee.* Referring to the calamities which he had, from time to time, brought on Jerusalem (see ch. lvii. 17). ¶ *But in my favour* (see Notes on ch. liv. 8).

11. *Therefore thy gates shall be open continually.* The main idea here is, probably, that the accession from the heathen world, and the consequent influx of converts, would be so great, that there would be a necessity that the gates should never be closed. It is *possible*, also, that the prophet meant to describe that time as a period of security and peace. The gates of cities were closed in time of war, and at night, to guard them from danger. But in those times, such would be the prevalence of peace, and such would be the purposes for which the multitude of strangers would come from all parts of the world, that the gates might be left open, and the city unguarded at all times. The sense is—1. That there will be immense multitudes that shall enter the true church from the heathen world. 2. That the gospel will be *constantly* and *unceasingly* offered to men. The doors of the church shall at no time be closed. By day and by night, at all seasons and in all places, men may come and obtain salvation. None shall be excluded because the gates shall be closed upon them; none because they are strangers and have come from distant lands; none because there will be no room; none because the conflux shall be so great that the provisions of mercy will be exhausted. 3. It will be a time of safety when the world shall be brought under the influence and the dominion of the Prince of Peace. There will be no need of closing the gates of cities, or of building walls around them. There will be no need to guard against hostile armies or the intrusions of hordes of

12 For the nation and kingdom that will not serve thee shall perish; yea, *those* nations shall be utterly wasted.

---

banditti. There will be no need of guarding against the fraud, oppressions, and dishonest arts of other men. If the principles of the true religion everywhere prevailed, there would be no need of walls to cities, or gates, or bars; no need of ramparts, of ships of war, and of fortifications; no need of bolts and locks and iron chests to guard our property. *No true Christian needs to guard himself or his property against another true Christian.* No lock, no bolt, no wall, no gate, no iron safe has been made in order to guard *against* a man who is the sincere friend of the Redeemer. They are made to guard against wicked men; and when universal truth and righteousness prevail, they may be suffered to rust and rot for want of use. Should the principles of Christianity be everywhere diffused, the walls of all cities might be suffered to fall down; their gates to stand open till they should decay; ships of war to lie in the dock till they should sink to the bottom; forts and fleets to be dismantled; and the whole business of making locks and shackles, and of building prisons and manufacturing instruments of war, would come to an end. ¶ *That* men *may bring unto thee.* So many shall be coming with the wealth of the Gentiles, that the gates shall be continually open. ¶ *The forces of the Gentiles.* The wealth of the heathen (see Notes on ver. 5). ¶ *And* that *their kings may be brought.* Lowth renders this, 'That their kings may come pompously attended.' Noyes, 'May come with their retinues.' The Chaldee renders it, 'And their kings be brought bound,' or in chains. But the Hebrew word used here (נְהוּגִים) denotes simply that they would be led or conducted in any way; and the idea is, that they would be induced, by the force of truth, to come and devote themselves to the service of God. They might be expected, indeed, to come, as Lowth says, pompously attended, but this idea is not in the Hebrew text.

12. *For the nation and kingdom.* Perhaps this is given as a reason for what is said in the previous verse—that kings and their subjects should come to Zion and embrace the true religion, *because* if it were not done they would perish. This is certainly one reason why sinners hasten to embrace the Saviour; and when this truth becomes deeply impressed on a community, it is one of the means of a revival of religion. An apprehension of danger; a certain anticipation of ruin if the gospel is not embraced; a conviction that 'there is salvation in no other,' is often a means of leading men to seek the Saviour. ¶ *That will not serve thee.* That will not become the servant of the church of God:—that is, that will not promote its interests, obey its laws, and maintain the true religion. ¶ *Shall perish.* This is applied particularly here to a 'nation' and a 'kingdom.' The idea is, that no nation can flourish that does not obey the law of God, or where the worship of the true God is not maintained. History is full of affecting illustrations of this. The ancient republics and kingdoms fell because they had not the true religion. The kingdoms of Babylon, Assyria, Macedonia, and Egypt; the Roman empire, and all the ancient monarchies and republics, soon fell to ruin because they had not the salutary restraints of the true religion, and lacked the protection of the true God. France cast off the government of God in the Revolution, and was drenched in blood. It is a maxim of universal truth, that the nation which does not admit the influence of the laws and the government of God must be destroyed. No empire is strong enough to wage successful war with the great JEHOVAH; and sooner or later, notwithstanding all that human policy can do, corruption, sensuality, luxury, pride, and far-spreading vice, will expose a nation to his displeasure, and bring down the heavy arm of his vengeance. There is no truth of more vital interest to *this* nation (America) than this; no declaration in any ancient writing expressive of the course of events in this world, that hangs with more portentous interest over this re-

13 The glory of Lebanon [a] shall come unto thee, the fir-tree, the pine-tree, and the box together, to beautify [b] the place of my sanctuary; and I will make the place of my feet [c] glorious.

14 The sons also of them that afflicted thee shall come bending unto thee; and all they that despised thee shall [d] bow themselves down at the soles of thy feet; and they shall call thee, The city of the LORD, The Zion [e] of the Holy One of Israel.

a Ho.14.6,7. b Ps.96.6. c Ps.132.7. d Re.3.9. e He.12.22.

public, than that 'THE NATION THAT WILL NOT SERVE GOD SHALL PERISH.' As a nation, we have nothing else to depend on but our public virtue, our intelligence, our respect for the laws of Heaven. *Our* defence is not to be in standing armies—but in God, as our living and ever-watchful protector and friend. *Our* hope is not in a vast navy, in strong ramparts, in frowning battlements, but in the favour of the Most High. No martial array, no strong fortresses, no line-of-battle-ships, can save a nation that has cast off the government of God, and that is distinguished for the violation of treaties and for oppression, bribery, and corruption. The nation that violates the Sabbath; that tramples on the rights of unoffending men and women; that disregards the most solemn compacts; and that voluntarily opens upon itself the floodgates of infidelity and vice, *must* expect to meet with the displeasure of the Almighty. And it is *as* true of an individual as it is of a nation. Of any human or angelic being; of any association or combination of men or angels that does not obey God, it is true that they shall be utterly destroyed.

13. *The glory of Lebanon.* The 'glory of Lebanon,' here means the trees that grew on Lebanon (see Notes on ch. xxxv. 2). ¶ *Shall come unto thee.* That is, thy beauty and glory will be as great as if those valuable trees were brought and planted around the temple. ¶ *The fir-tree* (see Notes on ch. xli. 19; lv. 13). ¶ *The box* (see also Notes on ch. xli. 19). ¶ *To beautify the place of my sanctuary.* The site of the temple, as if they were planted around it, and as if the magnificence of Lebanon was transferred there at once. The idea is, that the most valuable and glorious objects in distant nations would be consecrated to the service of the true God. ¶ *And I will make the place of my feet glorious.* Lowth renders this, 'I will glorify the place whereon I rest my feet;' and he supposes that the *ark* is meant as the place on which God rested his feet as a footstool. In support of this, he appeals to Ps. xcix. 5, 'Worship at his footstool;' and 1 Chron. xxviii. 2. So Rosenmüller understands it, and appeals further to Ps. cxxxii. 7. Doubtless the main idea is, that the temple was regarded as the sacred dwelling-place of God—and that he means to say, that every place in his temple, even where, to keep up the figure, he rested his feet when he sat on the throne, would be filled with magnificence and glory.

14. *The sons of them that afflicted thee.* In the previous verses the prophet had said that strangers and foreigners would become tributary to the true religion. Here, to give variety and interest to the description, he says, that even the descendants of those who had oppressed them would become tributary to them, and acknowledge them as favoured by JEHOVAH. ¶ *Shall come bending unto thee.* Shall come to thee in a posture of humiliation and respect. In regard to the fulfilment of this, we may observe—1. That there was a partial fulfilment of it in the conquest of Babylon. The *sons*, the descendants of those who had destroyed Jerusalem, and led the Jews into captivity, were constrained to acknowledge them, and, under Cyrus, to reconduct them to the land of their fathers (see Notes on ch. xiv. 1, 2). 2. It has often occurred, in times of persecution, that the immediate descendants of the persecutors, and that too by means of the persecution, became converted to the true religion, and acknowledged the God of those whom they had persecuted to be the true God. 3. It often occurs in times when there is no open and public persecution. Many of those now in the church are the chil-

15 Whereas thou hast been [a]for-
saken and hated, so that no man
went through *thee*, I will make thee
an eternal [c]excellency, a joy of
many generations.
16 Thou [d]shalt also suck the
milk of the Gentiles, and shalt suck
the breast of kings: and thou shalt
know that [e]I the LORD *am* thy
Saviour and thy Redeemer, the
Mighty One of Jacob.
17 For brass I will bring gold,
and for iron I will bring silver, and
for wood brass, and for stones iron:
I will also make thy officers peace,
and thine exactors righteousness.

[a] Ps.78.60,61. [b] La.1.4. [c] Re.3.12. [d] ch.66.11,12. [e] ch.43.3. [f] 2 Pe.3.13.

dren or descendants of those who had been the enemies of the gospel. They themselves did all that could be done, by their lives and examples, to train up their children in opposition to it. But the sovereign mercy of God interposed, and from such he selected heralds of salvation and preachers of righteousness to a lost world, or such as should become shining lights in the more obscure walks of the Christian life. ¶ *And all they that despised thee.* There shall yet be a universal acknowledgment of the true religion even in those nations that have spurned the gospel. This does not mean that *all* who have ever despised the true religion shall be converted and saved, but that there shall be a universal acknowledgement that it is of God, and that the church is under his care. See an explanation of this sentiment in the Notes on ch. xlv. 23. ¶ *At the soles of thy feet.* In a posture of the utmost reverence and submission (see Rev. iii. 9; comp. Notes on ch. xlix. 23). ¶ *And they shall call thee.* They shall honour thee as the favoured of the Lord; as the abode of the true God (see ch. ii. 3). ¶ *The Zion,* &c. The Zion, or the royal court where the holy God that is worshipped in Israel dwells.

15. *Whereas thou hast been forsaken.* Heb. 'Instead of (תַּחַת) thy being forsaken,' *i.e.*, thy subsequent prosperity shall come in the place of thy being formerly forsaken. The forsaking here refers to the various calamities, persecutions, and trials, which she had been called to endure. ¶ *So that no man went through* thee. When the country was desolate and abandoned, so that no caravan passed from one part of it to another, or made it a thoroughfare in going to other lands (comp. Lam. i. 4; see Notes on ch. xxxiv. 10). ¶ *I will make thee an eternal excellency.* Lowth, 'An everlasting boast.' Noyes, 'Glory.' I will make you for ever honoured or exalted, so that you shall no more be desolate and abased. ¶ *A joy of many generations.* A subject of joy from generation to generation; *i.e.*, one age after another.

16. *Thou shalt suck the milk of the Gentiles.* This expression means, 'Whatever is valuable and rich which they possess shall contribute to your welfare.' The idea is the same substantially which occurs in the previous parts of the chapter, that the riches of the heathen world would become tributary to the advancement of the true religion. ¶ *And thou shalt suck the breast of kings.* The Chaldee renders this, 'And thou shalt be satisfied with the riches of the people, and shalt delight thyself with the spoil of kings.' The phrase to suck the breast *of kings* is unusual; but the sense is simple and plain, that kings and their wealth should be made to contribute to sustain the church. See the sentiment explained in the Notes on ch. xlix. 23. ¶ *And thou shalt know.* By the protection which shall be extended to thee, and by the accession which shall be made to thee, thou shalt have full proof that JEHOVAH is thy protector and friend. The conversion of the heathen world shall demonstrate that JEHOVAH is the friend of his church and people.

17. *For brass I will bring gold.* This commences the description of the happy times when the Gentiles should be led to embrace the true religion, and when the wealth of the world would be consecrated to the service of the true God. The idea is, that all things would be changed for the better. The golden age should come; and a change from the calamities to which reference had

18 Violence shall no more be heard in thy land, wasting nor destruction within thy borders: for thou shalt call thy walls [a] Salvation, and thy gates Praise.

[a] ch.26.1.

been made by the prophet, would take place as great as if, in all purposes of life, gold should be used where brass is commonly used; and silver where iron is commonly used; and brass where wood is used; and iron where stones are used. Calvin supposes, not improbably, that allusion is here made to the temple, and that, in describing the future glory of the church, the prophet says that the change would be as glorious as if, in all places where brass and iron and wood and stone had been used, gold and silver and brass and iron should be respectively used in their places. The Chaldee renders this, 'Instead of the brass which they took away from thee, O Jerusalem, I will bring gold; and instead of the iron I will bring silver; and instead of the wood, brass; and instead of the stones, iron.' Jarchi, Kimchi, and Grotius, accord with this interpretation. But it is probably designed as a poetical description of the glory of the future age, and of the great changes which would take place in human society under the influence of the gospel. No one can doubt that the gospel produces these changes; and that the changes of society caused by the gospel are as beautiful and striking as though gold and silver should be substituted for brass and iron, and brass and iron for wood and stone. Such changes shall yet take place everywhere on the earth; and the world shall yet be beautified, enriched, and adorned by the prevalence of the true religion. ¶ *I will also make thy officers peace.* Thy officers shall be appointed to promote peace and shall secure it. The sense is, that wars would be ended, and that universal concord and harmony would prevail in the church under the guidance of those appointed to administer to its affairs (comp. ch. ii. 4; ix. 6). The word 'officers,' here denotes those who should be appointed to *superintend* the affairs of the church (from פָּקַד *pâkăd*, to visit, review, superintend, oversee), and refers here to all who should be appointed to *rule* in the church. The word itself may be applicable either to civil magistrates or to the ministers of religion. The LXX. render it, Ἄρχοντας—'Rulers,' and they translate the passage, 'I will give thy rulers in peace' (ἐν εἰρήνῃ). ¶ *And thine exactors.* They who should *exact*, or collect tribute or taxes. The word from which the noun here used is derived (נָגַשׂ), means to urge, impel, drive—hence the noun 'taskmaster'—ἐργοδιώκτης (Ex. iii. 7; Job iii. 18); then to urge a debtor, to exact a debt; then to rule or have dominion; to appoint and exact taxes, &c. Here it refers to magistrates, and it means that they would be mild and equal in their exactions. ¶ *Righteousness.* They shall not lay unequal or oppressive burdens; they shall not oppress in the collection of taxes. The idea is, that righteousness would prevail in every department of the church and the state.

18. *Violence shall no more be heard in thy land.* This is a most beautiful description of the peace and prosperity which would prevail in the times of the Messiah. If the gospel, in its purity, should prevail on earth, there would be no more scenes of violence and war. The battle-shout would be heard no more; the cry of violence, the clangour of arms, would resound no more. The pure gospel of the Redeemer has never originated one war; never produced one scene of bloodshed; never once prompted to violence and strife. There has been no war in any age or in any land which the principles of the gospel, if acted on by both the contending nations, would not have prevented; there have been no scenes of bloodshed which would not have been avoided if that had been suffered to control the hearts of men. And no one who believes the Bible to be a revelation from God, can doubt that the time *will* come when the mad passions of kings and nations shall be subdued, and when wars shall cease to be known except in the melancholy and disgraceful records of past events (comp. Notes on ch. ii. 4). ¶ *Wasting.* The waste of life and property; the burning of cities, towns, and villages; and the de-

19 The [a] sun shall be no more thy
light by day; neither for brightness
shall the moon give light unto thee:
but the LORD shall be unto thee an
everlasting light, and thy God [b] thy
glory.

20 Thy sun shall no more go down;
neither shall thy moon withdraw itself:
for the LORD shall be thine
everlasting light, and the days of
thy [c] mourning shall be ended.

a Re.21.23; 22.5. b Zec.2.5. c Re.21.4.

solation which spreads over farms and plantations on the march of a victorious enemy. ¶ *Nor destruction.* Heb. שֶׁבֶר—'Breaking.' The breaking or treading down caused by the march of a triumphant army. ¶ *In thy borders.* Within thy bounds or limits. Thy whole country shall be peace and prosperity; that is, wherever the gospel shall spread there shall be security and peace. ¶ *But thou shalt call thy walls Salvation.* Thou shalt live securely within thy walls, and shalt speak of them as furnishing protection or salvation. The time will come when the church shall have no reason to apprehend danger from abroad, and when all shall be peace within. ¶ *And thy gates Praise.* Because, says Grotius, those who are appointed to watch at their gates shall announce the approach of no enemy, but shall, with the highest security, celebrate the praises of God. Praise would be celebrated in all the places of public concourse, and perfect protection would be ascribed to all her walls; that is, in the church there would be entire security, and everywhere the praises of God would be celebrated.

19. *The sun shall be no more.* A similar expression denoting the great prosperity and happiness of the church, occurs in ch. xxx. 26 (see Notes on that place). The language here is exceedingly beautiful, and the idea is plain. It is designed to foretell the great glory which would exist in the church under the Messiah; a glory compared with which all that is furnished by the sun, moon, and stars, would be as nothing. Expressions similar to this, and probably derived from this, are used by John in describing the glory of heaven. 'And the city had no need of the sun, neither of the moon to shine in it; for the glory of God did lighten it, and the Lamb is the light thereof' (Rev. xxi. 23). 'And there shall be no night there; and they need no candle, neither light of the sun; for the Lord God giveth them light' (Rev. xxii. 5). The idea is, the light and beauty of truth would be so great; the Divine perfections shine forth so illustriously under the gospel, that the eye would be attracted to *that* light as superior to all the natural splendour of the sun and moon. All the wonders and beauties of the natural world would be lost in the superior brightness that would shine in the moral world. ¶ *Neither for brightness.* In order to give light; or, with her brightness she shall not shine on the night. ¶ *Shall the moon give light unto thee.* The beauty of the moon shall be lost in the superior effulgence of the rays of truth. ¶ *But the* LORD *shall be unto thee.* He will furnish a revelation that will disclose far more of his perfections and his glory, and that will be far more valuable to thee as a light and guide, than all the splendour of the heavenly bodies. ¶ *And thy God thy glory.* The honour of the church shall be that it has the true God for its protector. Its joys shall be found, not in the objects of nature—the beauty of created things—but in the glory of the Divine perfections, and in the laws and plans of the Redeemer. His name, his attributes, his laws, his protecting care, constitute her main glory. It is an honour to the church to have *such* a God and Redeemer; an honour to share his favour, and to be under his ever-watchful eye. The glory of the church is not her wealth, her numbers, her influence, nor the rank and talent of her ministers and members; it is the character of her sovereign Lord, and in his perfections it is right that she should exult and rejoice.

20. *Thy sun shall no more go down.* There shall be no total and long night of calamity, error, and sin. This is designed to describe the flourishing and glorious state of the church. It, of course, does not mean that there should be *no* times of calamity, no period of

21 Thy people also *shall be* all righteous: [a] they [b] shall inherit the land for ever, [c] the branch [d] of my planting, [e] the work [f] of my hands, that I may be glorified.

[a] ch.4.3; Re.21.27. [b] Mat.5.3. [c] ch.62.4. [d] Jn.15.2. [e] Ps.92.13. [f] Ep.2.10.

---

ignorance, no scenes of persecution; but it means that there should not be total night. Truth should reign on the earth, and there never would be a time when the light of salvation would be extinct. There never would be a time like that when Jerusalem was wholly destroyed, and a long total night came over the land. There never would be a time when the Sun of righteousness would not shine, or when the world would be wholly deprived of the illumination of his beams. The church would be perpetual. It would live through all changes, and survive all revolutions, and to the end of time the light of salvation would shine upon a darkened world. Since the Messiah came, the light of revelation has never been wholly withdrawn from the world, nor has there been a period in which total and absolute night has come over all the church of God. But the prophet, probably, referred to far more glorious times than have yet occurred. The period is coming when the light of salvation will shine upon the earth with unclouded and universal splendour, as if the sun having ascended to the meridian should stand there in a blaze of glory age after age; when there shall be no alternation of day and night; when the light shall not be obscured by clouds; and when there shall be no eclipse of his glory. ¶ *Neither shall thy moon.* This language is poetic, and means that there would be no such obscurity in the church as there would be in the world should the sun and moon be withdrawn. Light and beauty unobscured would fill the whole heavens, and the darkness of night would be henceforward unknown. ¶ *Withdraw itself.* Heb. יֵאָסֵף—'Be collected,' that is, shall not be withdrawn, or shall not wane. The LXX. Οὐκ ἐκλείψει—'Shall not be eclipsed,' or shall not fail. ¶ *The days of thy mourning* (see Notes on ch. xxv. 8). The description here, therefore, is one of great glory and happiness in the church. That period will yet arrive; and no friend of God and of the happiness of man can think of that time without praying most sincerely that it may soon come, when the Sun of righteousness, in the fulness of his glory, shall ascend to the meridian, and stand there without one obscuring cloud, and pour the splendour of the noontide beams all over a darkened world. Some of the ideas in this chapter, descriptive of the glorious times of the gospel, have been beautifully versified by Pope in his *Messiah:—*

Rise, crown'd with light, imperial Salem, rise!
Exalt thy tow'ry head, and lift thy eyes!
See a long race thy spacious courts adorn;
See future sons and daughters yet unborn,
In crowding ranks on every side arise,
Demanding life, impatient for the skies!
See barbarous nations at thy gates attend,
Walk in thy light, and in thy temple bend:
See thy bright altars throng'd with prostrate kings,
And heap'd with products of Sabean springs!
For thee Idumea's spicy forests blow,
And seeds of gold in Ophir's mountains glow;
See heaven its sparkling portals wide display,
And break upon them in a flood of day!
No more the rising sun shall gild the morn,
Nor evening Cynthia fill her silver horn;
But lost, dissolved in thy superior rays,
One tide of glory, one unclouded blaze,
O'erflow thy courts; the light himself shall shine
Reveal'd, and God's eternal day be thine!
The seas shall waste, the skies in smoke decay,
Rocks fall to dust, and mountains melt away;
But fix'd his word, his saving power remains;
Thy realm for ever lasts, thine own Messiah reigns!

21. *Thy people also* shall be *all righteous* (see Notes on ch. iv. 2). ¶ *They shall inherit the land for ever* (see Notes on ch. xlix. 8; liv. 3; comp. ch. lxv. 9; Matt. v. 5). ¶ *The branch of my planting.* On the meaning of the word *branch*, see Notes on ch. xi. 1; xiv. 19. Here it means a *scion* or shoot which JEHOVAH had planted, and which had sprung up under his culture. Grotius supposes it means *posterity*. The idea seems to be, that they would inherit the land and all which would grow up under the culture of the hand of JEHOVAH. ¶ *The work of my hands.* The *language* here is taken from the cultivation of the land of Canaan; but the sense is, that the church would inherit all that God had done for its welfare. Applied to the work of redemption, it means that the result

22 A little one shall become a thousand, and a small one a strong nation: I the LORD will hasten it in his time.

CHAPTER LXI.

ANALYSIS.

THIS chapter, in its design and structure, is intimately connected with the preceding. That it refers to the Messiah will be shown in the Notes on ver. 1–3, and the main scope and design of the chapter is to show some of the glorious results of his coming.

The chapter may be regarded as divided into the following parts, namely:—

I. The public address or proclamation of the Messiah, stating the design for which he had been appointed to his office, and the consolatory nature of his message (1–3).

II. The happy *effects* and privileges of his coming (4–9). 1. The effects of his coming in restoring the old wastes, and in building up the long-fallen ruins (4, 5). (1.) The aid of others would be called in for this. (2.) The sons of foreigners would become tributary to them, and feed their flocks and plough their fields, and dress their vines—that is, the heathen world would become subject to the church. 2. The *privileges*

---

of all the labours, self-denials, and sacrifices of the Redeemer, become the inheritance of the church. The comforts, joys, hopes, consolations of his people are the fruit of his self-denial, 'the work of his hands,' and they are permitted to enjoy it all—as if God should cultivate a fruitful field and give the avails entirely to them. ¶ *That I may be glorified* (see ch. xlix. 3; lxi. 3; Notes on ch. xlii. 8; xliii. 7). God would be glorified in having made so ample provision for their welfare, and in their being made happy by him. He is always glorified when others enjoy the fruits of his benevolence, and when they are made pure and happy as the result of his purposes and plans.

22. *A little one shall become a thousand.* There shall be a great increase, as if one, and that the smallest, should be multiplied to a thousand. The idea is, that the people, then small in number, would be greatly increased by the accession of the Gentile world. Lowth and Noyes render this, 'The little one.' Grotius, 'The least one.' So the LXX. 'O ὀλιγιστὸς. ¶ *I the* LORD *will hasten it in his time.* Noyes, 'Its time.' Lowth, 'Due time.' LXX. 'I will do it in the proper time' (κατα καιρὸν). The sense is, that this would be done at the proper time—called, in Gal. iv. 4, 'the fulness of time.' There was a proper season when this was to be accomplished. There were important preparations to be made before it could be done. The nations, under the Divine arrangement, were to be put into a proper position to receive the Messiah. He was not to come until—1. The experiment had been fairly made to show how weak and feeble man was without a revelation—to show that philosophy, and learning, and the policy of statesmen, could do nothing effectual for the salvation of men. 2. He was not to come until the world should be at peace, and until there would be facilities for the rapid propagation of religion in all lands. 3. Nor was he to come until all that had been said in prophecy should be fulfilled —until all the circumstances should combine, which had been foretold as favourable to the introduction of the reign of the Messiah. But *when* that period should arrive, then the LORD would 'hasten' it. There would be no unnecessary delay; none which the circumstances of the case did not call for. So it will be in the universal spread of the gospel referred to in this chapter. When the world shall be moulded into a proper state to welcome it; when the nations are *prepared* to receive it and profit by it; then the universal propagation shall be *hastened*, and a nation shall be born in a day (see Notes on ch. lxvi. 8). Meantime, for the coming of that day we should pray and labour. By the diffusion of truth; by schools; by the spread of the Bible; by preaching; by the translation of the Word of God into every language; by establishing the press in all the strong points of Pagan influence; by placing missionaries in all the holds of power in the heathen world; and by training up many to enter into the harvest, the Christian world should prepare for the universal conversion of the world to God. In due time it shall be hastened, and 'he that shall come, will come, and will not tarry' (Heb. x. 37).

which would result from his coming (6–9). (1.) *Absolutely.* They would be named friends of God, and enjoy the wealth of the heathen world. (2.) *Comparatively.* Their state would be far more than a recompence for all they had suffered. (3.) In the honour which would be put upon them. Their name would be known abroad, and their children be honoured as the blessed of the Lord.

III. The occasion of rejoicing which the church would have in this (10, 11). 1. In the beauty and honour with which she would be clothed. 2. In the abundant increase of righteousness and purity.

THE [a] Spirit of the Lord GOD *is* upon me; [b] because the LORD hath [c] anointed me to preach good tidings unto the meek: he hath sent me to bind up the broken-hearted, [d] to proclaim liberty [e] to the captives, and the opening of the prison to *them that are* [f] bound;

[a] Lu.4.16-21. [b] Jn.1.32; 3.34. [c] Ps.45.7. [d] Ps.147.3. [e] Jn.3.31,6. [f] Ro.7.23-25.

CHAPTER LXI.

1. *The Spirit of the Lord* GOD. Heb. 'The Spirit of the Lord JEHOVAH.' The Chaldee renders this, 'The prophet said, the spirit of prophecy from the presence of JEHOVAH God is upon me.' The Syriac, 'The Spirit of the Lord God.' The LXX. Πνεῦμα Κυρίου—'The Spirit of the Lord,' omitting the word *adonai* (אֲדֹנָי). So Luke quotes it in ch. iv. 18. That this refers to the Messiah is abundantly proved by the fact that the Lord Jesus expressly applied it to himself (see Luke iv. 21). Rosenmüller, Gesenius, and some others, suppose that it refers to Isaiah himself, and that the idea is, that the prophet proclaims his commission as authorized to administer consolation to the suffering exiles in Babylon. It cannot be denied that the language is such as may be applied in a subordinate sense to the office of the prophet, and that the work of the Redeemer is here described in terms derived from the consolation and deliverance afforded to the long-suffering exiles. But in a much higher sense it refers to the Messiah, and received an entire completion only as applied to him and to his work. Even Grotius, who has been said to 'find Christ nowhere in the Old Testament,' remarks, 'Isaiah here speaks of himself, as the Chaldee observes; but in him we see not an obscure image of Christ.' Applied to the Redeemer, it refers to the time when, having been baptized and set apart to the work of the Mediatorial office, he began publicly to preach (see Luke iv. 21). The phrase 'the Spirit of JEHOVAH is upon me,' refers to the fact that he had been publicly consecrated to his work by the Holy Spirit descending on him at his baptism (Matt. iii. 16; John i. 32), and that the Spirit of God had been imparted to him 'without measure' to endow him for his great office (John iii. 34; see Notes on ch. xi. 2). ¶ *Because the* LORD *hath anointed me.* The word rendered 'hath anointed' (מָשַׁח *mâshăhh*), is that from which the word *Messiah* is derived (see Notes on ch. xlv. 1). Prophets and kings were set apart to their high office, by the ceremony of pouring oil on their heads; and the idea here is that God had set apart the Messiah for the office which he was to bear, and had abundantly endowed him with the graces of which the anointing oil was an emblem. The same language is used in reference to the Messiah in Ps. xlv. 7 (comp. Heb. i. 9). ¶ *To preach good tidings.* On the meaning of the word (בַּשֵּׂר) here rendered 'to preach good tidings,' see Notes on ch. lii. 7. The LXX. render it, Εὐαγγελίσασθαι—'To evangelize,' to preach the gospel. ¶ *Unto the meek.* The word rendered 'meek' (עֲנָוִים) properly denotes the afflicted, the distressed, the needy. The word 'meek' means those who are *patient* in the reception of injuries, and stands opposed to revengeful and irascible. This is by no means the sense of the word here. It refers to those who were borne down by calamity in any form, and would be particularly applicable to those who had been sighing in a long captivity in Babylon. It is not improperly rendered by the LXX. by the word πτωχοῖς, 'poor,' and in like manner by Luke (iv. 18); and the idea is, that the Redeemer came to bring a joyful message to those who were oppressed and borne down by the evils of poverty and calamity (comp. Matt. xi. 5). ¶ *To bind up the broken-hearted* (see Notes on ch. i. 6). The

broken-hearted are those who are deeply afflicted and distressed on any account. It may be either on account of their sins, or of captivity and oppression, or of the loss of relations and friends. The Redeemer came that he might apply the balm of consolation to all such hearts, and give them joy and peace. A similar form of expression occurs in Ps. cxlvii. 3:

He healeth the broken in heart,
And bindeth up their wounds.

¶ *To proclaim liberty to the captives.* This evidently is language which is taken from the condition of the exiles in their long captivity in Babylon. The Messiah would accomplish a deliverance for those who were held under the captivity of sin similar to that of releasing captives from long and painful servitude. The gospel does not at once, and by a mere exertion of power, open prison doors, and restore captives to liberty. But it accomplishes an effect analogous to this: it releases the *mind* captive under sin; and it will finally open all prison doors, and by preventing *crime* will prevent the necessity of prisons, and will remove all the sufferings which are now endured in confinement as the consequence of crime. It may be remarked further, that the word here rendered 'liberty' (דְּרוֹר *dĕrōr*) is a word which is properly applicable to the year of Jubilee, when all were permitted to go free (Lev. xxv. 10): 'And ye shall hallow the fiftieth year, and proclaim liberty (דְּרוֹר) throughout all the land unto all the inhabitants thereof.' So in Jer. xxxiv. 8, 9, it is used to denote the manumission of slaves: 'To proclaim liberty (דְּרוֹר) unto them; that every man should let his man-servant, and every man his maid-servant, being an Hebrew, or an Hebrewess, go free.' So also ver. 15, 16, of the same chapter. So also in Ezek. xlvi. 17, it is applied to the year in which the slave was by law restored to liberty. Properly, therefore, the word has reference to the freedom of those who are held in bondage, or to servitude; and it may be implied that it was to be a part of the purpose of the Messiah to proclaim, ultimately, universal freedom, and to restore all men to their just rights. If this is the sense—and I see no reason to doubt it—while the main thing intended was that he should deliver men from the inglorious servitude of sin, it also means, that the gospel would contain principles inconsistent with the existence of slavery, and would ultimately produce universal emancipation. Accordingly it is a matter of undoubted fact that its influence was such that in less than three centuries it was the means of abolishing slavery throughout the Roman empire; and no candid reader of the New Testament can doubt that if the principles of Christianity were universally followed, the last shackle would soon fall from the slave. Be the following facts remembered—1. *No man ever made another originally a slave under the influence of Christian principle. No man ever kidnapped another, or sold another,* BECAUSE *it was done in obedience to the laws of Christ.* 2. No Christian ever manumitted a slave who did not feel that in doing it he was obeying the spirit of Christianity, and who did not have a more quiet conscience on that account. 3. No man doubts that if freedom were to prevail everywhere, and all men were to be regarded as of equal civil rights, it would be in accordance with the mind of the Redeemer. 4. Slaves are made in violation of all the precepts of the Saviour. The work of kidnapping and selling men, women, and children; of tearing them from their homes, and confining them in the pestilential holds of ships on the ocean, and of dooming them to hard and perpetual servitude, *is not the work to which the Lord Jesus calls his disciples.* 5. Slavery, in fact, cannot be maintained without an incessant violation of the principles of the New Testament. To keep men in ignorance; to withhold from them the Bible; to prevent their learning to read; to render nugatory the marriage contract, or to make it subject to the will of a master; to deprive a man of the avails of his own labour without his consent; to make him or his family subject to a removal against his will; to prevent parents from training up their children according to their own views of what is right; to fetter and bind the intellect and shut up the avenues to knowledge

2 To proclaim the acceptable year [a] of the LORD, and the day of vengeance [b] of our God; to comfort all that [c] mourn.

a Le.25.9,&c.; 2 Co.6.2. b 2 Th.1.9. c Mar.5.4.

as a necessary means of continuing the system; and to make men dependent wholly on others whether they shall hear the gospel or be permitted publicly to embrace it, is everywhere deemed essential to the existence of slavery, and is demanded by all the laws which rule over the regions of a country cursed with this institution. In the whole work of slavery, from the first capture of the unoffending person who is made a slave to the last act which is adopted to secure his bondage, there is an incessant and unvarying trampling on the laws of Jesus Christ. Not one thing is done to make and keep a slave in accordance with any command of Christ; not one thing which would be done if his example were followed and his law obeyed. Who then can doubt that he came ultimately to proclaim freedom to all captives, and that the prevalence of his gospel will yet be the means of universal emancipation? (comp. Notes on ch. lviii. 6). ¶ *And the opening of the prison.* This language also is taken from the release of those who had been confined in Babylon as in a prison; and the idea is, that the Redeemer would accomplish a work for sinful and suffering men like throwing open the doors of a prison and bidding the man who had been long lying in a dungeon to go free. On the grammatical structure of the verb here rendered 'opening of the prison' (פְּקַח־קוֹחַ), Gesenius (*Lex.*) and Rosenmüller may be consulted. According to Gesenius, it should be read as one word. So many MSS. read it. It occurs nowhere else. It means here *deliverance.* The LXX. render it, 'And sight to the blind,' which is followed by Luke. The *sentiment* which is found in the LXX. and in Luke, is a correct one, and one which elsewhere occurs in the prophets (see Isa. xxxiv. 5); and as the sentiment was correct, the Saviour did not deem it necessary to state that this was not the literal translation of the Hebrew. Or more properly the Saviour in the synagogue at Nazareth (Luke iv. 19) used the Hebrew, and when Luke came to record it, he quoted it as he found it in the version then in common use. This was the common practice with the writers of the New Testament. The Evangelist wrote probably for the Hellenists, or the Greek Jews, who commonly used the Septuagint version, and he quotes that version as being the one with which they were familiar. The sense is not materially varied whether the Hebrew be followed, or the version by the LXX. The Arabic version agrees nearly with the Evangelist. Horne (*Introduction,* ii. 403) is of opinion that the Hebrew formerly contained more than we now find in the manuscripts and the printed editions. Of that, however, I think there is no good evidence.

2. *To proclaim the acceptable year of the* LORD (see Notes on ch. xlix. 8). There is probably an allusion here to the year of Jubilee, when the trumpet was blown, and liberty was proclaimed throughout all the land (so Lev. xxv. 9, 10). In like manner the Messiah would come to proclaim universal liberty —liberty to all the world from the degrading servitude of sin. The time of his coming would be a time when JEHOVAH would be pleased to proclaim through him universal emancipation from this ignoble bondage, and to restore to all the privilege of being the freedmen of the Lord. ¶ *And the day of vengeance of our God* (see Notes on ch. xxxiv. 8). This is language adapted to the deliverance from Babylon. The rescue of his people would be attended with vengeance on their enemies. This was not quoted by the Saviour in his discourse at Nazareth, or if quoted, the fact is not recorded by Luke (see Luke iv. 19). The *text* which the Saviour took then as the foundation of his discourse (Luke iv. 21), seems to have ended with the clause before this. It is not to be inferred, however, that he did not consider the subsequent expressions as referring to himself, but it was not necessary to his purpose to quote them. Regarded as applicable to the Redeemer and his preaching, this doubtless refers to the fact that his coming

3 To appoint unto them that
mourn in Zion, to give unto them
beauty for ashes, the oil of joy
for [a] mourning, the garment of
praise for the spirit of heaviness:
that they might be called Trees of
righteousness, The planting [b] of the
LORD, that he might be glorified.

[a] Jn.16.20.

[b] ch.60.21.

would be attended with vengeance on his foes. It is a great truth, manifest everywhere, that God's coming forth at any time to deliver his people is attended with vengeance on his enemies. So it was in the destruction of Idumea—regarded as the general representative of all the foes of God (see Notes on ch. xxxiv., xxxv.); so it was in the deliverance from Egypt—involving the destruction of Pharaoh and his host; so in the destruction of Babylon and the deliverance of the captives there. So in like manner it was in the destruction of Jerusalem; and so it will be at the end of the world (Matt. xxv. 31–46; 2 Thess. i. 7–10). ¶ *To comfort all that mourn.* The expression, 'all that mourn,' may refer either to those who mourn over the loss of earthly friends and possessions, or to those who mourn over sin. In either case the gospel has afforded abundant sources of consolation (see Notes on ch. xxv. 8).

3. *To appoint unto them.* Heb. 'To place;' *i.e.*, to place happiness before them; to give them joy and consolation. ¶ *That mourn in Zion* (see Notes on ch. i. 8). The mourners in Zion mean those who dwelt in Jerusalem; then all those who are connected with the church of God—his poor and afflicted people. ¶ *To give unto them beauty for ashes.* In the Hebrew there is here a beautiful paronomasia, which cannot be transferred to our language—פְּאֵר תַּחַת אֵפֶר. The word rendered 'beauty' (פְּאֵר) means properly a head-dress, turban, tiara, or diadem; and the idea is, that the Redeemer would impart to his mourning people such an ornament instead of the ashes which in their grief they were accustomed to cast on their heads. For the use of the word, see Isa. iii. 20, and ver. 10 of this chapter; Ex. xxxix. 29; Ezek. xxiv. 17–23. It was common among the Orientals to cast dust and ashes upon their heads in time of mourning, and as expressive of their grief (comp. Notes on ch. lvii. 5; 2 Sam. xiii. 19). ¶ *The oil of joy.* The oil of joy denotes that which was symbolical or expressive of joy. Oil or ointment was employed on occasions of festivity and joy (see Notes on ch. lvii. 9); but its use was abstained from in times of public calamity or grief (see 2 Sam. xiv. 2). ¶ *The garment of praise.* That is, the garment or clothing which shall be expresive of praise or gratitude instead of that which shall indicate grief. ¶ *For the spirit of heaviness.* Instead of a heavy, burdened, and oppressed spirit. The word used here (כֵּהָה), usually means faint, feeble, weak (see Notes on ch. xlii. 3). It is applied to a lamp about to go out (ch. xlii. 3); to eyes bedimmed, or dull (1 Sam. iii. 2); to a faint or pale colour (Lev. xiii. 39). Here it denotes those of a faint and desponding heart. These expressions are figurative, and are taken from the custom which prevailed more in Oriental countries than elsewhere—and which is founded in nature—of expressing the emotions of the mind by the manner of apparel. These customs are stated in the book of Judith. She 'pulled off the sackcloth which she had on, and put off the garments of her widowhood, and washed her body all over with water, and anointed herself with precious ointment, and braided the hair of her head, and put on a tire upon it (Gr. mitre), and put on her garments of gladness wherewith she was clad during the life of Manasses her husband. And she took sandals upon her feet, and put about her her bracelets, and her chains, and her rings, and her ear-rings, and all her ornaments, and decked herself bravely to allure the eyes of all men that should see her' (ch. x. 3, 4). ¶ *That they might be called.* That is, those who had mourned in Zion. ¶ *Trees of righteousness.* In the Heb. 'Oaks,' or terebinth trees. By their being oaks of righteousness is meant men distinguished for righteousness or justice. The LXX. render it,

4 And they shall build [a] the old
wastes, they shall raise up the
former desolations, and they shall
repair the waste cities, the desolations of many generations.
5 And strangers shall stand and
feed your flocks, and the sons of
the alien *shall be* your plowmen
and your vine-dressers.
6 But ye shall be named the
priests [b] of the LORD; *men* shall
call you the [c] ministers of our God:
ye shall eat the riches of the Gentiles, and in their glory shall you
boast yourselves.

[a] ch.58.12. [b] Ex.19.6; 1 Pe.2.5,9; Re.1.6. [c] Eze.44.11; Ep.4.11,12.

Γενεαὶ—'Generations;' Jerome, *Fortes*—'Strong;' the Chaldee, 'Princes;' the Syriac, 'Rams;' but the word properly denotes the oak, or the terebinth tree—a lofty, strong, and magnificent tree. It is not uncommon to represent men by trees (see ch. i. 2), 30; Ps. xcii. 12–14):

The righteous shall flourish like the palm-tree;
He shall grow like a cedar in Lebanon,
Those that be planted in the house of the LORD,
Shall flourish in the courts of our God.
They shall still bring forth fruit in old age;
They shall be fat and flourishing.

See also the beautiful description in Ps. i. 3, and in Jer. xvii. 8. The idea here is, that they who had been oppressed and borne down by calamity and by a sense of sin, would become vigorous and strong; and would be such as aptly to be compared to majestic trees with far-spreading branches—an image everywhere of that which is truly beautiful. ¶ *The planting of the* LORD. Those whom JEHOVAH had truly planted; that is, those who were under his care and culture (see Notes on ch. lx. 21). The same figure is used by the Saviour. 'Every plant which my heavenly Father hath not planted shall be rooted up' (Matt. xv. 13). ¶ *That he might be glorified* (see Notes on ch. lx. 21).

4. *And they shall build the old wastes* (see Notes on ch. lviii. 12).

5. *And strangers shall stand* (see Notes on ch. xiv. 1, 2; lx. 10). ¶ *And feed your flocks.* The keeping of flocks constituted a very considerable part of the husbandry of those who dwelt in Palestine. Of course, any considerable prosperity of a spiritual nature would be well represented by an accession of foreigners, who should come to relieve them in their toil. It is not necessary to suppose that this is to be taken literally, nor that it should be so spiritualized as to suppose that the prophet refers to churches and their pastors, and to the fact, that those churches would be put under the care of pastors from among the heathen. The idea is, that it would be a time of signal spiritual prosperity, and when the accession would be as great and important *as if* foreigners were to come in among a people, and take the whole labour of attending their flocks and cultivating their fields. ¶ *Your ploughmen.* Heb. אִכָּר, *ikkâr*, from which probably is derived the Greek ἀγρός; the Gothic *akr;* the German *acker;* and the English *acre.* It means properly a digger or cultivator of the soil, or husbandman (Jer. li. 26; Amos v. 16). ¶ *And vine-dressers.* The sense here accords with that which has been so repeatedly said before, that the heathen world would yet become tributary to the church (see Notes on ch. lx. 5–7, 9, 10).

6. *But ye shall be named.* The idea here literally is, 'There will be no need of your engaging in the business of agriculture. All that will be done by others; and you, as ministers of God, may engage wholly in the duties of religion. The world shall be tributary to you, and you shall enjoy the productions of all lands; and you may, therefore, devote yourselves exclusively to the service of JEHOVAH, as a kingdom of priests.' A similar promise occurs in Ex. xix. 6: 'And ye shall be unto me a kingdom of priests, and an holy nation.' The idea is, that there would be a degree of spiritual prosperity, as great *as if* they were permitted to enjoy all the productions of other climes; *as if* all menial and laborious service were performed by others; and *as if* they were to be entirely free from the necessity of toil, and were permitted to devote themselves exclusively to the services of religion. ¶ *Ye shall eat the riches of the*

7 For your shame you *shall have*
double,[a] and *for* confusion they
shall rejoice in their portion: therefore in their land they shall possess
the double; everlasting joy shall be
unto them.

8 For I the LORD love judgment,
I hate robbery for burnt-offering;
and I will direct their work in
truth, and I will make an everlasting covenant [b] with them.

a ch.40.2; Zec.9.12. b ch.55.3; Ps.50.5.

Gentiles (see Notes on ch. lx. 5–11). ¶ *And in their glory.* In what constitutes their glory, or what they regard as valuable; that is, their wealth, their talents, and their power. ¶ *Shall you boast yourselves?* There has been considerable variety of interpretation in regard to the meaning of the word here used. Jerome renders it, *Et in gloria earum superbietis.* The LXX. 'In their wealth ye shall be admired' (θαυμασθήσεσθε). The Chaldee and Syriac render it, 'In their splendour ye shall glory.' The word used is יָמַר, *yâmăr*. It occurs nowhere else, it is believed, except in Jer. ii. 11, *twice*, where it is rendered 'changed.' 'Hath a nation *changed* (הַהֵימִיר) their gods, which are yet no gods? But my people have changed (הֵמִיר) their glory for that which doth not profit.' In the passage before us, it is used in Hithpael, and means properly *to exchange one's self with any one.* Here it means, 'In their splendour we shall take their places,' *i.e.*, we shall enjoy it in their stead. We shall avail ourselves of it *as if* we were to enter into their possessions, and *as if* it were our own. The sense is, it shall come to enrich and adorn the church. It shall *change places*, and shall all belong to the people of God—in accordance with that which has been so often said by Isaiah, that the wealth of the world would become tributary to the church.

7. *For your shame.* That is, instead of the reproach and humiliation which you have been called to experience. ¶ *You* shall have *double.* A double inheritance or reward (see Notes on ch. xl. 2). ¶ *And* for *confusion.* The word 'confusion' here means the same as a blush of shame, and refers to the scenes of humiliation and sorrow which the nation had passed through on account of its sins. ¶ *They shall rejoice.* There is here a change from the second to the third person—a change which is not unfrequent in Isaiah. The same persons, however, are intended. ¶ *In their portion.* That is, you shall be permitted to rejoice in the augmented privileges which you shall enjoy. They will be more than a compensation for all the calamities which you have been called to endure. ¶ *Therefore in their land.* This is to be regarded as addressed to the exiles in Babylon, and the promise is, that the people of God would be restored again to their own land, and to more than their former privileges and blessings there. ¶ *The double.* Double of what they formerly possessed; that is, their blessings would be greatly increased and multiplied. Applied to the times of the Messiah, to which the prophet undoubtedly refers, it means that the privileges of the friends of God would be far greater than had been enjoyed even in the most favoured times under the former dispensation. ¶ *Everlasting joy* (see Notes on ch. xxxv. 10).

8. *For I the* LORD *love judgment.* That is, 'I shall delight in rendering to my people what is right. It is right that they should enjoy my protection, and be favoured with the tokens of my kindness. Loving justice and right, therefore, I will confer on them the privileges and blessings which they *ought* to enjoy, and which will be a public expression of my favour and love.' ¶ *I hate robbery for burnt-offering.* There has been great variety in the interpretation of this phrase. Lowth renders it, 'Who hate rapine and iniquity.' Noyes, 'I hate rapine and iniquity.' Jerome, as in our translation, *Et odio habens rapinam in holocausto.* The LXX. Μισῶν ἁρπάγματα ἐξ ἀδικίας—'Hating the spoils of injustice.' The Chaldee, 'Far from before me be deceit and violence.' The Syriac, 'I hate rapine and iniquity.' This variety of interpretation has arisen from the different views taken of the Hebrew בְּעוֹלָה.

9 And their seed shall be known
among the Gentiles, and their offspring among the people: all that
see them shall acknowledge them,
that they *are* the seed *which* the
LORD hath blessed.
10 I will greatly rejoice [a] in the
LORD, my soul shall be joyful in
my God: for he hath clothed me
with the garments of salvation, he
hath covered me with the robe of
righteousness, [b] as a [1] bridegroom
decketh *himself* with ornaments,
and as a bride adorneth [c] *herself*
with her jewels.

a Ne.8.10; Hab.3.17,18; Ro.14.17. *b* Re.19.8. 1 *as a priest.* *c* Re.21.2.

The Syriac evidently prefixed the conjunction, ו *and,* instead of the preposition ב, *with* or *for;* and, perhaps, also the LXX. so read it. But this change, though slight, is not necessary in order to give a consistent rendering to the passage. The *connection* does not necessarily lead us to suppose that any reference would be made to 'burnt-offering,' and to the improper manner in which such offerings were made; but the idea is rather, that God hated rapine *and* sin; he hateth such acts as those by which his people had been removed from their land, and subjected to the evils of a long and painful captivity. And this is undoubtedly the sense of the passage. The Hebrew word עוֹלָה, usually without the ו, means properly a holocaust, or that which is *made to ascend* (from עָלָה, *to ascend*) from an altar. But the word here is the construct form for עַוְלָה, *evil, wickedness;* whence our word *evil* (see Job xxiv. 20; Ps. cvii. 42). And the sense here is, 'I hate rapine or plunder (גָּזֵל) *with* iniquity;' that is, accompanied, as it always is, with iniquity and sin. And hating that as I do, I will vindicate my people who have been plundered in this way; and who have been borne into captivity, accompanied with deeds of violence and sin. ¶ *And I will direct their work in truth.* Literally, 'I will give them work in truth or faithfulness;' that is, I will give them the reward of their work faithfully. They shall be amply recompensed for all that they have done and suffered in my cause. ¶ *And I will make* (see Notes on ch. lv. 3).

9. *And their seed.* The figure here is taken from the feelings of a parent who desires his children to be esteemed, and who regards it as an honour that they become so distinguished that their fame extends to distant lands. ¶ *Shall be known.* Shall be distinguished or honoured. For this use of the word 'known,' see Ps. lxvii. 2; lxxvi. 1; lxxix. 10. ¶ *And their offspring* (see Notes on ch. xlviii. 19). The Chaldee and the Syriac render this, 'Their children's children.' The sense is, that the true friends of the church shall be everywhere honoured. Distant lands shall be acquainted with them, and shall be disposed to show them distinguished respect. ¶ *Among the people.* The people of distant lands. ¶ *All that see them shall acknowledge them.* The time shall come when the true friends of the Redeemer will be universally honoured. They shall be regarded as the favoured of the Lord; and instead of being persecuted and despised, the nations of the earth will regard them as worthy of their confidence and esteem.

10. *I will greatly rejoice in the* LORD. This is the language of the prophet in the name of the church; or, as Vitringa supposes, the language of a chorus introduced here by the prophet. The Chaldee regards it as the language of Jerusalem, and renders it, 'Jerusalem said, I will surely rejoice in the LORD.' The sentiment is, that the prosperity and enlargement of Zion is an occasion of joy, and should lead to thanksgiving and praise. The phrase, 'I will rejoice *in the Lord,*' means that the joy would arise from the view of the faithfulness and perfections of JEHOVAH manifested in the redemption of his people. See similar expressions of joy in the song of Mary (Luke i. 46, 47). ¶ *For he hath clothed me with the garments of salvation.* That is, Jerusalem or the church. ¶ *He hath covered me with the robe of righteousness.* The word rendered 'robe' here means mantle, or a large and loose garment thrown over the other parts of the dress. Such

11 For as the earth bringeth forth her bud, and as the garden causeth the things that are sown in it to spring forth; so the Lord GOD will cause righteousness [a] and praise [b] to spring forth before all the nations.

a Ps.72.3; 85.11. b ch.62.7.

CHAPTER LXII.

ANALYSIS.

THE same general subject is pursued in this chapter which has been presented in the chapters which have gone before. The scope of the chapter is *consolatory*, and the design is to furnish such assurances of the Divine favour towards the afflicted people of God, as would uphold and comfort them in their trials. The language is such as would be addressed to the exiles in Babylon, but the main reference is undoubtedly to the times of the Messiah. The chapter may be conveniently regarded as comprising the following portions:

I. A speaker is introduced saying that he would have no rest until Zion should rise and obtain restoration from her degradation (1–5). This portion contains assurances of the Divine favour, and a promise of the future restoration and glory of Jerusalem. Who this speaker is, will be considered in ver. 1. The following are the assurances of the speaker. 1. He would give himself no peace until splendour and glory should spread over Zion (1). 2. The Gentiles would partake of the blessings conferred on Zion, and kings would come and unite with her (2). 3. Zion would be as beautiful and glorious as a royal crown in the hand of JEHOVAH (3). 4. She would be no more desolate and forsaken (4). 5. JEHOVAH would delight in Zion as a young married man delights in his bride (5).

II. The speaker says that he had set watchmen on the walls of Zion, and they are commanded to give him no rest—to be urgent and

garments are for protection and for ornament, and the image is that of the church defended and ornamented by God (see Notes on ch. xlix. 18). ¶ *As a bridegroom decketh* himself. Marg. 'As a priest.' The Hebrew is, 'As a bridegroom adorns himself as a priest' (יְכַהֵן); that is, as he makes splendid his head-dress in the manner of a priest. ¶ *With ornaments* (פְּאֵר). With a tiara, head-dress, diadem. See the word explained in ver. 3. The LXX. render it, Μίτραν—'Mitre.' The allusion is to the dress of the Jewish high-priest when he discharged the functions of his office, and particularly to the mitre and the plate or crown of gold which he wore in front of it (Ex. xxix. 6). It is not easy to give full force to the metaphor of the prophet in another language. The Hebrew, as near as we can express it, is, 'As a bridegroom attires himself as a priest with a crown or mitre.' The version by Aquila and Symmachus comes nearest to it—Ὡς νυμφίον ἱερατευόμενον στεφάνῳ. The sense is, that the church should be adorned with the highest ornament and beauty; not for the mere purpose of decoration, but as if it were a priest engaged in offering continually the sacrifice of prayer and praise. ¶ *And as a bride.* See this explained in the Notes on ch. xlix. 18. The word rendered 'jewels' here (כְּלִי) does not of necessity mean merely jewels. It properly means an apparatus, implement, utensil, vessel; and then dress, ornament of any kind; and would be better rendered here, in a more general sense, *bridal ornaments*.

11. *For as the earth bringeth forth.* This figure is several times used by the prophet (see Notes on ch. xlv. 8; lv. 10, 11). The idea is an exceedingly beautiful one, that, on the coming of the Messiah, truth and righteousness would spring up and abound like grass and fruits in the vegetable world when the earth is watered with rain. ¶ *Her bud.* The word 'bud' we now apply usually to the small bunch or protuberance on the branches of a plant, containing the rudiments of the future leaf or flower. The Hebrew word, however, (צֶמַח), rather means the germ, the shoot, or the young and tender plant as it comes up from the earth; that which first appears from the seed. ¶ *So the* LORD *God will cause righteousness to spring forth* (see Notes on ch. xlii. 19; xliii. 9; xliv. 4; xlv. 8). ¶ *Before all the nations.* The sense is, that righteousness would abound over all the earth, and that all the world would yet join in celebrating the praises of God.

importunate in prayer, until Jerusalem should be made glorious in the earth (6, 7).

III. The solemn assurance that JEHOVAH had sworn that there would be peace and security from the invasions of enemies (8, 9). The land would be no more subjected to plunder from abroad, but there would be that kind of safety and security which exists when a man sows and reaps without annoyance.

IV. The people are directed to prepare the way for the coming of JEHOVAH (10–12). A crier proclaims his approach, and directs that all obstructions should be removed.

FOR Zion's sake will I not hold my peace, and for Jerusalem's sake I will not rest, [a] until the righteousness thereof go forth as brightness, [b] and the salvation thereof as a lamp *that* burneth.

a ver. 6,7. *b* Pr.4.18.

CHAPTER LXII.

1. *For Zion's sake* (see Notes on ch. i. 8). On account of Zion; that is, on account of the people of God. ¶ *I will not hold my peace.* There have been very various opinions in regard to the person referred to here by the word 'I.' Calvin and Gesenius suppose that the speaker here is the prophet, and that the sense is, he would not intermit his labours and prayers until Zion should be restored, and its glory spread through all the earth. The Chaldee Paraphrast supposes that it is God who is the speaker, and this opinion is adopted by Grotius. Vitringa regards it as the declaration of a prophetic choir speaking in the name of the officers of the church, and expressing the duty of making continual intercession for the extension of the Redeemer's kingdom. Estius supposes it to be the petition of the Jewish people praying to God for their restoration. Amidst such a variety of interpretation it is not easy to determine the true sense. If it is the language of God, it is a solemn declaration that he was intent on the deliverance of his people, and that he would never cease his endeavours until the work should be accomplished. If it is the language of the prophet, it implies that he would persevere, notwithstanding all opposition, in rebuking the nation for its sins, and in the general work of the prophetic office, until Zion should arise in its glory. If the former, it is the solemn assurance of JEHOVAH that the church would be the object of his unceasing watchfulness and care, until its glory should fill the earth. If the latter, it expresses the feelings of earnest and devoted piety; the purpose to persevere in prayer and in active efforts to extend the cause of God until it should triumph. I see nothing in the passage by which it can be determined with certainty which is the meaning; and when this is the case it must be a matter of mere conjecture. The only circumstance which is of weight in the case is, that the language, 'I will not be silent,' is rather that which is adapted to a prophet accustomed to pray and speak in the name of God than to God himself; and if this circumstance be allowed to have any weight, then the opinion will incline to the interpretation which supposes it to refer to the prophet. The same thing is *commanded* the watchman on the walls of Zion in ver. 6, 7; and if this be the correct interpretation, then it expresses the appropriate solemn resolution of one engaged in proclaiming the truth of God not to intermit his prayers and his public labours until the true religion should be spread around the world. ¶ *I will not rest.* While I live, I will give myself to unabated toil in the promotion of this great object (see Notes on ver. 7). ¶ *Until the righteousness thereof.* The word here is equivalent to salvation, and the idea is, that the deliverance of his people would break forth as a shining light. ¶ *Go forth as brightness.* The word here used is commonly employed to denote the splendour, or the bright shining of the sun, the moon, or of fire (see ch. lx. 19; comp. ch. iv. 5; 2 Sam. xxiii. 4; Prov. iv. 18). The meaning is, that the salvation of men would resemble the clear shining light of the morning, spreading over hill and vale, and illuminating all the world. ¶ *As a lamp* that *burneth.* A blazing torch—giving light all around and shining afar.

2. *And the Gentiles shall see* (see ch. xi. 10; xlii. 1–6; xlix. 22; lx. 3, 5, 16).

2 And the Gentiles shall see thy
righteousness, and all kings thy
glory: and thou shalt be called by
a new [a] name, which the mouth of
the LORD shall name.
3 Thou shalt also be a crown [b] of
glory in the hand of the LORD, and
a royal diadem in the hand of thy
God.
4 Thou shalt no more be termed
Forsaken: [c] neither shall thy land
any more be termed Desolate; but
thou shalt be called [1] Hephzi-bah,
and thy land [2] Beulah: for the
LORD delighteth in thee, and thy
land shall be [d] married.

a Re.2.17. b Zec.9.16. c Ho.1.10; He.13.5. 1 i.e., *My delight is in her.* 2 i.e., *Married.* d Re.21.9,10.

¶ *And all kings thy glory* (see Notes on ch. xlix. 7, 23; lii. 15; lx. 3, 10, 11, 16). ¶ *And thou shalt be called by a new name.* A name which shall be significant and expressive of a greatly improved and favoured condition (see ver. 4). The idea is, that they would not be in a condition in which a name denoting humiliation, poverty, and oppression would be appropriate, but in circumstances where a name expressive of prosperity would be adapted to express their condition. On the custom of giving significant names, see Notes on ch. vii. 3; viii. 1. ¶ *Which the mouth of the* LORD *shall name.* Which shall be the more valuable because JEHOVAH himself shall confer it, and which must therefore be appropriate (see Notes on ver. 4, 12.

3. *Thou shalt also be a crown of glory.* On the application of the word 'crown' to a place, see Notes on ch. xxviii. 1, where it is applied to Samaria. Some difficulty has been felt by expositors in explaining this, from the fact that a crown or diadem was worn on the head and not held in the hand, and some have supposed that the word 'crown' here is equivalent to any ornament which might be either borne in the hand or worn on the head; others have supposed that the reference is to the custom of carrying a chaplet or garland in the hand on festival occasions. But probably the sense is this, 'Thou shalt be so beautiful and prosperous as to be appropriately regarded as a splendid crown or diadem. God shall keep thee as a beautiful diadem—the crown of beauty among the cities of the earth, and as that which is most comely and valuable in his sight.' This is the sense expressed by Gataker and Rosenmüller. ¶ *And a royal diadem.* Heb. 'A diadem of a kingdom.' The diadem is the wreath or chaplet, usually set with diamonds, which is *encircled* (צָנִיף from צָנַף *to roll* or *wind around, to encircle*) around the head. It here means such as was usually worn by monarchs; and the sense is, that Jerusalem would become exceedingly beautiful in the sight of God.

4. *Thou shalt no more be termed Forsaken.* That is, thou shalt be no more so forsaken as to make such an appellation proper. This refers to the new name which the prophet says (ver. 2) will be conferred on her. ¶ *Neither shall thy land.* Thy country shall no more be so wasted that the term desolation (שְׁמָמָה, Gr. ἔρημος) shall be properly applied to it. ¶ *But thou shalt be called Hephzi-bah.* Marg. as Heb. 'My delight is in her.' The idea is, that JEHOVAH would show her such favour, and he would have so much pleasure in his people, that this name of endearment would be appropriately given to her. The LXX. render this, Θέλημα ἐμόν—'My will,' or my delight. The sense is, that Jerusalem would be eminently the object of his delight. ¶ *And thy land Beulah.* Marg. as Heb. 'Married;' or rather, 'thou art married.' The LXX. render it, Οἰκουμένη—'Inhabited.' Lowth renders it, 'The wedded matron.' The figure is taken from a female who had been divorced, and whose appropriate name was 'Forsaken.' God says here that the appropriate name henceforward would not be the Forsaken, but *the married one*—the one favoured and blessed of God (see Notes on ch. l. 1). Language like this is common in the East. 'A sovereign is spoken of as married to his dominions; they mutually depend on each other. When a king takes possessions from another, he is said to be married to them.'—(Roberts.) ¶ *Thy*

5 For *as* a young man marrieth a virgin, *so* shall thy sons marry thee: and [1]*as* the bridegroom rejoiceth over the bride, *so* shall thy God rejoice [a]over thee.

1 *with the joy of the bridegroom.* a Je.32.41.

6 I have set watchmen upon thy walls, O Jerusalem, *which* shall never hold their peace day nor night; ye that [2]make mention of the LORD, keep not silence;

2 or, *that are the Lord's remembrancers.*

land shall be married. See Notes on ch. liv. 4–6, where this figure is extended to greater length. By a similar figure the church is represented as the beautiful bride of the Lamb of God (Rev. xxi. 9; xix. 7).

5. *For* as *a young man marrieth a virgin.* Roberts remarks on this, 'In general no youth marries a widow. Such a thing I scarcely ever heard of [in India], nor will it ever be except under some very extraordinary circumstances, as in the case of a queen, princess, or great heiress. Even widowers also, if possible, always marry virgins.' The idea here is, that JEHOVAH would have delight in his people, which would be properly represented by the affection which a young man has for his bride. ¶ So *shall thy sons marry thee.* Lowth renders this, 'So shall thy restorer wed thee.' He supposes that the word rendered in our common version, 'thy sons' (בָּנַיִךְ), should be pointed בֹּנַיִךְ, as a participle from בָּנָה, 'to build,' rather than from בֵּן, 'a son.' The parallelism requires some such construction as this; and the unusual form of expression, '*thy sons* shall be wedded to thee,' seems also to demand it. The LXX. render it, 'As a young man cohabits (συνοικῶν) with a virgin [bride] (παρθένῳ), so shall thy sons dwell with thee (κατοικήσουσιν οἱ υἱοί σου). So the Chaldee. The conjecture of Lowth has been adopted by Koppe and Döderlin. Rosenmüller supposes that there is here a mingling or confusion of figures, and that the idea is, that her sons should *possess* her—an idea which is frequently conveyed by the word בָּעַל *Bâăl*, which is here used. To me it seems that there is much force in the conjecture of Lowth, and that the reference is to God as the 'builder,' or the restorer of Jerusalem, and that the sense is that he would be 'married,' or tenderly and indissolubly united to her. If it be objected that the word is in the plural (בֹּנַיִךְ) it may be observed that the word commonly applied to God (אֱלֹהִים) is also plural, and that an expression remarkably similar to the one before us occurs in Isa. liv. 5, 'For thy Maker is thy husband' (Heb. בֹּעֲלַיִךְ, 'Thy husbands.') It is not uncommon to use a plural noun when speaking of God. It should be remembered that the points in the Hebrew are of no authority, and that all the change demanded here is in them. ¶ *And* as *the bridegroom.* Marg. as in Heb. 'With the joy of the bridegroom.' ¶ *Over the bride.* In the possession of the bride—probably the most tender joy which results from the exercise of the social affections.

6. *I have set watchmen upon thy walls* (see Notes on ch. xxi. 6–11). The speaker here is undoubtedly JEHOVAH; and by watchmen he means those whom he had appointed to be the instructors of his people—the ministers of religion. The name 'watchmen' is often given to them (Ezek. iii. 17; xxxiii. 7; see Notes on Isa. lii. 8; lvi. 10). ¶ Which *shall never hold their peace.* The watches in the East are to this day performed by a loud cry as they go their rounds. This is done frequently in order to mark the time, and also to show that they are awake to their duty. 'The watchmen in the camp of the caravans go their rounds, crying one after another, "God is one, he is merciful;" and often add, "Take heed to yourselves."'—(Tavernier.) The truth here taught is, that they who are appointed to be the ministers of religion should be ever watchful and unceasing in the discharge of their duty. ¶ *Ye that make mention of the* LORD. Marg. 'That are the LORD's remembrancers.' These are evidently the words of the prophet addressing those who are watchmen, and urging them to do their duty, as he had said (ver. 1) he was resolved to do his.

7 And give him no [1] rest, till he
establish, and till he make Jerusalem a praise in the earth.
8 The LORD hath sworn by his
right hand, and by the arm of his
strength: Surely [2] I will no more
give thy corn *to be* meat for thine
enemies; and the sons of the
stranger shall not drink thy wine
for the which thou hast laboured.
9 But they that have gathered it
shall eat it, and praise the LORD;
and they that have brought it together shall drink it in the courts
of my holiness.

1 *silence.* 2 *If I give.*

Lowth renders this, 'O ye that proclaim the name of JEHOVAH.' Noyes, 'O ye that praise JEHOVAH.' But this does not express the sense of the original as well as the common version. The Hebrew word הַמַּזְכִּירִים, from זָכַר, *to remember*) means properly those bringing to remembrance, or causing to remember. It is a word frequently applied to the praise of God, or to the celebration of his worship (Ps. xx. 7; xxxviii. 1; xlv. 17; lxx. 1; cii. 12). In such instances the word does not mean that they who are engaged in his service *cause* JEHOVAH to *remember*, or bring things to his recollection which otherwise he would forget; but it means that they would keep up his remembrance among the people, or that they proclaimed his name in order that he might not be forgotten. This is the idea here. It is not merely that they were engaged in the worship of God; but it is, that they did this in order to keep up the remembrance of JEHOVAH among men. In this sense the ministers of religion are 'the remembrancers' of the Lord. ¶ *Keep not silence.* Heb. 'Let there be no silence to you.' That is, be constantly employed in public prayer and praise.

7. *And give him no rest.* Marg. 'Silence.' In Heb. the same word (דֳּמִי) as in ver. 6. The idea is, 'Keep not silence yourselves, nor let him rest in silence. Pray without ceasing; and do not intermit your efforts until the desires of your hearts shall be granted, and Zion shall be established, and the world saved.' ¶ *Till he establish.* Until he shall establish Jerusalem, and restore it to its former rank and privileges. ¶ *Till he make Jerusalem a praise in the earth.* That it may be the subject of universal commendation and rejoicing, instead of being an object of reproach and scorn. The truth taught here is, that it is the privilege and duty of the ministers of God to pray unceasingly for the extension of his kingdom. Day and night the voice of prayer is to be urged, and urged as if they would give JEHOVAH no rest until the desires of their hearts should be granted (comp. Luke xviii. 1, *sq.*)

8. *The* LORD *hath sworn by his right hand.* An oath was taken in various forms among the ancients. It was usually done by lifting up the hand toward heaven and appealing to God. As God could swear by no greater (Heb. vi. 13), he is represented as swearing by himself (see Notes on ch. xlv. 23). Here he is represented as swearing by his right hand and by his arm—the strong instrument by which he would accomplish his purposes to defend and save his people. The sense is, that he solemnly pledged the strength of his arm to deliver them, and restore them to their own land. ¶ *Surely I will no more give.* Marg. as in Heb. 'If I give.' That is, I will not give. ¶ *Thy corn* to be *meat.* The word 'corn' in the Scriptures means all kinds of grain—especially wheat, barley, &c. The word 'meat' was formerly used to denote all kinds of food, and was not restricted as it is now usually to animal food. The meaning is, that they should not be subjected to the evils of foreign invasion and conquest. ¶ *And the sons of the stranger.* Foreigners, ch. lx. 10. ¶ *Shall not drink thy wine.* The productions of your toil shall be safe, and you shall enjoy them yourselves. All this denotes a state of safety and prosperity, such as there would be if they were allowed to cultivate the soil without interruption, and were permitted to enjoy the fruit of their labours.

9. *But they that have gathered it shall eat it.* There shall be a state of security, so that every man may enjoy the avails of his own labour. Nothing is a more certain indication of liberty and pros-

10 Go through, go through the gates; prepare [a] ye the way of the people; cast up, cast up the highway; gather out the stones; lift up a standard [b] for the people.

a ch.57.14. b ch.18.3; Ex.17.15.

perity than this—that every man may securely enjoy the avails of his own labour. Nothing more certainly marks the advance of civilization, and nothing so much tends to encourage industry and to promote prosperity. When a man has no security that what he sows shall be reaped by himself; when there is danger that it will be destroyed or consumed by foreign invaders; or, when it is liable to be taken by arbitrary power to minister to the wants and luxuries of the great, there will be no industry, no incitement to labour. Such is the condition always in war. Such is the condition now in the Turkish dominions; and such is the state in savage life, and in all uncivilized communities. And as the tendency of true religion is to repress wars, to establish order, and to diffuse just views of the rights of man, it everywhere promotes prosperity by furnishing security that a man shall enjoy the avails of his own productive industry. Wherever the Christian religion prevails in its purity, there is seen the fulfilment of this prophecy; and the extension of that religion everywhere would promote universal industry, order, and law. ¶ *And praise the* LORD. They shall not consume it on their lusts, nor shall they partake of it without gratitude. God shall be acknowledged as the bountiful giver, and they shall render him appropriate thanksgiving. ¶ *And they that have brought it together.* They who have gathered in the vintage. ¶ *Shall drink it in the courts of my holiness.* It would be drank with gratitude to God in the feasts which were celebrated at the temple (see Lev. vi. 16; Deut. xii. 17, 18; xiv. 23). The idea is, that the effect of true religion would be to produce security and liberty, and to make men feel that all their blessings came from God; to partake of them with gratitude, and to make them the occasion of praise and thanksgiving.

10. *Go through, go through the gates.* The connection of this with what goes before is not very apparent, and there has been a great diversity of opinion in regard to it among interpreters. Grotius supposes that it refers to the priests and Levites who are referred to also in the previous verses, and that it is a command for them to enter into the temple. Calvin supposes that it refers to the Christian church, and that the idea is, that the gates of it should be continually open for the return of penitent sinners. Rosenmüller supposes that it is an address to the cities lying between Babylon and Jerusalem, and that the idea is, that their gates would be thrown open for the return of the exiles, and that all obstacles would be taken out of the way. Others suppose that it refers to the Jews, and that the command is to them to go through the gates of Babylon, and an immediate order is added to the people to prepare the way for them. This last seems to me to be the sense of the passage. It is a direction to the exiles in Babylon to go forth and return to their own land. The gates so long closed against their return would be thrown open, and they would now have liberty to depart for their own country. Thus explained, the connection is apparent. The watchmen were commanded to pray until this was done (ver. 7); the prophet had said that he would not rest until it was done (ver. 1); JEHOVAH had promised this in a most solemn manner (ver. 8, 9); and now those prayers are heard, and that promise is about to be fulfilled, and they are commanded to leave the city and enter upon their journey to their own land (comp. Notes on ch. lii. 10–12). ¶ *Prepare ye the way of the people* (comp. Notes on ch. xl. 3). ¶ *Cast up, cast up the highway* (see Notes on ch. lvii. 14). ¶ *Gather out the stones.* Clear it from the stones—in other words, make a smooth path on which they can travel with ease. The word which is here used (סָקַל) commonly denotes to stone, or to pelt with stones, a species of capital punishment among the Hebrews (2 Sam xvi. 6–13). Hence it means to pile up stones in a heap; and it has also the signification of removing stones from a field

11 Behold, the LORD hath proclaimed unto the end of the world,
Say ye to the daughter of Zion,
Behold, thy [a] salvation cometh;
behold, his reward [b] *is* with him,
and his [1] work before him.
12 And they shall call them,
The holy people, The redeemed of
the LORD: and thou shalt be called,
Sought [c] out, A city not forsaken.

a Zec.9.9; Jn.12.14,15. b Re.22.12. 1 or, *recompence.* c Eze.34.11-16.

CHAPTER LXIII.

ANALYSIS OF CHAPTERS LXIII., LXIV.

THIS chapter and the following relate to the same general subject, and should not have been separated. The subject with which they are introduced is the destruction of the enemies of God (lxiii. 1–6), and this is followed by tender expressions of confidence in JEHOVAH, and by earnest supplications, on the part of his people, that he would interpose in their behalf. The prophet sees in vision a magnificent conqueror, stained with the blood of his enemies, returning from Edom, and from its capital Bozrah—a warrior flushed with victory, unsubdued, unweakened, and coming with the pride and stateliness of conquest. Who he is, is the object of inquiry; and the answer is, that he is a great and holy deliverer. *Why* his gorgeous robes are thus polluted with blood, becomes also a question of intense anxiety. The reply of the conqueror is, that he has been forth to subdue mighty foes; that he went alone; that there was none that could aid; and that he had trodden them down as a treader of grapes treads in the wine-press. The whole image here is that of a triumphant, blood-stained warrior, returning from the conquest of Idumea.

(Isa. v. 2), and here of removing them from the way when they are an obstruction to the traveller. Harmer supposes that the word here means to pile up stones at proper distances, as a kind of landmark in the deserts, in order to mark the way for travellers—a practice which, he says, is quite common in Arabia. But the more correct interpretation is, that they were to remove the stones from the way, in order that the journey might be made with ease. ¶ *Lift up a standard.* As when an army is about to march. They were about to be collected from their dispersions and restored to their own land, and the command is given, that the banner might be reared that they might rally around it (see Notes on ch. x. 18; lix. 19; xlix. 22).

11. *Behold the* LORD *hath proclaimed.* Proclamation is made to all nations that JEHOVAH is about to come and rescue his people. ¶ *Say ye to the daughter of Zion.* To Jerusalem (see Notes on ch. i. 8). ¶ *Thy salvation cometh.* Lowth renders this, 'Lo! thy Saviour cometh.' So the Vulgate, the LXX., the Chaldee, and the Syriac. The Hebrew word properly means *salvation,* but the reference is to God as the Deliverer or Saviour. The immediate allusion is probably to the return from Babylon, but the remote and more important reference is to the coming of the Redeemer (see Notes on ch. xl. 1–10). ¶ *Behold, his reward is with him.* See these words explained in the Notes on ch. xl. 10.

12. *And they shall call them.* It shall be the honourable and just name by which they shall be known, that they are a holy people, and that they are the redeemed of JEHOVAH. No name is so honourable as that; no one conveys so much that is elevated and ennobling as to say of one, 'he is one whom JEHOVAH has redeemed from sin and death and hell by atoning blood.' He who has a just sense of the import of this name, will desire no other record to be made of his life—no other inscription on his tomb—than that he is ONE WHO HAS BEEN REDEEMED BY JEHOVAH. ¶ *And thou shalt be called* (see Notes on ver. 2). ¶ *Sought out.* The city much sought after, or much desired—to wit, by converts who shall come from afar; by foreigners who shall come to do thee honour (see ch. ii. 3; xl. 5, 6, 10, 11; xlix. 18–22). Or it may mean that Jerusalem would be a city sought out and desired by JEHOVAH; *i.e.,* no more forsaken by him. So Gesenius understands it. ¶ *A city not forsaken.* No longer given up to the invasions of a foreign enemy, and abandoned to long desolation. The idea is, that the church and people of God would be the object of his kind protecting care henceforward, and would enjoy his continued smiles.

Who is referred to here has been a question in which interpreters have greatly differed in opinion. The following are some of the opinions which have been expressed.

1. Some have referred it to Judas Maccabeus. This was the opinion of Grotius, who supposed that it was designed to represent his conquest of Idumea (1 Mac. v. 1–5; Jos. *Ant.* xii. 8. 1). But against this interpretation there are insuperable objections. (1.) The attributes of the person here referred to do not agree with him. How could he announce that he was the proclaimer of righteousness and was mighty to save? (2.) The exploits of Judas Maccabeus were not such as to justify the language which the prophet here uses. He overcame the Idumeans, and slew twenty thousand men, but this event is by no means adequate to the lofty prediction of the prophet. (3.) There is another objection suggested by Lowth to this supposition. It is that the Idumea of the time of Isaiah was quite a different country from that which was laid waste by Judas. In the time of Isaiah, Idumea was known as the country south of Palestine, whose capital at one time was Petra, and at another Bozrah. But during the captivity in Babylon, the Nabatheans invaded and conquered the southern part of Judea, and took possession of a great part of what was the territory of the tribe of Judah, and made Hebron the capital. This was the Idumea known in later times, and this was the Idumea that Judas Maccabeus conquered (1 Mac. v. 65).

2. One writer, referred to by Poole (*Synopsis*), supposes that the allusion is to *Michael*, who came to assist Daniel against the Prince of the kingdom of Persia (Dan. x. 13).

3. Others have referred it to JEHOVAH subduing his enemies, and restoring safety to his people. This is the opinion of Calvin, Piscator, Junius, Noyes, and Gesenius.

4. The mass of interpreters have referred it to the Messiah. This is the opinion, among the ancients, of Origen, Jerome, Cyril, Eusebius, and Procopius; and among the moderns, of Lowth, Cocceius—*of course*, Calovius, &c. But to this opinion Calvin makes the following weighty objection; 'Christians,' says he, 'have violently distorted this passage by referring it to Christ, when the prophet simply makes an announcement respecting God. And they have feigned that Christ was red because he was covered with his own blood, which he poured out on the cross. But the simple sense is, that the Lord here goes forth in the sight of his people with red garments, that all might understand that he was their vindicator and avenger.'—(*Comm. in loc.*) The objections to an immediate and direct application to Christ, seem to me to be insuperable. (1.) There is no reference to it in the New Testament as applicable to him. (2.) The blood with which the hero was stained, was not his own blood, but that of his foes; consequently all the applications of the words and phrases here to the Messiah as stained with his own blood are misplaced. (3.) The whole image of the prophet is that of a triumphant warrior, returning from conquest, himself unharmed and unwounded, not that of a meek and patient sufferer such as the Messiah. It is, therefore, not without the greatest perversion that it can be referred to the Messiah, nor should it be so employed.—[These objections against the application of the passage to the Messiah, seem to be fatal only to one aspect of it, viz., that which presents the Messiah as stained with his *own* blood; but though the warrior here very clearly appears stained with the blood of *others*, not his own, but the blood of vanquished foes, still that warrior *may* be the Messiah, and this one of the numerous passages in which he is represented as a victorious conqueror (Ps. xlv. 3; Rev. vi. 2; xix. 11–16). The beautiful *accommodation* of the language in the third verse to the sufferings of Christ, seems to have led to the forced application of the whole passage to the Redeemer's passion. It certainly refers, however, to a *conquering*, not a suffering, Messiah. Alexander supposes the conqueror to be JEHOVAH, or the Messiah; Henderson, the Divine Logos, the Angel or Messenger of the Divine presence, who acted as the Protector and Saviour of ancient Israel. Edom is generally taken as the type of the enemies of Israel, or of the church; and this prophecy announces their overthrow.—ED.]

5. Vitringa supposes that there is described under the emblem used here, the final and peremptory manner with which the Messiah, the vindicator and avenger of his people, will take severe vengeance, with the shedding of much blood, on the princes, people, subjects, and patrons of idolatrous and apostate Rome; that the true church on the earth would be reduced to extremities; would be destitute of protectors; and that the Messiah would interpose and by his own power destroy the foes of his people.

The whole passage (1–6) has a striking resemblance to ch. xxxiv., where the prophet predicts the overthrow of Idumea, and the long desolations that would come upon that country and people, and probably the same idea is intended to be conveyed by this which was by that—that all the enemies of the Jews would be destroyed (see the Analysis to ch. xxxix., and the Notes on that chapter). It is to be remembered that Idumea was a formidable foe to the Jews; that there had been frequent wars between them; and especially that they had greatly provoked the anger of the Hebrews, and deserved the severest Divine vengeance for uniting with the Chaldeans when they took Jerusalem, and for urging them to raze it to its foundation (Ps. cxxxvii. 7). On these accounts, Idumea was to be destroyed. Vengeance was to be taken on this foe; *and the destruction of Idumea became a kind of pledge and emblem of the destruction of all the enemies of the people of God.* Thus it is used here; and the prophet sees in vision JEHOVAH returning in triumph from the complete overthrow of the capital of that nation, and the entire destruction of the inhabitants. He sees the mighty warrior return from the conquest; his raiment stained with blood; and he inquires who he is, and receives for answer that he has been *alone* to the conquest of the foes of his people. The idea is, that all those foes would be destroyed, and that it would be done by the power of God alone. The chapter, therefore, I do not regard as immediately referring to the Messiah, but to JEHOVAH, and to his solemn purpose to destroy the enemies of his people, and to effect their complete deliverance.

It may be further remarked that the portion in ch. lxiii. 1–6, is a *responsive song;* a species of composition common in the Bible (see Ps. xxiv.; cxxxiv.; Cant. iii. 6).

The two chapters (lxiii., lxiv.) may be divided into three parts.

I. The destruction of Edom (ch. lxiii. 1–6). 1. The view of the conquering hero coming from Bozrah, and the inquiry by the people who he is (ver. 1, first part). He comes with dyed garments, yet glorious, and with the state and air of a conqueror. 2. The response of JEHOVAH the conqueror, that it was he who was mighty to save (1, last part). 3. The inquiry of the people why he was thus red in his apparel, as if he had been treading in the wine-press (2). 4. The answer of JEHOVAH (3–6). (1.) He had indeed trod the wine-press, and he had done it alone. He had trod down the people in his anger, and their blood had been sprinkled on his raiment. (2.) The day of his vengeance had arrived, and the year of his redeemed had come. (3.) No one had been able to do it, and he had gone forth alone, and had trod down their strength in his fury.

II. A hymn of thanksgiving in view of the deliverance wrought, and of the many mercies conferred on Israel (ch. lxiii. 7–14). 1. A general acknowledgment of his mercy (7). 2. His choice of them as his people (8). 3. His sympathy for them in all their trials (9). 4. His kindness and compassion, illustrated by a reference to his leading them through the wilderness, notwithstanding their ingratitude and sin (10–14).

III. An earnest supplication in view of the condition of Israel (ch. lxiii. 15–19; lxiv.) The arguments are very beautiful and various for his interposition. 1. An appeal to JEHOVAH in view of his former mercies (15). 2. An argument from the fact that he was their Father, though they should be disowned and despised by all others (16.) 3. Earnest intercession from the fact that his enemies had trodden down the sanctuary, and that those who never acknowledged him, ruled in the land that he had given to his own people (17–19). 4. An earnest pleading with God, in view of the inestimable value of the favours which he conferred—the fact that there was nothing so much to be desired, that the world could confer nothing that was to be compared with his favour (ch. lxiv. 1–5). 5. An argument derived from the general prevalence of irreligion among the people (ch. lxiv. 6, 7). 6. Tender and affectionate pleading from the fact that they were his people (ch. lxiv. 8, 9). 7. A tender and affectionate argument from the fact that the holy city was waste; the temple in ruins; and the beautiful house where their fathers worshipped had been burned up with fire (ch. lxiv. 10–12).

This last passage (ch. lxiv. 10–12), proves that the scene of this prayer and vision is laid in Babylon. The *time* is after Jerusalem had been destroyed, the temple fired, and their sacred things transported; after Edom had joined with the Chaldeans in demanding the entire destruction of the city and temple, and had urged them on to the work of destruction (Ps. cxxxvii. 7); after the Idumeans had invaded the territories of Judea, and established a kingdom there. In their exile they are represented as calling upon God, and they are assured that the kingdom of their enemies would be wholly destroyed.

WHO *is* this that cometh from Edom, with dyed garments from Bozrah? this *that is* [1] glorious in his apparel, travelling in the greatness of his strength? I that speak in righteousness, mighty to save.

1 *decked.*

CHAPTER LXIII.

1. *Who is this.* The language of the people who see JEHOVAH returning as a triumphant conqueror from Idumea.

2 Wherefore [a]*art thou* red in thine apparel, and thy garments like him that treadeth in the wine-fat?

a Re.19.13,15.

Struck with his stately bearing as a warrior; with his gorgeous apparel; and with the blood on his raiment, they ask who he could be? This is a striking instance of the bold and abrupt manner of Isaiah. He does not describe him as going forth to war nor the preparation for battle; nor the battle itself, nor the conquests of cities and armies; but he introduces at once the *returning* conqueror having gained the victory—here represented as a solitary warrior, moving along with majestic gait from Idumea to his own capital, Jerusalem. JEHOVAH is not unfrequently represented as a warrior (see Notes on ch. xlii. 13).* ¶ *From Edom.* On the situation of Edom, and for the reasons of the animosity between that country and Judea, see the Aanlysis to ch. xxxiv. ¶ *With dyed garments.* That is, with garments dyed in blood. The word here rendered 'dyed' (חָמוּץ *hhâmûtz*), is derived from חָמֵץ *hhâmătz, to be sharp* and *pungent,* and is usually applied to anything that is sharp or sour. It is applied to *colour* that is bright or dazzling, in the same manner as the Greeks use the phrase *χρῶμα ὀξύ*—*a sharp colour*—applied to purple or scarlet. Thus the phrase *πορφύραι ὀξύταται* means a brilliant, bright purple (see Bochart, *Hieroz.* i. 2. 7). It is applied to the military cloak which was worn by a warrior, and may denote here either that it was originally dyed of a scarlet colour, or more probably that it was *made* red by the blood that had been sprinkled on it. Thus in Rev. xix. 13, the Son of God is represented as clothed in a similar manner: 'And he was clothed with a vesture dipped in blood.' In ver. 3, the answer of JEHOVAH to the inquiry why his raiment was red, shows that the colour was to be attributed to blood. ¶ *From Bozrah.* On the situation of Bozrah, see Notes on ch. xxxiv. 6. It was for a time the principal city of Idumea, though properly lying within the boundaries of Moab. In ch. xxxiv. 6, JEHOVAH is represented as having 'a great sacrifice in Bozrah;' here he is seen as having come from it with his garments red with blood. ¶ *This* that is *glorious in his apparel.* Marg. 'Decked.' The Hebrew word (הָדוּר) means *adorned, honourable,* or *glorious.* The idea is, that his military apparel was gorgeous and magnificent—the apparel of an ancient warrior of high rank. ¶ *Travelling in the greatness of his strength.* Noyes renders this, 'Proud in the greatness of his strength,' in accordance with the signification given by Gesenius. The word here used (צָעָה) means properly *to turn to one side,* to incline, to be bent, bowed down as a captive in bonds (Isa. li. 14); then to bend or toss back the head as an indication of pride (Gesenius). According to Taylor (*Concord.*) the word has 'relation to the actions, the superb mien or manner of a triumphant warrior returning from battle, in which he has got a complete victory over his enemies. And it may include the pomp and high spirit with which he drives before him the prisoners which he has taken.' It occurs only in this place and in ch. li. 14; Jer. ii. 20; xlviii. 12. The LXX. omit it in their translation. The sense is doubtless that JEHOVAH is seen returning with the tread of a triumphant conqueror, flushed with victory, and entirely successful in having destroyed his foes. There is no evidence, however, as Taylor supposes, that he is driving his prisoners before him, for he is seen alone, having destroyed all his foes. ¶ *I that speak in righteousness.* The answer of the advancing conqueror. The sense is, 'It is I, JEHOVAH, who have promised to deliver my people and to destroy their enemies, and who have now returned from accomplishing my purpose.' The assurance that he speaks in righteousness, refers here to the promises which he had made that he would rescue and save them. ¶ *Mighty to save.* The sentiment is, that the fact that he destroys the foes of his people is an argument that he can save those

* See Supplementary Note in the *Analysis.*

3 I have trodden the wine-press alone; and of the people *there was* none with me: for I will tread them in mine anger, and trample them in my fury; and their blood shall be sprinkled upon my garments, and I will stain all my raiment.

---

who put their trust in him. The same power that destroys a sinner may save a saint; and the destruction of a sinner may be the means of the salvation of his own people.

2. *Wherefore* art thou *red?* The inquiry of the people. Whence is it that that gorgeous apparel is stained with blood? ¶ *And thy garment like him that treadeth in the wine-fat?* Or rather the 'wine-press.' The word here used (גַּת) means the place where the grapes were placed to be trodden with the feet, and from which the juice would flow off into a vat or receptacle. Of course the juice of the grape would stain the raiment of him who was employed in this business, and would give him the appearance of being covered with blood. 'The manner of pressing grapes,' says Burder, 'is as follows:—having placed them in a hogshead, a man with naked feet gets in and treads the grapes; in about an hour's time the juice is forced out; he then turns the lowest grapes uppermost, and treads them for about a quarter of an hour longer; this is sufficient to squeeze the good juice out of them, for an additional pressure would even crush the unripe grapes and give the whole a disagreeable flavour.' The following statement of the Rev. I. D. Paxton, in a letter from Beyrout, March 1, 1838, will show how the modern custom accords with that in the time of Isaiah:—'They have a large row of stone vats in which the grapes are thrown, and beside these are placed stone troughs, into which the juice flows. Men get in and tread the grapes with their feet. It is hard work, and their clothes are often stained with the juice. The figures found in Scripture taken from this are true to the life.' This method was also employed in Egypt. The presses there, as represented on some of the paintings at Thebes, consisted of two parts; the lower portion or vat, and the trough where the men with naked feet trod the fruit, supporting themselves by ropes suspended from the roof (see Wilkinson's *Ancient Egyptians*, ii. 155). Vitringa also notices the same custom.

Huc, pater O Lenæ, veni; nudataque musto
Tinge novo mecum direptis crura cothurnis.
Georg. ii. 7, 8.

This comparison is also beautifully used by John, Rev. xiv. 19, 20: 'And the

TREADING THE WINE-PRESS.
From a Sculpture at Thebes.

angel thrust in his sickle into the earth, and gathered the vine of the earth, and cast it into the great wine-press of the wrath of God. And the wine-press was trodden without the city, and blood came out of the wine-press even unto the horses' bridles.' And in Rev. xix. 15, 'And he treadeth the wine-press of the fierceness of the wrath of Almighty God.' The comparison of blood to wine is not uncommon. Thus in Deut. xxxii. 14, 'And thou didst drink the pure blood of the grape.' Calvin supposes that allusion is here made to the wine-press, because the country around Bozrah abounded with grapes.

3. *I have trodden the wine-press alone.* I, Jehovah, have indeed trod the wine-press of my wrath, and I have done it alone (comp. Notes on ch. xxxiv. 5, 6). The idea here is, that he had completely destroyed his foes in Idumea,

4 For the day [a] of vengeance *is*
in mine heart, and the year of my
redeemed is come.
5 And I looked, and *there was*
none to help; and I wondered
that *there was* none to uphold:
therefore mine own arm brought
salvation unto me; and my fury,
it upheld me.
6 And I will tread down the
people in mine anger, and make
them drunk [b] in my fury, and I
will bring down their strength to
the earth.

a Zep.3.8.

b Je.25.26,27.

and had done it by a great slaughter. ¶ *For I will tread.* Or rather, I trod them. It refers to what he had done; or what was then past. ¶ *And their blood shall be sprinkled.* Or rather, their blood *was* sprinkled. The word here used (נֵצַח) does not commonly mean blood; but splendour, glory, purity, truth, perpetuity, eternity. Gesenius derives the word, as used here, from an Arabic word meaning to sprinkle, to scatter; and hence the juice or liquor of the grape as it is sprinkled or spirted from grapes when trodden. There is no doubt here that it refers to blood—though with the idea of its being spirted out by treading down a foe. ¶ *And I will stain all my raiment.* I have stained all my raiment—referring to the fact that the slaughter was extensive and entire. On the extent of the slaughter, see Notes on ch. xxxiv. 6, 7, 9, 10.

4. *For the day of vengeance* (see Notes on ch. xxxiv. 8). ¶ *And the year of my redeemed is come.* The year when my people are to be redeemed. It is a year when their foes are all to be destroyed, and when their entire liberty is to be effected.

5. *And I looked and* there was *none to help.* The same sentiment is expressed in ch. lix. 16 (see the Notes on that verse). ¶ *None to uphold.* None to sustain or assist. The design is to express the fact that he was entirely alone in this work; that none were disposed or able to assist him. Though this has no direct reference to the plan of salvation, or to the work of the Messiah as a Redeemer, yet it is true of him also that in that work he stood alone. No one did aid him or could aid him; but alone he 'bore the burden of the world's atonement.' ¶ *My fury, it upheld me.* My determined purpose to inflict punishment on my foes sustained me. There is a reference doubtless to the fact that courage nerves the arm and sustains a man in deadly conflict; that a purpose to take vengeance, or to inflict deserved punishment, animates one to make efforts which he could not otherwise perform. In ch. lix. 16, the sentiment is, 'his *righteousness* sustained him;' here it is that *his fury* did it. There the purpose was to bring salvation; here it was to destroy his foes.

6. *And I will tread them down.* Or rather, 'I *did* tread them down.' The allusion here is to a warrior who tramples on his foes and treads them in the dust (see Notes on ch. xxv. 10). ¶ *And made them drunk.* That is, I made them reel and fall under my fury like a drunken man. In describing the destruction of Idumea in ch. xxxiv. 5, JEHOVAH says that his sword was made drunk, or that it rushed intoxicated from heaven. See Notes on that verse. But here he says that the people, under the terrors of his wrath, lost their power of self-command, and fell to the earth like an intoxicated man. Kimchi says that the idea is, that JEHOVAH extended the cup of his wrath for them to drink until they became intoxicated and fell. An image of this kind is several times used in the Scriptures (see Notes on ch. li. 17; comp. Ps. lxxv. 8). Lowth and Noyes render this, 'I crushed them.' The reason of this change is, that according to Kennicott, twenty-seven MSS. (three of them ancient) instead of the present Hebrew reading וָאֲשַׁכְּרֵם, 'And I will make them drunk,' read וָאֲשַׁבְּרֵם, 'I will break or crush them.' Such a change, it is true, might easily have been made from the similarity of the letters כ and ב. But the authority for the change does not seem to me to be sufficient, nor is it necessary. The image of making them stagger and fall

7 I will mention the [a] loving-kindnesses of the LORD, *and* the praises
of [b] the LORD, according to all that
the LORD hath bestowed on us, and
the great goodness towards the house
of Israel, which he hath bestowed on
them according to his mercies, and
according to the multitude of his
loving-kindnesses.
8 For he said, Surely they *are*
my people, children *that* will not
lie: so he was their Saviour.

[a] Ho.2.19. [b] Ps.63.4.

like a drunken man, is more poetic than the other, and is in entire accordance with the usual manner of writing by the sacred penman. The Chaldee renders it, 'I cast to the lowest earth the slain of their strong ones.' ¶ *And I will bring down their strength.* I subdued their strong places, and their mighty armies. Such is the sense given to the passage by our translators. But Lowth and Noyes render it, more correctly, 'I spilled their life-blood upon the ground.' The word which our translators have rendered 'strength' (נֵצַח), is the same word which is used in ver. 3, and which is there rendered 'blood' (see Notes on that verse). It is probably used in the same sense here, and means that JEHOVAH had brought their blood to the earth; that is, he had spilled it upon the ground. So the LXX. render it, 'I shed their blood (κατήγαγον τὸ αἷμα) upon the earth.' This finishes the vision of the mighty conqueror returning from Edom. The following verse introduces a new subject. The sentiment in the passage is, that JEHOVAH by his own power, and by the might of his own arm, would subdue all his foes and redeem his people. Edom, in its hostility to his people, the apt emblem of all his foes, would be completely humbled; and in its subjugation there would be the emblem and the pledge that all his enemies would be destroyed, and that his own church would be safe. See the Notes on ch. xxxiv., xxxv.

7. *I will mention.* This is evidently the language of the people celebrating the praises of God in view of all his mercies in former days. See the analysis to the chapter. The design of what follows, to the close of ch. lxiv., is to implore the mercy of God in view of their depressed and ruined condition. They are represented as suffering under the infliction of long and continued ills; as cast out and driven to a distant land; as deprived of their former privileges, and as having been long subjected to great evils. Their temple is destroyed; their city desolate; and their whole nation afflicted and oppressed. The *time* is probably near the close of the captivity; though Lowth supposes that it refers to the Jews as scattered over all lands, and driven away from the country of their fathers. They begin their petitions in this verse with acknowledging God's great mercies to their fathers and to their nation; then they confess their own disobedience, and supplicate, by various arguments, the Divine mercy and favour. The Chaldee commences the verse thus, 'The prophet said, I will remember the mercy of the Lord.' But it is the language of the people, not that of the prophet. The word rendered 'mention' (אַזְכִּיר), means properly, I will *cause* to remember, or to be remembered (see Notes on ch. lxii. 6). ¶ And *the praises of the* LORD. That is, I will recount the deeds which show that he is worthy of thanksgiving. The repetitions in this verse are designed to be emphatic; and the meaning of the whole is, that JEHOVAH had given them abundant cause of praise, notwithstanding the evils which they endured.

8. *For he said.* JEHOVAH had said. That is, he said this when he chose them as his peculiar people, and entered into solemn covenant with them. ¶ *Surely they* are *my people.* The reference here is to the fact that he entered into covenant with them to be their God. ¶ *Children* that *will not lie.* That will not prove false to me—indicating the reasonable expectation which JEHOVAH might have, when he chose them, that they would be faithful to him. ¶ *So he was their Saviour.* Lowth renders this, 'And he became their Saviour in all their distress;' connecting this with the first member of

9 In all their afflictions he [a] was afflicted, and the angel [b] of his presence saved them: in his love and in his pity he redeemed them: and he bare [c] them, and carried them all the days of old.

a Ju.10.16; Zec.2.8; Mat.25.40.45; Ac.9.4. b Ex.14.19. c De.32.11,12.

the following verse, and translating that, 'it was not an envoy, nor an angel of his presence that saved them.' So the LXX. render it, 'And he was to them for salvation (εἰς σωτηρίαν) from all their affliction.' The Chaldee render it, 'And his word was redemption (פָּרִיק) unto them.' But the true idea probably is, that he chose them, and *in virtue* of his thus choosing them he became their deliverer.

9. *In all their affliction he was afflicted.* This is a most beautiful sentiment, meaning that God sympathized with them in all their trials, and that he was ever ready to aid them. This sentiment accords well with the connection; but there has been some doubt whether this is the meaning of the Hebrew. Lowth renders it, as has been already remarked, 'It was not an envoy, nor an angel of his presence that saved him.' Noyes, 'In all their straits they had no distress.' The LXX. render it, 'It was not an ambassador (οὐ πρέσβυς), nor an angel (οὐδὲ ἄγγελος), but he himself saved them.' Instead of the present Hebrew word (צָר *tzār*, 'affliction'), they evidently read it, צִיר *tzīr*, 'a messenger.' The Chaldee renders it, 'Every time when they sinned against him, so that he might have brought upon them tribulation, he did not afflict them.' The Syriac, 'In all their calamities he did not afflict them.' This variety of translation has arisen from an uncertainty or ambiguity in the Hebrew text. Instead of the present reading (לֹא, 'not') about an equal number of MSS. read לוֹ, 'to him,' by the change of a single letter. According to the former reading, the sense would be, 'in all their affliction, there was *no* distress,' —*i.e.*, they were so comforted and supported by God, that they did not feel the force of the burden. According to the other mode of reading it, the sense would be, 'in all their affliction, there was affliction to him;' that is, he sympathized with them, and upheld them. Either reading makes good sense, and it is impossible now to ascertain which is correct. Gesenius supposes it to mean, 'In all their afflictions there would be actually no trouble to them. God sustained them, and the angel of of his presence supported and delivered them.' For a fuller view of the passage, see Rosenmüller. In the uncertainty and doubt in regard to the true reading of the Hebrew, the proper way is not to attempt to change the translation in our common version. It expresses an exceedingly interesting truth, and one that is fitted to comfort the people of God;—that he is never unmindful of their sufferings; that he feels deeply when they are afflicted; and that he hastens to their relief. It is an idea which occurs everywhere in the Bible, that God is not a cold, distant, abstract being; but that he takes the deepest interest in human affairs, and especially that he has a tender solicitude in all the trials of his people. ¶ *And the angel of his presence saved them.* This angel, called 'the angel of the presence of God,' is frequently mentioned as having conducted the children of Israel through the wilderness, and as having interposed to save them (Ex. xxiii. 20, 31; xxxii. 34; xxxiii. 2; Num. xx. 16). The phrase, 'the angel of his presence,' (Heb. מַלְאַךְ פָּנָיו, 'angel of his face,' or 'countenance'), means an angel that stands in his presence, and that enjoys his favour, as a man does who stands before a prince, or who is admitted constantly to his presence (comp. Prov. xxii. 29). Evidently there is reference here to an angel of superior order or rank, but to whom has been a matter of doubt with interpreters. Jarchi supposes that it was Michael, mentioned in Dan. x. 13–21. The Chaldee renders it, 'The angel *sent* (שְׁלִיחַ) from his presence.' Most Christian interpreters have supposed that the reference is to the Messiah, as the manifested guide and defender of the children of Israel during their long journey in the desert. This is not the place to go

10 But they rebelled, and vexed his [a] Holy Spirit: therefore he was turned to be their enemy, [b] *and* he fought against them.

[a] Ac.7.51; Ep.4.30.

[b] La.2.5.

into a *theological* examination of that question. The sense of the Hebrew here is, that it was a messenger sent from the immediate presence of God, and therefore of elevated rank. The opinion that it was the Son of God is one that can be sustained by arguments that are not easily refuted. On the subject of angels, according to the Scripture doctrine, the reader may consult with advantage an article by Dr. Lewis Mayer, in the *Bib. Rep.*, Oct. 1388. ¶ *He redeemed them* (see Notes on ch. xliii. 1). ¶ *And he bare them.* As a shepherd carries the lambs of the flock, or as a nurse carries her children; or still more probably, as an eagle bears her young on her wings (Deut. xxxii. 11, 12). The idea is, that he conducted them through all their trials in the wilderness, and led them in safety to the promised land (comp. Notes on ch. xl. 11). ¶ *All the days of old.* In all their former history. He has been with them and protected them in all their trials.

10. *But they rebelled.* Against God. This charge is often made against the Jews; and indeed their history is little more than a record of a series of rebellions against God. ¶ *And vexed.* Or rather 'grieved.' The Heb. word עָצַב, in Piel, means *to pain, to afflict, to grieve.* This is the idea here. Their conduct was such as *was fitted* to produce the deepest pain—for there is nothing which we more deeply feel than the ingratitude of those who have been benefited by us. Our translators have supposed that the word conveyed the idea of *provoking to wrath* by their conduct (thus the LXX. render it παρώξυναν τὸ πνεύμα, κ.τ.λ.); but the more appropriate sense is, that their conduct was such as to produce pain or grief. Comp. Eph. iv. 30: 'Grieve not (μὴ λυπεῖτε) the Holy Spirit.' Ps. lxxviii. 40; xcv. 10. Heb. iii. 10–17. ¶ *His Holy Spirit.* The Chaldee renders this, 'But they were unwilling to obey, and they irritated (provoked, blasphemed רְגַז) against the words of the prophets.' But the reference seems rather to be to the Spirit of God that renewed, comforted, enlightened, and sanctified them. Grotius, Rosenmüller, and Gesenius, suppose that this means God himself—a Spirit of holiness. But, with the revelation of the New Testament before us, we cannot well doubt that the real reference here is to the third person of the Trinity—the renewer and sanctifier of the people of God. It may be admitted, perhaps, that the ancient Hebrews would refer this to God himself, and that their views of the offices of the different persons in the Divine nature were not very clearly marked, or very distinct. But this does not prove that the *real* reference may not have been to 'the Holy Ghost.' The renewer and sanctifier of the human heart at all times has been the same. And when any operations of the mind and heart pertaining to salvation are referred to in the Old Testament, nothing should forbid us to apply to the explanation of the expressions and the facts, the clear light which we have in the New Testament—in the same way as when the ancients speak of phenomena in the physical world, we deem it not improper to apply to the explanation of them the established doctrines which we now have in the physical sciences. By this we by no means design to say that the ancients had the same knowledge which we have, or that the language which they used conveyed the same idea to them which it now does to us, but that the events occurred in accordance with the laws which we now understand, and that the language may be explained by the light of modern science. Thus the word *eclipse* conveyed to them a somewhat different idea from what it does to us. They supposed it was produced by different causes. Still they described accurately *the facts in the case;* and to the explanation of those facts we are permitted now to apply the principles of modern science. So the Old Testament describes *facts* occurring under the influence of truth. The facts were

11 Then he remembered [a] the
days of old, Moses *and* his people,
saying, Where *is* he that brought
them up out of the sea with the
shepherd [1] of his flock? where *is*
he that put his Holy Spirit [b] within
him?

[a] Le.26.42. [1] or, *shepherds.* [b] Nu.11.17,25; Ne.9.20.

clearly understood. What shall hinder us, in explaining them, from applying the clearer light of the New Testament? Admitting this obvious principle, I suppose that the reference here was really to the third person of the Trinity; and that the sense is, that their conduct was such as was fitted to cause grief to their Sanctifier and Comforter, in the same way as it is said in the New Testament that this is done now. ¶ *He was turned.* He abandoned them for their sins, and left them to reap the consequences. ¶ And *he fought against them.* He favoured their enemies and gave them the victory. He gave them up to a series of disasters which finally terminated in their long and painful captivity, and in the destruction of their temple, city, and nation. The sentiment is, that when we grieve the Spirit of God, he abandons us to our chosen course, and leaves us to a series of spiritual and temporal disasters.

11. *Then he remembered.* He did not forget his solemn promises to be their protector and their God. For their crimes they were subjected to punishment, but God did not forget that they were his people, nor that he had entered into covenant with them. The object of this part of the petition seems to be, to recall the fact that in former times God had never wholly forsaken them, and to plead that the same thing might occur now. Even in the darkest days of adversity, God still remembered his promises, and interposed to save them. Such they trusted it would be still. ¶ *Moses* and *his people.* Lowth renders this, 'Moses his servant,' supposing that a change had occurred in the Hebrew text. It would be natural indeed to suppose that the word 'servant' would occur here (see the Hebrew), but the authority is not sufficient for the change. The idea seems to be that which is in our translation, and which is approved by Vitringa and Gesenius. 'He recalled the ancient days when he led Moses *and* his people through the sea and the wilderness.' ¶ *Where* is *he.* The Chaldee renders this, 'Lest they should say, Where is he?' that is, lest surrounding nations should ask in contempt and scorn, Where is the protector of the people, who defended them in other times? According to this, the sense is that God remembered the times of Moses and interposed, *lest* his not doing it should bring reproach upon his name and cause. Lowth renders it, 'How he brought them up;' that is, he recollected his former interposition. But the true idea is that of one asking a question. 'Where now is the God that formerly appeared for their aid?' And though it is the language of God himself, yet it indicates that state of mind which arises when the question is asked, Where is now the former protector and God of the people? ¶ *That brought them up out of the sea.* The Red Sea, when he delivered them from Egypt. This fact is the subject of a constant reference in the Scriptures, when the sacred writers would illustrate the goodness of God in any great and signal deliverance. ¶ *With the shepherd of his flock.* Marg. 'Shepherds.' Lowth and Noyes render this in the singular, supposing it to refer to Moses. The LXX., Chaldee, and Syriac, also read it in the singular. The Hebrew is in the plural (רֹעֵי), though some MSS. read it in the singular. If it is to be read in the plural, as the great majority of MSS. read it, it probably refers to Moses *and* Aaron as the shepherds or guides of the people. Or it may also include others, meaning that JEHOVAH led up the people with *all* their rulers and guides. ¶ *Where* is *he that put his Holy Spirit within him?* (see Notes on ver. 10). Heb. בְּקִרְבּוֹ—'In the midst of him,' *i.e.*, in the midst of the people or the flock. They were then under his guidance and sanctifying influence. The generation which was led to the land of Canaan was eminently pious, perhaps more so than any other of the people of Israel (comp. Josh. xxiv. 31; Judg. ii. 6–10).

12 That led *them* by the right
hand of Moses with his glorious
arm, dividing the [a]water before
them, to make himself an everlasting name?
13 That led them through the
deep, as an horse in the wilderness,
that they should not stumble?
14 As a beast goeth down into
the valley, the Spirit of the LORD
caused him to rest, so didst thou
lead thy people, to [b]make thyself
a glorious name.

a Ex.14.21,&c. b 2 Sa.7.23.

The idea here is, that God, who then gave his Holy Spirit, had seemed to forsake them. The nation seemed to be abandoned to wickedness; and in this state, God remembered how he had formerly chosen and sanctified them; and he proposed again to impart to them the same Spirit.

12. *That led* them *by the right hand of Moses* (see Notes on ch. xli. 10–13; xlv. 1). ¶ *Dividing the water before them* (Ex. xiv. 21). ¶ *To make himself an everlasting name.* He designed to perform a work which, it would be seen, could not be performed by any false god or by any human arm, and to do it in such circumstances, and in such a manner, that it might be seen everywhere that this was the true God (comp. Notes on ch. xlv. 6). The deliverance from Egypt was attended with such amazing miracles, and with such a sudden destruction of his foes, that none but the true God could have performed it. Egypt was at that time the centre of all the science, civilization, and art known among men; and what occurred there would be known to other lands. God, therefore, in this signal manner, designed to make a public demonstration of his existence and power that shall be known in all lands, and that should never be forgotten.

13. *That led them through the deep.* They went through the deep on dry land—the waters having divided and left an unobstructed path. ¶ *As an horse in the wilderness.* As an horse, or a courser, goes through a desert without stumbling. This is a most beautiful image. The reference is to vast level plains like those in Arabia, where there are no stones, no trees, no gullies, no obstacles, and where a fleet courser bounds over the plain without any danger of stumbling. So the Israelites were led on their way without falling. All obstacles were removed, and they were led along as if over a vast smooth plain. Our word 'wilderness,' by no means expresses the idea here. We apply it to uncultivated regions that are covered with trees, and where there would be numerous obstacles to such a race-horse. But the Hebrew word (מִדְבָּר) rather refers to *a desert*, a waste—a place of level sands or plains where there was nothing to obstruct the fleet courser that should prance over them. Such is probably the meaning of this passage, but Harmer (*Obs.* i. 161, *sq.*) may be consulted for another view, which may possibly be the correct one.

14. *As a beast that goeth down into the valley.* As a herd of cattle in the heat of the day descends into the shady glen in order to find rest. In the vale, streams of water usually flow. By those streams and fountains trees grow luxuriantly, and these furnish a cool and refreshing shade. The cattle, therefore, in the heat of the day, naturally descend from the hills, where there are no fountains and streams, and where they are exposed to an intense sun, to seek refreshment in the shade of the valley. The figure here is that of resting in safety after exposure; and there are few more poetic and beautiful images of comfort than that furnished by cattle lying quietly and safely in the cool shade of a well-watered vale. This image would be much more striking in the intense heat of an Oriental climate than it is with us. Harmer (*Obs.* i. 168, *sq.*) supposes that the allusion here is to the custom prevailing still among the Arabs, when attacked by enemies, of withdrawing with their herds and flocks to some sequestered vale in the deserts, where they find safety. The idea, according to him, is, that Israel lay thus safely encamped in the wilderness; that they, with their flocks and herds and riches, were suffered to remain unattacked by the king of Egypt; and that this was

15 Look down from heaven, and behold from the habitation [a] of thy holiness and of thy glory; where *is* thy zeal and thy strength, the sounding[1] of thy bowels [b] and of thy mercies towards me? are they restrained?

16 Doubtless thou *art* our Father, though Abraham be ignorant of us, and Israel acknowledge us not: thou, O LORD, *art* our Father, [2] our Redeemer: thy name *is* from everlasting.

[a] 2 Ch.30.27. 1 or, *multitude.* [b] Je.31.20; Ho.11.8. 2 or, *our Redeemer, from everlasting is thy name.*

a state of grateful repose, like that which a herd feels after having been closely pursued by an enemy, when it finds a safe retreat in some quiet vale. But it seems to me that the idea first suggested is the most correct—as it is, undoubtedly the most poetical and beautiful—of a herd of cattle leaving the hills, and seeking a cooling shade and quiet retreat in a well-watered vale. Such repose, such calm, gentle, undisturbed rest, God gave his people. Such he gives them now, amidst sultry suns and storms, as they pass through the world. ¶ *The Spirit of the* LORD (see on ver. 10). ¶ *So didst thou lead.* That is, dividing the sea, delivering them from their foes, and leading them calmly and securely on to the land of rest. So now, amidst dangers seen and unseen, God leads his people on toward heaven. He removes the obstacles in their way; he subdues their foes; he 'makes them to lie down in green pastures, and leads them beside the still waters' (Ps. xxiii. 2); and he bears them forward to a world of perfect peace.

15. *Look down from heaven.* This commences an earnest appeal that God would have mercy on them in their present calamities and trials. They entreat him to remember his former mercies, and to return and bless them, as he had done in ancient times. ¶ *And behold from the habitation* (see Notes on ch. lvii. 15). ¶ *Where* is *thy zeal.* That is, thy former zeal for thy people; where is now the proof of the interest for their welfare which was vouchsafed in times that are past. ¶ *And thy strength.* The might which was formerly manifested for their deliverance and salvation. ¶ *The sounding of thy bowels.* Marg. 'Multitude.' The word rendered 'sounding' (הָמוֹן), means properly a noise or sound, as of rain, 1 Kings xviii. 41; of singing, Ezek. xxvi. 13; of a multitude, 1 Sam. iv. 14, xiv. 19. It also means a multitude, or a crowd of men (Isa. xiii. 4; xxxiii. 3). Here it relates to an emotion or affection of the mind; and the phrase denotes compassion, or tender concern for them in their sufferings. It is derived from the customary expression in the Bible that the bowels, *i.e.*, the organs in the region of the chest—for so the word is used in the Scriptures—were the seat of the emotions, and were supposed to be affected by any strong and tender emotion of the mind (see Notes on ch. xvi. 11). The idea here is, 'Where is thy former compassion for thy people in distress?' ¶ *Are they restrained?* Are they withheld? Are thy mercies to be exercised no more?

16. *Doubtless.* Heb. כִּי—'For; verily; surely. It implies the utmost confidence that he still retained the feelings of a tender father. ¶ *Thou* art *our father.* Notwithstanding appearances to the contrary, and though we should be disowned by all others, we will still believe that thou dost sustain the relation of a father. Though they saw no human aid, yet their confidence was unwavering that he had still tender compassion towards them. ¶ *Though Abraham be ignorant of us.* Abraham was the father of the nation—their pious and much venerated ancestor. His memory they cherished with the deepest affection, and him they venerated as the illustrious patriarch whose name all were accustomed to speak with reverence. The idea here is, that though *even such a man*—one so holy, and so much venerated and loved—should refuse to own them as his children, yet that God would not forget his paternal relation to them. A similar expression of his unwavering love occurs in ch. xlix. 15: 'Can a woman forget her sucking child?' See Notes on that place. The language here expresses the

17 O LORD, why hast thou made
us to err [a] from thy ways, *and* hardened [b] our heart from thy fear? Return [c] for thy servants' sake, the
tribes of thine inheritance.

a Ps.119.10. *b* ch.6.10; Ro.9.17,18. *c* Ps.90.13.

unwavering conviction of the pious, that God's love for his people would never change; that it would live when even the most tender earthly ties are broken, and when calamities so thicken around us that we *seem* to be forsaken by God; and *are* forsaken by our *sunshine* friends, and even by our most tender earthly connections. ¶ *And Israel acknowledge us not.* And though Jacob, another much honoured and venerated patriarch, should refuse to recognize us as his children. The Jewish expositors say, that the reason why Abraham and Jacob are mentioned here and Isaac omitted, is, that Abraham was the first of the patriarchs, and that all the posterity of Jacob was admitted to the privileges of the covenant, which was not true of Isaac. The sentiment here is, that we should have unwavering confidence in God. We should confide in him though all earthly friends refuse to own us, and cast out our names as evil. Though father and mother and kindred refuse to acknowledge us, yet we should believe that God is our unchanging friend; and it is of more value to have such a friend than to have the most honoured earthly ancestry and the affections of the nearest earthly relatives. How often have the people of God been called to experience this! How many times in the midst of persecution; when forsaken by father and mother; when given up to a cruel death on account of their attachment to the Redeemer, have they had occasion to recall this beautiful sentiment, and how unfailingly have they found it to be true! Forsaken and despised; cast out and rejected; abandoned apparently by God and by men, they have yet found, in the arms of their heavenly Father, a consolation which this world could not destroy, and have experienced his tender compassions attending them even down to the grave. ¶ *Our Redeemer.* Marg. 'Our Redeemer, from everlasting is thy name.' The Heb. will bear either construction. Lowth renders it, very loosely, in accordance with the reading of *one* ancient MS., 'O deliver us, for the sake of thy name.' Probably the idea is that which results from a deeply affecting and tender view of God as the Redeemer of his people. The heart, overflowing with emotion, meditates upon the eternal honours of his name, and is disposed to ascribe to him everlasting praise.

17. *O* LORD, *why hast thou made us to err from thy ways?* Lowth and Noyes render this, 'Why dost thou suffer us to wander from thy way?' Calvin remarks on the passage, 'The prophet uses a common form of speaking, for it is usual in the Scriptures to say that God gives the wicked over to a reprobate mind, and hardens their hearts. But when the pious thus speak, they do not intend to make God the author of error or sin, as if they were innocent —*nolunt Deum erroris aut sceleris facere auctorem, quasi sint innoxii*—or to take away their own blameworthiness. But they rather look deeper, and confess themselves, by their own fault, to be alienated from God, and destitute of his Spirit; and hence it happens that they are precipitated into all manner of evils. God is said to harden and blind when he delivers those who are to be blinded to Satan (*Satanæ excæcandos tradit*), who is the minister and the executor of his wrath.'—(*Comm. in loc.*) This seems to be a fair account of this difficult subject. At all events, this is the doctrine which was held by the father of the system of Calvinism; and nothing more should be charged on that system, in regard to blinding and hardening men, than is thus avowed (comp. Notes on ch. vi. 9, 10; Matt. xiii. 14, 15). It is not to be supposed that this result took place by direct Divine agency. It is not by positive power exerted to harden men and turn them away from God. No man who has any just views of God can suppose that he exerts a positive agency to make them sin, and then punishes them for it; no one who has any just views of man, and of the operations of his own mind, can doubt that a sinner is voluntary in his transgression. It is true, at the same time,

18 The people of thy holiness have possessed *it* but a little while: our adversaries have trodden down thy[a] sanctuary.

a Ps.74.6-8.

that God foresaw it, and that he did not interpose to prevent it. Nay, it is true that the wickedness of men may be favoured by his abused providence—as a pirate may take advantage of a fair breeze that God sends, to capture a merchant-man; and true, also, that God foresaw it would be so, and yet chose, on the whole, that the events of his providence should be so ordered. His providential arrangements might be abused to the destruction of a few, but would tend to benefit and save many. The fresh gale that drove on one piratical vessel to crime and bloodshed, might, at the same time, convey many richly freighted ships towards the port. One might suffer; hundreds might rejoice. One pirate might be rendered successful in the commission of crime; hundreds of honest men might be benefited. The providential arrangement is not to *compel* men to sin, nor is it *for the sake* of their sinning. It is to do good, and to benefit many—though this may draw along, as a consequence, the hardening and the destruction of a few. He might, by direct agency, prevent it, as he might prevent the growth of the briers and thorns in a field; but the same arrangement, by withholding suns and dews and rains, would *also* prevent the growth of flowers and corn and fruit, and turn extended fertile lands into a desert. It is better that the thorns and briers should be suffered to grow, than to convert those fields into a barren waste. ¶ *Return.* That is, return to bless us. ¶ *The tribes of thine inheritance.* The Jewish tribes spoken of as the heritage of God on the earth.

18. *The people of thy holiness.* The people who have been received into solemn covenant with thee. ¶ *Have possessed* it *but a little while.* That is, the land—meaning that the time during which they had enjoyed a peaceable possession of it, compared with the perpetuity of the promise made, was short. Such is the idea given to the passage by our translators. But there is considerable variety in the interpretation of the passage among expositors. Lowth renders it:

> It is little, that they have taken possession of thy holy mountain;
> That our enemies have trodden down thy sanctuary.

Jerome renders it, 'It is as nothing (*quasi nihilum*), they possess thy holy people; our enemies have trodden down thy sanctuary.' The LXX. render it, 'Return on account of thy servants, on account of the tribes of thine inheritance, that we may inherit thy holy mountains for a little time' (*ἵνα μικρὸν κληρονομήσωμεν τοῦ ὄρους τοῦ ἁγίου*). It has been generally felt that there was great difficulty in the place. See Vitringa. The sense seems to be that which occurs in our translation. The design is to furnish an argument for the Divine interposition, and the meaning of the two verses may be expressed in the following paraphrase:—'We implore thee to return unto us, and to put away thy wrath. As a reason for this, we urge that thy temple—thy holy sanctuary—was possessed by thy people but a little time. For a brief period there we offered praise, and met with our God, and enjoyed his favour. Now thine enemies trample it down. They have come up and taken the land, and destroyed thy holy place (ch. lxiv. 11). We plead for thine interposition, because we are thy covenant people. Of old we have been thine. But as for them, they were never thine. They never yielded to thy laws. They were never called by thy name. There is, then, no reason why the temple and the land should be in their possession, and we earnestly pray that it may be restored to the tribes of thine ancient inheritance.' ¶ *Our adversaries.* This whole prayer is *supposed* to be offered by the exiles near the close of their captivity. Of course the language is such as they would *then* use. The scene is laid in Babylon, and the object is to express the feelings which they would have then, and to furnish the model for the petitions which they would then urge. We are not, therefore, to suppose that the temple when Isaiah lived and

19 We are *thine:* thou never barest rule over them; [1] they were not called by thy name.

1 or, *thy name was not called upon them.*

CHAPTER LXIV.

For an analysis of this chapter, see the Analysis prefixed to ch. lxiii. This chapter is closely connected with that in its design, and should not have been separated from it. This is one of the many instances where the division seems to have been made without any intelligent view of the scope of the sacred writer.

OH [a] that thou wouldest rend the heavens, that thou wouldest come down, that the mountains might [b] flow down at thy presence,

a Ps.144.5. *b* Ju.5.5.

---

wrote was in ruins, and the land in the possession of his foes. All this is seen in vision; and though a hundred and fifty years would occur before it would be realized, yet, according to the prophetic manner, he describes the scene as actually passing before him (see Introd. § 7; comp. Notes on ch. lxiv. 11).

19. *We are* thine. We urge it as a reason for thy interposition to restore the land and the temple, that we are thine from ancient times. Such I take to be the meaning of the passage—in accordance with the common translation, except that the expression מֵעוֹלָם, 'from ancient times,' rendered by our translators in connection with לֹא, 'never,' is thus connected with the Jewish people, instead of being regarded as applied to their enemies. The idea is, that it is an *argument* why God should interpose in their behalf, that they had been for a long time his people, but that his foes, who then had possession of the land, had never submitted to his laws. There has been, however, great variety in interpreting the passage. Lowth renders it:

We have long been as those whom thou hast not ruled;
We have not been called by thy name.

Noyes renders it better:

It has been with us as if thou hadst never ruled over us,
As if we had not been called by thy name.

Symmachus and the Arabic Saadias render it in the same manner. The LXX. render it, 'We have been as at the beginning when thou didst not rule over us, neither were we called by thy name;' that is, we have gone back practically to our former heathen condition, by rejecting thy laws, and by breaking thy covenant. Each of these interpretations makes a consistent sense, but it seems to me that the one which I have expressed above is more in accordance with the Hebrew. ¶ *Thou never barest rule over them.* Over our enemies—regarded in the prophetic vision as then in possession of the land. The idea is, that they have come into thy land by violence, and laid waste a nation where they had no right to claim any jurisdiction, and have now no claim to thy protection. ¶ *They were not called by thy name.* Heb. 'Thy name was not called upon them.' They were aliens and strangers who had unjustly intruded into the heritage of the Lord.

CHAPTER LXIV.

1. *Oh that thou wouldest rend the heavens.* That is, in view of the considerations urged in the previous chapter. In view of the fact that the temple is burned up (ver. 11); that the city is desolate; that the land lies waste, and that thine own people are carried captive to a distant land. The phrase 'rend the heavens,' implies a sudden and sublime descent of Jehovah to execute vengeance on his foes, as if his heart was full of vengeance, and the firmament were violently rent asunder at his sudden appearance. It is language properly expressive of a purpose to execute wrath on his foes, rather than to confer blessings on his people. The latter is more appropriately expressed by the heavens being gently opened to make way for the descending blessings. The word here rendered 'rend' (קָרַע), means properly *to tear asunder,* as, *e.g.*, the garments in grief (Gen. xxxvii. 29; 2 Sam. xiii. 31); or as a wild beast does the breast of any one (Hos. xiii. 8). The LXX., however, render it by a milder word—ἀνοίξῃς—'If thou wouldst *open* the heavens,' &c. So the Syriac renders it by 'O that thou wouldst *open*,' using a word that is usually applied to

2 As *when* the [1]melting fire burneth, the fire causeth the waters to boil; to make thy name known to thine adversaries, *that* the nations may tremble at thy presence!

[1] *the fire of meltings.*

---

the opening of a door. God is often represented as coming down from heaven in a sublime manner amidst tempests, fire, and storms, to take vengeance on his foes. Thus Ps. xviii. 9:

He bowed the heavens also and came down;
And darkness was under his feet.

Comp. Hab. iii. 5, 6. It should be remembered that the main idea in the passage before us is that of JEHOVAH coming down to destroy his foes. His people entreat him to descend with the proofs of his indignation, so that every obstacle shall be destroyed before him, Thus he is described in Ps. cxliv. 5, 6:

Bow thy heavens, O Lord, and come down;
Touch the mountains, and they shall smoke;
Cast forth lightning, and scatter them,
Shoot out thine arrows, and destroy them.

¶ *That the mountains might flow down at thy presence.* The idea here is, that the presence of JEHOVAH would be like an intense burning heat, so that the mountains would melt and flow away. It is a most sublime description of his majesty, and is one that is several times employed in the Bible. Thus in relation to his appearance on Mount Sinai, in the song of Deborah (Judg. v. 4, 5):

The earth trembled and the heavens dropped,
The clouds also dropped water.
The mountains melted from before JEHOVAH,
Even Sinai from before JEHOVAH, the God of Israel.

So Ps. xcvii. 5:

The hills melted like wax at the presence of JEHOVAH,
At the presence of JEHOVAH [the God] of the whole earth.

So also in Micah i. 3, 4:

Lo, JEHOVAH cometh forth out of his place,
And will come down and tread upon the high places of the earth,
And the mountains shall be molten under him.
And the valleys shall be cleft,
As wax before the fire,
And as the waters pour down a precipice.

2. *As* when *the melting fire burneth.* Marg. 'The fire of meltings.' Lowth renders it, 'As when the fire kindleth the dry fuel.' So Noyes, 'As fire kindleth the dry stubble.' The LXX. render it, Ὡς κηρὸς ἀπὸ προσώπου πυρὸς τήκεται—'As wax is melted before the fire.' So the Syriac renders it. The Hebrew word rendered here in the margin 'meltings' (הֲמָסִים), properly means, according to Gesenius, *brushwood, twigs.* So Saadias renders it. And the true idea here is, that the presence of JEHOVAH would cause the mountains to melt, as a fire consumes light and dry brushwood or stubble. Dr. Jubb supposes that the meaning is, 'As the fire of things *smelted* burneth'—an idea which would furnish a striking comparison, but there is much doubt whether the Hebrew will bear that construction. The comparison is a very vivid and sublime one, as it is in the view given above—that the presence of JEHOVAH would set on fire the mountains, and cause them to flow down as under the operation of an intense heat. I do not know that there is reason to suppose that the prophet had any reference to a volcanic eruption, or that he was acquainted with such a phenomenon—though Syria and Palestine abounded in volcanic appearances, and the country around the Dead Sea is evidently volcanic (see Lyell's *Geology*, i. 299); but the following description may furnish *an illustration* of what would be exhibited by the flowing down of the mountains at the presence of JEHOVAH, and may serve to show the force of the language which the prophet employs in these verses. It is a description of an eruption of Vesuvius in 1779, by Sir William Hamilton. 'Jets of liquid lava,' says he, 'mixed with stones and scoriæ, were thrown up to the height of at least 10,000 feet, having the appearance of a column of fire. The falling matter being nearly as vividly inflamed as that which was continually issuing forth from the crater, formed with it one complete body of fire, which could not be less than two miles and a half in breadth, and of the extraordinary height above mentioned, casting a heat to the distance of at least six miles around it.' Speaking of the lava which flowed from the mountain, he says, 'At the point where it issued from an arched chasm in the side of the mountain, the vivid torrent rushed with

3 When thou didst [a]terrible things
which we looked not for, thou camest
down, [b]the mountains flowed down
at thy presence.
4 For [c]since the beginning of the
world *men* have not heard, nor perceived by the ear, neither hath the
eye [1]seen, O God, besides thee,
what he hath prepared for him
that waiteth for him.

a Ps.65.5. b Ha.3.3,6. c 1 Co.2.9.

1 or, *seen a God beside thee* which *doeth so for him.*

the velocity of a flood. It was in perfect fusion, unattended with any scoriæ on its surface, or any gross material not in a state of complete solution. It flowed with the translucency of honey, in regular channels, cut finer than art can imitate, and glowing with all the splendour of the sun.'—(Lyell's *Geology*, i. 316.) Perhaps there can be conceived no more sublime representation of what was in the mind of the prophet than such an overflowing volcano. It should be observed, however, that Gesenius supposes that the word which is rendered (ver. 1–3), 'flow down' (נָזֹלּוּ), is derived, not from נָזַל *nâzăl, to flow*, to run as liquids do; but from זָלַל *zâlăl, to shake*, to tremble, to quake as mountains do in an earthquake. But it seems to me that the connection rather demands the former signification, as the principal elements in the figure *is fire*—and the office of fire is not to cause to tremble, but to burn or melt. The effect here described as illustrative of the presence of God, was that produced by intense burning heat. ¶ *The fire causeth the waters to boil.* Such an effect was anticipated at the presence of Jehovah. The idea is still that of an intense heat, that should cause all obstacles to be consumed before the presence of the Lord. To illustrate this, the prophet speaks of that which is known to be most intense, that which causes water to boil; and the prayer is, that Jehovah would descend in the manner of such intense and glowing fire, in order that all the foes of the people might be destroyed, and all the obstacles to the restoration of his people removed. The exact point of the comparison, as I conceive, is the *intensity* of the heat, as emblematic of the majesty of Jehovah, and of the certain destruction of his foes. ¶ *To make thy name known.* By the exhibition of thy majesty and glory.

3. *When thou didst terrible things.* In delivering the people from Egypt, and in conducting them to the promised land. ¶ Which *we looked not for.* Which we had never before witnessed, and which we had no right to expect. ¶ *Thou camest down.* As on Mount Sinai. ¶ *The mountains flowed down* (see Notes above). The reference is to the manifestations of smoke and fire when Jehovah descended on Mount Sinai (see Ex. xix. 18).

4. *For since the beginning of the world.* This verse is quoted, though not literally, by the apostle Paul, as illustrating the effects of the gospel in producing happiness and salvation (see Notes on 1 Cor. ii. 9). The meaning here is, that nowhere else among men had there been such blessings imparted, and such happiness enjoyed; or so many proofs of love and protection, as among those who were the people of God, and who feared him. ¶ Men *have not heard.* In no nation in all past time have deeds been heard of such as thou hast performed. ¶ *Nor perceived by the ear.* Paul (1 Cor. ii. 9) renders this 'neither have entered into the heart of man,' 'which,' says Lowth, 'is a phrase purely Hebrew, and which should seem to belong to the prophet.' The phrase, 'Nor perceived by the ear,' he says, is repeated without force or propriety, and he seems to suppose that this place has been either wilfully corrupted by the Jews, or that Paul made his quotation from some Apocryphal book—either the ascension of Esaiah, or the Apocalypse of Elias, in both of which the passage is found as quoted by Paul. The phrase is wholly omitted by the LXX. and the Arabic, but is found in the Vulgate and Syriac. There is no authority from the Hebrew MSS. to omit it. ¶ *Neither hath the eye seen.* The margin here undoubtedly expresses the true sense. So Lowth renders it, 'Nor hath the eye seen a God beside thee, which doeth such

5 Thou [a] meetest him that rejoiceth and worketh righteousness, *those that* remember thee in thy ways: behold, thou art wroth; for we have sinned: in those is continuance, [b] and we shall be saved.

a Ac.10.35.

b Mal.3.6.

things for those that trust in him.' In a similar manner the LXX. translate it, 'Neither have our eyes seen a God beside thee (*οὐδὲ οἱ ὀφθαλμοὶ ἡμῶν εἶδον θεὸν πλήν σου*), and thy works which thou hast done for those who wait for mercy.' The sense is, no eye had ever seen such a God as JEHOVAH; one who so richly rewarded those who put their trust in him. In the Hebrew, the word rendered 'O God,' may be either in the accusative or vocative case, and the sense is, that JEHOVAH was a more glorious rewarder and protector than any of the gods which had ever been worshipped by the nations. ¶ What *he hath prepared.* Heb. יַעֲשֶׂה—'He doeth,' or will do. So the LXX. Ἃ ποιήσεις—'What thou wilt do.' The sense given by our translators—'What he hath prepared,' has been evidently adopted to *accommodate* the passage to the sense given by Paul (1 Cor. ii. 9), ἃ ἡτοίμασεν, κ.τ.λ.—'What God has prepared.' But the idea is, in the Hebrew, not what God has *prepared* or *laid up* in the sense of preserving it for the future; but what he had already done in the past. No god had done what he had; no human being had ever witnessed such manifestations from any other god. ¶ *For him that waiteth for him.* Lowth and Noyes, 'For him who trusteth in him.' Paul renders this, 'For them that love him,' and it is evident that he did not intend to quote this literally, but meant to give the general sense. The idea in the Hebrew is, 'For him who *waits* (לִמְחַכֵּה) for JEHOVAH,' *i.e.*, who feels his helplessness, and relies on him to interpose and save him. Piety is often represented as an attitude of *waiting* on God (Ps. xxv. 3, 5, 21; xxvii. 14; xxxvii. 9; cxxx. 5). The sense of the whole verse is, that God in his past dealings had given manifestations of his existence, power, and goodness, to those who were his friends, which had been furnished nowhere else. To those interpositions the suppliants appeal as a reason why he should again interpose, and why he should save them in their heavy calamities.

5. *Thou meetest him.* Perhaps there are few verses in the Bible that have given more perplexity to interpreters than this; and after all that has been done, the general impression seems to be, that it is wholly inexplicable, or without meaning—as it certainly is in our translation. Noyes says of his own translation of the last member of the verse, 'I am not satisfied with this or any other translation of the line which I have seen.' Lowth says, 'I am fully persuaded that these words as they stand at present in the Hebrew text are utterly unintelligible. There is no doubt of the meaning of each word separately, but put together they make no sense at all. I conclude, therefore, that the copy has suffered by transcribers in this place.' And after proposing an important change in the text, without any authority, he says, 'perhaps these may not be the very words of the prophet, but, however, it is better than to impose upon him what makes no sense at all, as they generally do who pretend to render such corrupted passages.' Arch. Secker also proposed an important change in the Hebrew text, but there is no good authority in the MSS., it is believed, for any change. Without repeating what has been said by expositors on the text, I shall endeavour to state what seems to me to be its probable signification. Its *general* purpose, I think, is clear. It is to urge, as an argument for God's interposition, the fact that he was accustomed to regard with pleasure those who did well; yet to admit that he was now justly angry on account of their sins, and that they had continued so long in them that they had no hope of being saved but in his mercy. An examination of the words and phrases which occur, will prepare us to present at a single view the probable meaning. The word rendered 'thou meetest,' (פָּגַעְתָּ) means probably to strike upon, to impinge; then to fall upon in a hos-

tile manner, to *urge* in any way as with petitions and prayers; and then to *strike* a peace or league with any one. See the word explained in the Notes on ch. xlvii. 3. Here it means, as I suppose, to meet for purposes of peace, friendship, protection; that is, it was a characteristic of God that he met such persons as are described for purposes of kindness and favour; and it expresses the belief of the petitioners that whatever they were suffering, still they had no doubt that it was the character of God to bless the righteous. ¶ *That rejoiceth.* This translation evidently does not express the sense of the Hebrew, unless it be understood as meaning that God meets with favour those who rejoice *in* doing righteousness. So Gesenius translates it, 'Thou makest peace with him who rejoices to do justice; *i.e.*, with the just and upright man thou art in league, thou delightest in him.' So Noyes renders it, 'Thou art the friend of those who joyfully do righteousness.' Lowth, 'Thou meetest with joy those who work righteousness.' Jerome, 'Thou meetest him who rejoices and does right.' The phrase used (אֶת־שָׂשׂ) seems to me to mean, 'With joy,' and to denote the general habit of God. It was a characteristic of him to meet the just 'with joy,' *i.e.*, joyfully. ¶ *And worketh righteousness.* Heb. 'And him that doeth righteousness;' *i.e.*, 'thou art accustomed to meet the just with joy, *and* him that does right.' It was a pleasure for God to do it, and to impart to them his favours. ¶ Those that *remember thee in thy ways.* On the word 'remember,' used in this connection, see Notes on ch. lxii. 6. The idea is, that such persons remembered God in the modes which he had appointed; that is, by prayer, sacrifices, and praise. With such persons he delighted to meet, and such he was ever ready to succour. ¶ *Behold, thou art wroth.* This is language of deep feeling on the part of the suppliants. Notwithstanding the mercy of God, and his readiness to meet and bless the just, they could not be ignorant of the fact that he was now angry with them. They were suffering under the tokens of his displeasure; but they were not now disposed to blame him. They felt the utmost assurance that he was just, whatever they might have endured. It is to be borne in mind, that this is language supposed to be used by the exiles in Babylon, near the close of the captivity; and the *evidences* that God was angry were to be seen in their heavy sorrows there, in their desolate land, and in the ruins of their prostrate city and temple (see Notes on ver. 10, 11). ¶ *In those is continuance.* Lowth has correctly remarked that this conveys no idea. To what does the word 'those' refer? No antecedent is mentioned, and expositors have been greatly perplexed with the passage. Lowth, in accordance with his too usual custom, seems to suppose that the text is corrupted, but is not satisfied with any proposed mode of amending it. He renders it, 'because of our deeds; for we have been rebellious;'—changing *entirely* the text—though following substantially the sense of the Septuagint. Noyes renders it, 'Long doth the punishment endure, until we be delivered;' but expresses, as has been already remarked, dissatisfaction even with this translation, and with all others which he has seen. Jerome renders it, *In ipsis fuimus semper*—'We have always been in them,' *i.e.*, in our sins. The LXX. Διὰ τοῦτο ἐπλανήθημεν, κ.τ.λ.—'Because of this we wandered, and became all of us as unclean, and all our righteousness as a filthy rag.' It seems to me that the phrase בָּהֶם, 'in them,' or 'in those,' refers to sins understood; and that the word rendered 'continuance' (עוֹלָם) is equivalent to a *long former period*: meaning that their sins had been of long continuance, or as we would express it, 'we have been *always* sinners.' It is the language of humble confession, denoting that this had been the characteristic of the nation, and that this was the reason why God was angry at them. ¶ *And we shall be saved.* Lowth renders this, or rather *substitutes* a phrase for it, thus, 'For we have been rebellious'—amending it wholly by conjecture. But it seems to me that Castellio has given an intelligible and obvious interpretation by regarding it as a question: 'Jamdiu peccavimus, et servabimur?' 'Long time have we sinned,

6 But we are all as an unclean
thing, and all our [a]righteousnesses
are as filthy rags; and we all do fade
as a leaf; and our iniquities, like
the wind, have carried us away.
7 And [b]*there is* none that calleth
upon thy name, that stirreth up
himself to take hold of thee: for
thou hast hid [c]thy face from us,
and hast [1]consumed us, [2]because
of our iniquities.

a Phi.3.9. b Ho.7.7. c Ho.5.15.
1 *melted.* 2 *by the hand;* Job8.4.

and shall we be saved?' That is, we have sinned so long, our offences have been so aggravated, how can we hope to be saved? Is salvation *possible* for such sinners? It indicates a deep consciousness of guilt, and is language such as is used by all who feel their deep depravity before God. Nothing is more common in conviction for sin, or when suffering under great calamities as a consequence of sin, than to ask the question whether it is *possible* for such sinners to be saved.—I have thus given, perhaps at tedious length, my view of this verse, which has so much perplexed commentators. And though the view *must* be submitted with great diffidence after such a man as Lowth has declared it to be without sense as the Hebrew text now stands, and though no important *doctrine* of religion is involved by the exposition, yet some service is rendered if a plausible and probable interpretation is given to a much disputed passage of the sacred Scriptures, and if we are saved from the necessity of supposing a corruption in the Hebrew text.

6. *But we are all as an unclean* thing. We are all polluted and defiled. The word here used (טָמֵא), means properly that which is polluted and defiled in a Levitical sense; that is, which was regarded as polluted and abominable by the law of Moses (Lev. v. 2; Deut. xiv. 19), and may refer to animals, men, or things; also in a moral sense (Job xiv. 4). The sense is, that they regarded themselves as wholly polluted and depraved. ¶ *And all our righteousnesses.* The plural form is used to denote the *deeds* which they had performed—meaning that pollution extended to every *individual thing* of the numerous acts which they had done. The sense is, that all their prayers, sacrifices, alms, praises, were mingled with pollution, and were worthy only of deep detestation and abhorrence. ¶ *As filthy rags.* 'Like a garment of stated times' (עִדִּים)—from the root עָדַד (*obsol.*) to number, to reckon, to determine, *e.g.*, time. No language could convey deeper abhorrence of their deeds of righteousness than this reference—as it is undoubtedly—to the *vestis menstruis polluta.* 'Non est ambigendum,' says Vitringa, 'quin vestis עִדִּים notet *linteum* aut *pannum immundum* ex immunditie legali, eundemque fœdum aspectu; cujusmodi fuerit imprimis *vestis, pannus,* aut *linteum* feminæ menstruo profluvio laborantis; verisimile est, id potissimum hac phrasi designari. Sic accepit eam Alexandrinus, vertens, ὡς ῥάκος ἀποκαθημένης—*ut pannus sedentis;* proprie: ut pannus mulieris languidæ et desidentis ex menstruo παθήματι' (Lev. xv. 33; comp. xx. 18; Lam. i. 17). ¶ *And we all do fade as a leaf.* We are all withered away like the leaf of autumn. Our beauty is gone; our strength is fled (comp. Notes on ch. xl. 6, 7; l. 30). What a beautiful description this is of the state of man! Strength, vigour, comeliness, and beauty thus fade away, and, like the 'sere and yellow leaf' of autumn, fall to the earth. The earth is thus strewed with that which was once comely like the leaves of spring, now falling and decaying like the faded verdure of the forest. ¶ *And our iniquities like the wind.* As a tempest sweeps away the leaves of the forest, so have we been swept away by our sins.

7. *And* there is *none that calleth upon thy name.* The nation is corrupt and degenerate. None worship God in sincerity. ¶ *That stirreth up himself.* The word here used (מִתְעוֹרֵר) refers to the effort which is requisite to rouse one's self when oppressed by a spirit of heavy slumber; and the idea here is, that the nation was sunk in spiritual torpor, and that the same effort was needful to excite it which was requisite

8 But now, O LORD, thou *art* our
Father; we [a] *are* the clay, and
thou our potter; and we all *are*
the work of thy hand.
9 Be not wroth very sore, O
LORD, neither [b] remember iniquity
for ever: behold, see, we beseech
thee, we *are* all thy people.
10 Thy holy cities are a wilderness, Zion is a wilderness, Jerusalem a desolation.

[a] Je.18.6. [b] Ps.79.8,&c.

to rouse one who had sunk down to deep sleep. How aptly this describes the state of a sinful world! How much disposed is that world to give itself to spiritual slumber! How indisposed to rouse itself to call upon God! No man rises to God without effort; and unless men *make* an effort for this, they fall into the stupidity of sin, just as certainly as a drowsy man sinks back into deep sleep. ¶ *To take hold of thee.* The Hebrew word (חָזַק) means properly *to bind fast, to gird tight,* and then to make firm or strong, to strengthen; and the idea of *strengthening one's self* is implied in the use of the word here. It means, that with the consciousness of feebleness we should seek *strength* in God. This the people referred to by the prophet were indisposed to do. This the world at large is indisposed to do. ¶ *For thou hast hid thy face.* Thou hast withdrawn thy favour from us, as a people, on account of our sins. This is an acknowledgment that one effect of his withdrawing his favour, and one evidence of it was, that no one was disposed to call upon his name. All had sunk into the deep lethargy of sin. ¶ *And hast consumed us.* Marg. 'Melted.' The Hebrew word (מוּג) means *to melt, to flow down;* and hence, in Piel, *to cause* to melt or flow down. It is used to denote the fact that an army or host of men seem *to melt away,* or become dissolved by fear and terror (Ex. xv. 15; Josh. ii. 9–24; Job xxx. 22). 'Thou dissolvest (תְּמֹגְגֵנִי) my substance;' *i.e.*, thou causest me to dissolve before thy indignation. This is described as one of the effects of the wrath of God, that his enemies vanish away, or are dissolved before him. ¶ *Because of our iniquities.* Marg. as Heb. 'By the hand;' *i.e.*, our iniquities have been the *hand,* the agent or instrument by which this has been done.

8. *But now, O* LORD, *thou* art *our Father* (see Notes on ch. lxiii. 16). ¶ *We* are *the clay.* The idea seems to be, that their condition then had been produced by him as clay is moulded by the potter, and that they were to be returned and restored entirely by him—as they had no more power to do it than the clay had to shape itself. The sense is, that they were wholly in his hand and at his disposal (see Notes on ch. xxix. 16; xlv. 9). ¶ *And thou our potter.* Thou hast power to mould us as the potter does the clay. ¶ *And we all* are *the work of thy hand.* That is, as the vessel made by the potter is his work. We have been formed by thee, and we are dependent on thee to make us what thou wilt have us to be. This whole verse is an acknowledgment of the sovereignty of God. It expresses the feeling which all have when under conviction of sin; and when they are sensible that they are exposed to the Divine displeasure for their transgressions. Then they feel that if they are to be saved, it must be by the mere sovereignty of God; and then they implore his interposition to 'mould and guide them at his will.'

10. *Thy holy cities are a wilderness.* It is to be remembered that this is supposed to be spoken near the close of the exile in Babylon. In accordance with the usual custom in this book, Isaiah throws himself forward by prophetic anticipation into that future period, and describes the scene as if it were passing before his eyes (see Introd. § 7). He uses language such as the exiles would use; he puts arguments into their mouths which it would be proper for them to use; he describes the feelings which they would then have. The phrase, 'thy holy cities,' may either mean the cities of the Holy Land—which belonged to God, and were 'holy,' as they pertained to his people; or it may

11 Our holy and our beautiful house, [a]where our fathers praised thee, is burnt up with fire; and all our pleasant things are laid waste.

12 Wilt thou refrain [b]thyself for these *things*, O LORD? wilt thou hold thy peace and afflict us very sore?

[a] La.2.7.

[b] ch.43.14.

mean, as many critics have supposed, the different parts of Jerusalem. A part of Jerusalem was built on Mount Zion, and was called the 'upper city,' in contradistinction from that built on Mount Acra, which was called the 'lower city.' But I think it more probable that the prophet refers to the cities throughout the land that were laid waste. ¶ *Are a wilderness.* They were uninhabited, and were lying in ruins. ¶ *Zion is a wilderness.* On the name 'Zion,' see Notes on ch. i. 8. The idea here is, that Jerusalem was laid waste. Its temple was burned; its palaces destroyed; its houses uninhabited. This is to be regarded as being uttered at the close of the exile, after Jerusalem had been lying in ruins for seventy years—a time during which any forsaken city would be in a condition which might not improperly be called *a desert.* When Nebuchadnezzar conquered Jerusalem, he burnt the temple, broke down the wall, and consumed all the palaces with fire (2 Chron. xxxvi. 19). We have only to conceive what *must* have been the state of the city seventy years after this, to see the force of the description here.

11. *Our holy and our beautiful house.* The temple. It was called 'holy,' because it was dedicated to the service of God; and 'beautiful,' on account of its extraordinary magnificence. The original word more properly means *glorious.* ¶ *Where our fathers praised thee.* Few attachments become stronger than that which is formed for a place of worship where our ancestors have long been engaged in the service of God. It was now a great aggravation of their sufferings, that that beautiful place, consecrated by the fact that their forefathers had long there offered praise to God, was lying in ruins. ¶ *Is burned up with fire* (see 2 Chron. xxxvi. 19). ¶ *And all our pleasant things.* All that is precious to us (Heb.); all the objects of our desire. The reference is to their temples, their homes, their city—to all that was dear to them in their native land. It would be difficult to find a passage anywhere in the Bible—or out of it—that equals this for tenderness and true pathos. They were an exiled people; long suffering in a distant land with the reflection that their homes were in ruins; their splendid temple long since fired and lying in desolation; the rank grass growing in their streets, and their whole country overrun with wild beasts, and with a rank and unsubdued vegetation. To that land they longed to return, and here with the deepest emotion they plead with God in behalf of their desolate country. The sentiment here is, that we should go to God with deep emotion when his church is prostrate, and that *then* is the time when we should use the most tender pleadings, and when our hearts should be melted within us.

12. *Wilt thou refrain thyself.* Wilt thou refuse to come to our aid? Wilt thou decline to visit us, and save us from our calamities? ¶ *Wilt thou hold thy peace.* Wilt thou not *speak* for our rescue, and command us to be delivered? Thus closes this chapter of great tenderness and beauty. It is a model of affectionate and earnest entreaty for the Divine interposition in the day of calamity. With such tender and affectionate earnestness may we learn to plead with God! Thus may all his people learn to approach him as a Father; thus feel that they have the inestimable *privilege,* in times of trial, of making known their wants to the High and Holy One. Thus, when calamity presses on us; when as individuals or as families we are afflicted; or when our country or the church is suffering under long trials, may we go to God and humbly confess our sins, and urge his promises, and take hold of his strength, and plead with him to interpose. Thus pleading, he will hear us; thus presenting our cause, he will interpose to save.

CHAPTER LXV.

ANALYSIS.

It is generally supposed that this chapter is closely connected in sense with the preceding; and that its object is, to defend the proceedings of God in regard to the Jews, and especially with reference to the complaint in the preceding chapter. If so, it is designed to state the reasons why he had thus afflicted them, and to encourage the pious among them with the expectation of great future prosperity and safety. A general view of the chapter may be obtained by a glance at the following analysis of the subjects introduced in it.

I. God states in general that he had called another people who had not sought him, and extended the blessings of salvation to those who had been strangers to his name (1). This is evidently intended to show that many of his ancient people would be rejected, and that the blessings of salvation would be extended to others (Rom. x. 20). In the previous chapter they had pled (9), that they were 'all' his people; they had urged, because their nation had been in covenant with God, that he should interpose and save them. Here an important principle is introduced, that they were *not* to be saved of course because they were Jews; and that others would be introduced to his favour who belonged to nations which had not known him, while his ancient covenant people would be rejected. The Jews were slow to believe this; and hence Paul says (Rom. x. 20), that Isaiah was 'very bold' in advancing so unpopular a sentiment.

II. God states the true reason why he had punished them (2–7). It was on account of their sins. It was not because he was changeable, or was unjust in his dealings with them. He had punished them, and he had resolved to reject a large portion of them, though they belonged to his ancient covenant people, on account of their numerous and deeply aggravated crimes. He specifies particularly—1. That they had been a rebellious people, and that he had stretched out his hands to them in vain, inviting them to return. 2. That they were a people which had constantly provoked him by their idolatries; their abominable sacrifices; and by eating the things which he had forbidden. 3. That they were eminently proud and self-righteous, saying to others, Stand by yourselves, for we are holier than you. 4. That for these sins God could not *but* punish them. His law required it, and his justice demanded that he should not pass such offences by unnoticed.

III. Yet he said that the *whole* nation should not be destroyed. His elect would be saved; in accordance with the uniform doctrine of the Scriptures, that *all* the seed of Abraham should not be cut off, but that a remnant should be kept to accomplish important purposes in reference to the salvation of the world (8–10).

IV. Yet the wicked portion of the nation should be cut off, and God, by the prophet, describes the certain punishment which awaited them (11–16). 1. They would be doomed to slaughter. 2. They would be subjected to hunger and want, while his true servants would have abundance. 3. They would cry in deep sorrow, while his servants would rejoice. 4. Their destruction would be a blessing to his people, and the result of their punishment would be to cause his own people to see more fully the value of their religion, and to prize it more.

V. Yet there would be future glory and prosperity, such as his true people had desired, and such as they had sought in their prayers; and the chapter concludes with a glowing description of the glory which would bless his church and people (17–25). 1. God would create new heavens and a new earth—far surpassing the former in beauty and glory (17). 2. Jerusalem would be made an occasion of rejoicing (18). 3. Its prosperity is described as a state of peace, security, and happiness (19–25). (1.) Great age would be attained by its inhabitants, and Jerusalem would be full of venerable and pious old men. (2.) They would enjoy the fruit of their own labour without annoyance. (3.) Their prayers would be speedily answered—even while they were speaking. (4.) The true religion would produce a change on the passions of men *as if* the nature of wild and ferocious animals were changed, and the wolf and the lamb should feed together, and the lion should eat straw like the ox. There would be universal security and peace throughout the whole world where the true religion would be spread.

There can be no doubt, I think, that this refers to the times of the Messiah. Particular proof of this will be furnished in the exposition of the chapter. It is to be regarded, indeed, as well as the previous chapter, as primarily addressed to the exiles in Babylon, but the mind of the prophet is thrown forward. He looks at future events. He sees a large part of the nation permanently rejected. He sees the Gentiles called to partake of the privileges of the true religion. He sees still a remnant of the ancient Jewish people preserved in all their sufferings, and future glory rise upon them under the Messiah, when a new heavens and a new earth should be created. It is adapted, therefore, not only to comfort the ancient afflicted people of God, but it contains most important and cheering truth in regard to the final prevalence of the true religion, and the state of the world when the gospel shall everywhere prevail.

I [a] AM sought of *them that* asked
not *for me;* I am found of *them*
that sought me not: I said, Behold
me, behold me, unto a nation *that*
was not called by my name.

2 I [b] have spread out my hands
all the day unto a rebellious people,
which walketh in a way *that was*
not good, after their own thoughts.
3 A people that provoketh [c] me
to anger continually to my face;
that sacrificeth [d] in gardens, and
burneth incense upon [1] altars of
bricks;

[a] Ro.9.24,30. [b] Ro.10.21. [c] De.32.21. [d] Le.17.5 [1] *bricks.*

CHAPTER LXV.

1. *I am sought of* them that *asked not* for me. That is, by the Gentiles. So Paul applies it in Rom. x. 20. Lowth translates the word which is rendered, 'I am sought,' by 'I am made known.' Noyes, 'I have heard.' The LXX. render it, 'Ἐμφανὴς ἐγενήθην—'I became manifest.' Jerome, 'They sought me who had not before inquired for me.' The Chaldee, 'I am sought in my word by those who had not asked me before my face.' The Hebrew word דָּרַשׁ means properly *to frequent a place,* to search or seek; and in Niphal—the form here used—to be sought unto, to grant access to any one; hence to hear and answer prayer (Ezek. xiv. 3; xx. 3–31). Here there is not only the idea that he was *sought,* but that they *obtained* access to him, for he listened to their supplications. The phrase, 'That asked not for me,' means that they had not been accustomed to worship the true God. The idea is, that those had obtained mercy who had not *been accustomed* to call upon him. ¶ *I am found of* them. Paul has rendered this (Rom. x. 20), 'Ἐμφανὴς ἐγενόμην—'I was made manifest.' The idea is, that they obtained his favour. ¶ *I said, Behold me, behold me.* I offered them my favour, and invited them to partake of salvation. Paul has omitted this in his quotation. ¶ *Unto a nation.* This does not refer to any particular nation, but to people who had never been admitted to favour with God. ¶ That *was not called by my name* (see Notes on ch. lxiii. 19).

2. *I have spread out my hands.* To spread out the hands is an action denoting invitation or entreaty (Prov. i. 24). The sense is, that God had invited the Jews constantly to partake of his favours, but they had been rebellious, and had rejected his offers. ¶ *All the day.* I have not ceased to do it. The Chaldee renders this, 'I sent my prophets all the day to a rebellious people.' ¶ *Unto a rebellious people* (see Notes on ch. i. 2). Paul renders this, Πρὸς λαὸν ἀπειθοῦντα καὶ ἀντιλέγοντα—'Unto a disobedient and gainsaying people;' but the sense is substantially preserved. ¶ *Which walketh.* In what way they did this, the prophet specifies in the following verse. This is the *general* reason why he had rejected them, and why he had resolved to make the offer of salvation to the Gentiles. This, at first, was a reason for the calamities which God had brought upon the nation in the suffering of the exile, but it also contains a *general* principle of which that was only one specimen. They had been rebellious, and God had brought this calamity upon them. It would be also true in future times, that he would reject them and offer salvation to the heathen world, and would be found by those who had never sought for him or called on his name.

3. *A people.* This verse contains a *specification* of the reasons why God had rejected them, and brought the calamities upon them. ¶ *That provoketh me to anger.* That is, by their sins. They give constant occasion for my indignation. ¶ *Continually* (תָּמִיד). It is not once merely, but their conduct as a people is *constantly* such as to excite my displeasure. ¶ *To my face.* There is no attempt at concealment. Their abominations are public. It is always regarded as an additional affront when an offence is committed *in the very presence* of another, and when there is not even the apology that it was supposed

4 Which remain among the graves, and lodge in the monuments; which eat swine's flesh, and [1] broth of abominable *things is in* their vessels;

[1] or, *pieces*.

he did not see the offender. It is a great aggravation of the guilt of the sinner, that his offence is committed in the very presence, and under the very eye, of God. ¶ *That sacrificeth in gardens* (see Notes on ch. i. 29). ¶ *And burneth incense*. On the meaning of the word 'incense,' see Notes on ch. i. 13. ¶ *Upon altars of brick*. Marg. 'Bricks.' The Hebrew is simply, 'Upon bricks.' The command of God was that the altars for sacrifice should be made of unhewn stone (Ex. xx. 24, 25). But the heathen had altars of a different description, and the Jews had sacrificed on those altars. Some have supposed that this means that they sacrificed on the roofs of their houses, which were flat, and paved with brick, or tile, or plaster. That altars were constructed sometimes on the roofs of their houses, we know from 2 Kings xxiii. 12, where Josiah is said to have beaten down the 'altars that were on the top of the upper chamber of Ahaz, which the king of Judah had made.' But it is not necessary to suppose that such sacrifices are referred to here. They had disobeyed the command of God, which required that the altars should be made only of unhewn stone. They had built other altars, and had joined with the heathen in offering sacrifices thereon. The *reason* why God forbade that the altar should be of anything but unhewn stone is not certainly known, and is not necessary to be understood in order to explain this passage. It may have been, first, in order effectually to separate his people from all others, as well in the construction of the altar as in anything and everything else; secondly, because various inscriptions and carvings were usually made on altars, and as this tended to superstition, God commanded that the chisel should not be used at all in the construction of the altars where his people should worship.

4. *Which remain among the graves*. That is, evidently for purposes of necromancy and divination. They do it to appear to hold converse with the dead, and to receive communications from them. The idea in necromancy was, that departed spirits must be acquainted with future events, or at least with the secret things of the invisible world where they dwelt, and that certain persons, by various arts, could become *intimate* with them, or 'familiar' with them, and, by obtaining their secrets, be able to communicate important truths to the living. It seems to have been supposed that this acquaintance might be increased by lodging in the tombs and among the monuments, that they might thus be near to the dead, and have more intimate communion with them (comp. Notes on ch. viii. 19, 20). It is to be recollected, that tombs among the ancients, and especially in Oriental countries, were commonly excavations from the sides of hills, or frequently were large caves. Such places would furnish spacious lodgings for those who chose to reside there, and were, in fact, often resorted to by those who had no houses, and by robbers (see Matt. viii. 28; Mark v. 3). ¶ *And lodge in the monuments*. Evidently for some purpose of superstition and idolatry. There is, however, some considerable variety in the exposition of the word here rendered 'monuments,' as well as in regard to the whole passage. The word rendered 'lodge' (יָלִינוּ), means properly *to pass the night*, and refers not to a permanent dwelling in any place, but to remaining over night; and the probability is, that they went to the places referred to, to *sleep*—in order that they might receive communications in their dreams from idols, by being near them, or in order that they might have communication with departed spirits. The word rendered 'monuments' (נְצוּרִים) is derived from נָצַר, *nâtzăr*, to watch, to guard, to keep; then *to keep from view*, to hide—and means properly hidden recesses; and dark and obscure retreats. It may be applied either to the *adyta* or secret places of heathen temples where their oracles were consulted and many of their rites were performed;

or it may be applied to sepulchral caverns, the dark and hidden places where the dead were buried. The LXX. render it, 'They sleep in tombs and in caves (ἐν τοῖς σπηλαίοις) for the purpose of dreaming' (διὰ ἐνύπνια); in allusion to the custom of sleeping in the temples, or near the oracles of their gods, for the purpose of obtaining from them communications by dreams. This custom is not unfrequently alluded to by the ancient writers. An instance of this kind occurs in Virgil:

—— huc dona sacerdos
Cum tulit, et cæsarum ovium sub nocte silenti
Pellibus incubuit stratis, somnosque petivit:
Multa modis simulacra videt volitantia miris,
Et varias audit voces, fruiturque Deorum,
Colloquio, atque imis Acheronta affatur Avernis.
Æneid, vii. 86–91.

'Here in distress the Italian nations come,
Anxious to clear their doubts and earn their doom;
First on the fleeces of the slaughter'd sheep,
By night the sacred priest dissolves in sleep;
When in a train before his slumbering eye,
Their airy forms and wondrous visions fly:
He calls the powers who guard the infernal floods,
And talks inspired familiar with the gods.'
PITT.

In the temples of Serapis and Æsculapius, it was common for the sick and infirm who came there to be cured, to sleep there, with the belief that the proper remedy would be communicated by dreams. The following places may also be referred to as illustrating this custom:—Pausan. *Phoc.* 31; Cic. *Divin.* i. 43; Strabo vi. 3, 9; S. H. Meibom. *De incubatione in fanis Deorum olim facta.* Helmst. 1659, 4. Lowth and Noyes render it, 'In caverns.' The Chaldee renders it, 'Who dwelt in houses which are built of the dust of sepulchres, and abide with the dead bodies of dead men.' There can be no doubt that the prophet here alludes to some such custom of sleeping in the tombs, for the alleged purpose of conversing with the dead, or in temples for the purpose of communion with the idols by dreams, or with the expectation that they would receive responses by dreams (comp. Notes on ch. xiv. 9). ¶ *Which eat swine's flesh.* This was expressly forbidden by the Jewish law (Lev. xi. 7), and is held in abomination by the Jews now. Yet the flesh of the swine was freely eaten by the heathen; and when the Jews conformed to their customs in other respects, they doubtless forgot also the law commanding a distinction to be made in meats. Antiochus Epiphanes compelled the Jews to eat swine's flesh as a token of their submission, and of their renouncing their religion. The case of Eleazer, who chose to die as a martyr, rather than give such a proof that he had renounced his religion, and who preferred death rather than to dissemble, is recorded in 2 Macc. vi. 19–31. See also the affecting case of the mother and her seven sons, who all died in a similar manner, in 2 Macc. vii. Yet it seems that, in the time of Isaiah, they had no such devotedness to their national religion. They freely conformed to the nations around them, and thus gave public demonstration that they disregarded the commands of JEHOVAH. It is also to be observed, that swine were often sacrificed by the heathen, and were eaten in their feasts in honour of idols. The crime here referred to, therefore, was not merely that of partaking of the flesh, but it was that of joining with the heathen in idolatrous sacrifices. Thus Ovid says:

Prima Ceres avidæ gavisa est sanguine porcæ,
Ulta suas merita cæde nocentis opes.
Fastor, i. 349.

So Horace:

—— immolet æquis
Hic porcum Laribus—
Serm. ii. 164.

Thus Varro (*De Re Rustic.* ii. 4), says, 'The swine is called in Greek ὗς (formerly θῦς), and was so called from the word which signifies *to sacrifice* (θύειν), for the swine seem first to have been used in sacrifices. Of this custom we have vestiges in the fact, that the first sacrifices to Ceres are of the swine; and that in the beginning of peace, when a treaty is made, a hog is sacrificed; and that in the beginning of marriage contracts in Etruria, the new wife and the new husband first sacrifice a hog. The primitive Latins, and also the Greeks in Italy, seem to have done the same thing.' Spencer (*De Leg. Heb.* i. 7) supposes that this was done often in caves and dark recesses, and that the prophet refers to this custom here. If this view

6 Which say, Stand by thyself, come not near to me; for I am holier than thou. These *are* a smoke in my [1]nose, a fire that burneth all the day.

1 or, *anger*.

be correct, then the offence consisted not merely in *eating* swine's flesh, but in eating it in connection with sacrifices, or joining with the heathen in their idolatrous worship. ¶ *And broth of abominable* things. Margin, 'Pieces.' Lowth says that this was for 'lustrations, magical arts, and other superstitious and abominable practices.' The word here rendered 'broth,' and in the margin 'pieces' (פָּרָק), is derived from the verb פָּרַק, *pârăk, to break* (whence the Latin *frango;* the Goth. *brikan;* the Germ. *breoken;* and the English *break*), and means that which is broken, or a fragment; and hence broth or soup, from the fragments or crumbs of bread over which the broth is poured. The LXX. render this, 'And all their vessels are polluted.' It is not improbable that the broth or soup here used was in some way employed in arts of incantation or necromancy. Compare Shakspeare's account of the witches in Macbeth:

1. *Witch.* Where hast thou been, sister?
2. *Witch.* Killing swine. *Act* i. *Sc.* 3.

Hec. Your vessels and your spells provide,
Your charms, and everything beside.
Act iii. *Sc.* 5.

1. *Witch.* Round about the caldron go,
In the poison'd entrails throw,
Toad that under the cold stone,
Days and nights hath thirty-one,
Fillet of a finny snake,
In the caldron boil and bake,
Eye of newt, and toe of frog,
Wool of bat, and tongue of dog,
Adder's fork, and blind worm's sting,
Lizard's leg, and howlet's wing,
For a charm of powerful trouble,
Like a hell-broth boil and bubble.
Act iv. *Sc.* 1.

It seems probable that some such magical incantations were used in the time of Isaiah. Such things are known to have been practised in regions of idolatry (see Marco Polo, *De Region. Orient.*, iii. 24). 'When the priests of the idol,' says he, 'wish to engage in sacred things, they call the consecrated girls, and with them, in the presence of the idols, they engage in the dance, and sing aloud. These girls bear with them vessels of food, which they place on the table before the idols, and they entreat the gods to eat of the food, and particularly they pour out broth made of flesh before them, that they may appease them.' The whole scene here described by the prophet is one connected with idolatry and magical incantations; and the prophet means to rebuke them for having forsaken God and fallen into all the abominable and stupid arts of idolaters. It was not merely that they had eaten the flesh of swine, or that they had made broth of unclean meats—which would have been minor, though real offences—it was that they had fallen into all the abominable practices connected with idolatry and necromancy.

5. *Which say, Stand by thyself.* Who at the time that they engage in these abominations are distinguished for spiritual pride. The most worthless men are commonly the most proud; and they who have wandered farthest from God have in general the most exalted idea of their own goodness. It was a characteristic of a large part of the Jewish nation, and especially of the Pharisees, to be self-righteous and proud. A striking illustration of this we have in the following description of the Hindoo Yogees, by Roberts: 'Those men are so isolated by their superstition and penances, that they hold but little intercourse with the rest of mankind. They wander about in the dark in the place of burning the dead, or "among the graves;" there they affect to hold converse with evil and other spirits; and there they pretend to receive intimations respecting the destinies of others. They will eat things which are religiously clean or unclean; they neither wash their bodies, nor comb their hair, nor cut their nails, nor wear clothes. They are counted to be *most holy* among the people, and are looked upon as beings of another world.' ¶ *These* are *a smoke in my nose.* Marg. 'Anger.' The word rendered 'nose' (אַף) means sometimes nose (Num. xi. 20; Job xl. 24), and sometimes 'anger,' because anger

6 Behold, *it is* written before me;
I will not keep silence, but will recompense, even recompense into
their bosom.
7 Your iniquities, and the iniquities of your fathers together,
saith the LORD, which have burnt
incense upon the mountains, and
blasphemed me upon the hills:
therefore will I measure their former work into their bosom.

---

is evinced by hard breathing. The LXX. render this, 'This is the smoke of my anger.' But the correct idea is, probably, that their conduct was offensive to God, as smoke is unpleasant or painful in the nostrils; or as smoke excites irritation when breathed, so their conduct excited displeasure (Rosenmüller). Or it may mean, as Lowth suggests, that their conduct kindled a smoke and a fire in his nose as the emblems of his wrath. There is probably an allusion to their sacrifices here. The smoke of their sacrifices constantly ascending was unpleasant and provoking to God. ¶ *A fire that burneth all the day.* The idea here probably is, that their conduct kindled a fire of indignation that was continually breathed out upon them. A similar figure occurs in Deut. xxxii. 22: 'For a fire is kindled in mine anger,' or in my nose (בְּאַפִּי), 'and shall burn unto the lowest hell.' So in Ps. xviii. 8:

> There went up a smoke out of his nostrils,
> And fire out of his mouth devoured.

Compare Ezek. xxxviii. 18.

6. *Behold*, it is *written before me.* That is, the crimes of which they had been guilty, or the sentence which would be consequent thereon. The allusion is to the custom of having the decrees of kings recorded in a volume or on a table, and kept in their presence, so that they might be seen and not forgotten. An allusion to this custom of opening the books containing a record of this kind on trials, occurs in Dan. vii. 10, 'The judgment was set, and the books were opened.' So also Rev. xx. 12, 'And I saw the dead, small and great, stand before God; and the books were opened; and another book was opened, which is the book of life, and the dead were judged out of those things which were written in the books, according to their works.' So here. An impartial record had been made, and God would recompense them according to their deeds. ¶ *I will not keep silence.* Nothing shall compel me to desist from declaring a sentence which shall be just and right. ¶ *But will recompense, even recompense.* That is, I will *certainly* requite them. The word is repeated in accordance with the usual manner in Hebrew to denote emphasis. ¶ *Into their bosom* (see Ps. lxxix. 12; Jer. xxxii. 18; Luke vi. 38). The word *bosom*, here refers to a custom among the Orientals of making the bosom or front of their garments large and loose, so that articles could be carried in them, answering the purpose of our pockets (comp. Ex. iv. 6, 7; Prov. vi. 27). The sense here is, that God would *abundantly* punish them for their sins.

7. *Your iniquities.* Their idolatry and their forsaking God, and their arts of necromancy. ¶ *And the iniquities of your fathers together.* The consequences of your own sins, and of the long defection of the nation from virtue and pure religion, shall come rushing upon you like accumulated floods. This is in accordance with the Scripture doctrine everywhere, that the consequences of the sins of ancestors pass over and visit their posterity (see Ex. xx. 5; xxxiv. 7; Num. xiv. 18; Job xxi. 19; Luke xi. 50, 51; Notes on Rom. v. 19). The case here was, that the nation had been characteristically prone to wander from God, and to fall into idolatry. Crime had thus been accumulating, like pent-up waters, for ages, and now it swept away every barrier. So crime *often* accumulates in a nation. Age after age rolls on, and it is unpunished, until it breaks over every obstacle, and all that is valuable and happy is swept suddenly away. ¶ *Which have burnt incense upon the mountains* (see Notes on ver. 3). ¶ *And blasphemed me upon the hills.* That is, they have dishonoured me by worshipping idols, and by denying me in that public manner. Idols were usually worshipped on high places. ¶ *Will I measure their former*

8 Thus saith the LORD, As the
new wine is found in the cluster,
and *one* saith, Destroy it not; for
a blessing *is* in it: so will I do for
my servants' sakes, that I may not
destroy them all.
9 And I will bring forth a seed
out of Jacob, and out of Judah an
inheritor of my mountains: and
mine elect [a]shall inherit it, and
my servants shall dwell there.
10 And Sharon shall be a fold
of flocks, and the valley of Achor
a place for the herds to lie down
in, for my people that have sought
me.

[a] Ro.11.5,7.

work. I will recompense them; I will pour the reward of their work or of their doings into their bosom.

8. *Thus saith the* LORD. This verse is designed to keep their minds from utter despair, and to assure them that they should not be utterly destroyed. See the analysis of the chapter. ¶ *As the new wine.* The Hebrew word here used (תִּירוֹשׁ), means properly *must* or *new wine* (see Notes on ch. xxiv. 7). The LXX. render it here, ὁ ῥὼξ, a grain or berry; meaning probably a good grape. The Chaldee renders it, 'As Noah was found pure in the generation of the deluge, and I said I would not destroy them, that I might rise up a generation from him, so will I do on account of my servants, that I may not destroy all.' Jerome renders it, *Granum*—'A kernel,' or berry. ¶ *Is found in the cluster.* Expositors have differed in the interpretation of this passage. The true image seems to be taken from collecting grapes when a large part of them were in some way damaged or spoiled—either by the quality of the vine, or by a bad season, or by having been gathered too early, or being suffered to remain too long in a heap. In such a case the vine-dresser would be ready to throw them away. But in the mass he would find a few that were ripe and good. While he was throwing away the mass, some one would say that a part was good, and would entreat him not to destroy it. So with the Jews. The mass was corrupt, and was to be cut off. But still a portion should be left. This is in accordance with the doctrine everywhere occurring in Isaiah and elsewhere in the Scriptures, that the whole Jewish nation should not be cut off, but that a remnant should be preserved (see Notes on ch. vi. 13; comp. ch. i. 9; vii. 3; x. 21; xi. 11–16). ¶ *For a blessing.* That which is regarded as a blessing; that is wine (comp. Judg. ix. 13). ¶ *So will I do.* The whole nation shall not be cut off, but a remnant shall be kept and saved.

9. *And I will bring forth a seed.* I will give descendants to Jacob, who shall share my favour and repossess the land. ¶ *An inheritor of my mountains.* The mountains of Palestine—Jerusalem and the vicinity—called the mountains of God because he claimed that land as his peculiar residence, and the place where his holy religion was established. ¶ *And mine elect.* They who have been chosen by me to maintain my religion in the world.

10. *And Sharon.* Sharon was properly a district south of Mount Carmel, along the coast of the Mediterranean, and extending from Cæsarea to Joppa. In the Scripture, this is almost a proverbial name to denote extraordinary beauty and fertility (see Notes on ch. xxx. 9; xxxii. 5). ¶ *Shall be a fold of flocks.* At the time contemplated here by the prophet—the close of the exile—that whole country would have lain waste about seventy years. Of course, during that long period it would be spread over with a wild luxuriance of trees and shrubs. Once it was celebrated pasture-ground, and was exceedingly beautiful as a place for flocks and herds. Such a place it would be again when the exiles should return, and cultivate their native land. The following description of Sharon, in the spring of 1824, by the Rev. Mr. Thompson, an American Missionary, will give an idea of the natural appearance of that part of Palestine. The view taken was from a high tower in Ramla. 'The whole valley of Sharon, from the mountains of Jerusalem to the sea, and from the

11 But ye *are* they that forsake the LORD, that forget my holy mountain, that prepare a table for that [1]troop, and that furnish the drink-offering unto that [2]number.

1 or, *Gad.* 2 or, *Meni.*

foot of Carmel to the hills of Gaza, is spread before you like a painted map, and is extremely beautiful, especially at evening, when the last rays of the setting sun gild the distant mountain tops, the weary husbandman returns from his labour, and the bleating flocks come frisking and joyful to their fold. At such a time I saw it, and lingered long in pensive meditation, until the stars looked out from the sky, and the cool breezes of evening began to shed soft dews on the feverish land. What a paradise was here when Solomon reigned in Jerusalem, and sang of the *roses of Sharon!'* ¶ *And the valley of Achor.* This was a valley near to Jericho, and was distinguished as the place where Achan was put to death by stoning (Josh. vii. 24; xv. 7; Hos. ii. 15). The word 'Achor' (עָכוֹר), means properly *causing affliction,* and the name was probably given to that valley from the trouble or affliction which was there caused to the Israelites from the sin of Achan. The phrase, 'the valley of Achor,' would probably thence become a proverbial expression to denote that which caused trouble of any kind. And the sense here probably is, that that which had been to the nation a source of calamity should become a source of blessing—*as if* a place distinguished for causing trouble should become as celebrated for producing happiness. As that valley had been a source of great trouble on their first entering into the land of Canaan, so it would become a place of great exultation, peace, and joy, on their return from their exile. They would naturally enter Canaan near to that valley, and the place which to them had been once the occasion of so much distress, would be found a quiet and peaceful place where their herds might lie down in safety (comp. Hos. ii. 15).

11. *But ye are they that forsake the* LORD. Or rather, 'Ye who forsake JEHOVAH, and who forget my holy mountain, I will number to the sword.' The design of this verse is to remind them of their idolatries, and to assure them that they should not escape unpunished. ¶ *That forget my holy mountain.* Mount Moriah, the sacred mountain on which the temple was built. ¶ *That prepare a table.* It was usual to set food and drink before idols—with the belief that the gods consumed what was thus placed before them (see Notes on ver. 4). The meaning here is, that the Jews had united with the heathen in thus 'preparing a table;' that is, setting it before the idols referred to, and placing food on it for them. ¶ *For that troop.* Marg. 'Gad.' Perhaps there is nowhere a more unhappy translation than this. It has been made evidently because our translators were not aware of the true meaning of the word, and did not seem to understand that it referred to idolatry. The translation *seems* to have been adopted with some reference to the *paronomasia* occurring in Gen. xlix. 19; 'Gad, a troop shall overcome him'—גָּד גְּדוּד יְגוּדֶנּוּ—where the word Gad has some resemblance to the word rendered *troop.* The word *Gad* itself, however, never means *troop,* and evidently should not be so rendered here. Much has been written on this place, and the views of the learned concerning Gad and Meni are very various and uncertain. Those who are disposed to examine the subject at length, may consult Rosenmüller, Vitringa, and Gesenius on the passage; and also the following works. On this passage the reader may consult the Dissertation of David Mills, *De Gad et Meni,* and also the Dissertation of Jo. Goth. Lakemacher, *De Gad et Meni,* both of which are to be found in Ugolin's *Thesaurus,* xxiii. pp. 671–718, where the subject is examined at length. Mills supposes that the names Gad and Meni are two names for the moon—*sidus bonum,* and μηνη (*mēnē*). He remarks that 'on account of the power which the moon is supposed to exert over sublunary things, it was often called the goddess Fortune. It is certain that the Egyptians by Τύχη (*Fortune*), which they numbered among the gods who were present at

the birth of man, understood the moon.' Among the Arabians and Persians the moon is said to have been denominated *Sidus felix et faustum*—'The happy and propitious star.' See Rosenmüller *in loc.* Lakemacher supposes that two idols are meant—Hecate and Mana. Vitringa and Rosenmüller suppose that the sun and moon are intended. Grotius supposes that the name *Gad* means the same as the goddess Fortune, which was worshipped by the Hebrews, Chaldeans, and Arabians; and that *Meni* means a divinity of that name, which Strabo says was worshipped in Armenia and Phrygia. Other opinions may be seen in Vitringa. That two idols are intended here, there can be no doubt. For, 1. The circumstance mentioned of their preparing a table for them, and pouring out a drink-offering, is expressive of idolatry. 2. The connection implies this, as the reproof in this chapter is to a considerable extent for their idolatry. 3. The universal opinion of expositors, though they have varied in regard to the idols intended, proves this. Aben Ezra, Kimchi, and the Rabbins generally suppose that by *Gad* the planet Jupiter was intended, which they say was worshipped throughout the East as the god of fortune, and this is now the prevalent opinion. The word גַּד (*Gad*), says Gesenius, means *fortune*, especially the god Fortune, which was worshipped in Babylon. He supposes that it was the same idol which was also called Baal or Bel (comp. Notes on ch. xlvi. 1), and that by this name the planet Jupiter—*Stella Jovis*—was intended, which was regarded throughout the East as the genius and giver of good fortune, hence called by the Arabians *bona fortuna major*—'the greater good fortune.' The word 'Meni,' on the other hand, Gesenius supposes to denote the planet Venus, called in the East *bona fortuna minor*—'the lesser good fortune.' The Vulgate renders this, *Fortunæ*—'To Fortune.' The LXX., Τῷ δαιμονίῳ—'To a demon;' though, in the corresponding member, *Meni* is rendered by τῇ τύχῃ—'To Fortune,' and it is possible that the *order* of the words has been inverted, and that they meant to render the word *Gad* by Fortune. The Chaldee renders it simply, לְטַעֲוָן—'To idols.' It is agreed on all hands that *some* idol is here referred to that was extensively worshipped in the East; and the general impression is, that it was an idol representing *Fortune*. But whether it was the Sun, or the planet Jupiter, is not easy to determine. That it was customary to place a table before the idol has been already remarked, and is expressly affirmed by Jerome. 'In all cities,' says he, 'and especially in Egypt, and in Alexandria, it was an ancient custom of idolatry, that on the last day of the year, and of the last month, they placed a table filled with food of various kinds, and a cup containing wine and honey mixed together—*poculum mulso mistum*—either as an expression of thankfulness for the fertility of the past year, or invoking fertility for the coming year.' Thus Herodotus (iii. 18) also describes the celebrated table of the sun in Ethiopia. 'What they call the table of the sun was this: A plain in the vicinity of the city was filled, to the height of four feet, with roasted flesh of all kinds of animals, which was carried there in the night under the inspection of magistrates; during the day, whoever pleased was at liberty to go and satisfy his hunger. The natives of the place affirm that the earth spontaneously produces all these viands; this, however, is what they call the table of the sun.' ¶ *And that furnish the drink-offering.* In all ancient worship, it was customary to pour out a libation, or a drink-offering. This was done among idolaters, to complete the idea of a repast. As they placed food before the idols, so they also poured out wine before them, with the idea of propitiating them (see Notes on ch. lvii. 6). ¶ *To that number.* Marg. 'Meni.' The phrase, 'to that number' evidently conveys no idea, and it would have been much better to have retained the name *Meni*, without any attempt to translate it. The rendering, 'to that number' was adopted because the word מְנִי *mĕnī* is derived from מָנָה *mânâ*, to allot, to appoint, to number. Various opinions also have been entertained in regard to this. Rosenmüller and many others suppose that the moon is intended, and it has been supposed

12 Therefore [a] will I number you to the sword, and ye shall all bow down to the slaughter: because when [b] I called, ye did not answer; when I spake, ye did not hear; but did evil before mine eyes, and did choose that wherein I delighted not.

a Zep.1.4-6. b 2 Ch.36.15.

---

that the name *Meni* was given to that luminary because it *numbered* the months, or divided the time. Bynæus and David Mills have endeavoured to demonstrate that this was the moon, and that this was extensively worshipped in Eastern nations. Vitringa supposes that it was the same deity which was worshipped by the Syrians and Philistines by the name of *Astarte*, or *Ashtaroth*, as it is called in the Scripture; or as οὐρανίης, the queen of heaven; and if the name *Gad* be supposed to represent the sun, the name *Meni* will doubtless represent the moon. The goddess Ashtaroth or Astarte, was a goddess of the Sidonians, and was much worshipped in Syria and Phenicia. Solomon introduced her worship in Jerusalem (1 Kings xi. 33). Three hundred priests were constantly employed in her service at Hierapolis in Syria. She was called 'the queen of heaven;' and is usually mentioned in connection with Baal. Gesenius supposes that the planet Venus is intended, regarded as the source of good fortune, and worshipped extensively in connection with the planet Jupiter, especially in the regions of Babylonia. It seems to be agreed that the word refers to the worship of either the moon or the planet Venus, regarded as the goddess of good fortune. It is not very material which is intended, nor is it easy to determine. The works referred to above may be consulted for a more full examination of the subject than is consistent with the design of these Notes. The leading idea of the prophet is, that they were deeply sunken and debased in thus forsaking JEHOVAH, and endeavouring to propitiate the favour of idol-gods.

12. *Therefore will I number you to the sword.* There is undoubtedly an allusion here to the idol *Meni* mentioned in ver. 11, and a play upon the name, in accordance with a custom quite common in the sacred Scriptures. The word מָנִיתִי, *mânîthî*, 'I will number,' is derived from מָנָה, *mânâ*, the same word from which מְנִי, *mĕnî*, is derived. The idea is, since they worshipped a god whose name denoted *number*—perhaps one who was supposed to number or appoint the fates of men—God would *number* them. He would determine their destiny. It would not be done by any idol that was supposed to preside over the destinies of men; not by blind fate, or by any one of the heavenly bodies, but it would be by an intelligent and holy God. And thus *numbering* or *determining* their lot would not be in accordance with their expectations, imparting to them *a happy fortune*, but would be devoting them to the sword; that is, to destruction. The allusion is, probably, to the calamities which God afterwards brought on them by the invasion of the Chaldeans. ¶ *And ye shall all bow down to the slaughter.* This is evidently strong, and probably hyperbolic language, meaning that a large portion of the nation would be cut off by the sword. The allusion here is, I think, to the slaughter of the Jewish people in the invasion of the Chaldeans. The evil of idolatry prevailed, in the time of Isaiah, under the reign of Manasseh; and in the time of Zedekiah it had increased so much even in Jerusalem, that it was said, 'All the chief priests and the people transgressed very much after all the abominations of the heathen; and polluted the house of the Lord which he had hallowed in Jerusalem .... And they mocked the messengers of God, and despised his words, and misused his prophets, until the wrath of the Lord arose against his people, till there was no remedy. Therefore he brought upon them the king of the Chaldeans, who slew their young men with the sword, in the house of their sanctuary, and had no compassion upon young man or maiden, old man or him that stooped for age; he gave them all into their hand' (2 Chron. xxxvi. 14, 16, 17). It is possible, also, that this is intended to express a more general

13 Therefore thus saith the Lord
GOD, Behold, my servants shall eat,
but ye shall be hungry: behold, my
servants shall drink, but ye shall be
thirsty: behold, my servants shall
rejoice, but ye shall be ashamed:
14 Behold, my servants shall
sing for joy of heart, but ye [a]shall
cry for sorrow of heart, and shall
howl for [1]vexation of spirit.
15 And ye shall leave your name
for a curse [b]unto my chosen: for
the Lord GOD shall slay thee, and
call his servants by another name:

[a] Mat.8.12. [1] breaking. [b] Zec.8.13.

truth, and to intimate that when his people forsake him he will punish them; but the primary reference, it is proable, was to the slaughter caused by the Babylonians when they destroyed Jerusalem. ¶ *Because when I called.* When I called you by the prophets to repentance and to my service (see Prov. i. 24, *sq.*) ¶ *Ye did not answer.* You showed the same disregard and contempt which a child does who suffers a parent to call him, and who pays no attention to it. One of the chief aggravations of human guilt is, that the sinner pays no attention to the calls of God. He pretends not to hear; or he hears to disregard it. No more decided contempt can be shown to the Almighty; no deeper proof of the stupidity and guilt of men can be furnished. ¶ *But did evil before mine eyes* (see Notes on ver. 3).

13. *Therefore, thus saith the Lord* GOD. The design of this verse is to show what would be the difference between those who kept and those who forsook his commandments. The one would be objects of his favour, and have abundance; the other would be objects of his displeasure, and be subjected to the evils of poverty, grief, and want. ¶ *My servants shall eat.* Shall have abundance. They shall be objects of my favour. ¶ *But ye.* Ye who revolt from me, and who worship idols. ¶ *Shall be hungry.* Shall be subjected to the evils of want. The idea is, that the one should partake of his favour; the other should be punished.

14. *Shall sing for joy of heart.* They who serve me shall have abundant occasion of rejoicing. *But ye—shall howl.* You shall shriek under the anguish and distress that shall come upon you. ¶ *For vexation of spirit.* Marg. as in Hebrew, 'Breaking.' That is, your spirit shall be broken and crushed under the weight of the calamities that shall come upon you.

15. *And ye shall leave your name for a curse unto my chosen.* To my people; to those whom I have selected to be my friends. The word here rendered 'curse' (שְׁבוּעָה) means properly an oath, or *a swearing;* and then an imprecation or a curse (see Num. v. 21; Dan. ix. 11). The sense here seems to be, that their punishment would be so great that it would become the subject of imprecation when others wished to bind themselves in the most solemn manner by an oath. The pious, who wished to confirm a promise or a covenant in the most solemn manner, would say, 'If we do not perform the promise, then let us experience the same punishment at the hand of God which they have done' (comp. Jer. xxix. 22). Or it may mean, that their name would be used proverbially, like that of Sodom, as a signal example of wickedness and of the abhorrence of God. ¶ *And call his servants by another name.* So disgraceful and dishonourable shall be that name, that JEHOVAH will apply another name to his people. Is there not an allusion here to the designed change of the *name* by which the people of God are known? Has it not been by the special providence of God that his true people are now known by another appellation? Is there any name on earth now that is more the subject of reproach and execration than all the appellations by which his ancient people were known? The name *Jew*—what ideas does it convey to all the nations of the earth? It is connected with reproach; a name regarded as belonging to a people accursed by God; a name more universally detested than any other known among men. And was it not *because* this name would be thus dishonoured, reproached, and despised, that another

16 That he who blesseth [a] himself in the earth, shall bless himself in the God of truth; and he that sweareth [b] in the earth, shall swear by the God of truth; because the former troubles are forgotten; and because they are hid from mine eyes.

17 For behold, I create new heavens, [c] and a new earth: and the former shall not be remembered, nor [1] come into mind.

a Je.4.2. b De.6.13; Ps.63.11. c 2 Pe.3.13; Re.21.1. 1 *upon the heart.*

was given to the true people of God—the name CHRISTIAN — an honoured name—denoting true attachment to the Messiah?

16. *That he who blesseth himself in the earth.* That is, he who shall invoke blessings on himself. ¶ *Shall bless himself in the God of truth.* Or by the true God. He shall not seek a blessing from a false god; but he shall come before the true God, and seek a blessing at his hand. ¶ *And he that sweareth.* Every oath that is taken in the land shall be by the true God. There shall be no swearing by idols; but the true God shall be everywhere acknowledged. ¶ *Because the former troubles are forgotten.* The former punishments and calamities shall be passed away. The favour of God shall be restored. His pure worship shall be re-established, and his name shall be celebrated again in the land. The image here is one of returning prosperity and favour; a state when the happiness will be so great that all the former trials will be regarded as not worthy of recollection.

17. *For behold.* The idea in this verse is, that there should be a state of glory as great as if a new heaven and a new earth were to be made. ¶ *I create new heavens.* Calamity and punishment in the Bible are often represented by the heavens growing dark, and being rolled up like as a scroll, or passing away (see Notes on ch. xiii. 10; xxxiv. 4). On the contrary, prosperity, happiness, and the Divine favour, are represented by the clearing up of a cloudy sky; by the restoration of the serene and pure light of the sun; or, as here, by the creation of new heavens (comp. Notes on ch. li. 16). The figure of great transformations in material things is one that is often employed in the Scriptures, and especially in Isaiah, to denote great spiritual changes (see ch. xi.; li. 3; xxxv. 1, 2, 7; lx. 13, 17). In the New Testament, the phrase here used is employed to denote the future state of the righteous; but whether on earth, after it shall have been purified by fire, or in heaven, has been a subject of great difference of opinion (see 2 Pet. iii. 13; Rev. xxi. 1). The passage before us is highly poetical, and we are not required to understand it literally. There is, so far as the language is concerned, no more reason for understanding this literally than there is for so understanding the numerous declarations which affirm that the brute creation will undergo a change in their very nature, on the introduction of the gospel (ch. xi.); and all that the language necessarily implies is, that there would be changes in the condition of the people of God as great *as if* the heavens, overcast with clouds and subject to storms, should be re-created, so as to become always mild and serene; or *as if* the earth, so barren in many places, should become universally fertile and beautiful. The immediate reference here is, doubtless, to the land of Palestine, and to the important changes which would be produced there on the return of the exiles; but it cannot be doubted that, under this imagery, there was couched a reference to far more important changes and blessings in future times under the Messiah—changes as great *as if* a barren and sterile world should become universally beautiful and fertile. ¶ *For the former shall not be remembered.* That is, that which shall be created shall be so superior in beauty as entirely to eclipse the former. The sense is, tha[t] the future condition of the peop[l]e [of] God would be as superior to what it w[as] in ancient times as would be a ne[wly] created earth and heaven superi[or in] beauty to this—where the heave[ns are] so often obscured by clouds, and the earth is so extensively des[olate]

18 But be ye glad and rejoice
for[a] ever *in that* which I create:
for, behold, I create Jerusalem a
rejoicing, and her people a joy.
19 And [b] I will rejoice in Jerusalem, and joy in my people: and
the voice of weeping [c] shall be no
more heard in her, nor the voice
of crying.
20 There shall be no more
thence an infant of days, nor an
old man that hath not filled his
days; for the child shall die an
hundred years old; but the [d] sinner *being* an hundred years old
shall be accursed.

a ch.51.11; 1 Th.5.16. b ch.62.5. c Re.7.17. d Ec.8.12.13.

barren. ¶ *Nor come into mind.* Marg. as Heb. 'Upon the heart.' That is, it shall not be thought of; it shall be wholly forgotten. On this verse, comp. Notes on ch. li. 16.

18. *But be ye glad and rejoice* (see Notes on ch. li. 11). ¶ *For ever.* It is not to be momentary happiness—like a bright morning that is soon overcast with clouds. The joy of God's people is to endure for ever, and they shall have ceaseless cause of praise and thanksgiving. ¶ *I create Jerusalem a rejoicing.* A source of rejoicing; or a place of rejoicing. ¶ *And her people a joy.* That is, in themselves joyful, and a source of joy to all others. The idea is, that the church would be a place of the highest happiness, and that they who were redeemed would have occasion of perpetual joy. The Saviour did not come to minister gloom, nor is the true effect of religion to make his people melancholy. Religion produces seriousness; but seriousness is not inconsistent with permanent happiness. Religion produces deep thought and soberness of deportment and conversation; but this is not inconsistent with a heart at ease, or with a good conscience, or with permanent joy. Religion fills the mind with hope of ETERNAL LIFE; and the highest happiness which the soul *can* know must be in connection with the prospect of unchanging blessedness beyond the grave.

19. *And I will rejoice in Jerusalem* (see Notes on ch. lxii. 5). ¶ *And the voice of weeping shall no more be heard* (see Notes on ch. xxv. 7, 8).

20. *There shall be no more thence.* The LXX., the Syriac, and the Vulgate read this, 'There shall not be *there.*' The change requires the omission of a single letter in the present Hebrew text, and the sense seems to demand it. The design of the prophet here is, to describe the times of happiness and prosperity which would succeed the calamities under which the nation had been suffering. This he does by a great variety of images, all denoting substantially the same thing. In ver. 17, the change is represented to be as great as if a new heaven and a new earth should be created; in this verse the image is, that the inhabitants would reach a great age, and that the comparatively happy times of the patriarchs would be restored; in ver. 21, the image is taken from the perfect security in their plans of labour, and the fact that they would enjoy the fruit of their toil; in ver. 25, the image employed is that taken from the change in the nature of the animal creation. All these are poetic images designed as illustrations of the general truth, and, like other poetic images, they are not to be taken literally. ¶ *An infant of days.* A child; a sucking child. So the Hebrew word, עול, denotes. The LXX. render it, 'Nor shall there be there any more an untimely birth (ἄωρος), and an old man who has not filled up his time.' The idea is not that there should be no infant in those future times—which would be an idea so absurd that a prophet would not use it even in poetic fiction—but that there will not be an infant *who shall not fill up his days*, or who will be short-lived. All shall live long, and all shall be blessed with health, and continual vigour and youth. ¶ *Nor an old man that hath not filled his days.* They shall enjoy the blessings of great longevity, and that not a longevity that shall be broken and feeble, but which shall be vigorous and happy. In further illustration of this sentiment, we may remark, 1. That there is no reason to suppose that it will be *literally* fulfilled

even in the millenium. If it is to be regarded as literally to be fulfilled, then for the same reason we are to suppose that in that time the nature of the lion will be literally changed, and that he will eat straw like the ox, and that the nature of the wolf and the lamb will be so far changed that they shall lie down together (ver. 25). But there is no reason to suppose this; nor is there any good reason to suppose that *literally* no infant or child will die in those times, or that no old man will be infirm, or that *all* will live to the same great age. 2. The promise of long life is regarded in the Bible as a blessing, and is an image, everywhere, of prosperity and happiness. Thus the patriarchs were regarded as having been highly favoured men, because God lengthened out their days; and throughout the Scriptures it is represented as a proof of the favour of God, that a man is permitted to live long, and to see a numerous posterity (see Gen. xlv. 10; Ps. xxi. 4; xxiii. 6; cxxviii. 6 (Heb.); xci. 16; Prov. iii. 2–14; xvii. 6. 3. No one can doubt that the prevalence of the gospel everywhere would greatly lengthen out the life of man. Let any one reflect on the great number that are now cut off in childhood in heathen lands by their parents, all of whom would have been spared had their parents been Christians; on the numbers of children who are destroyed in early life by the effects of the intemperance of their parents, most of whom would have survived if their parents had been virtuous; on the numbers of young men now cut down by vice, who would have continued to live if they had been under the influence of the gospel; on the immense hosts cut off, and most of them in middle life, by war, who would have lived to a good old age if the gospel had prevailed and put a period to wars; on the millions who are annually cut down by intemperance and lust, and other raging passions, by murder and piracy, or who are punished by death for crime; on the millions destroyed by pestilential disease sent by offended Heaven on guilty nations; and let him reflect that these sources of death will be dried up by the prevalence of pure virtue and religion, and he will see that a great change *may* yet take place literally in the life of man. 4. A similar image is used by the classic writers to denote a golden age, or an age of great prosperity and happiness. Thus the Sybil, in the *Sybilline Oracles*, B. vii., speaking of the future age, says, Στήσει δὲ τὸ γένος, ὡς πάρος ἦν σοι—'A race shall be restored as it was in the ancient times.' So Hesiod, describing the silver age, introduces a boy as having reached the age of an hundred years, and yet but a child:

'Αλλ' ἑκατὸν μὲν παῖς ἔτεα παρὰ μητέρι κεδνῃ,
'Ετρέφετ' ἀτάλλων μέγα νήπιος ᾧ ἐνὶ οἴκῳ.

¶ *For the child shall die an hundred years old.* That is, he that is an hundred years old when he dies, shall still be a child or a youth. This is nearly the same sentiment which is expressed by Hesiod, as quoted above. The prophet has evidently in his eye the longevity of the patriarchs, when an individual of an hundred years of age was comparatively young—the proportion between that and the usual period of life then being about the same as that between the age of ten and the usual period of life now. We are not, I apprehend, to suppose that this is to be taken literally, but it is figurative language, designed to describe the comparatively happy state referred to by the prophet, *as if* human life should be lengthened out to the age of the patriarchs, and as if he who is now regarded as an old man, should then be regarded as in the vigour of his days. At the same time it is true, that the influence of temperance, industry, and soberness of life, such as would exist if the rules of the gospel were obeyed, would carry forward the vigour of youth far into advancing years, and mitigate most of the evils now incident to the decline of life. The few imperfect experiments which have been made of the effect of entire temperance and of elevated virtue; of subduing the passions by the influence of the gospel, and of prudent means for prolonging health and life, such as the gospel will prompt a man to use, who has any just view of the value of life, show what *may* yet be done in happier times. It is an obvious reflec-

21 And [a] they shall build houses,
and inhabit *them;* and they shall
plant vineyards, and eat the fruit
of them.
22 They shall not build, and
another [b] inhabit; they shall not
plant, and another eat; for as the
days of a tree [c] *are* the days of my
people, and mine elect shall [1] long
enjoy the work of their hands.

a Am.9.14. b Le.26.16; De.28.30. c Ps 92.12.

1 *make them continue long,* or, *wear out.*

tion here, that if such effects are to be anticipated from the prevalence of true religion and of temperance, then he is the best friend of man who endeavours most sedulously to bring others under the influence of the gospel, and to extend the principles of temperance and virtue. The gospel of Christ would do more to prolong human life than all other causes combined; and when that prevails everywhere, putting a period, as it must, to infanticide, and war, and intemperance, and murder, and piracy, and suicide, and duelling, and raging and consuming passions, then it is impossible for the most vivid imagination to conceive the effect which shall be produced on the health and long life, as well as on the happiness of mankind. ¶ *But the sinner* being *an hundred years old shall be accursed.* The sense of this appears to be, 'not all who reach to a great age shall be judged to be the friends and favourites of God. Though a sinner shall reach that advanced period of life, yet he shall be cursed of God, and shall be cut down in his sins. He shall be held to be a sinner and shall die, and shall be regarded as accursed.' Other interpretations of this expression may be seen in Poole and in Vitringa. The above seems to me to be the true exposition.

21. *And they shall build houses* (see Notes on ch. lxii. 8, 9).

22. *They shall not build, and another inhabit.* Every man shall enjoy the avails of his labour. ¶ *For as the days of a tree* are *the days of my people.* That is, in that future time, such *shall be* the length of the lives of the people (see ver. 21). The LXX. render this, 'The days of the tree of life.' The Syriac, 'As the days of trees.' The Chaldee as the LXX. The idea is, that the lives of his people would be greatly prolonged (see Notes on ver. 20). A *tree* is among the most long-lived of material objects. The oak, the terebinth, the cypress, the cedar, the banyan, attain to a great age. Many trees also live to a much longer period than a thousand years. The Baobab tree of Senegal (*Adansonia digitata*) is supposed to attain the age of several thousand years. Adanson inferred that one which he measured, and found to be thirty feet in diameter, had attained the age of 5150 years. Having made an incision to a certain depth, he first counted three hundred rings of annual growth, and observed what thickness the tree had gained in that period. The average rate of growth of younger trees, of the same species, was then ascertained, and the calculation made according to a supposed mean rate of increase. De Candolle considers it not improbable that the celebrated Taxodium, of Chapultepec, in Mexico, which is 117 feet in circumference, may be still more aged. In Macartney's *Embassy to China*, i. 131, an account is given of a tree of this description, which was found to be at the base no less than fifty-six feet in girth. On the longevity of trees, see *Bibliotheca Univ.*, May 1831, quoted in Lyell's *Geology*, ii. 261. The idea here is, simply, that his people would attain to an age like that of the trees of the forest; that is, that the state of things under the Messiah would be *as if* human life were greatly prolonged (see Notes on ver. 20). ¶ *And mine elect shall long enjoy the work of their hands.* Marg. 'Make them continue long,' *or* 'wear out.' The word here used (יְבַלּוּ from בָּלָה) means properly to fall, to fall away, to fail; to wear out, to wax old (Deut. viii. 4; xxix. 4; Isa. l. 9; li. 6); hence in Piel, *to consume.* The idea here is, that they would live to consume; *i.e.*, to enjoy the productions of their own labour. Their property should not be wrested from them by injurious taxation, or by plunder; but they would be permitted long to possess it, until they

23 They shall not labour in vain; nor bring forth for trouble: for they *are*[a] the seed of the blessed of the LORD, and their offspring with them.

24 And it shall come to pass, that before they call, I will answer; and [b] while they are yet speaking, I will hear.

[a] ch.61.9; Ro.9.7,8.

[b] Ps.32.5; Da.9.20,21.

should *wear it out,* or until it should be consumed. Vulg. 'The works of their hands shall be of long continuance (*inveterabunt*),' or shall be kept a long time. The LXX. 'For the works of their labours (των πόνων) shall become old, or of long continuance (παλαιώσουσιν).' See Notes on ch. lxii. 8, 9.

23. *They shall not labour in vain.* That is, either because their land shall be unfruitful, or because others shall plunder them. ¶ *Nor bring forth for trouble.* Lowth renders this, 'Neither shall they generate a short-lived race.' Noyes, 'Nor bring forth children for an early death.' The LXX. render it, Οὐδὲ τεκνοποιήσουσιν εἰς κατάραν—'Nor shall they bring forth children for a curse.' The Chaldee, 'Nor shall they nourish them for death.' There can be no doubt that this refers to their posterity, and that the sense is, that they should not be the parents of children who would be subject to an early death or to a curse. The word here rendered 'bring forth' (יֵלְדוּ) is a word that uniformly means to bear, to bring forth as a mother, or to beget as a father. And the promise here is, that which would be so grateful to parental feelings, that their posterity would be long-lived and respected. The word here rendered 'trouble' (בֶּהָלָה) means properly *terror,* and then the effect of terror, or that which causes terror, sudden destruction. It is derived from בָּהַל *bâhăl,* to trouble, to shake, to be in trepidation, to flee, and then to punish suddenly; and the connection here seems to require the sense that their children should not be devoted to sudden destruction. ¶ *For they* are *the seed of the blessed of the* LORD (see Notes on ch. lix. 21).

24. *Before they call, I will answer.* That is, their desires shall be anticipated, God will see their wants, and he will impart to them the blessings which they need. He will not wait to be applied to for the blessing. How many such blessings do all his people receive at the hand of God! How ready is he to anticipate our wants! How watchful is he of our necessities; and how rich his benevolence in providing for us! Even the most faithful and prayerful of his people receive numerous favours and comforts at his hand for which they have not directly asked him. The prayer for the supply of our daily food, 'Give us this day our daily bread,' God had anticipated, and had prepared the means of answering it, long before, in the abundant harvest. Had he waited until the prayer was offered, it could not have been answered without a miracle. Ever watchful, he anticipates our necessities, and in his providence and grace lays the foundation for granting the favour long before we ask him. ¶ *And while they are yet speaking, I will hear.* So it was with Daniel (Dan. ix. 20, 21; comp. Ps. xxxii. 5). So it was with the early disciples when they were assembled in an upper room in Jerusalem, and when the Spirit of God descended with great power on the day of Pentecost (Acts ii. 1, 2). So when Paul and Silas, in the prison at Philippi, 'prayed and sang praises to God,' he heard them and came for their rescue (Acts xvi. 25, 26). So it has often been—and especially in revivals of religion. When his people have been deeply impressed with a sense of the languishing state of religion; when they have gone unitedly before God and implored a blessing; God has heard their prayers, and even while they were speaking has begun a work of grace. Hundreds of such instances have occurred, alike demonstrating the faithfulness of God to his promises, and fitted to encourage his people, and to excite them to prayer. It is one of the precious promises pertaining to the blessings of the reign of the Messiah, that the answer of prayer shall be IMMEDIATE—and for this his people should look, and this they should expect. God can as easily answer prayer at once as to

25 The [a] wolf and the lamb shall feed together, and the lion shall eat straw like the bullock: and dust [b] *shall be* the serpent's meat. They shall not hurt nor destroy in all my holy mountain, saith the LORD.

a ch.11.6-9. *b* Ge.3.14.

CHAPTER LXVI.

ANALYSIS.

IT is generally supposed that this chapter is a continuation of the subject of the foregoing (Lowth). The general design is to reprove the hypocritical portion of the nation, and to comfort the pious with the assurance of the favour of God, the accession of the Gentile world, and the destruction of the foes of the church. The Jews valued themselves much upon the pomp of their temple-worship and the splendour of their ritual; they supposed that that was to be perpetual; and they assumed great merit to themselves for the regular services of their religion. Before the captivity in Babylon they were prone to fall into idolatry; afterwards they were kept from it, and to the present time they have not been guilty of it—so effectual was that heavy judgment in correcting this national propensity. But after their captivity their national proneness to sin assumed another form. That love of form and strict ceremony; that dependence on mere rites and the external duties of religion; that heartless and pompous system of worship commenced, which ultimately terminated in Pharisaic pride, and which was scarcely less an object of abhorrence to God than gross idolatry. To that state of things the prophet probably looked forward; and his object in this chapter was to reprove that reliance on the mere forms of external worship, and the pride in their temple and its service which he saw would succeed the return from the exile in Babylon.

It is generally agreed that the reference here is to the state of things which would follow the return from Babylon. Lowth supposes that it refers to the time when Herod would be rebuild-

delay it; and when the proper state of mind exists, he is as ready to answer it now as to defer it to a future time. What encouragement have we to pray! How faithful, how fervent should we be in our supplications! How full of guilt are we if one single blessing is withheld from our world that *might* have been imparted if we had prayed as we ought; if one single soul shall be lost who might have been saved if WE had not been unfaithful in prayer!

25. *The wolf and the lamb shall feed together* (see Notes on ch. xi.) ¶ *And the lion shall eat straw.* Shall eat hay or provender like the ox. The food of the lion now is flesh. Changes shall take place as great *as if* his nature were changed, and he should graze with the herds of the field. See a full illustration of this sentiment from the classic writers in the Notes on ch. xi. 6. ¶ *Like the bullock.* Or the ox—the cattle that *herd* together—for so the Hebrew word (בָּקָר) means. The word may be applied to a bullock, an ox, or a cow. ¶ *And dust* shall be *the serpent's meat.* There is evidently here an allusion to the sentence pronounced on the serpent in Gen. iii. 14. The meaning of the declaration here is, probably, that dust should *continue* to be the food of the serpent. The sentence on him should be perpetual. He should not be injurious to man—either by tempting him again, or by the venom of his fangs. The state of security would be as great under the Messiah *as if* the most deadly and poisonous kinds of reptiles should become wholly innoxious, and should not attempt to prey upon men. It is to be remembered that many of the serpent kind included under the general word used here (נָחָשׁ), were dangerous to men; and indeed a large portion of them are deadly in their bite. But in future times there will be a state of security as great *as if* the whole serpent tribe were innocuous and should live on the dust alone. There can be no doubt that the prophet means here to describe the passions and evil propensities of men, which have a strong resemblance to the ferocity of the wolf, or the lion, and the deadly poison of the serpent, and to say that those passions would be subdued, and that peace and concord would prevail on the earth (see Notes on ch. xi. 8). ¶ *They shall not hurt nor destroy.* See this explained in the Notes on ch. xi. 9. All this is partially realized wherever the gospel prevails, but it will be more fully realized when that gospel shall exert its full power and shall be spread around the world.

ing the temple in the most magnificent manner, and when, notwithstanding the heavy judgment of God was hanging over their heads, the nation was formal in its worship, and proud and self-confident, as if it was the favourite of God. Vitringa supposes that it refers to the time of the introduction of the new economy, or the beginning of the times of the Messiah.

That it refers to times succeeding the captivity at Babylon, and is designed to be at once a prophetic description and a reproof of the sins which would prevail after their return, is apparent from the whole structure of the chapter, and particularly from the following considerations: 1. There is no one description, as in the former chapters, of the land as desolate, or the city of Jerusalem and the temple in ruins (see ch. lxiv. 10, 11). 2. There is no charge against them for being *idolatrous*, as there had been in the previous chapters (see especially ch. lxv. 3, 4, 11). The sin that is specified here is of a wholly different kind. 3. It is evidently addressed to them when they were either rebuilding the temple, or when they greatly prided themselves on its service (see ver. 1). 4. It is addressed to them when they were engaged in offering sacrifice with great formality, and with great reliance on the mere external services of religion; when sacrifice had degenerated into mere form, and when the spirit with which it was done was as abominable in the sight of God as the most odious of all crimes. From these considerations, it seems to me that the chapter is designed to refer to a state of things that would succeed the return from the exile at Babylon, and be a *general* description of the spirit with which they would then engage in the worship of God. They would indeed rebuild the temple according to the promise; but they would manifest a spirit in regard to the temple which required the severe reproof of JEHOVAH. They would again offer sacrifice in the place where their fathers had done it; but though they would be effectually cured of their idolatrous tendencies, yet they would evince a spirit that was as hateful to God as the worst form of idolatry, or the most heinous crimes. A large portion, therefore, of the nation would still be the object of the Divine abhorrence, and be subjected to punishment; but the truly pious would be preserved, and their number would be increased by the accession of the Gentile world.

As an additional consideration to show the correctness of this view of the time to which the chapter refers, we may remark, that a large part of the prophecies of Isaiah are employed in predicting the certain return from the exile, the re-establishment of religion in their own land, and the resumption of the worship of God there. It was natural, therefore, that the spirit of inspiration should glance at the character of the nation *subsequent* to the return, and that the prophet should give, in the conclusion of his book, *a summary graphic description of what would occur in future times.* This I take to be the design of the closing chapter of the prophecies of Isaiah. He states in general the character of the Jewish people after the return from the exile; condemns the sins with which they would then be chargeable; comforts the portion of the nation that would be disposed in sincerity to serve God; predicts the rapid and glorious increase of the church; declares that the enemies of God would be cut off; affirms that all the world would yet come at stated seasons to worship before God; and closes the whole book by saying that the people of God would go forth and see all their enemies slain. This general view may be more distinctly seen by the following analysis of the chapter:—

I. JEHOVAH says that heaven was his throne, and the earth his footstool, and that no house which they could build for him would adequately express his glory; no external worship would suitably declare his majesty. He preferred the homage of an humble heart to the most magnificent external worship; the tribute of a sincere offering to the most costly outward devotion (1, 2).

II. He declares his sense of the evil of mere external worship, and threatens punishment to the hypocrites who should engage in this manner in his service (3, 4). In these verses it is implied that in the service of the temple after the return from the exile, there would be a spirit evinced in their public worship that would be as hateful to God as would be murder or idolatry, or as would be the cutting off a dog's neck or the sacrifice of swine; that is, that the spirit of hypocrisy, self-righteousness, and pride, would be supremely odious in his sight. They were not therefore to infer that *because* they would be restored from the exile, therefore their worship would be pure and acceptable to God. The fact would be that it would become so utterly abominable in his sight that he would cut them off and bring all their fears upon them; that is, he would severely punish them.

III. Yet even then there would be a portion of the people that would hear the word of the Lord, and to whom he would send comfort and deliverance. He therefore promises to his true church great extension, and especially the accession of the Gentiles (5–14). 1. A part of the nation would cast out and persecute the other, under pretence of promoting the glory of God and doing his will (5). Yet JEHOVAH would appear for the joy of the persecuted portion, and the persecutors would be confounded. 2. A sound is heard as of great agitation in the city; a voice indicating great and important revolutions (6). This voice is designed to produce consolation to his people; dismay to his foes. 3. A promise is given of the great and sudden enlargement of Zion—an increase when conversions would be as sudden as if a child were born without the ordinary delay and pain of parturition; as great as if a nation were born in a day (7–9). 4. All that love Zion are called on to rejoice with her, for the Gentile nations would come like a flowing stream, and the church would be comforted, as when a mother comforteth her child (10–14).

IV. God would punish his foes. He would devote idolaters to destruction (15–17).

V. He would send the message of salvation to those who were in distant parts of the world (19–21).

VI. At that time, the worship of God would everywhere be regularly and publicly celebrated. From one new moon to another, and from one Sabbath to another, all flesh would come and worship before God (23).

VII. The friends of God would be permitted to see the final and interminable ruin of all the transgressors against the Most High (24). Their destruction would be complete; their worm would not die, and their fire would not be quenched, and the whole scene of the work of redemption would be wound up in the complete and eternal salvation of all the true people of God, and in the complete and eternal ruin of all his foes. With this solemn truth—a truth relating to the final retribution of mankind, the prophecies of Isaiah appropriately close. Where more properly could be the winding up of the series of visions in this wonderful book, than in a view of the complete destruction of the enemies of God; how more sublimely than by representing the whole redeemed church as going forth together to look upon their destruction, as victors go forth to look upon a mighty army of foes slain and unburied on the battle-field?

THUS saith the LORD, The heaven [a] *is* my throne, and the earth *is* my footstool: where *is* the house that ye build unto me? and where *is* the place of my rest?

a 2 Ch.6.18; Mat.5.34; Ac.17.24.

CHAPTER LXVI.

1. *The heaven* is *my throne* (see Notes on ch. lvii. 15). Here he is represented as having his seat or throne there. He speaks as a king. Heaven is the place where he holds his court; whence he dispenses his commands; and from whence he surveys all his works (comp. 2 Chron. vi. 18; Matt. v. 34). The idea here is, that as God dwelt in the vast and distant heavens, no *house* that could be built on earth could be magnificent enough to be his abode. ¶ *The earth* is *my footstool.* A footstool is that which is placed under the feet when we sit. The idea here is, that God was so glorious that even the earth itself could be regarded only as his footstool. It is probable that the Saviour had this passage in his eye in his declaration in the sermon on the mount, 'Swear not at all; neither by heaven, for it is God's throne; nor by the earth, for it is his footstool' (Matt. v. 34, 35). ¶ *Where* is *the house that ye build unto me?* What house can you build that will be an appropriate dwelling for him who fills heaven and earth? The same idea, substantially, was expressed by Solomon when he dedicated the temple: 'But will God indeed dwell on the earth? Behold, the heaven, and heaven of heavens cannot contain thee; how much less this house that I have builded!' (1 Kings viii. 27.) Substantially the same thought is found in the address of Paul at Athens: 'God, that made the world, and all things therein, seeing that he is Lord of heaven and earth, dwelleth not in temples made with hands' (Acts xvii. 24). ¶ *And where* is *the place of my rest?* It has already been intimated (in the analysis) that this refers probably to the time subsequent to the captivity. Lowth supposes that it refers to the time of the rebuilding of the temple by Herod. So also Vitringa understands it, and supposes that it refers to the pride and self-confidence of those who then imagined that they were rearing a structure that was *worthy* of being a dwelling-place of JEHOVAH. Grotius supposes that it refers to the time of the Maccabees, and that it was designed to give consolation to the pious of those times when they were about to witness the profanation of the temple by Anti-

2 For all those *things* hath mine
hand made, and all those *things*
have been, saith the LORD: but to
this *man* will I look, *even* to *him*
that is poor [a] and of a contrite
spirit, [b] and trembleth [c] at my word.
3 He that killeth an ox *is as if*
he slew a man; he that sacrificeth
a [1] lamb, *as if* he cut off a dog's
neck; he that offereth an oblation,
as if he offered swine's blood; he
that [2] burneth incense, *as if* he
blessed an idol. Yea, they have
chosen their own ways, and their
soul delighteth in their abominations.

[a] Mat.5.3. [b] ch.57.15. [c] Ezr.9.4; 10.3.

1 or, *kid*. 2 *maketh a memorial of*, Le.2.2.

ochus, and the cessation of the sacrifices for three years and a half. 'God therefore shows,' says he, 'that there was no reason why they should be offended in this thing. The most acceptable temple to him was a pious mind; and from that the value of all sacrifices was to be estimated.' Abarbanel supposes that it refers to the times of redemption. His words are these: 'I greatly wonder at the words of the learned interpreting this prophecy, when they say that the prophet in this accuses the men of his own time on account of sacrifices offered with impure hands; for lo! all these prophecies which the prophet utters in the end of his book have respect to future redemption.' See Vitringa. That it refers to some future time when the temple should be rebuilt seems to me to be evident. But what precise period it refers to—whether to times not far succeeding the captivity, or to the times of the Maccabees, or to the time of the rebuilding of the temple by Herod, it is difficult to find any data by which we can determine. From the whole strain of the prophecy, and particularly from ver. 3–5, it seems probable that it refers to the time when the temple which Herod had reared was finishing; when the nation was full of pride, self-righteousness, and hypocrisy; and when all sacrifices were about to be superseded by the one great sacrifice which the Messiah was to make for the sins of the world. At that time, God says that the spirit which would be evinced by the nation would be abominable in his sight; and to offer sacrifice then, and with the spirit which they would manifest, would be as offensive as murder or the sacrifice of a dog (see Notes on ver. 3).

2. *For all those* things *hath mine hand made*. That is, the heaven and the earth, and all that is in them. The sense is, 'I have founded for myself a far more magnificent and appropriate temple than you can make; I have formed the heavens as my dwelling-place, and I need not a dwelling reared by the hand of man.' ¶ *And all those* things *have been*. That is, have been made by me, or for me. The LXX. render it, 'All those things are mine.' Jerome renders it, 'All those things *were made*;' implying that God claimed to be the Creator of them all, and that, therefore, they all belonged to him. ¶ *But to this* man *will I look*. That is, 'I prefer a humble heart and a contrite spirit to the most magnificent earthly temple' (see Notes on ch. lvii. 15). ¶ That is *poor*. Or rather 'humble.' The word rendered 'poor' (עָנִי), denotes not one who has no property, but one who is down-trodden, crushed, afflicted, oppressed; often, as here, with the accessory idea of pious feeling (Ex. xxiv. 12; Ps. x. 2, 9). The LXX. render it, Ταπεινὸν—'Humble;' not πτωχόν (*poor*). The idea is, not that God looks with favour on a poor man merely *because* he is poor—which is not true, for his favours are not bestowed in view of external conditions in life—but that he regards with favour the man that is humble and subdued in spirit. ¶ *And of a contrite spirit*. A spirit that is broken, crushed, or deeply affected by sin. It stands opposed to a spirit that is proud, haughty, self-confident, and self-righteous. ¶ *And that trembleth at my word*. That fears me, or that reveres my commands.

3. *He that killeth an ox* is as if *he slew a man*. Lowth and Noyes render this, 'He that slayeth an ox, killeth a man.' This is a literal translation of the Hebrew. Jerome renders it, 'He who sacrifices an ox is *as if* (*quasi*) he

slew a man.' The LXX., in a very free translation—such as is common in their version of Isaiah—render it, 'The wicked man who sacrifices a calf, is as he who kills a dog; and he who offers to me fine flour, it is as the blood of swine.' Lowth supposes the sense to be, that the most flagitious crimes were united with hypocrisy, and that they who were guilty of the most extreme acts of wickedness at the same time affected great strictness in the performance of all the external duties of religion. An instance of this, he says, is referred to by Ezekiel, where he says, 'When they had slain their children to their idols, then they came the same day into my sanctuary to profane it' (ch. xxiii. 39). There can be no doubt that such offences were often committed by those who were very strict and zealous in their religious services (comp. ch. i. 11–14, with ver. 21–23. But the generality of interpreters have supposed that a different sense was to be affixed to this passage. According to their views, the particles *as if* are to be supplied; and the sense is, not that the mere killing of an ox is as sinful in the sight of God as deliberate murder, but that he who did it in the circumstances, and with the spirit referred to, evinced a spirit as odious in his sight as though he had slain a man. So the LXX., Vulgate, Chaldee, Symmachus, and Theodotion, Junius, and Tremellius, Grotius, and Rosenmüller, understand it. There is probably an allusion to the fact that human victims were offered by the heathen; and the sense is, that the sacrifices here referred to were no more acceptable in the sight of God than they were. The prophet here refers, probably, first, to the *spirit* with which this was done. Their sacrifices were offered with a temper of mind as offensive to God as if a man had been slain, and they had been guilty of murder. They were proud, vain, and hypocritical. They had forgotten the true nature and design of sacrifice, and such worship could not but be an abhorrence in the sight of God. Secondly, It may also be implied here, that the period was coming when all sacrifices would be unacceptable to God. When the Messiah should have come; when he should have made by one offering a sufficient atonement for the sins of the whole world; then all bloody sacrifices would be needless, and would be offensive in the sight of God. The sacrifice of an ox would be no more acceptable than the sacrifice of a man; and all offerings with a view to propitiate the Divine favour, or that implied that there was a deficiency in the merit of the one great atoning sacrifice, would be odious to God. ¶ *He that sacrificeth a lamb.* Marg. 'Kid.' The Hebrew word (שֶׂה) may refer to one of a flock, either of sheep or goats (Gen. xxii. 7, 8; xxx. 32). Where the species is to be distinguished, it is usually specified, as, *e.g.*, Deut. xiv. 4, שֵׂה כְשָׂבִים וְשֵׂה עִזִּים (*one of the sheep and one of the goats*). Both were used in sacrifice. ¶ As if *he cut off a dog's neck.* That is, as if he had cut off a dog's neck for sacrifice. To offer a dog in sacrifice would have been abominable in the view of a Jew. Even the price for which he was sold was not permitted to be brought into the house of God for a vow (Deut. xxiii. 18; comp. 1 Sam. xvii. 43; xxiv. 14). The dog was held in veneration by many of the heathen, and was even offered in sacrifice; and it was, doubtless, partly in view of this fact, and especially of the fact that such veneration was shown for it in Egypt, that it was an object of such detestation among the Jews. Thus Juvenal, *Sat.* xiv. says:

Oppida tota canem venerantur, nemo Dianam.

'Every city worships the dog; none worship Diana.' Diodorus (B. i.) says, 'Certain animals the Egyptians greatly venerate (σέβονται), not only when alive, but when they are dead, as cats, ichneumons, mice, and dogs.' Herodotus says also of the Egyptians, 'In some cities, when a cat dies all the inhabitants cut off their eyebrows; when a dog dies, they shave the whole body and the head.' In Samothracia there was a cave in which dogs were sacrificed to Hecate. Plutarch says, that all the Greeks sacrificed the dog. The fact that dogs were offered in sacrifice by the heathen is abundantly proved by Bochart (*Hieroz.* i. 2. 56). No kind of sacrifice could have been regarded with higher detestation by a pious Jew. But

4 I also will choose their [1] delusions, [a] and will bring their fears upon them; because [b] when I called, none did answer; when I spake, they did not hear: but they did evil before mine eyes, and chose *that* in which I delighted not.

5 Hear the word of the LORD, ye that tremble [c] at his word; Your brethren that hated you, that cast you out for my name's sake, said, Let the LORD be glorified: but he shall appear to your joy, and they shall be ashamed.

1 or, *devices*. a 2 Th.2.11. b ch.65.12; Je.7.13,14. c ver.2.

God here says, that the spirit with which they sacrificed a goat or a lamb was as hateful in his sight as would be the sacrifice of a dog; or that the time would come when, the great sacrifice for sin having been made, and the necessity for all other sacrifice having ceased, the offering of a lamb or a goat for the expiation of sin would be as offensive to him as would be the sacrifice of a dog. ¶ *He that offereth an oblation.* On the word here rendered 'oblation' (מִנְחָה) see Notes on ch. i. 13. ¶ As if he offered *swine's blood.* The sacrifice of a hog was an abomination in the sight of the Hebrews (see Notes on ch. lxv. 4). Yet here it is said that the offering of the *mĭnhhâ*, in the spirit in which they would do it, was as offensive to God as would be the pouring out of the blood of the swine on the altar. Nothing could more emphatically express the detestation of God for the spirit with which they would make their offerings, or the fact that the time would come when all such modes of worship would be offensive in his sight. ¶ *He that burneth incense.* See the word 'incense' explained in the Notes on ch. i. 13. The margin here is, 'Maketh a memorial of.' Such is the usual meaning of the word here used (זָכַר), meaning to remember, and in Hiphil to cause to remember, or to make a memorial. Such is its meaning here. Incense was burned as a *memorial* or a remembrance-offering; that is, to keep up the remembrance of God on the earth by public worship (see Notes on ch. lxii. 6). ¶ As if *he blessed an idol.* The spirit with which incense would be offered would be as offensive as idolatry. The sentiment in all this is, that the most regular and formal acts of worship where the heart is wanting, may be as offensive to God as the worst forms of crime, or the most gross and debasing idolatry. Such a spirit often characterized the Jewish people, and eminently prevailed at the time when the temple of Herod was nearly completed, and when the Saviour was about to appear.

4. *I also will choose their delusions.* Marg. 'Devices.' The Hebrew word here rendered 'delusions' and 'devices' (תַּעֲלוּלִים) properly denotes petulance, sauciness; and then vexation, adverse destiny, from עָלַל, *âlăl*, to do, to accomplish, to do evil, to maltreat. It is not used in the sense of delusions, or devices; and evidently here means the same as calamity or punishment. Comp. the Heb. in Lam. i. 22. Lowth and Noyes render it, 'Calamities;' though Jerome and the LXX. understand it in the sense of illusions or delusions; the former rendering it, '*Illusiones*, and the latter ἐμπαίγματα—'delusions.' The parallelism requires us to understand it of calamity, or something answering to 'fear,' or that which was dreaded; and the sense undoubtedly is, that God would choose out for them the kind of punishment which would be expressive of his sense of the evil of their conduct. ¶ *And will bring their fears upon them.* That is, the punishment which they have so much dreaded, or which they had so much reason to apprehend. ¶ *Because when I called* (see Notes on ch. lxv. 12). ¶ *But they did evil before mine eyes* (see Notes on ch. lxv. 3).

5. *Hear the word of the* LORD. This is an address to the pious and persecuted portion of the nation. It is designed for their consolation, and contains the assurance that JEHOVAH would appear in their behalf, and that they should be under his protecting care though they were cast out by their brethren. To whom this refers has been a question with expositors, and it

is perhaps not possible to determine with certainty. Rosenmüller supposes that it refers to the pious whom the 'Jews and Benjaminites repelled from the worship of the temple.' Grotius supposes that it refers to those 'who favoured Onias;' that is, in the time of Antiochus Epiphanes. Vitringa supposes that the address is to the apostles, disciples, and followers of the Lord Jesus; and that it refers to the persecution which would be excited against them by the Jewish people. This seems to me to be the most probable opinion: 1. Because the whole structure of the chapter (see the analysis) seems to refer to the period when the Messiah should appear. 2. Because the state of things described in this verse exactly accords with what occurred on the introduction of Christianity. They who embraced the Messiah were excommunicated and persecuted; and they who did it believed, or professed to believe, that they were doing it for the glory of God. 3. The promise that Jehovah would appear for their joy, and for the confusion of their foes, is one that had a clear fulfilment in his interposition in behalf of the persecuted church. ¶ *Your brethren that hated you.* No hatred of others was ever more bitter than was that evinced by the Jews for those of their nation who embraced Jesus of Nazareth as the Messiah. If this refers to his time, then the language is plain. But to whatever time it refers, it describes a state of things where the pious part of the nation was persecuted and opposed by those who were their kinsmen according to the flesh. ¶ *That cast you out.* The word here used is one that is commonly employed to denote excommunication or exclusion from the privileges connected with the public worship of God. It is language which will accurately describe the treatment which the apostles and the early disciples of the Redeemer received at the hand of the Jewish people (see John xvi. 2, and the Acts of the Apostles generally). ¶ *For my name's sake.* This language closely resembles that which the Saviour used respecting his own disciples and the persecutions to which they would be exposed: 'But all these things will they do unto you for my name's sake, because they know not him that sent me' (John xv. 21; comp. Matt. x. 22; xxiv. 9). I have no doubt that this refers to that period, and to those scenes. ¶ *Said, Let the* Lord *be glorified.* That is, they profess to do it to honour God; or because they suppose that he requires it. Or it means, that even while they were engaged in this cruel persecution, and these acts of excommunicating their brethren, they professed to be serving God, and manifested great zeal in his cause. This has commonly been the case with persecutors. The most malignant and cruel persecutions of the friends of God have been originated under the pretext of great zeal in his service, and with a professed desire to honour his name. So it was with the Jews when they crucified the Lord Jesus. So it is expressly said it would be when his disciples would be excommunicated and put to death (John xvi. 2). So it was in fact in the persecutions excited by the Jews against the apostles and early Christians (see Acts vi. 13, 14; xxi. 28–31). So it was in *all* the persecutions of the Waldenses by the Papists; in all the horrors of the Inquisition; in all the crimes of the Duke of Alva. So it was in the bloody reign of Mary; and so it has ever been in all ages and in all countries where Christians have been persecuted. The people of God have suffered most from those who have been *conscientious persecutors;* and the most malignant foes of the church have been found *in* the church, persecuting true Christians under great pretence of zeal for the purity of religion. It is no evidence of piety that a man is full of conscientious zeal against those whom he chooses to regard as heretics. And it should always be regarded as proof of a *bad* heart, and a *bad* cause, when a man endeavours to inflict pain and disgrace on others, on account of their religious opinions, under pretence of great regard for the honour of God. ¶ *But he shall appear to your joy.* The sense is, that God would manifest himself to his people as their vindicator, and would ultimately rescue them from their persecuting foes. If this is applied to

6 A voice of noise from the city,
a voice from the temple, a voice of
the LORD that rendereth recompence to his enemies.

Christians, it means that the cause in which they were engaged would triumph. This has been the case in all persecutions. The effect has always been the permanent triumph and establishment of the cause that was persecuted. ¶ *And they shall be ashamed.* How true this has been of the Jews that persecuted the early Christians! How entirely were they confounded and overwhelmed! God established permanently the persecuted; he scattered the persecutors to the ends of the earth!

6. *A voice of noise from the city.* That is, from the city of Jerusalem. The prophet sees in a vision a tumult in the city. He hears a voice that issues from the temple. His manner and language are rapid and hurried—such as a man would evince who should suddenly see a vast tumultuous assemblage, and hear a confused sound of many voices. There is also a remarkable abruptness in the whole description here. The preceding verse was calm and solemn. It was full of affectionate assurance of the Divine favour to those whom the prophet saw to be persecuted. Here the scene suddenly changes. The vision passes to the agitating events which were occurring in the city and the temple, and to the great and sudden change which would be produced in the condition of the church of God. But to whom or what this refers has been a subject of considerable difference of opinion. Grotius understands it of the sound of triumph of Judas Maccabeus, and of his soldiers, rejoicing that the city was forsaken by Antiochus, and by the party of the Jews who adhered to him. Rosenmüller understands it of the voice of God, who is seen by the prophet taking vengeance on his foes. There can be no doubt that the prophet, in vision, sees JEHOVAH taking recompence on his enemies—for that is expressly specified. Still it is not easy to determine the exact time referred to, or the exact scene which passes before the mind of the prophet. To me it seems probable that it is a scene that immediately preceded the rapid extension of the gospel, and the great and sudden increase of the church by the accession of the heathen world (see the following verses); and I would suggest, whether it is not a vision of the deeply affecting and agitating scenes when the temple and city were about to be destroyed by the Romans; when the voice of JEHOVAH would be heard in the city and at the temple, declaring the punishment which he would bring on those who had cast out and rejected the followers of the Messiah (ver. 5); and when, as a result of this, the news of salvation was to be rapidly spread throughout the heathen world. This is the opinion, also, of Vitringa. The phrase rendered here 'a voice of noise' (קוֹל שָׁאוֹן), means properly the voice of a tumultuous assemblage; the voice of a multitude. The word 'noise' (שָׁאוֹן) is applied to a noise or roaring, as of waters (Ps. lxv. 8); or of a crowd or multitude of men (Isa. v. 14; xiii. 4; xxiv. 8); and of war (Amos ii. 2; Hos. x. 14). Here it seems probable that it refers to the confused clamour of war, the battle cry raised by soldiers attacking an army or a city; and the scene described is probably that when the Roman soldiers burst into the city, scaled the walls, and poured desolation through the capital. ¶ *A voice from the temple.* That is, either the tumultous sound of war already having reached the temple; or the voice of JEHOVAH speaking from the temple, and commanding destruction on his foes. Vitringa supposes that it may mean the voice of JEHOVAH breaking forth from the temple, and commanding his foes to be slain. But to whichever it refers, it doubtless means that the sound of the tumult was not only *around* the city, but *in* it; not merely in the distant parts, but in the very midst, and even at the temple. ¶ *A voice of the* LORD *that rendereth recompence.* Here we may observe—1. That it is recompence taken on those who had cast out their brethren (ver. 5). 2. It is vengeance taken within the city, and on the *internal*, not the *external* enemies. 3. It

7 Before she travailed, she
brought forth; before her pain
came, she was delivered of a man
child.
8 Who hath heard such a thing?
who hath seen such things? Shall
the earth be made to bring forth
in one day? *or* shall a nation be
born at once? for [a] as soon as
Zion travailed, she brought forth
her children.

a Ac.2.44,47.

is vengeance taken in the midst of this tumult. All this is a striking description of the scene when the city and temple were taken by the Roman armies. It was the vengeance taken on those who had cast out their brethren; it was the vengeance which was to precede the glorious triumph of truth and of the cause of the true religion.

7. *Before she travailed, she brought forth.* That is, Zion. The idea here is, that there would be a great and sudden increase of her numbers. Zion is here represented, as it often is, as a female (see ch. i. 8), and as the mother of spiritual children (comp. ch. liv. 1; xlix. 20, 21). The *particular* idea here is, that the increase would be *sudden*—as if a child were born without the usual delay and pain of parturition. If the interpretation given of the 6th verse be correct, then this refers probably to the sudden increase of the church when the Messiah came, and to the great revivals of religion which attended the first preaching of the gospel. Three thousand were converted on a single day (Acts ii.), and the gospel was speedily propagated almost all over the known world. Vitringa supposes that it refers to the sudden conversion of the Gentiles, and their accession to the church. ¶ *She was delivered of a man child.* Jerome understands this of the Messiah, who was descended from the Jewish church. Grotius supposes that the whole verse refers to Judas Maccabeus, and to the liberation of Judea under him before any one could have hoped for it! Calvin (*Comm. in loc.*) supposes that the word *male* here, or *man-child,* denotes the manly or generous nature of those who should be converted to the church; that they would be vigorous and active, not effeminate and delicate (*generosam prolem, non mollem aut effeminatam*). Vitringa refers it to the character and rank of those who should be converted, and applies it particularly to Constantine, and to the illustrious philosophers, orators, and senators, who were early brought under the influence of the gospel. The Hebrew word probably denotes a *male,* or a man-child, and it seems to me that it is applied here to denote the character of the early converts to the Christian faith. They would not be feeble and effeminate; but vigorous, active, energetic. It *may,* perhaps, also be suggested, that, among the Orientals, the birth of a son was deemed of much more importance, and was regarded as much more a subject of congratulation than the birth of a female. If an allusion be had to that fact, then the idea is, that the increase of the church would be such as would be altogether a subject of exultation and joy.

8. *Who hath heard such a thing?* Of a birth so sudden. Usually in child-birth there are the pains of protracted parturition. The earth brings forth its productions gradually and slowly. Nations rise by degrees, and are long in coming to maturity. But here is such an event as if the earth should in a day be covered with a luxurious vegetation, or as if a nation should spring at once into being. The increase in the church would be as great and wonderful as if these changes were to occur in a moment. ¶ *Shall the earth be made to bring forth in one day?* That is, to produce its grass, and flowers, and fruit, and trees. The idea is, that it usually requires much longer time for it to mature its productions. The germ does not start forth at once; the flower, the fruit, the yellow harvest, and the lofty tree are not produced in a moment. Months and years are required before the earth would be covered with its luxuriant and beautiful productions. But here would be an event as remarkable *as if* the earth should bring forth its productions in a single day. ¶ Or *shall a nation be born at once?* Such

9 Shall I bring to the birth, and
not cause [1]to bring forth? saith
the LORD: shall I cause to bring
forth, and shut *the womb?* saith
thy God.
10 Rejoice [a]ye with Jerusalem,
and be glad with her, all ye that
love her: rejoice for joy with her,
all ye that mourn for her:
11 That ye may suck, [b]and be
satisfied with the breasts of her
consolations; that ye may milk
out, and be delighted with the
abundance [2] of her glory.

1 or, *beget.* a Ps.26.8; 84.1-4; 122.6. b 1 Pe.2.2. 2 or, *brightness.*

an event never *has* occurred. A nation is brought into existence by degrees. Its institutions are matured gradually, and usually by the long process of years. But here is an event as remarkable *as if* a whole nation should be born at once, and stand before the world, mature in its laws, its civil institutions, and in all that constitutes greatness. In looking for the fulfilment of this, we naturally turn the attention to the rapid progress of the gospel in the times of the apostles, when events occurred as sudden and as remarkable *as if* the earth, after the desolation of winter or of a drought, should be covered with rich luxuriance in a day, or as if a whole nation should start into existence, mature in all its institutions, in a moment. But there is no reason for limiting it to that time. Similar sudden changes are to be expected still on the earth; and I see no reason why this should not be applied to the spread of the gospel in heathen lands, and why we should not yet look for the rapid propagation of Christianity in a manner as surprising and wonderful as would be such an instantaneous change in the appearance of the earth, or such a sudden birth of a kingdom.

9. *Shall I bring to the birth?* The sense of this verse is plain. It is, that God would certainly accomplish what he had here predicted, and for which he had made ample arrangements and preparations. He would not commence the work, and then abandon it. The figure which is here used is obvious; but one which does not render very ample illustration proper. Jarchi has well expressed it: 'Num ego adducerem uxorem meam ad sellam partus, *sc.* ad partitudinem, et non aperirem uterum ejus, ut fœtum suum in lucem produceret? Quasi diceret; an ego incipiam rem nec possim eam perficere?' ¶ *Shall I cause to bring forth?* Lowth and Noyes render this, 'Shall I, who begat, restrain the birth?' This accurately expresses the idea. The meaning of the whole is, that God designed the great and sudden increase of his church; that the plan was long laid; and that, having done this, he would not abandon it, but would certainly effect his designs.

10. *Rejoice ye with Jerusalem.* The idea which is presented in this verse is, that it is the duty of all who love Zion to sympathize in her joys. It is one evidence of piety to rejoice in her joy; and they who have no true joy when God pours down his Spirit, and, in a revival of religion, produces changes as sudden and transforming as if the earth were suddenly to pass from the desolation of winter to the verdure and bloom of summer; or when the gospel makes rapid advances in the heathen world, have no true evidence that they love God or his cause. Such scenes awaken deep interest in the bosoms of angels, and in the bosom of God the Saviour; and they who love that God and Saviour *will* rejoice in such scenes, and will mingle their joys and thanksgivings with the joys and thanksgivings of those who are thus converted and saved. ¶ *All ye that mourn for her.* That sympathize in her sorrows, and that mourn over her desolations.

11. *That ye may suck.* The same figure occurs in ch. lx. 16; and substantially in ch. xlix. 23. See the Notes on those places. ¶ *That ye may milk out.* The image is an obvious one. It means that they who sympathized with Zion would be nourished by the same truth, and comforted with the same sources of consolation. ¶ *And be delighted with the abundance of her glory.* Marg. 'Brightness.' Lowth renders this, 'From her abundant stores.' Noyes, 'From the fulness of her glory.'

12 For thus saith the LORD, Behold, I will extend peace to her like a river, and the glory of the Gentiles like a flowing stream: then shall ye suck, ye [a]shall be borne upon *her* sides, and be dandled upon *her* knees.

[a] ch.60.4,16.

Jerome (Vulg.), 'And that you may abound with delights from every kind of her glory.' The LXX. 'That sucking ye may be nourished from the commencement' (Thompson); 'or the entrance of her glory' (ἀπὸ εἰσόδου δόξης αὐτῆς). This variety of interpretation has arisen from the uncertain meaning of the word זִיז, *zīz*, rendered 'abundance.' Gesenius supposes that it is derived from זוּז, *zūz*, meaning, 1. *To move;* 2. *To glance, to sparkle, to radiate*, from the idea of rapid motion; hence, to flow out like rays, to spout like milk; and hence the noun זִיז, *zīz*, means *a breast*. This derivation may be regarded as somewhat fanciful; but it will show why the word 'brightness' was inserted in the margin, since one of the usual significations of the verb relates to brightness, or to sparkling rays. Aquila renders it, Ἀπὸ παντοδαπίας—'From every kind of abundance.' Symmachus, Ἀπὸ πλήθους—'From the multitude.' The word probably refers to the abundance of the consolations which Zion possessed. Lowth proposes to change the text; but without any authority. The Chaldee renders it, 'That ye may drink of the wine of her glory;' where they probably read יַיִן (*wine*), instead of the present reading, ¶ *Of her glory.* The abundant favours or blessings conferred on Zion. The glory that should be manifested to her would be the knowledge of Divine truth, and the provisions made for the salvation of men.

12. *For thus saith the* LORD. This verse contains a promise of the conversion of the Gentiles, and the fact that what constituted their glory would be brought and consecrated to the church of God. ¶ *I will extend.* The word rendered 'I will extend' (נֹטֶה) means properly *to stretch out,* as the hand or a measure; then to spread out or expand, as a tent is spread out, to which it is often applied (Ge. xii. 8; xxvi. 5); or to the heavens spread out over our heads like a tent or a curtain (Isa. xl. 22). Here it may mean either that peace would be *spread out* over the country as the waters of an overflowing river, like the Nile or Euphrates spread out over a vast region in an inundation; or it may mean, as Gesenius supposes, 'I will *turn* peace upon her like a river; *i.e.*, as a stream is turned in its course.' To me it seems that the former is the correct interpretation; and that the idea is, that God would bring prosperity upon Zion like a broad majestic river overflowing all its banks, and producing abundant fertility. ¶ *Peace.* A general word denoting *prosperity* of all kinds—a favourite word with Isaiah to describe the future happiness of the church of God (see ch. ix. 6, 7; xxvi. 12; xxxii. 17; xlv. 7; xlvi. 18; lii. 7; liv. 13; lv. 12; lvii. 19). ¶ *Like a river.* That is, says Lowth. like the Euphrates. So the Chaldee interprets it. But there is no evidence that the prophet refers *particularly* to the Euphrates. The image is that suggested above—of a river that flows full, and spreads over the banks—at once an image of sublimity, and a striking emblem of great prosperity. This same image occurs in ch. xlviii. 18. See Notes on that place. ¶ *And the glory of the Gentiles* (see Notes on ch. lx. 5, 11). ¶ *Like a flowing stream.* Like the Nile, says Vitringa. But the word נַחַל is not commonly applied to a *river* like the Nile; but to a torrent, a brook, a rivulet—either as flowing from a perennial fountain, or more commonly a stream running in a valley that is swelled often by rain, or by the melting of snows in the mountain (see Reland's *Palestine*, ch. xlv.) Such is the idea here. The peace or prosperity of Zion would be like such a swollen stream—a stream overflowing (שׁוֹטֵף) its banks. ¶ *Then shall ye suck;* ver. 11. ¶ *Ye shall be borne upon* her *sides.* See this phrase explained in the Notes on ch. lx. 4. ¶ *And be dandled upon* her *knees.* As a child is by its nurse or mother. The idea is, that the tender-

13 As one whom his mother
comforteth, so will I comfort you;
and ye shall be comforted in Jerusalem.
14 And when ye see *this*, your
heart shall rejoice, [a] and your bones
shall [b] flourish like an herb: and
the hand of the LORD shall be
known towards his servants, and
his indignation towards his enemies.
15 For [c] behold, the LORD will
come with fire, and with his chariots
like a whirlwind, to render his anger
with fury, and his rebuke with
flames of fire.

[a] Jn.16.22. [b] Pr.3.8; Eze.37.1-14. [c] 2 Th.1.8.

est care would be exercised for the church; the same care which an affectionate mother evinces for her children. The insertion of the word '*her*' here by our translators weakens the sense. The meaning is, not that they should be borne upon the sides and dandled upon the knees of Zion or of the church; but that God would manifest to them the feelings of a parent, and treat them with the tenderness which a mother evinces for her children. As a mother nurses her children at her side (comp. Notes on ch. lx. 4), so would God tenderly provide for the church; as she affectionately dandles her children on her knees, so tenderly and affectionately would he regard Zion.

13. *As one whom his mother comforteth.* See the Notes on ch. xlix. 15, where the same image occurs.

14. *And when ye see* this. This great accession to the church from the Gentile world. ¶ *Your bones shall flourish like an herb.* This is an image which is often employed in the Scriptures. When the vigour of the body fails, or when it is much afflicted, the bones are said to be feeble or weakened, or to be dried (Ps. vi. 2; li. 8; xxii. 14, 17; xxxviii. 3; Lam. i. 13; Prov. xiv. 30; xvii. 22). In like manner, prosperity, health, vigour, are denoted by making the bones fat (see Notes on ch. lviii. 11; Prov. xv. 20), or by imparting health, marrow, or strength to them (Prov. iii. 8; xvi. 24). The sense here is, that their vigour would be greatly increased. ¶ *The hand of the* LORD *shall be known.* That is, it shall be seen that he is powerful to defend his people, and to punish their enemies.

15. *For behold, the* LORD *will come with fire.* The LXX. read this 'As fire' (ὡς πῦρ). Fire is a common emblem to denote the coming of the Lord to judge and punish his enemies (Ps. l. 3):

Our God shall come, and shall not keep silence;
A fire shall devour before him,
And it shall be very tempestuous round about him.

So Habak. ii. 5:

Before him went the pestilence,
And burning coals went forth at his feet.

So Ps. xcvii. 3:

A fire goeth before him,
And burneth up his enemies round about.

So it is said (2 Thess. i. 8), that the Lord Jesus will be revealed 'in flaming fire, taking vengeance on them that know not God' (comp. Heb. x. 27; 2 Pet. iii. 7). So JEHOVAH is said to breathe out fire when he comes to destroy his foes:

There went up a smoke out of his nostrils,
And fire out of his mouth devoured;
Coals were kindled by it.
Ps. xviii. 8.

Comp. Notes on ch. xxix. 6; xxx. 30. This is a *general* promise that God would defend his church, and destroy his foes. To what this *particularly* applies, it may not be possible to determine, and instead of attempting that, I am disposed to regard it as a promise of a general nature, that God, in those future times, would destroy his foes, and would thus extend protection to his people. So far as the *language* is concerned, it may be applied either to the destruction of Jerusalem, to any mighty overthrow of his enemies, or to the day of judgment. The single truth is, that all his enemies would be destroyed as if JEHOVAH should come amidst flames of fire. That truth is enough for his church to know; that truth should be sufficient to fill a wicked world with alarm. ¶ *And with his chariots like a whirlwind.* The principal idea here is, that he would come with immense *rapidity*, like a chariot that was borne forward as on the whirlwind, to destroy his foes. God is often represented as coming in a chariot

16 For by fire and by his sword will the LORD plead with all flesh: and the slain of the LORD shall be many.

—a chariot of the clouds, or of a whirlwind. Ps. civ. 3:

> Who maketh the clouds his chariot,
> Who walketh upon the wings of the wind.

Comp. Ps. xviii. 10; see Note on ch. xix. 1. See also Jer. iv. 13:

> Behold, he shall come up as clouds,
> And his chariots shall be as a whirlwind.

Chariots were commonly made with two wheels, though sometimes they had four wheels, to which two horses, fiery and impetuous, were attached; and the rapid movement, the swift revolving wheels, and the dust which they raised, had no slight resemblance to a whirlwind (comp. Notes on ch. xxi. 7, 9). They usually had strong and sharp iron scythes affixed to the extremities of their axles, and were driven into the midst of the army of an enemy, cutting down all before them. Warriors sometimes fought standing on them, or leaping from them on the enemy. The chariots in the army of Cyrus are said to have been capacious enough to permit twenty men to fight from them. The following cut is a representation of the wooden war-chariot of the Parthians, and will give an idea of the general appearance and uses of the chariots of ancient times.

CHARIOT FROM SCULPTURES AT PERSEPOLIS.

¶ *To render his anger with fury.* Lowth renders this, 'To breathe forth his anger.' Jerome translates it, *Reddere, i.e.*, to render. The LXX. Ἀποδοῦναι, to give, or to render. Lowth proposes, instead of the present text, as pointed by the Masorites, לְהָשִׁיב—*lĕhâshībh*, to read it לְהַשִּׁיב—*lĕhăssībh*, as if it were derived from נָשַׁב—*nâshăbh*. But there is no necessity of a change. The idea is, that God would recompense his fury; or would cause his hand to turn upon them in fury. ¶ *With fury.* Lowth renders this, 'In a burning heat.' The word used (חֵמָה) properly means *heat*, then anger, wrath; and the Hebrew here might be properly rendered 'heat of his anger;' that is, glowing or burning wrath, wrath that consumes like fire. ¶ *With flames of fire.* His rebuke shall consume like fiery flames; or it shall be manifested amidst such flames.

16. *For by fire and by his sword.* The sword is an instrument by which punishment is executed (see Notes on ch. xxxiv. 5; comp. Rom. xiii. 4). ¶ *Will he plead with all flesh.* Or rather, he will judge (נִשְׁפָּט), that is, he will execute his purposes of vengeance on all the human race. Of course, only that part is intended who *ought* to be subject to punishment; that is, all his foes. ¶ *And the slain of the* LORD *shall be many.* The number of those who shall be consigned to woe shall be immense—though in the winding up of the great drama at the close of the world, there is reason to hope that a large proportion of the race, taken as a whole, will be saved. Of past generations, indeed,

17 They [a] that sanctify themselves, and purify themselves in the gardens, [1] behind one *tree* in the midst, eating swine's flesh, and the abomination, and the mouse, shall be consumed together, saith the LORD.

[a] ch.65.3,4.

1 or, *one after another.*

there is no just ground of such hope; of the present generation there is no such prospect. But brighter and happier times are to come. The true religion is to spread over all the world, and for a long period is to prevail; and the hope is, that during that long period the multitude of true converts will be so great as to leave the whole number who are lost, compared with those who are saved, much less than is commonly supposed. Still the aggregate of those who are lost, 'the slain of the Lord,' will be vast. This description I regard as having reference to the coming of the Lord to judgment (comp. 2 Thess. i. 8); or if it refer to any other manifestation of JEHOVAH for judgment, like the destruction of Jerusalem by the Romans, it has a strong resemblance to the final judgment; and, like the description of that by the Saviour (Matt. xxiv.), the language is such as naturally to suggest, and to be applicable to, the final judgment of mankind.

17. *They that sanctify themselves.* That is, who attempt to purify themselves by idolatrous rites, by ablutions, and lustrations. The design here is, to describe those who will be exposed to the wrath of God when he shall come to execute vengeance. ¶ *And purify themselves in the gardens* (see Notes on ch. lxv. 3). ¶ *Behind one* tree *in the midst.* This passage has not a little exercised the ingenuity of commentators. It is quite evident that our translators were not able to satisfy themselves with regard to its meaning. In the margin they have rendered it, 'one after another,' supposing that it may mean that the idolaters engaged in their sacrifices in a solemn procession, walking one after another around their groves, their shrines, or their altars. In the translation in the text, they seem to have supposed that the religious rites referred to were celebrated behind one particular selected tree in the garden. Lowth renders it, 'After the rites of Achad.' Jerome renders it, *In hortis post januam intrinsecus*—'In the gardens they sanctify themselves behind the gate within.' The LXX. 'Who consecrate and purify themselves (*εἰς τοὺς κήπους, καὶ ἐν τοῖς προθύροις ἔσθοντες, κ.τ.λ.*) for the gardens, and they who, in the outer courts, eat swine's flesh,' &c. The Chaldee renders the phrase סִיעָא בָּתַר סִיעָא *turba post turbam*—'Multitude after multitude.' The vexed Hebrew phrase used here, אַחַר אַחַד *āhhăr āhhădh*, it is very difficult to explain. The word אַחַר means properly *after;* the after part; the extremity; behind—in the sense of following after, or going after any one. The word אַחַד, *āhhādh*, means properly *one;* some one; any one. Gesenius (*Comm. in loc.*) says that the phrase may be used in one of the three following senses: 1. In the sense of one after another. So Sym. and Theo. render it —*ὀπίσω ἀλλήλων.* Luther renders it, *Einer hier, der andere da*—'one here, another there.' 2. The word אַחַד, *āhhăhd*, may be understood as the name of a god who was worshipped in Syria, by the name of Adad. This god is that described by Macrobius, *Sat.*, i. 23: 'Understand what the Assyrians think about the power of the sun. For to the God whom they worship as Supreme they give the name Adad, and the signification of this name is *One.*' That the passage before us refers to this divinity is the opinion of Lowth, Grotius, Bochart, Vitringa, Dathe, and others. 'The image of Adad,' Macrobius adds, 'was designated by inclined rays, by which it was shown that the power of heaven was in the rays of the sun which were sent down to the earth.' The same god is referred to by Pliny (*Hist. Nat.* xxxvii. 71), where he mentions three gems which received their names from three parts of the body, and were called 'The veins of Adad, the eye of Adad, the finger of Adad;' and he adds, 'This god was worshipped by the Syrians.' There can be no doubt that such a god was worshipped; but it is by no means certain that this idol is here referred to. It is not improbable, Vitringa

18 For I *know* their works and their thoughts: it shall come, that I will gather all nations and tongues; and they shall come, and see my glory.

---

remarks, that the name *Adad* should be written for *Ahhadh*, for the ease of pronunciation—as a slight change in letters was common for the purpose of euphony. But it is still not quite clear that this refers to any particular idol. 3. The third opinion is that of Gesenius, and accords substantially with that which our translators have expressed in the text. According to that, it should be rendered 'Those who sanctify and purify themselves in the [idol] groves after one in the midst;' *i.e.*, following and imitating the one priest who directed the sacred ceremonies. It may mean that a solemn procession was formed in the midst of the grove, which was led on by the priest, whom all followed; or it may mean that they imitated him in the sacred rites. It seems to me probable that this refers to some sacred procession in honour of an idol, where the idol or the altar was encompassed by the worshippers, and where they were led on by the officiating priest. Such processions we know were common in heathen worship. ¶ *In the midst.* In the midst of the sacred grove; that is, in the darkest and obscurest recess. Groves were selected for such worship on account of the sacred awe which it was supposed their dark shades would produce and cherish. For the same reason, therefore, the darkest retreat—the very middle of the grove—would be selected as the place where their religious ceremonies would be performed. I see no evidence that there is any allusion to any *tree* here, as our translators seem to have supposed; still less, that there was, as Burder supposes, any allusion to the tree of life in the midst of the garden of Eden, and their attempts to cultivate and preserve the memory of it; but there *is* reason to believe that their religious rites would be performed in the centre, or most shady part of the grove. ¶ *Eating swine's flesh.* That is, in connection with their public worship (see Notes on ch. lxv. 4). ¶ *And the abomination.* The thing which is held as abominable or detestable in the law of God. Thus the creeping thing and the reptile were regarded as abominations (Lev. xi. 41, 42). They were not to be eaten; still less were they to be offered in sacrifice (comp. Ex. viii. 26; Deut. xx. 16; xxix. 17; see Notes on ch. lxv. 3). ¶ *And the mouse.* The Hebrew word here used means the *dormouse*—a small field-mouse. Jerome understands it as meaning the *glis*, a small mouse that was regarded as a great delicacy by the Romans. They were carefully kept and fattened for food (see Varro, *De Rust.*, iii. 15). Bochart (*Hieroz.*, i. 3, 34) supposes that the name here used is of Chaldaic origin, and that it denotes a field-mouse. Mice abounded in the East, and were often exceedingly destructive in Syria (see Bochart; comp. 1 Sam. v. 4). Strabo mentions that so vast a multitude of mice sometimes invaded Spain as to produce a pestilence; and in some parts of Italy, the number of field-mice was so great that the inhabitants were forced to abandon the country. It was partly on account of its destructive character that it was held in abomination by the Hebrews. Yet it would seem that it was eaten by idolaters; and was, perhaps, used either in their sacrifices or in their incantations (see Notes on ch. lxv. 4). Vitringa supposes that the description in this verse is applicable to the time of Herod, and that it refers to the number of heathen customs and institutions which were introduced under his auspices. But this is by no means certain. It may be possible that it is a general description of idolatry, and of idolaters as the enemies of God, and that the idea is, that God would come with vengeance to cut off all his foes.

18. *For I know their works.* The word 'know,' says Lowth, is here evidently left out of the Hebrew text, leaving the sense quite imperfect. It is found in the Syriac; the Chaldee evidently had that word in the copy of the Hebrew which was used; and the Aldine and Complutensian editions of the LXX. have the word. Its insertion is necessary in order to complete the sense; though the proof is not clear

19 And I will set a sign [a] among them, and I will send those that escape of them unto the nations, *to* Tarshish, Pul, and Lud, that draw the bow, *to* Tubal and Javan, *to* the isles afar off that have not heard my fame, neither have seen my glory; [b] and they shall declare my glory among the Gentiles.

a ch.18.3,7; Lu.2.34. b Mal.1.11; Mat.28.19.

that the word was ever in the Hebrew text. The sense is, that though their abominable rites were celebrated in the deepest recesses of the groves, yet they were not concealed from God. ¶ *That I will gather all nations and tongues.* They who speak all languages (comp. Rev. vii. 9; x. 11; xi. 9). The sense is, that the period would come when JEHOVAH would collect all nations to witness the execution of his vengeance on his foes. ¶ *And see my glory.* That is, the manifestation of my perfections in the great events referred to here—the destruction of his enemies, and the deliverance of his people. To what particular period this refers has been a point on which expositors are by no means agreed. Grotius says it means, that such shall be the glory of the Jewish people that all nations shall desire to come and make a covenant with them. The Jewish interpreters, and among them Abarbanel (see Vitringa), suppose that it refers to a *hostile* and *warlike* assembling of all nations in the time of the Messiah, who, say they, shall attack Jerusalem with the Messiah in it, and shall be defeated. They mention particularly that the Turks and Christians shall make war on Jerusalem and on the true Messiah, but that they shall be overthrown. Vitringa supposes that it refers to the assembling of the nations when the gospel should be at first proclaimed, and when they should be called into the kingdom of God. Many of the Fathers referred it to the final judgment. It is difficult to determine, amidst this variety of opinion, what is the true meaning. Opinions are easily given, and conjectures are easily made; and the opinions referred to above are entitled to little more than the appellation of conjecture. It seems to me, that there is involved here the idea of the judgment or punishment on the enemies of God, and at about the same time a collecting of the nations not only to witness the punishment, but also to become participants of his favour. In some future time, JEHOVAH would manifest himself as the punisher of his enemies, and all the nations also would be permitted to behold his glory, as if they were assembled together.

19. *And I will set a sign among them* (see Notes on ch. xi. 12; xviii. 3). On the meaning of the word 'sign' (אוֹת), see Notes on ch. vii. 11. What is its meaning here is to be determined by the connection. That would seem to me to require some such interpretation as this: That when God should come (ver. 17, 18) to take vengeance on his foes, and to manifest his glory, he would establish some *mark* or *memorial;* would erect some standard, or give some signal, by which his true friends would escape, and that he would send them to distant nations to proclaim his truth and gather together those who had not seen his glory. What that sign should be, he does not here say. Whether a standard, a secret communication, or some intimation beforehand, by which they should know the approaching danger and make their escape, is not declared. It is by no means easy to determine with certainty on this passage; and it certainly becomes no one to speak dogmatically or very confidently. But it seems to me that the whole passage may have been intended, by the Holy Spirit, to refer to the propagation of the gospel by the apostles. The heavy judgments referred to may have been the impending calamities over Jerusalem. The glory of God referred to, may have been the signal manifestation of his perfections at that period in the approaching destruction of the city, and in the wonders that attended the coming of the Messiah. The gathering of the nations (ver. 18) *may* possibly refer to the collecting together of numerous people from all parts of the earth about that time; that is, either the assembled people at the time of the Saviour's death (Acts ii. 8, 11), or the gathering of the armies

of the Romans—a commingled multitude from all nations—to inflict punishment on the Jewish nation, and to behold the manifestation of the Divine justice in the destruction of the guilty Jewish capital. The 'sign' here referred to, *may* denote the intimations which the Redeemer gave to his disciples to discern these approaching calamities, and to secure their safety by flight when they should be about to appear (Matt. xxiv. 15–18). By these warnings and previous intimations they were to be preserved. The sign was 'among them,' *i.e.*, in the very midst of the nation; and the object of the intimation was, to secure their safety, and the speedy propagation of the true religion among all nations. Deeply sensible that there is great danger of erring here, and that the above view may be viewed as mere conjecture, I cannot, however, help regarding it as the true exposition. If there is error in it, it may be pardoned; for it will probably be felt by most readers of these Notes that there has not been a *too frequent* reference in the interpretation proposed to the times of the Christian dispensation. ¶ *And I will send those that escape of them.* According to the interpretation suggested above, this refers to the portion of the Jewish nation that should escape from the tokens of the Divine displeasure; that is, to the apostles and the early disciples of the Redeemer. The great mass of the nation would be abandoned and devoted to destruction. But a remnant would be saved (comp. ch. i. 9; xi. 11, 16). Of that remnant, God would send a portion to make his name known to those who had not heard it, and they would lead distant nations to the knowledge of his truth. The whole passage is so accurately descriptive of what occurred in the times when the gospel was first preached to the pagan world, that there can be little danger of error in referring it to those times. Compare Vitringa on the passage for a more full view of the reasons of this interpretation. The names of the places which follow are designed to specify the principal places where the message would be sent, and stand here as representatives of the whole heathen world. ¶ To *Tarshish* (see Notes on ch. ii. 16; xxiii. 1; lx. 19). Tarshish was one of the most distant seaports known to the Hebrews; and whether it be regarded as situated in Spain, or in the East Indies, or south of Abyssinia (see Notes above) it equally denotes a distant place, and the passage means that the message would be borne to the most remote regions. ¶ *Pul.* This is supposed to denote some region in Africa. Jerome renders it, 'Africa.' The LXX. Φοὺδ—'Phud.' Bochart, *Phaleg.* iv. 26, supposes that it means *Philae*, a large island in the Nile, between Egypt and Ethiopia; called by the Egyptians *Pilak, i.e.*, the border, or far country (see Champollion, *l'Egypte*, i. 158). There are still on that island remains of some very noble and extensive temples built by the ancient Egyptians. ¶ *And Lud.* Jerome renders this, 'Lydia.' The LXX. 'Lud.' There was a Lydia in Asia Minor—the kingdom of the celebrated Crœsus; but it is generally supposed that this place was in Africa. Ludim was a son of Mizraim (Gen. x. 13), and the name *Ludim*, or Lybians, referring to a people, several times occurs in the Bible (Jer. xlvi. 9; Ezek. xxvii. 10; xxx. 5). These African Lybians are commonly mentioned in connection with Pul, Ethiopia, and Phut. Bochart supposes that Abyssinia is intended, but it is by no means certain that this is the place referred to. Josephus affirms that the descendants of Ludim are long since extinct, having been destroyed in the Ethiopian wars. It is clear that some part of Egypt is intended, says Calmet, but it is not easy to show exactly where they dwelt. ¶ *That draw the bow* (מֹשְׁכֵי קֶשֶׁת). The LXX. here render the Hebrew phrase simply by Μοσὸχ—'Mosoch,' understanding it of a place. Lowth supposes that the Hebrew phrase is a corruption of the word Moschi, the name of a nation situated between the Euxine and the Caspian seas. But there is no authority for supposing, as he does, that the word 'bow' has been interpolated. The Chaldee renders it, 'Drawing and smiting with the bow.' The idea is, that the nations here referred to were distinguished for the use of the bow. The bow was in common use in wars; and it is by no means improbable that at that time they had acquired peculiar

20 And they shall bring all your brethren *for* an offering [a] unto the LORD, out of all nations, upon horses, and in chariots, and in litters,[1] and upon mules, and upon swift beasts, to my holy mountain Jerusalem, saith the LORD, as the children of Israel bring an offering in a clean vessel into the house of the LORD.

a Ro.15.16.

1 or, *coaches*.

celebrity in the use of this weapon. ¶ To *Tubal.* Tubal was the fifth son of Japhet, and is here joined with Javan because they were among the settlers of Europe. The names before mentioned together relate to Africa, and the sense there is, that the message should be sent to Africa; here the idea is, that it should be sent to Europe. Tubal is commonly united with Meshech, and it is supposed that they peopled countries bordering on each other. Bochart labours to prove that by Meshech and Tubal are intended the Muscovites and the Tibarenians. The Tibarenians of the Greeks were the people inhabiting the country south of the Caucasus, between the Black Sea and the Araxes. Josephus says, that 'Tubal obtained *the Thobelians* (Θωβήλους) who are reckoned among the Iberians.' Jerome renders it, 'Italy.' It is not possible to determine with certainty the country that is referred to, though some part of Europe is doubtless intended. ¶ *And Javan.* Jerome renders this, 'Greece.' So the LXX. Εἰς τὴν Ἑλλάδα—'To Greece.' Javan was the fourth son of Japhet, and was the father of the Ionians and the Greeks (Gen. x. 2–4). The word 'Ionia,' Gr. Ἰων, Ἰωνία, is evidently derived from the word here rendered 'Javan' (יָוָן), and in the Scriptures the word comprehends all the countries inhabited by the descendants of Javan, as well in Greece as in Asia Minor. Ionia properly was the beautiful province on the western part of Asia Minor—a country much celebrated in the Greek classics for its fertility and the salubrity of its climate—but the word here used includes all of Greece. Thus Daniel (xi. 2), speaking of Xerxes, says, 'He shall stir up all against the realm of Javan.' Alexander the Great is described by the same prophet as 'king of Javan' (viii. 21; x. 20). The Hindoos call the Greeks Yavanas—the ancient Hebrew appellation. It is needless to say, on the supposition that this refers to the propagation of the gospel by the apostles, that it was fulfilled. They went to Greece and to Asia Minor in the very commencement of their labours, and some of the earliest and most flourishing churches were founded in the lands that were settled by the descendants of Javan. ¶ *To the isles afar off* (see Notes on ch. xli. 1). ¶ *That have not heard my fame.* Heb. 'Who have not heard my report,' *i.e.*, who were ignorant of the true God. ¶ *Neither have seen my glory.* The glory which he had manifested to the Hebrews in giving his law, and in the various exhibitions of his character and perfections among them.

20. *And they shall bring all your brethren.* That is, as great success shall attend them *as if* they should bring back all who had gone there when scattered abroad, and should present them as an offering to JEHOVAH. The image here is taken from the scene which would be presented, should the distant nations be seen bringing the scattered exiles in all lands on horses, and on palanquins, and on dromedaries, again to Jerusalem, and presenting them before JEHOVAH in the city where they formerly dwelt. It is the image of a vast caravan, conducted by the heathen world when they had become tributary to the people of God, and when they united to return them to their own land. The *spiritual* signification is, that all they who should be appropriately called 'brethren,' all who should be the true friends of God, should be brought and offered to JEHOVAH; that is, there should be a great accession to the people of God from the heathen world. ¶ *For an offering unto the* LORD. Heb. מִנְחָה *mĭnhhâ*—not a bloody offering or sacrifice: but an offering such as was made by flour, oil, &c. (see Notes on ch. i. 13.) ¶ *Out of all nations.* The truth shall be proclaimed in all lands, and a vast accession shall be made from all parts

of the world to the true church of God. To understand this description, we must form an idea of immense caravans proceeding from distant parts of the world to Jerusalem, bearing along the converts to the true religion to be dedicated to the service of JEHOVAH. ¶ *Upon horses.* Horses were little used by the Hebrews (see Notes on ch. ii. 7), but they are much used by the Arabs, and form an important part of the caravan that goes to distant places. ¶ *And in chariots* (comp. Notes on ver. 15). It is, however, by no means certain that the word here used refers to a wheeled vehicle, Such vehicles were not used in caravans. The editor of the *Ruins of Palmyra* tells us that the caravan they formed to go to that place, consisted of about two hundred persons, and about the same number of beasts of carriage, which were an odd mixture of horses, camels, mules, and asses; but there is no account of any vehicle drawn on wheels in that expedition, nor do we find an account of such things in other eastern journeys (Harmer). Coaches, Dr. Russel assures us, are not in use in Aleppo, nor are they commonly used in any of the countries of the East. The Hebrew word here used (רֶכֶב, *rêkhĕbh*), means properly *riding*—riders, cavalry (see it explained in the Notes on ch. xxi. 7); then *any* vehicle for riding—whether a waggon, chariot, or litter. Lowth renders it, 'In litters.' Pitts, in his account of the return from Mecca, describes a species of litter which was borne by two camels, one before and another behind, which was all covered over with searcloth, and that again with green broadcloth, and which was elegantly adorned. It is not improbable that some such vehicle is intended here, as it is certain that such things as waggons or chariots are not found in oriental caravans. ¶ *And in litters.* Marg. 'Coaches.' But the word *litters* more properly expresses the idea. Lowth renders it, 'Counes.' Thevenot tells us that *counes* are hampers, or cradles, carried upon the backs of camels, one on each side, having a back, head, and sides, like great chairs. A covering is commonly laid over them to protect the rider from wind and rain. This is a common mode of travelling in the East.

LITTERS FOR TRAVELLING IN THE EAST.—From Laborde.

The coune, or hamper, is thrown across the back of the camel, somewhat in the manner of saddle-bags with us. Sometimes a person sits on each side, and they thus balance each other, and sometimes the end in which the person is placed is

21 And I will also take of them
for priests, [a] *and* for Levites, saith
the LORD.
22 For as the new [b] heavens and
the new earth, which I will make,
shall remain before me, saith the
LORD, so shall your seed and your
name remain.
23 And [c] it shall come to pass,
that from one [1] new moon to another, and from one sabbath to
another, shall all [d] flesh come to
worship before me, saith the LORD.

a Re.1.6. b ch.65.17. c Zec.14.14.
1 *new moon to his new moon, and from sabbath to his sabbath.* d Ps 65 2.

balanced by provisions, or articles of furniture in the other. 'At Aleppo,' says Dr. Russel, 'women of inferior condition in long journeys are commonly stowed, one on each side of a mule, in a sort of covered cradles.' The Hebrew word here used (צָב *tzâbh*), means properly a *litter*, a *sedan coach*—what can be lightly or gently borne. The LXX. render it, Ἐν λαμπήναις ἡμιόνων μετὰ σκιαδίων—'In litters of mules, with shades or umbrellas.' Perhaps the following description of a scene in the khan at Acre, will afford an apt illustration of this passage. 'The bustle was increased this morning by the departure of the wives of the governor of Jaffa. They set off in two coaches of a curious description, common in this country. The body of the coach was raised on two parallel poles, somewhat similar to those used for sedan chairs—only that in these the poles were attached to the lower part of the coach—throwing consequently the centre of gravity much higher, and apparently exposing the vehicle, with its veiled tenant, to an easy overthrow, or at least to a very active jolt. Between the poles strong mules were harnessed, one before and one behind; who, if they should prove capricious, or have very uneven or mountainous ground to pass, would render the situation of the ladies still more critical.'—(Jowett's *Christian Researches in Syria*, pp. 115, 116, Am. Ed.) ¶ *And upon swift beasts.* Dromedaries. So Lowth and Noyes render it; and so the word here used—כִּרְכָּרוֹת—properly denotes. The word is derived from כָּרַד *kârăd*, to dance; and the name is given to them for their bounding or dancing motion, their speed being also sometimes accelerated by musical instruments (Bochart, *Hieroz.* i. 2, 4). For a description of the dromedary, see Notes on ch. lx. 6. ¶ *As the children of Israel.* As the Jews bear an offering to JEHOVAH in a vessel that is pure. The utmost attention was paid to the cleanliness of their vessels in their public worship.

21. *And I will also take of them for priests.* I will give to them an honourable place in my public service; that is, I will make them ministers of religion *as if* they were priests and Levites. This cannot be taken *literally*—because the priests and Levites among the Jews were determined by law, and by regular genealogical descent, and there was no provision for substituting any in their place. But it must mean that under the condition of things described here, those who should be brought from the distant pagan world would perform the same offices in the service of God which had been performed formerly by the priests and Levites—that is, they would be ministers of religion. The services of God would no longer be performed by the descendants of Aaron, or be limited to them, but would be performed by others who should be called to this office from the heathen world.

22. *For as the new heavens and the new earth* (see Notes on ch. lxv. 17). ¶ *Shall remain before me.* They shall not pass away and be succeeded by others. The idea is, that the state of things here described would be permanent and abiding. ¶ *So shall your seed and your name remain* (see Notes on ch. lxv. 15).

23. *And it shall come to pass.* As the prophet closes the book and winds up his whole prophecy, he directs the attention to that future period which had occupied so much of his attention in vision, when the whole world should be acquainted with the true religion, and all nations should worship JEHOVAH. Of *such* a book there could be no more appropriate close; and such a contemplation peculiarly became the last pro-

24 And they shall go forth, and look upon the carcasses of the men

phetic moments of the 'evangelical prophet' Isaiah. ¶ *From one new moon to another.* Marg. 'New moon to his new moon.' The Hebrew literally is, 'As often as the month cometh in its month;' *i.e.*, in its time, every month, every new moon (Gesenius, *Lex.*, on the word מִדֵּי). The Hebrews held a festival on the return of each month, or at every new moon (see Notes on ch. i. 14). A similar prophecy occurs in Zech. xiv. 16: 'And it shall come to pass, that every one that is left of all the nations which came up against Jerusalem, shall even go up from year to year to worship the King, the Lord of hosts, and to keep the feast of tabernacles.' In regard to the meaning of this, it is evident that it cannot be taken literally. In the nature of things it would be impossible for all nations to go literally before JEHOVAH in Jerusalem once a month, or once a year, to worship. It must then be meant that at *periodical seasons*, all the human family would worship JEHOVAH. The festivals of the new moon, the feast of tabernacles, and the Sabbaths, were the *set time* among the Hebrews for the worship of God; and the idea is, that on set times, or at regularly recurring intervals, the worship of God would yet be celebrated in all lands. I see no evidence, therefore, that this means that there should be established on the earth the habit of meeting for prayer, or for the worship of God once a month—any more than the passage above quoted from Zechariah proves that a feast like that of tabernacles would be celebrated once a year. But the idea is clear, that the time would come when JEHOVAH would be worshipped regularly and periodically everywhere; that in all nations his worship would be established in a manner similar in some respects to that which prevailed among his people in ancient times. ¶ *And from one Sabbath to another* (comp. Notes on ch. lviii. 13, 14). There can be no permanent worship of God, and no permanent religion on earth, without a Sabbath; and hence it was, that while the observance of the feasts of tabernacles, and of the Passover, and of the new moons, made a part of the *ceremonial* law, the law respecting the Sabbaths was incorporated with the ten commandments as of moral and perpetual obligation; and it will be literally true that all the race shall yet be brought to worship God on the return of that holy day. It was instituted in paradise; and as one design of the plan of redemption is to bring man back to the state in which he was in paradise, so one effect of the true religion everywhere will be, and *is*, to make men reverence the Sabbath of the Lord. No man becomes truly pious who does not love the holy Sabbath. No nation ever has been, or ever can be converted which will not, and which *does* not, love and observe that day. Every successful effort to propagate the true religion is a successful effort to extend the practice of observing it; and just as certain as it is that Christianity will be spread around the world, so certain will it be that the Sabbath will be observed in all lands. The period is, therefore, yet to arrive when the delightful spectacle will be presented of all the nations of the earth bowing on the return of that day before the living God. The plans of this life will be suspended; toil and care will be laid aside; and the sun, as he rolls around the world, will rouse nation after nation to the worship of the true God; and the peace and order and loveliness of the Christian Sabbath will spread over all the hills and vales of the world. Who that loves the race will not desire that such a period may soon come? Who can wonder that Isaiah should have fixed his eye in the close of his prophetic labours on a scene so full of loveliness, and so replete with honour to God, and with goodwill to men? ¶ *Shall all flesh.* All the human family, all nations—a most unequivocal promise that the true religion shall yet prevail around the world. ¶ *Come to worship before me.* That is, they shall assemble for the worship of God in their respective places of devotion.

25. *And they shall go forth.* The sense of this verse evidently is, that the pious and happy worshippers of God shall see the punishment which he will execute on his and their foes, or shall

that have transgressed against me; for their worm shall [a] not die, neither shall their fire be quenched; and they shall be an abhorring [b] unto all flesh.

a Da.12.2. b Mar.9.44-48.

see them finally destroyed. It refers to the time when the kingdom of God shall be finally and perpetually established, and when all the mighty enemies of that kingdom shall be subdued and punished. The image is probably taken from a scene where a people whose lands have been desolated by mighty armies are permitted to go forth after a decisive battle to walk over the fields of the slain, and to see the dead and the putrifying bodies of their once formidable enemies. ¶ *And look upon the carcasses of the men.* The dead bodies of the foes of God (see ver. 15, 16). ¶ *For their worm shall not die.* This image is evidently taken from the condition of unburied bodies, and especially on a battle-field. The Hebrew word (תּוֹלַע) properly refers to the worms which are generated in such corrupting bodies (see Ex. xvi. 20; Notes on Isa. xiv. 11). It is sometimes applied to the worm from which the crimson or deep scarlet colour was obtained (Notes on ch. i. 18); but it more properly denotes that which is produced in putrid substances. This entire passage is applied by the Saviour to future punishment; and is the fearful image which he employs to denote the final suffering of the wicked in hell. My views on its meaning may be seen in the Notes on Mark ix. 44, 46. ¶ *Neither shall their fire be quenched.* The fire that shall consume them shall burn perpetually. This image is taken evidently from the fires kindled, especially in the valley of Hinnom, to consume putrid and decaying substances. That was a valley on the south side of Jerusalem, into which the filth of the city was thrown. It was the place where, formerly, an image of brass was raised to Moloch, and where children were offered in sacrifice (2 Kings xvi. 3; 2 Chron. xxviii. 3). See a description of this in the Notes on Matt. v. 22. This place was subsequently regarded as a place of peculiar abomination by the Jews. The filth of the city was thrown there, and it became extremely offensive. The air was polluted and pestilential; the sight was terrific; and to preserve it in any manner pure, it was necessary to keep fires continually burning there. The extreme loathsomeness of the place, the filth and putrefaction, the corruption of the atmosphere, and the lurid fires blazing by day and by night, made it subsequently one of the most appalling and loathsome objects with which a Jew was acquainted. It was called the GEHENNA OF FIRE, and was the image which the Saviour often employed to denote the future punishment of the wicked. In that deep and loathsome vale it seems to have been the common expectation of the Jews that some great battle would be fought which would establish the supremacy of their nation over all others. Hence the Chaldee renders this, 'They shall go forth, and shall look upon the dead bodies of the sinners who have rebelled against my word; because their souls shall not die, and their fire shall not be extinguished; and the wicked shall be judged IN GEHENNA (בְּגֵיהִנָּם), until the righteous shall say, We have seen enough.' It is, however, by no means certain that Isaiah refers here especially to the valley of Hinnom. The image in his mind is evidently that of a vast army slain, and left to putrify on the field unburied, and where fires would be kindled in part to consume the heaps of the slain, and in part to save the air from pestilential influences. All the enemies of God and his church would be like such a vast host strewed on the plains, and the perpetuity of his kingdom would be finally established. ¶ *And they shall be an abhorring.* An object of loathing. So the Hebrew word דֵּרָאוֹן, means. It is derived from דָּרָא, an obsolete root, signifying, in Arabic, to thrust away, to repel. Jerome renders it, *Ad satietatem visionis*—understanding by it, that all flesh should look upon those dead bodies until they were satisfied. The LXX., Εἰς ὅρασιν—'For a vision;' or that all flesh might look upon them. It is evident that the LXX. read the word as if it were derived from the verb רָאָה, *to see.* ¶ *Unto all flesh* (see ver. 23). The sense is, that so entire would be their overthrow, and such objects of loathing would they become, that all the friends of God would turn from them in abhorrence. All the enemies of God would be destroyed; the pure religion would triumph, and the people of God would be secure.

It may be made a question, perhaps, to what period this refers. The Saviour (Mark ix. 44, 46), applied *the language* to the future punishment of the wicked, and no one, I think, can doubt that in Isaiah it *includes* that consummation of worldly affairs. The radical and essential idea in the prophet is, as it seems to me, that such would be the entire overthrow and punishment of the enemies of God; so condign their punishment; so deep their sufferings; so loathsome and hateful would they be when visited with the Divine vengeance for their sins, that they would be an object of loathing and abhorrence. They would be swept off as unworthy to live with God, and they would be consigned to punishment—loathsome like that of ever-gnawing worms on the carcasses of the slain, and interminable and dreadful like ever-consuming and extinguishable fires.

This is the consummation of the series of bright visions that passed before the mind of Isaiah, and is an appropriate termination of this succession of wonderful revelations. Where could it more appropriately close than in the final triumph of the true religion, and in the complete and final destruction of all the enemies of God? The vision stretches on to the judgment, and is closed by a contemplation of those scenes which commence there, but which never end. The church is triumphant. Its conflicts cease. Its foes are slain. Its Redeemer is revealed; and its everlasting happiness is founded on a basis which can never be shaken.

Here I close my labours in endeavouring to elucidate the visions of this wonderful prophet. I thank God—the source of every right feeling and every holy desire, and the suggester of every plan that will in any way elucidate his word or promote his glory—that he ever inclined my heart to these studies. I thank him for the preservation of my life, and the continuance of my health, until I am permitted to bring this work to a close. I record, with grateful emotions, my deep conviction, that if in any way I have been enabled to explain that which was before dark; to illustrate that which was obscure; or to present any views which have not before occurred to those who may peruse this work, it is owing to the gracious influences of his Holy Spirit. And I desire to render thanks to the Great Source of light and truth, if I have been enabled to throw any light on the prophecies recorded here more than 2500 years ago; or to confirm the faith of any in the truth of the inspiration of the Bible by tracing the evidences of the fulfilment of those predictions. And I now commend the work to the blessing of God, and devote it to the glory of his name and to the advancement of the Redeemer's kingdom, with a humble prayer that it may be useful to other minds; —but with the deep conviction, that whatever may be its effect on other minds, I have been abundantly compensated for all my labour in the contemplation of the inimitable beauties, and the sublime visions of Isaiah. Thanks to God for this book;—thanks for all its beauties, its consolations, its promises, its views of the Messiah, its predictions of the certain triumph of truth, and its glowing descriptions of the future conquest of the church, when God shall extend to it 'peace like a river, and the glory of the Gentiles like a flowing stream.' Come soon that blessed day, when 'the ransomed of the Lord shall return to Zion, with songs and everlasting joy upon their heads' (ch. xxxv. 10); when 'the wilderness and the solitary place shall be glad, and the desert shall rejoice and blossom as the rose' (ch. xxxv. 1); and when it shall be announced to the church, 'thy sun shall no more go down; neither shall thy moon withdraw itself; for JEHOVAH shall be thine everlasting light, and the days of thy mourning shall be ended' (ch. lx. 20). May I be permitted to close my labours on this book in the beautiful language of Vitringa?* 'These words (ver. 23,

* Hæc extrema sunt (sc. ver. 23, 24) utriusque oppositi hominum generis piorum et impiorum, in quibus post varia prolusoria Dei judicia, fata

24) express the final doom of the two opposite classes of men, the righteous and the wicked, when, after various preparatory judgments of God, the fates of all ages, and our own also, shall be determined; with which also this Divine book of Isaiah itself is terminated. Be it our lot, with those who are holy; with those who fear God and love the truth; with the humble, meek, and merciful, and with those who persevere in every good work to the end of life, from the gracious sentence of our great Lord, Saviour, and Judge, Jesus Christ, to obtain, by the will of the Father, the same portion with them. In which hope, I also, now deeply affected, and prostrate before his throne, give humble thanks to God the Father, and his Son Christ Jesus, through the Spirit, for the grace and light with which he has endowed me, his unworthy servant, in commencing and completing the commentary on this book; entreating, with earnest prayer, of his grace and mercy, that, pardoning those errors into which erroneously I may have fallen, he will employ this work, such as it is, to the glory of his name, the use of the church, and the consolation of his people; and to Him be the glory throughout all ages.'

---

sæculorum omnium, et nostra quoque terminabuntur; quibusque ipse quoque hic Divinus Liber Iesaiæ, magni Prophetæ, terminatur. Esto sors nostra cum sanctis, Dei reverentibus; veritatis amantibus; humilibus, mansuetis, misericordibus, et in bono opere ad finem vitæ perseverantibus, ex sententia gratiæ magni nostri Domini, Servatoris, ac Judicis Christi Jesu, sortes hasce ex voluntate Patris diribituri. Qua spe ego quoque hoc tempore affectus, prostratusque ante thronum ejus, Deo PATRI, in FILIO ejus CHRISTO JESU per SPIRITUM, submisso animo gratias ago pro gratia et lumine, quibus me indignum servum suum in commentatione hujus Libri inchoanda et absolvenda prosequutus est; supplici prece ab ejus gratia et misericordia contendens, ut aberrationibus in quas imprudens inciderim, ignoscens, hoc Opus quale est, vertere velit in maximam gloriam sui Nominis, usum Ecclesiæ, et solatium piorum.

'Αὐτῷ ἡ δόξα εἰς τοὺς αἰῶνας τῶν αἰώνων.'

FROM Donald Morrison
To Donald Stewart